THE LEXICOGRAPHY OF ENGLISH

THE LEXICOGRAPHY OF ENGLISH

FROM ORIGINS TO PRESENT

Henri Béjoint

OXFORD

UNIVERSITY PRESS

OXFORD
UNIVERSITY PRESS

Great Clarendon Street, Oxford OX2 6DP

Oxford University Press is a department of the University of Oxford.
It furthers the University's objective of excellence in research, scholarship,
and education by publishing worldwide in

Oxford New York

Auckland Cape Town Dar es Salaam Hong Kong Karachi
Kuala Lumpur Madrid Melbourne Mexico City Nairobi
New Delhi Shanghai Taipei Toronto

With offices in

Argentina Austria Brazil Chile Czech Republic France Greece
Guatemala Hungary Italy Japan Poland Portugal Singapore
South Korea Switzerland Thailand Turkey Ukraine Vietnam

Oxford is a registered trade mark of Oxford University Press
in the UK and in certain other countries

Published in the United States
by Oxford University Press Inc., New York

© Henri Béjoint 2010

First published 2010 by Oxford University Press

An earlier and much shorter version of this book was published by
Oxford University Press in 1994 as
Tradition and Innovation in Modern English Dictionaries
and reissued in paperback in 2000 as
Modern Lexicography: An Introduction

British Library Cataloguing in Publication Data
Data available
Library of Congress Cataloging-in-Publication Data
Data available
Typeset by SPI Publisher Services, Pondicherry, India
Printed and bound in Great Britain by
CPI Antony Rowe, Chippenham, Wiltshire
ISBN 978–0–19–829967–7

1 3 5 7 9 10 8 6 4 2

CONTENTS

CONTENTS WITH SUBHEADINGS

ACKNOWLEDGEMENTS

I would like to thank my masters in lexicography Guy-Jean Forgue, Josette Rey-Debove, Jean Tournier, and Sue Atkins; my colleagues at Université Lyon 2 Pierre Arnaud, Claude Boisson, François Maniez, and Philippe Thoiron for checking a first draft of the text and correcting errors; Jeremy Harrison for help on many occasions; the anonymous reviewer whose remarks vastly improved the book; my students who taught me as much as I taught them; the dictionary publishers who provided me with dictionaries; John Davey at OUP for his patience during all those years when the book was 'almost finished'; Jake Hicks, the photographer, who took immense pains to get everything right when photographing the dictionary pages for the plate section; Katrin Thier, the OUP librarian, for finding the books in the OED library; Beverley Hunt, the OUP archivist, for finding the photographs of the early OED offices; and Peter Gilliver of the OED (and its official historian) for advice on what and whom they contained. And my wife Dominique.

I have drawn freely on the writings of the best linguists and metalexicographers I know: Sue Atkins, Jean-Claude Boulanger, Tony Cowie, Charles Fillmore, Dirk Geeraerts, Patrick Hanks, Franz-Josef Hausmann, Robert Ilson, Sidney Landau, Tom McArthur, Rosamund Moon, Noel Osselton, Bernard Quemada, Alain Rey, Josette Rey-Debove, Michael Rundell, John Sinclair, Gabriele Stein, Laurence Urdang, Anna Wierzbicka, Ladislav Zgusta, and others who will forgive me if their name is not included here, who know more than I do and write more elegantly than I could. Much of the content comes from them, and some of the form, in the guise of numerous quotations: 'The ability to quote is a serviceable substitute for wit' (W. Somerset Maugham). To that extent, the book is a compilation, in the sense that the word had in the fifteenth century of a work composed by collecting the best of various authors. I have done my best throughout to indicate where I found my inspiration, and I extend my apologies for any omissions that might have slipped through.

Henri Béjoint

Lyon, June 2009

LIST OF PLATES

Acknowledgements

Plate 19 is reproduced by permission of Harper Collins Ltd; Plates 20a and 20b are reproduced by permission of Pearson Ltd; Plate 21 is reproduced by permission of Cambridge University Press; plates 22 and 23 are reproduced by permission of Macmillan Ltd; plate 25 is reproduced by permission of the Wikipedia Foundation Inc.; plates 24 and 26–29 are reproduced by permission of the Secretary to the Delegates of Oxford University Press. All other plates are taken from copies of books in the OED library: these were photographed by Jake Hicks.

1. Title page of *The Dictionary of Syr Thomas Eliot Knyght* (1538).

2. Title page of *The New World of Words*, by E. P. (Edward Phillips) (1671 edition).

3. Page showing the entries from *dictionary to dike-grave* in *The New World of Words*, by E. P. (Edward Phillips) (1671 edition).

4. Title page of Cawdrey's *A Table Alphabeticall* (1604).

5. Title page of Johnson's *A Dictionary of the English Language* (first edition 1755).

6. Page showing the entries *F* to *face* in Johnson's *A Dictionary of the English Language* (first edition 1755).

7. Page showing the entries *hal* to *ham* in Richardson's *A New Dictionary of the English Language* (1836 edition).

8. Page showing the entries *deliver* to *demagogue* in Webster's *An American Dictionary of the English Language* (1828).

9. Page showing the entries *didelphyidæ* to *die* from *The Century Dictionary* (1889–91).

10. Page showing entries for *pursue* from *A New English Dictionary on Historical Principles* (OUP 1928).

11. Page showing the entries for *purpureal* to *purtenance* from *The Shorter Oxford English Dictionary* (1933).

ABBREVIATIONS

ACD	*American College Dictionary*
ACQUILEX	Acquisition of Lexical Knowledge
AFRILEX	African Association for Lexicography
AHD	*American Heritage Dictionary*
AHD1	*American Heritage Dictionary*, First edition
AHD2	*American Heritage Dictionary*, Second edition
AHD3	*American Heritage Dictionary*, Third edition
AHD4	*American Heritage Dictionary*, Fourth edition
ALD	*Advanced Learner's Dictionary*
ALD1	*Advanced Learner's Dictionary*, First edition
ALD2	*Advanced Learner's Dictionary*, Second edition
ALD3	*Advanced Learner's Dictionary*, Third edition
ALD4	*Advanced Learner's Dictionary*, Fourth edition
ALD5	*Advanced Learner's Dictionary*, Fifth edition
ALD6	*Advanced Learner's Dictionary*, Sixth edition
ALD7	*Advanced Learner's Dictionary*, Seventh edition
ALDE	*Advanced Learner's Dictionary*, Encyclopedic edition
ARCHER	A Representative Corpus of Historical English Registers
ASIALEX	Asian Association for Lexicography
AUSTRALEX	Australasia Association for Lexicography
BBI	*The BBI Combinatory Dictionary of English*
BBI2	*The BBI Dictionary of English Word Combinations*
BNC	British National Corpus
BoE	Bank of English
C20D	*Chambers' Twentieth Century Dictionary*
C21D	*Chambers 21st Century Dictionary*
CANCODE	Cambridge and Nottingham Corpus of Discourse in English
CED	*Collins English Dictionary*
CED1	*Collins English Dictionary*, First edition

CED4	*Collins English Dictionary,* Fourth edition
CED9	*Collins English Dictionary,* Ninth edition
CES	Corpus Encoding Standard
CIC	Cambridge International Corpus
CIDE	*Cambridge International Dictionary of English*
CIDE1	*Cambridge International Dictionary of English,* First edition
CIDE2	*Cambridge International Dictionary of English,* Second edition
CIDE3	*Cambridge International Dictionary of English,* Third edition
CL	computational lexicography
CLAWS	Constituent Likelihood Automatic Word-tagging System
COB	*Collins COBUILD English Language Dictionary*
COB1	*Collins COBUILD English Dictionary,* First edition
COB2	*Collins COBUILD English Dictionary,* Second edition
COB3	*Collins COBUILD English Dictionary for Advanced Learners,* Third edition
COB4	*Collins COBUILD English Dictionary for Advanced Learners,* Fourth edition
COB5	*Collins COBUILD English Dictionary for Advanced Learners,* Fifth edition
COB6	*Collins COBUILD English Dictionary for Advanced Learners,* Sixth edition
COBUILD	Collins Birmingham University International Language Database
COD	*Concise Oxford Dictionary*
COD1	*Concise Oxford Dictionary,* First edition
COD2	*Concise Oxford Dictionary,* Second edition
COD4	*Concise Oxford Dictionary,* Fourth edition
COD5	*Concise Oxford Dictionary,* Fifth edition
COD6	*Concise Oxford Dictionary,* Sixth edition
COD7	*Concise Oxford Dictionary,* Seventh edition
COD8	*Concise Oxford Dictionary,* Eighth edition
COD9	*Concise Oxford Dictionary,* Ninth edition
COD10	*Concise Oxford Dictionary,* Tenth edition
COD11	*Concise Oxford Dictionary,* Eleventh edition
CPA	Corpus Pattern Analysis
CQS	corpus query system

CWR	*Cambridge Word Routes*
DARE	*Dictionary of American Regional English*
DEC	dictionnaire explicatif et combinatoire
DFC	*Dictionnaire du français contemporain*
DOST	*Dictionary of the Older Scottish Tongue*
DSNA	Dictionary Society of North America
DTD	Document Type Definition
DWS	dictionary writing system
EAGLES	Expert Advisory Group on Language Engineering Standards
ECD	explanatory and combinatory dictionary
EEBO	Early English Books Online
ELRA	European Language Resources Association
EMEDD	Early Modern English Dictionaries Database
EURALEX	European Association for Lexicography
EWED	*Encarta World English Dictionary*
FSD	full sentence definition
GID	*The Reader's Digest Great Illustrated Dictionary*
GLLF	*Grand Larousse de la langue française*
GPD	general-purpose dictionary
GR	*Grand Robert de la langue française*
ICE	International Corpus of English
ICECUP	ICE Corpus Utility Program
ICLE	International Corpus of Learner English
IJL	*International Journal of Lexicography*
IPA	International Phonetic Alphabet
ISV	International Scientific Vocabulary
KWIC	key word in context
LDEL	*Longman Dictionary of the English Language*
LDEL1	*Longman Dictionary of the English Language*, First edition
LDEL2	*Longman Dictionary of the English Language*, Second edition
LDELC	*Longman Dictionary of English Language and Culture*
LDOCE	*Longman Dictionary of Contemporary English*
LDOCE1	*Longman Dictionary of Contemporary English*, First edition
LDOCE2	*Longman Dictionary of Contemporary English*, Second edition

LDOCE3	*Longman Dictionary of Contemporary English,* Third edition
LDOCE4	*Longman Dictionary of Contemporary English,* Fourth edition
LDOCE5	*Longman Dictionary of Contemporary English,* Fifth edition
LEME	Lexicons of Early Modern English
LLA	*Longman Language Activator*
LLC	London Lund Corpus
LLCE	Longman Lexicon of Contemporary English
LOB	Lancaster Oslo Bergen corpus
LOCNESS	Louvain Corpus of Native English Essays
LRM	Lexical Reference Media
LU	lexical unit
M	million (words)
MEDAL	*Macmillan English Dictionary for Advanced Learners*
MEDAL1	*Macmillan English Dictionary for Advanced Learners,* First edition
MEDAL2	*Macmillan English Dictionary for Advanced Learners,* Second edition
MI	mutual information
MLD	monolingual learner's dictionary
MRD	machine-readable dictionary
MWC1	*Merriam-Webster's Collegiate Dictionary,* First edition
MWC2	*Merriam-Webster's Collegiate Dictionary,* Second edition
MWC7	*Merriam-Webster's Collegiate Dictionary,* Seventh edition
MWC8	*Merriam-Webster's Collegiate Dictionary,* Eighth edition
MWC9	*Merriam-Webster's Collegiate Dictionary,* Ninth edition
MWC10	*Merriam-Webster's Collegiate Dictionary,* Tenth edition
MWC11	*Merriam-Webster's Collegiate Dictionary,* Eleventh edition
NLP	Natural Language Processing
NOAD	*New Oxford American Dictionary*
NODE	*New Oxford Dictionary of English*
NSC	necessary and sufficient conditions
NSD	native speaker's dictionary
NSM	natural semantic metalanguage
ODCIE	*Oxford Dictionary of Current Idiomatic English*
ODE	*Oxford Dictionary of English*
OED	*Oxford English Dictionary*

OED1	*Oxford English Dictionary*, First edition
OED2	*Oxford English Dictionary*, Second edition
OED3	*Oxford English Dictionary*, Third edition
OEDS	*Oxford English Dictionary, Supplement*
OPD	*Oxford Paperback Dictionary*
OUP	Oxford University Press
PED	*Penguin English Dictionary*
PED	pocket electronic dictionary
PL	*Petit Larousse Illustré*
POD	*Pocket Oxford Dictionary*
POS	part of speech
PR	*Petit Robert*
PT	prototype theory
RHC	*Random House College Dictionary*
RHD	*Random House Dictionary of the English Language*
RHD1	*Random House Dictionary of the English Language*, First edition
RHD2	*Random House Dictionary of the English Language*, Second edition
RHW	*Random House Webster's Unabridged Dictionary*
RHWC	*Random House Webster's College Dictionary*
SGML	standard generalized markup language
SND	Scottish National Dictionary
SOED	*Shorter Oxford English Dictionary*
SOED4	*Shorter Oxford English Dictionary*, Fourth edition
SOED5	*Shorter Oxford English Dictionary*, Fifth edition
SOED6	*Shorter Oxford English Dictionary*, Sixth edition
TEI	Text Encoding Initiative
TG	transformational generative grammar
TLF	*Trésor de la langue française*
TLFI	*Trésor de la langue française informatisé*
UKWAC	United Kingdom Web Archiving Consortium
W2	*Webster's New International Dictionary of the English Language*, Second edition
W3	*Webster's Third New International Dictionary of the English Language*
WAT	Woordeboek van die Afrikaanse Taal

WBD	*World Book Dictionary*
WNW	*Webster's New World Dictionary of the American Language*, College edition
WNW1	*Webster's New World Dictionary of the American Language*, First edition
WNW2	*Webster's New World Dictionary of the American Language*, Second edition
WNW3	*Webster's New World Dictionary of the American Language*, Third edition
WNW4	*Webster's New World Dictionary of the American Language*, Fourth edition
WSD	word sense disambiguation
XML	extensible markup language

INTRODUCTION

IN 1994, when Oxford University Press published my book *Tradition and Innovation in Modern English Dictionaries*, lexicography was entering a period of intense activity. Many new dictionaries had been published, as well as an abundant metalexicographic literature, an 'efflorescence of metalexicography' (Ilson 1997: 351), specialized journals had been launched,[1] publishers had created special series of books, international associations of lexicographers had been formed,[2] conferences organized, and specialized courses were beginning to be offered by universities. Now, fifteen years later, lexicography is more active than ever: the quantity of dictionaries and of metalexicographic literature has kept increasing, other associations have been created[3] and conferences are organized all over the world. The French have coined the term *dicomania*[4] to qualify the period. A request for the word *dictionary* on the web via Google can return 500,000,000 occurrences in 0.05 seconds.

But the lexicography of 2010 is not the lexicography of 1994. Dictionaries have changed in many ways. More are now published in electronic format, on CD-ROM or online. All lexicographers now use computers, and many also use corpora. Many linguists have produced work that is relevant to dictionary making and that has begun to have an influence on dictionaries. Neither the computer nor the corpus or the use of linguistics have solved all the problems of lexicography—a dictionary is still the produce of the competence of the lexicographer and of his pedagogical skills—but they have brought about profound changes in the dictionary text and in the job of the lexicographer.

---

[1] *Cahiers de lexicologie* (1959), *Dictionaries* (1979), *Lexique* (1982), *Lexicographica* (1985), *International Journal of Lexicography* (1988), *Lexikos* (1991).
[2] DSNA (1975), EURALEX (1983), AUSTRALEX (1990).
[3] AFRILEX (1995), ASIALEX (1997).   [4] *Dico* is short for *dictionnaire*.

The dictionary has always been a highly popular genre in all countries. In 1985 in Britain, 'over 90 per cent of households possess[ed] at least one, making the dictionary far more popular than cookery books (about 70 per cent) and indeed significantly more widespread than the Bible (which was to be found in 80 per cent of households in England in 1983, according to the Bible Society)' (Ilson 1985b: 1). In a survey investigating the notion of deprivation in Britain, a dictionary was among the items judged to be 'a necessity' by 53 per cent of the respondents, 'above cars, dressing-gowns, newspapers, evenings out, VCRs, and Internet access' (Moon 2002: 629). In the USA in 1989, 87 per cent of American homes had a dictionary (Algeo 1989a: 37). In France, there is an average of more than one dictionary per household[5] and prison directors 'do not like to buy dictionaries for their libraries: it is a kind of book that is immediately stolen, they say' (Collinot and Mazière 1997: 175).

The dictionary is a strange commercial object. The same dictionary is often published in different versions: concise, college, desk, school, or mini; for the family, for the teenager, for schoolchildren, for particular countries, sometimes for specific American states. The exact same dictionary text is often published under different guises, bound in plastic or leather, with or without pictures, in colour or in black and white, with a thumb-index or without, in bigger print, etc. A dictionary can have different titles on the dust jacket, on the back of the book, on the title page, etc. Also, some dictionaries are produced by obscure publishers and have very short life spans, few copies being produced and sold. Some are marketed only in bookshops specializing in books at reduced prices, in railway-station bookstalls or in supermarkets, some are sold only by mail (Landau 1994a: 318). Some dictionaries are old texts with only minor adjustments, and some are still sold years after their replacements were published. And it is often difficult to know how new a dictionary is: there are new editions, revised editions, updated editions, new printings, but the labels do not mean much and the details are often obscure, or absent (Landau 2001: 453).

This is a book about lexicography, as the title indicates, more particularly about the lexicography of English. There are so many dictionaries published in English-speaking countries that it is impossible to list—let alone examine—them all, and the book focuses on the monolingual general-purpose dictionary, the most popular type, the one that has the closest connections with the society in which it is produced, and probably the most interesting to study from the points of view of sociology and of linguistics. Many dates have been important for English lexicography: 1604, the publication of *A Table Alphabeticall*, the first

---

[5] http://www.u-cergy.fr/dictionnaires/

monolingual dictionary; 1755, the publication of Johnson's *Dictionary*; 1828, the publication of Webster's *American Dictionary*; 1929, the *Oxford English Diction-ary*; 1960, the first conference on lexicography in the English-speaking world at Bloomington, Indiana; 1961, *Webster's Third New International Dictionary*; 1963, the *Advanced Learner's Dictionary*, the first major learner's dictionary; 1978, the *Longman Dictionary of Contemporary English*, the first dictionary with a con-trolled vocabulary and available on magnetic tape; 1987, the *COBUILD Diction-ary of the English Language*, the first dictionary based on a corpus. The most interesting monolingual general-purpose dictionaries of English will be exam-ined chronologically, within the lexicographic tradition to which they belong: what are the continuities, if any, between the first dictionaries of hard words and the dictionaries of the early twenty-first century? What are the similarities and the differences between Britain and the USA? The object is not to list all the features of all dictionaries but to show the evolution, or absence of evolution, that constitutes the history of lexicography. The dictionaries will also be exam-ined synchronically in the context of what Hausmann (1984) has called the *paysage dictionnairique* of the two countries since 1950.

The first part of the book is about what the dictionaries of English have been and are, and the second about what dictionaries are and could be. The first part is about dictionaries, the second about compiling processes to produce dic-tionary text to be published in paper or electronic format. The main thesis is that three factors have been influencing dictionaries since the last decades of the twentieth century and will continue to influence them—user studies, linguis-tics, and the use of the computer—and that progress in those three domains will determine the quality of the dictionaries of the future. A secondary thesis is that English dictionaries are a good example, probably the best example, of the evolution of lexicography from the seventeenth to the twenty-first century and beyond.

The book is not a manual of practical lexicography. It is not a history of lexicography nor a treatise on how linguistics can be applied to dictionaries, but a bit of all that. It will be found weak or wanting on many aspects, but as Johnson wrote in his *Preface*, 'In this work, when it shall be found that much is omitted, let it not be forgotten that much likewise is performed.'

The book examines the general-purpose dictionaries of English from the point of view of someone who is not a native speaker. Being an outsider is obviously a disadvantage, but it may also procure angles that the native speaker does not have: 'When one wants to study men, one must look at one's neighbours; but to study man, one must learn to cast one's look afar; one must first observe the differences in order to discover the properties,' Jean-Jacques Rousseau noted in his *Essay on the Origin of Languages*. Dictionaries are so familiar to us all, such faithful companions, such subtle mirrors of the characteristics of ourselves and our societies that it may be easier for the outsider to see how strange they are, and how different they could have been. The dictionaries that we know are the result of a complex interaction between what the public needs and wants and what the publishers and the lexicographers are capable of producing, and the lexicographic traditions that have solidified over the centuries are now so deeply ingrained in our societies as to go unnoticed.

A full comparison between the lexicographies of English and of French was beyond the scope of the book, but I wanted to bring in some of the concepts and methods of French metalexicography and apply them to English dictionaries. Also, it was interesting to compare the French lexicographic tradition with the traditions of Britain and the USA, to see how close they were and how different. In the process other local traditions—the Spanish, the German, the Italian, the Dutch—that would have been equally interesting, had to be left unexplored.

Much of metalexicography is simply descriptive, and a lot of this book certainly is. But description may not be enough. I have tried to delve a little further whenever I could, keeping in mind all the time that I needed to avoid the two extremes of seeing faults everywhere and excusing all weaknesses. Linguists often expose the faults of dictionaries but rarely propose any viable solutions to improve them. Their writings exhibit a profusion of *shoulds* and *shouldn'ts*, as if they had all the answers, but they never consider the language as a whole, as lexicographers must. The other extreme attitude is to excuse all the foibles of dictionaries with the argument that lexicographers do not have the time, or the money, or both, to take on board what linguists, psycholinguists, sociolinguists, and specialists of all sorts have written. This may be true, but it is an explanation, not an excuse, if dictionaries are to evolve and adapt to the societies that produce them. The linguists who criticize dictionaries are useless if they indulge in what some have called *lexicographiction* (Descamps and Vaunaize 1983: 109), and the lexicographers who hide behind their working conditions, the poor skills of the average dictionary user, the weight of social pressures, or the dire realities of business to excuse their shortcomings are no better.

The terms used in lexicography are tricky. As in all the branches of linguistics, many are difficult to define: *sense, meaning, referent* and *reference, denotation* and *connotation, word, concept, idiom, collocation, phrase, synonym, register, dialect,* etc. The English of lexicography also has its own hesitations on form: what are the plurals of *corpus,* of *index,* of *thesaurus*? Is it *thesauruses* or *thesauri* (Landau 2001: 438)? Should I say *lexicographic* or *lexicographical, monosemous* or *monosemic, unilingual* or *monolingual, multilingual* or *plurilingual, collocate* or *collocator*?

And there are difficulties of translation: how does one say '*dictionnaire de langue*' in English? And '*dictionnaire analogique*', '*dictionnaire de mots*', '*dictionnaire de choses*'?

The origin of this book is a passionate love of dictionaries, perhaps the trace of a childhood during which they were adored because they were rare and because they represented a social status that seemed unattainable. It is the pleasure of holding those thick and heavy volumes, those treasures of the knowledge of others, of opening them at random, of discovering the riches of a language and a culture, those impressively resourceful tools that have the answers to—almost— all our questions. Dictionaries are an endless source of enjoyment, and perhaps the most important object of this book is to try to persuade the reader that lexicography is a fascinating domain. 'I have never met a person who is not interested in language,' writes Steven Pinker to begin *The Language Instinct*; I have hardly ever met anyone who is not interested in dictionaries.

DICTIONARIES AND THE DICTIONARY

1.1 DEFINITIONS

THE word *dictionary* was coined on the basis of the Latin forms *dictionarius* or *dictionarium*, from *dictio*, 'action of saying', or 'word', itself from the verb *dicere*, 'say'. According to the *Oxford English Dictionary* (*OED*), *dictionarius* was used for the first time *c.*1225 by the poet and grammarian Joannes de Garlandia, or John of Garland(e) (*c.*1195–*c.*1272) as the title of his compilation of Latin vocables, sayings, and maxims arranged according to their subjects, with glosses in French or English, published in Paris, for the use of learners. The first recorded use of *dictionarium* was in 1340 as the title of part 3 of the *Reductorium, repertorium et dictionarium morale utriusque testamenti* of Pierre Bersuire, or Peter Bercharius, or Berchorius (*c.*1290–1362), a friend of Petrarch. This was an alphabetically arranged glossary of more than 3,000 words from the Bible, with moral expositions, 'moralizations on the chief words of the Vulgate for the use of students in theology' (*OED*).

The first use of *dictionary* recorded by the *OED* is almost two centuries later, in 1526, by W. Bonde in *A Pilgrimage of Perfection*: 'And so Peter Bercharius in his dictionary describeth it.' In 1538 it was used for the first time as a title by Thomas Eliot, or Elyot, for his collection of Latin words with English equivalents, *The Dictionary of Syr Thomas Eliot Knyght* (Plate 1): 'About a yere passed I beganne a Dictionarie, declaryng latine by englishe' (*Preface*). In French, the word *dictionaire*[1] was first used in *Le Jardin de Plaisance et fleur de rhétorique*, a collection of texts

---

[1] The modern spelling with two *n*'s appeared later. In 1763, Féraud still used *Dictionaire*. On the use of *diction(n)aire* in French, see Brunet (1992) and Boulanger (2003).

published *c.*1501 by Antoine Vérard. It was first used as a title in 1538, the same year as in England, by Robert Estienne for his *Dictionaire francois-latin.*

Other Indo-European languages have words from the same Latin origin: Spanish has *diccionario,* Italian *dizionario,* Portuguese *dicionário,* Romanian *dictionar,* Catalan *diccionari.* Another pattern is English *wordbook,* Dutch *woordenboek,* German *Wörterbuch.* Swedish and Norwegian have *ordbok,* Danish *ordbog.* Russian has *slovar* and Polish *slovnik,* from *slov,* 'word'.

The concept of the dictionary remained vague for a long time (Matoré 1968: 58–60). The words *dictionary* and *diction(n)aire* have been used 'for all sorts of presentations of information about "words", however conceived' (McArthur 1986*b*: 79), works that would not be considered as dictionaries now. Some were encyclopedias, the most famous example being the illustrious *Encyclopédie ou Dictionnaire raisonné des sciences, des arts et des métiers* in 35 volumes, published between 1751 and 1772 by Denis Diderot and Jean Le Rond d'Alembert. Some were books containing various alphabetically arranged items, such as Voltaire's *Dictionnaire philosophique, ou la raison par l'alphabet* (1764), Flaubert's *Dictionnaire des idées reçues* (1847) or Ambrose Bierce's *Devil's Dictionary* (1906). Some were simply books about words: in 1830, David Booth published *An Analytical Dictionary of the English Language,* which was a continuous text, a sort of treatise explaining the words of philosophy (Hüllen 2004*a*/2005: 315–19). And there is even a 'lexicon novel' by Milorad Pavic called *Dictionary of the Khazars* (1988).

On the other hand, dictionaries in the modern sense have been published under many other names. Early European dictionaries were called *abecedarium, alphabetum, alvearium, biblioteca, declaratio, descriptio, glossarium, (h)ortus, lexicon, liber floridus, manipulus, medulla, promptuarium, promptorium, repertorium, summa, tabula, terminarius, thesaurus, vocabularius, vocabularium, vulgaria,* etc. (McArthur 1998: 195–6; Boulanger 2003: 428 *ff.*). In French, they were *alphabet, vocabulaire, glossaire, syllabaire,* even *préservatif* or *omnibus du langage* (Matoré 1968: 117). The word *thrésor,* or *trésor,* modelled on the Latin *thesaurus,* 'treasure-house' in Greek, was used by Jean Nicot[2] for his *Thresor de la langue françoise* (1606). In English, early dictionaries have been called *alveary, expositor, glossary, lexicon, table alphabetical, thesaurus, treasury,* etc. (Murray 1993: 106).[3] Some dictionaries had titles that used none of these words: a strange

---

[2] Jean Nicot (1530–1600), named Jacques Nicot in my edition of the *New Shorter Oxford English Dictionary,* was the French ambassador to Lisbon who sent tobacco (*l'herbe à Nicot,* 'Nicot's grass') to Catherine of Medicis in France in 1560. His dictionary can be consulted on the website of the University of Toronto.

[3] On picturesque dictionary titles, see Rey (1982: 12–16).

example is *Dieu, l'homme et la parole*, a highly original etymological dictionary published in 1853 by J. Azaïs. Dictionaries in manuscript form often did not have any titles at all.[4]

1.1.1 *What is a dictionary?*

All modern dictionaries have a definition of *dictionary*—although it is difficult to imagine someone consulting a dictionary to know what a dictionary is.[5] In English, the first was E. P.'s *New World of Words*, published in 1658, which said (Plate 3)

a Book wherein hard words and names are mentioned, and unfolded.

For French, the first was Richelet's *Dictionnaire francois*, published in 1680:

Livre qui contient les mots d'une langue, d'un art ou d'une science par ordre alphabétique.[6]

Clearly, there were already differences between the two countries. For Matoré (1968: 20), the only good definition of *dictionnaire* in a dictionary was in the *OED*:[7]

A book dealing with the individual words of a language (or certain specified classes of them), so as to set forth their orthography, pronunciation, signification and use, their synonyms, derivation, and history, or at least some of these facts: for convenience of reference, the words are arranged in some stated order, now, in most languages, alphabetical; and in larger dictionaries the information given is illustrated by quotations from literature.

But Rey (1977: 57) did not like it: 'words are not the only eligible units, single words unduly eliminate coded phrases, the definition is restricted to monolingual dictionaries, definitions and word histories characterize only one particular type of dictionary.' For him, it was only a definition of the *OED* itself: 'In fact, what is described, rather than defined, is a socio-cultural dictionary type which did not exist before 1860 and is outdated one century later' (Rey 1977: 57).

---

[4] They are referred to by their first entry or entries.
[5] Nagy (2004: 115) mentions 'a cartoon [in a newspaper] depicting a curious reader who wants to find out what the dictionary says about itself' and finds the following definition: '1. what are you, some sort of wise guy? You know &*%$ well what a dictionary is, you're holding one you dumb @#$*! Now put me down and stop goofing off.
[6] 'A book that contains the words of a language, an art or a science, in alphabetical order.'
[7] This is the main definition in a longer entry.

The *Encarta World English Dictionary* (1999) has six meanings for *dictionary*, the *Reader's Digest Great Illustrated Dictionary* (1984) five, the *OED* (1989) four, the *Collins English Dictionary* (1979) three. The *New Oxford Dictionary of English* (1998) sees only two, perhaps one and a half. The first is the usual meaning:

a book that lists the words of a language in alphabetical order and gives their meaning, or that gives the equivalent words in a different language.

and the second is more general:

a reference book on any subject, the items of which are arranged in alphabetical order.

Lexicographers,[8] when they are not writing dictionaries, and metalexicographers[9] have their own definitions, which do not have to be as concise as dictionary definitions. Quemada, in his study of French dictionaries from the origins to 1863, was confronted with their diversity over more than three centuries and he proposed a broad definition: 'A dictionary is above all a catalogue of words which is designed to give easy access to items of information whose quantity and nature are left to the appreciation of the author' (1968: 14). Mel'čuk (1992: 332) also had a vague formula: 'A specific list of lexical units of a language, arranged in a specific way and supplied with specific information, the whole being designed for a specific purpose.' Zgusta (1971: 17) was more precise:

A dictionary is a systematically arranged list of socialized linguistic forms compiled from the speech-habits of a given speech-community and commented on by the author in such a way that the qualified reader understands the meaning...of each separate form, and is informed of the relevant facts concerning the function of that form in its community.

Rey's definition (1970*a*: 165) was written in a language that was typical of the 1960s and 1970s in the history of French linguistics: 'an ordered list of graphic and didactic statements about sign-units which function in the system of one natural language or several.' The best definition of *dictionnaire* is in Rey-Debove's study

---

[8] The word *lexicographer*, meaning 'someone who writes dictionaries', was first used in 1658, according to the *OED*. English also had *dictionarist* and *lexicographist*. Instead of *lexicographe*, French had the word *dictio(n)nariste* until at least the middle of the eighteenth century, for example in Trévoux (1732) and Féraud (1763).

[9] The word *métalexicographie* may have been coined by Rey and Delesalle (1979), but Hausmann (1988: 80) alludes to an earlier source that I have been unable to trace. Hausmann (1989*b*: 216) defines it (in German) as 'a complex of activities concerned with the dictionary as an object of reflection and research rather than the production of dictionaries' (translated by Hartmann 2001: 28). *Metalexicographer* may have a pejorative connotation when it is used by lexicographers to refer to people who criticize their activities but have never compiled a dictionary.

of French dictionaries (1971: 27), again written in typical French linguistic terminology of the times:

A dictionary is a didactic book that describes a (generally structured) set of linguistic elements and presents them in separate and ordered units, thus allowing for consultation. The elements, which range from the letter to elements that are above sentence-length, are usually followed by paragraphs (two structures, or only one). The information, whether implicit (one structure) or explicit (two structures), follows a pre-determined program and is always, at least in part, about the sign; in the explicit information that seems to be only about the referent, the presence of a definition is taken as information about the sign.

We will take the main points of this definition one after the other to list the main features of dictionaries.

1.1.1.1 A dictionary is a series of separate paragraphs

Dictionaries, like phone books, mail-order catalogues, and some encyclopedias are strings of independent paragraphs called *articles* or *entries*.[10] A dictionary is 'a collection of fragments' (Hitchings 2005: 103) that are not meant to be read in succession, as only the different parts of each entry are related. The rare cases where succeeding entries are semantically related, as with *cigar* and *cigarette*, are the exception rather than the rule in English and French—although they may be more common in other languages.

One of the big challenges of lexicography is to ensure that the text of the dictionary is consistent, even though it is made up of so many unconnected pieces. The different entries must not disagree, and each entry must be treated in a way that corresponds as much as possible to its position and relative importance in the language.

1.1.1.2 A dictionary is meant to be consulted, not read

The text of a dictionary, being a succession of unconnected paragraphs, is normally consulted rather than read, as in all reference works, which are 'for consultation rather than perusal' (Ilson 1997: 353). Typically only one entry or part of an entry is consulted at a time. Of course, some dictionaries are more readable, or 'browsable', than others: Johnson's *Dictionary* has been described as the 'first dictionary that could be read with pleasure' (Macaulay, in Downie 1918: 22), and the *OED* has been called 'first class reading' (Considine 1998: 580). One finds stories of people who said that they had read a dictionary from cover to

---

[10] The term *entry* is sometimes also used to refer to the lexical item heading the paragraph.

cover, either because they thought it was a good way of acquiring knowledge, or simply because they found it pleasant: 'William Pitt, the First Earl of Chatham, found Bailey's dictionary[11] both entertaining and profitable reading' (Starnes and Noyes 1946: 100), and Robert Browning read all of Johnson's dictionary to '"qualify" himself as an author' (Hitchings 2005: 3).

The consultation of a dictionary was despised by D'Alembert (1763/1965: 122), who thought that alphabetized dictionaries—not the *Encyclopédie*—could only be used by people who did not have enough education to read primary sources, or who were too lazy.

These collections can only procure some enlightenment to those who would not be perseverant enough to secure it for themselves without such help; but they will never replace true Books for those who seek to educate themselves; dictionaries being designed as they are can only be consulted, and do not lend themselves to proper reading.

In his *Dictionnaire des idées reçues*, Flaubert 'defined' *dictionnaire* as 'En dire: "N'est fait que pour les ignorants."'[12] Dictionaries are indeed repositories of small fragments of information that can be digested quickly. That is one of the reasons why lexicographers have tended to be considered as specialists of the trivial detail, people who delight in negligible minutiae, curio collectors, obsessive nitpickers, at best humble, dull, serious, hard-working artisans, the harmless drudges evoked by Johnson (see below, 2.3.2) and many others, and at worst severe, pompous, and futile schoolmasters.

1.1.1.3 Dictionaries have a double structure

The terms *macrostructure* and *microstructure*, now commonly used in French and in English, were introduced by Rey-Debove (Lehmann 2006: 202).[13] Macrostructure, she said, is the arrangement of the list of entry words[14] in each dictionary, 'the complete set of entries arranged in some order, part of which is always used for vertical scanning when the user is looking for a particular piece of information. The macrostructure is commonly called "nomenclature"' (Rey-Debove 1971: 21). *Macrostructure* can indeed be used as a synonym of *nomenclature*, or *wordlist*, but it may be useful to distinguish the two: *nomenclature* to refer to the list of lexical items that are treated in a dictionary, and *macrostructure* for the same list

[11] It was Bailey's *Universal Etymological English Dictionary* (1721).
[12] 'Say: "Is only meant for the ignorant"'.
[13] In English, they are sometimes spelt *macro-structure* and *micro-structure*.
[14] The entry word (or *entry-word*) is also called *entry, entry-form, main entry, headword*, or *look-up form*.

once it has been organized to constitute the 'architecture' of the dictionary.[15] The macrostructure organizes the nomenclature in entries and sub-entries.[16]

The word *microstructure* refers to 'the set of pieces of information as they are ordered in every article,... which are meant to be read horizontally after the entry word' (Rey-Debove 1971: 21). The microstructure of a dictionary is composed of a certain number of information items, or fields, which vary in nature according to the type of dictionary (pronunciation, etymology, synonyms, etc.) and in arrangement according to each individual dictionary. My edition of *Petit Robert*[17] dated 1995, for example, has spelling, pronunciation, part of speech (POS), etymology, usage label,[18] definition, example, and cross-reference[19] in simple entries, always in the same order. In complex entries, some of the microstructural information, such as the definition and sometimes the syntactic behaviour, is specific to each sub-entry or part of the entry but other elements such as pronunciation, etymology, etc. are given only once for the whole entry, at the beginning or at the end.

The terms *microstructure* and *macrostructure* were coined in the 1970s at a time when the word *structure* and the corresponding concept were very popular among scientists, and every scientific notion had to be structural. In Rey-Debove's view, *structure* referred to a pre-established organization in which none of the constituting elements could be modified without modifying the whole. This is fairly clear in the case of the microstructure, which is a programme systematically applied to all the entries, with the same information, *mutatis mutandis*, always given in the same order. This is what modern dictionaries do, but those of earlier periods were often less systematic. There was very little structure in the articles of, for example, the earliest editions of the *Dictionnaire de l'Académie* (Leroy-Turcan 1996),[20] and Samuel Johnson's dictionary was not rigidly structured in the modern sense either.

---

[15] The word *nomenclature* is also used in French with both meanings: the wordlist of a dictionary before its elements are organized, and the ordered list. Bogaards (1996: 281), like Rey-Debove, uses *macrostructure* for 'the total number of entries'.

[16] A *sub-entry* is the treatment of a lexical item within another entry.

[17] PR. First published 1967.

[18] A usage label is a noun or adjective indicating the kind of context in which the word is normally used: *slang, literary, American, Medicine*, etc. Usage labels are usually abbreviated (*sl, lit, US, med*, etc.). They are of different kinds, social, geographical, stylistic, etc., corresponding to different varieties of language.

[19] A *cross-reference* is a reference from an entry to another in the same dictionary: 'see x', 'cf x', etc.

[20] The *Dictionnaire de l'Académie française*, first conceived in 1636, was published for the first time in 1694, with editions in 1718, 1740, 1762, 1798, 1835, 1878, and 1932. The ninth edition is under way: as of May 2007, 2 volumes have been published (A–Enz and Éoc–Map), and entries as far as *patte* can be consulted on the web.

In the case of the macrostructure, the structure is less clear than for the microstructure. The lexical items are organized according to their morphology and to their meaning, but the macrostructure is at best a loose structure: items can be added or subtracted without causing major problems to the whole. However, the same type of macrostructure (see below, 8.2.2.1) must be used in all entries.

It is impossible to imagine a dictionary without a macrostructure: all dictionaries have a list of entry words, and if the list is not organized the book is not a dictionary. Some dictionaries, for example spelling dictionaries, crossword dictionaries, etc., seem to have no microstructure, but this is an illusion. No dictionary can avoid giving, at the very least, two pieces of information about a lexical item: the fact that it belongs to the language or variety of language that the dictionary represents—this is macrostructural information—and how it is spelt—this is microstructural information. In the larger dictionaries, those sub-entries that are just listed and only have implicit microstructural information are called *run-ons*, or *run-on entries*.[21]

Many other types of documents, cookery books, guidebooks, phone books, or mail-order catalogues have two structures. In all of them, the entries that make up the nomenclature are organized in a macrostructure and are given a microstructural treatment: price, description, address, ingredients, telephone number, etc. In the dictionary, however, the macrostructure is made up of the words of a language, the microstructure gives information about those words, not about the things that the words refer to (see below), and the two structures are connected: all the words of the macrostructure have a microstructure and all the words used in the microstructure are included in the macrostructure: the dictionary is closed (see below, 8.2.5.4).[22]

The notions of macrostructure and microstructure are useful, because they organize the dictionary neatly in two intersecting directions, vertical (or paradigmatic) for the macrostructure and horizontal (or syntagmatic)[23] for the microstructure. But they are not as simple as they look. The question is: what is the macrostructure made of? The simple answer is that the macrostructure is

---

[21] *Run-on entries* are often used for derivatives: for example, the entry *understand* may also contain *understandable, understandably*, etc.

[22] 'Closedness' normally applies to the whole dictionary, but Allen (1986: 1) notes that the Fowler brothers, compilers of the *Concise Oxford Dictionary* (1911), used the word *telegraphese* in their *Preface* to qualify their defining style though it was not defined in the dictionary.

[23] The terms *syntagmatic* and *paradigmatic* were introduced by Saussure. *Syntagmatic* refers to the arrangement of the elements of discourse (phoneme, morpheme, lexical item, etc.) one after the other; it is a relation *in presentia*. *Paradigmatic* refers to the set of elements that can be inserted in any given slot of the syntagmatic chain; it is a relation *in absentia*.

the list of headwords, the lexical items that begin each entry. But what about those that head the sub-entries, for example *liaise* in the entry *liaison*, or *walk the plank* at *plank*? What about run-on entries such as *electrically* in the entry *electrical*? And why not every single meaning in polysemous entries that is given some microstructural treatment, even if minimal? The answers to those questions will determine the number of 'words' that the publishers of the dictionary will advertise (see below, 4.3.2), but more importantly they rest on the question of the nature of the lexical item: is it a form, a word, a meaning? We will see that individual meanings are even more difficult to identify than words (see below, 8.2.3), and that their organization requires more sophisticated methods than the organization of words.

The meaning of *microstructure* depends on the meaning one gives to *macrostructure*, and vice versa. If the macrostructure is the list of headwords, all the information in the entries, including complex ones, is microstructural, the division into sub-entries and into separate senses; if it is a list of individual meanings, then distinguishing meanings in polysemous lexemes is the job of the macrostructure, and the microstructure is the information given about each meaning. This means that the compilation of a dictionary cannot deal with macrostructure first and then move on to microstructure: the two are inseparable.

Because of those difficulties, the concepts of macrostructure and microstructure are not as useful as was first thought. Some metalexicographers have proposed the notion of *address*, which refers to any element, headword, sub-headword, run-on, meaning, etc. to which microstructural information—a definition, an explanation, an illustration, an example, etc.—applies.[24] The notion of address shifts the emphasis on the relation between macrostructure and microstructure and sidesteps the problem of the unit of macrostructure. It is, Ilson says enthusiastically, 'a conceptual tool of breathtaking power for the analysis of the parts of dictionary entries and how they are related' (Ilson 1997: 354), but it has not been widely adopted.

Other terms using *-structure* have recently appeared (Hartmann and James 1998): *megastructure* for the organization of the different parts of a dictionary, from the first to the last page, including the A–Z text; *mediostructure* for the system of cross-references; *iconostructure* for the organization of pictorial illustrations (Boulanger 2003: 13), etc.

---

[24] *Address* is not much used in this sense in English and is not even in the *OED*. *Adresse* is sometimes used in French lexicography, probably from the English, in the sense of entry or headword.

1.1.1.4 A dictionary is an ordered list of items

Because the dictionary is designed for consultation, the text must be arranged in such a way that all the items of the macrostructure have a precise position, so that the users can quickly find what they need (Rey-Debove 1971: 20). The entries must be classified according to simple criteria, so that the users will have no difficulty mastering the rules. All reference works, catalogues, directories, indexes, atlases, etc. also organize their contents to make them accessible.

Some of the earliest ancestors of modern dictionaries were so short, a few hundred words, that they had no classification at all: old Tibetan dictionaries (Goldstein 1991) and probably some dictionaries in Sumer (Boisson *et al.* 1991) were just lists of words in no particular order. The need for classification appeared when glossaries contained too many words for easy consultation, a step towards the modern dictionary (Boulanger 2003: 259).

Words can be classified either by their forms, sound or spelling, or by their meanings. Classification by sound has been used in some dictionaries: in *Le Robert oral-écrit, L'orthographe par la phonétique* (1989), for example, *doute* is before *doigt*, because [dut] comes before [dwa]. But such dictionaries are difficult to use. In most dictionaries words are classified by graphic form. Different languages have different rules for classifying words graphically: Sumerian, Chinese, Japanese, Arabic, etc. use, or used, keys, roots, radicals, etc. (Zgusta 1989*b*, 2006: 198 *ff.*; Haywood 1986), and Indo-European languages use their own versions of the alphabet containing their letters with diacritics: *á, ç, è, î* in French, *ñ* in Spanish, *ö* in Norwegian, the *haček* in Czech, etc.

Since the beginnings of alphabetical ordering, words have been classified by their first letter or letters—ordering by the last letters is possible but has never been popular.[25] The use of the beginning of the word was common practice for Greek lexicographers in ancient times and was then forgotten, to be re-discovered in Europe in the Middle Ages (Boulanger 2003: 276, 415).[26] When lexicographers began using the alphabet in bilingual glossaries, it was firmly established, and there was little hesitation on letters and their order. The only differences with the modern alphabet were for U and V, which were considered as the same letter for a long time, and for I and J. The first dictionary to distinguish them in English was

---

[25] That is what reverse dictionaries do. They are useful for crossword puzzles, for writing poetry and for linguists studying suffixation. See A. F. Brown's *Normal and Reverse English Word List*, 8 volumes (Philadelphia: University of Pennsylvania, 1963), Martin Lehnert's *Reverse Dictionary of Present-Day English* (Leipzig: Verlag Enzyklopädie, 1971), Richard C. Herbst's *Backword Dictionary for Puzzled People* (New York: Alamo Publishing Company, 1979), etc.

[26] On the history of alphabetic ordering, see Boulanger (2002, 2003).

William Perry's *The Royal Standard English Dictionary*, published in 1778 (Ossel-ton 2005: 548), and in French it was Jean-François Féraud's *Dictionnaire critique de la langue française* in 1787.[27]

In the beginning, lexicographers used only the first letter of the entry word: this was an 'a-order' (Stein 2002: 8). Then, the second letter was used (an 'ab-order'), then the third ('abc-order'), as in Papias' *Elementarium doctrinae rudi-mentum*, composed around 1050 (Boulanger 2003: 273 *ff.*, 411). Sometimes only the first consonant and the first vowel were considered: if the word began with two consonants the second was disregarded (Boulanger 2002: 12–13; 407 *ff.*). In 1690, Furetière's *Dictionnaire* still used a system that did not include all the letters of the headword (Boulanger 2002: 23) but many lexicographers had by then adopted the new system (McArthur 1986*b*: 76; Boulanger 2003: 259, 373 *ff.*, 415). In 1602, John Withals, in the introduction to a later edition of his dictionary, *A shorte Dictionarie of English and Latin for Yonge Beginners*, originally published in 1553, noted that all lexicographers had adopted a complete alphabetical order (Hüllen 1999/2006: 176), which was not quite true, since Johnson's *Dictionary*, in 1755, was still not strictly alphabetical in the modern sense (Landau 2001: 19), but it shows what the general tendency was. Johnson was aware of it: in the *Preface* to Richard Rolt's *New Dictionary of Trade and Commerce*, published in 1761, he wrote: 'it has lately been the practice of the learned to range knowledge by the alphabet.'

The adoption of a complete alphabetical order using all the letters of the word was an important step in the development of dictionaries. Yet the whole process took a long time, extending over seven centuries. There were several reasons: one is that many of the glosses collected from manuscripts to compile the very first dictionaries (see below, 2.1.2) were in abbreviated form (Boulanger 2003: 417); another is that for a long time languages did not have a unified spelling; and a third, perhaps, is that some religious authorities disapproved of alphabetical ordering, because it failed to reflect God's perfect organization of the world. At least, that is what Boulanger (2003: 409, 422) says, although he does not provide the evidence.

Arranging the headwords in alphabetical order is standard procedure in modern lexicography, but the operation is far from simple. There are many problems that cannot be solved satisfactorily and consistently, and the whole thing is still 'a quagmire' for lexicographers preparing a paper dictionary (Atkins and Rundell 2008: 190). Difficult areas are the positioning of words with diacritics, of words with capital letters (which should come first, *wash*, or *Wash*?), of

---

[27] François Gaudin, personal communication.

abbreviations, of multiword items, not to mention the formulations that do not use letters (9/11) (Landau 2001: 107–9). Abbreviations can be placed according to the letters that are used or according to the letters of the words that they stand for: *DIY* between *divulge* and *dizzy* or, because the *D* stands for *do*, between *do* and *docile*. The former is by far the commoner, and the more reasonable, solution. Multiword items pose a double problem: the choice of the entry word and the treatment of the space between the words: *ice cream* can be in the letter I for *ice*, or in the letter C for *cream*. Most dictionaries use the first word, but not all, and not always. The best solution is to place multiword items at all the entries for each of their constituent words, but this is too space consuming in most paper dictionaries. If one word must be chosen, it should be the word that the users are most likely to use—except that no one really knows, in spite of the research that has been carried out on the subject (see below, 7.2.3.4). In electronic dictionaries, or *e-dictionaries*, however, many of those problems are easily solved, since the users can type in a word and the machine will locate it wherever it has been placed (Jackson 2002: 159). If a multiword item has a separate entry, the problem is what to do with the space between the words: one can have, for example, *post*, *postilion*, *post office*, etc., or *post*, *post office*, *postilion*, etc. Roughly, the first solution is typical of American, and the second of British, dictionaries (Landau 2001: 107). Again, the problem no longer exists in e-dictionaries.

Alphabetical ordering does not account for the semantic relations between words: it separates those that are related and puts side-by-side words that have no relation. In an alphabetical dictionary, meaning is at the end of the process for the compiler and for the user: the dictionary is semasiological, i.e. to be used from the form of a lexical item to its meaning, as in reception, or comprehension, or decoding, rather than onomasiological, i.e. going from the meaning to the sign, as in expression, or encoding.[28] A more satisfactory solution from the point of view of semantics and for expression is the grouping of words by meaning, in themes, families, fields, domains, categories, networks, sets, types, etc., permitting onomasiological consultation. Dictionaries organized by meaning have been called *non-alphabetical, conceptual, ideographic, ideological, notional, onomasiological, semantic, systematic, thematic, topical*, etc. (McArthur 1998: 149 *ff.*), or again *thesaurus* or *lexicon* (Hüllen 1999/2006). Pruvost (2006: 111 *ff.*) distinguishes four subtypes: '*synonymique*' for dictionaries that organize words in groups of synonyms,

<hr/>

[28] 'Christian K. Reisig used the term *Semasiologie, semasiologisch* for the first time in his lectures on Latin philology in 1825' (Hüllen 1999/2006: 16, referring to Davies 1998: 311–14) in German; *onomasiologie* and *onomasiologisch* were first used in 1903 by A. Zauner 'in a study of the names of body parts in the Romance languages' (Babini 2000: 70).

'*analogique*' for those that group words having common semantic features, '*méthodique*' for those that group words in themes and '*idéologique*' for those that organize words according to a vision of the universe. But those labels are not clear, and the choice of a title seems to be as much a question of usage, tradition, and commercial prospects as of contents or presentation.

Dictionaries whose contents are organized by meaning are more ancient than dictionaries using formal classifications, because they are better adapted to the description of a technical or scientific domain, and to learning by heart (Boulanger 2003: 129, 374 *ff*.). They have been traced to the clay tablets of Sumer (Boisson *et al.* 1991), and there are many early examples in Egypt, China, India, and the Middle East (Boulanger 2003; Hüllen 1999/2006: 30 *ff*.). In English, the earliest example is the glossary of Ælfric, Abbot of Eynsham, near Oxford (*c*.955–*c*.1010), *Nomina multarum rerum anglice*, produced around the year 1000, which had eighteen sections beginning with 'God, heaven, angels, sun, moon, earth, sea' (Hüllen 1999/2006: 62). John Withals' *A shorte Dictionarie of English and Latin for Yonge Beginners*, published in 1553 and edited several times for more than eighty years, eventually contained about 18,400 English words with their equivalents in Latin, arranged by themes, in an organization where religion was not pre-eminent (Hüllen 1999/2006: 168 *ff*.). In 1668, John Wilkins' *Essay Towards a Real Character, And a Philosophical Language* was completed by an *Alphabetical Dictionary* by William Lloyd, bishop of Worcester, which, despite its title, was really an onomasiological dictionary (McArthur 1986*b*: 117). It had about 13,000 entries, which carefully distinguished word senses (Read 2003: 209) and 'all words used for the purpose of definition had themselves to be defined' (Read 2003: 209). It was a highly elaborate work that Johnson admired and consulted (Dolezal 1985; Hüllen 1999/2006: 244 *ff*.). However, it was difficult to use: the authors 'had perversely contrived to make the riches of their book inaccessible to the ordinary man,' argued Sledd and Kolb (1955: 168).

The most illustrious example of a non-alphabetical dictionary in English is *Roget's Thesaurus of English Words and Phrases* by Peter Mark Roget, a co-author of the seventh edition of the *Encyclopaedia Britannica*. The *Thesaurus*, begun in 1810 and published in 1852, contained about 40,000 words. It has been re-edited several times since then in many different forms, paper or electronic, with additions and deletions but the same organization.[29] *Roget* is not a registered trademark any more, and many versions have been produced by different publishers

---

[29] There were six main British editions (1879, 1925, 1962, 1982, 1987, and 1998) and seven American (1886, 1911, 1922, 1946, 1962, 1977, and 1992)—the version available on the Internet is 'based on the copyright-free 1911 edition' (Nesi 2000*b*: 840)—plus many imitations.

that do not have much in common with the original, except the name. *Roget's Thesaurus* has also inspired many similar publications in other languages, among them Prudence Boissière's *Dictionnaire analogique de la langue française*, published in Paris in 1862.

Roget's Thesaurus was a dictionary of synonyms combined with an onomasiological dictionary (Hüllen 2004a/2005). It was in the lineage of John Locke's revolutionary philosophy of language, 'where the assumption that vocabulary follows reality in the way in which a name follows a thing turns into the assumption that vocabulary identifies and gives order to reality because it provides the inalienable signs for the expression of ideas' (Hüllen 2004a/2005: 170). It took inspiration from Withals and Lloyd and their predecessors, and from Johannes Amos Comenius, the famous author of *Janua Linguarum Reserata*[30] (1631) and *Orbis Sensualium Pictus* (1658), both written for the teaching of Latin to young students and remarkable for the organization of their lexical material (Hüllen 1999/2006: 361 *ff.*). Comenius had been inspired by the *Nomenclator omnium rerum* of Hadrianus Junius (1567), which had equivalents in Latin, Greek, French, and English. *Janua Linguarum Reserata*, a dictionary of sentences, went through 101 editions in all European languages and even in Arabic, Turkish, Persian, and Mongolian during the whole of the seventeenth century. It was even used in the brand new university of Harvard. In all, probably 30,000 copies were produced (Hüllen 1999/2006: 385).[31] *Orbis Sensualium Pictus*, a collection of pictures with numbered elements with comments, went through 245 editions. *Roget's Thesaurus* was also inspired by the tradition of the dictionary of synonyms, born in France with Abbé Girard's work, *La justesse de la langue françoise* (1718) and *Synonymes françois* (1736), and then adopted by other European countries (see below, 3.3.2.2 and 4.2.3.1).

All onomasiological dictionaries of the *Thesaurus* type group words in sections arranged in a hierarchy, taxonomy, a Porphyrian tree, or a system of Chinese boxes. They suppose an organization of the words of a language[32] that represents to some extent the organization of the world as conceived by their authors. *Roget's Thesaurus* had a five-level hierarchy, presented in the first pages of the book: six

[30] This (*The Gate of Tongues Unlocked*) was a response to *Janua Linguarum* (*The Gate of Tongues*), published in 1611 in Salamanca by the Irish Jesuit William Bathe, which was a Latin-to-Spanish manual, religiously orientated, with 'twelve great themes and some 5,000 items accompanied by 1,200 illustrative sentences' (McArthur 1998: 157).

[31] Comenius himself turned it into a stage-play (Hüllen 1999/2006: 391), probably a unique case in the history of lexicography.

[32] Normally only of one language, though some authors, among whom Wilkins (Hüllen 1999/2006: 244 *ff.*), have aimed at producing an organization that would be valid for all languages, a step towards the creation of a universal language. See also Hallig and von Wartburg (1952).

classes (Abstract relations, Space, Matter, Intellect, Volition, and Affections), divided into sections (for example, in Abstract relations: Existence, Relation, Quantity, Order, Number, Time, Change, Causation, etc.), divided into sub-sections (for example, in Existence: Abstract, Concrete, Formal, Modal, etc.), divided in sub-sub-sections organized in one column or two (for example, in Abstract: Existence, Inexistence; in Concrete: Substantiality, Unsubstantiality; in Formal: Intrinsicality, Extrinsicality, etc.), in all about 1,000 categories. Each main entry contained lists of words organized by part of speech (POS).

The position of an entry word in such a macrostructure is in itself a piece of semantic information: it tells the user what domain the word belongs to, what other words it is related to and the nature of the relation. From the names of the different categories to which a word belongs—and those to which it does not—one can work out an approximate definition: for example, in *Roget's Thesaurus*, *river* is 'liquid inorganic matter in motion', together with *brook*, *stream*, etc.

The organization in *Roget's Thesaurus* is partly similar to that of his predecessors, but also partly different. Each author, each dictionary has its own organization: 'a thematic layout promotes the compiler's eccentricity while an alphabetic layout inhibits it' (McArthur 1998: 153). Because there is no generally accepted organization, onomasiological dictionaries are usually difficult to use. Rey (1977: 16) tells the following anecdote:

Having noticed a copy of Boissière's analogical dictionary on Gide's desk, and having wondered whether this was the explanation for Gide's vast vocabulary and lexical felicities, Martin du Gard set about finding the precious book. He eventually found a copy, and paid a dear price for it. When Gide next came to visit him, 'I see, he said, you have Boissière's dictionary? What do you think of it?' 'Wonderful!' 'Really? I bought a copy a long time ago myself; but I have never been able to use these dictionaries.'

He concludes sadly that onomasiological dictionaries are unconvincing: 'The practical value of such books is debatable and their theoretical value is based on the naive illusion that the lexical sign and the concept are absolutely equivalent—not to say identical' (Rey 1977: 16). Onomasiological dictionaries have usually been equipped with an alphabetical index to facilitate consultation, including *Roget's Thesaurus*, to which Roget's son John L. added an index for the 1879 edition. Some of the modern variations of the *Thesaurus* are even totally alphabetized, somehow defeating the whole purpose.

The compilation of onomasiological dictionaries should have been encouraged by field theory in linguistics, which appeared in the 1930s in Germany (see Ullmann 1962; Lyons 1977), as it aimed at grouping words in networks according to semantic criteria (Hüllen 2004a/2005: 40–50), and by componential analysis, which developed in the 1950s (Lyons 1977) and tried to establish lists of semantic features that could be used for comparing word meanings.[33] But this theoretical support was not enough, and onomasiological dictionaries have remained a minor genre, generally neglected by dictionary users and by metalexicographers, no doubt unjustly (Hüllen 1994; McArthur 1998). They may become popular again in the era of electronic lexicography: 'Indeed, it [onomasiological lexicography] is a covert influence on much of current reference-book practice, and is enjoying a modest overt renaissance among "print" dictionaries, and could also have a useful future as lexicography moves into the electronic era' (McArthur 1998: 150).

Some lexicographers have invented techniques to give semasiological dictionaries some of the advantages of onomasiological dictionaries without the disadvantages. The old system of 'derivation', used since at least the eleventh century in many dictionaries, for example in Nicot's *Thresor*, grouped related words together in the same entries (Boulanger 2003: 277, 342, 388 *ff.*) In the first edition of the *Dictionnaire de l'Académie* (1694), headwords were ordered alphabetically but each entry also had the words that were related etymologically—even in the absence of any semantic relation in synchrony: for example, *chien, chenêt, canine* were in the entry for *chien* and *duëment, indu, induëment, dette, endetter, débiter, redevable, redevance, débiteur* were in the entry for *devoir* (Matoré 1968: 84; Pruvost 2006: 38). This was meant to show the richness of the French language: 'We thought that it would be agreeable and instructive to arrange the Dictionary by Roots,' wrote the 'Académiciens' in the *Preface*.[34] In England, Richardson had a similar system in his *New Dictionary of the English Language* (1836/7): for example, he had *host, hostess, hostless, hosteller*, etc. in the same entry. This is good for acquiring information about words and their history, but not for expression or comprehension. More recently, *A Thesaurus Dictionary of the English Language*, published in the USA in 1903 by Francis March,[35] was an alphabetical dictionary with 'a reference to the main synonym–antonym[36] "studies" or groups, similar to the treatment in Roget' (Urdang 1996b: 70); the

---

[33] See Crystal (1985) for a quick definition and Leech (1974) for more detail.

[34] The system was the object of so much criticism, particularly by Furetière, that it was abandoned in the second edition (1718) and replaced by a more classical solution.

[35] March, an American Professor, was in charge of the American reading programme for the *OED* (see below, 3.1.1).

[36] An antonym is a word whose meaning is the 'opposite' of the meaning of another. There are graded antonyms (*big/small*) and ungraded antonyms (*single/married*) (Crystal 1985); or polar antonyms (*long/short*), equipollent antonyms (*hot/cold*), and overlapping antonyms (*good/bad*) (Cruse 2000a: 169 *ff.*).

Reader's Digest Great Encyclopedic Dictionary (1972) had 'two conventional "dictionary" volumes plus a volume of thematically-arranged alphabetic glossaries' (McArthur 1998: 163); and many dictionaries are now published with a thesaurus as a companion volume in paper form or on CD-ROM.

Many alphabetical dictionaries have information showing semantic relations between words, with cross-references[37] leading to other entries treating synonyms, antonyms, hypernyms,[38] etc. Ephraim Chambers in his *Cyclopaedia* (1728) constructed a sophisticated system of cross-references that sent the reader back to an organization of knowledge, after the Baconian model, presented in the *Preface* in the form of a taxonomy. The *Grand Robert* (*GR*),[39] marketed as an *analogical dictionary*, has an extensive system of cross-references: the entry for *cheval*, for example, mentions *jument, poulain, pouliche*, etc. and has cross-references to *étalon, cavalier, haras, monter, trot, galop*.[40] This is extremely useful for expression. In the 'explanatory and combinatory' dictionaries (ECDs) developed by Mel'čuk,[41] entry words are ordered alphabetically but each word is the centre of a complex network of syntagmatically and paradigmatically related words, the *lexical functions* of the headword (see below, 8.2.6.1).

E-dictionaries allow searches that were difficult or impossible in paper dictionaries: for example, they can return all words whose definitions contain a certain word, *plant*, or *flower, fruit*, etc., all definitions whose genus word (see below, 8.2.5.1) is *implement*, or *device*, all words whose entries contain the label *Physics*, or *Music*, etc. The computerization of dictionaries is blurring the line between onomasiological and semasiological lexicography (McArthur 1998: 159).

On the whole, the alphabetical arrangement is clearly the easier and the faster system for the user (Zgusta 1971: 282; Rey 1977: 20–1). Also, it gives the owners and users of a dictionary the impression that they have all the lexis of the language, from *aardvark* to *zyzomys*, or *zyzzogeton*, at their disposal, in a form whose completeness is immediately apparent. Because of this, alphabetical ordering has become part of the common concept of dictionary: 'though strictly conventional,

---

[37] On cross-references in dictionaries, see Rey-Debove (1989c). They were used as early as the thirteenth century in Johannes Januensis de Balbis' *Catholicon* (Boulanger 2003: 297). On the different types of cross-references, see Gouws and Prinsloo (1998).

[38] A *hypernym* (or *hyperonym*) is a word that includes the meaning of another (the hyponym): for example, *animal* is a hypernym of *cat*, and *cat* is a hyponym of *animal*. Hypernyms are used in intensional definitions (see below, 8.2.5.1) (see *hyponymy* in Crystal 1985).

[39] *Dictionnaire alphabétique et analogique de la langue française*, Paul Robert, 6 volumes, 1953–70, 1985, 2001. It is now constantly updated in electronic form.

[40] *mare, colt, filly; stallion, cavalier, stud farm, to ride, trot, gallop.*

[41] In French *DEC*, for *Dictionnaire explicatif et combinatoire* (Montréal: Presses de l'Université de Montréal), I 1984, II 1988, III 1992, IV 1999, etc. Similar dictionaries exist for Russian and English.

[it] is so overwhelmingly dominant that the ordinary person associates with this familiar sequence the very genre of the dictionary' (Malkiel 1962: 17).

1.1.1.5 A dictionary lists linguistic units

Every entry in a dictionary is headed by an entry word, or headword, which is the element used for macrostructural arrangement. In simple entries, the headword is also the object of the microstructural treatment—in complex ones, some of the information may apply to parts of the entry. Headwords, sub-headwords as well as run-ons are linguistic units: they are signs in the Saussurean sense, i.e. double-faced entities with a form (the 'signifiant') and a meaning (the 'signifié').[42] They can be defined, and they are memorized by the members of the linguistic community. They are the building blocks of phrases and sentences. Dictionaries treat simple words,[43] the units that appear in a text as uninterrupted sequences of letters, and also items made up of several words such as compounds, phrases, idioms, etc. (see below, 8.2.4). Even when the entry treats a multiword item, it is often headed by a single word: for example, *leg* or *pull* for *pull someone's leg*. In that case, the headword is only the form that determines the position of the entry in the macrostructure but it is not the object of the microstructural information.

Many dictionaries also list affixes, prefixes, suffixes, etc. Dictionaries listing only the building blocks of words may please some linguists, but they could never be popular because they are not what the general public needs. A few have been published for Latin and German (Hüllen 1999/2006: 250), and in France the *Robert Méthodique* (1982), compiled by Rey-Debove,[44] lists all the 'morphemes' that are used in more than one word and can be said to have meaning: for example *cabr-* as in *cabrer, cabri, cabriole*, etc., *cand-* as in *candélabre, candide, incandescent, incendie, chandelle*, etc.

---

[42] The 'signifié' is somehow linked to a referent, i.e. 'the entity (object, state of affairs, etc.) in the external world to which a linguistic expression refers; for example, the referent of the word *table* is the object "table"' (Crystal 1985). Some linguists (not Crystal 1985) also say that a word is linked to a concept, i.e. what the language users have in their minds that corresponds to a word. The concept may be considered as part of the signifié.

[43] On the complex notion of 'word', see Cruse (1986), Di Sciullo and Williams (1987), Lipka (1990), Grefenstette and Tappanainen (1994), Jackson and Zé Amvela (2000), Polguère (2003), Halliday (2004). *Word* is not a technical term that can be defined with any precision, even in Indo-European languages, let alone across languages. But it is useful in any discussion of language: 'the word is undoubtedly difficult to define, but it is unavoidable, a central notion in the mechanism of language' (Saussure 1968: 154). The graphic word has lately become more important than ever in the exploration of corpora (see below, 9.1). I will use the term *lexical item* to refer to any lexical unit that is eligible for inclusion and treatment in a dictionary.

[44] It became *Le Robert Brio* in 2004, with a few changes.

The books that list quotations or proverbs are marginal dictionaries, because quotations and proverbs can hardly be said to be linguistic units. And how should those that list proper names be considered? Proper names have some characteristics of linguistic units, but not all: they are signs used to refer to something, but they do not normally represent categories (Kleiber 1996).[45]

1.1.1.6 A dictionary is a didactic book

A dictionary contains information that is offered to its users; it is a 'teacher who cannot talk', as the Chinese say (Chi 1998: 565). Like all didactic books, it must be knowledgeable, objective, scientific, impersonal, authoritative, and user-friendly.

Lexicographers do their best to make the information contained in the dictionary readily available. The text is divided into paragraphs, and the longer paragraphs are divided in sections that are numbered or at least identified. It uses various fonts, sometimes colours, to indicate the different sorts of information. It gives examples, pictorial illustrations, etc. The only restriction on user-friendliness in a dictionary comes from the need to save space: contrary to other didactic books, the dictionary tries to eliminate repetition and to cram as much information as possible into the available space, hence the use of codes, abbreviations, tildes, parentheses, etc. (see below).

Dictionaries also have some of the characteristics of scientific writings: they contain definitions, they use learned words, sentences in the passive voice, they sometimes (not always) provide evidence for what they say and they do not have explicit marks of hesitation or doubt.

Modern dictionaries are impersonal: they ban all traces of the personalities of their compilers (Rey-Debove 1971: 23): they are authorless. Earlier dictionaries were more tolerant, and their authors often mentioned details of their personal lives. Richelet named his doctor and one of his neighbours in some of his examples (Lehmann 2005: 327–8), and Furetière alluded to recent events in many entries, to provide relief to the reader, he said, because the dictionary is 'dry and boring in its very nature'.[46] Some of Samuel Johnson's definitions have been quoted so often that a couple of examples will suffice here:[47]

[45] Proper names, or proper nouns, are usually contrasted with common nouns (Crystal 1985). Oddly enough, neither French nor English has a term for all the lexical items of a language excluding proper names, i.e. common nouns, verbs, adjectives, etc.

[46] In *Projet et fragment d'un dictionnaire critique* (1692) (Genève: Slatkine, 1970).

[47] They are not typical of Johnson, whose definitions are mostly serious, contrary to what many metalexicographers have written (see below 2.3.2).

excise 'A hateful tax levied upon commodities, and adjudged not by the common judges of property but wretches hired by those to whom excise is paid'

pension 'An allowance made to anyone without an equivalent. In England it is generally understood to mean pay given to a state hireling for treason of his country'[48]

To the entry for *lich*, he added a comment on *Lichfield*, his birthplace: *Salve magna parens*. The practice was usual at the time and nobody seemed to mind (Sledd and Kolb 1955: 36). In his *American Dictionary of the English Language*, published in 1828, Noah Webster mentioned his daughter, his travels in Europe, and various little episodes of his life. He also expressed his personal views on slavery, drunkenness, etc. (Schulman and Lepore 2008: 49). In France, Pierre Larousse had articles in his *Grand Dictionnaire Universel* (1864–90) that expressed his personal opinions clearly (Enckell 2005: 140). One at least is well known:

Bonaparte 'mort...le 18 brumaire, an VIII de la République française, une et indivisible'[49]

Some of Johnson's definitions are clearly satirical, or humorous, the 'Johnsonian effect' (Algeo 1990a: 214), and this would not be tolerated in modern dictionaries. However, one finds examples of whimsical definitions, comments, or examples, whether deliberate or not. The first edition of the *Concise Oxford Dictionary* (1911) defined *it stands to reason* by ' "It is logically demonstrable (that)" or popularly "I shall lose my temper if you deny (that)" ' (see also Allen 1986). Wyld's *Universal Dictionary* (1932) defined *currant bun* by 'with few or no currants'. Even the *OED* had, for example

abbreviator 'an officer of the court of Rome, appointed...to draw up the Pope's briefs'

This was not intentional, according to Winchester (2003: 149), but Craigie 'was very pleased with the now famous last quotation for the word *moron*, when he saw it in the first proof of the *Supplement*... "See the happy moron. He doesn't give a damn. I wish I were a moron. My God! Perhaps I am!" ' (Brewer 2007: 42). Recent editions of *Chamber's Twentieth Century Dictionary* had:[50]

---

[48] Johnson's well-known definition of *oats* as 'A grain, which in England is generally given to horses, but in Scotland supports the people' was possibly a joke at the expense of his amanuenses, five of whom were Scottish. A.W. Read argues that it comes from Skinner's *Etymologicon Linguae Anglicanae*, 1671 (*in* Congleton and Congleton 1984: 64).

[49] 'died on Brumaire 18, in the 8th year of the French Republic, one and indivisible'. Needless to say, Brumaire 18 is the date of the *coup d'état*. Bonaparte became Emperor in 1805 as Napoléon I and died in St Helens in 1821.

[50] Rosamund Moon, personal communication. I have been unable to find when these definitions were introduced: my 1929 edition does not have them; my 1959 edition does.

civil 'polite (in any degree short of discourtesy)'
éclair 'a cake long in shape, but short in duration'
he-man 'a man of exaggerated or extreme virility, or what some women take to be virility'
jaywalker 'a careless pedestrian whom motorists are expected to avoid running down'
middle-aged 'between youth and old age, variously reckoned to suit the reckoner'
noose 'a snare or bond generally, esp. hanging or marriage'
Welsh rabbit 'melted cheese with or without ale, etc., poured over hot toast—sometimes
    written "Welsh rarebit" by wiseacres'

American dictionaries have been more serious, but the *American College Dictionary* (1947) once had

unicorn 'A fabulous animal with a single horn, said to elude every captor save a virgin, and seldom caught[51]

and *W3* defined *wolf n.*, among other definitions, as (Morton 1994: 178)

a man forward, direct, and zealous in amatory attentions to women

Geeraerts (1989: 290) gives the following example, translated from the Van Dale Dutch dictionary of 1976:

kosmonaut 'a somewhat hyperbolic designation for persons who make a tiny jump in cosmic space, for example by having themselves shot to the moon or a planet of our solar system'

Modern dictionaries are expected to provide serious and impersonal knowledge, the knowledge of the society as a whole rather than the opinions or humour of an individual. Meschonnic (1991: 63–4), however, always an original observer of things lexicographic, thinks that no dictionary is simply didactic, that the didacticism of the dictionary is an illusion.

One can only see didacticism in the dictionary if one sees it as a model, thus unduly extending a particular conception of the dictionary and a stage in its historical develop-ment....And the delay with which dictionaries reflect their times finally makes it impossible for them to be seen as educators, though such a role remains as a fantasy in the minds of some.

This is debatable. He then goes on to note that of the two sorts of dictionaries, those that are only informative and those that are polemical, only the latter are remembered, while the others are forgotten, and endlessly replaced: 'The purely informative, transparent, discourse goes the way of all bad translations, those that

---

[51] *DSNA Newsletter* 26/1: 5.

have to be redone' (Meschonnic 1991: 63). If this is true, and I believe it is, then modern societies have chosen the informative sort, those that have to be endlessly rewritten, the more objective but also the more boring.

1.1.1.7 A dictionary gives information about linguistic signs

A dictionary, Rey-Debove says, gives information about the lexical items of a language rather than about their referents, the 'things', objects, ideas, feelings, phenomena, etc. that those items refer to. Unquestionably, most of the micro-structural information in a dictionary article applies to the word: spelling, POS, pronunciation, etymology, syntactic behaviour, synonymy, etc. That is why a dictionary cannot be translated. If a list of words does not have such information, it is not a dictionary. But there is a problem with the definition: what does it define, the word, or the thing, or both?

French lexicographers have long distinguished 'définition de mot' (definition of the word) and 'définition de chose' (definition of the thing).[52] The two types can be distinguished, Rey-Debove (1970a: 10) says, if the underlying verb is made explicit: the verb *be* introduces a definition of the thing ('a cat is an animal that . . .'), whereas *refer to* introduces a definition of the word ('the word *cat* refers to an animal that . . .'). The problem is that many dictionary definitions can be read as either the one or the other.

To distinguish between 'définition de mot' and 'définition de chose', one needs to distinguish between 'mot' and 'chose', word and thing, and what it means to know a word and to know a thing.[53] The distinction between *linguistic knowledge* or *lexical knowledge, word knowledge* or *dictionary knowledge*, and *encyclopedic knowledge* or *world knowledge, cultural knowledge* or *non-linguistic knowledge* is one of the important issues of modern linguistics (Peeters 2000), and it is highly relevant to semanticists (what is meaning?), to syntacticians (what should the lexical component of a theory of language contain?), to specialists of machine translation (what does the machine need to know?), to psycholinguists (what is involved in the acquisition of a word?) as well as to lexicographers. Until the 1980s, most linguists agreed that the two types of knowledge should be distinguished, and could be (Kegl 1987). Recently, however, some linguists have suggested that the distinction between the two types is not as clear as was once thought. An important date in this evolution was the publication of a paper by

---

[52] At least since Pascal's *Opuscules*, 'De l'esprit géométrique', published *c.*1657 (Rey 1990: 16), and the Port-Royal grammarians. The French Academy alluded to the distinction in the preface of their *Dictionnaire* (1694).

[53] On these highly complex questions, see Le Guern (2003).

Haiman in 1980, 'Dictionaries and encyclopedias', which argued that there is no theoretical basis to separate lexical knowledge from encyclopedic knowledge. Other linguists followed, particularly psycholinguists, cognitive linguists,[54] and corpus linguists: for them, there is no reason to distinguish what is linguistic and what is encyclopedic. Prototype linguists (see below, 8.2.5.7) 'blur (or erase) the line between the definitional and the encyclopedic, and call into question the separation of linguistic and conceptual semantic knowledge' (Murphy 2003: 17). Similarly, 'the conflation of linguistic knowledge with encyclopedic knowledge is one of the major axioms of corpus linguistics' (Teubert and Čermakova 2004: 156). Research by psycholinguists, neurolinguists, and specialists of the pathology of language has been scarce (Peeters 2000: 35), but it also indicates that 'knowing a word' includes having information about the 'thing' that the word refers to, hence that linguistic knowledge and encyclopedic knowledge are mixed (Aitchison 1994: 43 *ff.*).[55] This is probably the majority view now: contemporary linguistics tends to 'emphasise the similarities and continuities between linguistic and non-linguistic knowledge' (Lamb 1973; see also Taylor 1995: 81–98).

But the advocates of a clear distinction have not abandoned the field (Peeters 2000: 2). For Wierzbicka (1985: 40–1), linguistic knowledge is 'shared knowledge', what every language user knows about a thing, without which the use of the word in communication would be impossible, and all the rest is encyclopedic. Linguistic knowledge, she says, can be attained by introspection, but 'there are some types of information about denotata which can never become part of the folk concept' (Wierzbicka 1996: 336). If the distinction is not always clear-cut, she says, this does not call into question the necessity of drawing a line, and the possibility of doing so.

What conclusions can lexicographers draw? A clear distinction between word knowledge and world knowledge would make it possible to distinguish word and thing, 'définition de mot' and 'définition de chose', and to decide what goes into the dictionary, leaving the rest for the encyclopedia (see below, 1.1.2.3). This is important, because dictionary definitions have to be compact, for practical reasons, and should aim at being consistent throughout the dictionary—even though the users rarely notice the inconsistencies. But the practice of lexicography does not help to distinguish the two types of knowledge. Every day, lexicographers have occasion to agree with the linguists who argue that it is difficult, if not impossible, to write a definition without saying anything about

---

[54] Much of modern linguistics is cognitive, i.e. interested in the relations between language and the mind, but the label is rather loose. See Croft and Cruse (2004), Evans and Green (2006), Evans (2007), Evans *et al.* (2007), Geeraerts and Cuyckens (2007), Geeraerts (2006*b*).

[55] Indeed, the two are often mixed in the experiments carried out by psycholinguists.

the world, to define the word without describing the thing. If all information about the world were banned, a definition would be reduced to virtually nothing, along the lines of *horse* 'an animal called "horse"' (Wierzbicka 1972: 54), or *elephant* 'that animal of the species "elephant"' (Leech 1974: 88). And even then one might wonder how far the concepts corresponding to *animal* and *species* are encyclopedic. Haiman (1980: 342) suggested that the 'most impeccable definition' of *elephant* would be 'elephant NP'![56] There is no such thing as a pure 'définition de mot', at least for content words:[57] there is 'no sharp line drawn between the two types' (Rey-Debove 1989a: 308–9). Rey agrees: 'Contrary to what an excessively simplifying semiotic model has implied, the frontier is extraordinarily fuzzy' (Rey 1977: 171). As a consequence, dictionary definitions (see below, 8.2.5) lie somewhere between the brief statement that contains only what is necessary and sufficient to distinguish the word from all the other words of the language and the extensive description that gives details much beyond what the language users should know about the thing in order to be able to use the word. They are all 'définition de mot', with more or less encyclopedic knowledge added.

The distinction between 'dictionnaire de mots' (dictionary of words), a dictionary that gives as little encyclopedic information as possible and that has no proper names, and 'dictionnaire de choses' (dictionary of things), a dictionary with proper names that is more generous in encyclopedic knowledge, appeared in France in the seventeenth century and was firmly established by the French Academy. Furetière writes in his *Preface* (1690): 'It was not my design to write a dictionary of words', meaning, of course, that the *Dictionnaire de l'Académie* was only a 'dictionnaire de mots' while his was a *Dictionnaire universel*, both a 'dictionnaire de mots' and a 'dictionnaire de choses'.[58] The distinction has been used since then in France (Quemada 1968: 77; Rey-Debove 1971: 188) and in Germany (*Sprachwörterbücher* and *Sachwörterbücher*; see Wiegand 1998a). In modern French lexicography, *Petit Robert* is a 'dictionnaire de mots',[59] *Petit Larousse*[60] is a 'dictionnaire de choses'. In English, the *OED* is a 'dictionnaire de

---

[56] Semanticists have tended to concentrate on concrete nouns: *chat* (Rey 1977), *libraire* (Rey-Debove 1970a), *pomme de terre* (Rey-Debove 1971: 228), *carrot* (Weinreich 1962: 33), *cup* (Labov 1973, Wierzbicka 1985), *wolf* (Leech 1974), etc. But concrete nouns are not the most difficult words in lexicography: 'most of the words one has to deal with when working through the alphabet turn out to be more recalcitrant than those chosen as examples in works on semantic theory' (Atkins 1993: 19).

[57] Content words, or lexical words, or full words, are words with 'stateable lexical meaning' (Crystal 1985): nouns, verbs, and adjectives; as opposed to *function words*, or *grammatical words*, or *closed-category words*, whose role is to 'express grammatical relationships': prepositions, conjunctions, etc.

[58] The *Dictionnaire de l'Académie* was completed by a 'dictionnaire de choses', the *Dictionnaire des Arts et des Sciences* of Thomas Corneille (1694).

[59] Though the later editions have more and more terms, hence more and more world knowledge.

[60] First edition published 1905, dated 1906, with a new edition every year.

mots' and *Webster's Third* more a 'dictionnaire de choses'. On the whole, British dictionaries of the twentieth century have been 'dictionnaires de mots' while American dictionaries have always been 'dictionnaires de choses'.[61] Of course, the larger a dictionary is the more encyclopedic information it has, and the opposition is not binary: there are many intermediate cases.

1.1.1.8 A dictionary represents a lexical set

A dictionary is necessarily a dictionary **of** a language, or of a variety or subset of a language. There are dictionaries of Polish, of medieval English, of the language of the French underworld, of Italian idiomatic phrases, etc. The wordlist must correspond to a pre-existing set of words, a lexis,[62] an entity that must be perceived as the word stock of a linguistic code used by the members of a community. If it did not, the dictionary users would never know if they stand a reasonable chance of finding what they are looking for. This, we shall see, is a recent development: the glossaries that preceded modern dictionaries were lists of words used in a text (see below, 2.1.2), and early dictionaries did not aim at collecting all the words of a language (see below, 2.2.1).

In every dictionary project the number of words in the wordlist is adjusted to the practical constraints of time, space, cost of production, and cost of the finished product for the buyers. But even the larger dictionaries cannot have all the words of a language. The *OED* with its more than 400,000 words excluded many scientific words, taboo words, dialect words, Americanisms, etc. (see below, 3.1.1).

The half-million entries in a so-called 'unabridged' dictionary are but the tip of the lexicographical iceberg, for it is estimated that fifty thousand chemical compounds are discovered and named every year. There is not—and may never be—a complete inventory of all the slang words that have been used in English since printing was developed.

(McDavid 1973*b*: 259)

There are '500,000 possible carbon compounds and some 600,000 zoological species', Morton (1994: 149) says. According to Barnhart, English creates 'an average of 800 new words every year' (in Ilson 1993: 20), and of course he means words that stand a chance of being recorded in a dictionary. Whatever the figures, the task is impossible within the limits of traditional lexicography: 'a

---

[61] Interestingly, English has no common equivalent for 'dictionnaire de mots', probably because *dictionary* means 'dictionnaire de mots'. *Lexical dictionary* has been suggested. Ilson (1990*b*: 1970) uses 'dictionnaire de langue'.

[62] I will use *lexis* to refer to the set of lexical items that are part of a particular language, and *lexicon* to refer to lexical items in general, the lexical constituent of any language, as opposed to grammar (see Neef and Vater 2006).

work with a million entries would not completely cover the lexicon' (Urdang 1993: 132). And there are other reasons why no dictionary can have all the words of a language. The limits of the language are not clear, particularly in a language such as English, with all its varieties, social, regional, situational, modal, etc. Should one include all the words used by teenagers, by children, by poets, the words that have been used but are not used anymore, the foreign words used in English texts, all the words used on the Internet? Also, the lexis of a language keeps changing. Words are abandoned, and some are invented every minute, so that dictionaries are partly obsolete[63] at the time of publication: 'around a dozen new lexical items' appear in each day's edition of *The Times* (Sinclair 2004*b*: 21). In fact, the number of words is infinite: 'if you suffer from sesquipedaliaphobia, you can think of your *great-grandmother*, your *great-great-grandmother*, your *great-great-great-grandmother*, and so on, limited only in practice by the number of generations since Eve' (Pinker 1994: 130). The 'notion of an inventory of *all* the words in a language is incoherent. When we have recorded all the known words, there is always one more' (Hanks 2002: 157). Johnson had already noted in his *Preface*: 'no dictionary of a living tongue can ever be perfect, since while it is hastening to publication, some words are budding, and some falling away.'[64] Chasing up the words of a language, Winchester writes, is very much like 'herding cats' (2003: 25).

As a consequence, it is easy to find examples of words used in newspapers, on the radio, in conversation, etc. that are not recorded in any dictionary: 'I had occasion recently to look up all the names used in the classification of dinosaurs, and found only 70% of them in the largest dictionaries; similarly, only about 75% of the terms defined in my linguistics dictionary were included' (Crystal 1986: 75).

Many dictionaries have used the adjective *complete*: *The Complete English Dictionary* of Frederick Barlow (1772), *A Complete and Universal English Dictionary*, by James Barclay (1774), the *New and Complete Dictionary of the English Language* of John Ash (1775), John Boag's *Popular and Complete English Dictionary* (1848), etc. (see Mugglestone 2005: 70), and many others used it in their subtitles. But does anyone need a complete dictionary? One could imagine a thesaurus of all, say almost all, the lexical items in the language, a huge ongoing lexical data bank, but who, apart from the linguists, would use it? A dictionary can only be a collection of the more important words (see below, 8.2.1.2), those that are taught and learnt, whose sum constitutes the word stock of the language.

---

[63] An obsolete word is a word that is no longer used; an archaic word is an old word that is no longer in common use but still used occasionally for effect.

[64] Note that for Johnson, having 'all' the words of a language was equivalent to being perfect.

If exhaustiveness is unattainable, a dictionary should at least try to be representative: the wordlist should be a faithful portrait of the lexis of the language. 'The aim is obviously not to propose a randomly chosen section of the whole set, but to prepare a reduction that will contain the most representative elements,' says Rey-Debove (1971: 30). 'Wordlists are never arbitrary. They are not exhaustive, but they cannot be lists of items chosen at random' (Rey-Debove 1969a: 188). In practice, the nomenclatures of dictionaries lie somewhere between the whole lexis, which is unattainable, and the 'common' lexis, i.e. the words that are shared by all the members of the community, the words 'in common use in the public press and in ordinary speech in both informal and reserved styles (such as those used in business), as distinguished from specialized vocabularies such as those of law, medicine, or the physical sciences' (Landau 2001: 30). It is often difficult to decide whether a word deserves to be included in a particular dictionary. Mugglestone (2005) gives an interesting account of the compilation of the *OED*: the new term *radium*, for example, was excluded after some deliberation because the compilers thought that it would not last (see below, 3.1.1). In fact, it is always possible to add or delete a word without much harm to the overall quality of the nomenclature, as we have seen, since the lexical set that the dictionary represents is never defined with precision. Dictionary reviewers always have a hard time assessing the quality of the wordlist—unless there are really gross mistakes—because the model is not completely known: 'Many people mistakenly imagine that languages "exist" in dictionaries and grammars, but such books are only limited attempts to describe some of the more obvious features of a language. Languages really exist only in people's minds' (Nida 1997: 267). Saying that the wordlist of a dictionary is representative of a language is no doubt true very generally, but impossible to verify and demonstrate. Representativeness is an act of faith rather than a reality.

1.1.1.9 A dictionary is a special kind of text

All the defining features of *dictionary* can be summed up in a formula: the dictionary is a special kind of text, or rather a particular collection of text types. Dictionaries usually have different sections in addition to the dictionary proper, the A–Z section, each with its own textual features. This 'ancillary matter' (Urdang 1993: 133) can be *front matter*, or *fore matter*, which is placed at the beginning, before the first entry: an introduction, a preface, a foreword, a list of abbreviations, a list of contributors, a text on 'How to use the dictionary', an essay on the history of the language, etc.; *back matter*, at the end of the dictionary: irregular verbs, Christian names, a grammar, maps, etc.; or *mid-matter*, or *middle matter*, a central section with pictorial illustrations, notes, etc. Both front matter and back matter are old traditions (Hüllen 1999/2006: 210). They can be tables, lists, pictures, or just text.

The style of early dictionaries was free and discursive, but it became formalized in the eighteenth century and it is now almost the same in all societies.

> In our days the presentation of lexicographical information has become rather conventionalized and one often wonders whether lexicographers are not just following suit without asking themselves what these conventions stand for.... And the question that has been neglected but that is central to lexicography is whether there are any intrinsic interdependencies between the linguistic data given and the methods used to present them.   (Stein 1984*a*: 124)

The A–Z section in modern dictionaries is a combination of two systems: each item of information can be read both horizontally in its entry together with the other elements of the same entry, and vertically within all the other items of information of the same kind in the other entries.

The dictionary text excludes non-linear presentations such as graphs or tables, even when those would be clearer. The order in which the different items of information of the entry are given is standardized to some extent: pronunciation comes first, etymology next, or at the end of the entry, definitions almost always come before examples or citations, if any. There are dictionaries in which the examples are given before the definitions, as in the *Dictionnaire du Français Contemporain* (1966), and Hausmann (1990*a*: 230–1) argues that this might be more effective than the traditional order, but it is rarely used, except in children's dictionaries.

The use of typography is standardized to a large extent:

> Thus, bold-face type may indicate a main entry or sub-entry; (small) capitals, a cross-reference to another entry; square brackets may enclose information about etymology or codes giving information about inflectional patterns or patterns of grammatical use; round brackets (parentheses) within a definition may enclose the typical object of a transitive verb.   (Ilson 1993: 27)

Dictionaries have a special style. They use words such as *relating, characterized, marked, stated, specified*, etc. and some constructions such as *of or pertaining to, any of, as of*, etc. are typical, 'although it may well be that their full significance is lost on many readers' (Hanks 1987: 116). Definitions have no verbs, no deictics;[65]

---

[65] A deictic is a word that refers 'directly to the personal, temporal or locational characteristics of the situation within which an utterance takes place, whose meaning is thus relative to that situation: e.g. *now/then, here/there, I/you, this, that*' (Crystal 1985). *You* is now used in many definitions.

they often use the passive with unspecified agents; many items of information are abbreviations or symbols: *a., adj., adv., Amer., arch., Archit., Astron., attrib., Austr.,* etc. Parentheses have been used in definitions at least since Elisha Coles's *An English Dictionary* in 1676, although they are sometimes difficult to interpret: 'it requires considerable sophistication to work out precisely what each set of parentheses is doing' (Hanks 1987: 116). For example, *fuse* in the *Longman Dictionary of Contemporary English* (1978) is 'to (cause (metal) to) melt in great heat', and *gallop* in the *Advanced Learner's Dictionary of Current English* until 1995 was '(of a horse) to go at a gallop'. Landau (2001: 175), commenting on the definition of *doff* in the *Random House Dictionary* (*RHD*), 'to remove or tip (the hat), as in greeting', writes: 'Is one to assume that the word *hat* is the usual object of *doff*, or that *hat* means "any hat"? Dictionaries should have some way of distinguishing between *hat* and "the class of objects denoted by *hat*" '.

The dictionary is one of the most complex texts, with a large number of information types and many items belonging to more than one type. Many earlier dictionaries had a 'contorted' style (Hanks 1988: 43) that has been called *dictionarese*, and user studies have shown that the users often find it difficult (see below, 7.2.3). A lot of work has been done recently to improve user-friendliness and modern dictionaries are much more easily accessible. E-dictionaries can afford to have a more relaxed style, closer to ordinary prose, and they can use charts, tables, graphs, etc. that would take too much space in paper dictionaries (see below, 9.2.1).

1.1.1.10 Can anyone define *dictionary*?

Let us sum up: A dictionary is a reference tool, in paper or electronic form, that provides information on the meaning and use of a representative sample of the lexical items of a language or of a variety of a language, where each item is treated in a separate paragraph and all the paragraphs are ordered for easy consultation.

The difficulty, in the definition of the word *dictionary* is that dictionaries are produced in an infinite variety. Boulanger (2003: 462) compares their production to a forest with all sorts of trees, shrubs, and plants of all shapes and dimensions that keep appearing and disappearing, some living longer than others, some species becoming dominant in an area for a period, etc. There are so many varieties of dictionaries that anybody trying to define the word is condemned to polish and re-polish their definitions in an eternal quest for the unattainable perfect formulation. And with e-lexicography, the task has become even more difficult: 'our concept of the dictionary is under great pressure' (van Sterkenburg 2003*b*: 5). Our definition will have to be reconsidered at the end of this book.

1.1.2 *The dictionary and other types of books*

1.1.2.1 Various types of dictionaries

Libraries are full of dictionaries that do not have all of our defining features. Dictionaries of quotations or of linguistic difficulties are about language and their contents are arranged in short articles in a formal way for consultation, but they are not about the meanings of words. There are also dictionaries that provide encyclopedic information on a given subject in the form of alphabetically ordered articles, anywhere between a few lines and a few pages in length: dictionaries of economics, of the Celts, of perennial plants, of whisky, of Cézanne, or dictionaries of biographies. Those are only about things; they may be called *dictionaries* but they are encyclopedic.

Some linguistic theories need a *lexicon*, or *dictionary*, which is the list of words to be attached to their sentence-building rules in order to account for the production of adequate discourse. It is usually very short, because a few example words are enough for the discussion of the theory. Also, the specialists of data banks have lists of words that are used to locate pieces of information in the bank. Those lists are also called *dictionaries*, sometimes *thesauri*, and *anti-dictionaries* are the lists of the words that are *not* used in this way. Computers are also sold with dictionaries that are lists of the forms of the language that the system uses to check spelling and, to some extent, grammar in the texts written on the computer (Fontenelle 2008c).

1.1.2.2 The dictionary and other lists of words

There are many other terms to refer to books of words, or wordbooks, i.e. books 'containing a list or lists of systematically (esp. alphabetically) arranged words' (*Shorter Oxford English Dictionary*): *index, concordance, glossary, vocabulary, lexicon, thesaurus, gazetteer*, etc., and they are not easy to distinguish. A gazetteer is a list of geographical names. An index is a list of words in alphabetical order, usually at the end of a book, containing some of the words mentioned in the book and indicating the places where they are mentioned (Sappler 1990). The only microstructural information is the number of the page or paragraph where the word can be found in the text. An index contains only the words or names that are important in the book. It does not represent anything apart from the source text to which it is attached. Most of the words in indices—or *indexes*—are nouns. A concordance is also a list of words in alphabetical order containing the words used in a book or by an author, each with a reference to the places where it occurs, or quotations of the relevant passages. Unlike the index, it is typically a book. The first concordance was compiled for the Latin Vulgate in 1230, and there have been many others for the Bible (Hanon 1990: 1563) and for literary works, in many languages. A concordance may contain only the important words, or every single word, as in modern concordances in electronic form.

Glossary, vocabulary, and *lexicon* have largely overlapping meanings. A glossary is usually a list of rare, obsolete, dialectal, or technical words used in a particular domain or text. Early glossaries were lists of glosses added to manuscripts in order to clarify the meanings of difficult Latin words, and were the ancestors of our dictionaries (see below, 2.1). Some glossaries are attached to a particular book, others are separate volumes containing the terms of a domain, in which case they give definitions or explanations. A vocabulary is a list of words, usually in alphabetical order, with definitions or translations, typically used in the teaching of a foreign language. The word *lexicon*, used by some linguists to refer to the lexical component of a language, can also be a list of the words of a domain or of a region, like a *glossary*. *Vocabulary* and *lexicon* are also often used interchangeably (Landau (2001: 35). A thesaurus is a collection of words arranged according to meaning, as in *Roget's Thesaurus*.

1.1.2.3 The dictionary and the encyclopedia

The Latin form *encyclopaediam* was drawn, erroneously it seems, from the Greek *enkuklios* ('drawing a circle') and *paideia* ('teaching') by an Italian monk in a gloss dated 1476,[66] and used in the title of a book by Jakob Locher in 1508 (Boulanger 2003: 186). The word *encyclopédie* was used for the first time in 1522 by Guillaume Budé in a manuscript for *L'Institution du prince*, dedicated to Francis I, to be published in 1547. Rabelais used it in 1532 in *Pantagruel* in the sense of 'all human knowledge': '...qu'il m'a ouvert le vray puys and abysme de Encyclopedie'.[67] In English, Eliot, who was the first to use *dictionary* in a title, defined *encyclopedia* in 1531 as 'that lernynge whiche comprehendeth all lyberall science and studies', a sense later defined by the *OED* as 'circle of learning'. The first occurrences of the word in the sense of 'book containing all human knowledge', according to the *OED*, are dated 1644 in a verse by T. Diconson accompanying John Bulwer's *Chirologia*, under the form *encycloped*, and 1662 by John Evelyn, the diarist, as *encyclopedia*. The variant *cyclopaedia* was only used by Ephraim Chambers in the title of his encyclopedic dictionary (1728; see below, 2.2.2).

It may seem futile to list the differences between a dictionary and an encyclo-pedia: everybody knows what each looks like and what it can be used for. An

---

[66] Chambers, in his *Cyclopaedia* (1728), says: 'It is mistakenly that some derive the word from *chain*, or *fetter*, that holds by the feet'!

[67] 'That he opened the true well and abyss of encyclopedia' (Chapter 20).

encyclopedia has pictures, it can have long articles, sometimes several pages, the articles are always headed by nouns,[68] common nouns or proper names, they are typically arranged by domain, and above all the microstructural information is about things, not about words: while the dictionary contains 'lexical information about words', the encyclopedia contains 'non-lexical information about things' (Fillmore 1969: 124), and that is why the encyclopedia can be translated. The headwords of an encyclopedia are just labels pointing to a piece of relevant information: for example, an article *garden* will contain a history and geography of gardening, an explanation of its techniques, etc. rather than a definition of the word with the features of the 'signifié'. In many cases, a different entry word might have been chosen for the same entry.

The encyclopedia article, which aims at describing the world, uses the entry word as a means of access to the domain of description. The entry word is not used as a sign, but only for its contents: any neighbouring word in the same semantic field could be used in its place. On the contrary, the dictionary, which aims at describing words, has entry words which are, as signs, the objects of description . . . and every entry word, which is taken as a form, is unique: it cannot be replaced by a synonym or an equivalent in another language.   (Rey 1982: 19)

Yet the differences between the contents of the dictionary and the contents of the encyclopedia are unclear, as we have seen. In fact, the two types of book were not distinguished for a long time: both evolved from a common origin (Boisson *et al.* 1991; Boulanger 2003). Even today, many linguists think that 'many a work that is called a "dictionary" could just as easily be called an "encyclopedia"' (McArthur 1998: 152), and often this is not a compliment at all: 'so-called dictionaries are rather impoverished encyclopedias' writes Eco (1984: 47). All dictionaries contain information that is more or less clearly encyclopedic, either in their nomenclature (proper names and specialized terms) or in their microstructure (definitions and examples), as we have seen. The *Concise Oxford Dictionary*, fifth edition (1964),[69] had (see Leech 1974: 204):

wolf 'Erect-eared, straight-tailed, harsh-furred, tawny-grey, wild, gregarious, carnivorous quadruped allied to dog preying on sheep, etc. or combining in packs to hunt larger animals'

Such definitions, that go much beyond the meaning of the word for the average user, are also often used in American dictionaries.

---

[68] With a few exceptions: an encyclopedia of wine, for example, may use adjectives like *acid, alcoholic, amabile, bianco, brut,* etc.

[69] The definition in the sixth edition was slightly modified.

However the two genres, the dictionary and the encyclopedia, must be distinguished as much as possible, if only for practical reasons. Even Haiman admits that the distinction is necessary, and that it works 'very well in practice' (Haiman 1980: 355). For Wierzbicka (1996: 336), the dictionary has the shared knowledge, the encyclopedia has the encyclopedic knowledge, and failing to distinguish them 'leads to stagnation in lexical semantics'. Let us say that the presence of encyclopedic information does not identify the encyclopedia, but the absence of linguistic information does.

A dictionary that has entries for proper names is called *encyclopedic*. Those come in various sub-types: some have two sections, one linguistic and one encyclopedic, usually in that order, like *Petit Larousse*; some have lists of geographical or biographical names, with minimal microstructure, at the end, while other proper names are in the main list, like *Webster's New Collegiate Dictionary* (1973); some have only one macrostructure, like the *Collins English Dictionary* (1979) and many American dictionaries; some separate the encyclopedic from the linguistic in each entry, like *Larousse Trois Volumes en couleurs* (1965), which has small essays headed ENCYCL in some entries, after the definitions. The entry for *chat*, for example, says, after the definition:

ENCYCL. *chat.* Le chat jouit d'une excellente vision nocturne, d'une bonne ouïe, d'une grande sensibilité tactile au niveau des vibrisses*. Son approche est silencieuse, son saut puissant; ses griffes, rétractiles, sont toujours acérées, ses crocs redoutables, ses molaires tranchantes...[70]

The *New Oxford Dictionary of English* (1998) has a similar, two-layered, arrangement. For example, the entry for *climbing perch* runs:

climbing perch ▶ noun a small edible freshwater fish which is able to breathe air and move over land, native to Africa and Asia.
• Family Anabantidae: three genera and several species, including *Anabas testudinens*.

The presentation of information in more than one 'layer' is easily done in e-dictionaries.

1.1.2.4 The dictionary and the grammar

Dictionaries and grammars also have certain features in common: they are both metalinguistic descriptions with a didactic purpose, designed to facilitate

---

[70] 'The cat enjoys excellent nocturnal vision, good hearing, fine tactile sensitivity in its vibrissae.* It moves silently and is a powerful jumper; its claws are retractile and always sharp, its fangs are formidable, its molars are cutting...'

linguistic communication. They are usually thought of as complementary, the two basic tools of 'grammatization', the process 'whereby a language is described and equipped', they are 'the bases of our metalinguistic knowledge' (Auroux 1994: 110). 'The dictionary is a poet's breviary,' writes George Steiner (1997: 32), 'a grammar is his missal'.

Yet everyone knows a dictionary from a grammar book, and not only because the words *dictionary* or *grammar* are usually mentioned in the titles. The differences are obvious: the text of the grammar is not divided into unconnected articles, and thus it is normally read, not consulted; the grammar accounts for clauses and sentences, the dictionary explains words; above all, the grammar is unambiguously about the language, not about the world.

Many linguists have tried to distinguish what belongs in the dictionary and what belongs in the grammar. Saying that the dictionary is about words while the grammar is about clauses and sentences is basically true, but it is not enough. There are many statements about how to construct clauses and sentences in a dictionary, in the entries for function words, in POS labels and also implicitly in the examples and quotations. Also, grammars do have things to say about words, particularly on the rules of morphology. Gleason (1962: 90) suggests another difference: '[t]he grammatical statement deals with form, the dictionary with meaning'. But this is untenable: the dictionary contains many statements that are about form, and the grammar—despite the efforts of some—has never been able to do without considerations of meaning. A more serious suggestion has been that '[a]ll matters that apply to a considerable number of items would belong to the grammatical statement, those which apply to a single item to the dictionary' (Gleason 1962: 92). This corresponds to a period when grammar was thought to be regular and lexis irregular, when Bloomfield (1933: 274) defined lexis as 'a list of basic irregularities'.[71] It is typical of the linguistic schools that focused on the grammar, seen as the more important aspect, and the more amenable to study. But how does one count the number of items to which a statement applies, and where is the limit beyond which a feature can be said to be regular enough to be considered grammatical?

There are facts that one hesitates to classify as grammatical or lexical. For example, what about the *-er* endings in agent nouns? 'Is this a lexical rule, because it relates words of different major classes, or is it a transformation—or more generally a non-lexical rule—on the grounds that it is relatively productive and regular?' (Hudson 1988: 292). What about the *un-* prefix in adjectives? What

---

[71] A position later reasserted by Chomsky (1995: 235): 'I understand the lexicon in a rather traditional sense: as a list of "exceptions", whatever does not follow from general principles.'

about word order in 'someone nice' and *'nice someone' (Hudson 1988: 292–5)? Or in *glad person, *glad occasion? What about the rules of nominal composition (Levi 1983: 194)?

Since the 1970s, many linguists have advocated a 'rapprochement' between the grammar and the lexicon, saying that the border between the two was fuzzy (Halliday 2004: 3), that they were two different perspectives on the same phenomena: 'grammar and vocabulary are not two different things; they are the same thing seen by different observers' (Halliday 1992: 63). They are complementary: 'their respective patches turn out to be like the north end and the south end of the same field, rather than like different fields separated by a hedge' (Hudson 1988: 295). For corpus linguists, syntax and the lexicon are inseparable, because the meaning of a word can only be grasped if one examines the contexts in which it is used, and the way it is used is in its turn determined by its meaning (Hunston and Francis 2000; Teubert and Čermakova 2004; see below, 8.2.6).

For lexicographers, the distinction between syntax and lexicon is important because it determines what goes into the dictionary, as opposed to what should be left to the grammar, and the current rapprochement is not much help: if there is no difference between lexical information and grammatical information, then the dictionary can contain anything, and the limit is only practical. Perhaps the only answer is in what the dictionary users need. This varies with each dictionary type and with each individual dictionary. For example, information on the syntagmatic behaviour of words and on the building of sentences and discourse is important if the dictionary is to serve as a tool for expression (see below, 5.1.1).

Modern dictionaries record more information that used to be considered as grammatical (Apresjan 2002: 91): they have become 'grammaticalized' (Stein 2002: 12).

1.2 TYPES OF DICTIONARIES

1.2.1 Dictionary typologies

Many people have tried to classify dictionaries, at least since the entry *dictionnaire* in the French *Encyclopédie* in the eighteenth century, but the task is not easy and the results often disappointing. Creating categories in theory, as all true typologies should, is fine, but then one discovers that they cannot accommodate all existing dictionaries. And constructing categories on the basis of the observation of real dictionaries, strictly speaking a classification rather than a typology, is a never-ending task that has to be redone every time a new dictionary is published.[72] The two approaches are illustrated below. Perhaps the main interest of the exercise is that it provides an extensional definition of the word *dictionary*, a complement to our intensional definition, and an opportunity to explore the outer limits of the concept.

1.2.1.1 Formal typologies

The simplest way to categorize dictionaries is to use their apparent features. Librarians use their titles: dictionary of the English language, dictionary of synonyms, of South African English, etc. (see Besterman 1943; Whittaker 1966). American lexicographers use their size: unabridged (more than 250,000 words), semi-unabridged (between 130,000 and 250,000 words), and abridged dictionaries (less than 130,000 words) according to Kister (1977: 4), but Landau (2001: 30) has different figures: '[i]n practice, *unabridged* has meant a dictionary of 400,000 to 600,000 entries'. Also, the label *unabridged* is ambiguous: strictly speaking, an unabridged dictionary is a dictionary that is 'not abridged from a larger source' (Urdang 1997: 77), but it is also a dictionary that gives 'full coverage to the lexicon in general use at a particular time in the history of a language and substantial coverage to specialized lexicons' (Landau 2001: 30), so that a dictionary can be unabridged in one sense but not in the other. In addition, the figures do not work in other languages: the *Grand Robert* (1953) is not abridged, gives full coverage of the French lexicon, but has only about 100,000 entries. Even the *Trésor de la langue française* (*TLF*),[73] the most comprehensive dictionary of French, would only be a semi-unabridged by American standards.

The American market also has college dictionaries, with anywhere between 160,000 and 180,000 words according to Landau (2001: 30), one-fourth to one-third of an unabridged dictionary, 'about 3 million words'[74] or in the neighborhood of 16.5 million characters' (Landau 2001: 385); desk dictionaries, 'one step below the college dictionaries', having 60,000 to 80,000 entries (Landau 2001: 31); paperback dictionaries, etc. All these categories are vague: Landau writes in the same book that desk dictionaries 'include the American college dictionaries'

---

[72] For a recent classification of existing dictionaries, see the table of contents of Hausmann *et al.* (1989–91).

[73] Sixteen volumes published between 1971 and 1994, edited by Paul Imbs until 1977 (volumes 1–7) then by Bernard Quemada (volumes 8–16), 90 million examples treated, 150 staff, about 100,000 words and their histories, 270,000 definitions, and 430,000 examples. Available as *TLFI* (*Trésor de la Langue Française Informatisé*) since 2000 online free of charge and on CD-ROM since 2004.

[74] This is not the number of headwords, obviously, but the number of words used in the dictionary text (see below, 4.3.2).

(Landau 2001: 95), but for Urdang (2000: 38) *desk dictionary* is a synonym of *college dictionary*. British lexicographers have their own categories: *shorter, concise, compact, essential, pocket, little, mini*, etc. They recently began speaking of desk dictionaries, the 'British equivalent, in terms of size, of the American collegiate dictionary' (Jackson 2002: 67), or desktop dictionaries.

1.2.1.2 More sophisticated typologies

Shcherba (1940), in one of the most often quoted typologies, uses six binary oppositions: academic vs. informative dictionaries, the former being designed to give guidance on usage and the second to describe usage; encyclopedic vs. linguistic dictionaries; concordances vs. ordinary dictionaries, the former being thesauri of all the recorded words of a language; alphabetical vs. ideological dictionaries; defining vs. translating dictionaries; and non-historical vs. historical dictionaries.

Malkiel (1962) uses three main features: 'range', 'perspective', and 'presentation'. Range distinguishes between dictionaries according to the number of entries, the number of languages, and the importance of linguistic information. Perspective differentiates between historical dictionaries, describing the evolution of the language over a certain period and containing obsolete and archaic words as well as information on the history of words, and synchronic dictionaries, describing the language as it is used in the present period. Presentation, in Malkiel's typology, is a measure of the precision of the definitions, the nature of the examples, of the presence of pictures, phonetic transcription and usage labels. Malkiel also distinguishes between detached, preceptive, or facetious dictionaries, although as we have seen facetiousness is hardly compatible with modern lexicography. Finally, Malkiel mentions the type of arrangement: the entries can be alphabetic, semantic, or ... casual!

Sebeok (1962) opposes dictionaries produced by their compilers and dictionaries abstracted from a corpus. Indeed, 'many dictionaries (the cheapest kind) are written entirely by INTROSPECTION' (Atkins 1993: 14), except that they also use other dictionaries: 'All commercial dictionaries are based to some extent on pre-existing works' (Landau 2001: 346), so that 'the purely generated dictionary scarcely exists' (Rey 1977: 77).

Guilbert (1969: 28–9) proposes to base his typology on the kind of linguistic approach used by the lexicographer.

Submitting to tradition or following scientific linguistic analysis: those are the two extremities of the scale on which the ideas of modern lexicographers can be positioned. A typology of modern French dictionaries must therefore be an analysis of each dictionary in the light of the achievements of linguistics, allowing each to be placed on the scale that goes from the linguistic to the non-linguistic.

He then proceeds to distinguish five types: the encyclopedia, the scientific and technical dictionary, the linguistic and encyclopedic dictionary, the *dictionnaire de langue*, and the linguistic dictionary, the latter being a dictionary written by linguists. He also distinguishes between commercial dictionaries and academic (or scholarly) dictionaries, a distinction later used by Atkins (1993: 5), who opposed the trade dictionary and the scholarly and historical dictionary.[75] The former has a wider public, is smaller and cheaper, and above all it is compiled by non-linguists, she says. But the distinction is not entirely convincing: 'it is pointless to oppose "commercial" dictionaries and "scientific" dictionaries. ... The larger "diction-naires de langue" are thought to be more "scientific", probably because they are more extensive and more austere' (Quemada 1987: 237), because they are compiled by highly skilled professionals who work with less time pressure than lexico-graphers working in publishing houses preparing dictionaries for a wider public, because they are financed by inexhaustible public funds, etc. Bigger is almost always better in lexicography. But commercial dictionaries are not necessarily bad, and many are excellent: 'any opposition between "commercial" dictionaries (i.e. those that are produced by publishers who are openly trying to make a profit) and "disinterested" descriptions, which are allegedly more "scientific", is simply untenable' (Rey and Delesalle 1979: 9). How indeed should one consider *PR*, for example? It is undoubtedly commercial, but the care with which it is compiled, the nature of its contents, and the quality of its editors make it a scholarly dictionary as well.

Landau (2001: 7–42) proposes ten classifying features: number of languages (monolingual, bilingual, or multilingual dictionaries); variety of English (UK, US, etc.); primary language of the users (native-speakers, foreign learners); form of presentation (alphabetic or thematic); manner of financing (scholarly or commercial); age of users (adults or children); period of time covered (general or period dictionaries); size (unabridged, desk, concise, compact, pocket, mini, etc.); scope of coverage by subject (general or specialized); limitations in the aspects of language covered (dialect, etymological, pronunciation, synonym, etc.); nature of the entries (dictionaries of abbreviations, of collocations, etc.). It is difficult to do better. Interestingly enough, the 1984 version of his book had another distinction, prescriptive vs. descriptive dictionaries (see below, 4.3.3), that was dropped in the 2001 edition.

---

[75] Note that for Atkins a scholarly dictionary can only be historical.

1.2.1.3 Functional typologies

Some have argued that a typology should not be based on the characteristics of dictionaries but on the linguistic tasks that they are designed for, 'the relatively varying purposes achieved by the dictionary for the benefit of different groups of users' (Hartmann 1987: 16). Of course, there is a close correlation between the characteristics of dictionaries and how they are meant to be used. Wagner (1967: 94, 123–6) distinguished extensive dictionaries (*dictionnaires extensifs*) for reception and selective dictionaries (*dictionnaires sélectifs*) for expression or for vocabulary building. Dubois and Dubois (1971) also used *extensive*, which they opposed to *intensive*: extensive dictionaries emphasize macrostructure (as many words as possible—good for Scrabble!) while intensive dictionaries focus on microstructure (fewer lexical items but more information on each, good for text production).

Dictionaries are said to be *extensive* when their wordlist coincides more or less with the set of all the lexical items that ideally exist in the language, the dialect, the functional lexicon of a particular technique, etc. Dictionaries are said to be *intensive* when, having chosen some of those items on the basis of various criteria, they then provide more information on each.   (Dubois and Dubois 1971: 13).[76]

Matoré (1968: 190) also distinguished between quantitative dictionaries, designed for a vast public looking for quick and superficial information about many different sorts of things, and qualitative dictionaries, for people who want precise information about the language.

1.2.1.4 Genetic typologies

Rey (1977: 54–80) proposed yet another classification, a genetic typology based on the chronologically ordered choices that the lexicographer has to make when compiling a dictionary. Dubois and Dubois (1971: 14), reacting to an earlier version (Rey 1970*b*), called it 'the most detailed that has ever been produced'. Among other things, Rey opposed observed dictionaries, based on the observation of discourse, and observed and generated dictionaries, which use language produced by the lexicographers and their informants; functional and non-functional information, i.e. information that is meant to facilitate communication as opposed

---

[76] Read (1973*a*) uses *extensive* and *intensive* differently. For him, an extensive dictionary distinguishes as many senses as possible in the entries for polysemous words, whereas an intensive dictionary reduces the number of different meanings to a minimum. Thus, an extensive dictionary has many polysemous entries and many different senses in each, whereas an intensive dictionary has few polysemous entries and few senses in each entry (see below, 8.2.3.5).

to information that is only there to educate the user on some linguistic or non-linguistic point; and functional and non-functional macrostructures: if all the entry words belong to the same code, if they can all function together in discourse, the macrostructure is called *functional*. Rey (1977: 80) noted that his typology failed to accommodate all the dictionaries that have been published: it was, he said, 'too narrow in practice, though it may seem too loose to linguists'. At least, it showed that the compilation of a dictionary is the result of a chain of connected choices (Atkins 1993: 10 *ff.*; Atkins and Rundell 2008).

1.2.1.5 The basic types of dictionaries

There are many other binary, tertiary, or scalar distinctions that can be used to classify dictionaries (Pruvost 2006: 119 *ff.*; Atkins and Rundell 2008: 24). But the conclusion is clear: it is impossible to classify dictionaries in a way that would be both orderly and realistic. Dictionaries come in more varieties than can be accounted for in a simple taxonomy. For Rey (2003: 89), the typology of dictionaries is 'almost as complex as that of leguminous plants or of arthropods, and it still awaits its Linné or its Cuvier'. Galisson (2001: 118) even suggested using the term *dictionnaires intersticiels* ('interstitial dictionaries') to refer to those dictionaries that do not belong to any recognized category but are created to bridge a gap. On the whole, however, the following broad distinctions will be found useful and relatively easy to use.

Monolingual and bilingual dictionaries. The distinction between the bilingual, or multilingual (or plurilingual) dictionary and the monolingual (or unilingual)[77] dictionary is usually clear enough. Monolingual dictionaries are those in which the language of description is the same as the language being described: the microstructural information is given in the language from which the words of the macrostructure are drawn. A bilingual dictionary uses two different languages, one as the object of description and one as the instrument of description. Typically, bilingual dictionaries are designed for translation and provide equivalents, although some dictionaries are bilingual without being translation dictionaries: for example, the best etymological dictionary of French, the *Französisches Etymologisches Wörterbuch* of Walter von Wartburg (1922–28), has Latin headwords and explanations about French words written in German.

---

[77] *Monolingual* is the preferred form, although some use *unilingual* (see for example, Weinreich 1962: 26–7). *OED2* had neither in the sense that can be applied to a dictionary, though it did have *monolingual* (antedated recently to 1879 from 1953: *OED News*, December 2002). *OED Online* has one example of *monolingual* that applies to a dictionary dated 1968, but still does not mention the dictionary sense for *unilingual* (or *multilingual* or *plurilingual*). French also has *monolingue* and *unilingue*, equally ignored by most French dictionaries.

There are many intermediate types. *Bilingualized,* or *semi-bilingual* or *hybrid* dictionaries (James 1994; Marello 1996*a*) can be bilingual dictionaries to which short definitions have been added: for example the *Robert and Signorelli Dictionnaire français–italien italien–français,* 1981 (Marello 1998). Or they are monolingual dictionaries in which each word, sometimes each meaning, has a translation into the other language added to the definition. Those have recently become popular in some countries as learners' dictionaries (see below, 5.2.2.5), but are actually an old genre: many of the earliest monolingual dictionaries of European vernacular languages had Latin equivalents. The *Dictionnaire de Trévoux,*[78] published in 1704, still did. There is also at least one dictionary that has two monolingual dictionaries of two languages printed in two columns facing one another on each page: the *Diccionario Inglès, for Spanish Speakers,*[79] in which each English word has an English definition (for the more advanced users) and a definition in Spanish (for the less advanced), with examples of usage and equivalents in Spanish.

The dialect dictionary and, to a lesser extent, the slang dictionary, can be considered as monolingual because their explanations are given in the language of the headwords, or bilingual because the entry words do not belong to the same functional code as the language of explanation. The answer is obviously in the evaluation of the distance between the language variety described in the macrostructure and the standard language. A dictionary defining Americanisms in British English might, given a certain definition of language, be considered bilingual (Geeraerts 1989: 294–5). Such dictionaries have been called *quasi-bilingual* or *homogloss,* the true bilinguals being *heterogloss.*

General and specialized dictionaries. A dictionary can be *general* or *specialized* (or *special-purpose,* or *special* or *restricted*) in its macrostructure or in its microstructure or in both (Landau 2001: 35). The macrostructure of a dictionary can be called *general* if it is representative of the lexis of a language. The macrostructure of the *OED,* for example, is general and so is the *Pocket Oxford Dictionary.* A specialized macrostructure, on the other hand, is one that is restricted to one variety, a dialect, technical jargon, slang, etc., or to one type of entry word, phrasal verbs, idioms, etc.

---

[78] The *Dictionnaire universel françois et latin* or '*Dictionnaire de Trévoux*', compiled by Jesuit scholars in the village of Trévoux, had a first edition in 1704, mostly drawn from Furetière's *Dictionnaire universel* of 1690. This was generally considered mediocre but the numerous editions that followed, with a final one in 8 volumes in 1771, were much better. It was very much influenced by religion, and was very popular, particularly as an encyclopedia. It was used by Johnson (see below, 2.3.2).

[79] de Mello Vianna, F. (1982) (Skokie, IL: Voluntad Publishers, Inc.).

A general microstructure is one that gives a full programme of information for each lexical item, including at least an explanation of the meaning, a definition in a monolingual dictionary, or an equivalent in a bilingual dictionary. If the dictionary gives only one type of information (pronunciation, etymology, collocations, synonyms, idioms, pictorial illustrations, etc.), the microstructure is specialized. A dictionary such as the *Concise Oxford Dictionary* has a general macrostructure and a general microstructure; dictionaries of etymology[80] or dictionaries of pronunciation have a general macrostructure and a specialized microstructure; dictionaries of slang, or of dialects, have a specialized macrostructure and usually a general microstructure. A dictionary giving the etymology of dialect words, for example, would have a specialized macrostructure and a specialized microstructure, clearly an infrequent type.

Encyclopedic and linguistic dictionaries. Dictionaries that have proper names (names of countries, regions, rivers, towns, mountains, etc., names of famous people, of the places of famous battles, names of famous fictional characters, of planets, etc.) are called *encyclopedic*, while dictionaries that do not have proper names can be called *linguistic*, or *language dictionaries*—nobody knows what to call them. Encyclopedic dictionaries also have a microstructure that gives more information on things, while linguistic dictionaries will focus more on information on words.

Foreign learners' and native speakers' dictionaries. Many early dictionaries were designed for foreign learners or tourists (see below, 2.2.3), and the dictionary for native speakers appeared later in many cultures. Recently, dictionaries for foreign learners have been flourishing again, in Britain first and then in other countries (see below, Chapter 5).

Dictionaries for adults and dictionaries for children. Dictionaries can be designed for different ages, from small children to adults. Dictionaries for adolescents are designed for the needs of the school or college: their wordlists are based on what is found in schoolbooks, and their microstructural information is what teenagers need for their schoolwork. Dictionaries for children 'range from the large-format work with pictures and an imaginative use of colour, aimed at those just beginning to learn to read, to school dictionaries that look like the adult version' (Jackson 2002: 83). The latter have a shortened wordlist with only the most important words of the language, or those that the lexicographer thinks the children will need. Some also use different techniques for the explanation of meaning, with pictorial illustrations and illustrative examples before, or even in

---

[80] On etymological dictionaries of English, see Liberman (1998).

lieu of, definitions (see below, 8.2.5.9). They are interesting for the metalexico-grapher, although they have rarely been the objects of research (but see Corbin 2001). Ilson (1986*b*: 70) notes that American children's dictionaries are more innovative than dictionaries for adults:

The American children's dictionary as a genre is a remarkable achievement. There is a marvellously creative use of illustrations in such books. They have experimented with unorthodox defining techniques and sometimes with the replacement of definitions by examples only, as C.K. Ogden did in *Basic by Examples* (1933). Even more interesting, some have done in practice what many semanticists have advocated in theory: grouped senses by semantic categories across part-of-speech boundaries, as when the military senses of charge are explained next to each other even though some are nominal and some are verbal.[81]

One of the peculiarities of children's dictionaries is that they have to please three populations, the children for whom they are intended, the teachers who recom-mend them, and the parents who buy them.

Alphabetized and non-alphabetized dictionaries. Most dictionaries are alphabet-ized, but there is a wide spectrum of dictionaries that use a system of classifica-tion based, as we have seen, on the contents of the entry words.

Electronic and paper dictionaries. More and more dictionaries are published in electronic form. Some are on CD-ROM, some are available on the Internet and some are sold as hand-held devices (see below, 9.2). Some are the same text as the corresponding paper dictionaries, like the *TLF informatisé* (*TLFI*), some are temporary versions of dictionaries that will later be published on paper, like *OED3*, and some are dictionaries that will never be published on paper, like *Wiktionary.*

1.2.2 *The monolingual general-purpose dictionary*

Among all these types of dictionaries, one occupies a particular position in all societies: the monolingual general-purpose dictionary (GPD). It is the dictionary that every household has, that most people think of first when the word *diction-ary* is mentioned, it is the type that is most often bought, most often consulted, and the one that plays the most important role in the society that produces it. It sells in large numbers everywhere, and it is also the one that metalexicographers describe most, sometimes exclusively. In fact, some of the definitions of *dictionary*

---

[81] The idea of grouping senses semantically rather than grammatically, Ilson says, goes back to Thorndike in the 1930s.

that we have seen are only definitions of that particular type in a particular society at a particular period: the general-purpose dictionary is the prototypical dictionary for every one of us.

The typical GPD is monolingual, alphabetical, has a general macrostructure, a representative wordlist, a general microstructure with at least a definition for each meaning of each entry word, and is designed for adults. Geeraerts (1989: 293–4) expresses this as a specialist of prototype semantics (see below, 8.2.5.7):

The prototypical dictionary... is monolingual rather than multilingual, provides linguistic rather than encyclopedic information, contains primarily semasiological rather than onomasiological or non-semantic data, gives a description of a standard language rather than restricted or marked language varieties, and serves a pedagogical purpose rather than a critical or scholarly one.

The general-purpose dictionary comes in an infinite number of sub-types in different societies and different periods. The study of those variations will be one of the main objects of this book.

A BRIEF HISTORY OF
ENGLISH DICTIONARIES

2.1 PRE-HISTORY: FROM GLOSSARIES TO DICTIONARIES

2.1.1 *The origins*

SUMERIAN lists of up to 14,000 words on clay tablets dating back to the third millennium BC have been found, and these can be considered as ancestors both of our dictionaries and our encyclopedias (Boisson *et al.* 1991: 263).[1] They have been called *pre-dictionaries*, or *proto-dictionaries*, although they were very different from the modern type. Even societies without a writing system seem to have had oral compilations of words that may be considered as pre-dictionaries: there is at least one contemporary African society that has been shown to have lists of words among its oral records used in traditional village recitations. Those lists are either bilingual or monolingual, sometimes with short definitions, half way between poetry and lexicography (Boisson *et al.* 1991: 292). And there must have been others, including perhaps our closest ancestors on the European continent, although no traces have been found. Most societies, and probably all language communities with writing systems have dictionaries, produced either by themselves or by outsiders.

In Ancient Greece, Aristophanes of Byzantium created a school of lexicography for the study of dialects in the third century BC. In Rome, Varro, called the

---

[1] On the history of dictionaries, see Rey (1982), McArthur (1986*b*), Hausmann *et al.* (1989–91), Boulanger (2003). On the history of British dictionaries, see Starnes and Noyes (1946, 1991), Starnes (1954), Sledd and Kolb (1955), Schäfer (1980, 1989), Osselton (1983, 1989), Stein (1985), Green (1996), Read (2003), Cowie (2008). On the history of dictionaries in the USA, see Friend (1967), Wells (1973), and Burkett (1979).

most learned of the Romans by his contemporaries, compiled a thematic dictionary, part of *De Lingua Latina*, in the first century BC, and in the second century AD Julius Pollux wrote the *Onomasticon*, a dictionary of Attic synonyms and phrases in ten volumes, arranged by subject matter. The Romans also produced many Greek–Latin glossaries. In the seventh century, Isidore of Seville published his famous *Etymologiae*, a sort of encyclopedia that remained influential until the fifteenth century, and several encyclopedias were compiled during the Middle Ages (Rey 1982; McArthur 1986*b*), among which was the *Liber de proprietatibus rerum* by Barthélemy l'Anglais (or Bartholomeus Anglicus), written *c*.1230.

The development of dictionaries was facilitated by the introduction of the *codex*, i.e. a text in book form, with separate pages bound together and a cover, which gradually replaced the *volumen*, or scroll, i.e. a roll of parchment or paper, between the second and the fourth century (Boulanger 2003: 218). The *codex* made consultation easier; because it could be opened on a table, it made it possible to compare two pages, it provided precise references by page numbers,[2] and it allowed the use of free hands to take notes (Pruvost 2000: 1). It was therefore much better suited than the *volumen* to works of reference.[3] But the decisive step was the introduction of printing in Europe in the fifteenth century, imported to England by Caxton in 1476. This changed the whole attitude to knowledge: until then, 'reference books such as dictionaries were nonexistent ... — indeed incompatible with the medieval educational spirit of achieving an active oral command of knowledge through constant *repetitio*' (Ostler 2007: 172). The first book 'that bore a date of publication (1460) was the *Catholicon...*, a Latin grammar and dictionary intended for those in holy orders that had been compiled in 1286 by Johannes Januensis de Balbix' (Ostler 2007: 251). Printing multiplied the number of books made available to the public: 'By 1500, 20 million printed volumes had been produced' (Ostler 2005: 326).[4] And as more books became available to an ever-increasing public the more need there was for reference books.

Early dictionaries were compiled for various reasons (Boisson *et al.* 1991). Some were monolingual lists of names of things ordered by themes, produced for the instruction of future administrators, perhaps to be learnt by heart, as in

---

[2] Ostler (2007: 121) speculates that the *codex* was popularized—though not invented—by early Christians who needed to quote from holy texts in their sermons.

[3] Reading off the screen of a computer is, oddly enough, closer to using a *volumen* than it is to using a *codex*.

[4] The figure comes from Febvre, L. and Martin, H.-J. (1958), *L'Apparition du livre* (Paris: Albin Michel): 248–9.

Sumer or Egypt, some were bilingual lists designed to facilitate commercial or administrative relations with neighbouring societies, some were prepared to help Christian missionaries in their attempts at converting the local populations in Africa, America, or Asia. And many dictionaries were not designed to meet the needs of a public but to satisfy the compilers themselves: they were lists of names to embrace the world, to impose some order on the chaos. This diversity of purposes is reflected in the classification of dictionaries in libraries, Boulanger (2003: 356) notes: in the Middle Ages they were sometimes with the grammars, sometimes with schoolbooks, sometimes with religious books and Bibles.

Most histories of lexicography say that the first dictionaries were bilingual, but this was true only in Europe and a few other societies where bilingual glossaries or dictionaries were necessary to clarify the meaning of religious texts. In most societies, the first dictionaries were monolingual, because each community was preoccupied by its own existence, certain of its superiority over its barbaric neighbours and saw little interest other than commercial in other languages and cultures (Boisson *et al.* 1991).

2.1.2 *Glosses and early bilingual dictionaries*

The direct ancestors of European dictionaries were handwritten glosses added to Latin manuscripts in the Middle Ages, in order to help readers who did not have enough Latin to understand the more difficult words.[5] These glosses, written in the margins (marginal glosses) or between the lines (interlinear glosses), were in Latin at first, but by 'the seventh century they were appearing in English' (Halliday 2004: 14), and after that they could be in one or the other, or both, whichever seemed to be clearest. Soon, they were collected, first at the end of the manuscript and then to form separate volumes, called *glossaries*. Glossaries introduced the decontextualization that was to be one of the main characteristics of dictionaries: in glosses, every piece of information applied to a word or group of words in a unique context, but when the collections of glosses were produced independently, they had to give information that was valid for all contexts.

A famous example of an early bilingual glossary is the eighth-century[6] *Reichenau glossary*, or *Glosses of Reichenau*, discovered in the eponymous monastery on

---

[5] Glossing is an old technique. The tablets of Tell-el-Amarna, in Canaanite, were glossed in Akkadian *c.*1350 BC (Claude Boisson, personal communication). 'In India as early as the third to second century BC, glossaries were drawn up to explain the difficult words in the Vedas, which by that time were already a thousand years old' (Halliday 2004: 11). The same had been done in the Roman Empire for Greek texts explained in Latin (Boulanger 2003: 213).

[6] Many sources give the year 768. *Encyclopedia Universalis* says tenth century.

an island on Lake Constance, which had two lists: one of 3,152 difficult words from the Vulgate and another of 1,725 hard words, i.e. unusual and difficult words of various origins with glosses in Romance or easy Latin (Boulanger 2003: 314–15). Ælfric's *Glossary* or *Nomina multarum rerum anglice*, with about 1,300 thematically ordered Latin words with Old English equivalents, was produced *c*.1000 (Hüllen 1999/2006: 62), probably the oldest glossary giving English equivalents (Boulanger 2003: 240). John Garland's *Dictionarius*, famous for its pioneering use of the word *dictionarius*, as we have seen, appeared *c*.1225.[7]

With the increase of the commerce of goods and ideas between nations, multilingual lists soon appeared. Early examples are the *Codex comanicus*, a Persian–Latin–Kipchak[8] dictionary written *c*.1350, found in Petrarch's library, and the *Vocabularius quadriidiomaticus* of Dietrich Engelhus, published *c*.1400, which had Latin translations of Greek, Hebrew, and German words (Boulanger 2003: 376). Ambrogio Calepino, an Augustinian monk from Bergamo, published his *Dictionarium latinarum e grecopariter derivantium* in 1502, which became the best-known dictionary of the period. It contained Latin and a few Greek entries, but later editions also had Italian and French, and it was eventually expanded to eleven languages, including Polish and Hungarian. His *Dictionarium decem Linguarum*, published in 1585, was a huge folio which was soon known by the name of its author,[9] the first in the history of lexicography, to be followed by Furetière, Johnson, Webster, Littré, Hornby, Robert, etc. 'François Garon's *Vocabulary of five languages: Latin, Italian, French, Spanish and German* proved so popular after its publication in Venice in 1526 that by the 1546 edition it had been extended to cover eight languages' (Hale 1994: 159). John Baret's *An Alvearie or Triple Dictionarie, in Englishe, Latin, and French* was published in London in 1573 and there was a *Quadruple* edition with Greek in 1580. All were based on Eliot's *Dictionary*.

In England, many bilingual Latin to English glossaries were published in the sixteenth century. The *(H)ortus Vocabulorum* (Garden of Words), was published by Wynkyn de Worde, the famous printer and publisher, *c*.1500.[10] The *Dictionary*

---

[7] Modern dictionaries were also inspired by thematic dictionaries (Hüllen 1999/2006) or vocabularies (Starnes and Noyes 1946: 197 *ff.*) and specialized dictionaries (Read 2003), that both existed long before language dictionaries.

[8] A language spoken in the Crimea.

[9] Interestingly, *calepin*, derived from *Calepino*, which had come to mean *dictionary*, means 'small notebook' in modern French.

[10] These early dictionaries of English are listed on the catalogue of the Cordell Collection of the Indiana State University Library. Many are available in full or in part on *Early English Books Online* (EEBO) and/or on *Early Modern English Dictionaries Database* (EMEDD; Lancashire 2004), lately renamed *Lexicons of Early Modern English* (LEME), which are accessible via many library systems. Many also exist as facsimile reprints.

of Syr T. Eliot Knyght (1538), the first to use the word *dictionary*, 'completed at Henry VIII's instance'[11] (Lancashire 2004: 19), was the first dictionary ever to be published with pictures (McDermott 2005: 174). It went through several editions. Thomas Cooper's *Thesaurus Linguae Romanae et Britannicae* (1565) had 2,000 pages, much material taken from Eliot and quotations[12] from classical authors. It was probably used by the young Shakespeare (Starnes and Noyes 1946: 242). Thomas Thomas's *Dictionarium Linguae Latinae et Anglicanae*, 1,000 pages and 'nearly 40,000 headwords', including 'common function words as well as content words', with 'information on grammar and usage' (Moon 2004b: 639), was published in 1587.

The first glossaries went from Latin to the vernacular language, but glossaries from the vernacular language to Latin soon appeared, and were handy tools for learning Latin. Some were the same text reversed, a complex operation with modern dictionaries but easier with glossaries that had minimal microstructural information, a short, often one-word, explanation. The earliest example of an English to Latin glossary was probably the *Promptorium Parvulorum, sive Clericorum* ('A Storehouse for Children or Clerics'), an alphabetical list of about 12,000 words collected for English schoolboys by the Dominican monk Galfridus Grammaticus[13] (Geoffrey the Grammarian), compiled around 1440 (Green 1996: 39) and printed by Caxton in 1499.[14] The *Catholicon Anglicum*, published *c.*1480, had about 8,000 entries and provided many Latin synonyms. Richard Huloet's (or Howlet's) *Abecedarium Anglo-Latinum* was published in 1552. *A Shorte Dictionarie of English and Latin for Yonge Beginners*, by John Withals[15] (1553), which had pictures, was 'the best-selling dictionary of the century' (Green 1996: 92), 'wildly popular ..., remaining in print for more than 70 years, at least until 1634' (Winchester 2003: 21). John Rider's *Biblioteca Scholastica* was published in 1589.

Other European languages had their bilingual glossaries or dictionaries at approximately the same time. German had a Latin–German *Vocabularius brevilogus* compiled in the fourteenth century. For Italian, the first Latin–Italian

---

[11] Many dictionaries have been compiled 'at the instance' of sovereigns.
[12] *Citation* seems to be the preferred term in American English, while British authors prefer *quotation* (Simpson 2003: 267). Ramson (2002: 27) uses *citation* in the sense of an appeal to an authority to establish the meaning of a word and *quotation* in the sense of the actual text fragment. Both should be distinguished from examples: 'Those that serve as textual or authentic evidence to document the use of a specific sense or construction by a specific writer at a specific time are commonly termed *quotations*. Those which have an exemplificatory function and for which the source has no attesting rôle are regarded as examples' (Stein 1999: 45).
[13] The author of the *Promptorium* is presented as anonymous in many sources.
[14] It was used by the editors of *OED*, who extracted over 5,500 quotations from it (Brewer 2004: 13).
[15] Of whom virtually nothing is known, except that he was a schoolmaster (Starnes 1954: 167–8; Hüllen 1999/2006: 168).

dictionary was published in 1470/5 by Nicodemo Tranchedino and for Spanish, it was Antonio de Nebrija's *Lexicon ex sermone latino in hispaniensem*, published in Salamanca in 1492. In France, the *Dictionarium latino-gallicum* of Robert Estienne, published in Paris in 1513, was highly successful and was reprinted several times. Estienne later reversed it to compile the *Dictionaire Françoislatin contenant les motz et manieres de parler François, tournez en latin*, published in 1539, the same year as François I produced the famous ordinance of Villers-Cotterêts making French obligatory in all official documents. It was a *folio* volume with about 10,000 French entries ordered alphabetically, each provided with translations in Latin and sometimes explanations in French, compiled for students. It laid the foundations of dictionary typography: headwords were set on separate lines, in a larger font and indented and examples of usage were also indented (Luna 2004). There was an augmented edition in 1549, which was to become the basis of Jean Nicot's *Thresor*, published in 1606, six years after Nicot's death, which had about 16,000 words—a considerable figure if one considers that the first edition of the *Dictionnaire* of the French Academy in 1694 had about 18,000. Nicot's *Thresor* had extended explanations in French, and is therefore often considered as the first monolingual dictionary of French, although it also provided Latin equivalents.

The next step was bilingual glossaries between two vernacular languages. They were preceded by textbooks containing lists of equivalents such as *The Introductory to Wryte and to Pronounce French* by Alexander Barclay (1521), the famous translator of *The Ship of Fools*, and *Lesclarcissement de la langue françoyse* (1530), by John Palsgrave, who was Mary Tudor's tutor, which gave definitions and illustrated some meanings with quotations, proverbs, etc. (Williams 2000: 42). The first French–English dictionary was *A dictionarie French and English*, published in 1567 or 1568 (but the only surviving edition is dated 1570), compiled by Thomas Chaloner (Eccles 1986: 52) or by Claude de Sainliens, or Desainliens, a French Huguenot who signed his English books Claudius Hollyband, or Holliband.[16] It was largely copied from the many editions of the *Dictionaire Françoislatin* of Robert Estienne. The second was *The Treasurie of the French tong*, published in 1580 by Claudius Hollyband, actually a new edition of the preceding dictionary. Yet another edition, published in 1593, was called *A Dictionarie French and English*. The *Dictionary of the French and English Tongues: Brief Directions for such as desire to learne the French Tongue*, by Randle Cotgrave (1611), often considered as the first French–English dictionary, was extensively copied from those predecessors. It had many illustrative quotations, including Rabelais

---

[16] Sainliens signed his books in Latin Claudius a Sancto Viculo.

(Hitchings 2005: 48). John Florio's[17] *A Worlde of Wordes, or Dictionarie in Italian and English* (1598), a dictionary of Italian words drawn from a corpus of literary texts, with English definitions and translations, had many different editions (Starnes 1965).

2.2 DICTIONARIES FROM THE RENAISSANCE TO THE EIGHTEENTH CENTURY

2.2.1 *Dictionaries of hard words*

The first monolingual dictionaries in Europe appeared in the early seventeenth century, as part of the grammatization of vernacular languages, when it became clear that they also, like Latin, could have a grammar and be codified. An early example was, for Flemish, the *Tresor der Duytsscher talen*, by Jan Van den Werve, 1553. In France, Jean Nicot published his *Thresor de la langue françoise* in 1606. In Spain, the first monolingual was the *Tesoro de la lengua castellana o española* by Covarrubias, published in 1611. In Italy, after many glossaries of Tuscan, the first monolingual dictionary was the *Vocabolario della Crusca* published in Venice in 1612 by the Italian Academy, a normative dictionary designed to fix the language in a form that could be used by the literary authors of the time, the first normative dictionary, later to be imitated in Spain and in France.

For English, the first true monolingual dictionary was *A Table Alphabeticall, conteyning and teaching the true writing, and vnderstanding of hard vsuall English wordes, borrowed from the Hebrew, Greeke, Latine, or French. etc.*, published by Robert Cawdr(e)y in 1604 (Plate 4). Cawdrey, a schoolmaster, collected his 2,560 words, mostly from Thomas's *Dictionarium Linguae Latinae et Anglicanae*, published in 1587 (Starnes and Noyes 1991: 15) and from earlier grammar books. Among those, there was Edmund Coote's *The English Schoole-Maister*, published in 1596, which was the first grammar book to include a list of difficult words with their definitions, mostly copied from Richard Mulcaster's *The First Part of the Elementarie*, 1582, which had 8,000 terms without definitions, including function words and other common words, i.e. words used in current usage such as *centre*, *national*, and *real* (Moon 2004b: 642). Coote went through sixty-four printings

---

[17] John Florio was the author of the first translation of Montaigne's *Essais* (1595) into English in 1603, which is famous among translators for having changed French geographical names into English ones.

until 1737, and some think he was the true father of English lexicography: 'If the English dictionary can be said to have an "inventor", that man is in no sense Cawdrey, but is Edmund Coote' (Read 2003: 194).[18]

The *Table Alphabeticall* contained 'hard usual' words, words that were used, not 'inkhorn terms' (Moon 2004*b*), but words that were difficult. They were arranged in an order that was not exactly alphabetical, despite the title. It was as simple in its microstructure as the title suggests: each headword was explained by a synonym or two, sometimes three or four, or a short gloss.

Abandon 'cast away, or yield up, to leave, or forsake'
Abash 'blush'
abba 'father'

It went through four editions until 1617.[19] It is interesting to note that the first edition was published seven years before the publication of the Authorized Version of the Bible, at a time when 'Shakespeare, John Donne and others were laying . . . the foundations of English literature' (McArthur 1998: 89). Shakespeare was 40, and therefore 'had no access to a [monolingual] dictionary during most of his writing career' (Winchester 2003: 19).

Next came *An English Expositor, Teaching the Interpretation of the Hardest Words Used in Our Language* by John Bullokar, another schoolmaster. It was also a dictionary of hard words, mostly words borrowed from other languages or based on Latin or Greek. It was published in 1616, the year of Shakespeare's death. Bullokar had already published a *Brief Grammar for English* in 1586—the same authors often wrote dictionaries and grammar books. The *Expositor* had about 5,000 words, twice as many as Cawdrey, and a few pictures. It was the first dictionary to indicate 'to what profession or special field of knowledge a term belongs' (Starnes and Noyes 1946: 21). It went through three editions during Bullokar's lifetime, and then several others until 1731, each new edition enlarged by free borrowings from other dictionaries.

The English Dictionarie: or, An Interpreter of Hard English Words by H. C., Henry Cocker(r)am,[20] of whom virtually nothing is known, published in 1623, was the first monolingual to use the word *dictionary* in its title, almost a century after the bilingual *Dictionary* of Elyot. It had about 5,000 words arranged in three

---

[18] On early English grammar-books, their use of lexicographic techniques, and how they were used by lexicographers, see Mitchell (2005).

[19] It is available on the website of the University of Toronto. Of the first edition there is apparently only one surviving copy, in the Bodleian Library at Oxford.

[20] The title pages of early dictionaries were extremely copious, but often did not give the name of the author, just initials.

books, many borrowed from Bullokar. The second book was original in that it included 'vulgar' words, glossed by more refined equivalents, clearly intended as a help for those users who wanted to express themselves elegantly. Cockeram also had some proper names and a few pictures in the third book, which introduced an encyclopedic tradition in lexicography. It went through twelve editions until 1670.

Glossographia: or, A Dictionary Interpreting all such Hard Words...as are now used in our refined English Tongue,[21] published in 1656 by T.B. (Thomas Blount, a barrister), had about 10,700 entries. It had quotations and pictures, and was the first dictionary to supply etymologies. Blount was also 'the first English lexicographer to cite the authorities he had consulted' (Starnes and Noyes 1946: 47). His dictionary went through four editions until 1681.

The early monolingual dictionaries of English had poor wordlists compared to the bilingual dictionaries that had preceded them (Osselton 1983: 14). Read (2003: 207) notes that 'the compilers of English dictionaries, strangely enough, never took advantage of these sources [i.e. the bilinguals]', and he even doubts that the ones were really derived from the others. The first monolinguals recorded only, or mostly, hard words, perhaps because they were influenced by the glossaries and dictionaries that had preceded them (Osselton 1990: 1944), probably because the English language felt the need to assert itself by enlisting more words, particularly learned words from Greek and Latin. This happened only in Britain and in no other European country (Dolezal 2007), and English dictionaries of hard words would continue being published well into the eighteenth century. McArthur (1998: 202) calls them *crypto-bilingual,* 'because they served to explain many foreignisms that were pouring into English at the time'. Many of their words had simpler synonyms of Germanic origin and were hardly ever used: Read (2003: 197) lists *adpugne, adstupiate, defust, depex, bulbitate, catillate, fraxate, glabretall, noxious, plumative, prodigity,* etc.[22] But they were included in dictionary after dictionary, because the lexicographers just copied their predecessors, and no doubt because there was a public demand for such lists.[23]

[21] A *glossographer,* for Blount, was 'he that interprets strange words.'

[22] Read (2003: 196) mentions that 'in *The Duchess of Malfi,* produced about 1616, a physician speaks of "A very pestilent disease, my lord, they call it lycanthropia." The Marquis of Pescara then answers, "What's that? I need a dictionary to't"'. One feels that there is more amusement, perhaps contempt, than admiration for the dictionary as a repository of hard words.

[23] However, there were people who thought that those words should be eliminated from the language. The resulting battle, that raged in the late sixteenth and in the seventeenth century, came to be known as the 'ynkhorne controversy' (Hüllen 2004b: 85).

2.2.2 *The inclusion of common words*

The New World of English Words: or a General English Dictionary by E. P., Edward Phillips, who was Milton's nephew and student, was published in 1658, the first English dictionary to be published as a folio (Plate 2).[24] It had about 11,000 words, including proper names. Phillips 'claimed the right to judge good words and bad' (Lancashire 2005: 166), which made him one of Johnson's favourite lexicographers. He started the practice of 'branding' words that he thought were unsuitable for polite use by a dagger sign (Osselton 1958). He did not have pictures, but had field labels and included a history of the English language, a first in English lexicography (Sledd and Kolb 1955: 11). His dictionary went through five editions until 1700, although several authors had 'exposed his etymological howlers' (Lancashire 2005: 157) and lexical blunders, and shown that he had 'scandalously plagiarized much of Blount's own *Glossographia* (1656)' (Lancashire 2005: 157) without once mentioning Blount's work, which made him Blount's archenemy.[25] Phillips also probably lied when he named '34 "learned Gentlemen and Artists" as if they had assisted him' (Lancashire 2005: 165; see also Landau 2001: 214). It was published in a revised and expanded form in 1706 under the title *The New World of Words, or Universal English Dictionary* by J. K. (John Kersey),[26] who almost doubled its size, 'from 14,000 in 1671 to 26,000 word-entries in 1706' (Lancashire 2005: 158), 38,000 according to Starnes and Noyes (1946: 84), including common words. This was highly successful, and it was also the first dictionary 'in which it was announced as an aim to give words pertaining to remarkable things in "our *American* Plantations"' (Read 2003: 223).

Elisha Coles's *An English Dictionary* (1676), with about 25,000 words, mostly hard words, also corrected many of Phillips' errors. It included slang and dialect words, a first in general lexicography, and proper names with encyclopedic developments. Coles was a 'school-master and teacher of the English tongue to foreigners', as the title page said. His *Dictionary* was very popular, going through eleven editions until 1732.

The *Gazophylacium Anglicanum*, published in 1689, considered anonymous by some but attributed to Stephen Skinner, the famous author of the *Etymologicon Linguae Anglicanae* (1671) by others, with a second edition called *A New English Dictionary Showing the Etymological Derivation of the English Tongue* in 1691,

[24] I.e. with a page half the size of the printing page.
[25] In 1673, Blount published *A World of Errors Discovered in the New World of Words*.
[26] 'The almost unknown John Kersey' (Lancashire 2005: 158), 'son of the famous algebraist' (Read 2003: 222), but also 'the most gifted early eighteenth-century English lexicographer' (Lancashire 2005: 166).

explained the etymology of 'all the common English words', and it had a second part with proper names. *A New English Dictionary: Or, a Compleat Collection of the Most Proper and Significant Words, Commonly Used in the Language; With a Short and Clear Exposition of Difficult Words and Terms of Art*, by J. K.'s (probably John Kersey[27]) was published in 1702, with a new edition in 1713. It had about 28,000 words, including 'Difficult Words and Terms of Art', i.e. technical terms, as well as more common words, 'the Most Proper and Significant Words, Commonly used in the Language', than any other dictionary before. Those words were just glossed, but their presence made the *New English Dictionary* one of the first dictionaries in 'the tradition of comprehensive lexical coverage' (Barnbrook 2005: 194). It 'held its popularity for seventy years' (Starnes and Noyes 1946: 78). John Kersey later compiled a *Dictionarium Anglo-Britannicum: or, a general English Dictionary, comprehending a brief... explication of all sorts of difficult words* (1708), which had about 35,000 words and was 'an abridgment of the Kersey-Phillips *New World of Words* of 1706' (Starnes and Noyes 1946: 96). It was important in the history of English lexicography because it was the first abridged dictionary. Other dictionaries of the same period were Edward Cocker's *English Dictionary*, 1704, about 22,000 words, with a last edition in 1724, and *Glossographia Anglicana Nova* (1707), which was, according to Starnes and Noyes (1946: 94), the 'first English dictionary to make any considerable use of woodcuts'.

For French, the first true monolingual dictionary was the *Dictionnaire françois contenant généralement tous les mots français tant vieux que modernes et les termes des sciences et des arts*, published in Geneva[28] by César-Pierre Richelet, a former schoolteacher, in 1680. It was a dictionary of about 25,000 entries in two volumes compiled 'in order to give some help to gentlemen who love our language'. This means that Molière, who died in 1673, never had a monolingual dictionary and Corneille could only use one during the last four years of his life. The *Dictionnaire françois* was a 'dictionnaire de mots', it indicated pronunciation and had quotations from the best authors. Ten years later, in 1690, the *Dictionnaire universel, contenant généralement tous les mots françois tant vieux que modernes et les termes de toutes les Sciences et des Arts* of Antoine Furetière was published. It had three volumes and about 40,000 entries. Furetière had been attending the meetings of the Academy but was dissatisfied with the results and decided to produce his own dictionary, with specialized terms carefully explained. It was a

[27] Landau (2001: 429) mentions a source that shows 'skepticism about the attribution'.
[28] The French Academy, which had been granted a monopoly on dictionaries, had forbidden its publication in France.

'dictionnaire de choses', although it also had a few literary quotations and did not have pictures. His entry for *poire* (pear), for example, contains a long list of all the different kinds of pear, with their colour, taste, time of maturity, etc.

At the same time, the first encyclopedic dictionaries and encyclopedias appeared. John Harris' *Lexicon Technicum* (1704–10) was a dictionary of specialized, mostly scientific, terms, later to be used by Johnson. In 1728, Ephraim Chambers[29] published his *Cyclopaedia, or an Universal Dictionary of Arts and Sciences*, the first encyclopedia in English, but organized in alphabetically ordered short articles. It aimed at summing up all human knowledge, drawing on Pierre Bayle's *Dictionaire historique et critique* (1696), a dictionary of proper names with a highly elaborate macrostructure, itself a reaction to Moreri's *Grand Dictionaire historique ou Le mélange curieux de l'histoire sacrée et profane* (1683), a very popular dictionary[30] that was translated into English by Jeremy Collier in 1674.[31] Chambers presented human knowledge in a rationally organized hierarchy, with an extensive system of cross-references explained at length in his *Preface*, making his dictionary half onomasiological. He was also in favour of the creation of an authority on language, as in France and in Italy, but protested that this was not the lexicographer's job, as a dictionary could only record usage (*Preface*). The *Cyclopaedia* was a huge success, going through several editions, and was used by Johnson. It was also the main source of inspiration for Diderot and d'Alembert's *Encyclopédie*.[32] Encyclopedic dictionaries and encyclopedias were henceforth to be used by all lexicographers for the compilation of general-purpose dictionaries.

Dictionaries containing common words became dominant in the course of the eighteenth century, while the dictionary of hard words all but disappeared, undoubtedly the sign of a change in the role of the dictionary. It is probably not a coincidence that the word *lexicography* appeared during the seventeenth century: the first occurrence recorded in the *OED* is 1680, in *Deaf and Dumb Man's Tutor*, by George Dalgarno, 'I shall therefore only make some few reflexions upon Etymology and Syntax, supposing Orthography to belong to Lexicography'.[33]

[29] Ephraim Chambers should not be confused with the Chambers brothers, authors of *Chambers' Encyclopaedia* (10 volumes) published between 1860 and 1868. The *Cyclopaedia* can be consulted on the Internet: http://www.cyclopaedia.org/

[30] Victor Hugo used it for historical notations in *La Légende des siècles* (Matoré 1968: 91), though he did his best to hide the fact (Brunet 1992: 39).

[31] The dictionary of names disappeared from the English scene after the seventeenth century.

[32] Diderot had been asked to translate the *Cyclopaedia* into French after Chambers himself, who spoke French fluently, had refused, for obscure reasons, perhaps his declining health. But the project eventually developed into the much larger *Encyclopédie* (Darnton 1979).

[33] It was long thought that *lexicography* had been first used by Samuel Johnson in 1755. In French, *lexicographie*, from *lexicography*, was first used in the *Encyclopédie*.

2.2.3 The role of the first monolingual dictionaries

Monolingual dictionaries were popular right from the start. There is no record of a lexicographer having ever made a fortune, but many dictionaries were very successful, going through several editions over extended periods of time, often several decades, sometimes more than a century. As dictionaries were a profitable market, there was ferocious competition between authors and between publishers.

All lexicographers made heavy use of the work of their predecessors, at a time when copyright laws did not exist:[34] they all borrowed extensively from other dictionaries, sometimes with little new material, whatever the titles of their dictionaries said, and often did not name their sources. Such practices continued well into the eighteenth century (Sledd and Kolb 1955: 4; Reddick 1990/1996: 26).

> The use of previous or contemporary authors' work, parts of work or ideas without acknowledging the source, that is, the practice known as plagiarism nowadays, was not considered dishonest, base or deceitful in the eighteenth century. On the contrary, it was an extended practice which dated back to the Renaissance 'commonplace book'.[35]
>
> (Rodriguez-Álvarez and Rodriguez-Gil 2006: 296)

Most of those early dictionaries were compiled by schoolmasters, and they were didactic tools, for young native speakers or foreigners, all those who suffered from an education gap and who needed to improve their mastery of the language, particularly those people who did not have access to the traditional means of education (Dolezal 1986; see also Curzan 2000: 96).

> The cultural and educational function of the earliest English dictionaries—down to 1750 at least—was to enable a wider, unlatined, reading public to understand and to learn to use the new technical and abstract vocabulary of learned words, which in many cases thus became less 'hard' and were assimilated into the language.   (Osselton 1983: 16)

This was clear in their prefaces or in their title pages that often occupied all of the front pages: for example, the *Preface* to the 1586 edition of Withals' *A shorte Dictionarie in Latine and English, Verie Profitable for Yong Beginners*[36] explained that the dictionary was to 'preserve the tender youth ... from the infection of barbarousness'. Cawdrey's *Table Alphabeticall* was 'for the benefit and helpe of

---

[34] The first law on copyright in England is dated 1710 ('Statute of Queen Anne').

[35] The commonplace book was a collection of notable passages and quotations gathered by students for future use.

[36] The exact wording of the title could be changed with each new edition. This still occasionally happens.

Ladies, Gentlewomen, or any other unskilfull persons'; Bullokar's *English Expositor* was for 'the ignorant'; the aim of Cockeram's *Dictionarie* was 'Enabling as well Ladies and Gentlewomen, young Schollers, Clarkes, Merchants, as also Strangers of any Nation, to the understanding of the more difficult Authors... and the more speedy attaining of an elegant perfection of the English tongue'; Blount's *Glossographia* was 'chiefly intended for the more-knowing Women, and less-knowing Men'; E. P.'s *General English Dictionary* was 'very necessary for Strangers, as well as our own Countrymen; or for all persons that would rightly understand what they discourse, Write, or Read'; Kersey's *New English Dictionary* (1702) was for 'young Scholars, Tradesmen, Artificers,[37] and the Female Sex, who would learn to spell truely', and the *Dictionarium Anglo-Britannicum* (1708) added that 'it may be a continual help to all that want an Instructor'.

Perhaps it is this public of users that explains the evolution of dictionaries: for such people, even the easy words of the language were hard.

In a situation where the standard national language, as these languages developed in Europe in the centuries that preceded the Dictionary of the French Academy, is not the native dialect of many of its users, many seemingly 'easy words' of such a standard language are 'hard words' for such non-native users of it, so that many of the users seek advice in the dictionary.   (Zgusta 1986*b*: 75–6)

2.3 THE TURNING POINT OF THE EIGHTEENTH CENTURY

2.3.1 *The precursors*

The eighteenth century was a period of rapid evolution for monolingual dictionaries, at a time when many other things were also changing in European societies. Because of the general fascination for knowledge and its dissemination, because of the development of science and technology, because there were more people writing, to a wider public, because periodicals appeared in many countries at that time, there was a need for reference works of all kinds, and particularly a need for authority on what words meant (Nunberg 1994). Zgusta (1986*b*: 74) argues that the great change in lexicography was initiated by the first edition of the *Dictionnaire de l'Académie* in 1694, and the dates proposed by Collison (1982) and Osselton (1983) are close: 1702, the publication of J. K.'s *New English*

---

[37] Artificers were engineers, skilled practitioners of an art or trade.

Dictionary, and 1708, the publication of Kersey's *Dictionarium Anglo-Britannicum*. The first decade of the eighteenth century was certainly remarkable in England: it produced five new dictionaries, with the first universal dictionary, the first abridged, and the largest dictionary ever—all by John Kersey (Starnes and Noyes 1946: 98).

The *Universal Etymological English Dictionary* (1721) of Nathan Bailey, yet another schoolmaster, had about 40,000 words and 'claimed to be a complete inventory of the English language' (van Sterkenburg 2003*b*: 13). It used earlier dictionaries, particularly Kersey's *Dictionarium Anglo-Britannicum* (1708) and was designed 'for the Entertainment of the Curious, as the Information of the Ignorant, and for the benefit of young Students, Artificers, Tradesmen and Foreigners'—ladies were not mentioned. It included the most common words as well as words from Chaucer, Spenser, and Shakespeare, and obsolete expressions, proverbs and 'a wealth of phraseological information', marking 'a change in thinking about the lexicon and about what dictionaries should treat' (Moon 2000: 512). It also had four-letter words (see below, 6.1.1.3), but it marked them by a dagger, together with all 'low' words that were best avoided, dialect words, obsolete words, while approved words were marked by an asterisk (Benson 2001: 72). It had illustrative quotations, more than five hundred cuts, or woodcuts, and was the 'first English dictionary to treat etymology with consistent purpose and seriousness' (Landau 2001: 128), showing 'the true meaning of words' (Silva 2000: 77). Common words were given short definitions. For example:

dog 'a Mongrel or Mastive, a Creature well known'
cat 'A creature well known'
goat 'A beast'

It remained in print until 1802, the thirtieth edition, and the later editions, with about 50,000 words, were serious competitors for Johnson's dictionary (Starnes and Noyes 1946: 106).

Bailey published a second volume in 1727, referred to as *Volume II*, which contained items omitted from the first volume as well as new material, hard words, specialized terms, with woodcuts. It also 'marked where the stress should fall in the pronunciation of a word' (Morton 1994: 121). This also had several editions, showing 'considerable rearrangement' (Starnes and Noyes 1946: 112).

Bailey's *Dictionarium Britannicum: or a more compleat universal etymological English dictionary than any extant...*, published in 1730, was a book of almost 900 pages containing about 48,000 words. It aimed at being exhaustive, including 'hard and technical words' as well as the names of people and places and

four-letter words, with 'the professed purpose of entertaining as well as informing the reader' (Starnes and Noyes 1946: 118). It dropped the proverbs of the
earlier volume (although many were re-introduced in later editions) but included
provincialisms. It gave etymologies, for the first time set off in square brackets
(Luna 2004), advice on pronunciation, and also had woodcuts to illustrate the
words that the author thought could not be satisfactorily defined. Later editions
numbered about 60,000 words. Johnson used the second, published in 1736. The
Britannicum was 'the most serious rival [of Johnson's *Dictionary*] throughout the
eighteenth century' (Sledd and Kolb 1955: 147). A later edition revised by J. N.
Scott and often called the *Scott–Bailey*, drawing much of its material from
Johnson (Morton 1994: 28), was published at the same time as Johnson's second
edition in 1755. It was sold in fascicles and was very successful, which infuriated
Johnson.

Thomas Dyche's *New General English Dictionary* (1735), edited by William
Pardon after Dyche's death, had only about 20,000 words, mostly taken from
Bailey, and addressed schoolchildren and the less educated adults. It was possibly
the first English dictionary to include a grammar of the language (Sledd and Kolb
1955: 12). It was reprinted until 1794 (eighteenth edition). A later, enlarged,
version much inspired by the *Dictionnaire de Trévoux* and therefore by Furetière
was later translated into French by Esprit Pézenas and Jean-François Féraud to
produce a *Nouveau Dictionnaire des Sciences et des Arts* (1753–54). B. N. Defoe's[38] *A
Compleat English Dictionary* was published in 1735, and (almost) the same text
was published under three other titles in 1737, 1739, and 1741 (Starnes and Noyes
1991: 139–46). The *Complete English Dictionary* of John Wesley, the founder of the
Methodist movement, a small dictionary that announced the innumerable
abridged dictionaries of the twentieth century, was published in 1753 (Starnes
and Noyes 1946: 172 *ff.*; McArthur 1986*b*: 134).

Benjamin Martin's *Lingua Britannica Reformata*, published in 1749, had a
'wordlist of approximately 24,500', 'considerably smaller than those of its predecessors'. Clearly, 'the sheer size of the dictionary did not form part of its claim to
pre-eminence' (Benson 2001: 85). It was the first monolingual dictionary 'to use
numbered definitions' (Osselton 1988: 246), although some argue that Martin
drew the idea from Johnson's *Plan*, published in 1747,[39] and to adopt a 'logical'
order for the senses of polysemous words (Starnes and Noyes 1946: 152), with the
etymological or original sense first, and then the figurative or metaphorical. This

---

[38] No parent of Daniel Defoe the novelist.
[39] Atkins and Rundell (2008: 271) thank Rosamund Moon for the suggestion. The first French
lexicographer to number meanings may have been Féraud (1763).

was modelled on the Latin dictionary of Robert Ainsworth (Sledd and Kolb 1955: 43), published in 1736, and it greatly impressed Johnson (Hitchings 2005: 76). Martin was a mathematician, and he included 'figures and diagrams, particularly for geometrical terms' (McDermott 2005: 185). His dictionary was very interesting, but it only had a second edition, in 1754.

2.3.2 Samuel Johnson

The main event in the evolution of English lexicography in the eighteenth century was the publication of Samuel Johnson's *Dictionary* in 1755. Johnson, 'wholly unknown to the public, because all his work had been published anonymously' (McAdam and Milne 1963: vii), had taken up an idea that was current among many intellectuals of the time and that some publishers were ready to back: to produce an authoritative dictionary of the English language. He started work in 1746, and in 1747 he published his *Plan of a Dictionary of the English Language*, addressed to 'the Right Honorable Philip Dormer, Earl of Chesterfield'.[40] He had signed a contract with a consortium of booksellers that granted him money to pay his expenses, including six amanuenses,[41] whose job was to copy his notes and annotations of the texts he consulted. He had been allowed a period of preparation of three years, but the dictionary was published after nine years, on 15 April 1755, under the title *A Dictionary of the English Language, in which the Words are deduced from their Originals, and illustrated in their Different Significations by Examples from the best Writers...By Samuel Johnson, A.M.* (Plate 5).[42] It was bound 'in two large folio volumes, each the size of a lectern Bible' (McAdam and Milne 1963: viii) or in four volumes (Hitchings 2005: 192).[43] The first page of the dictionary text (not the cover) bore the title *A General Dictionary of the English Language*. It had about 42,000 entries, a *Preface* that has been almost unanimously praised as one of the best expressions of the problems of lexicography, a brief history of the English language and a grammar. A copy was sent to the French Academy—which gives an idea of the ambitions of the author—and

---

[40] Reproduced in Fontenelle (2008a).

[41] One of whom had worked on the fourth and fifth editions of Chambers' *Cyclopaedia* (Hitchings 2005: 62).

[42] For *Artium Magister*. Johnson is often called *Dr Johnson*, but he never took a university degree. He was awarded an M.A. by the University of Oxford on 20 February 1755, when the text of the dictionary was finished and ready to be published. The sixth edition (1785) has 'By Samuel Johnson, LL.D.' (Congleton and Congleton 1984: 79).

[43] The dictionary is available on a CD-ROM edited by Anne McDermott in 1996 at Cambridge University Press (see Osselton 2005). There are also abridged paper editions (McAdam and Milne 1963/1982; Lynch 2004; Crystal 2005).

the Academy in turn 'promised to repay with a new edition of its own masterpiece as soon as the new edition should appear', which it did in 1761 (Sledd and Kolb 1955: 146).

Johnson's dictionary has been closely examined and extensively commented upon. Some have claimed that Johnson was the inventor of modern lexicography, others that he was only following in the steps of his predecessors; some have said that he exerted a profound influence on the evolution of the English language while for others that influence was negligible. As usual, the truth is probably somewhere in between: Johnson did not invent much, but he brought together different elements that had never been assembled before in any single dictionary of English, and he added generous portions of his immense culture and strong personality. In that sense he is undoubtedly one of the leading figures—if not *the* leading figure—in the history of English lexicography.

Johnson's *Dictionary* had two clearly defined objectives: to explain 'the words and phrases used in the general intercourse of life, or found in the works of those whom we commonly style polite writers' (*Preface*), and 'to preserve the purity, and ascertain the meaning of our English idiom' (*Preface*). Thus it was both descriptive and prescriptive (see below). Johnson had all the words that he could find in acceptable sources, hard words and common words, except those that he considered improper, and he also had compounds, phrasal verbs, phrases, etc., which he treated with particular care, one of the features for which his dictionary was remarkable (Osselton 1986). He had many technical and scientific terms as well as dialect words (Plate 6).

Johnson added comments and labels in many entries to indicate what he thought was good usage. Cassidy (1997: 105–6) counted the number of times various labels expressing disapproval[44] were used: he found 217 occurrences of *low*,[45] 96 of *improper*, 94 of *corrupt*, 94 of *cant*, 38 of *barbarous*, 32 of *ludicrous*, 27 of *erroneous*, etc. There were also *affected, bad, burlesque, colloquial, inelegant, provincial, uncircumstantial, vile, vitious, wanton*, etc. together with *impropriety, without authority, ignorantly, scarce English*, and the occasional picturesque phrase such as *neither elegant nor necessary*, or *not yet received, nor is it wanted, colloquial barbarism, ought not to be admitted into the language, unworthy of use*, etc. (Hitchings 2005: 132–4). The words that were condemned included *to belabour, to budge, to cajole, cheery, to coax, conundrum, to doff, to dumbfound, extraordinary, fuss, gambler, glum, ignoramus, nowadays, posse, shabby, simpleton,*

---

[44] Osselton (2006) notes that Johnson had envisaged indicating register and approval/disapproval via a set of typographical signs (*, ‡, °, etc.) like some of his predecessors, but eventually chose to use labels.

[45] Osselton (2006: 100) finds 223.

spick and span, to squabble, tiny, touchy, trait, to volunteer, width, etc. (see Sledd and Kolb 1955: 37). There were also laudatory labels: *a good word, elegant and useful, elegant and expressive,* etc. (Hitchings 2005: 135).

Yet Johnson's influence on language was limited (Sledd and Kolb 1955: 27 *ff.*). In spite of his personal prestige and of the prestige of his dictionary, the words that he had condemned did not all suffer: some disappeared from usage, but neither more nor less than other words that he had not condemned, and some have survived: *abominable, antiquity,* etc. His only influence was in the domain of spelling, and even this was limited (Sledd and Kolb 1955: 33, 137): he had entries for *aile, dasy, sithe,* etc.

Like all lexicographers, Johnson used earlier dictionaries: Phillips's *New World of Words* (Lancashire 2005: 157), Bailey's *Dictionarium Britannicum,* Ainsworth's Latin *Thesaurus* (mentioned 584 times),[46] Bailey's *Universal* (197 times), and there were occasional references to the *Dictionnaire de Trévoux,*[47] Chambers' *Cyclopaedia* (for which his father was among the early subscribers)[48] and many others. He also consulted Martin's *Lingua Britannica Reformata,* which had been published in 1749 when he had already started work. Many of his entries and definitions were inspired by those dictionaries, though his debts were not always acknowledged: there are '1,144 references to "Dict."... especially common in the first few letters' (Hitchings 2005: 247, who refers to De Vries 1994).[49]

Johnson's definitions were considered 'terse, stylish, and sometimes witty, as well as factual, clear, and comprehensible (with a few exceptions, some of them deliberate)' (Hanks 2005: 243), although he admitted the difficulty of defining some words, particularly the simplest ones: 'to interpret a language by itself is very difficult... simple ideas cannot be described' (*Preface*).

Johnson illustrated most meanings by quotations, that were assembled via a systematic reading of all the great—particularly literary—works written in English between 1586, the year of the death of Sir Philip Sidney, and 1660, the Restoration. He eventually used later writers, so that he had 'the usage of writers from the golden age of Elizabeth to the best usage of his own day' (Brewer 2000: 40). He was, according to all observers of the time, a prodigious reader. He selected about 250,000 passages, about half of which he eventually used, yielding about 110,000 illustrative passages (Hitchings 2005: 70) of varying lengths from about 500 authors (Hitchings 2005: 97), including himself, quoted thirty-three times, he

---

[46] The figures are from Hitchings (2005: 247).   [47] Probably the 1743 edition.
[48] Johnson may have used Chambers' *Preface* as a model for his own (Sledd and Kolb 1955: 19 *ff.*). Sledd and Kolb suggest that he also owned one of the later editions.
[49] On Johnson's work habits as a lexicographer, see Reddick (1990).

reckoned, but this may be an underestimate (Hitchings 2005: 99).[50] He cited only the authors he liked, and refused to quote from 'any wicked writer's authority for a word, lest it should send people to look in a book that might injure them for ever' (*Preface*). He did not cite, for example, Samuel Richardson who was only a novelist (Hitchings 2005: 102), or the philosopher Thomas Hobbes because he 'did not like his principles' (Mugglestone 2005: 70). He arranged his quotations in chronological order when there was more than one in an entry, to reflect the evolution—Johnson said 'progress'—of meaning (Kolb and Kolb 1972: 61–72; Reddick 1990: 97). Noah Webster, commenting on Johnson's *Dictionary* later, thought that too much space had been devoted to quotations, particularly for the illustration of common words, but they were what made it so entertainingly readable. Johnson was not the first lexicographer to illustrate meanings with quotations, but he was certainly more systematic than any of his predecessors. The use of quotations 'was one of the features that most distinguished' his dictionary (Landau 2005: 219).

Johnson used quotations for attestation, to 'prove the bare existence of words' (*Preface*), 'to illustrate the meaning of words in context, to establish that a word had been used by a reputable authority, to display how words were used by the best authors, to show the language as it was at an earlier era before it was contaminated by foreign influences, and to impart useful lessons and moral instruction' (Morton 1989: 154–5; see also Reddick 1990: 9). 'It is not enough that a dictionary delights the critic,' Johnson wrote in the *Preface*, 'unless at the same time it instructs the learner'. He wanted his dictionary to be an 'arbiter of standards' (Hitchings 2005: 68) and his quotations to 'give pleasure or instruction, by conveying some elegance of language, or some precept of prudence, or piety' (*Plan*).

Johnson's treatment of polysemy was another of his achievements, some say his greatest (Sledd and Kolb 1955: 193). He accounted for subtle nuances of meaning with a precision that was unknown in English lexicography, announcing the *OED*: *world* had sixteen meanings, *take* 134, *set* about 90, etc. Sometimes he had to acknowledge defeat: 'kindred sense may be so interwoven, that the perplexity cannot be disentangled' (*Preface*). The different meanings were ordered 'logically', perhaps after Martin's dictionary of 1749.

Of course, Johnson's *Dictionary* had its weaknesses. Its etymologies were often faulty, its definitions sometimes obscure, its choice of words debatable, its indication of pronunciation sketchy (Congleton and Congleton 1984). It had

---

[50] He had a few quotations from other living authors. And he did have a few quotations from earlier authors, for example Chaucer (Hitchings 2005: 97).

many words that nobody ever used (Sledd and Kolb 1955: 135), in the tradition of the dictionaries of hard words: *abactor, to ablactate, to ablegate, abliguration, abnodation, absinthiated, absonous, to absume, accubation, to accumb, acroamatical, to adcorporate, anatiferous* 'producing ducks', etc. It missed a few important words: *to ambush, annulment, athlete, authoress, average* (adj.), *bank-note, blond, to chirrup, civilization engineering, euphemism, inaugural, irritable, malaria, nemesis, to orphan, palimpsest, shibboleth, ultimatum, underdone, virus, zebra, zinc* (see Hitchings 2005: 165 and Mugglestone 2005: 37). Some definitions were just strings of synonyms (Hitchings 2005: 121):

plague 2 'to trouble; to teaze; to vex; to harass; to torment; to afflict; to distress; to torture; to embarrass; to excruciate; to make uneasy; to disturb'

Others were extremely short: *archery* was 'the use of a bow', *backbone* 'the bone of the back', *cabbage-worm* 'an insect', *savingly* 'from saving', *slider* 'he who slides', *unheated* 'not made hot', and *defluxion* was . . . 'a defluxion'. The words of music were 'for the most part quickly dispatched' (Hitchings 2005: 160): *hautboy* was 'a wind instrument'.

Some words were treated at length, many names of animals (Hitchings 2005: 186), most names for chemical substances, etc.: *elephant,*[51] *camel,*[52] *opium, rose, air-pump,* or *parsnep* (Hitchings 2005: 161) were lavishly defined. There were 150 words for *eagle,* and *armadillo* had a long paragraph, apparently inspired by the *Trévoux* dictionary:

A four-footed animal of Brasil, as big as a cat, with a snout like a hog, a tail like a lizard, and feet like a hedge-hog. He is armed all over with hard scales like armour, whence he takes his name, and retires under them like the tortoise. He lives in holes, or in the water, being of the amphibious kind. His scales are of a bony or cartilaginous substance; but they are easily pierced . . .

The reasons why some articles were so short and some so long are obscure. A number of articles were long because there were few sources of encyclopedic knowledge at the time and Johnson wanted to give information that was

---

[51] This included the famous description of its mating habits, found in various forms in Aristotle, Pliny, and many others: 'In copulation the female receives the male lying upon her back; and such is his pudicity, that he never covers the female so long as anyone appears in sight.' This had been denied by Browne as early as 1646 in his *Pseudodoxia Epidemica*, but it was still in Furetière's *Dictionnaire* (1690), in Buffon's *Histoire naturelle* (1749–89), and even in the *Encyclopédie*, perhaps from Furetière: 'Some say that the female prepares a great number of leaves with her trunk, makes it a sort of bed on which she lies on her back when she needs to receive the male, and calls him; that their coupling only takes place in the remotest and most solitary places, and that the females carry for ten years.'

[52] Webster also had a long entry for *camel.*

otherwise unavailable (Sledd and Kolb 1955: 35). In other cases, he simply liked the word, or the concept, or had found an interesting source. Some articles were short because Johnson could not find suitable sources, or because he felt that a long definition was not necessary. Murray, when he compiled the *OED*, tried to avoid such discrepancies (Rand Hoare and Salmon 2000: 159), although he did not completely succeed (Burnett 1989: 139).

Some definitions were difficult to understand. The often-quoted *network* ('Any thing reticulated or decussated, at equal distances, with interstices between the intersections'[53]) may have been deliberate: perhaps Johnson just wanted to astonish the reader. Certainly, some of his definitions seem to have been written more for the effect they produced than for their usefulness. In some entries, he expressed personal preferences or detestations, as we have seen. Here are a few other examples:

cockney 'effeminate, ignorant, low, mean, despicable citizen'
compliment 'an act, or expression of civility, usually understood to include some hypocrisy'
leader 'One at the head of any party or faction: as the detestable Wharton was the *leader* of the Whigs'
patron '. . . commonly a wretch who supports with insolence, and is paid with flattery'.[54]

Johnson's quotations were only vaguely identified: he often gave only the name of the author (Dryden, Addison, Bacon, Swift, etc.) without further details, so that it was difficult to verify, and he used abbreviations: '"M" means Milton, "Dr" Dryden, but it is difficult to know who are "Br." or "W__n."' (Hitchings 2005: 250). Also Johnson was not consistent: he used *Shakesp.*, but also *Shakes.*, *Shak.*, *Shake.*, and *Sha.* (Hitchings 2005: 251). He assumed that the users of his dictionary would know their great literature, or just wouldn't care, as long as the quotation had been chosen under his authority. Some quotations were given from memory, because, he complained, he could not afford to buy the books. As a consequence, there are many errors. Hitchings (2005: 78) mentions the illustration for *learn*: 'Johnson has Caliban say, "You taught me language, and my profit on't / Is, I know not how to curse: the red plague rid you / For *learning* me your language." The "not" is Johnson's addition; Caliban actually says he *does* know how to swear'.[55] Some of the quotations from his own writings are even

---

[53] He defined *to decussate* as 'To intersect at acute angles', and *reticulated* as 'Made of network; formed with interstitial vacuities.'

[54] This may have been an echo of his quarrel with Lord Chesterfield who, he thought, had not supported him when he needed it most (Sledd and Kolb 1955).

[55] In Shakespeare's *The Tempest*, Act I, Scene ii.

labelled *Anonymous* (Hitchings 2005: 99)! But the 'most noteworthy misattribu-tion appears at **Island** *n.*, where he attributes a quotation from Pope's *Essay on Man* to himself' (Silva 2005: 238).

Johnson's etymologies have generally been judged poor, even though they were important to him, as he believed, like Bailey, that the etymology of a word revealed its true meaning. One of the reasons for his shortcomings was that he was familiar with only a limited number of languages, and he was particularly weak in the languages of Northern Europe (Hitchings 2005: 92). Of course, there were not many reliable sources of etymological information at the time, and collecting Johnson's 'fanciful etymologies' is a 'cheap sport' (Sledd and Kolb 1955: 40). The *Dictionary* had no pictures, and as a consequence, McDermott (2005: 176) argues, was not much use for technical and scientific words.[56] Johnson, after Bailey's *Volume II* of 1727 or perhaps after Dyche and Pardon (1735),[57] indicated word stress (*fla'pdragon, me'rrythought, respira'tion*), but his indication of pro-nunciation was judged inadequate by some, among whom Webster. It was later corrected 'when an abridged version of Johnson's dictionary was combined with Walker's popular pronouncing dictionary in 1827, an edition edited by Joseph Worcester' (Landau 2005: 219).

Johnson also had occasional weaknesses. He used different spellings for the same word in different parts of the text, for example *dutchess* but *archduchess* (Osselton 2005: 547). He had 'entries for *nought* and *naught*... but not for *zero*, which he may have felt to be too French' (Stanley 2004: 162). The definition of *pastern* was 'the knee of a horse', whereas 'everyone knows that it is a horse's ankle' (Hanks 2005: 254). There is a—possibly apocryphal though often repeated—story that when a lady asked him why he got it wrong, he cheerfully replied: 'Ignorance, madam, pure ignorance'. In some cases, Johnson just can-didly confessed his puzzlement in the dictionary text itself, as in:

etch 'a country word, of which I know not the meaning'
to swelt 'To puff in sweat, if that be the meaning'
trolmydames 'Of this word I know not the meaning'
sleeveless 'This sense, of which the word has been long possessed, I know not well how it
    obtained... though I know not what better to suggest'
tatterdemalion 'tatter and I know not what'

---

[56] McDermott notes that the dictionary was richer in technical and scientific terms in the first letters of the alphabet. After that, Johnson either recognized that the book would be too long if he continued (Hitchings 2005: 109), or he lost interest, or perhaps the change was due to the fact that he could not replace one of his amanuenses, who had specialized in the exploitation of Chambers' *Cyclopaedia*.
[57] I thank the anonymous reviewer who pointed this out as 'the more likely model'.

The strangest example is probably *to worm*:

to deprive a dog of something, nobody knows what, under his tongue, which is said to prevent him, nobody knows why, from running mad.   (quoted by Hitchings 2005: 165)

He had warned the reader in the *Preface*: 'Some words there are which I cannot explain, because I do not understand them'. Such candidness is unthinkable in modern dictionaries.

Johnson had no illusions about the perfection of his achievement: 'to pursue perfection was, like the first inhabitants of Arcadia, to chase the sun',[58] he wrote in the *Preface*, and 'Every other author may aspire to praise, the lexicographer can only hope to escape reproach'. Still, he thought that on the whole his dictionary was as good as any other: dictionaries, he said, are 'like watches, the worst is better than none, and the best cannot be expected to go quite true' (Piozzi 1925, in Docherty 2000).[59]

Johnson was a grumpy and melancholy person. He suffered different ailments from an early age and he was not happily married.[60] Hitchings (2005: 114) claims that many of his chosen texts 'are morbid, many of the quotations bleak or disturbing. More than 1% of the *Dictionary*'s illustrative quotations refer explicitly to death, around 300 mention disease, and "melancholy" and its cognates appear more than 150 times'. Some of his definitions do betray a certain pessimism. The well-known definition of *lexicographer* was

a writer of dictionaries, a harmless drudge, that busies himself in tracing the original, and detailing the signification of words

A *drudge* was 'One employed in mean labour; a slave; one doomed to servile occupation'. *Grubstreet* was

Originally the name of a street in Moorfields in London, much inhabited by writers of small histories, dictionaries, and temporary poems; whence any mean production is called grubstreet

And the entry for *dull* has the following example: 'Not exhilarating; not delightful; as, *to make dictionaries is* dull *work*.'[61]

---

[58] Hence the title of Green's book (1996). Chambers had said almost the same in his own *Preface*.

[59] This is in his *Letters*, IV, 379. It may have been based on lines 9 and 10 of Pope's *An Essay on Criticism*: 'Tis with our judgments as our watches, none / Go just alike, yet each believes his own'.

[60] During the rehearsal of his play *Irene*, he 'told Garrick that he would have to stay away: "the white bubbies and the silk stockings of your actresses excite my genitals"' (Hitchings 2005: 105).

[61] This is an old theme. Scaliger the Younger (1540–1609), a lexicographer whom Johnson admired, composed the following quatrain, quoted in the Preface of the Trévoux dictionary (1721), here translated by an anonymous contemporary: 'If a man hath committed some hideous crime, for

Despite its imperfections, Johnson's *Dictionary* was greeted as a great achievement, although it was hardly a commercial success, selling 'fewer than 4,000 copies in its first 10 years' (Benson 2001: 87). The Accademia Della Crusca pronounced it 'a perpetual Monument of Fame to the Author' (Sledd and Kolb 1955: 110), Coleridge called it 'a most instructive and entertaining book',[62] and Adam Smith agreed in the *Edinburgh Review* (1755): 'when we compare this book with other dictionaries, the merit of its author appears very extraordinary' (Congleton and Congleton 1984: 15). It was deemed equal, if not superior, to the *Dictionnaire* of the French Academy. David Garrick, a former pupil of Johnson's, wrote admiringly:

Johnson, well-arm'd like a hero of yore
Has beat forty French, and will beat forty more![63]   (in Mugglestone 2000*b*: 4).

Pellissier, in the *Encyclopédie*, judged it 'one of the best dictionaries in any language. There are few examples of such an extensive work produced by one man with such authority' (1867 edition, article *dictionnaire*).

Yet Johnson was not admired by all. Horne Tooke (see below) pronounced the *Dictionary* 'one of the most idle performances ever offered to the public: compiled by an author who possessed not one single requisite for the undertaking' (Sledd and Kolb 1955: 9). He criticized Johnson's taste for rare words: 'Nearly one third of this Dictionary is as much the language of the Hottentots as of the English' (in Sledd and Kolb 1955: 35). And Walpole wrote: 'In Johnson's Dictionary I can hardly find anything I look for' (in Sledd and Kolb 1955: 137).

A second edition was offered, only two months after the first, in weekly numbers, 165 instalments in all,[64] to 'attract those who could not afford to purchase the entire text in one go' (Hitchings 2005: 210). It was 'essentially a reprint of the first' (Sledd and Kolb 1955: 111) and was not very successful either. The subsequent editions were folios or quartos: the third (1765) was 'essentially a reprint of the second' (Sledd and Kolb 1955: 111), the fourth (1773) was 'considerably revised' (Sledd and Kolb 1955: 114), and the fifth, in 1784, the year of Johnson's

shame/Betrayed his father, or ta'en God's name in vain/Set him to make a lexicon—if there be torture on this earth/Can punish him more, I know it not and am nothing worth'. Considine (2007: xii) quotes the following, from an unknown Danish author: 'At the dictionary's letter A / Mr. Brandt is young and gay— / When he finally arrives at Zed, / he's in his wheelchair, nearly dead.'

[62] *Biographia Literaria*, Part I, quoted by Hitchings (2005: 180).

[63] He referred to the third edition of the *Dictionnaire de l'Académie* (1740). Chambers had already mocked the slowness of the French Academy in the *Preface* of his *Cyclopaedia* (1728). For a longer excerpt of Garrick's poem, see Congleton and Congleton (1984: 11).

[64] Also advertised for sale in fascicles at the same time was the Scott–Bailey edition of Bailey's *Dictionarium*, also published in 1755 (Morton 1994: 27).

death, the last to be prepared under Johnson's authority, was 'an unimportant reprint of the fourth' (Sledd and Kolb 1955: 127). There were also several revisions by other lexicographers, an octavo abridgement, 'which appeared, from 1756 to 1786, in eight editions' (Sledd and Kolb 1955: 114), adaptations for the American market, etc. There was an abridged encyclopedic edition 'published not long after his [i.e. Johnson's] death that includes weights and measures, a table of heathen deities, Archbishop Ussher's history of the world with principal dates from the creation in 4004 BC, and the market days in the principal towns of England and Wales' (Richard Bailey, personal communication). H. J. Todd's four-volume enlargement was first published in 1815, with improved etymologies and corrected quotations. Chalmer's abridged edition appeared in 1820, Latham's revised version in 1866–70, and there was another abridgement in 1876, when 'the first fascicle of the *OED* was less than ten years away' (Sledd and Kolb 1955: 155). Johnson's *Dictionary* remained in common use for more than a century.

Johnson came to be known as *Dictionary Johnson*, and his *Dictionary* soon became *the* dictionary in the English-speaking world. It was used by all later lexicographers, in Britain and in other countries, who deemed it 'lawful plunder' (Walker, in Sledd and Kolb 1955: 182), including some who were very critical of his achievement. Webster even regretted that, like all works of genius, it 'interrupted' the 'progress' of lexicography (Sledd and Kolb 1955: 1). It also remained a favourite of amateurs, for reasons that are well expressed by Hitchings (2005: 182):

Dictionaries do contain sketches and miniature histories, and Johnson's, produced by a single man rather than by committee, is furbished with numerous spicy oddments and sugared nuggets. More than any other English dictionary, it abounds with stories, arcane information, home truths, snippets of trivia, and lost myths. It is, in short, a treasure house.

It 'was superseded only by the Philological Society's historical dictionary and by the "utility dictionary" of the Merriam Company' (Sledd and Kolb 1955: 205; see below, 3.1.1 and 4.1.1).

Johnson has never been considered an important figure of the Enlightenment. He certainly was a believer in reason and in tolerance, and he was committed to education and the dissemination of knowledge, but he was too pessimistic to believe in the improvement of man and of society. Still, his *Dictionary* was a landmark in the history of English lexicography—if not in the history of lexicography in general—because of its intrinsic qualities and also because it appeared at the right time. Even though it was not very successful at first, 'Johnson's *Dictionary* was what its age demanded—a standard and standardizing dictionary which included...an extensive list of words selected with some care, explained by divided and classified definitions, and illustrated with quotations from authorities' (Sledd and Kolb 1955: 44). It 'appealed to the newly affluent and the upwardly mobile. ... The *Dictionary* succeeded thanks in no small part to the shift from Restoration elitism to a more middle-class Britain, characterized by a mercantile consciousness' (Hitchings 2005: 207).

After 1755, English dictionaries were never again exactly the same (McDermott and Moon 2005: 153). Osselton (1983: 17) sees four main aspects in the change:

> The century down to 1850 saw great changes in the notion of what a dictionary should be: it came to be seen as a scholarly record of the whole language; in method, it became inductive—that is, based on or derived from a corpus; the emphasis came to lie far more than hitherto on the literary rather than the technical language; and the dictionary now assumed an authoritarian or normative function.

2.3.3 *The birth of a tradition*

2.3.3.1 **The dictionary as a 'scholarly record of the whole language'**

The early monolingual dictionaries of English had only a few thousand words, but their wordlists increased rapidly, with the inclusion of more and more dialect or regional words, technical, scientific or esoteric terms from medicine, chemistry, astronomy, heraldry, the law, the arts, etc., and common words. With Johnson, the inclusion of common words became an essential feature of the dictionary. This was a major step: while the dictionaries of hard words were humble reference books for occasional use, the dictionary after Johnson became a thesaurus of the language, its most easily accessible portrait. As such, it could begin to play a social and political role by materializing the language of a social group or of a nation (see below).

The first dictionaries to include common words treated them with great economy of style: Kersey's *New English Dictionary* (1702) defined *dog* as 'a beast', his *Dictionarium Anglo-Britannicum* (1708) defined it as 'a well-known creature'. This continued well into the eighteenth century, for example in Martin's *Lingua Britannica Reformata* (1749), which defined *badger* as 'the name of a wild beast', *beaver* as 'an amphibious animal, like an otter', *elephant* as 'the biggest of all beasts', and *hare* as 'a well-known animal' (Hitchings 2005: 185), in Bailey's dictionaries, as we have seen, and in Johnson's, where *fish* was 'an animal that inhabits the water' and *whale* was 'the largest of fish'.[65] This was justified by the fact that the public knew what those words meant.

---

[65] The meaning of *fish* was broader then, just like the French *poisson*. In an (apocryphal?) anecdote, when Cuvier was received at the Académie française in 1818, he discovered that the definition of *crayfish* in the *Dictionnaire de l'Académie* was 'petit poisson rouge qui marche à reculons' ('little red

The introduction of common words transformed the work of lexicographers. The skills required of them were of a different nature. They could no longer be content with adding as many words as they could and defining them cursorily. They had to think of reasons to include or exclude a word other than their own fancy or the imagined needs of their public. They had to come to grips with the notions of exhaustiveness and of representativeness. Also, they had to refine their solutions for identifying polysemy and presenting polysemous entries. It is difficult now to imagine a general monolingual dictionary that would not have entries for the common words of the language, even though the users might never consult them (see below, 7.2.2).

2.3.3.2 The dictionary using a corpus

With Johnson, lexicographers started using a corpus (Osselton 1983: 17): they found the words of their nomenclature in texts rather than in dictionaries and a major criterion for inclusion was usage. Of course it was not called *corpus* at the time, and it was different from what we now call *corpus* (see below, 9.1). The corpus of eighteenth-century lexicographers was an open collection of mostly literary texts from reputable authors, from which words were drawn, together with quotations to prove that a word was used by these authors and to illustrate its use. It was typically made up of texts written in the prestige variety of the language. Johnson was not 'the first to base his dictionary closely on actual examples of usage' (McDermott and Moon 2005: 153), but his corpus was more extensive, more precisely defined than any other before him and he explored it more systematically.

Osselton called Johnson's method 'inductive', because the material for his dictionary came from his corpus, but this may be slightly exaggerated: in fact, Johnson drew many of his headwords and his microstructural information 'from already-published dictionaries' (Lancashire 2005: 164), and he used his corpus as much to illustrate the words that he had decided to include as to find eligible words. The corpus was often used *a posteriori*, to confirm his intuitions and to give to his pronouncements the authority of the great authors of the texts that he used.

2.3.3.3 A dictionary of the literary language

Because he wanted his dictionary to record the best linguistic usage, Johnson based it on the literary texts of the best authors of the past. The compilers of the *Tesoro* in Spain in 1611 and of the *Vocabolario* in Italy in 1612 had shown the way in

---

fish that moves backwards') and he said 'My dear fellow Academicians, the crayfish is not a fish, it is not red and it does not move backwards. But apart from that your definition is perfect'.

their descriptions of Spanish and Italian. Richelet had done the same for his *Dictionnaire françois* (1680): the title page said that it was 'drawn from the usage of the best authors of the French language'. Interestingly, the French Academy had decided otherwise for the first edition of its dictionary in 1694:

> Chapelain's plan of 1636 had envisaged systematic recourse to great authors of the past. . . . But this purist and literary orientation was rejected by important elements at Court and in the cultivated classes, and the Academy abandoned the notion of including citations from literary texts—the opposite course, it will be noted, to that taken later by Samuel Johnson. (Cowie 2002: 80)

The *Dictionnaire de l'Académie* aimed at describing the language of the present, the language of the courtiers and of the most distinguished people: it was 'synchronic and mundane', rather than 'passéist and literary' (Collinot and Mazière 1997: 24).

The literary basis of Johnson's dictionary and of many dictionaries that followed led to a more generous use of quotations than before, in France and in England (Read 1986: 32). Literary quotations had been used in English lexicography as early as 1598 by Florio in his *Worlde of Wordes* (Landau 1984: 55), but Johnson had more of them than preceding lexicographers, and he used them more systematically, for every word and meaning. Oddly enough, in the early stages, in France, the practice was not approved by all: 'The inflation of quotations in monolingual and bilingual Latin dictionaries in the sixteenth century was seen as a substitute for the reading of ancient texts, and argued against as such' (Collinot and Mazière 1997: 34).

Literary quotations have remained a feature of all the larger dictionaries since then: 'A dictionary without examples is only a skeleton', Larousse said much later.[66] They are still used for various reasons, to show that a word exists, to show that it is used by great authors, to show in what sort of context it is used, to introduce extra information, encyclopedic, pragmatic, cultural, to mention famous literary passages, to serve as vehicles for values and opinions, or to make the dictionary more attractive. For Littré, they were 'scraps of the purple' (Leschiera 1990: 85).

The use of literary quotations in a dictionary that has the common words of a language had consequences that some—including Samuel Johnson himself (Read 1986: 38)—have found absurd:

---

[66] The formula was adapted from a comment by Voltaire on the *Dictionary* of the French Academy (Pruvost 2004: 8).

The literary bias has marked lexicography since the eighteenth century; so much so that it would seem sacrilegious in France for a large dictionary (and this is true of the *G.L.L.F.* [*Grand Larousse de la Langue Française*, 1978] as well as of the *T.L.F.*) not to illustrate the most common use of the most frequent verb by a quotation from Victor Hugo, J. K. Huysmans, Paul Claudel or André Malraux.   (Wagner 1975: 94)

The practice has continued: *PR* illustrates the adjective *ferme* by a quotation from Pierre Mac Orlan, 'Prends encore ces tomates. Elles sont fermes et fraîches';[67] *SOED* has a quotation by Anthony Burgess to illustrate the adjective *kind*, 'Mother Andrea had a sweet face and was kind and gentle', and there are thousands of similar examples.

2.3.3.4 The normative function of the dictionary

A few lexicographers before Johnson had indicated their approval or disapproval of words or expressions by using labels or various typographical symbols (Osselton 2006), but the idea that dictionaries could have a regulatory influence on language appeared only in the eighteenth century. It was an issue in 1728, as this passage from Chambers' *Preface* for his *Cyclopaedia* shows:

The Dictionarist, like an Historian, comes after the Affair, and gives a Description of what has pass'd. [He] is not supposed to have any hand in the Things he relates; he is no more concerned to make the Improvements, or establish the Significations, than the Historian to atchieve the Transactions he relates.   (*Preface* XII)

In many European countries at the time, people thought that language was deteriorating, and that dictionaries could help arrest the evolution and protect the language from decay: 'One of the devices used by society to impose uniformity of meaning and usage is the dictionary' (Hanks 1979: 38). The movement had started in Spain and Italy in the sixteenth and seventeenth centuries, where official regulatory bodies, the Academies, had been created. Their dictionaries were compiled at the request of the sovereigns to record the whole language and to establish a standard to be followed (Zgusta 1989a: 75). The same anxiousness to fix the language reached the intelligentsia in France and in Britain in the seventeenth and early eighteenth centuries (Sledd and Kolb 1955: 5 *ff.*). In France, it led to the creation of the French Academy in 1635, which soon started work on its dictionary. In England, Locke had pleaded for the creation of an authority on language in his *Essay Concerning Human Understanding* in 1690,[68] and some, like Daniel Defoe or Jonathan Swift, wanted to emulate the French

---

[67] 'Take these tomatoes, they are firm and fresh'.
[68] Book III, Chapter xi, section 25. On this, see Starnes and Noyes (1946: 146 *ff.*).

(Benson 2001: 84)—Johnson was against the idea.[69] It never materialized, but one consequence was the publication of a large number of grammar books which, together with dictionaries, could be expected to participate in the sifting of the good grain from the chaff (Read 1986: 32) and which were extremely popular: 'The tremendous interest in grammar in the eighteenth century is exemplified by the publication of about fifty grammars in the first half of the century and more than 200 in the second half' (Landau 2001: 244). Robert Lowth's *A Short Introduction to English Grammar* (1762), for example, went through hundreds of editions.

The dictionary that was needed to establish a standard was one that would enjoy enough prestige to impress its users, and that would be clearly prescriptive, indicating what was good and what was bad usage. Dryden pleaded for the compilation of such a dictionary in 1693 (Benson 2001: 84), and for some time, Addison planned to compile one (Sledd and Kolb 1955: 7); Pope also 'had drawn plans for a dictionary' (Sledd and Kolb 1955: 51), but it was Samuel Johnson who was eventually entrusted with the task.

A prescriptive dictionary is a dictionary that includes the 'good' words in its wordlist and that omits the bad words, or expresses its disapproval of the 'bad' words that it has not been able to omit; a descriptive dictionary records usage as it is, good or bad. The two types use different norms. Descriptive dictionaries use a quantitative norm based on the observation of the use of language in the community: any form is good as long as it is used by a sufficient number of users. The difficulty is to determine the minimum number of users, or of uses, required for a linguistic form to be considered acceptable. The quantitative norm corresponds to the modern corpus (see below, 9.1). Prescriptive dictionaries use a qualitative norm based on the use of language by the best users. The difficulty here is the choice of the model. It is always written rather than spoken, and literary, and typically from some time before the compilation of the dictionary. The qualitative norm corresponds to the eighteenth-century type of corpus, giving priority to aesthetic judgement over frequency.

No dictionary can be purely descriptive, because the lexicographer has to choose what to include. All dictionaries exclude some words, dialect words, obsolete words, children's words, taboo words, etc. (see below, 8.2.1). However liberal in their macrostructure and microstructure, they always embody a model of linguistic usage through what they choose to record and to omit (Rey 1982: 30). That is why many metalexicographers prefer to say that dictionaries are normative, a label that does not have the negative connotations of the term *prescriptive*. The normative aspect of dictionaries is best seen in the indication of spelling. The dictionary, even if it gives

---

[69] On the movement in the USA, see Read (1936).

the different spellings of a word, has to choose a form for use as an entry or sub-entry, and therefore shows a preference. Pure descriptivism is impossible.

A dictionary can be purely prescriptive, but its prescriptions are hopeless if they are too far removed from the realities of usage, if they are pure 'Canutism'. When Johnson started work on his *Dictionary*, he was anxious 'that the English language would change beyond recognition' (Mitchell 2005: 208), and he wanted to play a part in the effort to save it from decay: 'Every language,' he wrote in the beginning of his *Preface*, 'has ... improprieties and absurdities, which it is the duty of the lexicographer to correct or proscribe'. He wrote to Lord Chesterfield: 'This, my Lord, is my idea of an English dictionary; a dictionary by which the pronunciation of our language may be fixed, and its attainment facilitated; by which its purity may be preserved, its use ascertained, and its duration lengthened'.

[He was] imbued with prescriptivism, both in his choice of sources and in his judgement on the usages his sources illustrated. He censored usage in choosing his quotation sources from a clearly defined and limited range of literary giants and of writers of established stature in selected other fields, for example, theological or philosophical, and he censured these writers' usage even while recording it in his dictionary.   (Brewer 2000: 41)

He was, Green (1996: 3) writes with the hyperbole that has become usual when it comes to discussing Johnson's achievements, 'playing God. Or, if not God, then at least Moses, descending from Sinai with the tablets of the law'. But Johnson later realized, like Chambers and Martin before him, that no one can prevent language from changing, and that the best the lexicographer can do is to record those changes. By 1755, he had abandoned his prescriptivist hopes:

Those who have been persuaded to think well of my design, require that it should fix our language, and put a stop to those alterations which time and chance have hitherto been suffered to make in it without opposition. With this consequence I will confess that I flattered myself for a while; but now begin to fear that I have indulged expectation which neither reason nor experience can justify.... And with equal justice may the lexicographer be derided, who being able to produce no example of a nation that has preserved their words and phrases from mutability, shall imagine that his dictionary can embalm his language, and secure it from corruption and decay, that it is in his power to change sublunary nature, or clear the world at once from folly, vanity, and affectation.
(*Preface*)

It is probably unreasonable to see the eighteenth century as a radical change from earlier times in lexicography. The history of dictionaries is more a series of gradual changes in several directions, with the occasional leap and bound, than a straightforward linear and regular evolution. Still, the eighteenth century and

Johnson above all were the beginning of modern lexicography, when dictionaries became formalized and began being designed as portraits of a language and considered as such by the public. One can say that the effects of Johnsonian lexicography, the use of literary quotations and the historical method, culminated in the first edition of the *OED*, and that they are still felt today. Modern dictionaries still aim at recording the 'whole' language, they use a corpus, and the larger GPDs still illustrate every word and sense by quotations from authentic, if not always literary, texts. But the history of lexicography was not finished.

> [S]ome departments of lexicography had not even appeared by 1755; most notable among these were probably synonymy and the phonetic treatment of pronunciation. Other departments urgently called for improvement. Etymology cried out for a complete revision, definitions were unequal, and grammatical annotations were needed for irregular conjugations, plurals, and comparisons. All of these improvements were, however, to be introduced in some form by the close of the century.
>
> (Starnes and Noyes 1946: 281)

2.4 EIGHTEENTH- AND NINETEENTH-CENTURY DICTIONARIES

2.4.1 *British dictionaries after Johnson*

After Johnson, there were further editions of Bailey's *Universal Etymological English Dictionary* and of the Scott–Bailey of 1755. John Entick's *The New Spelling Dictionary*, published in 1764 for 'young People, Artificers, Tradesmen and Foreigners', much inspired by the two Bailey dictionaries, had about 22,000 words (Rodriguez-Álvarez and Rodriguez-Gil 2006: 301) and went through several editions. It was later used by Noah Webster as the basis of his *Compendious Dictionary* of 1806 (see below). Other dictionaries were Frederick Barlow's *The Complete English Dictionary* (1772); William Kenrick's *New Dictionary of the English Language*, 1773; the *Complete and Universal English Dictionary* (1774) of James Barclay, a clergyman; John Ash's *The New and Complete Dictionary of the English Language*, 1775;[70] Thomas Sheridan's *A General Dictionary of the*

---

[70] Ash became famous for saying that the word *curmudgeon* came from *coeur* meaning 'unknown' and *mechant* meaning 'correspondent'. The error came from a faulty reading of Johnson, who had an 'entry for *curmudgeon* saying "It is a vitious manner of pronouncing *coeur mechant*, Fr. An unknown correspondent"'. (Hitchings 2005: 90). Dictionary plagiarism . . .

English Language, 1780, which was particularly good on pronunciation (Sledd and Kolb 1955: 175).

Charles Richardson, a fierce enemy of Johnson (Sledd and Kolb 1955: 191), published his *New Dictionary of the English Language* in 1836/7. Richardson was, like Johnson, a strong personality who used his dictionary to provide education, instruction, and moral advice. He applied the highly controversial philological principles that John Horne Tooke had developed in *The Diversions of Purley* (1786, then 1798–1805 for the revised edition). Horne Tooke was 'one of the most systematically frantic etymologists who ever lived' (Sledd and Kolb 1955: 183). He argued that all words could be traced back to an original monosyllabic form with a simple concrete meaning:[71] *bar*, for example, with the meaning 'defence' could be seen in words like *barn, barge, bark, baron, bargain*, etc. (Zgusta 2006: 21), a 'fabric of conjectures' according to Murray (Mugglestone 2005: 224) (Plate 7). Horne Tooke was the last 'linguist' 'for whom the word "etymology" had the meaning it had since antiquity, namely the search for the genuine... meaning of the word' (Zgusta 2006: 21).[72] Richardson even said that every single letter had a meaning of its own. He was strangely out of touch with the developments in historical linguistics that were beginning to take place at the time (see below, 3.1.1). He defined words in groups under strange headwords: for example, he had an entry ADULTER in which he treated together *adulterate, adulteration, adulterator, adulterer, adulteress, adulterine, adulterous, adulterously*, and *adultery*. His definitions were often cursory, and he relied on his many chronologically arranged quotations to clarify meanings. For example, at *knuckle*, he said

It seems to countenance Tooke's etym. that the word is comm. app. to the *knee*-joint of a calf ;—a *knuckle* of veal ;—also the bending joints of the fingers

followed by several quotations. Because of these quotations, and because of his desire to write the history of each word, Richardson was one of the precursors of the *OED*.

The Imperial Dictionary, English, Technological, and Scientific; Adapted to the Present State of Literature, Science, and Art of John Ogilvie, in two volumes, was published in 1850. It was an encyclopedic dictionary based on Webster's 1828 dictionary (see below) and was much praised for its pictures, not only of concrete objects or people but also of verbs, an innovative practice later adopted by other

---

[71] Horne Tooke believed, after John Locke, that every word had a concrete meaning first, and then only could develop abstract meanings (Zgusta 1989c: 203, 2006: 21). The idea has origins in Isidore of Seville.

[72] The belief obviously survived among non-linguists. Morton (1994: 86) mentions Ambrose Bierce, who argued that *dilapidated* 'should be applied only to rundown *stone* structures'.

dictionaries. There was a revised edition by Charles Annandale in 1882, and the text was later used for the American *Century Dictionary* (see below). Hunter's large *Encyclopaedic Dictionary* was published between 1879 and 1888. It had 5,629 pages, while the *Imperial* only had 2,922 (Bailey 2000: 214), and it introduced the use of bold for headwords in English dictionaries (Luna 2004). The British could also use a two-volume edition of Webster's *American Dictionary of the English Language* (see below) published in 1832 under the title *A Dictionary of the English Language*.

2.4.2 *American dictionaries before Noah Webster, and after*

The first dictionaries used in America were produced in Britain. 'For Americans in the second half of the eighteenth century, Johnson was the seminal authority on language, and the subsequent development of American lexicography was coloured by his fame' (Hitchings 2005: 224). The first dictionary ever to be published in America was a revised edition of William Perry's *Royal Standard Dictionary* in 1788, and the first to be compiled by an American was a *School Dictionary*, published in 1798 by Samuel Johnson Jr., no relative of the British lexicographer (Friend 1967),[73] a 'small dictionary of about 4,000 vocabulary items' (Landau 2001: 432). It was soon followed by Caleb Alexander's *The Columbian Dictionary of the English Language*, published in 1800, also a small dictionary, and not very successful.

Noah Webster was a schoolmaster, 'lawyer, lecturer, journalist, crusader for copyright legislation and the unlikely author of a two-volume work entitled the *History of Pestilential Diseases*, which was considered the standard work in the field' (Morton 1994: 41). He was also the author of popular readers and spelling-books. He entered the lexicographic scene with the publication of *A Compendious Dictionary of the English Language* in 1806, a 'modest, small-sized dictionary of about 400 pages,... the first dictionary of any significance produced by an American' (Landau 2005: 217). It had 'some 37,000 entries,[74] including 5,000 words that Webster claimed were not included in any other English dictionary' (Morton 1994: 41). It was based on Entick's *New Spelling Dictionary* of 1764, 'with an addition of about 5,000 words' (Landau 2005: 217), including many technical and scientific terms. In it, Webster 'repudiated the authority of Johnson and set out a wide range of reform' (Hitchings 2005: 225), particularly in spelling: he

---

[73] Or was it one of those dictionaries that used Johnson's name for commercial reasons? The practice of using the names of well-known authors was not uncommon in the eighteenth century (Rodriguez-Álvarez and Rodriguez-Gil 2006: 312).

[74] More than 90 entries per page?

proposed such changes as *center, honor, program*, etc. The dictionary had 'very brief definitions and no etymologies' (Landau 2005: 217; though see Morton 1994: 41) but extensive back matter, with tables of currencies used in different countries, weights and measures ancient and modern, a history of the world, divisions of time, the Jewish, Greek, and Roman calendars, the number of inhabitants in the USA, with export figures, remarkable events, and discoveries, and a list of all the post-offices of the USA (Marckwardt 1963/1967: 34). This was to become part of the American lexicographic tradition.

The true beginning of American lexicography was the publication of *An American Dictionary of the English Language* in 1828, when Noah Webster, who had worked on the project for 28 years, was already 70. It was the first dictionary to use the word *American* in its title (Plate 8). It came in two quarto volumes, with about 1,600 pages and about 70,000 entries (remember that Johnson had about 42,000) and was designed to compete with Todd's revision of Johnson, published in 1818. Webster was very critical of his predecessors in general and of Johnson in particular: he disapproved of 'the limited scope of the vocabulary, the etymologies, and the pronunciations', as well as of 'the use of too many illustrative quotations' (Morton 1994: 42). But then Webster was very critical of everybody except himself, Sledd and Kolb (1955: 191) write, 'just the man to be stern with everyone but Noah Webster'. He professed 'amazement at how obvious some of Johnson's blunders were' (Landau 2005: 218), and decided to concentrate on etymologies and definitions instead, 'with quotations being assigned a relatively minor role' (Singleton 2000: 197). Still, Webster made copious use of existing dictionaries, particularly of Johnson's ninth edition (1805): for example, about one-third of his definitions in the letter L were 'culled from Johnson or show unmistakeable signs of Johnson's influence' (Reed, in Landau 2005: 220).

Webster wanted to produce a distinctively American dictionary, and said in his *Preface* that he wanted to illustrate usage by quoting only from American literature. He did quote Franklin, Washington, Adams, Jay, Madison, etc.—not Jefferson, whom he hated, or Fenimore Cooper—but he also relied extensively on British authors and poets (Landau 2005: 227). The etymologies in the *American Dictionary* were strange. Webster was obviously unaware of the research that was being carried out in Europe on the history of Indo-European languages (Morton 1994: 45; see below, 3.1.1). Blinded by his 'stubborn belief in his own infallibility' (Morton 1994: 42), he had devised his own system of derivation of meanings, which turned out to be catastrophic, his 'most glaring failure', 'a fiasco' (Morton 1994: 42).[75]

---

[75] For example, he derived *ginseng* from the Chinese and the Iroquois (Schulman and Lepore 2008: 53).

Webster focused on common contemporary usage rather than on the literary usage of the past. He was more interested in science than in the arts, and his scientific definitions may be seen as ancestors of the style of American dictionaries to this day (see below, 4.2.2). He was also prescriptive, like the early Johnson, although the social contexts were very different. He had strong opinions on what was proper and what was not (Schulman and Lepore 2008: 57), and he succeeded in influencing spelling to some extent, although many opposed the changes that he proposed (Landau 2005: 226):[76]

His spelling triumphed in American usage, at least in many words ending in *-our* in British usage, along with *theater* as against *theatre*, *center* as against *centre*; he cut *musick* and *publick* down to *music* and *public*, although he failed in his equally sensible *imagin*, *primitiv*, and *thum*.   (Laird 1970: 278)

But on the whole his influence on the language was limited (Sledd and Kolb 1955: 198). Later, he lost his faith in prescriptivism, like Johnson before him, when he realized how hopeless the task was (Laird 1970: 263 *ff.*).

An American Dictionary was the first in a long lineage of Webster dictionaries that were immensely successful, selling almost as well in Britain as in the USA (Sledd and Kolb 1955: 202). 'By 1837 the dictionary was already out of print, and in 1840 Webster pledged his home to secure a bank loan to help pay for a new edition' (Landau 2005: 226). The second edition appeared in 1841, 'Corrected and Enlarged', with 5,000 new words, when Webster was then more than 80. The dictionary was sent to Queen Victoria with a message: 'Our common language is one of the ties that bind the two nations together; I hope the works I have executed will manifest to the British nation that the Americans are not willing to suffer it to degenerate on this side of the Atlantic' (Rollins in Hitchings 2005: 225).

After Noah Webster's death in 1843, the rights to the name *Webster* were bought by the Merriam brothers, who employed Webster's son-in-law, Chauncey A. Goodrich, to prepare a revised edition. A third 'New Revised Edition' in one volume was produced in 1847, with 85,000 entries and pictures. There was a fourth in 1859, also edited by Goodrich, called *Pictorial* because it had sections of pictorial illustrations: it was 'touted as the first illustrated American dictionary' (Morton 1994: 48).

A substantially improved and enlarged, 'highly-regarded' (Morton 1994: 45) edition by Goodrich and Noah Porter came out in 1864, in which the etymologies had been totally revised by the German scholar C. A. F. Mahn, and 3,000 pictorial illustrations inserted. It is often called *The Webster–Mahn*, or *The Unabridged*. It had about 115,000 entries, a huge number that made it the first unabridged

---

[76] Webster also claimed to have invented one word for the dictionary: *demoralize*.

dictionary ever, and it also had abundant ancillary matter with the names of fictional characters and places in literature, names in the Bible, foreign quotations, etc., 171 pages in all. Its methods bore some resemblance to what was being done at the same time in Britain for the preparation of the *OED*: 'Thirty professors in scientific and humanistic fields served as editors, and other scholars and literary figures were encouraged to send in new words and citations' (Morton 1994: 50). It was heavily used during the compilation of the *OED* (see below, 3.1.1).

The G. and C. Merriam Company published their famous *Webster's International Dictionary*, called *The International*, in 1890. It was a big dictionary with 175,000 entries, with a change of title that expressed the desire of the publishers to establish the dictionary as an authority on all varieties of English. It 'attempted to include the English of Australia and Canada' (Morton 1994: 50), an innovation that announced the dictionaries of the twentieth century.

Webster's New International Dictionary[77] was published in 1909. It was a thoroughly revised edition, with a large number of pictures and about 400,000 entries, more than double the preceding edition, which made it one of the largest dictionaries ever produced. It made room for the new entries by introducing the 'device of the divided page—placing below a horizontal line near the bottom of each page less important, obsolete, or highly technical entries, which were more briefly treated and printed in smaller type' (Morton 1994: 61). The *New International* competed in a battle of the giants with the *Funk and Wagnalls Standard Dictionary of the English Language* by Isaac Funk (see below, 4.1.2), published in 1890–93, another big encyclopedic dictionary about which Mark Twain wrote 'I have found that one can do without principles, but not without the *Funk and Wagnalls Standard Dictionary*', and with the *Century Dictionary*, which had appeared in 1891 (see below).

The success of Webster's *American Dictionary of the English Language* was due to its qualities, to the fact that, like Johnson's *Dictionary*, it answered a social need and to the fact that it was cleverly commercialized. Webster had a modern view of lexicography, seeing it 'as a commercial enterprise to make money by representing a product as having novel value that customers want', in which he was radically different from Johnson, who saw his task as conducing 'wherever possible to moral improvement and the advancement of piety' (Landau 2005: 219).

For a long time, the commercial success of Webster's dictionaries was challenged only by Joseph Emerson Worcester, also a schoolteacher turned lexicographer, who had been Webster's assistant during the preparation of the first

---

[77] Dictionary publishers often use the adjective *new* in dictionary titles (sometimes only on the dust-jackets) to avoid making the date of publication too visible and to preserve the appeal of the dictionary for as long as the dictionary buyers are ready to believe what they are told.

edition of the *American Dictionary*. Worcester, contrary to Webster, was a great admirer of Johnson (Sledd and Kolb 1955: 139). After having published in 1827 a revised edition of Chalmer's abridgement of Johnson's *Dictionary* improved by Todd that incorporated Walker's pronouncing dictionary, then an abridgement of Webster's *American Dictionary* in 1829, he published his own *Comprehensive Pronouncing and Explanatory Dictionary of the English Language* in 1830, a small dictionary for schoolchildren, which was judged by some to be superior to Webster's dictionary of 1828 (Sledd and Kolb 1955: 203), but was not very successful. Worcester then published his *Universal and Critical Dictionary of the English Language* in 1846, with 27,000 additional words, 'some etymologies, illustrative quotations, and notes' (Morton 1994: 47) and a remarkable treatment of idioms. This had many subsequent editions, but Worcester's masterpiece was *A Dictionary of the English Language*, published in 1860, the last dictionary he ever published, designed to be a competitor for Webster's *Pictorial* of 1859. It was a big dictionary of 1,786 pages and more than 100,000 entries, with a large number of illustrative quotations, and it was the first to include a large number of usage notes on near synonyms (Landau 2001: 134). It was 'widely viewed upon publication as the best English dictionary in the world' (Morton 1994: 39). Worcester is remembered in the history of dictionaries as having 'established the pattern of larger and ever more comprehensive dictionaries' (Landau 2001: 84).

Hostilities 'began when Webster accused Worcester of plagiarism' (Morton 1994: 46) in his *Comprehensive* dictionary, and rapidly escalated into a war that went on for decades (Laird 1970: 286), until the last edition of Worcester in 1886. Webster was infuriated by the fact that a British edition of Worcester's *Universal* indicated, mistakenly, that it was 'compiled from the materials of Noah Webster…' The period has been called 'the War of the Dictionaries' (Morton 1994: 45).

Noah Webster was 'a typical Yankee of the period: industrious, self-reliant, pious, frugal' (Morton 1994: 40), and he was much praised for his intellect. He had 'a clearness of mind, soundness of judgment and catholicity of interest that puts him intellectually in the same class with Franklin' (Krapp 1925: 352). But he was also a curmudgeon, 'egotistical, opinionated, close-minded, and quarrelsome' (Morton 1994: 40), of 'a fiercely competitive nature, quick to take offense, disputatious, and aggressive in argument to the point of truculence' (Landau 2005: 218). He could not accept that the commercial success of his dictionaries was challenged by Worcester's, and he did not die a happy man (Green 1996: 327 *ff.*; Micklethwait 2000: 246 *ff.*).

The six-volume *Century Dictionary and Cyclopedia* of William Dwight Whitney[78] was published in instalments between 1889 and 1891, with a revised edition in 1895.

---

[78] A linguist who had worked on the 1864 edition of Webster (Mugglestone 2000*a*: 251).

With 7,046 pages, about 215,000 entries, 500,000 definitions, 300,000 illustrative quotations, and 8,000 cuts, it was the largest dictionary of the times, even bigger than Webster's *International* (Plate 9). Oddly enough, it was somehow derived from Webster's work. The text of the *American Dictionary of the English Language* of 1828, in its 1841 edition, 'was acquired by a Scottish publisher to be turned into the four-volume encyclopedic *Imperial Dictionary*' (Hartmann 2001: 45) and published in Britain. The *Imperial* was later used as the basis for the *Century Dictionary* after it had been revised by Annandale, a fine example of 'lexicographic archaeology', or circulation of dictionary texts back and forth across the Atlantic, one of the many stories of mutual influences that are not always acknowledged. The *Century* was synchronic and descriptive. In it, 'meanings are induced from the uses of words', where Johnson had declared that 'the words are deduced from their originals' (Bailey 1996: 7). It was good in its definitions and in the organization of polysemous entries, and particularly rich in scientific and technical words. It was very popular and still has admirers: 'As a general user's dictionary—that is, one not deliberately historical in purpose—the *Century* is probably the best dictionary of English ever produced' (Urdang 1997: 82). It was later published in ten volumes as part of *The Century Dictionary and Cyclopedia* (1901), which had 'much encyclopedic material even in its A–Z section, many thousands of illustrative quotations, and numerous fine pictorial illustrations. Beautifully printed and bound, it is surely one of the handsomest dictionaries ever made' (Landau 2001: 85). An edition in twelve volumes was published in 1911, and a last one in 1914.[79]

On the whole, the nineteenth century was a prosperous time for American lexicography. British dictionaries of the same period have been mostly forgotten, because they were too much under the influence of Johnson to be innovative, but American dictionaries flourished, and established a tradition that was different from the British tradition on which they were originally based. Rather than tools for the well educated to read their literature or enjoy sharing their culture with their peers, American dictionaries were all-purpose guides and reference works accessible to American citizens of all social classes and all levels of education.

2.4.3 *The nineteenth-century dictionary and its social roles*

In the eighteenth century, dictionaries became part of the range of regulating instruments used by societies to ensure the smooth functioning of the linguistic code, to prevent it from deteriorating and becoming a myriad of sub-codes. In

[79] See *Dictionaries* (1996), special issue n°17.

the nineteenth century, dictionaries were instrumental in the maintenance of the social hierarchy, sometimes in its subversion. Their normativity reinforced social order: in America, Smith (1979: 56) says, 'the real goals of language teaching [have] been to engineer the maintenance of the social classes as they solidified in the nineteenth century [and] much of what passes for education in American schools has, whatever the intention, even now the same result'. But on the other hand dictionaries could also be subversive, by allowing the middle classes to talk like their 'betters' and by helping the under-privileged acquire education and improve their social status.

2.4.3.1 Dictionaries for the middle classes

The American emerging middle classes had the same needs in the nineteenth century as in Britain when Johnson's *Dictionary* was published: 'As the bourgeoisie increased their wealth and power, they began to wish to talk like their betters' (McDavid 1979: 24), and for this they needed a prescriptive, authoritative dictionary. McDavid (1973*a*: 5) writes:

[The dictionary was a] response to the rise of the middle classes, the dissemination of knowledge and literacy, and the general ferment of intellectual curiosity arising from the Renaissance and the Reformation—to say nothing of the perhaps less admirable but thoroughly comprehensible ambitions of the newly risen and affluent to use without stumbling the kind of language to which the traditional upper classes had been accustomed. The need to provide information about language for the uninformed and socially insecure underlies all subsequent lexicography.

The history of dictionaries is a story of the widening of their public. Since the sixteenth century, lexicographers have produced dictionaries that had more and more words but were also cheaper and more accessible, so that more people could buy them. Some of the larger dictionaries were sold in cheap fascicles to make them accessible to an increasing portion of the population, and there were also abridged editions. There is no clear record of a dictionary having been instrumental in the elevation of social status of a middle-class family or individual, but that is certainly one of the powerful motives for which dictionaries were produced and bought.

2.4.3.2 Dictionaries to educate the uneducated

Early dictionaries were designed to help foreigners, or youngsters, or ladies, as we have seen. American dictionaries of the nineteenth century were also compiled for a vast public that did not have access to proper schooling. The dictionary became, together with the Bible, one of the two guides that all American households had to possess, and it was particularly important for those who lived far from the urban sources of knowledge and culture: 'most rural estates, be they ever so humble, boasted a dictionary' (McDavid 1979: 17).

The growth of population and of public education as a means of self-improvement in a free society created an enormous demand for books that would teach immigrants and others how to speak and write correctly.... Dictionaries naturally assumed large import-ance as authorities to be relied on to settle questions of usage, pronunciation, and etymology.   (Landau 2001: 85).

The immigrant population needed guides to the culture that was necessary for their assimilation and social advancement.

There was a similar movement in Europe at the same time. During the nineteenth century, lexicographers compiled dictionaries designed to combat ignorance and its social consequences. The Grimm brothers in Germany were probably the first to paint the well-known family scene in which the poor father teaches his children with the help of a dictionary:

In a memorable passage in his *Preface* Grimm has a vision of his dictionary finding a place in every household not unlike that of the Family Bible: he sees the *pater-familias* presiding in the evening over the family circle, picking out and discussing words from it for the (linguistic) betterment of his sons, while the mother listens attentively.
(Osselton 2000: 64)

In France, Maurice Lachâtre, probably the most original nineteenth-century French lexicographer (see below), who has been totally forgotten, evoked the same scene in the *Preface* of his dictionary in 1858—except that for him the mothers also participated and daughters were taught as well as the sons: 'Now, the mothers and fathers of poor families, with the *Dictionnaire français illustré*, can educate their children, boys or girls, without having to resort to a master or professor and without sending the children to a school or college' (Pruvost 2001*b*: 71). And his dictionary was indeed used that way—sometimes without the mother: 'The head of the family wanted to educate the children....[H]e had them learn by heart the first volume of La Châtre's dictionary, in which several pages were missing' writes Henri Calet in his memoirs.[80] Most dictionaries may have been difficult for the children—'the Latin definitions and the learned etymologies hardly fit in with this cosy domestic scene' (Osselton 2000: 64)—but the idea was precisely to teach them what was difficult.

---

[80] *Le Tout sur le tout* (Paris: Gallimard) (1948/1980: 159).

That sort of zeal for the education of the people was very much alive in France in the nineteenth century. It certainly motivated Pierre Larousse:

[W]hile he wanted sound vulgarization and simplicity at all costs in order to better serve the people, Larousse worked towards the accomplishment of a work whose scientific quality would be worthy of the public of lower middle class people, school teachers and petty 'fonctionnaires' who used it to improve their education and to help them work more efficiently towards a lay and democratic society. Thus, *mutatis mutandis*, the role of the first Larousse dictionary was similar to that played by the Encyclopédie in the eighteenth century: both were sorts of summations of human knowledge, as well as instruments for the liberation of mankind.   (Matoré 1968: 127)

This led him to lay particular emphasis on expression, so that his users could learn to write properly (Pruvost 2002*b*: 66). He also adopted a linguistic standard that was not literary: 'The Larousse dictionary is . . . the dictionary that broke free from the literary reference that was so powerful in Littré's to establish a sort of normality of common opinion on meaning' (Collinot and Mazière 1997: 46). Larousse was admired for his dedication to social advancement: he was 'an admirable servant of social knowledge, a tireless "schoolmaster" of progressive thinking, aggressively engaged in the diffusion of information' (Collinot and Mazière 1997: 46). He was also keen on teaching moral values, like Johnson but with more explicitly social aims, playing the part of the defender of society against vice.[81]

In English lexicography, such efforts mostly came from Scotland, not England. Wesley's small dictionary, published in 1753, aimed at educating the working classes (McArthur 1986*b*: 134). The Chambers brothers in Edinburgh saw their *Encyclopedia, A Dictionary of Universal Knowledge for the People* (1859–68) as a means to help those who needed education: 'When they set up in business, the brothers called themselves "publishers for the people", expressing through this slogan a particularly Scottish and Presbyterian desire to spread learning to all men and women' (McArthur 1986*b*: 134). Later, the *Chambers' English Dictionary* (1872) was 'intended with a crusade-like zeal for *everybody*' (McArthur 1998: 135).

Education means linguistic and ideological standardization, and the dictionary, like the educating system, was seen by some as more tyrannical than liberating.

---

[81] In his *Grand Dictionnaire* (1873) he evoked the scandalous case of Count Libri, a friend of Prosper Mérimée, who had used his position at the 'Bibliothèque nationale' to steal valuable books and manuscripts. See Manguel, A. (1996/8), *Une Histoire de la lecture* (Paris: Babel): 284–87.

When Becky Sharp leaves Miss Pinkerton's academy for young ladies in the first chapter of Thackeray's *Vanity Fair*, her final action is to throw a presentation copy of Johnson's *Dictionary* out of the window of her carriage ... Becky Sharp saw Johnson's *Dictionary* as a symbol of oppressive and hateful erudition.   (Considine 1998: 579)[82]

Be it for the middle classes or for the people, the dictionaries of the eighteenth and nineteenth centuries were tools for the dissemination of knowledge, because knowledge was seen as a means of improving one's social status and because knowledge meant happiness: 'Felicity can only be obtained by becoming knowledgeable,' Chambers had written in the *Preface* of his *Cyclopaedia* (1728), an idea that was the hallmark of the Enlightenment.

2.4.3.3 Dictionaries to submit the people or to liberate the masses?

The educating zeal of many nineteenth-century lexicographers was a zeal for integration. Their aim was to help the underprivileged join society as it was, not to change it. In Europe, though not in America, some lexicographers went one step further and compiled dictionaries that would subvert the social order. Pierre Bayle was one of their ancestors. Though not a revolutionary, he was in favour of reason against religious belief, and his *Dictionaire historique et critique* (1696) was considered subversive. Stendhal, in his autobiography, speaking of his monarchist father around 1796 (Stendhal was 13), wrote: 'Around that period my father did not buy Bayle's *Dictionnaire* ... in order not to compromise my religion, so he said to me'.[83] Clearly, some people in the society of Stendhal's family were still buying Bayle, although it had been published a hundred years before and it was still felt to be dangerous. Victor Hugo found dictionaries too conservative, and he declared emphatically that he wanted to put a 'red bonnet'[84] on them.

Lachâtre, again, 'who is as unknown today as he was subversive during his lifetime' (Gaudin 2002: 43), hated all forms of authority, including schools and teachers—but not dictionaries—and was openly revolutionary. He ridiculed the Church and all those who wielded some sort of power in some of the illustrative sentences of his *Dictionnaire universel* (1852): 'Le pape est affecté d'incontinence d'urine', 'Crions haro sur le despotisme', 'La lubricité de Louis XV effrayait ses

---

[82] See also Congleton and Congleton (1984: 44–5). There is similar evidence in France: 'I questioned the Russian writer on his method of work, wondering why he did not do his own translations, since he spoke very pure French.... He confessed that the Academy and its dictionary froze him' (Alphonse Daudet, *Trente ans à Paris*, quoted as an epigraph by Andreï Makine, 1995, *Le testament français*, Paris: Mercure de France).

[83] *Vie de Henry Brulard* (Paris: Garnier) (1890/1961: 272).

[84] 'In 'Réponse à un acte d'accusation', *Les Contemplations*; an allusion to the red hat worn by French revolutionaries (against the white that symbolized Royalty).

maîtresses',[85] etc. (Gaudin 2002: 50). Even Larousse's *Grand dictionnaire universel du XIXe siècle* was judged to be dangerously liberal by some, and was listed in the Vatican's Index in 1873.

Of course there is a limit to how anti-social a dictionary can be: it has to sell well to have any influence. Lachâtre's *Dictionnaire universel* never did, and the adventure was soon ended: its 'career was stopped by a court ruling ordering that it be seized and destroyed' (Gaudin 2006: 241). Lachâtre tried again, but his other dictionary, the *Dictionnaire français illustré*, was also seized and destroyed, and Lachâtre was sentenced to 5 years in prison and a fine of 6,000 francs.

2.4.3.4 The dictionary as a patriotic emblem

In America, the nineteenth-century dictionary was an emblem of the new nation. Until Webster, the Americans had imported their dictionaries, but 'importing a British dictionary...ruffled national pride' (Bailey 1996: 6). Webster did not like the British, despite his message to Queen Victoria on the occasion of the publication of his second edition, and he was against the use of their dictionaries (Laird 1970: 263 *ff.*). He saw the dictionary as a means to signify that America was mature enough to break free from the influence of the mother country, a sign of national existence, a symbol of the unification of the community. 'It is not only important, but, in a degree necessary, that the people of this country, should have *An American Dictionary of the English Language,*' he wrote in the *Preface*. He wanted his dictionary to establish a new standard suited to the new country, which is why he proposed new words and new spellings:

As an independent nation our honour requires us to have a system of our own, in language as well as government. Great Britain, whose children we are, and whose language we speak, should no longer be our standard. For the taste of her writers is already corrupted, and her language is on the decline. But if it were not so, she is at too great a distance to be our model and to instruct us in the principles of our own tongue.

(Webster 1789; see also Green 1996: 256)

The dictionary has also been a patriotic emblem in other countries. In seventeenth-century France, the *Dictionnaire de l'Académie* was published at a time of great commercial and military expansion, and it was presented as an instrument in the service of the nation.[86] The *OED* was financed to the end, despite the colossal expense (see below, 3.1.1), because it was seen as a symbol of the power of

---

[85] 'The Pope is incontinent', 'Let us do away with despotism', 'The lewdness of Louis XV frightened his mistresses'.

[86] See the 'Epitre au Roi' ('Epistle to the King'), in the first edition (1694).

Victorian Britain (Benson 2001: 68). More recently, dictionaries played a part in the independence of some nations under the domination of others: 'the publication of specifically New Zealand dictionaries is part of a continuing development of national awareness, a process that has been underway from about the beginning of the century and that has slowly gathered momentum' (Scott 1986: 319). The patriotic role of the monolingual dictionary may have been one of its major functions (Zgusta 2006: 186 *ff.*).

> The spirit of nationalism has often proved a driving force in the making of dictionaries. Scholars were quick to recognize that the compilation of a reliable and comprehensive dictionary was one sign of the achievement of their country's maturity, just as the lack of grammars and dictionaries indicated the dominance of a foreign power or the weakness of a truly national feeling.   (Collison 1982: 18)

The dictionary is still an emblem for nations or communities, for the Basque, the Brazilians, the Catalans, the Slovenians, the Swahilis, the Zulus, and many others, as countries are born or struggle for recognition.

    In the course of three centuries, the dictionary became an extraordinarily varied and popular genre. Dictionaries to help travellers, dictionaries to understand hard words, dictionaries to fix the language, dictionaries to help the middle classes imitate the aristocracy, dictionaries to educate the working classes, dictionaries to change the world and even dictionaries to make people happy.... Instruments of tyranny, and of liberation. By the end of the nineteenth century, it seemed that dictionaries had run the whole gamut of their possible roles.

3

THE BRITISH TRADITION OF THE SCHOLARLY DICTIONARY

3.1 THE *OXFORD ENGLISH DICTIONARY*

3.1.1 *The first edition,* OED1

IN November 1857, Richard Chenevix Trench, Dean of Westminster who would later become Archbishop of Dublin, presented before the London Philological Society a paper in two parts, published afterwards as a single document under the title *On Some Deficiencies in Our English Dictionaries,*[1] in which he deplored the state of English lexicography. According to him, as summed up by Landau (2001: 78):

1. They failed to include obsolete terms by any consistent method.
2. Families and groups of words were inconsistently entered.
3. Earlier and later examples of illustrative quotations could be found.
4. Coverage of important early meanings was defective, especially important for understanding the historical development of the word.
5. Synonym discriminations were neglected.
6. The literature had been inadequately surveyed for apt quotations to illustrate the first use of a word, its etymology, and its meaning.
7. A miscellany of irrelevant and redundant information—mythological characters, encyclopedia articles, and so on—was cluttering up dictionaries needlessly.

---

[1] Available on the *OED Online* website and in Hartmann and Smith (2003).

Trench said that England could do much better, and his suggestions were taken up by members of the Society, who produced a *Proposal for a Publication of a New English Dictionary* in 1859, that would make use of the most recent developments in linguistics.

Almost a century before, in 1786, William Jones, who had worked for Samuel Johnson and was serving as a judge in India, had given a lecture in Calcutta in which he spoke of his intuition that Sanskrit, Greek, and Latin all came from the same source. Sanskrit, he said, bears to Greek and Latin 'a stronger affinity... than could possibly have been produced by accident;... no philologer could examine them all three without believing them to have sprung from some common source, which, perhaps, no longer exists'. This aroused the interest of philologists, Rasmus Rask in Denmark, who published an essay on the origins of Old Norse in 1818, and in Germany Franz Bopp, author of a comparative study of verbs in 1816, and Jacob Grimm, who compiled a grammar of German between 1819 and 1837. They were laying the foundations of what later came to be known as comparative linguistics. Franz Passow, a German lexicographer, published an essay in 1812 in which 'he strongly advocated the provision of chronologically arranged citations in the service of showing forth the history of each word' (Singleton 2000: 198), its *Lebensgeschichte*. He put his theory into practice in his *Handwörterbuch der griechischen Sprache* (1831), and this in turn influenced the work of H. G. Liddell and R. Scott for their *Greek–English Lexicon Based on the Work of Franz Passow* (1845), with a *Preface* that the *OED* would later quote from: 'Our Plan has been that marked out and begun by Passow, viz. to make each article a History of the usage of the word referred to'. In the 1830s in Germany, the Grimm brothers, Jacob and Wilhelm, had started working on their *Deutsches Wörterbuch* that was later, much later, published,[2] to show the origins of German words and provide a unified language for Germany.

The dictionaries used in Britain in the 1850s were H. J. Todd's four-volume enlargement of Johnson's *Dictionary* (1818 and 1827), Richardson's *Dictionary* (1836/7), the editions of Webster's *American Dictionary* of 1848 and 1859, and Ogilvie's *Imperial Dictionary* (1850). Later came Webster's *Unabridged* (1864), Latham's enlarged edition of Johnson (1866–70), *Chambers English Dictionary* (1872), *Cassell's Encyclopaedic Dictionary* (1879), Hunter's *Encyclopædic Dictionary* (1879–88), Annandale's revised edition of the *Imperial* (1882), and Whitney's *Century Dictionary* (1891). Trench lamented their weaknesses, 'their lack of rigour, their inconsistency, and their absence of systematic investigation' (Mugglestone 2004: 146),

---

[2] It was published in 1961, in 32 volumes, with 350,000 words.

The work of compilation for a better dictionary started slowly and amidst all sorts of difficulties, which have been described at length in the literature.[3] They continued until the day of publication, as the editors were 'pushing through uncharted territory' (Mugglestone 2005: 23). The project was eventually saved by the feeling that Britain had to have its dictionary, like Germany: 'We do but follow the example of the Grimms, when we call upon Englishmen to come forward and write their own dictionary,' the *Proposal* had proclaimed in 1859 (Mugglestone 2005: xiv) and that the most powerful nation on earth had to have the largest dictionary ever produced (Mugglestone 2005: 183 *ff.*). By the end of the nineteenth century, there was no longer any doubt that the dictionary was going to be completed, whatever the cost: the *OED* was to be the production of the triumphant Britain of the Victorian era.

It was in 1878, when James A. H. Murray accepted the editorship, that the compilation of the new dictionary began in earnest. Murray, born in a poor family in a Scottish village in 1837, had left school at the age of 14, but became a schoolteacher (Plate 26). He was an autodidact who could read in at least twenty languages (Hitchings 2005: 92), had been active in the Philological Society and had been awarded an honorary doctorate by the University of Edinburgh in 1874. In the contract, the dictionary was to take 10 years to produce and it was to be published in four volumes, 8,400 pages in all (Mugglestone 2005: 131).

Murray started working full time with a team of helpers in surroundings that have often been described, particularly his 'Scriptorium', built for the purpose in his gardens at Oxford (Plate 27). His first decision was to launch a worldwide appeal for unpaid volunteers to read books and documents that would eventually constitute the *OED*'s corpus, and select words and the appropriate passages. The appeal was renewed in 1879: 'A thousand readers are wanted, and confidently asked for, to complete the work as far as possible within the next three years . . .'.[4] There were seventy-six readers in 1857, over a hundred in 1859 (Mugglestone 2005: 8), 754 in 1880, and eventually about 2,700 sent in contributions in the form of slips, one for every suggested word or meaning. Murray also issued several lists of particular books that people could usefully read, and he requested help on difficult words.[5]

Among the readers there were many Americans—who were not asked to specialize in American texts (Ramson 2002: 4), and there were interesting figures: Francis March, author of the *Thesaurus Dictionary of the English Language*, William Dwight Whitney, the editor of the *Century Dictionary*, and Dr Minor,

---

[3] See Murray (1977), Mugglestone (2000*a*, 2005), Winchester (2003).
[4] The different appeals to readers can be found on the *OED* website (see also Simpson 2003: 263–4).
[5] *OED News*, March 2006.

the mad American surgeon, who worked very hard for Murray while he was in jail for murder (Winchester 1998; see also Bailey 2004).

The dictionary was first published in parts (47 in all), then in 118 paper-backed sections called *fascicles* of 64 pages each delivered to subscribers every three months. The first part was published in 1884 and the last fascicle on 19 April 1928.[6] Publication by fascicles, which had been used in the eighteenth century for Johnson's and Bailey's dictionaries and in France for the *Encyclopédie*, ensured adequate financing of the project, but it also had unfortunate consequences on the dictionary text. Some words used in definitions were elucidated much later: Mugglestone (2005: 123) mentions the example of the word *omentum*, used in the definition of *anepiploic* ('Having no epiploon, or omentum'), which 'was not to be defined until twenty years later when the fascicle O–Onomastic appeared in 1902'.[7] In some cases also, a word was used in a definition although it had not been defined in that sense, or it had been given a derogatory label (Mugglestone 2005: 160).

Murray died in 1915, when the work was at letter T, having 'spent thirty-three of his seventy-eight years supplying copy to the printer' and editing '7207 pages, or almost half' (Ramson 2002: 2) of the total dictionary. The general editorship then went to Henry Bradley, who also had little formal education but was a remarkable philologist. He had been working on the *OED* since 1886 and had become second editor in 1888.[8] Two other editors joined the team later: William Craigie, who taught Latin at the University of St Andrews, had started working on the *OED* in 1897 and became an editor in 1901, and Charles Onions, who started in 1895 and became fourth editor in 1914 (Plate 28). Together, they 'edited just over half of the entire OED' (Gilliver 2000: 166),[9] although Murray always insisted on being editor-in-chief as long as he was present, and the dictionary is remembered as Murray's.

The successive editors were plagued by financial problems and by the diktats of the delegates of Oxford University Press through the entire period of preparation, but the lexicographic method was clear right from the start, and never changed. One of the problems was that the editors found it difficult to stick to the original plan of 5.5 pages of text for one in Webster's *Dictionary* of 1864: the ratio never

[6] Part I, published on 29 January 1884, *A* to *Ant*, had 352 pages and 8,365 words. The last fascicle was *Wise–Wyzen* (*X–Zyxt* had come out in 1921). Part II (*Ant* to *Batten*) was published in November 1885. See Mugglestone (2000a: 228–31) for the complete list.

[7] 'A fold or duplication of the peritoneum connecting the stomach with certain of the other viscera, as the liver, spleen, and colon'.

[8] He came to Murray's attention when he published a penetrating review article on the first part of the *OED*.

[9] Bradley edited E, F, G, L, M, part of S, and part of W, Craigie edited N, Q, part of R, part of S, U, V, and part of W, Onions edited part of S, part of W, and all of XYZ.

stopped growing, and towards the end of the alphabet it reached sixteen (Brewer 2004: 36), in part because Webster was less thorough with the last letters of the alphabet, a case of 'alphabet fatigue' (Osselton 2007). And the work of compilation advanced at a pace that was much slower than planned: 'Three years before the dictionary had originally been expected to be finished, not even the second letter of the alphabet had been completed' (Mugglestone 2005: 24).

The dictionary was published in 1928, about 40 years behind schedule, a familiar story of inadequate planning that repeats itself with every ambitious lexicographic project, 44 years after the publication of the first fascicle, about 70 years after compilation had started, exactly 100 years after Webster's main dictionary and almost 200 after Johnson's. It was entitled *A New English Dictionary on Historical Principles, Founded Mainly on Materials Collected by the Philological Society* (Plate 10). It had twelve volumes, 15,490 pages, almost twice the planned number, three columns of text on each page, 252,000 entries, 414,800 defined words and 1,827,306 quotations, the largest language dictionary of English ever.[10] The event was celebrated by a huge dinner on 6 June 1928, and the first two sets to come off the press were presented to King George V and to Calvin Coolidge, the American President (Winchester 2003: xxiii), a clear sign that the *OED* meant to play, 'in relation to the English language, the role of custodian to the world' (Ramson 2002: 5). Incidentally, the gift may not have been fully appreciated by the King, who 'regarded his set of the *Oxford English Dictionary* simply as a very suitable ornament for the library at Windsor Castle' (Considine 1998: 580).

In 1933, a *Supplement* of 866 pages, edited by Onions and Craigie, was published. It contained 'words which were born too late for inclusion' (Winchester 2003: 239), 'changes in the earlier volumes' (Landau 2001: 83), which were almost 50 years old, and corrections of the mistakes of the first edition. The *Supplement* included *automobile, chromosome, cinema, cubism, lip-stick, pacifist, psycho-analysis, radium, relativity, surrealist, television,* etc. (Mugglestone 2005: 204 *ff.*), more scientific and technical words, military words that had appeared during World War One (Mugglestone 2005: 198 *ff.*) and many words from non-British varieties of English (Ogilvie 2004: 652). By then, the dictionary had come to be known as *The Oxford English Dictionary,* and it was under that title that the 13 volumes were then sold: *The Oxford English Dictionary on Historical Principles.*[11] It now had 16,500 pages.

[10] Precise figures were obtained by the computerization of the text. Compared to Johnson, the *OED*, for example, had 47,648 words in Volume 1 where Johnson had 3,740 (Ramson 2002: 1). Littré's *Dictionnaire* had about 4,000 pages, the *Century* had 7,000.

[11] The title *Oxford English Dictionary* had been used informally before that date. It appeared for the first time on the cover of the fascicle *Deceit–Deject* on 1 January 1895.

Like all dictionaries, the *OED* made use of its predecessors (Zgusta 1989c). It used Johnson, particularly 'in the earlier part of the alphabet' (Silva 2005: 235), and even included words simply because Johnson had included them, for example *astroscopy, besputter, carrotiness, carcelage*, etc. (Silva 2005: 234), despite Murray's declaration that the *OED* would 'insert no word because it is in another Dictionary' (Mugglestone 2005: 45). The *OED* also 'reproduced around 1,700 of Johnson's definitions, marking them simply "J"' (Hitchings 2005: 228). It used Webster 1864, the *Century Dictionary*, which was 'cited 2,118 times' (Bailey 1996: 13), Richardson (1836/7), Martin (1749), etc. It also used dictionaries of other languages, among which Littré's *Dictionnaire*.[12] But the *OED* went far beyond what any of its predecessors had done, both in macrostructure and in microstructure. Its methodology was explained in the *Plan* published in 1884 in the first fascicle and in the *Preface* of Volume I in 1888.

1. The *OED* was a historical dictionary,[13] sometimes referred to as a *philological* dictionary (Rey and Delesalle 1979: 16). It was historical in three ways: the wordlist, the arrangement of information, and the etymologies. The wordlist covered a huge period: the *OED* aimed at listing 'words now in use, or known to have been in use since the middle of the twelfth century' (*OED*: xxviii). No dictionary of English had covered such a period before: Johnson only went from 1586 to 1660, with a few additional more recent words.

The *OED* arranged information in chronological order whenever possible: for example, it listed the different spellings of a word in the order in which they had appeared. In polysemous entries, the meanings were also arranged chronologically, to retrace the historical development of the word, in accordance with the new orientation in linguistics: every word 'should be made to tell its own story' (Singleton 2000: 198).[14] In fact, there were many entries where the arrangement was not strictly chronological, either because there was not enough evidence or because the evidence did not make sense. For example, the traditional distinction between the transitive and the intransitive meanings of verbs, as practised by

---

[12] It had been published between 1863 and 1873.

[13] The *OED* was not the first dictionary to use the word *historical* in its title. French examples were Moreri's *Grand Dictionaire historique* (1671), and Bayle's *Dictionaire historique et critique* (1696). But this referred to history in its usual sense, not the history of words. The French Academy started a *Dictionnaire historique de la langue française* in 1835, which was never finished (Pruvost 2002a: 48). Recently the Robert publishers produced a two-volume etymological dictionary, the *Dictionnaire Historique de la Langue Française* (1992).

[14] In France, Louis Dochez had published a *Nouveau dictionnaire de la langue française* in 1859 in which meanings were ordered chronologically to illustrate the history of each word (Pruvost 2006: 67).

Craigie—but frowned upon by Murray—disrupted chronological ordering: it was 'counter-historical' (Silva 2000: 84). Meanings, when not chronologically ordered, were arranged in 'a logical chain of development' (Murray 1977: 203): 'concrete precedes abstract; single precedes generalized; religious precedes secular; literal precedes figurative; simple verb precedes phrasal verb' (Silva 2000: 93). Eventually, in many entries, the ordering was a compromise between chronology and logic (Silva 2000: 80). Zgusta (1989c: 200, 2006: 68) even argues that strict chronological ordering was 'extremely rare'. In most cases, however, the first meaning in an entry was an old, often extinct, meaning, generally the oldest.

The third manifestation of the historical perspective was in the provision of etymological information. This was given in a special paragraph at the beginning of each entry, and it was the most detailed ever published for English. It gave the 'derivation of each word, that is, taking back the current shape or spelling of each word to its earliest form in English, and the establishment of its cognates in other Germanic languages, or, if it is a loan word, of its form in the borrowed-from language' (Burchfield 1986: 19). The *OED*, however, contrary to some of its predecessors, did not use etymology to establish the 'true' meaning of each word but only to reconstruct its semantic evolution. It focused on the historical development of words more than on their origin (Silva 2000: 78). The *OED* also gave the date of the earliest recorded occurrence of each meaning, and pre-dating an *OED* entry then became a favourite sport of students of English (Schäfer 1980, 1989).

2. The *OED* was a descriptive dictionary. The corpus contained non-fiction, technical and scientific sources, even popular newspapers and magazines, a feature for which the editors were criticized during the period of compilation (Mugglestone 2000b: 13, 2005: 121), and the aim was to record the words that it contained, all of them: 'What goes in determines what comes out' (Brewer 2007: 129). 'Philology and the lexicography that is attached to it ... rest on the observation of discourse; the "philological" dictionary aims at constructing a linguistic model purely based on observation' (Rey and Delesalle 1979: 16). The editors wanted to cast 'aside the prescriptive resistance to change and variation which had long hallmarked its predecessors' (Mugglestone 2000c: 190), notably Richardson and Todd (Bailey 2000: 208). They made it clear that they did not intend to pass judgement on usage, true to what Dean Trench had recommended:

A Dictionary, then, according to that idea of it which seems to me alone capable of being logically maintained, is an inventory of the language. ... It is no task of the maker of it to select the good words of a language. ... The business which he has undertaken is to collect and arrange all words... whether they do or do not commend themselves to his judgment.... He is an historian... not a critic. (n.p.)

Murray's attitude reflected the descriptivism of modern linguistics, for which all types of discourse were worthy of study. Murray held on to this principle throughout the compilation of the dictionary, as much as he could, despite fierce opposition, even from academic circles (Mugglestone 2005: 21 *ff.*). He even refused to condemn some forms that were considered as signs of bad education, for example *different to* (Mugglestone 2005: 145) or *averse to* (Mugglestone 2005: 170).

However, like all dictionaries, the *OED* could not help choosing words, usages and spellings when there were variants. Sometimes it chose forms that were not the most common, '*ax, Shakspere, tire* (of motor cars), and *rime*' (Winchester 2003: 235)—but this did not influence usage any more than Johnson or Webster had, despite the prestige of the *OED*. Some words were excluded, although 'every decision to exclude a word [was] a departure from the purist ideal of descriptive lexicography so confidently stated by Trench and the others' (Brewer 2000: 41). The *OED* excluded taboo words—after much hesitation (Mugglestone 2007: 5 *ff.*)—regardless of their frequency in usage. The story of their exclusion is interesting: it was recently revealed that the team carried out all the research and the collection of quotations, but eventually yielded to pressures to omit them, 'in deference to Victorian sensibilities' (Mugglestone 2000*b*: 10; see also Mugglestone 2005: 84 *ff.*), although they were all in Farmer and Henley's seven-volume *Slang and its Analogues*, published between 1890 and 1904. A few were included after the letter N, after a slight change in policy, so that *quaint*, explained by a quotation from Florio's *Worlde of Wordes*, 'a woman's quaint or privities', as well as *shit* and *twat* were included, although *cunt* and *fuck* had not been.[15] The change of policy cannot be explained by the death of Queen Victoria, since the compilation had not reached the letter N in 1901; the *OED* was still at M in 1906 (Brewer 2004: 24).

The *OED*, despite its declared descriptiveness, also used derogatory labels, *low*, *vulgar, illiterate*, etc., although it was far more parsimonious than Johnson: *enthuse* was 'ignorant' (Mugglestone 2005: 168 *ff.*), *pants* (instead of *drawers*) was 'shoppy', etc. The label *erroneous* or *erron.* was used in nearly 2,000 entries. The label *catach.* (catachrestic) or the symbol ¶, indicating '"incorrect" or contentious usage of one sort or another' (Brewer 2004: 29), was 'by far the

---

[15] *Cunt* was 'later included in the 1972 *Supplement*' (Mugglestone 2000*a*: 11). Oddly enough, Murray kept *ballock*.

most important circumstance in which the *OED* was straightforwardly prescriptive' (Burchfield 1989: 91). There were also more extensive comments: *a blunder,
often improperly used, certainly faulty, a bad use*, etc. (Mugglestone 2000*d*). One
sense of *avocation* was 'improperly foisted upon the word', *caucus* was 'generally
misused', etc.

3. The *OED* was an exhaustive dictionary, at least the most comprehensive
dictionary of English ever produced. It aimed at including 'the whole world of
English words' (Murray, in Mugglestone 2000*b*: 2), all the words of English for
which there was enough acceptable evidence, i.e. 'three citations from different
sources over a five-year span' (Sheidlower 1995: 38). This was the original plan,
but of course there had to be limits (Mugglestone 2005: 104). The *OED* excluded
taboo words, as we have seen, for reasons of propriety, but also proper names and
the adjectives derived from them, foreign borrowings if they were not fully
naturalized, slang words, many derivatives[16] (Mugglestone 2005: 93), many
scientific and technical terms (Mugglestone 2005: 110 *ff.*) if they were too exclusively scientific,[17] because of 'a distaste for such special subjects, as for commerce
and industry, as being profoundly incompatible with the generalist orientation of
the upper classes' (Landau 2001: 83). It also excluded many words from regional
English or from non-British varieties of English: there were virtually no Americanisms or Australianisms. Some have argued that the policy of the *OED* 'with
regard to all kinds of regional words was ill-defined from the beginning' (Görlach
1990: 1478), but Ogilvie (2004) convincingly shows on the basis of *OED* files that
there was no deliberate policy, only a lack of evidence or evidence not properly
noticed.

The editors of the *OED* had to struggle between two conflicting imperatives:
the principled pledge to include all the words of the English language, and the
commercially motivated need to leave out words because they would have made
the dictionary unacceptable to some people or because they would have made it
too bulky. Murray '(and his co-editors) would be haunted by the sense of the
ideal—and its elusiveness' (Mugglestone 2005: 36).

The *OED* was also 'exhaustive' in another way: it was extremely thorough in its
distinction of the meanings of polysemous words (see below, 8.2.3): it had 'eighteen
main senses and twenty-six sub-senses, including numerous phrases and attributive uses, and fifty-four combinations' for *cat* (Silva 2000: 80–1). The entry for *set*

---

[16] A *derivative* is a word derived from another word by an affix. Derivation should be distinguished
from inflexion: the former produces a new word, the latter a form of the same word.

[17] At first, it was proposed that technical and scientific terms be grouped in a special section of the
dictionary, but the idea was abandoned (Rand Hoare and Salmon 2000: 159).

had '154 main divisions' (Ramson 2002: 2), took 40 days to assemble, used about 60,000 words and covered 'more than eighteen pages'. The entry for *pass* was given 16 columns (Mugglestone 2005: 187), *point* 21, *candle* 'occupied four columns and 376 lines' where Johnson had fourteen lines and Webster twenty (Mugglestone 2005: 26).

4. The *OED* was a literary dictionary. As we have seen, other lexicographers had sought evidence and a linguistic model in literature before, but the *OED* carried the practice to unprecedented dimensions. 'From the very beginning the dictionary was conceived as a dictionary of English literature in print. An aesthetic literary judgement guided the editors to some extent in their selection of quotations' (Stanley 2000: 137). The corpus of the *OED* contained all the great literary authors of the past, and a word found in a famous book had a good chance of being included, even if it was infrequent: 'Words of marginal import- ance used by these preferred authors are rarely omitted' (Schäfer 1980: 13). The *OED* even had *hapax legomena* (Greek for 'words that are used only once'): *devilship*, used by Thomas Nashe (Brewer 2007: 115), *embracive*, used by Thack- eray (Mugglestone 2005: 119), *fringent*, used by Emerson in his poem 'The daemonic love', *to gimlet*, used by De Quincey (Mugglestone 2005: 137), *literata* and *linguipotence*, used by Coleridge (Mugglestone 2005: 97, 101), *ochidore*, used by Kingsley in *Westward Ho!*,[18] *riverrun*, used by Joyce in *Finnegan's Wake*, *unleaving*, used by Hopkins in his poem 'Spring and fall', *vermigrade*, used by Beckett and found 'nowhere except in another dictionary' (Burchfield 1992: 249), *whiskerage*, used by Carlyle (Brewer 2007: 116), etc. It even had *juvescence*, used by mistake by T. S. Eliot instead of *juvenescence* (see Gilliver *et al.* 2006). All of those were hard to define, because of the lack of evidence. A counter example, of a word that was omitted though found in a great book was *abashless*, used by Browning (Mugglestone 2005: xii).

5. The *OED* was illustrated by quotations for every sense of every word. The readers had sent 'around 2.5 million slips in 1880' (Mugglestone 2005: 15) and eventually 6 million (Mugglestone 2005: 64), from more than 5,000 sources, covering a period of more than 700 years. Many of those, Murray discovered, were not of very good quality, and some were totally useless. Eventually, 1,861,212 quotations were selected for publication, 1,827,306 for the first twelve volumes, an average of 4.2 citations per entry. The original idea was to have roughly one quotation per century whenever possible, but there were many departures from this: 'two periods in particular were vastly better represented in the dictionary

[18] *OED News*, March 2002.

than others—the late-sixteenth century and the nineteenth century' (Brewer 2000: 52), perhaps because they were periods of literary excellence, but the eighteenth century was badly represented, for reasons that are not totally clear.[19] In some cases, Murray 'happily invented additional examples... where he deemed existing evidence to be inadequate' (Mugglestone 2005: 130), some-times giving information on his personal life, as for *arrival*: 'the new arrival is a little daughter' (Brewer 2007: 225).

Murray had asked the readers to concentrate on 'remarkable words', words that struck them as 'rare, obsolete, old-fashioned, new, peculiar, or used in a peculiar way' (*OED Introduction*), but this had unfortunate consequences. The compilers had many quotations for rare words or meanings, but few, sometimes none, for the more common. It was discovered, for example, that there were 'over fifty citations... for *abusion*, fewer than five for *abuse*' (Mugglestone 2000b: 8), none for *glass* in its main sense (Mugglestone 2005: 41), two 'for *rape* meaning sexual assault' (Brewer 2004: 32), but ten for *runcible*, a nonsense word invented by Edward Lear. In the final text, the number of quotations was not directly proportional to the importance of the word or sense.

Figures published after the text of the *OED* was computerized indicate that the most often quoted writers were Shakespeare (32,886 times),[20] Walter Scott (15,499), Wycliffe (11,971), Milton (11,967), Chaucer (11,000), Dryden (9,000), Dickens (7,500), Tennyson (6,972), Macaulay (5,575), Southey (4,741), Coleridge (3,702), Ruskin (3,323), Wordsworth (2,055), Froude (2,006), etc. If these figures are set against the number of pages read for each author, 'Coleridge is the most heavily quoted of the named writers' (Brewer 2000: 43), and the work that had the most quotations was *Cursor Mundi*, a 'fourteenth-century northern poem' (Winchester 2003: 111),[21] with about 11,000 quotations (Brewer 2004: 13). The Bible is quoted 20,160 times (Willinsky 1994: 99), slightly less than Shakespeare but more than any other author. A 'total of 2,976 quotations are attributed to Johnson's dictionary' (Silva 2005: 237).[22] Some authors were neglected: 'William Blake is quoted 112 times, Christina Rossetti 133 times, Emily Brontë 68 times' (Brewer 2004: 13).

---

[19] Among possible reasons, Brewer (2007: 129) suggests that eighteenth-century sources had been allotted to readers who 'failed to deliver the slips they had promised'.

[20] Precise figures can vary, because the same author could be cited in different forms, or because they were obtained via different methods (Brewer 2000: 43, 2004: 12).

[21] *Cursor Mundi* is a long religious epic relating the history of the world as recorded in the Old and New Testaments. Written by an anonymous author *c.*1300, it is in the northern English dialect.

[22] With some of Johnson's mistakes, later discovered by the compilers of *OED3* (Silva 2005).

Quotations were perfectly accurate, including the spelling, and were given with full bibliographic details, except when they were taken from Johnson, in which case Murray acknowledged he lacked the time, energy, and money to check. They were grouped at the end of each entry or sub-entry in chronological order, so that reading the paragraph of quotations gives a good idea of the evolution of the word. In some rare cases, words were even offered without a definition, with the note 'See quotations': for example *morindin* (Winchester 2003: 143).

Because of the numerous quotations and the historical ordering of the meanings of polysemous words and of the quotations, the *OED* is one of the more readable dictionaries ever produced. It was, and still is, first class reading:

[It] would be as good a companion on a desert island as a man could hope for,[23] as apart from the history of the words, the quotations are endlessly entertaining in themselves. It is like having all the birthday books and literary calendars ever written rolled into one.

(Considine 1998: 580)

As it was published in fascicles or parts, it was also described as 'the longest sensational serial ever written' (Arnold Bennett, quoted in Considine 1998: 584).

6. The *OED* was a language dictionary, a dictionary of words, not of things. A dictionary, Murray said, is not an encyclopedia, and the primary purpose of the dictionary is 'to illustrate the *word*, and not tell us about the *thing*' (Rand Hoare and Salmon 2000: 159). Originally, there was to be a special section for proper names (Rand Hoare and Salmon 2000: 159), but the idea was dropped. Some were retained in the *OED*, some were not: *East Indies, England, Holland, Iceland, Lapland, Poland, Portugal,* etc. are in, but *France, Germany, Ireland, Scotland, Wales,* etc. are not. '[I]t has been suggested that some of them were included in the *OED* for the simple reason that readers had registered these names on their slips' (Schäfer 1980: 29). The *OED* did not have a single picture, although there was a long tradition of pictorial illustrations in British dictionaries, going back to Blount's dictionary (1656), and although recent dictionaries such as the *Imperial Dictionary* (1850) and Hunter's *Encyclopaedic Dictionary* (1879–88) had woodcuts or other illustrations (Bailey 2000: 214). Even the word *colour* only had a definition in the *OED*.

Because he did not want proper names, Murray decided to exclude the adjectives derived from them, such as *African, Alaskan, Albanian, Aristotelian,*

---

[23] 'Lord Oxford once said that if he were cast on a desert island, and could only choose one author for company, he would have the forty volumes of Balzac. I choose the Dictionary every time. . . . Our histories, our novels, our poems, our plays—they are all in this one book' (Stanley Baldwin, Prime Minister 1923–1929, in *OED News*, June 2003).

or *Virgilian, Ptolemaic, Miltonic, Johnsonian.* But a few slipped through, such as *Acadian, American, Australian, Canadian, Egyptian,* etc. (Curzan 2000: 99), some because they were necessary to explain other words (Ogilvie 2004: 654): *American* was necessary to define *Americanize* and *Americanism. African* had to wait until the 1933 *Supplement.*

Even though it did not aim at being encyclopedic, the *OED,* like all big dictionaries, is rich in information on the world at the end of the nineteenth and beginning of the twentieth century, particularly on Victorian society. There is an entry, for example, for *Conservative Party* (Brewer 2004: 23); the entry for *when* has 'The Oxford Dictionary of the English Language will have to be revised and enlarged when this war is over'.[24] Among thousands of examples, Osselton notes the definition of the phrase *to turn cart-wheels*:

to execute a succession of lateral summersaults ... street-boys do this by the side of a moving omnibus, etc., for chance coppers thrown to them

'All dictionaries bear the tincture of the age in which they are compiled,' Osselton (1993: 125) concludes.

7. The *OED* was objective: 'Neutrality and impartiality remained the aim' (Mugglestone 2005: 59) throughout the period of compilation. It tried to avoid any trace of the likes and dislikes of the editors or compilers, and of their moral judgements (Mugglestone 2005: xxi). Craigie once mentioned a definition of *retreat* from a *Dictionary of Marine* illustrating the kind of lack of objectivity that he did not want in the *OED*: at *retreat,* it had 'Retreat is the order in which a French fleet retires before an enemy. As it is not properly a term of the British marine, any fuller account would be out of place' (Winchester 2003: 236). Of course there are traces of moral judgements in some entries: the definition of *masturbate* was 'to practise self-abuse', the entry for *orgasm* was 'obfuscated' (Mugglestone 2005: 87), etc. Perfect neutrality is another 'unattainable ideal' (Mugglestone 2005: 87; see below, 6.1.1).

8. The *OED* was a scholarly dictionary. It was in touch with the latest developments in linguistics, as had been advocated by Dean Trench. It was historical, in a period where linguists were interested in the evolution of languages and the delineation of language families, it was descriptive, as was the linguistics of the time, it was thorough in its microstructural information and serious in tone, with little regard for user-friendliness. It was a dictionary for well-educated people.

---

[24] A rare case of the use of a deictic, *this,* in a dictionary example.

The *OED* has been the object of many articles, reviews, and books, probably more than any dictionary in the world. Some early readers were shocked by the inclusion of words that they thought should not have been allowed in a proper dictionary: 'I am not the editor of the English language,' Murray is reported to have replied once, in an unusual bout of irritation. More serious reviewers exposed errors or inconsistencies, many of which were simply the consequence of the fact that the compilation took such a long time and was carried out by so many people. Some parts were better than others: Murray himself 'expressed the belief that A and E (the latter being Bradley's first volume) were the two weakest letters' (Silva 2000: 87). There were omissions and mistakes in the selection of words and meanings, as we have seen: 'the verb *juggle* in the most usual transitive sense of keeping several items (balls, clubs, etc.) in the air at once ... was over-looked in both the first edition and the Supplement' (Paton 1995: 84); *bondmaid*, first used in 1526, was omitted (Curzan 2000: 100) for reasons that, according to Winchester (2003: 103), reveal the working conditions of the time: 'its slips had fallen down behind some books, and the editors had never noticed that it was gone' (see also Mugglestone 2005: 82). Other omissions included *radium*,[25] *chromosome, appendicitis,*[26] *proof-reading, anaerobic* (Mugglestone 2005: 140) and many technical compounds (Curzan 2000: 106). The 'shoe-size sense' was only mentioned for *nine, six, twelve,* and perhaps *thirteen.*

Temperatures cannot be up in the eighties—only, on OED evidence, in the nineties, and implicitly, through a quotation, in the twenties. One can be aged eighty, but not eight, eighteen, or eleven—nor explicitly, later in the alphabet, two, four, five, nine, thirteen, fourteen, fifteen, nineteen or ninety.   (Burnett 1989: 140)

On the other hand, the *OED* had a few spurious words:

[They] gained entry but in error, chiefly as a result of misprints or misreadings. Examples are *hugesum*, an erroneous spelling for *ugsome, cook-mate*, an erroneous spelling for the questionable *cock-mate*, and the nonce-word *featherly*, a misreading for *feathery*, which as an unfortunate result of an unfortunate lexicographical practice, survived in a number of other dictionaries.   (Ramson 2002: 3)

On the whole, the *OED*, with its comprehensive and scholarly contents, was an extraordinary dictionary. Its entries were wonderfully learned and enjoyable. But

---

[25] Though *radioactivity* was in, as was *X-rays*. Radium had just been discovered, but Craigie thought the word was an 'ephemeral coinage' (Mugglestone 2005: 113).

[26] 'Murray was advised in 1891 not to admit "all the crack-jaw medical and surgical words." After Edward VII's coronation was delayed by surgery for the removal of his appendix, the word became common parlance and was accepted in the *OED*' (Morton 1994: 299; see also Murray 1977: 222).

it was designed more for the learned than for a wide public. It had something to teach to everybody, but it was more likely to be used by the elite. It carried to unprecedented heights the concept of the dictionary as a record of the literary language. It was modern in its interest in linguistics, in its exhaustiveness, in its systematic use of quotations, its historical ordering of meanings and quotations, its descriptivism and its scientific approach to lexicography. It was also modern in the way it was generated, by pooling the knowledge of thousands of learned readers, and produced, by a large team of lexicographers, marking the end of the period when dictionaries were written by single authors. And it was unequalled in its systematic exploration of a body of written sources covering several centuries.

The *OED* was extremely influential, especially in Britain but also in other language communities. It was a model for many lexicographers, a monument for the public and a supreme reference for writers: 'The OED has been to me a teacher, a companion, a source of endless discovery. I could not have been a writer without it,' said Anthony Burgess.[27] It modified the reference habits of the English-speaking world over the following decades: Murray, Bailey (2000: 225) notes wryly, 'had educated people into wanting something from a dictionary that most of them did not want at all—for instance, the historical list of variant spellings—and denying them what they did want—for instance, insight into what an *angel-fish* might look like'. It also, like Johnson, reduced the competition to a trickle: the only large dictionary published after the *OED* was Henry Cecil Wyld's *Universal Dictionary of the English Language* in 1932, about 1,400 pages, that was good on pronunciation and etymology, and could have been successful if it had been published in other circumstances.

3.1.2 *The* Supplements

The thirteen volumes of the first edition of the *OED* with the *Supplement* went unmodified for almost 40 years. Oxford University Press had considered a complete revision, but could not face the time and expense. It was eventually decided that there would be a new supplement, and work started in 1957, 100 years exactly after Dean Trench's seminal papers, under the editorship of Robert Burchfield, a scholar from New Zealand. The agenda was to correct and complement the first edition and to record the changes that had taken place in the vocabulary of English since the 1920s. The compilation was scheduled to take

---

[27] *OED News*, March 2006.

7 years, but eventually it was a four-volume *Supplement to the OED* (*OEDS*), 5,730 pages, 69,300 entries,[28] which took 29 years to prepare: A–G came out in 1972, H–N in 1976, O–Scz in 1982, and Se–Z in 1986.[29]

OEDS followed *OED* methodology, with a few changes. Some were minor: for example, the entry words were no longer capitalized. Others were more important. The corpus included more non-literary documents, television scripts, etc. (Brewer 2004: 4): *OEDS* had *bonkers, head-on, hobbit, iffy, Nazi, quark, usherette, video*, etc. (Mugglestone 2005: 206 *ff.*). It had many technical and scientific terms (Rand Hoare and Salmon 2000: 162), many adjectives derived from proper names, and a 'fairly large number of names of trademarks . . . because they turn up in fiction or in poetry . . . *H.P. sauce, Jello, Kleenex, Polaroid, Portakabin, Walkman and Weetabix*' (Burchfield 1992: 248). It had many taboo words that had been omitted in the *OED* (Brewer 2007: 204), and it made 'bold forays into the written English of regions outside the British Isles, particularly that of North America, Australia, New Zealand, South Africa, India, and Pakistan' (*Preface* to the 1972 volume: xiv).[30] *OEDS* was received with almost unanimous praise, but it had many flaws. The task of correcting the *OED* was almost impossible, and *OEDS* 'left the myriad errors and imperfections of the parent dictionary . . . virtually untouched' (Brewer 2004: 5). It had too many unnecessary quotations, too many transparent combinations as well as too many *OED* entries that were not changed for the best (Brewer 2007: 176 *ff.*).

Up until the mid 1980s, everything in the dictionary division of Oxford University Press had been done by hand. The lexicographers worked at their desks with the million slips provided by the readers (Hulbert 1955; Murray 1977). But in the 1980s, even such a venerable institution as the *OED* had to adapt to the times. All the data contained in the first thirteen volumes plus the four supplements was transferred onto a CD-ROM, which came out in 1988. There was a worldwide survey of users of the dictionary to determine their preferences (Benbow *et al.* 1990), and the results were used to organize a complex consultation system. The entries could be accessed by language of origin, by year or century of first occurrence, by author in the list of quotations, by individual book used as a source, by word contained in the definitions or in the examples, by label of domain, or through any combination of these. This allowed searches that

---

[28] Almost the size of an unabridged dictionary of French.

[29] On *OEDS*, see Brewer (2007).

[30] With inevitable omissions: Forgue (1981: 91) notes that *Chicano* was not in. Ogilvie (2008) argues that Burchfield was not as bold as he says in his inclusion of words from other varieties, and that the person to praise on that count was actually Craigie.

would have been impossible or too time-consuming with the paper version and considerably enhanced the value of the *OED* for research purposes. Some reviewers expressed dissatisfaction with the earlier versions of the interface: the data could only be accessed through a word, not a phrase, the sign ¶ could not be used, and the program did not differentiate between lower-case and capital letters, so that typing ON for Old Norse would also return all the occurrences of the preposition *on* (Kaye 1989: 85). But later versions were improved.

3.1.3 *The second edition:* OED2

The second, more important, step in the updating of the *OED* was the publication on paper of the second edition (*OED2*) by John Simpson and Edmund Weiner in 1989, only three years after the publication of the last volume of the *Supplements*. The idea was to incorporate *OED1* and *OEDS*, 'the monitoring of new words and the making good of deficiencies in the dictionary's coverage of the English vocabulary' (Weiner 1987: 39), again with the help of many unpaid helpers worldwide. *OED2* had 20 volumes, 21,728 pages, a 'total of 616,500 forms' (xxiii), 59 million words, 291,500 entries, 615,164 defined words, 2,436,600 quotations and ... occupied 1.20 metres of shelf room, 'more than five times the size of any other dictionary of English,' the publicity said. It was dedicated to Queen Elizabeth II.

    OED2 had some 5,000 new words and senses, 'amounting to one percent of the dictionary's total of half a million or more' (Brewer 2004: 5): *ageism, aids, beta-blocker, biryani, bonk, break-dancing, CD-ROM, cling film, cruise missile, deregulation, fuzzy logic, glasnost, hands-on, legionnaire's disease, page three girl, passive smoking, perestroika, televangelism, toy boy, yuppification,* etc. Many of the new words were from non-standard or non-British varieties of English, particularly Americanisms (Simpson 1988: 440). Some other improvements were made: for example, the pronunciation was indicated in IPA (International Phonetic Alphabet[31]), which had been used for the first time by Wyld for his *Universal Dictionary of the English Language* in 1932 (Ilson 1986b: 55), instead of the complex transcription system invented by Murray.

    OED2 was advertised as a new dictionary but it retained most of the original text of *OED1*. Thousands of its entries dated back to the end of the nineteenth century: for example, Brewer (2004: 23) notes that the entry for *Conservative Party,* 'one of the two great English political parties', hides the fact that when the

---

[31] IPA originally stood for International Phonetic Association, founded in France in 1886 (Association Phonétique Internationale), which popularized the alphabet.

definition was first written the other party was the Liberal Party. In addition to this, it was impossible to see what belonged to *OED1*, what belonged to *OEDS* and what was new (Brewer 2004: 5), and as a consequence it was difficult to know whether the absence of a modern quotation in an entry meant that the word was obsolete or whether this had been overlooked. Some words were not given their modern meanings: *balloon* was 'An air-tight envelope of paper, silk, or similar material...' (Mugglestone 2005: 210), *clerk* 'one employed to make fair copies of documents', *fire-engine* 'a machine for throwing water to extinguish fires', and *typewriter*, 'one who does typewriting...'. In some cases, even the old spellings were retained, as in *beet-root* or *fire-work*. And it was difficult to interpret such labels as *now*: did it mean in 1989 or in 1928 (or earlier)? Osselton (1993: 128) concluded that 'as a historical dictionary OED2 is...greatly inferior to its predecessor'.

OED2 was made available on CD-ROM as a result of the computerization program carried out by Oxford University Press with IBM at the University of Waterloo in Canada. The first version came out in 1992 and it was regularly edited, each version adding new words and improving the interface. The CD-ROM edition of *OED2* has been acclaimed as 'the most sophisticated example of a dictionary on CD-ROM presently available on the market' (Brunet 1997: 18).[32]

3.1.4 *Towards a third edition:* OED3

A thorough updating of the text of the *OED* was started in 1993, at last, beginning at letter M because the first letters of *OED1* had been less consistent in their application of Murray's principles. *OED3* was scheduled to cost '£35 million/US$55 million'[33] and to 'take 500 person-years' (Landau 2001: 88), with an estimated completion date in 2010—that in 2004 had already been deferred (Brewer 2004: 17).[34] 'Some sixty-five lexicographers, aided and abetted by an army of readers, library researchers, and editorial assistants, are beavering away' (Hanks 2005: 261), working with corpora and the Internet, in conditions that have little to do with Murray's (Weiner 1994) (Plate 29). They update and sometimes completely transform existing entries with the new evidence that has surfaced since 1929 (Brewer 2004: 21), they reword the definitions in more modern language, they insert earlier quotations for many meanings, some sent in by thousands of identified or anonymous contributors, they re-organize complex entries, trying

---

[32] Brunet compared *OED2* on CD-ROM with the *Encyclopedia Universalis*, the *Robert électronique* and *TLFI* in terms of contents and user-friendliness.

[33] *OED News*, December 2002.

[34] Compilation was at letter R, about one-quarter of the way, in December 2008.

to reconcile logical and chronological ordering of meanings, applying 'the histor-ical method more rigorously' (Silva 2000: 93), alphabetically first and then in groups as of March 2008. Of course, they also insert new entries, particularly more scientific and technical words and more words from other varieties of English.[35] Eventually, the *OED* is hoping to become a dictionary of 'World English' (Weiner 1986).

OED3 'maintains four major reading programs' (Ramson 2002: 5), one for Britain, one for America, one historical, and one scholarly. Pending completion of the third edition, three volumes called the *Oxford English Dictionary Additions Series* were published, two in 1993 and a third in 1997. They contained the material that would later be incorporated into *OED3*, in disjointed alphabetical sequences according to the order in which the entries were revised and com-pleted. Here was *juggle*, at last! Osselton (1998: 246), reviewing Volume 3 of the *Addition Series*, found much to be dissatisfied with, 'common spelling illiteracies such as *accomodation*', stress-marks 'where none are needed . . . and left out when they should be put in', wrong pronunciations, etc. Also, the volumes could not be used independently and were 'not broadly entertaining for the popular audience' (Sheidlower 2000: 148). The publication of the *Additions Series* has been discon-tinued, and the updatings are now made available on the Internet, directly incorporated into the main text.

Since March 2000, *OED Online* has been available by subscription. The text contains the whole of *OED2* plus the three volumes of *Additions*, and is being constantly enriched by the quarterly releases of the new and revised material of *OED3*, a modern version of the fascicles for the publication of *OED1*, at the rate of about 6,000 words per year.[36] The layout is splendid, pleasant to the eye and easy to use, and the interface is full of possibilities for research. The user can turn off part(s) of the entry, or combine two words for an onomasiological search: for example, if you want to know what the word is for 'fear of spiders', you can type in *fear* and *spider* and you get *arachnophobia*.[37] There are currently about 700,000 words and 2.5 million quotations. Unfortunately, one does not always know when a particular entry was written or revised: before 1928 for *OED1*, or before 1933 for the *Supplement*, or before 1976 for *OEDS*, or after. Even the entries that

---

[35] Weiner (in Abley 2009: 44) says that Singapore English is not covered properly, perhaps because it is full of Chinese words.

[36] *OED News* for March 2006 announces new or updated entries for *philosopher, phlebotomist, photographer, photojournalist, phrenologer, physician, physicist, physiotherapist, pianist, piece-broker, pigeoneer,* and *pilot*.

[37] Admittedly an easy case, because there is only one word that has both *fear* and *spider* in its definition.

have been modified or added recently are changed as new information becomes available, so that preceding strata are irretrievably lost, giving the dictionary a 'disconcerting volatility' (Brewer 2007: 245). There is now, however, an option for users who want to consult *OED2* separately.

The story of the *OED* began in 1857 with Dean Trench's papers, which looked at earlier dictionaries and outlined the features of the dictionaries of the future. It extended over the whole of the twentieth century and will reach beyond, when *OED3* will be published and used, linking Johnson's lexicography with the lexicography of the twenty-first century. Some think that it is a thing of the past, 'along with the Albert Memorial and the British Empire' (Willinsky in Osselton 2002: 332), and others regret that it is part of 'a dictionary-making tradition which is no more' (Osselton 2002: 333).

3.2 THE FAMILY OF THE *OXFORD ENGLISH DICTIONARY*

3.2.1 *The* Shorter Oxford English Dictionary

Shortly after *OED1* had been published, work that had started in 1902 on an abridged version was accelerated, and the *Shorter Oxford English Dictionary on Historical Principles* (*SOED*) came out in 1933. It was based on the same principles as the parent dictionary: historical, descriptive, exhaustive, literary, linguistic, objective, and scholarly, with quotations, no pictorial illustrations and no proper names, but it had fewer entries, was less detailed, and had fewer quotations. It had the dates of first occurrence but not the full history of words (Plate 11). It did not have words from before 1700 except words from Shakespeare, Spencer, and the Bible. There was a second edition in 1936 and a third in 1944, which was updated several times until a major revision in 1973, which had 80,000 entries and 163,000 words, including 5,000 new ones. The 1993 edition, published after *OEDS*, was entirely revised and was called the *New Shorter Oxford English Dictionary* (*SOED4*). It had '83,000 quotations from 7,000 authors', and 'more than half a million definitions'. It was made available on CD-ROM in 1999.

SOED5, published in 2002, dropped the *New* in its title. It had 'one third the coverage of the *Oxford English Dictionary* in one tenth of the size' (OUP brochure). It was richer in non-British words, although it still failed to mark Briticisms. Its layout was thoroughly redesigned, with new fonts, space between the entries, etc. (Luna 2004). On the whole, it was not very different from *SOED4*, because the nine-year interval 'is not sufficient for a new edition' (Görlach 2004: 88). *SOED6*, with '2,500 new words and meanings' and 85,000 quotations (OUP website), was published in 2007. *SOED*, in its successive editions, has been a 'phenomenally successful work' (Brewer 2007: 23), evidence that there is a demand for a lighter and cheaper version of the *OED*.

3.2.2 *The* Concise Oxford Dictionary

The first edition of the *Concise Oxford Dictionary of Current English* (*COD1*), compiled by the brothers H. W. and F. G. Fowler,[38] is dated 1911, antedating *OED1* by seventeen years. When it was published, the *OED* was reaching the letter R, so the compilers could use it as a source of material from A to R but were on their own for the end of the alphabet (Allen 1986). The methodological principles were not quite the same as those of the *OED*, because *COD* was meant to be a small popular dictionary of current English. McArthur (1986b: 136) lists five objectives:

1. not to be encyclopedic;
2. to give adequate space to common words and their idioms;
3. to supplement the definitions with illustrative phrases only when really necessary to clarify the meaning;
4. to order the senses of words according to casual logic and present-day appropriateness...;[39]
5. to have a layout involving 'the severest economy of expression—amounting to telegraphese—that readers can be expected to put up with.' (*COD Preface*).

No source explains in detail how the contents of the *OED* were reduced to fit the 1,064 pages of *COD*. The *Preface* said that the new dictionary excluded all obsolete and archaic words as well as most scientific and technical terms. It was also poor in dialect words and words from other English-speaking countries (Read 1962: 222). The quotations were replaced by short examples invented by the compilers (Allen 1986: 1), and the etymologies were simplified (Plate 12a).

The most striking feature of *COD* was its style. Its metalanguage was telegraphic, to the point where it was sometimes difficult to understand.

---

[38] H. W. Fowler later worked for *SOED*. In 1926, when he was sixty-eight, and still at work, OUP offered to pay for a servant to help him, but he refused, saying that he was keen on physical exercise (he took a swim every morning) and accusing OUP of trying to force on him 'the means of slow suicide and quick lexicography'. (*The New Yorker*, 3 April 1989: 92)

[39] Actually, the order varied, and in some entries the first meaning was the oldest current meaning, and obsolete meanings were given at the end.

Definitions are written in a compressed but flowing style that is very different from American styles of defining. COD covers many more senses than one would expect in a dictionary of this size, but its definitions are therefore often very brief amounting sometimes to a kind of shorthand reminder rather than a definition. When it works, it works very well indeed; one feels in private converse with a friend. When it fails, one is utterly lost and feels by turns stupid and abandoned.   (Landau 1984: 338)

COD also used a form of nesting, i.e. grouping semantically related headwords in an article[40] even if it disorganizes alphabetical order, a practice that was to continue over several editions, although it makes it difficult for the user to find a word: for example, *carnation* was in the entry for *carnal* (Hanks 2008: 91). It also used the swung dash: for example, the entry for *hawk* contained ~*-eyed* . . . ~*-moth* . . . ~*-nosed* . . . ~*'s bill* . . . Hence ~ISH, ~LIKE. *COD* was referred to at OUP as the 'Cramped Oxford Dictionary' (Plate 12b).[41]

In a way, *COD* was a friendly dictionary. It contained highly compressed information available to anyone ready to make an effort to get it. It also had the right amount of eccentricity required of a friend, no doubt the mark of the two main compilers. Some entries had traces of a sort of macabre humour: *minus* was illustrated by 'returned minus an arm' and *wind up* by 'shot his wife and child and wound up by stabbing himself' (Allen 1986: 2).

COD2 appeared in 1929, compiled by H. W. Fowler alone. There was a third edition in 1934, a fourth in 1951, a fifth in 1964. *COD6*, published in 1976, was the first in the series to give American spellings. *COD7*, published in 1982, had 'over 40,000 headwords with a total of 75,000 vocabulary items'. It introduced the use of the letter **R** to mark offensive or controversial language (see below, 6.1.1.2). *COD8*, published in 1990 by Robert E. Allen, announced 120,000 entries (including 20,000 new ones) and 190,000 definitions, although I cannot reconcile this with the figures given for preceding editions—obviously the result of a different method of counting (see below, 4.3.2).[42] Its entries were still nested, but all the lexical items, including derived forms, were listed in full, so that the text was clearer. It was also the first in the series to make a real effort to give prominence to current English, as its title had indicated since the first edition. For example *obtrusive*, which had been 'obtruding oneself; unduly noticeable', became

---

[40] *Nesting* is often opposed to *niching*, the grouping of headwords in an article in strict alphabetical order if they share their first letters, even if they are not semantically related. A form of nesting is used in many dictionaries for derivatives: for example, *dryness* in the entry for *dry* (see below, 8.2.2.2).

[41] *The New Yorker*, 3 April 1989: 93.

[42] Higashi *et al.* (1992: 130) observe that 'there is no substantially great change in number' between *COD8* and *COD7*, only 'an increase of about 1.9 per cent'!

1 unpleasantly or unduly noticeable 2 obtruding oneself

COD8 had front matter with an essay on 'English over fifteen centuries' and another on 'Eighty years of the *Concise Oxford Dictionary*'. It used the IPA for its (rare) indications of pronunciation. It was also the first to be 'computer-based': the text had been 'compiled from the extensive records of words and usages held by the Oxford Dictionary Department,' the book cover said. Did 'computer-based' mean 'corpus-based'? It is difficult to find examples of changes attributable to the use of the computer.

COD9, published in 1995, was called *The Concise Oxford Dictionary*, omitting the 'Current English' of preceding editions. It abandoned the front matter and the nesting tradition. It listed compounds as headwords, regardless of their spelling (one word, two independent words, or two words linked by a hyphen). The entry for *hawk* had a special section for derived forms (fully spelt), with *hawkish, hawkishly,* and *hawkishness*, and there were separate entries for *hawkmoth, hawknosed*, etc. *COD9* was the first in the series to be sold as a CD-ROM.

COD10, published in 1999, had 'over 240,000 words, phrases, and definitions', the dust jacket said, another quantum leap from the preceding edition. It used the British National Corpus (BNC; see below, 9.1.7.1) to determine 'the most frequently used meanings of common words', but the meanings of polysemous words were still in the traditional order, concrete original first and figurative second, not in the order of frequency: *bastard, bitch, column, passage, pursue, torrent*, etc. (see below, 8.2.3.10). It did not use any labels for the syntax of verbs, such as *transitive* or *intransitive*, and it had abundant encyclopedic back matter (Countries of the world, Alphabets, accents, and punctuation marks, Weights and measures, Groups of animals, etc., Proofreading marks, Games and puzzles wordbuilder, SMS, and Guide to good English), forty pages in all, a move towards the American tradition of encyclopedic knowledge in dictionaries.

COD11, published in 2004 by C. Soanes and A. Stevenson (who also edited the *Oxford Dictionary of English*; see below, 4.4.2), changed its title again: it is the *Concise Oxford English Dictionary*. It naturally insists on its up-to-date lexical coverage:

COD1 had no entry for *computer, radio, television,* or *cinema*, although it did have *cockyolly bird* ('nursery phrase for a bird') and *impaludism* ('morbid state—found in dwellers in marshes'). It defined *beverage* as 'drinking-liquor', *cancan* as 'indecent dance', and *neon* as 'lately discovered atmospheric gas'. *Gay* meant 'full of or disposed to or indicating mirth; light-hearted, sportive', while *Lesbian* was simply 'of Lesbos'. (OUP website)

It has usage notes on synonyms, paronyms, etc. and 'extended word histories that examine the origins and development of hundreds of words' in addition to the traditional etymologies (OUP website). More interestingly, it uses patterns (see below, 8.2.6) in its definitions and identification of meanings. For example, *afraid* is

afraid of/to do feeling fear or anxiety; frightened. (**afraid for**) anxious about the well-being of

COD has been a best seller on the British market since 1911, but it has completely changed in the course of its history. It has changed so much that it has become difficult to distinguish the continuities from one edition to the next. It is currently a handy, easy-to-use, reliable small dictionary for everyday usage.

There is an endless series of smaller dictionaries more or less directly derived from the *OED*. The earliest and smallest was the *Pocket Oxford Dictionary of Current English*, published for the first time in 1924, with a ninth edition in 2002. There are also a *Little Oxford Dictionary* (1930, eighth edition 2002), a *Compact* (second edition 2002), a *Mini*, etc. The public needs small dictionaries. Of course, the smaller the dictionary the more remote it is from the methodology of the *OED*.

3.2.3 *Other relatives of the* OED

The *OED* was used by many dictionaries, in Britain and elsewhere, as a source of material or as a model of lexicographic methodology. It inspired many historical dictionaries compiled on similar principles, so that the category of historical dictionaries came to be considered as a major category in the English-speaking world (Read 1986: 28)—although not in many other countries. Dictionaries of English compiled with an *OED*-influenced methodology include dictionaries for earlier periods and dictionaries of local varieties of English. The *Early Modern English Dictionary* was started in 1928 but was then suspended. Hans Kurath's *Middle English Dictionary* was started in the 1930s because 'the *OED*'s treatment of medieval words and senses is patchy and unreliable' (Brewer 2000: 44) and was published by the University of Michigan between 1952 and 2001, after 71 years. The *Dictionary of Old English*, started in 1969 at the University of Toronto (D was published in 1986, C in 1988), is not yet complete. Joseph Wright's *English Dialect Dictionary* was started in 1898 and the six volumes were published in 1905.

Craigie's *Dictionary of the Older Scottish Tongue from the Twelfth Century to the End of the Seventeenth* (*DOST*), begun in 1921 at the University of Wisconsin, while Craigie was still working on *OED1*, started publication in 1937 and the twelve volumes were completed in 2002. Grant's *Scottish National Dictionary*

(*SND*) in ten volumes covering Scots since 1700 was begun in 1929 and the last volume was published in 1976.[43] The *Dictionary of American English*, also compiled by Craigie, in four volumes, was begun in 1925 and finished in 1944. *A Historical Dictionary of American English* has been in progress since the 1920s and has not yet been published. The *Dictionary of Canadianisms on Historical Principles*, started in the 1940s, was continued by Walter S. Avis, and published in 1967. 'Work has begun on a fully revised and expanded edition'.[44] The *Dictionary of Americanisms* of Mitford M. Mathews was published in 1951. There is also a *Dictionary of Newfoundland English* (1982) and a *Dictionary of Prince Edward Island English* (1988), both published by the University of Toronto; an *Australian National Dictionary, A Dictionary of Australianisms on Historical Principles* (1989), with 10,000 Australianisms and 60,000 quotations from 9,000 Australian sources (Ramson 1987, 2002); a *Dictionary of South African English on Historical Principles*, which was started in 1969 and published in 1996 (Delbridge 1983: 31–4; Gold 1989); a *Dictionary of New Zealand English: A Dictionary of New Zealandisms on Historical Principles*, published in 1997 after 40 years of work, which has about 6,000 entries. Random House published the first two volumes of the *Random House Historical Dictionary of American Slang* but then abandoned the project, and the last two volumes will be published by Oxford University Press.[45]

Dictionaries inspired by the *OED* are scholarly, ambitious projects typically carried out by academics and published by universities. They take a long time to prepare and cost a lot of money, sometimes so much that they have slack periods for lack of funding, or are just abandoned. They are 'languishing dictionaries' (Ramson 2002: 13), typical of what Atkins (1993: 5) calls the 'scholarly and historical dictionary... with a tendency to run out of money around letter C'. Historical dictionaries are invaluable tools for a language community, but once they have been compiled they may not have to be done again, only updated when new information becomes available. Because of this, because they are so bulky and costly, the historical dictionaries of the future, if there are any, will be e-dictionaries.

The *OED* is also related to a large family of dictionaries of other languages, some of which had been started before Murray began collecting material, all 'products of a nineteenth century philological tradition in which the past was seen as the best means of informing us about the present' (Osselton 1993: 131). The *Deutsches Wörterbuch* of the Grimm brothers, begun in 1840 and completed

---

[43] Both *DOST* and *SND* are available free of charge on the Internet as the *Dictionary of the Scots Language*.
[44] *DSNA Newsletter*, Spring 2006.   [45] *OED News*, September 2003.

in 1964, also used volunteers to read the literature and collect quotations in order to trace the evolution of German words. The *Woordenboek der Nederlandsche Taal* of Matthias de Vries, started in 1851, with a first volume published in 1882, was only finished in 1998, probably the record time taken to complete a dictionary: 147 years between the initial impulse and the publication of the final part (Osselton 2000: 60)! It has '40 volumes, 45,800 pages, around 1,600,000 citations and around 400,000 headwords' (van Sterkenburg 2003*b*: 15).[46] The Swedish *Ordbok öfver Svenska Språket utgifven af Svenska Akademien* had a first volume in 1898 and its completion may be expected in 2017. The Danish *Ordbog over det Danske Sprog*, begun in 1919, was completed in 1954. The *Geiriadur Prifysgol Cymru* (*Dictionary of the Welsh Language*), begun in 1921, finished in 2003, has about 100,000 headwords and 323,000 definitions. The Buro van die Woordenboek van die Afrikaanse Taal (WAT) has been working on a dictionary of Afrikaans since 1926. The Academy of Sciences in Budapest has been working on a historical dictionary of Hungarian since the late 1980s, etc. Even the *TLF* belongs to the same tradition, to some extent: it is also linguistic rather than encyclopedic, it is literary, it uses a corpus, it has no pictorial illustrations, and above all it traces the histories of words. However, the *TLF*, although originally designed to record French words since their origins, was later reduced to nineteenth- and twentieth-century sources.

3.3 OTHER TRADITIONAL BRITISH DICTIONARIES

3.3.1 *General-purpose dictionaries*

Many other dictionaries have been published in Britain in the course of the twentieth century that share some features with the *OED*. Oxford University Press has produced the *Oxford Illustrated Dictionary* (1962, etc.), the *Oxford Senior Dictionary* (1982, etc.), the *Oxford Paperback Dictionary* (1979), which was adapted for the American market under the title of *Oxford American Dictionary* (1980), not a great success in the USA, perhaps because 'in the modern British tradition, it is unyieldingly lexical, with none of the encyclopedic content Americans have come to expect' (Ilson 1990*b*: 1969).

Chambers, the Scottish publishers, produced the *Chambers's Twentieth Century Dictionary* (*C20D*), with a first edition in 1901 and several others with slightly

---

[46] It has been available online free of charge since January 2007.

changed titles, the *Chambers English Dictionary* first and then *Chambers Dictionary* (Brookes *et al.* 2001). It had a few pictures, appendices with Latin, Greek, and foreign quotations, the Greek and Russian alphabets, Roman figures, mathematical symbols, etc. and was particularly rich in Scotticisms and in literary words. It was advertised as the ideal companion of the crossword addict. It was also remarkable for the humorous tone of many of its definitions, as we have seen.[47] It was, like *COD*, a 'friendly' dictionary, talking to you as a friend would (Landau 1984: 338), but not always easy to understand. The print was very small, the different meanings in polysemous entries were separated by a colon, compounds and derived words were nested, and there was not a single quotation or even example. The definitions were compact, sometimes enigmatic, as in

Volume 'a roll, or scroll, which was the form of ancient books : a book, whether complete in itself or part of a work : a rounded mass, convolution : cubical content : a quantity : dimensions : fullness of voice'

Yet it was an endearing dictionary, because it was rich and somewhat unpredictable. The later editions have been the official reference dictionary for Scrabble competitions in Britain. The most recent one continues using nested entries, refuses to use the IPA, and has no proper names. It has kept the quirky definitions, such as that of *éclair* or *middle-aged,* and added a few, such as *paneity,* 'the state of being bread', or

taghairm '(in the Scottish highlands) divination; especially inspiration sought by lying in a bullock's hide behind a waterfall'[48]

A ninth edition was published in 2003.

In 1996, Robert Allen, who had edited *COD8,* published the *Chambers 21st Century Dictionary* (*C21D*), not a direct successor to *C20D* despite its title. It was much more modern in design, with some encyclopedic entries, though not many, concentrating on 'the language that people use everyday'. There was a revised edition in 2000.

3.3.2 *Specialized dictionaries*

3.3.2.1 Dictionaries of pronunciation

Guidance on proper pronunciation has always been important in Britain, where accent is an indicator of social class, as illustrated in Bernard Shaw's play

---

[47] Incidentally, the 1901 *Preface* recognized two great American dictionaries, the *Century* and the *Funk & Wagnalls Standard.* No mention of Webster.

[48] In a review of *Chambers Dictionary* on Michael Quinion's website, World Wide Words.

Pygmalion and its cinema version *My Fair Lady.* Thomas Dyche's *A Guide to the English Tongue,* published in 1707, more a spelling-book than a dictionary, 'provided help with word stress by placing a mark after the stressed syllable' (McArthur 1998: 134). General-purpose dictionaries have given some pronunciations of words since Bailey's *Volume II* of *An Universal Etymological Dictionary* in 1727, for example James Buchanan's *Lingua Britannicae* in 1757, but the first serious treatment of pronunciation in a GPD was in Sheridan's *A General Dictionary of the English Language* in 1780 (Landau 1984: 57). Dictionaries of pronunciation appeared in the second half of the eighteenth century: William Johnston's *Pronouncing and Spelling Dictionary* in 1764, Thomas Spence's *Grand Repository of the English Language* in 1775 (Beal 2004), etc. John Walker's *Critical Pronouncing Dictionary of the English Language* in 1791, the most successful, that remained influential for more than a century (Morton 1994: 122), was incorporated into late editions of Johnson's dictionary.

The most prestigious modern dictionary of pronunciation in Britain is Daniel Jones's *English Pronouncing Dictionary,* with a first edition in 1917 and a seventeenth in 2006, of course with a CD-ROM, 'one of the most influential ELT books ever published' (McArthur 1998: 138). It gives both RP and General American. A serious competitor is the *Longman Pronunciation Dictionary,* 1990, by J. C. Wells, which also includes American pronunciations.

3.3.2.2 Dictionaries of synonyms and thesauruses

The first dictionary of synonyms may have been Julius Pollux's dictionary in ancient Rome (second century AD), and dictionaries of Latin synonyms were produced until the fifth or sixth centuries (Boulanger 2003: 448). But they were abandoned after that, to reappear only in the eighteenth century. The first modern example, *La justesse de la langue françoise,* was published in France in 1718 by Abbé Girard, and it was one of the main inspirations for *Roget's Thesaurus.* In English, the first was John Trusler's *Difference between Words Esteemed Synonymous in the English Language* (1766),[49] soon followed by *British Synonymy: or an Attempt to regulate the Choice of Words in Familiar Conversation,* published in 1794 by Hester Lynch Piozzi (or Thrale), William Perry's *The Synonymous, Etymological, And Pronouncing Dictionary* in 1805 and William Taylor's *English Synonyms Discriminated* in 1813. George Crabb's *English Synonyms Explained,* published in 1816, was probably the best of them all (Hüllen 2004b: 85), although his 'claim to be the first in the field of scientific English

---

[49] On the history of synonym dictionaries, see Hausmann (1990d) and Hüllen (2004a).

synonymy is obviously false' (Stanley 2004: 160). The production of dictionaries of synonyms has continued, and many of them have remained in print for very long periods.

Dictionaries of synonyms and thesauruses are close genres: a thesaurus organizes synonyms by meaning while a dictionary of synonyms lists headwords alphabetically and groups words by meaning as well, or else every word would have to be mentioned several times. After *Roget's Thesaurus*, the ancestor of all thesauruses in English, published in 1852, there have been countless publications using the word *thesaurus* in their titles. Modern examples are Urdang's *Oxford Thesaurus. An A–Z Dictionary of Synonyms* 1991, then 1997; the *Concise Oxford Thesaurus: A Dictionary of Synonyms*, 1995; the *Penguin Thesaurus*, 2004, etc.

3.3.2.3 Dictionaries of slang

There is a long tradition of dictionaries of slang in Britain, dating back to the beginning of the seventeenth century. A famous early example is Francis Grose's *Classical Dictionary of the Vulgar Tongue*, published in 1785, which went through three editions until 1796 (Coleman 2004). J. S. Farmer and W. E. Henley's *Slang and its Analogues, Past and Present* was published between 1890 and 1904. Eric Partridge's *A Dictionary of Slang and Unconventional English* was published in 1937, with an eighth edition in 1984 and a concise edition in 2007. Other examples are T. Thorne's *Bloomsbury Dictionary of Contemporary Slang*, 1997; Jonathon Green's *The Cassell Dictionary of Slang*, 1998, second edition 2005, 'over 65,000 entries'; John Ayto's *The Oxford Dictionary of Slang*, 1998, 'over 10,000 words and phrases', etc. Dictionaries of slang have always been a minor genre in Britain, but they are still alive. One may wonder who uses them: detective-story writers? Or are they read rather than consulted?

3.3.2.4 Dictionaries of new words

Dictionaries of new words are a recent development. They appeared in the late twentieth century in many countries, because of the acceleration of lexical changes, and because the general-purpose dictionaries could not keep up with the evolution. They are fun to consult, but their usefulness for the general public is so limited in time and scope that one may marvel that there is indeed a market for them. Examples are the *Longman Register of New Words*, 1989/90 (Algeo 1990*a*); the *Oxford Dictionary of New Words: A Popular Guide to Words in the News*, 1991, compiled in Britain but also marketed in the USA and another *Oxford Dictionary of New Words* published in 1997, but 'the relationship between the two is not immediately apparent' (Ayto 2000: 47). Although a new genre, the dictionary of new words in paper form is disappearing, because new words can be recorded much faster on the Internet: 'The spate of the mid- to late 1980s has contracted to a trickle' (Ayto 2000: 50).

3.3.2.5 Other dictionaries

In Britain as in many other countries, there are dictionaries for crossword enthusiasts, where words are arranged by number of letters as well as by alphabetical order, direct and reverse, with or without definitions. There are also dictionaries of abbreviations: the *Oxford Dictionary of Abbreviations*, 1998, the *New Penguin Dictionary of Abbreviations*, 2000; dictionaries of proverbs: the *Concise Oxford Dictionary of Proverbs*, 1998, the *Penguin Dictionary of Proverbs*, 2001; dictionaries of etymology, although the field is more than adequately covered by the *OED*: the *Oxford Dictionary of English Etymology*, 1966, by G. W. S. Friedrichsen, R. W. Burchfield, and C. T. Onions, no less, which had several reprints, the *Chambers Dictionary of Etymology*, 1999, etc.

3.3.3 *Dictionaries of other English-speaking countries*

3.3.3.1 Dictionaries of new Englishes

Britain has been a major source of dictionaries for all English-speaking countries. South African GPDs have all been based on British dictionaries: the *South African Pocket Oxford Dictionary* (1987), 30,000 entries (Allen 1986: 7), the *South African Concise Oxford Dictionary* (2002), an enriched version of *COD*, etc.[50]

The lexicographic history of Australia began in 1898 with the publication of *Austral English, A Dictionary of Australian Words, Phrases and Usages*, by Edward E. Morris (Delbridge 1983), a compilation of the notes taken by the author as a reader for the *OED* (Benson 2001: 124 *ff.*). The first dictionaries published in Australia were inspired by British models: the *Australian Pocket Oxford Dictionary* (1976), the *Australian Concise Oxford Dictionary* (1986), or the *Heinemann Australian Dictionary* (1976). The first genuinely Australian dictionary was the *Macquarie Dictionary*, edited by Arthur Delbridge (1981), originally based on the British *Hamlyn's Encyclopedic World Dictionary* (1971), itself based on the *American College Dictionary* (1947)—another example of the circulation of dictionary texts across seas and continents. It is a general dictionary with about 80,000

---

[50] South Africa has an association of lexicography (AFRILEX), which is particularly active in the lexicography of Afrikaans and of African languages, and has published a yearly journal, *Lexikos*, since 1991.

entries, with encyclopedic material and quotations. Australia now has a full-fledged lexicographic production, with a *Macquarie Thesaurus* (1984, 1986), a *Macquarie Dictionary of New Words*, 1990 (Ayto 1992), an *Australian Learner's Dictionary* (1997), a *Slang Dictionary* (2004), etc. and Macquarie has even started producing special editions 'for Singapore, Malaysia and Brunei' (Benson 2001: 129).

The *Heinemann New Zealand Dictionary* (1979, 1982) was the first specifically New Zealand dictionary. After that, several others were published, all inspired by British models: the *New Collins Concise Dictionary of the English Language, New Zealand Edition*, in 1982, the *Collins New Zealand Compact English Dictionary* in 1984, the *New Zealand Pocket Oxford Dictionary*, published in 1986 by Burchfield and based on the seventh edition of the *POD* (1984). The *New Zealand Oxford Dictionary* (2005) has 1,500 pages, 'over 100,000 definitions...and a wide range of encyclopedic information. It is the most extensive, authoritative, and accessible dictionary ever published in New Zealand' (OUP publicity).

Canada did not start producing dictionaries until the 1960s (Considine 2003). Before that, the dictionaries available in Canada had been imported from Britain or from the USA (Drysdale 1979: 37). It now has its own dictionaries, some of which are closer to the American tradition than they are to the British. The *Canadian Senior Dictionary* (1979), published later under the title *Gage Canadian Dictionary* (1983), used material from the *Thorndike-Barnhart* line of American dictionaries, to which it added elements from the *Dictionary of Canadianisms on Historical Principles*. The *Penguin Canadian Dictionary*, published in 1990, with 75,000 entries, was advertised as 'the first dictionary to be compiled with entirely Canadian material'. The *Canadian Oxford Dictionary*, published in 1998, a general, non-historical, encyclopedic dictionary, had 130,000 entries, over 23,000 illustrative examples, over 7,000 idioms, 6,000 place names, 6,000 biographies, etc. It is based on the *COD* and on 'an analysis of over 20 million words of Canadian text'.

Jamaica has a *Dictionary of Jamaican English* (1967), with 15,000 entries, which pioneered the use of spoken material in lexicography (Ilson 1990*b*: 1967), the Bahamas have a *Dictionary of Bahamian English* (1982), the whole of the Caribbeans a *Dictionary of Caribbean English Usage* published in 1996 (Allsopp 1987), sub-Saharan Africa has a *Dictionary of Africanisms: Contributions of Sub-Saharan Africa to the English Language* published in 1982. But the project of a *Dictionary of West African English* has not been brought to completion (Görlach 1990: 1490).

Some English-speaking countries are still missing from the list. India is active in the domain of the lexicography of Indian languages, particularly bilingual dictionaries (Singh 1982) and has produced small dictionaries of English, but there is no general dictionary of Indian English: 'Efforts by the Oxford University Press to publish a dictionary of Indian English resulted in abject failure since customers in India preferred the "proper" British dictionary,' somebody wrote in *Wikipedia*. India does not even have its dictionary on historical principles that so many countries have produced or are producing, perhaps 'because of the lack of a local norm' (Görlach 1990: 1490).

3.3.3.2 The two types of dictionaries

There are two types of dictionaries in Australia, New Zealand, Canada, and South Africa: dictionaries of regionalisms and localized general-purpose dictionaries, the former always preceding the latter (Benson 2001: 105 *ff.*). Many of the dictionaries of regionalisms were based on the methodology of the *OED*, sharing with the parent dictionary the use of a corpus, a chronological ordering of meanings, a large number of quotations, mostly from literature, a descriptive attitude, etc., but they were more encyclopedic, laying particular emphasis on the local, mostly rural, culture: they were cultural dictionaries in the particular sense of historical dictionaries, showing how the creation and the evolution of words accompanied the development of a culture.

The first step in the localization of GPDs imported from the USA or Great Britain was to insert regionalisms, sometimes in the form of separate lists (Benson 2001: 126), but the simple addition of a few regionalisms is not enough to do justice to the local variety (Delbridge 1983: 39), and each country had to produce its own dictionaries. Those were part of a general movement towards political and cultural independence from the mother country, a necessary step to assert the identity of the community, as we have seen.

Like historical dictionaries, dictionaries of regionalisms cost a lot of money, because they use time-consuming methods, they necessitate a lot of research, field studies, etc. and few people or institutions now have enough resources or energy to complete them, at least in the form of paper dictionaries. No doubt future dictionaries of regionalisms, if any, will be electronic.

3.4 THE TRADITION OF THE SCHOLARLY DICTIONARY

The dictionaries that we have grouped under the banner of the British scholarly tradition are all different, but they share some characteristics—although no dictionary has them all and no single characteristic is present in all dictionaries:

1. a linguistic orientation, with a focus on words rather than on things, with little encyclopedicity and no pictorial illustrations (the encyclopedic trend in British lexicography ended with Ogilvie's *Imperial Dictionary* in 1850—only to be born again more than a century later, with the *Collins English Dictionary* (see below, 4.4.1));
2. a descriptive, detached attitude to usage;
3. the use of a corpus of written documents as the source of information for the macrostructure and the microstructure;
4. a focus on the literary language, although the language of reference has gradually broadened to include non-literary documents;
5. a relative poverty in the representation of scientific and technical terms;
6. a relative poverty in the representation of words from regional varieties of English in and outside Britain, although the more recent dictionaries have been more comprehensive;
7. a focus on the use of the dictionary as an aid to reading, and very little help provided for expression;
8. synthetic entries, with a tendency to group several related words, derived forms, compounds, etc. in the same entry;
9. a relative elitism in form and content, with no particular efforts to ease the consultation process for the less educated user.

Landau (2001: 95), remembering his early years, sums up those characteristics elegantly, and finds a lot to praise:

Learning to use such a dictionary took some practice and trial-and-error, but one often found the effort was worthwhile. The style of presentation was dense but efficient, to cram as much information as possible into the least space. Thus, entries were generally nested rather than listed separately. There were few or no numbered senses; often only a semicolon separated definitions. Stress and vowel quality were sometimes indicated by diacritics in the headword, and no respelling was offered. No encyclopedic information was given, and there was little coverage of the scientific and technical vocabulary. No pictorial illustrations were included.

On the whole, British traditional dictionaries are designed to provide knowledge on the words of a language. They demand a lot from their users, and only provide their riches to those who deserve them, either because of their birth or because of their efforts.

THE AMERICAN TRADITION OF THE UTILITY DICTIONARY

4.1 UNABRIDGED DICTIONARIES

4.1.1 Webster's Third New International Dictionary

WEBSTER's *New International Dictionary, Second Edition* (W2), published in 1934, one year after the 13-volume *OED*, continued the tradition of *Webster's International Dictionary* of 1890 and *Webster's New International Dictionary* of 1909. It had about 600,000 'entries' and nearly 3,400 pages, more than its predecessor, one of the largest dictionaries ever published. Its launching was celebrated lavishly (Morton 1994: 148), as for the *OED* a few years before. W2 had a historical arrangement of meanings and it had the 'divided page' invented for the 1909 edition for rare terms (Plates 13a and 13b). It had proper names in two appendices, one for the names of people and one for the names of places, it had many obsolete words and pictorial illustrations, and a separate section for abbreviations. It was a formidable achievement, and was very successful, widely admired, praised for its coverage, for the quality of its definitions, and for its treatment of pronunciation. It was 'more than respected. It was accepted as the ultimate authority on meaning and usage, and its pre-eminence was virtually unchallenged in the USA' (Morton 1994: 2).[1] It 'dominated the market for unabridged dictionaries until the

---

[1] *W2* is unfortunately also remembered for the story of the spurious entry for *dord* 'n. *Physics and Chem.* Density', which was mistakenly recorded because the slip noting the use of 'D or d' for *density* had been misdirected to the main wordlist instead of the section for abbreviations. The error went 'undetected for five years' (Morton 1994: 119).

1960s' (Morton 1994: 39) and even continued to be used after the publication of its successor (see below).

Webster's Third New International Dictionary (*W3*) was published in 1961, after about 10 years of preparation. Although the lexicographers at Merriam-Webster never stopped collecting material after the publication of *W2*, compilation proper started in the early 1950s.[2] *W3* had 2,726 pages and 450,000 vocabulary entries, about 100,000 of which were new compared to *W2* (Landau 2001: 87), meaning that about 250,000 had been dropped (Morton 1994: 202) (Plate 14a). It drew on a body of about 6 million quotations. Its editor, Philip B. Gove, wanted it to be 'a scholar's dictionary as well as one that would be accessible to the average reader' (Morton 1994: 130).

Like all dictionaries, *W3* made heavy use of preceding dictionaries: the Webster line, particularly *W2* that it was meant to replace, the *OED* in many entries (Burchfield 1989),[3] the *Century Dictionary*, etc. But it was also a truly innovative dictionary in many respects: it was 'a completely new work.... Every line of it is new,' the *Preface* said.

1. *W3* was descriptive, at least more descriptive than its American predecessors. 'For us to attempt to prescribe the language would be like *Life* reporting the news as its editors would prefer it to happen,' Gove wrote in the *Preface*. 'Lexicography should have no traffic with ... artificial notions of correctness and superiority. It must be descriptive and not prescriptive' (Gove 1967a: 7). *W3* recorded all common expressions, even those that were disputed, often with no explicit condemnations. It used fewer usage labels than *W2*—although it did have some labelling, contrary to what some critics said (Morton 1994: 138). The label *slang* was used 'less than half as often' (Morton 1994: 251) as in *W2*, so that some slang words were not labelled at all, and evaluative labels such as *correct* and *incorrect, proper* and *improper, erroneous, humorous, jocular, ludicrous, contemptuous, popular, loosely*, etc. were dropped (Morton 1994: 138). The label *colloquial* was also dropped, because it was, Gove said, consistently misinterpreted, and it was replaced by *substandard* or *non-standard*. Gove thought that the evidence provided by the quotations would be enough for the dictionary user to decide what register the word belonged to, a position that corresponded to the views of such contemporary linguists as Charles C. Fries (Morton 1994: 139). Unfortunately, this might have worked for the scholar, but not for the average reader, and it irritated many reviewers (see below).

In his effort to be descriptive, Gove had even decided to include the more common taboo words, which had been absent from *W2*, and accordingly

---

[2] On the story of *W3* see Morton (1994).
[3] Burchfield, when he was preparing *OEDS*, offered to pool resources with Gove but the arrangement was later cancelled (Brewer 2007: 168).

prepared the entries, but they were rejected by the publishers (Morton 1991: 24), on the grounds that they were unacceptable for the general public.

2. *W3* was a dictionary of words more than a dictionary of things. Most of the encyclopedic material of *W2* was dropped, because Gove disapproved of other dictionaries for their tendencies to be 'gazetteers'. But there were also practical reasons, although Gove was reluctant to admit it (Morton 1994: 274): space was needed to accommodate all the new words that had appeared since 1934. Whatever the reasons, he discarded biographical appendices and all proper names (Morton 1994: 63), except when they were parts of compounds as in *achilles' heel* or *macadam road*, or when they were used as common nouns, for example *hercules* ('man of great strength'), *hamlet* ('brooding, indecisive person'), *einstein* ('genius'), or *crusoe* ('solitary castaway') (Morton 1994: 64), and of course there were proper names in the definitions and quotations.

In fact, there were no capitalized entries in *W3*: even such words as *frigidaire*, *kleenex*, or *scotch tape* were written without capitals (Morton 1994: 215). The only capitalized headword was *God*, 'presumably in fear of divine retribution,' Urdang (1996*a*: 32) mused (there was another entry for *god*). *Jesus, Jesus Christ,* and *Christ* were absent, even as expletives, and many entries had the label *usu. cap.*, for example *american, canada goose*, etc. The policy of *W3* on that point changed in later editions (Morton 1994: 222): 'Much to his justified chagrin, Gove was forced to violate several of his lexicographic convictions, and in printings after the first the noun *kodak* became *Kodak*, although the verb, which was not protected, remained *kodak*' (Chapman 1996: 369).

The absence of proper names was against the American tradition and was regretted by many, even inside Merriam-Webster (Morton 1994: 61 *ff.*). What the critics deplored was the absence of the information that helps integrate the dictionary user into American society, the names of characters in the Bible, of American heroes, of places in American history or geography, etc.

Think, if you can, of an unabridged dictionary from which you cannot learn who Mark Twain was, or what were the names of the apostles, or that the Virgin was Mary, the mother of Jesus of Nazareth, or what and where the District of Columbia is.

(Follett 1962, in Laird 1970: 503)

One can think of the *OED* as a good example of an unabridged dictionary that had none of these: in fact, *W3* was only following another lexicographic tradition, illustrated by Johnson's *Dictionary* and defended by Dean Trench, but the reading publics were different on the two sides of the Atlantic.

Gove also wanted to drop all the pictorial illustrations of *W2*, but he had to accept the publishers' instructions for the first printings, which eventually included colour plates for flags, birds, etc. scattered through the text, about one-quarter of the illustrations of *W2* Gove won in the end, but for the wrong reasons: all illustrations were withdrawn in the 1975 impression, because of the cost, except the one for the word *color* (Algeo 1990*b*: 1995).

Naturally, there is plenty of encyclopedic information in *W3*, as in all large dictionaries. Apart from the four highly technical pages for *color* and the five pages for *dye*, many of the illustrative phrases contain information on American, or world, culture. One example among thousands: the entry *wall* had 'The Great Chinese ~ was 1500 miles long' (Morton 1994: 64).

3. *W3* was not a historical dictionary, although it ordered meanings chronologically. It omitted archaisms not used since 1755—*W2* had thousands of them—except for those that were used in past literature that was still read (Morton 1994: 209). The space was occupied by scientific and technical words, for which *W3*'s coverage and treatment were remarkable, thanks to the help of about 200 consultants (Morton 1994: 131) on all sorts of specialized subjects, 'Camp Fire Girls', 'Pipes and Tobacco' (another one for 'Tobacco'), 'Knots', 'Pipe Organs', 'Girl Guiding', 'Soft Drinks', 'Cocktails', 'Liquors and Cordials', 'Tea', 'Girl Scouts', 'Shoes', etc.

4. *W3* was illustrated by quotations, many more than in *W2*. There were about 100,000, anywhere between two words and a few lines in length, by about 14,000 different authors. Some were prestigious: the most often quoted was Shakespeare, 'with 2,143 quotations,[4] and Milton was second, with 446' (Morton 1994: 101). There were no literary hapax: 'The single appearance of a word in a highly reputable publication has never ensured its appearance in a Merriam dictionary' (Morton 1994: 97). *W3* also had quotations from more unexpected authors: politicians such as Harry Truman, Richard Nixon, Dwight Eisenhower, popular writers such as James T. Farrell, Corey Ford, Mickey Spillane, or public figures such as Polly Adler (madam and author), Fred Allen (comedian), Art Linkletter (host of radio and TV shows), Al Capp (cartoonist), etc. Gove chose those passages 'not for literary flavor or for lending authority to a definition', nor to 'impart moral instruction' but because of their 'usefulness in "clarifying meaning"' (Morton 1994: 99–100, 209). Eisenhower was (briefly!) quoted in the entry for *goof*, *n.* 2: 'made a ~', a good illustration of the unreasonable desire of lexicographers to quote a well-known figure even when the quotation is totally useless. Gove was criticized for retaining popular but non-prestigious authors:

---

[4] More than 15,000 in *OED1*.

Morton (1994: 6) mentions a quotation for the verb *drain*, 'Three shows a day drain a girl', by Ethel Merman, a musical comedy star, noting that the criticism bore not on the lexicographic inadequacy of the quotation but on the personality of its author, the sort of person that the American public refused to regard as a linguistic model.

5. W3 was interested in the spoken language, although almost all of its evidence was written. It gave as many pronunciation variants as possible: 'five for *aunt* instead of two' in W2, 'seven for *idea* instead of three', etc. (Morton 1994: 257). There was so much detail in some entries that they were confusing, especially with the complex system used for the notation (Morton 1994: 257). W3 used the schwa symbol of the IPA (ə) for the unstressed vowel sound in words such as *familiar, paragraph,* etc., which had been used by the *American College Dictionary* in 1947 (see below) but not in W2.

6. W3 aimed at being objective. Gove wanted to eliminate all subjectivity from its definitions and examples. For instance, in W2, *apache* had been defined as 'of warlike disposition and relatively low culture', *maori* had '. . . pleasing in features, and brave and warlike' and *cure* 4 was illustrated by 'cure girls of running after officers' (Morton 1991: 26). All this was excluded from W3. Sometimes, the desire to be objective may have been pushed too far: Urdang (1996*a*: 33) notes that the W3 definitions for words such as *nazi* ('a member of the former National Socialist German Workers' party...') or *stalinism* ('the theories of Joseph Stalin') are 'clinically bland, innocuous'.

7. W3 used a new style of definition. Gove thought the definitions in W2 were too imprecise, and invented a 'single-statement defining style' (Morton 1991: 25) that he was particularly proud of. He wrote 'completely analytical one-phrase definitions' (*Preface*) that aimed at giving a complete description of the referent. In some cases, as in the definitions of the names of plants, animals or artefacts, this resulted in long, complex paragraphs that were not easy to read. The definitions for *groan* or *door* have often been quoted (Algeo 1990*b*: 1995; Morton 1991: 25). The verb *groan* was defined by

To make a deep, usu. inarticulate and involuntary often strangled sound typically abruptly begun and ended and usu. indicative of pain or grief or tension or desire or sometimes disapproval or annoyance

The definition of *door* went:

A movable piece of firm material or a structure supported usu. along one side and swinging on pivots or hinges, sliding along a groove, rolling up and down, revolving as one of four leaves, or folding like an accordion by means of which an opening may be closed or kept open for passage into or out of a building, room or other covered enclosure or a car, airplane, elevator or other vehicle.

Clearly, the compiler was trying to list all the possible doors that exist or could exist. This style of definition did not meet with general approval. It was 'highly controversial' (Morton 1991: 25) right from the start, 'opposed by some staff members' (Morton 1994: 87) and outside observers. The most obvious reproach was that the definitions were difficult to understand: they were, Urdang (1996a: 34) wrote much later, 'couched in a cabalistic style that seems deliberately bent on excluding any not privy to the shibboleths of the genre'. Also, Hanks (1979) convincingly argues, definitions that try to describe the referent in all its possible variations are self-defeating, because they can never be exhaustive. Still, the definitions of W3 were maintained in later reprints, and the style was even adopted by the Merriam-Webster Collegiate dictionaries (see below).

8. W3 had completely new etymologies, compiled by Charles Sleeth, that were found admirable and are still admired. They were placed in a special paragraph at the beginning of the entry, as in a historical dictionary. Sleeth also introduced the label *ISV* for *International Scientific Vocabulary*, to categorize scientific and technical words based on Latin and Greek roots and having variants in many languages, a sort of 'Lingua Franca transcending national idioms, and where the nationality of coiners was not always known nor very crucial'. This was to 'avoid the quagmire of pinning down the exact language of origin for every term and element of the scientific vocabulary' (Chapman 1996: 368).

Some of the innovations of W3, particularly its descriptivism and lack of proper names, enraged those of the users who liked their dictionaries to be encyclopedic and prescriptive, true to the Merriam-Webster tradition (see below). The disapproval 'touched off the stormiest controversy in the annals of lexicography' (Morton 1994: 1), that started even before the dictionary went on sale, and in which Gove 'bore the brunt of the attack' (Morton 1994: 2). The optimists noted that the violence of the criticism at least attracted the attention of linguists, at a time in the history of linguistics when they were just beginning to look more carefully at the lexicon (Morton 1994: 279; see below, 8.1.1.4), and showed that the dictionary was important for the American public. Despite its imperfections and the hostility of some, W3 was eventually a commercial success, selling more than 2.5 million copies (Morton 1994: 281), and 'an important achievement in the history of lexicography' (Morton 1994: 9).

Merriam-Webster published three supplements to W3 (*6,000 Words* in 1976, *9,000 Words* in 1983, *12,000 Words* in 1986) containing words that had appeared since 1961: *acid, jawbone, leverage, Man, yo-yo* in 1976, *end user, golden handshake, natural gas, on-air, underperform, world-class* in 1986, etc. Most of those new words were scientific and technical, but there were also a few words that had been omitted from *W3*: an example mentioned in the introduction to *6,000 Words* was *frog*, 'a spiked or perforated holder used to keep flowers in position in a vase' (*6,000 Words*: 17a).

An edition of *W3* was published in 1993 that contained the text of the 1961 edition plus the text of the supplements, still under Gove's editorship. It had 'more than 472,000 vocabulary entries' according to the book jacket. A really new edition (*W4*) is said to be in preparation, starting with the transformation of the text of *W3* into a machine-readable text: it was still 'in fairly early stages' in February 1999 (Landau 2001: 449). Pending this, Merriam-Webster has made the entire text of *W3* available on a CD-ROM and online, with regular updatings.

4.1.2 Other large dictionaries

The *Funk and Wagnalls Standard Dictionary of the English Language*, a big encyclopedic dictionary, first appeared in 1893, then changed its title to *New Standard* in 1913, and was produced until 1963. The first edition, with 458,000 words, was bigger than the *New International* of 1909, to be outnumbered only by *W2*. It inaugurated the practice of placing the etymology after the definition, adopted afterwards by other American dictionaries, and more recently by some British dictionaries as well. It did not have chronological or logical ordering, but gave 'the most important current definition *first* and the obsolescent and obsolete meanings last,' it said in a pre-publication document dated 1891. Unfortunately, it 'has never been entirely reset' (Landau 1984: 341).

The *Random House Dictionary of the English Language, Unabridged Edition* (*RHD*) was first published in 1966, in the wake of the controversy over *W3*, and as a competitor. It was based on the files of the *American College Dictionary* (see below) and gave 'considerable attention to usage notes as well as labels in its effort to make the new dictionary "fully descriptive"—a phrase suggesting faith in descriptive lexicography but dissatisfaction with *Webster's Third*' (Morton 1994: 284). Despite the use of *unabridged* in the title, it was about half the coverage of *W3*, but it had 'thousands of names of people and places, and other encyclopedic entries' (Landau 2001: 427), making it useful more as a general reference work than as a language dictionary. It was the first dictionary of English to use computers in its compilation, mainly, it seems, to ensure consistency (see below, Chapter 9). The 1987 edition (*RHD2*) claimed 315,000 words, 50,000 of which were new compared with the 1975 impression of the first edition, plus almost 300 pages of encyclopedic appendices. It also 'increased the number of usage notes and revised and expanded the earlier ones' (Landau 2001: 427) and had dates for the first occurrences of words, like the *OED*. Its text was entirely on tape in machine-readable form. The CD-ROM, *Random House Unabridged Electronic Dictionary*, was first published in 1994. In 1996, when the new paper edition was published, the name *Webster* was 'by judicial determination, in the public domain' (Abate 1991: 153), and the dictionary was called *Random House Webster's Unabridged Dictionary (RHW)*,[5] no doubt to give it an extra aura of respectability. This was later imitated by many other American dictionaries.

4.2   SMALLER AMERICAN DICTIONARIES

4.2.1   *Desk dictionaries*

The *American Heritage Dictionary of the English Language (AHD)*, with 'about 200,000 definitions', is a desk dictionary, somewhere between the unabridged and the college dictionary in size. It was first published in 1969, eight years after *W3* and, like *RHD*, as a reaction against it. The circumstances have often been described:

The President of the American Heritage Publishing Company, James Parton, convinced that Merriam-Webster had abandoned all standards of traditional lexicography and sold out to a bunch of radical descriptivists who would trample all our principles of correct usage, determined to rescue English from the academic long-hairs, marihuana smokers, foreigners, and other pernicious influences by creating a wholesome new unabridged dictionary that would set matters right. At one time he considered buying the Merriam-Webster company in order to destroy all copies of MW3 [= *W3*], but Merriam had been uncooperative.   (Landau 1994*a*: 314–15; see also Morton 1994: 228 *ff*.)

The editor-in-chief of *AHD*, William Morris, made the point forcefully in the *Introduction*: the new dictionary would, he wrote, 'faithfully record our language, the duty of any lexicographer, but it would not, like so many others in these permissive times, rest there. On the contrary, it would add the essential dimension of guidance, that sensible guidance toward grace and precision which intelligent people seek in a dictionary'. *AHD* banked on the aspirations of the American public: 'insecurity about usage is good business' (Landau 2001: 249). In order to give authority to their prescriptions, the compilers asked a panel of 105

---

[5] On the story of the loss of copyright, see Morton (1994: 216): 'By 1904, at least a dozen firms were using *Webster* in their dictionary titles'. In 1977, Kister listed 69 dictionaries using the name *Webster* in their titles; in 1991, Abate (1991: 153) wrote that the name 'appeared in the titles of scores of different dictionaries'. See also Landau (2001: 91, 410 *ff*.).

journalists, editors, authors, and college professors, 'to furnish the guidance which we believe to be an essential responsibility of a good dictionary' (*AHD*: vii). The panel's task was 'to pass judgment on what was acceptable and what was not' (Morton 1994: 229). The dictionary eventually had 502 usage notes, about 250 of which contained the opinions of the panel, with percentages representing the votes of the members. For example, the entry for *flammable* had

Flammable is as acceptable as *inflammable* in all areas of speech and writing, according to 61% of the Usage Panel, though *inflammable* is more common outside technical contexts

'The closest the panel came to unanimity was the vote on *ain't*: 99 percent disapproved of it in writing and 84 percent in speech' (Morton 1994: 229), clearly a response to *W3* (see below). Some entries disregarded the opinions of the panel, no doubt because the editors found the panel too permissive: *shakedown, n.* ('extortion') was labelled *informal*, 'although 80 percent of the panel approved its use' (Morton 1994: 231).

The Usage Panel was criticized, because it included people who had been critical of *W3* and because 'teachers of English and specialists in the study of language and lexicography were woefully underrepresented', as were women (90 men and 10 women), coloured people and younger people (average age 'about sixty-four') (Morton 1994: 230). For Landau (1994*a*: 315), the panel was 'putative "good writers" whose judgments about disputed usages are supposed to provide guidance for the rest of the benighted English-speaking world, who must otherwise struggle along with nothing to light our way but our own woefully imperfect Sprachgefühl'. The idea of a usage panel was even called 'a marketing gimmick, not a source of serious information about usage' (Cresswell and McDavid 1986: 83).

But *AHD* had other commendable features: it had taboo words, which had been avoided in American dictionaries before, its definitions were good, its etymologies were detailed, its graphic design was attractive, there was a third column with a large number of pictorial illustrations including photographs and it carried a useful Appendix on Indo-European roots.[6]

The second edition (1982, *AHD2*) dropped the Appendix on Indo-European roots and eliminated almost all proper names and abbreviations from the main wordlist to shift them to special sections. The third edition (1992, *AHD3*), by A. H. Soukhanov, who had also worked for Merriam-Webster, was advertised as 'a lexicon of more than 200,000 boldface forms', over 350,000 entries and meanings, 34,000 examples and nearly 4,000 photographs and drawings. It reintroduced the Appendix on Indo-European roots and inserted many more

---

[6] Which was later published as a separate volume.

quotations. It also simplified the metalanguage: for instance, 'pertaining to' was changed to 'having to do with'. It had 400 notes on word histories, 900 synonym paragraphs, more than 500 notes and comments on matters of grammar, diction, pronunciation, registers, and nuances of usage. It used the label *Usage Problem*, like the **R** of *COD7* (1982), for words such as *chicano*.[7] It continued the tradition of the Usage Panel, with 175 people, including 60 women. The conclusions were written by Geoffrey Nunberg in such a subdued tone that Landau (1994*a*: 316) wonders 'exactly what the role of the Usage Panel is'. On the whole *AHD3* was judged to be 'a perfectly good, serviceable dictionary' (Urdang 1993: 133). It had a CD-ROM edition called *The American Heritage Talking Dictionary* (1994), and was made available online. *AHD4* (2000) has 'over 200,000 entries', including 10,000 new words and meanings. It retains most of the features of the preceding edition, with notes on synonyms and usage or word histories (including the history of some taboo words), and the Appendix on Indo-European roots, with a new one on Semitic roots. The Usage Panel, 200 scholars and writers, is still there, to show the current linguistic usage of 'the educated middle-classes'.

The *World Book Dictionary* (*WBD*), about 200,000 words, first published in 1963, was based on the *Century Dictionary* (Landau 2001: 89) and edited by Clarence L. Barnhart and his son Robert K. as a supplement to the *World Book Encyclopedia*. It had no proper names and aimed at being usable by all, even children. The definitions were simple, in clear contrast with the definitions in *W3*. For example, *door* was:

1. a movable part to close an opening in a wall. A door turns on hinges or slides open and shut. A room has at least one door; a house or building may have several or many doors. 2. any movable part that suggests a door...3. an opening where a door is; doorway...

It was particularly useful for its extensive quotations—not a frequent feature in American dictionaries of that size. The 1981 edition had 264,000 words. *WBD* was updated every year and is now sold as a CD-ROM.

4.2.2 *College dictionaries*

College dictionaries are not only for students but for a broader public: 'Although *college* is an essential selling tool, and college and university students remain an important segment of their audience, college dictionaries are not written for college students...they are intended to be *the* basic dictionary for every literate

---

[7] Defined as 'A Mexican-American', followed by a usage note. *Mexican-American* was not defined, a 'dead-end'.

person in the United States' (Landau 1994*a*: 317–18). They sell well: 'about 2 million are currently sold each year' (Landau 2001: 90). And they are updated at regular intervals: 'College dictionaries are revised every ten years or so, but they are updated every year or every other year, chiefly in order to provide themselves with an up-to-date copyright date' (Landau 2001: 396). The major ones are all very similar 'in trim size, heft, thickness, entry count, price, and color [and] only the most discerning buyers could possibly detect a difference' (Abate 1991: 154).

There is a long lineage of college dictionaries by Merriam Webster, called *Collegiate*, a property of the Merriam-Webster Company. They have always been the most successful of all college dictionaries, and are considered by many as the model of the genre. The first, published in 1898, was called *Webster's Collegiate Dictionary*. There was a seventh edition in 1965, famous for having *make love* as a guide word, no doubt inserted at the last minute by a lexicographer to replace *make fast*, since there was no entry *make love*. The eighth edition, in 1975 (*MWC8*), like its predecessors, kept the defining style of *W3*. Most of its definitions were very brief: for example, *volume* was

1 : SCROLL 1a 2 a : a series of printed sheets bound typically in book form : BOOK b : a series of issues of a periodical c : ALBUM 1c 3 etc.

But the definitions of scientific words were detailed and used specialized terms. For example, *peach* was

a low spreading freely branching Chinese tree (*Prunus persica*) of the rose family that is cosmopolitan in cultivation in temperate areas and has lanceolate leaves, sessile usu. pink flowers borne on the naked twigs in early spring, and a fruit which is a single-seeded drupe with a hard endocarp, a pulpy white or yellow mesocarp, and a thin downy epicarp

MCW8 was also the first in the series to include taboo words, probably because *AHD* had included them a few years before.

Webster's Ninth New Collegiate Dictionary (1983, *MWC9*) had 160,000 entries and 200,000 definitions. It had usage notes and gave the dates of first occurrences. The tenth edition, *Merriam-Webster's Collegiate Dictionary* (1993, *MWC10*), changed its title to emphasize the heritage of the Webster family of dictionaries in the face of the free use of the name *Webster* by the competition (Morton 1994: 217). It was very much like its predecessors. It had the same defining style; it had separate entries for each POS of the same form: for example, *front* had three entries, noun, verb, and adjective; it had a chronological ordering of meanings in polysemous entries, a 'marketing gimmick' for some (Abate 1994: 186); it had biographical, geographical names, abbreviations, and foreign words and phrases in separate sections, a practice that had been abandoned by all its competitors; and it gave cross-references in small capitals. *MWC10* was a bestseller, like its predecessors: 'Recent estimates... suggest that the Merriam–Webster dictionary has at least 50% of the college edition market' (Abate 1994: 175). There was an electronic version in 1994. *MWC11*, published in 2003, has 1,664 pages and comes with a CD-ROM containing a thesaurus, an encyclopedia, and a Spanish–English dictionary. It is also available via a free one-year subscription, an innovation that may be imitated by other publishers. It has 165,000 entries and 225,000 definitions, with a total of '100,000 changes' (how does one count 'changes'?) from the preceding edition, 2,700 illustrative quotations and 700 pictorial illustrations, including 200 black-and-white line drawings. It still has separate sections for geographical and biographical names, although this time the abbreviations have been integrated into the main wordlist.

The Funk and Wagnalls line of college dictionaries began with the *New College Standard* in 1947, and continued with the *Funk and Wagnalls Standard College Dictionary* in 1963. The latest edition was published in 1977, and it has never been updated. The text was used for the compilation of the *Reader's Digest Great Encyclopedic Dictionary*, published in 1966. Once a very successful line of dictionaries, Funk and Wagnalls has now disappeared.

American Heritage also produced college editions, which are simplified versions of *AHD*: the *American Heritage Dictionary, Second College Edition* was published in 1982 (Landau 1984: 335), the third edition, in 1993, was a 'slightly abridged version of AHD3' (Landau 1994a: 315), the fourth came out in 2004.

The *American College Dictionary* (1947, *ACD*), compiled under the direction of Clarence Barnhart, was the first dictionary published by Random House. It had about 132,000 entries and used the *New Century* (1927), an abridgement of the *Century Dictionary*, but it was a new dictionary in its own right. Barnhart was interested in the ideas of the psychologist Edward L. Thorndike,[8] who advocated the use of frequency lists to choose the words of the wordlist, argued that examples should be invented by the lexicographer to complement the definitions and that definitions should be adapted to the competence of the users. *ACD*, under Thorndike's influence, emphasized the quality of the treatment of each word rather than the number of words in the wordlist (Barnhart 1949). Some of these ideas had been expressed by Henry Sweet in *The Practical Study of Languages* (1899: 139 *ff*.) and were later to be used by the compilers of dictionaries for foreign students (see below, Chapter 5), but they had little influence on the American lexicographic tradition. Barnhart recruited linguists to help him (Barnhart 1949), particularly for the etymologies, as well as outside experts for the treatment of

---

[8] Who edited dictionaries for schoolchildren and authored a large number of books (see below, 8.1.1.1).

specialized entries. *ACD* had a single alphabetical list for common and proper names, ordered meanings by frequency, contrary to the Merriam-Webster dictionaries, and was the first American dictionary to use the schwa symbol. It was descriptive, but this did not prevent it from being a very successful dictionary, selling in huge numbers, no doubt because it was aimed at a public of students. For some, it 'has come to define the modern genre' of the college dictionary (Landau 1994a: 312) as much as the Merriam-Webster collegiates. It was used as a basis for the compilation of other dictionaries: the *RHD* (a case of expansion rather than abridgement), *Hamlyn's Encyclopedic World Dictionary*, published in Britain in 1971 and the *Macquarie Dictionary* published in Australia in 1981. *ACD* was regularly updated until 1970, but is no longer available.

The *Random House College Dictionary* (*RHC*), based on *RHD*, was first published in 1968. The 1984 edition had 'more than 170,000 words' and was noted for its extensive use of the computer in the preparation stages, to ensure consistency across entries. The title of the 1991 edition was changed to *Random House Webster's College Dictionary* (*RHWC*): 'The addition of *Webster's*, that "time-honored designation", to the title, was said by the editor-in-chief to affirm "quality in dictionary making"' (Abate 1991: 153).[9] *RHWC* continued the Random House tradition of listing all entries in a single list, of ordering meanings by frequency and of providing dates in the etymologies at the end of entries. There was a new edition in 1997 and another in 2000, with 'over 207,000 definitions'.

Webster's New World Dictionary of the American Language, College Edition (*WNW*) was published in 1953 by David Guralnik, following the publication of a desk version called *Webster's New World Dictionary of the American Language, Encyclopedic Edition* in 1951. *WNW* had 'over 157,000 entries', including proper names, in a single alphabetical list. Its definitions were more discursive and less obscure than in *MWC*: for example, *volume* was

1. orig., a roll of parchment, a scroll, etc. 2. *a)* a collection of written, typewritten or printed sheets bound together; book *b)* any of the separate books making up a matched set or a complete work 3. a set of the issues of a periodical etc.

and *peach* was

1. a small tree (*Prunus persica*) of the rose family, with lance-shaped leaves, pink flowers, and round, juicy, orange-yellow fruit, with a fuzzy skin and a single, rough pit

---

[9] Merriam-Webster sued (Landau 2001: 91, 411) and the court ordered Random House to pay them $4 million, not so much because of the use of the word *Webster* but because the cover design was too similar to that of a Merriam-Webster dictionary (Abate 1991: 153). Interestingly, the following edition of *RHWC* had an entry for *Webster* defined as 'a dictionary of the English language' (Landau 2001: 410).

WNW was praised for its 'coverage of the vocabulary, etymologies, pronunciations, and appearance' (Read, in Morton 1994: 217) and was very successful. It became, after *ACD*, 'Merriam-Webster's most formidable competitor, replacing the once mighty Funk and Wagnalls in that role' (Landau 1994*a*: 314). The second edition (*WNW2*, 1970) used a star (☆) to indicate Americanisms, defined as those words and usages that originated in the USA, no doubt to underline the Americanness of the dictionary. It also became famous for its squeamishness, for fear of being banned from schools (see below, 6.1.1.3). Guralnik's defence has often been derided, but it makes good commercial, if not lexicographic, sense.

The absence from this dictionary of a handful of old, well-known vulgate terms for sexual and excretory organs and functions is not due to a lack of citations for these words from current literature. On the contrary, the profusion of such citations in recent years would suggest that the terms in question are so well known as to require no explanation.
                                                                                            (*Foreword*: viii)

The third edition (*WNW3*), published in 1989, included the taboo words. It also had a single alphabetical list, and gave meanings in chronological order. There was an edition on CD-ROM in 1995 but, like many electronic editions, it was not much more than 'a screen display of the entries in the printed dictionary. The use of electronic search capabilities is minimal, and little effort seems to have been devoted to tailoring these resources to the contents or the uses of a dictionary' (Ford 1996: 212). The fourth edition, *Webster's New World College Dictionary* (*WNW4*), with 163,000 entries (5,000 new), 'over 800 illustrations' and a four-colour atlas, was published in 1998. It had boxed synonym notes and came with a CD-ROM. It was later included in the online dictionary yourdictionary.com. A revised edition came out in 2004.

   The American college dictionary is a successful genre, because every American college freshman is required to buy one, but it is not very innovative: 'The American college dictionary market is highly competitive, and no publisher wants to introduce a feature that might make his dictionary harder to use' (Landau 2001: 122), or more difficult to sell.

4.2.3 *Specialized American dictionaries*

4.2.3.1 Dictionaries of synonyms and thesauruses

In the *Preface* to his *American dictionary* of 1828, Webster wrote that he hoped it would 'to a great extent, supply the place of a book of synonyms', as he had synonym discriminations in many entries. For example, *anguish* was

Extreme pain, either of body or mind. As bodily pain, it may differ from agony, which is such distress of the whole body as to cause contortion, whereas anguish may be a local pain as of an ulcer, or gout. But anguish and agony are nearly synonymous. As pain of the mind, it signifies any keen distress from sorrow, remorse, despair and kindred passions.

The 1859 edition, the *Pictorial*, also had lists of synonyms, and this was imitated, even improved by Worcester. The *Funk and Wagnalls Standard* of 1893 did the same and added antonyms. Also, most American dictionaries after Webster gave synonyms in many definitions, often in lieu of a definition. Perhaps that is why, for a long time, no dictionary of synonyms or thesaurus was produced in America.

This began to change in the middle of the twentieth century, and all the big dictionary publishers now have their own: the *Webster's New Dictionary of Synonyms* (1942); Funk and Wagnalls *Modern Guide to Synonyms* (1968), compiled by S. I. Hayakawa, reprinted as *Use the Right Word: The Reader's Digest Modern Guide to Synonyms and Related Words* (1987) and published in England as *Cassell's Modern Guide to Synonyms* (1971), with a second edition also published as *Choose the Right Word: A Modern Guide to Synonyms* (1987), and as the *Penguin Modern Guide to Synonyms* (1987); the *Webster's New World Dictionary of Synonyms* (1984); the *Merriam-Webster's Dictionary of Synonyms* (1993); the *Reader's Digest Oxford Wordfinder* (1993), created from *COD8* and Urdang's *Oxford Thesaurus*, etc.

Roget's Thesaurus has sold in huge numbers in America, in its various guises, some of them alphabetically arranged, for ease of consultation but still called *thesauruses*. Their commercial success is clear: my own copy of the *New American Roget's College Thesaurus in Dictionary Form* (1962) says that the book has gone through 66 new editions! Others, with alphabetical or conceptual arrangements, are the *New World Thesaurus* (1971), the *Webster's Collegiate Thesaurus* (1976), now *Merriam-Webster's Collegiate Thesaurus* (1988), the *Random House College Thesaurus* (1984), the *Oxford Thesaurus: American Edition* (1992), edited by Laurence Urdang, 'certainly the most sophisticated of the current lot of alphabetical thesauruses' (Landau 2001: 140), because it includes example sentences, etc. Some of these, whose criteria for inclusion are obscure, lean towards the picturesque rather than the useful (Landau 2001: 140).

American lexicography has also produced various other dictionaries providing guidance on usage. The *Random House Webster's Word Menu* (1992) organizes about 65,000 words by themes, and contains traditional definitions for each and an index. It 'has the earmarks of an immensely dedicated but eccentric individual effort, filled with oddities that are peculiar to it and that no doubt make it endearing to some of its users' (Landau 2001: 22). The *Word Finder* (1947) by Rodale, not a dictionary of synonyms in the traditional sense, provides the user with thousands of collocations (see below, 8.2.4) classified by POS. It is huge, dense, and somewhat chaotic, but useful because it has so much information. Finally, Henry Burger's *The Wordtree* (1985), a highly original dictionary which took 27 years to compile, gives 24,600 English transitive verbs, some of them invented to fill a gap, organized in a strict hierarchy, designed to provide ways to master the language and the world and impose one's point of view on others, no less! It is a fascinating construction, but proves difficult to use.

4.2.3.2 Dictionaries of slang

There is a marked interest in America for the language of the underworld (Landau 2001: 38–9). The *American Thesaurus of Slang*, by Lester Berrey and Melvin van den Bark, 1,174 pages, was published in 1942 and re-edited several times; the *Dictionary of American Slang*, by Harold Wentworth and Stuart Flexner, 1960 (1975, 1998), 669 pages, was later used as the basis for the *New Dictionary of American Slang* (Robert Chapman, 1986, 1995). The *Random House Historical Dictionary of American Slang* is noteworthy for its size, 'the largest work on English slang, and I assume, the largest work on the slang of any language . . . roughly three times the size of R. L. Chapman's' (Spears 1995: 186) and its *OED*-inspired dated quotations. The first two volumes (1, A–G, 1994; 2, H–O, 1997) have been published, but the project has now been handed over to Oxford University Press for the last two. It is 'immensely helpful' (Landau 2001: 240).

4.2.3.3 Dictionaries of regionalisms

American lexicographers have produced a number of dictionaries of regionalisms. The main early productions have already been mentioned as part of the *OED* historical tradition: Mathews' *Dictionary of Americanisms* (1951), and Craigie's *Dictionary of American English* (1938–44). The *Dictionary of American Regional English* (*DARE*; 1985–2002), edited under the direction of Frederic Cassidy from the early 1960s to his death in 2000, is the result of long and detailed dialectological fieldwork begun in 1963, with 2,700 informants in more than 1,000 communities in all of the 50 states, with around 1,600 questions and nearly 2,5 million responses (Cassidy 1987a, 1987b). It brings together words and phrases that refer to the elements of daily life in rural America that had to be collected because they risked being wiped off the surface of the earth. The dictionary is remarkable, both very scholarly, breaking new lexicographic ground by providing maps ('Spot Maps') showing the areas where words are used, and highly entertaining.

Many dictionaries, or glossaries, of Americanisms have been published since the end of the eighteenth century but dictionaries of Briticisms were unknown for a long time (see, however, Schur 1980). The word *Briticism* itself is rare.[10] Oddly enough, no comprehensive dictionary of Black English has ever been produced or even envisaged in the USA (Görlach 1990: 1479).

4.2.3.4 Other dictionaries

The *Pronouncing Dictionary of American English* of John Kenyon and Thomas Knott, first published in 1944 was very successful and remained the best pronouncing dictionary of American English for several decades. Unfortunately, it has never been revised. More recent productions are S. Noory's *Dictionary of Pronunciation* (1965) and the *NBC Handbook of Pronunciation* (1984), but none has had the prestige and the influence of Daniel Jones' *English Pronouncing Dictionary* in Britain, no doubt because American English is more tolerant of regional accents.

American dictionaries of idioms (see below, 8.2.4) have tended to specialize in metaphorical, picturesque, phrases: *a pig in a poke, a one-horse town, to spill the beans*, etc. They include the *Kenkyusha Dictionary of Current English Idioms* (1964), the *Dictionary of American Idioms* of Maxine Boatner, Edward Gates, and Adam Makkai, first published in 1966 as *A Dictionary of Idioms for the Deaf*, then under its new title in 1975, mainly designed for foreign learners, etc. Also worthy of mention are *NTC's American Idioms Dictionary* (1987), *NTC's Dictionary of Phrasal Verbs and Other Idiomatic Verbal Phrases* (1993), the *American Heritage Dictionary of Idioms* (1997), with 10,000 entries, the *Longman American Idioms Dictionary* (1999), etc. (see Landau 2001: 40).

The USA has also had a few dictionaries of new words (Barnhart and Barnhart 1990; Algeo 1995).[11] The supplements to *W3* (*6,000 Words, 9,000 Words*, and *12,000 Words*) have been mentioned. Clarence Barnhart's *Dictionary of New English* in three volumes (1973, 1980, 1990) was designed to update all existing dictionaries of English, including the *OED*. Naturally, almost all the entries are nouns, and most of them are scientific and technical (see Algeo 1990*a*). All entries are provided with generous quotations, etymologies, and usage information.

---

[10] Allen Walker Read worked for a long time on a dictionary of Briticisms that has never been completed (Read 1987). Algeo is preparing one (*DSNA Newsletter*, Spring 2003; see also Algeo 1987).

[11] See also the special issue of *Dictionaries* (16, 1995).

4.3 THE TRADITION OF THE UTILITY DICTIONARY

4.3.1 *The main characteristics of American GPDs*

All American dictionaries have been influenced by the Merriam-Webster dictionaries (Landau 2001: 94), one way or another, by *W2, W3,* and the collegiate line, just like all British dictionaries have been influenced by the *OED.* Traditional American GPDs are characterized by the following features (see also McArthur 1986*b*: 137).

1. They are encyclopedic more than linguistic, because the first dictionaries in the nineteenth century had to answer the needs of a public that did not have many other sources of knowledge to turn to. They have proper names (*W3* being one of the few exceptions), sometimes mixed with other types of lexical items in only one wordlist (*RHC*), sometimes in two or three different lists (*MWC*). Most recent American dictionaries also have pictorial illustrations, except again *W3.* Their definitions tend to be encyclopedic, and they have always had, either before or after the dictionary proper, pages of ancillary matter, a tradition that goes back to Webster's *Compendious Dictionary* of 1806: weights and measures, moneys and currencies, the population of the cities of the USA, lists of post-offices, of Presidents, the Declaration of Independence, etc. *WNW* (1969 edition) and *RHC* (before 1991) had a list of all the colleges and universities in Canada and the USA, now abandoned by all dictionaries, *WBD* (1973 edition) had 124 pages with vocabulary tests, a guide to forms of address, etc., *RHD2* had nearly 300 pages including a four-language dictionary (French–German–Spanish–Italian), etc. The reasons for such additions to the main dictionary text can be trivial, to avoid blank pages at the end of a signature, but there is also a desire to outdo the competition by having more material (see below) as much as to satisfy the needs of the American public for that type of information.

Among unabridged dictionaries we see no end yet to the 'encyclopedic', whether it be practical information or a miscellany of appended facts and addenda, e.g. the 29 'specialist' dictionaries of the *Reader's Digest Great Encyclopedic Dictionary* (1966) or the non-lexical supplements such as 'Wines of the Presidents' and 'How to start a club and run its meetings' in *Funk and Wagnalls Standard International,* bicentennial edition (1973). Non-lexical and encyclopedic supplements swell *The Random House Dictionary of the English Language* (1966) by nearly one-fourth its total volume.   (Roe 1982: 20)

2. They are more prescriptive than descriptive, except for *W3* and a few others (see below). The American society has a '"yearning for certainty"' that

'developed from the nation's early reliance on "a book standard to learn what they thought prevailed in England. This linguistic colonialism lasted a long time and set the pattern of accepting the dictionary as a lawgiver,"' Read wrote (in Morton 1994: 199). He went on: 'Rather than observe the language around them, as Englishmen do, Americans give up their autonomy and fly to a dictionary to settle questions of language'. For that reason, and also because dictionaries were used in schools and colleges, American dictionaries were long reluctant to include marginal, particularly taboo, words.

3. They provide guidance on usage: they have 'always been intimately associ-ated with questions of usage and the standard' (Algeo 1990b: 2005). They have notes on register and on synonym discrimination: for example, the entry for *importance* in *AHD* has a note explaining the difference between *importance*, *consequence*, *moment*, *significance*, *import*, and *weight*. *MWC9* has 'a very helpful usage note discriminating the connotations of *ghastly*, *grisly*, *gruesome*, *macabre*, and *lurid*' (Abate 1991: 168). 'Over the years usage notes . . . have become increas-ingly visible features' (Morton 1994: 285).

4. They are more focused on technical and scientific words than on literary language. They are synchronic rather than historical, even though some, includ-ing the Merriam-Webster line, order the meanings of polysemous words in chronological order. They tend to give few obsolete or archaic words, partly because in the beginning American lexicographers wanted to produce specifically American dictionaries but had little native literature to draw from (Simpson 1990: 1958).

5. They give headword status to many compounds and all sorts of phrases. For example, one page of *MWC8* chosen at random has entries for *ground ball*, *ground bass*, *ground cloth*, *ground cover*, *ground-effect machine*, *ground floor*, *ground glass*, etc., all of which would probably be included in the entry for *ground* in otherwise equivalent British dictionaries, or would be omitted because they are semantically regular (see below, 8.2.4). Some American dictionaries even have entries for the names of associations, of colleges, of books, foreign quotations, etc.: *MWC10* had *Jefferson Davis's Birthday*, *Riemannian geometry*, etc. (Landau 2001: 358), a practice that boosts the number of 'words' announced by the dictionary.

The 1934 Webster announces 400,000 words. But then one realizes that the count includes such entries as *Home Owner's Loan Corporation*, *Angle of incidence* (as well as 49 entries of the type *Angle of-*), *Blenheim Spaniel*, *Book of Common Prayer*, *Characteristic of a surface*, *Engagement ring*, *Ils ne passeront pas*, *Lex Talionis*, *Tobacco brown*, *Poor in spirit*, etc.   (Rey-Debove 1971: 63)

6. They give etymological information (Zgusta 1971: 251–2), probably because the lexicographers think that knowing the origins of words, for the American public, is part of the mastery of language that is necessary for acculturation.

7. They indicate pronunciation in a 'respelling system' using diacritics rather than the IPA, because 'American publishers identify their market as people who do not know, and will not learn, the IPA' (Landau 1999: 252). Only the more recent EFL/ESL American dictionaries have adopted the IPA.

8. They are not generous in their inclusion of words from other varieties of English, probably because they aim at providing a linguistic model, in which other varieties of English are not welcome. British spellings and pronunciations are rarely indicated, the number of Briticisms is limited, and even Canadianisms were often omitted until recently (Read 1962: 221–2). Interestingly, many American GPDs call themselves dictionaries of American English, while none of the dictionaries produced in Great Britain say that they are dictionaries of British English.

Dictionaries have always been popular in America (Algeo 1990*b*: 1987). 'Clearly, dictionaries are in demand, and play an important role in American society—a society that is not notorious for the purchasing of books' (McDavid 1979/1980: 296), either because the demand genuinely comes from the public or because 'the publishing industry has succeeded in convincing every family that their continuing literacy depends crucially on owning a dictionary' (Landau 2001: 30). But the popularity of dictionaries has led the publishers to reproduce old recipes rather than invent new solutions. American dictionaries of the twentieth century, contrary to those of the nineteenth, have not been characterized by their innovations. Even after the 1960s, when dictionaries were changing so rapidly all over the world, the evolution was more timid in the USA: 'the American dictionaries have been the most resistant to change' (Landau 1994*a*: 348). They are prisoners of their prosperity, which encourages them to maintain the traditions that have made them successful: 'competition has done more to suppress innovation than to encourage excellence' (Landau 2001: 30). Landau (1994*a*: 348–9) speculates that lexicographic innovation in America could only be caused by a major earthquake, 'competition from a new source—that is, the introduction in the American market of a major new dictionary from abroad . . . or because one of the four [major dictionary publishers] is acquired by a foreign company which is not saddled with the package of the hidebound American companies'.

The differences between the British and the American traditions are clear, though some dictionaries produced in Britain have always sold well in the USA and some dictionaries produced in America have been popular in Britain—the tastes of the public do not always coincide with the leading lexicographic traditions. The British dictionary is an *aide-mémoire* or a source of philological information for the educated user; the American dictionary is an all-purpose reference tool for anyone who needs guidance on usage and on the culture. The British dictionary is for an elite; the American dictionary is for the general public. The British dictionary is 'scholar-driven', i.e. determined by what the specialists think should feature in a dictionary; the American dictionary is 'public-driven', i.e. determined by what the public wants, or what the lexicographers think that the public wants. It is a 'utility' dictionary, a serviceable, reliable, and simple work of reference on all sorts of linguistic and cultural questions. The British dictionary is a learned friend; the American dictionary is a schoolmaster.

4.3.2 *The numbers game*

The history of lexicography is a 'story of more' as much as a 'story of better'. Every lexicographer, every dictionary publisher has wanted to produce a dictionary that had more than the predecessors, more entries, more words, more pages, more information. This started with the collection of hard words, which could be added *ad libitum*, and perhaps even invented (Dolezal 2007). It continued with the addition of common words, then of regional, dialect, slang words, proper names, idioms, of technical and scientific terms, and of words from other Englishes, all in everlasting supply. Some dictionaries also increased their wordlists by adding neologisms—what the popular reviewers always check when a new dictionary is published (see below, 7.1.2.2)—and a fair sprinkling of transparent derivatives and word combinations.

Modern dictionary publishers, in their pursuit of spiraling marketing claims to have 'more' entries than competitors, have lighted on . . . analogical formations as a rich source of additional 'entries', which take up very little space, since, as Johnson suggests, they can be listed without the trouble of a definition.   (Hanks 2005: 249)

Many dictionaries have also added ancillary matter of all kinds, for good measure, particularly in America: 'Almost every new work was expected to be bigger than its predecessors, and little thought was given to the criteria for selecting additional material' (Morton 1994: 60). All the successive editions of the same dictionary tend to grow in size, and not only because the language keeps growing.

American dictionaries, designed for people in need of linguistic advice, should have had a limited number of entries with a thorough treatment of each word, but that is not what happened. American lexicographers have been particularly active in the race for quantity. The competition began with the Webster–Worcester war in the nineteenth century and reached a peak with the publication of *W2* in 1934, with its 600,000 entries. It was encouraged by the American federal government, which used mainly quantitative criteria to select dictionaries for adoption in schools and colleges. The main criterion was the inclusion of a certain number of words, to the despair of lexicographers: 'The federal government's standards for selecting dictionaries are laughable. For over 30 years the government has selected dictionaries primarily by the number of entries in them, regardless of the quality of definitions' (Barnhart 1962: 177).

Even when a new dictionary is not bigger than its competitors, there are ways of making it look bigger. American lexicographers, after boosting the number of entries by giving headword status to all sorts of items, started counting not only entries but other things as well: the items that were defined, or somehow treated in the dictionary, the run-ons, all the possible forms of a word, the words in lists, etc. If *W2* had 3,400 pages and 600,000 entries, even disregarding the fact that some of those pages were not the dictionary proper, there was an average of about 180 entries per page! In the early 1930s, the US Department of the Treasury together with the Merriam Company set up regulations to facilitate the governmental purchase of dictionaries for the education system (Urdang 2000: 35). The verdict was: headwords, inflected forms, variant forms, idioms and phrases, run-on entries, and words in lists were OK; the rest was not. But the publishers soon started bending the rules in all sorts of ways, counting 'regular plurals...., regular comparative and superlative forms...for adjectives', etc. (Urdang 2000: 36).[12]

To confuse the potential buyers, the publishers use various terms, *word*, of course, but also *entry, reference, definition, form, item*, etc., none of which is precisely defined. *Entry* is ambiguous, as we have seen, *form* and *reference* are obscure. Ilson (2000: 327) notes that some of the dictionaries that use *reference* in their blurb do not even define the word in that sense in the dictionary. If you count definitions, every single meaning of a polysemous word can be counted, which encourages the lexicographers to distinguish as many meanings as possible, not necessarily the best solution for the users (see below, 8.2.3.5).

Inevitably, these questions have been the source of conflicts. Landau (2001: 427) tells the story of a lawsuit between Random House and Bantam Books: the latter had claimed that one of their dictionaries had 80,000 entries, but Random House judged it to be about 56,000. 'The two publishers eventually reached an out-of-court settlement and Bantam withdrew its advertising'.

---

[12] On this question, Landau (2001: 436) sends the reader back to one of his earlier publications (Landau 1964), 'the only published account describing in any detail how dictionaries count entries'.

It is difficult, if not impossible, for a metalexicographer to check the figures given by the publishers, but their counts do seem to be consistently exaggerated (Landau 1984: 84). For example, the dust jacket of the 1973 edition of *WNW* announced 157,000 entries, but a rapid calculation based on the number of entries on twenty pages chosen at random indicates that there could not be more than 80,000 entries in the sense of 'headword beginning a new article'. The same calculation for *AHD* (1969 edition) gives 75,000 instead of 155,000! The least unreliable—but not the easiest—way of evaluating the contents of a dictionary is to count all the words that it contains: for example, the *Collins English Dictionary* (1979; *CED*) has 3 million words, the *Reader's Digest Great Illustrated Dictionary* (1984) 4 million (Ilson 1986b: 54), *CED4* has 3.6 million and the *New Oxford Dictionary of English* (1998; *NODE*) 4 million, according to their publishers.

British dictionaries were long published without any quantitative claims, but they have recently begun to boast about quantity as well: they 'have begun to play the numbers game of claiming more of *something* than anyone else' (Landau 2001: 110).

4.3.3 *Prescriptive dictionaries*

America, like all colonial societies, looked to the mother nation for a long time for guidance on linguistic usage, and Americans imported British dictionaries until the early nineteenth century. When they began to produce their own, those had to provide advice on what to say and what not to say: they had to be prescriptive (Wells 1973). They had to be arbiters of linguistic usage, like the schoolmarm of American fame, like her revered by some and dreaded by others.

For people who do not like to be told what to do, the pressure was too strong, and the reactions were violent: in *The Devils' Dictionary*, Ambrose Bierce defined *dictionary* as 'A malevolent literary device for cramping the growth of a language and making it hard and inelastic', and lashed at the *lexicographer*. The passage is worth quoting in full.

A pestilent fellow who, under the pretense of recording some particular stage in the development of a language, does what he can to arrest its growth, stiffen its flexibility and mechanize its methods. For your lexicographer, having written his dictionary, comes to be considered 'as one having authority,' whereas his function is only to make a record, not to give a law. The natural servility of the human understanding having invested him with judicial power, surrenders its right of reason and submits itself to a chronicle as if it were a statue. Let the dictionary (for example) mark a good word as 'obsolete' or 'obsolescent' and few men thereafter venture to use it, whatever their need of it and however desirable its restoration to favor—whereby the process of impoverishment is accelerated and speech decays. On the contrary, recognizing the truth that language must grow by innovation if it grow at all, makes new words and uses the old in an unfamiliar sense, has no following and is tartly reminded that 'it isn't in the dictionary'—although down to the time of the first lexicographer (Heaven forgive him!) no author ever had used a word that *was* in the dictionary. In the golden prime and high noon of English speech; when from the lips of the great Elizabethans fell words that made their own meaning and carried it in their very sound; when a Shakespeare and a Bacon were possible, and the language now rapidly perishing at one end and slowly renewed at the other was in vigorous growth and hardy preservation—sweeter than honey and stronger than a lion—the lexicographer was a person unknown, the dictionary a creation which his Creator had not created him to create.

Bierce added a poem by Sigismund Smith for good measure:

> God said: 'Let Spirit perish into Form,'
> And lexicographers arose, a swarm!
> Thought fled and left her clothing, which they took,
> And catalogued each garment in a book.
> Now, from her leafy covert when she cries:
> 'Give me my clothes and I'll return,' they rise
> And scan the list, and say without compassion:
> 'Excuse us—they are mostly out of fashion.'

The agitation that followed the publication of *W3* is the most spectacular episode in the history of prescriptivism in American lexicography, and it shows that in the early 1960s the issue was still hot. Many reviews, comments, and books have been published about it.[13] On one side were the descriptivists, the compilers of *W3* and their allies, including most linguists, and on the other were the prescriptivists, that Bolinger (1980: 164) called the 'shamans', many journalists, some teachers and a few lexicographers. The battle was a quarrel of the Ancients and the Moderns,[14] with the descriptivists being the Moderns, and the prescriptivists the Ancients. Public opinion was massively behind the latter.

---

[13] See Sledd and Ebbitt (1962), Marckwardt (1963/1967), Gold (1985), Haebler (1989), and Morton (1994). The bibliography in Haebler has 567 items, from 1961 to 1988, all American, and there were more to come.

[14] The phrase (*querelle des anciens et des modernes*) was first applied to a quarrel between two sides of the *Académie française* in the early 1690s: the Ancients, led by Boileau, supported the merits of ancient writers and advocated the imitation of ancient texts while the Moderns, led by Perrault, supported contemporary authors. Racine was an Ancient, Fontenelle a Modern. The quarrel was the subject of Swift's *A Tale of a Tub*, published in 1704.

The stakes were clear: what is the role of the dictionary? But it is not easy to understand why the battle was so ferocious. There were long-standing oppositions that suddenly crystallized because of other things that were happening at the same time in the USA. Part of the American public felt that authority in general, particularly in the education of children at home and at school, was being challenged, and *W3* was seen as an instrument of the new permissiveness. What the prescriptivists could not admit, what caused the torrent of reproach that all but carried away *W3*,[15] was that in their eyes it had forfeited its role as an indicator of good usage. The critics were infuriated by the treatment of some objectionable words and phrases, not many, just 'a few disputed usages' and 'a handful of quotations' (Morton 1994: 174). An editorial in the *New York Times* of 12 October 1961 had: 'Webster's has, it is apparent, surrendered to the permissive school that has been busily extending its beachhead on English instruction in the schools' (Morton 1994: 173). For Wilson Follett (1962: 77), author of *Modern American Usage*, a dictionary was no use if it did not provide usage guidance:

The rock-bottom practical truth is that the lexicographer cannot abrogate his authority if he wants to. He may think of himself as a detached scientist reporting the facts of language, declining to recommend use of anything or abstention from anything; but the myriad consultants of his work are not going to see him so.... The fact that the compilers disclaim authority and piously refrain from judgments is meaningless; the work itself, by virtue of its inclusions and exclusions, its mere existence, is a whole universe of judgments received by millions as the Word from on high.

The most often discussed case was the entry for *ain't*. *W3* said (Plate 146):

though disapproved by many and more common in less educated speech, used orally in most parts of the USA by many cultivated speakers

which merely described current usage but was judged too permissive. The dictionary was designed, the critics said, to 'comfort the ignorant, confer approval upon the mediocre, and subtly imply that proper English is the tool only of the snob' (Morton 1994: 157), no less. *W3* 'was portrayed as a revolutionary document that would corrupt our speech and undermine our cultural traditions' (Morton 1994: xii). There were charges that *W3* was the work of dangerously liberal structuralist linguists—though Gove himself wrote that it owed virtually nothing to linguistics (see below, 8.1.1.2)—and even that the dictionary was 'Communist-inspired' (Morton 1994: 6), under 'the influence of the "bolshevik spirit"' (Morton 1994: 183).

---

[15] Many reviewers told their readers to keep their old *W2* and boycott *W3* (see Morton 1994).

Yet *W3* was not particularly permissive compared with similar dictionaries: the language proposed as a model was not 'anything goes' as its enemies said, but cultivated usage, formal and informal. And *W3* was certainly not the first American dictionary to proclaim its desire to describe the language as it was really used rather than prescribe: *W2*, in 1934, had been at least as descriptive, and there had been an entry for *ain't* in the 1890 and 1909 editions as well as in *W2*. Even before that, for the 1864 edition, Goodrich had declared that a dictionary could only describe usage (Marckwardt 1963/1967: 33), as Johnson had done before him.

The battle was extremely violent, and it is a matter of metalexicographic interest that a new dictionary could arouse almost as much passion in the USA as, if not more than, apparently far weightier issues:

In 1961 there was far more newspaper concern, editorial and otherwise, with the Merriam-Webster's *Third New International Dictionary* than with American policy toward Southeast Asia, and the good grey *New York Times* objected far more strenuously to the real or imagined defects of the *Third* than it did to Mr. Kennedy's taking what turned out to be irretrievable commitments to South Viet Nam.   (McDavid 1979/1980: 297)

Things eventually calmed down after a few years, and *W3* was accepted by the American public as a great dictionary. In the meantime, a new word had been created during the *W3* turmoil, *dictionary-bashing*, for 'violent, vicious assault against a dictionary, aimed at destroying it', that was later applied to other contexts.

On the British side, dictionaries have been more descriptive than prescriptive, true to the heritage of Samuel Johnson and the *OED*, and the British public was never really interested in the opposition. *W3* was considered as a good dictionary in Britain right from the start: the reviews 'all treated the new edition respectfully, and most were written by scholars who praised it' (Morton 1994: 197). In France, the questions of the purity of the language and of the need to use language properly have always been important, and most lexicographers have been prescriptivists since the 'Académie française' and its *Dictionnaire* in 1694, with a few exceptions like Richelet or Furetière.[16] Littré wanted to describe the language of the best language users of the past as a model for contemporary usage: 'It is respect for the past which will save us from current errors' (Osselton 2000: 67). The idea that a dictionary must be prescriptive is still present in the French public, and remains one of the reasons why people buy dictionaries.

If the dictionary reflects exactly my own language, mixed up with thousands of others, I will find it useless. What I want is examples of what to say, what not to say, rules that will

---

[16] Richelet, at his entry for *langue*, says: 'it is as much possible to fix the French LANGUAGE as it is to fix the humour of the French'; and at the entry for *gens*: 'what should be done is to consult the ears and the men who are nimble in the use of the language' (Corneri 1990: 48).

make me more respectable if I follow them. Lovers of purist works, in 1694 as well as in the twentieth century, have no other motivation; lovers of all 'dictionnaires de langue' have this motivation as well, among others.   (Rey 1970*c*: 24)

But it is hard to imagine in France a battle with the violence of the battle around *W3* in the USA.

Evidence from journals, conferences, and books on lexicography suggests that prescriptivism is no longer a hot issue, even in America. The consensus among lexicographers and metalexicographers seems to be that dictionaries should describe usage as well as attitudes to usage, including disapproval when it is shared by enough people, whoever they are (Morton 1994: 276). But some modern dictionaries, such as the *Encarta World English Dictionary* (see below), are still prescriptive, with a vengeance—although it is hard to assess the impact of prescriptive features on the public—and there are traces of prescriptivism, or at least normativism, in the most innovative dictionaries of our times, the dictionaries for foreign learners (see below, Chapter 5). It is reasonable to think that the situation will change with the e-dictionary, which does not embody authority in the same way as the paper dictionary (see below, 9.2).

4.4 DICTIONARIES FOR BRITAIN AND THE USA, AND BEYOND

There have always been relations between the lexicographers of Britain and of the USA. Webster took part of his inspiration from Johnson, and his dictionaries were known in Britain, used and even copied (Sledd 1972: 122). The compilers of the *OED* used Webster's 1864 edition as a benchmark, and the *OED* was sold in America in large numbers. The efforts of British publishers to sell dictionaries in the USA have not always been successful: the 1927 American edition of the *POD* 'soon went out of print and was not revived' (Allen 1986: 7). They never stopped trying: the *Longman Dictionary of American English*, for example, was published in 1983. Recently, some British publishers have established headquarters in the USA from which they have produced dictionaries, among which was the *New Oxford American Dictionary* (*NOAD*; see below), published in 2001.

4.4.1 The American dictionary in Britain

Hamlyn's Encyclopedic World Dictionary, compiled by Patrick Hanks with the help of the linguist Simeon Potter and published in 1971, was one of the first

American-style dictionaries published in Britain. It was based on *ACD*—which was based on the *Century Dictionary*—and the same size. A few years before, in 1968, Longman had produced the *Longman's English Larousse* (60,000 words), an adaptation of the French tradition of *Petit Larousse*, a medium-sized encyclopedic dictionary with proper names and pictorial illustrations, later published under the title *Longman Modern English Dictionary* (1976), perhaps because mentioning *Larousse* in the title was not a good idea. Neither of those dictionaries was very successful for reasons that are not clear.

4.4.1.1 The *Collins Dictionary of the English Language*

The American tradition gained a foothold in Britain in 1979 with the publication of the *Collins English Dictionary* (*CED*),[17] compiled by Hanks, William McLeod, and Urdang on the basis of a dictionary text that had been used for *ACD* and *RHD* (McArthur 1992: 308). It was similar in size to American college dictionaries, 162,000 words, a figure obtained through the same sort of calculation.[18] Like most college dictionaries, *CED* had etymologies, usage notes, an encyclopedic wordlist, many technical and scientific words, and entries for various phrases, such as *Copernican system* and *listed building* (Landau 2001: 358), *ideas of reference, ignition key, fencing wire*, etc. as well as 'thousands of rarely used derivatives, such as *oppressingly, sluggardliness*, and *idioticalness*' (Landau 2001: 102). *CED* indicated the century when a word appeared in print for the first time, and gave semantically related words, like *aqueous* in the entry for *water*. But it had neither cultural addenda nor pictorial illustrations, both standard features of American college dictionaries, and it was not openly prescriptive (Plate 15).

Many of *CED*'s definitions were by synonyms (see below, 8.2.5): for example *obtrusive* was

1. Obtruding or tending to obtrude. 2. Sticking out; protruding; noticeable

For concrete words they were encyclopedic and technical, as in many American dictionaries, in the style of *MWC* but perhaps less daunting: *elephant* was

either of the two proboscidean mammals of the family *Elephantidae*. The **African elephant** (*Loxodonta Africana*) is the larger species, with large flapping ears and a less humped back than the **Indian elephant** (*Elephas maximus*), of S and SE Asia[19]

---

[17] Collins had published a totally different *Collins English Dictionary* in 1974, a learners' dictionary.
[18] 'It [*CED*] has also caught the American disease of entryitis, boasting of 162,000 entries' (Landau 1984: 338).
[19] Strangely, the definition does not give any idea of size. *COD7* (1982), of similar size and period, had 'largest living land animal, of which two species survive, with a trunk and long curved ivory tusks'.

The definition of *peach* started with a description of the tree, not the fruit, where *COD* had the 'fruit' definition first, even before the use of a corpus. But on the whole the defining style of *CED* was considered to be reasonably user-friendly.

CED was very successful, evidence that by the late 1970s the British public was ready for American-style encyclopedic dictionaries. It has gone through several editions at close intervals, called *Collins Dictionary of the English Language*, or *The Collins English Dictionary*, according to whether you look at the dust jacket or the title page. The most recent editions use the Bank of English (BoE; see below, 9.1.7). It was 'the leading American-style, British desk dictionary' in 2001 (Landau 2001: 95) and it now competes with *COD11*. The latest edition, *CED9* (2007), is available online, on a CD-ROM with a thesaurus, and also has an edition for Palm OS.

4.4.1.2 British dictionaries influenced by the American tradition

Many dictionaries published in Britain after 1979 have borrowed features from American dictionaries, because of the success of *CED*. They were encyclopedic, they began playing the numbers game, and '[e]ven thumb-index tabs, that useless American appurtenance that disfigures the edges of a book's pages, is now a standard feature of British desk dictionaries' (Landau 2001: 95).

The *Oxford Encyclopedic English Dictionary*, 200,000 definitions, and 100 pages of cultural addenda on countries of the world, music, money (and—someone had to start—ecology!), was published in 1991. The *Longman New Universal Dictionary* (1982), based on *MWC8*, was the first product of an agreement between Longman and Merriam (Ilson 1990*b*: 1970). It had 90,000 entries and 225,000 definitions and was designed to compete with *CED* and *COD*. The *Oxford English Reference Dictionary*, published in 1996, was based on the text of *COD8* to which encyclopedic entries and encyclopedic information were added. A second edition was published in 2002.

All those dictionaries share some features with the American college or desk dictionary but not all:

[T]here isn't a single dictionary in the British list that has all the major design features of the American dictionaries. For example, CED hasn't got pictures or synonym essays. LDEL [*Longman Dictionary of the English Language*; see below] hasn't got pictures or orthographic syllabification. GID *has* got pictures, and lots of them, but for reasons of space omits the full-fledged synonym essay, contenting itself with lists of near-synonyms. So there is as yet no British dictionary with all the features one associates with the American college dictionary. The British lexicographic scene is still fluid.

(Ilson 1986*b*: 58)

Why did the British public discover a liking for American dictionaries in the end of the twentieth century? Is it a change in tastes? Is it just a hankering for novelty? Is it that the public eventually emerged from the episode of the *OED* during which they had been led to believe that they did not need encyclopedic dictionaries? Is it that dictionary publishers reached new categories of users, hitherto untouched by the traditional dictionaries? Who knows?

4.4.2 NODE *and* NOAD, *or two traditions in one dictionary*

The Reader's Digest Great Illustrated Dictionary (*GID*), compiled by Robert Ilson and published in 1984, with 180,000 entries, based on *AHD*, was perhaps the first dictionary to have a British and an American edition published at the same time, but it was not very successful. *The New Oxford Dictionary of English* (*NODE*), by Judy Pearsall and Hanks, was published in 1998. It had 'over 350,000 words, phrases and definitions', about a quarter of which were scientific, technical, or encyclopedic (Landau 1999: 253). It used the BNC (see below, 9.1.7) and claimed to have explored 'previously neglected fields as diverse as computing, complementary medicine, antique collecting, and winter sports' (*Preface*).

NODE was encyclopedic in the sense that it had proper names, but it did not have pictorial illustrations, like *CED* (Plates 17a and 17b). Like learner's dictionaries, it gave information for encoding, preferred patterns, the countability of nouns, etc. Like *COD10*, it did not use the labels *vt* and *vi*, which it replaced by *with obj.* and *without obj.*, but it used *figurative*, long abandoned in other dictionaries. It did not indicate the pronunciation of the 'easier words', a policy that, according to Landau 'opens the door to the argument that simple words or definitions, too, might be omitted. But no one is ready to turn back the clock to re-embrace the "hard words" tradition of the eighteenth century' (Landau 2001: 126). *NODE* gave some etymologies, in a style that used few abbreviations.

NODE was innovative in its treatment of polysemous words. It incorporated the idea, put forward by prototype theory (see below, 8.2.5.7), that they have a 'core' meaning, or a few core meanings, around which the other meanings can be grouped. The core meaning is not necessarily the oldest meaning nor the most frequent, it is the meaning that native speakers think of as the most central, the one from which the other meanings can be derived. *NODE* accordingly divided its long entries into as many numbered parts as there were core meanings, each beginning a new line, and then arranged all the other, less important meanings in the relevant part, in a paragraph printed in smaller type. For example, the entry for *column* had three core meanings:

1 an upright pillar, typically cylindrical and made of stone or concrete, supporting an
  arch, entablature, or other structure or standing alone as a monument
2 a vertical division of a page or text
3 one or more lines of people or vehicles moving in the same direction

The first of those core meanings had a paragraph attached to it saying:

■ a similar vertical, roughly cylindrical thing: *a great column of smoke* ■ an upright
shaft forming part of a machine and typically used for controlling it: *a Spitfire control
column*

This was an attempt to give a more faithful picture of the polysemy of the word
than the usual listing of meanings (see below, 8.2.3), representing the endless
variations of discourse, and it also made the long entries more readable. On the
whole, the technique has been found convincing.

   NODE can be bought with a CD-ROM under the title *Oxford Talking Dictionary*, which has a dictionary of proper names, maps, pictures, pronunciation, etc.
The new edition, published in 2003, has unfortunately changed its title to *Oxford
Dictionary of English* (*ODE*), so that the old edition is *new* and the new edition is
not, but it has retained the characteristic features. *ODE* has 3,000 new words,
12,000 encyclopedic entries on people and places, and 500 usage notes.

   One of the interesting things about *NODE* is that it had an edition for the
American market, where it was called *The New Oxford American Dictionary*
(*NOAD*). This was published in 2001 under the editorship of Erin McKean
(Algeo 2003) (Plate 18). It also has proper names and encyclopedic information and the same presentation of polysemy, but with usage notes and black
and white illustrations it is closer to the American tradition than *NODE*. It
drew on the corpus resources of Oxford University Press (see below, 9.1.7). A
second edition was published in 2005, with a CD-ROM and a Palm OS
version. The whole text is also available to the users of Macintosh computers
OSX 10.4. *NOAD* sells well compared to its direct competitors, *MWC10*,
AHD4 and *SOED*.[20]

4.4.3 EWED: *A dictionary of global English?*

The *Encarta World English Dictionary* (*EWED*) was published in 1999 by Microsoft as a complement to the Encarta encyclopedia. For the first time in the history
of English-language lexicography, there were three editions published at the same
time: one for the USA (by Anne Soukhanov, a former editor of *AHD*), one for the

---

[20] It ranked fourth on the Amazon website on 29 October 2007.

UK, and one for Australia. The three differed in wordlist, wording of definitions, and addenda, but they were very similar in size and style. All had about 100,000 headwords, 'over 400,000 references'[21] and 'over 3,500,000 words of text', which places them in direct competition with *AHD*, *CED*, *NODE*, and *NOAD*. *EWED* had American features: encyclopedic entries for people and places (about 10,000), notes on usage and synonyms, pictorial illustrations (about 3,000), including photographs, and syllabication. It also had extensive front matter, with essays that, Ilson (2000: 330) writes about the UK edition, are 'masterpieces of fatuity'.

EWED claimed to be the first dictionary of global English, and boasted of its coverage of regional varieties, although it is not exemplary in the labelling of regionalisms, and not even in their inclusion (Landau 2000: 113): 'EWED's coverage of US English is not good' (Ilson (2000: 329). It drew its wordlist from a corpus of 50 million words of world English developed specifically for it, the Bloomsbury Corpus of Words (Introduction: xiii; see below, 9.1.7.5), but Landau (2000: 113) notes that most of the examples of the US edition are invented rather than authentic, and that *EWED* is not particularly rich in idioms and phrases.

EWED arranges meanings by frequency, and heads every meaning in long entries by a short gloss, called 'quick definition', in bold capitals, to facilitate scanning, an adaptation of the 'sign-posting' used in some learner's dictionaries (see below, Chapter 5). It is the only native speakers' dictionary to do that. Sometimes the gloss is exactly, or almost, the same as the definition, 'an unjustified waste of precious dictionary space' (Ilson 2000: 330). Consider the entry for *q* in the UK edition:

2. SPEECH SOUND CORRESPONDING TO LETTER 'Q' the speech sound that corresponds to the letter 'Q'

or *fly* in the US edition (Landau 2000: 114):

13. PASS QUICKLY to pass very fast

EWED is also characterized by its 'determination to avoid giving offense to any group' (Landau 2000: 114), probably because it is the product of a big corporation that has 'many clients to please' (Landau 2000: 116). Many words are considered suspect:

EWED considers almost any word offensive that has to do with mental or physical incapacity, mental mistakes, sex, age, or race. It considers the word *madness* offensive,

---

[21] 'I do not know what this refers to' (Landau 2001: 453).

and one can't call someone a *nut* or a *nutcase* in its book without being offensive. *Weirdo* is off limits, and no one can be a *basket case* or a *vegetable* or *off his* (or *her*) *rocker, screwed up, schizoid,* or *handicapped*. EWED makes no distinction between words used humorously or affectionately and words used to insult. So among the words it labels offensive are *jerk, slob, schnook, klutz, loony,* and *crazy*. It views the language as a fortified castle of virtue, and every battlement is equipped with a cannon loaded with warnings.

(Landau 2001: 234)

EWED uses heavy artillery to warn the user:

Sometimes even telling us three times that a word is offensive isn't deemed enough. Here is definition 4 of **minority**: 'OFFENSIVE TERM offensive term for minority member, now avoided by careful speakers because it can cause offense (*offensive*).' Of the 18 words used, two define it—'minority member'—and the rest warn us not to use it.

(Landau 2000: 115)

The entry for *fuck*—there is one—contains 35 mentions of the label *offensive* in various guises.

   EWED is also available as a CD-ROM or sold with computer software. There is a second edition called *Encarta Webster's Dictionary of the English Language* (2004).

   On the whole, *EWED* has not been well received, partly, perhaps, because the arrival of Microsoft in the small world of dictionary publishing was not welcome. Its coverage, its use of short definitions and its extreme efforts to avoid offensiveness have not impressed the critics.

EWED could have been a marvellously innovative dictionary in many ways. It could have been keyed to the Encarta encyclopaedia. But it wasn't. It could have offered a coverage of English vocabulary unrivalled in a dictionary of its class. But it doesn't. It could have offered an unrivalled coverage of the diatopically restricted items that English has spawned or picked up in its pilgrimage throughout the world. But it appears not to do so, despite its title. It could even have aspired to be the first-ever monolingual dictionary designed specifically for native speakers. But those who produced it appear to have harboured no such lofty ambition.   (Ilson 2000: 329)

Ilson (2000: 328) even found traces of 'carelessness', the mortal sin of lexicography: in the UK edition, there is one entry for *Black, Shirley* and another for *Temple, Shirley*, with different texts. Landau (2000: 115) is equally severe for the US edition, speaking of 'ignorance of American culture as well as of its language'.

   The *Encarta* dictionaries are less interesting than *NODE*, but they are symptomatic of the period. They illustrate the arrival of new publishers, including companies specializing in software, and the simultaneous production of dictionaries for several English-speaking countries. Another example of this globalizing tendency is the *Longman Dictionary of the English Language* (*LDEL*), first published in 1984, with the collaboration of Randolph Quirk, which blended 'the expertise and databases of Merriam-Webster in the US with Longman in the UK, to produce a work that is close to nation-neutral' (McArthur 1998: 40). It was based on the *New Universal* of 1982 and made use of material in the Survey of English Usage (see below, 9.1). The second edition (1991), the largest Longman dictionary ever, had 'over 220,000 meanings' in a single wordlist incorporating abbreviations, biographical and geographical names, about 600 usage notes and 400 boxed synonym comparisons, pronunciation in non-IPA symbols, but no pictorial illustrations. Meanings were ordered by frequency: 'Meanings that are current throughout the English-speaking world are shown first; they appear in the order in which they are first recorded in English' (xvi). Are we ready for a single dictionary for all English-speaking countries?

5

A NEW TRADITION:
THE DICTIONARY FOR
FOREIGN STUDENTS

D ICTIONARIES are for people who need help in the use of language, and
lexicography is a form of teaching. All bilingual and some monolingual
dictionaries have been designed for students learning a foreign language. Monolingual dictionaries for foreign learners of English became a distinctive genre in
Britain in the second half of the twentieth century, with the worldwide boom of
the teaching of English as a foreign language.[1] They took inspiration from
research on the teaching of languages that had begun in the early years of the
century, particularly Harold Palmer's *The Scientific Study and Teaching of Languages*, published in 1917. Palmer tried to organize the acquisition of the lexis in
stages. The most important words, he said, around 3,000, could be determined by
an experienced teacher. At the same time, in the USA, Thorndike was also trying
to grade words in the learning process, but through frequency counts in texts. He
published *The Teacher's Word Book* in 1921, which listed the 10,000 words that
American children should know. Several dictionaries with controlled vocabularies were published in the following decades. In 1935, Michael West and J. G.
Endicott, siding with Palmer's subjective approach rather than with the quantitative approach of Thorndike, published their *New Method English Dictionary*,
with about 24,000 words defined by a defining vocabulary of 1,923 words. The
General Basic English Dictionary, on which C. K. Ogden had been working since
the 1920s, came out in 1940. It had about 20,000 words, all defined with the 850

[1] For a history, description, and analysis of English learners' dictionaries, see McArthur (1998),
Cowie (1999a), Stein (2002).

words of Basic English. Michael West's *General Service List of English Words* appeared in 1953. Its entries were defined by 1,490 easy words (Cowie 1999a: 14 ff.). At the same time, there was research on the formalization of syntax in sentence patterns to facilitate teaching. In 1938, Palmer published *A Grammar of English Words*, in which each syntactic construction was represented by a code with letters and figures.

Monolingual dictionaries for foreign learners have been called *EFL*[2] *dictionaries*, *ELT*[3] *dictionaries*, *pedagogical dictionaries*, *learners' dictionaries*,[4] the most common term, or *MLDs*,[5] in which case dictionaries for native speakers are called *NSDs*.[6] Learners' dictionaries were ignored by metalexicographers for decades, in a lexicographic world that was dominated by the prestige of the *OED* and of *W3* and their families of dictionaries, but they would eventually turn out to be immensely successful commercially and also important in the history of lexicography. Because of their prosperity, because of the fierce competition between them, and because they were extensively analysed and commented upon by armies of metalexicographers and teachers all over the world, they have constantly improved and have had an influence on all dictionaries.

5.1. THE 'BIG FIVE'

Dozens of learners' dictionaries have been published, but there are five, from five different publishers, that are usually considered to be of major importance, and referred to as 'the Big Five'.

5.1.1 The Oxford *Advanced Learner's Dictionary*

The dictionary that was to become the *Advanced Learner's Dictionary of Current English* was published first in Japan in 1942 under the title *Idiomatic and Syntactic English Dictionary*,[7] by A. S. Hornby, E. V. Gatenby, and H. Wakefield,

---

[2] For 'English as a foreign language'.   [3] For 'English language teaching'.
[4] A somewhat misleading denomination, since all dictionaries are designed for people who have something to learn. Also, the users of these dictionaries are 'often not learners in the prototypical sense of the word but non-native speakers of English' (Varantola 2001: 238).
[5] For 'monolingual learners' dictionaries'.
[6] In France, where the tradition is less clearly identified, they are called *dictionnaire pédagogique*, *dictionnaire pour apprenants*, *dictionnaire d'apprentissage*, *dictionnaire de français langue étrangère*, or *dictionnaire pour étrangers*.
[7] Still available from Kaitakusha, the Japanese publisher.

who had taught English as a foreign language in Tokyo, where Palmer had worked and carried out his research on the teaching of lexis and grammar. The text was brought back to Britain during the Second World War and taken over by a new department of Oxford University Press, the dictionary department having refused to touch what was not, in their eyes, a true dictionary (Strevens 1978: ix) (Plate 16). It was reproduced photographically and published in 1948 as *A Learner's Dictionary of Current English*, which was to become the *Advanced Learner's Dictionary of Current English* in 1963 and the *Oxford Advanced Learner's Dictionary of Current English* in 1974. It was characterized by the following features.

1. *Vocabulary control*: *ALD* limited its wordlist to the most important words, i.e. the more frequent, on the assumption that foreign students needed information on those words more than they did rare literary, learned, technical, or scientific words. This limitation of the wordlist entailed the need to use only those words in the definitions, hence the notion of a defining vocabulary. *ALD* did not restrict itself to a precise defining vocabulary but its definitions were couched in simple language. For example, *peach* was

(tree with) juicy round fruit with delicate yellowish-red skin and a rough stone-like seed

2. *Grammatical and syntactic information*: *ALD* gave information on the plurals of nouns, the comparatives of adjectives, irregular verbal forms and distinguished countable and uncountable nouns. It was the first dictionary to provide 'patterns' for verbal constructions by means of a coding system designed by Hornby on the basis of Palmer's *Grammar* of 1938. For example, the entry for the verb *regard* had four meanings, three of which (1, 3, and 4) were marked P 1 while number 2 was marked P10, and P10 was explained in a table in the front matter of *ALD* that said (adapted):

Pattern 10 Verbs marked P 10 may be followed by an object and an adverb or an adverb phrase (including adverbial infinitives meaning *in order to*)

	Subject × Verb	Object	Adverb, Adverb Phrase, etc.
1	*Put*	*it*	*here.*
2	*He took*	*his hat*	*off.*
3	*He has given*	*it*	*away.*
4	*Mr Smith showed*	*me*	*to the door.*
5	*We employed*	*her*	*as a cook.*
etc.			

This was certainly the most innovative feature in *ALD*, and it would be adopted by all learners' dictionaries to become a standard feature of the genre.

3. *Numerous examples*: *ALD* illustrated every meaning with at least one example, more than in any other dictionary of comparable size. All were fabricated, representing current usage rather than literary styles, clearly meant as models to imitate. They were often truncated: at *hard*, *ALD* had *to go for a hard gallop, a subject that is hard to learn, to be hard on a person, the hard discipline of army life*, and *Regular physical exercises soon make a soldier hard*, etc.

4. *A focus on phraseology*: The study of phraseology was just beginning to attract the attention of some linguists when *ALD* was published, and *ALD* recorded a great number of phrases. For example, the entry *peace* treated *make peace, at peace with, the King's peace, keep the peace, break the peace, a breach of the peace, at peace, hold one's peace, make one's peace with*.[8] It is not always easy to draw the line between phrases, i.e. groups of words in a more or less frozen form (see below, 8.2.4) and plain examples.

5. *A focus on current English*: *ALD* did not have obsolete or archaic words, and it gave the meanings of polysemous words in order of descending 'currency', estimated intuitively. For example, *bitter adj.*

1. sharp; acrid; tasting like quinine[9] 2. painful; causing sorrow; hard to bear 3. severe; filled with envy or caused by envy or hate

ALD had black ink drawings: in C, for example, there were pictures for *cabbage, cabin* (a log cabin), *cabinet* (a china cabinet), *cacao, cactus, cage, calendar, camel, cameo, camera, can* (an oil can), *canary, cancel* (cancelled stamps), *candlestick, cane chair, cannon* (and cannon-balls), *canoe, canopy, cap* (a cap on a bottle), etc., concrete nouns mostly. It indicated pronunciation in IPA.[10] *ALD* also had extensive front matter ('How to use the dictionary', 24 pages, including 14 on verb patterns), and back matter: lists ('Irregular verbs', 'Common abbreviations', 'Measures', 'Weights', 'Geographical names', 'Counties and shires', 'The United States of America', 'Ranks in the armed forces', 'Ranks in the merchant marine') and pictures ('Full-rigged sailing ship', 'Sailing dinghy', 'Motor-car (exterior)', 'Motor-car (interior)', 'Aeroplane', 'Cricket', 'Football (soccer)', 'Rugby union football (rugger)', 'Baseball', 'Music', etc.).

---

[8] *ALD2* (see below) added *a peace rally* (marked 'offensive'), *treaty of peace*, etc.

[9] Was quinine a substance that foreign learners were likely to have tasted? *ALD2* added *beer*, which is almost equally problematic if the dictionary is to be used by children.

[10] The IPA was used only in learners' dictionaries for several decades. The *OED* only began in 1989. It is now used in almost all British dictionaries, but in America only in recent learners' dictionaries.

ALD was extremely successful, because the public of students learning English was immense and growing fast, because it had virtually no competitor and because the teaching community managed to persuade everybody that it was indispensable to use a monolingual learners' dictionary.

The second edition (*ALD2*), published in 1963, fifteen years after *ALD1*, had fewer proper names, different pictures[11] and saved space by introducing the tilde, or *swung dash* (~), in place of the entry word and by nesting entries: for example, the main entry for *shock* (there were two others, for 'hair' and for 'corn') included ~ *absorber*, ~ *tactics*, ~ *troops*, ~ *brigade*, ~ *workers*, ~ *treatment*, and ~ *therapy* as well as ~*er*, ~*ing*, and ~*ingly*. The commercial success continued: 'the first two editions alone had sales of 7 million copies' (Jackson 2002: 130). The third edition, published in 1974 under the title *Oxford Advanced Learner's Dictionary of Current English* (*ALD3*) announced, for the first time, a number of entries (50,000) and of words (100,000). It unfortunately changed the order and numbering of the syntactic patterns, making things hard 'for teachers and students who had taken the trouble to memorize the patterns of the 1963 edition' (Hanks 2008: 96). It had fewer pictorial illustrations, but many of them were photographs: *cactus, camera, cannon, canoe*, etc. It also used a new system for the notation of pronunciation, but in 1978, when the *Longman Dictionary of Contemporary English* (*LDOCE1*; see below) came out, the publishers produced a revised edition with a more traditional system. The fourth edition (*ALD4*), by Anthony P. Cowie, the compiler of the two-volume *Oxford Dictionary of Current Idiomatic English* (see below), was published in 1989 after the publication of the *LDOCE1* in 1978 and *LDOCE2* and the *Collins COBUILD English Language Dictionary* (*COB1*) in 1987 (see below). It had '57,100 words and phrases', and '81,500 examples'—new ways of measuring the contents. It simplified the coding system for syntactic patterns, gave more detail on the syntax of nouns and adjectives, and put yet more emphasis on collocations. Its main innovation was that it listed phrases under all their content words, with a cross-reference to the entry where they were defined, the mark of Cowie's editorship.

ALD5 was published in 1995, the same year as *COB2*, *LDOCE3*, and the *Cambridge International Dictionary of English* (*CIDE1*; see below). It had

---

[11] Van der Meer and Sansome (2001: 286), noting that the choice of items to be illustrated varies greatly between successive editions, conclude that 'these pictures are not really an essential part of the dictionary, but rather one of its selling points, chosen at random, used to advertise...The unpredictability of their occurrence...will probably ensure that their role will remain marginal...essentially something users stumble upon rather than expecting them.'

'63,000 references'[12]—yet another unit of measure, and the words were defined by 'just under 3,000 words'. It used the BNC (100 million words at the time; see below, 9.1.7) and the Oxford American English Corpus (40 million words; see below, 9.1.7), although it is not clear how this affected the contents. It did not give frequencies. Many examples were full sentences rather than truncated phrases as in previous editions, but some were obviously invented, to show interesting collocations: at *folly*, there was '*It's utter folly to go swimming in this weather*', illustrating a meaning that is rare in the BNC, and at *torrent* '*After the winter rains, the stream becomes a raging torrent*', '*The rain was coming down in torrents*', where *ALD4* had '*raging mountain torrents*', '*rain pouring down in torrents*'. Perhaps the influence of the BNC is also in entries such as *pursue*: *ALD4* had

1 follow (sb/sth.), esp in order to catch or kill; chase ... 2 (continue to) be occupied or busy with (sth.); go on with ...

but it was changed in *ALD5*, perhaps to account for the relative frequency of the meanings, to

1 to do sth or try to achieve sth over a period of time ... 2 to continue to discuss, find out about or be involved in sth 3 to follow or chase sb/sth, especially in order to catch them ...

ALD5 changed the coding again to make it clearer: Ipr, Tn.p, etc. in *ALD4*, were now [V + adv./prep.], [VN + adv./prep.], etc. Like *LDOCE3*, *ALD5* had boxed usage notes on near synonyms or often confused words: for example, at *close v*, a note said

Close and **shut** often have the same meaning although **close** can be a quieter action: *Close/shut the door behind you* ...

Like *LDOCE*, *ALD5* listed its defining vocabulary. The word *volcano*, which had been defined in *ALD4* as

mountain or hill with an opening or openings through which lava, cinders, gases, etc., come up from below the earth's surface (*an active volcano*), may come up after an interval (*a dormant volcano*), or have ceased to come up (*an extinct volcano*)

was defined in *ALD5* as

a mountain with a large opening on the top, and sometimes others on the side, through which melted rocks and gases escape with great force, or have done so in the past

---

[12] Bogaards (1996: 282) guesses that it actually had '70,000 or 75,000 items'. A case of a dictionary having more than it claims?

Whether or not this is an improvement is another story.

ALD6 was published in 2000, after LDOCE3, COB2, and CIDE1 (see below). It had '80,000 references'[13] and '90,000 examples of language in use'. The defining vocabulary now had only 3,000 words, and some of the definitions were inspired by the definitions in COB (see below): *satisfaction*, which had been 'a feeling of pleasure because one has sth or has achieved sth' in ALD5 was now

the good feeling that you have when you have achieved sth

ALD6, like COB, also had some attitudinal labels in the definitions, as in

pass away People say 'pass away' to avoid saying 'die'

where ALD5 had '(*euph*) to die' (van der Meer and Sansome 2001: 290). The usage labels were given in full: for example, in the entry *wimp, infml derog* in ALD5 became *informal, disapproving* in ALD6. ALD6 abandoned nested entries, following the de-nesting trend started by COD9 in British dictionaries: for example, there were different entries for *shock n, shock v.* (with a sub-entry *shocked*), *shock absorber, shocker, shocking, shocking pink, shock tactics*, and *shock therapy.* As usual in such cases, some of the choices were debatable: van der Meer and Sansome (2001: 284) noted that *waste disposal* was treated in the entry *waste n.* but *waste disposal unit* was a main entry, that *mortgage rates* and *mortgage repayments* were in the entry *mortgage, interest rates* in the entry *interest* but *interest group* was a main entry. Having different entries for different POS is probably a good thing in a learner's dictionary, because 'the easiest minimum thing for a learner to inference about an unknown word is its part of speech, rather than anything of its meaning' (Scholfield 1999: 26).

Like LDOCE3 and CIDE1, ALD6 introduced short glosses in capitals for each meaning of polysemous words, which it called *short cuts*, a practice that had been introduced by ALD4 only for a handful of highly polysemous verbs. As in other dictionaries, those glosses were sometimes dangerously close to the definitions: for example, one short cut for *dead* (meaning 12) was COMPLETE/EXACT, and the definition was 'complete or exact'. Sometimes, there was no definition at all, as in *do* 2 BEHAVE. Also, some short cuts used words that were not part of the defining vocabulary, as in *mark* (noun) 10: TARGET. ALD6 also had usage boxes of different kinds, an effort to match the competition in the provision of information on usage. There were 'Grammar points', for example at *dare*

---

[13] An increase of 17,000, or 26%, over the preceding edition, really?

Dare (sense 1) usually forms negatives and questions like an ordinary verb and is followed by an infinitive with to ...

Some boxes were called 'Which word', for example, at *deep*

The adverbs **deep** and **deeply** can both mean a long way down or into something ...

Some were 'British / American', for example at *different*

Different from is the most common structure in both *BrE* and *AmE*. **Different to** is also used in *BrE* ...

Some were 'Vocabulary building', for example at *do*

Household jobs: do or **make**? To talk about jobs in the home you can use such phrases as **wash the dishes, clean the kitchen floor, set the table**, etc. In conversation the verb **do** is often used instead ...

Some boxes were called 'Word family': for example at *defy* '*defy v., defiance n.* and *defiant adj.*'. And there were 'Language study' pages: Linking words together, Collocation, Nouns and adjectives, Verbs, etc., 'Topic pages' with text and pictorial illustrations on Computing, Cooking, Health, Musical instruments, and Sport, 'Origin notes', etc. *ALD6* was available on a CD-ROM that gave access to 'lexical fields' placing each word in a network of relations with other words. In 2001, OUP declared that, all editions together, *ALD* had sold 'over 33 million copies'.[14]

   ALD7, published in 2005 after *LDOCE4* in 2000, *COB3* and *CIDE2* in 2001, and the *Macmillan English Dictionary for Advanced Learners* (*MEDAL*) in 2002 (see below), has '183,500 words, phrases and meanings', '85,000 example sentences', '7,000 synonyms and opposites', '5,000 study words', '2,000 words illustrated', etc., figures that are impossible to compare with those of the preceding edition or of the competition. Like *LDOCE4* and *MEDAL*, it distinguishes the 3,000 most important words, which are printed in larger type. It has the same array of usage boxes as *ALD6*, with information on collocations (see below, 8.2.4): for example, at *damage v*

to damage/hurt/harm/impair/prejudice sb's **health/chances**
to damage/hurt/harm/prejudice sb's **interests**
to damage/hurt/harm sb's **reputation**
to **seriously/severely/greatly/irreparably** damage etc.

Interesting collocations are also shown in bold in the examples. *ALD7* also has notes on synonyms: for example, at *damage*, the same note explicitly compares

----

[14] OUP brochure, 2001.

hurt, harm, impair, and *prejudice. ALD7* continues the race towards more information given in back matter: 8 pages in *ALD1,* 30 in *ALD2,* 33 in *ALD3,* 49 in *ALD4,* 36 in *ALD5,* 30 in *ALD6,* 94 in *ALD7. ALD* is now available online.

5.1.2 *The* Longman Dictionary of Contemporary English

The *Longman Dictionary of Contemporary English* (*LDOCE*) was launched in 1978, after *ALD3.* It was the same size, announcing 'over 55,000 entries, over 69,000 example sentences and phrases and over 100,000 pronunciations', and shared many features with its predecessor: vocabulary control, grammatical information, many examples, emphasis on phraseology, pronunciation indicated in IPA, pictures, meanings ordered by frequency, front matter and abundant back matter (Plates 20a and 20b). But it also had original points.

1. *LDOCE* coded not only verbal constructions but also nouns and adjectives: for example [S] was for 'nouns that are special singular nouns and can be used with *a* or *an* but not with *one*', Example: *Have a* **think** *about it*'; [Wa1] was for 'usually short adjectives and adverbs that form their COMPARATIVE and SUPERLATIVE in one of the following 3 ways ...', Example: **nice, nice***r***, nice***st*'. The codes were very abstract, too abstract for the user's comfort: for example, the verb *mock* was coded '[Wv4; T1; I∅ (*at*)]'.

2. *LDOCE* had usage notes on difficult points. The technique had been used for a long time in American dictionaries, beginning with Worcester, a 'very convenient tool for breaking up the alphabetical order and overcoming other formal constraints of traditional dictionary entries' (Herbst 1996a: 338), and it was later adopted by all learners' dictionaries. *LDOCE,* for example, had at the end of the entry *horse*

USAGE: Note the word order in this fixed phr.: **horse and cart:** *I'll go and get it with the horse and cart.*

3. *LDOCE* was more generous in its inclusion of American English than *ALD,* 'in terms of lexis,[15] but also of pronunciation, morphology, and even syntax' (Rundell 1998: 319). American pronunciations were based on *MWC9.*

4. Above all, *LDOCE* went one step further than *ALD* in the use of a defining vocabulary. Like West and Endicott in their *New Method English Dictionary* in 1935, it listed the words that were used in the definitions, 2,000,[16] it said,

---

[15] With the occasional mistake: *Am. fender* was *Br. bumper* instead of *wing* (Stein 2002: 37).
[16] Palmer's list had 3,000 words.

actually 2,147 words and 52 affixes, in an Appendix bizarrely called 'List of words used in the dictionary': *a, ability, able, -able, about, above, abroad, absence, absent* adj, *accept, accident,* etc. The definitions could use words that were not in the list, but those were printed in small capitals and explained. For example, *elephant* was

the largest 4-footed animal now living, with 2 long curved teeth (TUSKS) and a long nose called a TRUNK with which it can pick things up.[17]

Most of the words in the list were frequent, polysemous words and the number of meanings was far beyond 2,000: each word in the list had 'about twelve senses', and 'over 24,000 of the 74,000 senses defined in *LDOCE* are senses of these words' (Wilks *et al.* 1989: 201). But the dictionary said, rather vaguely, that only the most central meanings were used. Bogaards (1996: 289) noted that some definitions used the word *independence*, although the list contained only *depend, in-,* and *–ence.* Rundell (1998: 319) mentions the definition for *disreputable,* 'having a bad name', which used a 'non-central or (worse) idiomatic meaning' of the word *name.* But, he said, that was simply 'a bad definition', not a serious argument against the use of a defining vocabulary (see also Atkins and Rundell 2008: 449).

One problem with the use of a controlled vocabulary is that it affects the 'chain of definitions': if *cat* is defined as 'a mammal . . . ', one can look up *mammal,* etc., thus enlarging one's knowledge, but if *cat* is defined as 'an animal . . . ', the chain is short-circuited (see below, 8.2.5.3). Another, more serious, drawback of the defining vocabulary is that it sometimes forces the definers towards formulations that are stilted, unnatural or excessively simple. In *LDOCE, quail* was 'a kind of small bird', and *volcano* was

a mountain with a large opening (CRATER) at the top

This sounded like child-language.[18] In some cases, Stein (1979: 6) argues, the definitions were simply wrong. For example *bemoan* 'to be very sorry because of' missed the point, which is that *bemoan* is a 'way of *expressing* sorrow': the word cannot be used of someone who is silently sorry.[19] Of course such errors occur in all dictionaries, but in that case it may have been due to the fact that *moan* was not in the defining vocabulary (*sorrow* was).

Some metalexicographers concluded that *LDOCE*'s defining vocabulary was less useful than it appeared at first (Michiels and Noël 1984; Jansen *et al.* 1987), but most thought that all things considered it was a good idea

---

[17] Note the use of figures as a space-saving device.

[18] Compare the definition in *MWC8*: 'a vent in the planetary crust from which molten or hot rock and steam issue'. Which is better depends on who the user is and what the information is needed for.

[19] Compare the definition in *ALD3*: 'moan for, show great sorrow for'.

(Herbst 1996*a*: 324). The question was, and still is: does a defining vocabulary produce better definitions?

It has yet to be demonstrated that a limited defining vocabulary produces definitions that are easier to understand than those produced without one by conscientious lexicographers striving for simplicity, or that any limited defining vocabulary can do without supplementation by certain appropriate words ... , or that a gain in simplicity is necessarily worth the sacrifice of appropriate technical defining words ... and technical information entailed.   (Ilson 1993: 29; see below, 8.2.5)

Several studies of dictionary use have addressed this question since the publication of *LDOCE* (see below, 7.2.4.1).

 LDOCE indicated stress shifts in compounds used in discourse, in what may have been excessive and confusing detail: for example *hornet's nest* /, .ʹ .|ǀ.. ./. It had only authentic examples drawn from the Survey of English Usage (see below, 9.1). *LDOCE* tended to split the meaning of polysemous words in many subsenses, sometimes to absurd lengths: the most often quoted example is the entry for the verb *walk*, in which *LDOCE* distinguished seven different meanings, beginning with

1 (of people and creatures with 2 legs) ... 2 (of creatures with 4 legs)

Why not a special definition for creatures with six legs, some said, and one for spiders? And how about millipedes?[20]
 LDOCE had a much more analytic macrostructure[21] than *ALD*, giving entry status to homographs, compound nouns, phrasal verbs[22] and even some derived words: for example, there were separate entries for *shock absorber, shocker, shockheaded, shocking* (with *shockingly*), *shockproof, shock treatment*, and *shock troops*, and the adjectival uses of *good* were scattered over more than fifteen entries: *good book, good-humoured, good looker, good-looking, good looks, good-natured, good offices, good sense*, etc. This sometimes made it difficult to locate a word, when closely related words were separated by totally different ones, as on page 899, which had *put over, put over on, putrefaction, putrefactive, putrefy, putrescent, putrid, putsch, putt 1, putt 2, puttee, putter 1, putter 2, putter about, putter away, put through*, etc.
 LDOCE, like *ALD*, was a great commercial success, and it was the object of many review articles and papers. It was also made available on magnetic tape,

---

[20] On polysemy in *LDOCE*, see Landau (2001: 201–2).
 [21] An analytic macrostructure is a macrostructure with many short entries (see *homographic macrostructure* below, 8.2.2.1).
 [22] With the inevitable difficulties: for example, is *eat out* a phrasal verb or a special sense of *eat*?

which allowed research that had hitherto been impossible, especially as the tape had information on register, type of object, etc. that was not in the printed dictionary (see below, 9.3.1).

LDOCE2, edited by Della Summers, was published in 1987 (Carter 1989; Fillmore 1989; Hausmann and Gorbahn 1989). It had '56,000 words and phrases', '75,000 examples', many 'Language notes' on difficult points of usage and pictorial illustrations for verbs (*decorate, diffuse, dissolve*), for adjectives (*jagged*), adverbs (*just*), and prepositions (*for*). It simplified the coding of syntactic patterns and returned to a more synthetic macrostructure: for example, all the phrasal verbs with *put* were sub-entries in the entry for *put*. There was less differentiation of meanings in the treatment of polysemous words: *walk* did not have different meanings according to the number of legs. And the meanings of polysemous words were now ordered by frequency rather than by 'logic'. LDOCE2 also improved its definitions: *bemoan* was defined by

to express sorrow or disappointment because of

although *volcano* remained (almost) the same

a mountain with a CRATER (= large opening) at the top

LDOCE3, also edited by Della Summers, was published in 1995, after COB1 in 1987 and ALD4 in 1989, and the same year as COB2, ALD5, and CIDE1 (see below). It had 'over 80,000 words and phrases'.[23] It was based on the BNC and other corpora compiled by Longman (see below, 9.1.7) from which it drew 'the frequency of words in spoken and written English, British and American usage, and frequency of collocations, grammar patterns and synonyms'. There were 150 graphs comparing frequencies: for example, at *indicate*

This graph shows that **show** is much more common than **indicate** in both spoken and written English. This is because **show** is much more general in meaning and is more commonly used in informal English than **indicate**

LDOCE3 marked the 3,000 most frequent words in the margin, S1 for words that were among the 1,000 most common words in spoken English, W1 for written English, S2 or W2 for words in the 1,000–1,999 range, etc. There were 'Usage Notes' discussing near synonyms, various problem words and collocations: for example, at *war*, a graph headed 'This graph shows some of the words most commonly used with the noun **war**' compared the frequencies of *war with, win/ lose a war, fight a war, war between, war breaks out, war against, at war*, and

---

[23] Bogaards (1996: 282) says 'between 90,000 and more than 100,000 lexical units'.

nuclear war (in that order), 'all of this ... potentially valuable for language production' (Rundell 1999: 46). Examples were a mixture of authentic and invented sentences: at *torrent,* '*After five days of heavy rain the Telle river was a raging torrent*', at *neat* '*The new lodger was fortunately a neat person*', etc. The grammatical notation was simplified again (Aarts 1999): for example, *indoor,* which had been noted *adj* [A] in *LDOCE2,* sending the user back to page F40, which explained that [A] stood for 'Used only before the noun it describes', now had '*adj* [only before noun]' in the entry. Homographs were grouped in the same entries by POS, perhaps under the influence of *COB* (see below): there was only one entry for *bank n.* or *bay n. LDOCE3* avoided parentheses in its definitions: one meaning of *save,* which had been 'to make unnecessary (for)' in previous editions became

to help someone by making it unnecessary for them to do something unpleasant or inconvenient

in *LDOCE3* (Rundell 1999: 43). Some of the definitions were in the style of *COB* (see below): *neigh* was 'if a horse neighs, it makes a long loud noise', and *dainty* was 'dainty movements are small and careful' (Herbst 1996a: 326); *exclusive,* which had been defined by '1 that excludes people considered to be socially unsuitable and charges a lot of money' in *LDOCE2*,[24] was now

1 exclusive places, organizations, clothes, etc are so expensive that not many people can afford to use or buy them

Pain, defined by 'suffering; great discomfort of the body or mind' in *LDOCE2* was defined in *LDOCE3* by 'the feeling you have when part of your body hurts' (Rundell 1998: 332).[25] When necessary, *LDOCE3* defined patterns rather than words:

Compare the open-ended 'meaning' at **spot**[1] 6 in *LDOCE1*: 'an area of mind or feelings: *I have a soft spot for my old school*' with the treatment in *LDOCE3, COBUILD2* [*COB2*; see below] and *ALD5,* all of which (correctly) focus on the typical instantiation of this meaning in the phrase **have a soft spot for.**   (Rundell 1998: 338)[26]

LDOCE3 used glosses, called *signposts* (the *short cuts* of ALD6, later called *Guide words* in *CIDE*), for the meanings of polysemous words, and each meaning started a new line. The signposts were printed in bold small capitals: for example,

---

[24] Neither *exclude* nor *socially,* or *unsuitable* were in the defining vocabulary; *include, social,* and *suitable* were.

[25] And *hurt* was defined by *pain,* a case of circularity (see below, 8.2.5.3).

[26] There was already an entry for *soft spot* in *LDOCE1* and *LDOCE2.*

the entry *indicate* had six signposts: 1 FACTS, 2 POINT AT, 3 YOUR WISHES/ INTENTIONS, 4 A SIGN FOR, 5 IN A CAR, and 6 TREATMENT. In addition to this, *LDOCE3* also had 'menus' at the beginning of some of the longer entries, with 'super signposts', the main headings: for example, the entry *place* had a menu of five super signposts:

1 PLACE, POSITION, OR AREA	4 FIRST/SECOND PLACE
2 TAKE PLACE	5 OTHER MEANINGS
3 IN PLACE	

Each of these headed a group of meanings, and in each group the meanings were headed by their signposts. Here the first menu item, 1 PLACE, POSITION, OR AREA, commanded a group of seven meanings: 1 POINT/POSITION, 2 PLACE FOR DOING STH, 3 BUILDING / TOWN / COUNTRY ETC, 4 SB'S HOUSE, etc. Both the signposts and the menus were useful innovations,[27] and they are now used in other dictionaries, particularly electronic dictionaries where the amount of text that the user can see is limited by the screen and a summary of the entry is helpful. But they were criticized, because they assume that the users have some idea of the meaning of the word they are looking for, because they are heterogeneous in nature (collocates, synonyms, hypernyms, names of domain, etc.) and because many of them use very frequent, highly polysemous words that are 'sometimes too ambiguous or vague to facilitate effective searching' (Rundell 1998: 327).

LDOCE4 was published in 2000, the same year as *ALD6*. It has '106,000 words and phrases' and '220,000 word combinations'—yet another unit of measure. It continues the traditions of the half-invented, half-authentic examples, the defining vocabulary, the usage notes, and the signposts but has abandoned the menus, which in the meantime have been adopted by *MEDAL* (see below). The 3,000 most important words of its wordlist are printed in red, the others in blue. It introduced a new type of definition for some nouns, the 'single clause *when*-definition', as in

planned obsolescence 'when a product is deliberately made so that it will soon be replaced ... '

or

sensitivity 'when someone is easily upset or offended by things that people say'

---

[27] It is not clear whether signposts were invented by *LDOCE* or by *CIDE*. Menus had been used in Japanese and Korean dictionaries before, Atkins and Rundell (2008: 204) write.

This was based on folk definitions, used to explain the meaning of words, especially by adults to children,[28] and perhaps on the operational definitions used by scientists (see below, 8.2.5.1), and it had been used by lexicographers before, as in Cawdrey's *Table Alphabeticall* (1604):

homonimie 'when divers things are signified by one word'

But it has not been generally adopted (Atkins and Rundell 2008: 444). *LDOCE4* was made available online. *LDOCE5*, published in 2009, gives access to a DVD-ROM with thousands of additional examples and collocations.

5.1.3 *The* Collins COBUILD English Language Dictionary

The *Collins COBUILD English Language Dictionary* (*COB*) was compiled by a group of lexicographers working in Birmingham under the direction of John Sinclair and published in 1987, the same year as *LDOCE2*.[29] It had 'over 70,000 references' and had been prepared with the help of the computer: 'What makes *COB* especially remarkable is that the compilation process for COBUILD used the computer in all the four traditional lexicographic stages of data-collecting, entry-selection, entry construction and entry arrangement' (Ooi 1998: 33). It used a corpus that was the joint property of Collins and of the University of Birmingham, 20 million words by the time the dictionary was finished (see below, 9.1.7). The front flap said that it had been 'specially developed for learners and teachers of English', and it did have some features of the learner's dictionary, a limited wordlist, meanings arranged by frequency, coding of syntactic patterns, etc. (Plate 19). But it differed from *ALD* and *LDOCE* in many ways: it did not have a list of words used in the definitions; it did not have any usage boxes, pictures, or addenda—not even linguistic ones, not even a list of irregular verbs. Its most interesting features were the following.

1. *COB* was the first dictionary to draw all its headwords and examples from an electronic corpus: it was 'the very first study in corpus-driven lexicography' (Tognini-Bonelli 2001: 85; see below, 9.1.4.2). Its examples were taken from the

---

[28] On folk definitions, see Iris *et al.* (1988), Richards and Taylor (1992).

[29] COBUILD, for Collins Birmingham University International Language Database, was a department of HarperCollins Publishers specializing in the preparation of reference works for language learners in English. It was based at the University of Birmingham. Throughout the 1980s, following the computational, corpus-based approach to language analysis of John Sinclair, COBUILD developed a large corpus of modern English as well as software tools to manipulate and analyse the corpus data, and trained a team of corpus linguists and lexicographers. (Sweeney Linden, personal communication, 13 June 2000).

corpus, with only minor adaptations (Fox 1987: 138), especially for length or 'to remove distracting, obscure or possibly offensive elements' (Potter 1998: 357). This ensured their authenticity, which is why the dust jacket said that *COB* would help learners 'with real English'—'perhaps on the analogy of "real ale"' (McArthur 1998: 147). It was actually a reaction against the invented, often stilted, examples of other dictionaries: 'Using invented examples is like fixing a horse race: the lexicographer invents an example to justify his definition instead of devising a definition to fit the examples' (Landau 2001: 210).[30] But the *COB* technique also had its unfortunate consequences. Some examples hardly made sense out of their original contexts, or were useless: meaning **6** of *every* was illustrated by '*One woman in every two hundred is a sufferer*' (Hausmann and Gorbahn 1989: 46); *gravitate* was illustrated by '*He gravitated naturally to New-market*' (Rundell 1998: 335) and *topsy-turvy* by '*That's rather a topsy-turvy way of looking at things*'.

2. *COB*'s macrostructure grouped all homographs in the same entries, as if the dictionary had been designed only for elucidating isolated, context-free forms, which was strange in a dictionary that laid such emphasis on words in context. For example, there was only one entry for the form *w i n d*, that began

wind, winds, winding, winded, wound. The word **wind** is pronounced /wɪnd/ for paragraphs 1–10 and /waɪnd/ for paragraphs 11–13 and the phrasal verbs. **Winded** is the past tense and past participle of the verbs in paragraphs 4 and 6, and **wound** is the past tense and past participle of the verbs in paragraphs 11–13 and the phrasal verbs. 1. A **wind** is a current of air . . .

This was probably meant to facilitate consultation, but it rested on the (false) assumption that the users know nothing of the word they are looking up.

3. The syntactic patterns of verbs, nouns, and adjectives which, Sinclair (1987b: 114) said, provided 'a link between the broad generalities of grammar and the individualities of particular words', were given in coded form in a special column to the right of the main text, so that they did not clutter it. The code used only abbreviations that were easy to understand: ADV, PREP, VB, ADJ, AFTER, -ING, etc., and all the metalinguistic labels were included in their proper alpha-betical place in the macrostructure and defined: '*to-INF*, for instance, comes between *toilet water* and *to-ing and fro-ing*' (Ilson 1992: 276). But the system was

---

[30] In fact, invented examples are usually based on actual usages and corpus examples are usually adapted for use in a dictionary, so that the distinction between the two types is 'somewhat blurred' (Atkins and Rundell 2008: 457). The best treatment of examples is in Atkins and Rundell (2008: 328 *ff*. and 453 *ff*.). See also Drysdale (1987) and Humblé (2001).

still criticized for being too complex (Carter 1989: 36): for example, verbs such as *cook* were coded V-ERG, for 'ergative'.

4. Because it was based on a corpus, *COB* indicated the most frequent, common patterns in which every word was used, which probably explains why the dust jacket said that *COB* would help learners 'with real English'.

5. *COB* also used the extra column to indicate the lexical relations of the headword (synonyms, antonyms, or hypernyms) in coded form: for example, for *gravel* the extra column had '⇑ stone' (where the ⇑ means *hypernym*), for *gravestone* '⇑ monument', '= headstone' (where = means *synonym*), for *poor* '≠ rich' (where ≠ means *antonym*).

6. The most innovative feature of *COB* was its definitions, which were based on Sinclair's work on the idiomaticity of language (see below, 8.2.6.3) and probably inspired by the study of folk definitions. Instead of the traditional verbless formulae, they were complete sentences in which the word to be defined was used in a typical pattern and accompanied by its typical collocates, 'as though the dictionary were answering its users' question "What does this word mean?"' (Atkins and Rundell 2008: 38). The definitions, called *FSDs* for *full sentence definitions*, were in two parts: to the left was the entry word in a typical context, and to the right a defining phrase that reformulated the contents of the first half. Such definitions underline a distinction that is always present, though rarely mentioned, between the unit of treatment and the unit of classification in a dictionary: the unit of classification in *COB* is the graphic word, for obvious practical reasons, but the unit that is defined in the entry is the pattern in which it is normally used. There were various formulations according to the character-istics of the word to be defined (Hanks 1987). For nouns one finds:

- an X is a ... : 'A **passageway** is a long, narrow space ... ';
- if someone V + X, you/they ... : 'If someone gives you a **pasting**, they criticize you severely ... ';
- if you are a X, ... you ... : 'If you are a **past master** at something, you are very skilful at it ... ';
- your X is ... : 'Your **pate** is the top of your head ... ';
- if someone has X, ... : 'If a man has **paternity leave**, his employer allows him some time off work ... '.

For adjectives:

- someone who is X + V ... : 'Someone who is **passionate** expresses very strong feelings ... '.

- an X + N is: '**Pastel** colours are pale, light and soft ... ';
- if something is X, it is ... : 'If something is **patchy**, it is not spread evenly ... '.

For verbs:

- to X someone means to ... : 'To **bewitch** someone or something means to cast a spell ... '.
- if you X something, you ... : 'If you **passivize** a verb or a structure that contains a verb, you make the verb passive'.
- when something is Xed, ... : 'When milk or cream is **pasteurized**, bacteria are removed from it'.
- someone who Xs ... : 'Someone who **peddles** goods goes from place to place selling small objects ... '.

COB also used metalinguistic formulations such as 'If you say X you mean Y', 'If you refer to someone as X, you mean Y', or 'X is a word ... ',[31] clearly a 'définition de mot', for words like *abject, ablutions, actually, blues, deep, bridal, rascal,* etc. Of course, any association of the pronoun *you* with disagreeable things or actions was avoided, for example for verbs like *kill,* or *rob,* or *strangle*: a definition beginning 'If you **strangle** someone ... ' 'could conceivably be read as carrying the implication that in the English-speaking world it is acceptable to go around strangling people. "When you **strangle** someone ... " is even worse: it sounds as if we do it every day!' (Hanks 1987: 126). Yet the definition for *electrocute* was 'If you **electrocute** yourself, or if you **are electrocuted** ... ', and the definition for *steal* began 'If you **steal** something from someone ... ' (Barnbrook 2002: 7–9). The reasons for the choice of a particular formulation are not clear (Rundell 2006: 333).

FSDs were presented as revolutionary by the compilers, but they had been used before. Osselton (1991: 316) notes that some (not many) of the definitions in Florio's *Worlde of Wordes*, published in 1598, remind the reader 'of defining techniques recently introduced in the *Collins COBUILD English Language Dictionary*': for example

Ancheggiare, is when a horse doth coruet with a quicke time, carying himself altogither vpon his hanches

Rundell (2006: 324) found similar examples in Bailey's *Dictionarium Britannicum* (1730):

---

[31] Fillmore (1989: 63) noted that *cunt* was defined by 'a **cunt** is a very rude and offensive word that refers to a woman's vagina', admittedly a mistake by an individual lexicographer rather than a problem with the method—other taboo words were satisfactorily defined.

TRANSCENDENTAL *Curves* [in the *higher Geometry*] are such as cannot be defined by Algebraical Equations, or which, when expressed by Equations, one of their Terms is a variable of flowing Quantity

In France, the technique was used in the *Dictionnaire de l'Académie* (Lehmann 2002: 79):

On dit qu'*un homme*, qu'*un cheval est en nage, tout en nage*, pour dire qu'il est tout trempé, tout mouillé de sueur[32]

It was also used in some children's dictionaries, as in *Petit Robert des enfants* (1988), which defined *saboter* by

Saboter une chose, c'est l'abîmer pour qu'on ne puisse plus s'en servir[33]

The *COB* compilers claimed that FSDs were better than traditional definitions for reception because complete sentences are easier to understand than the traditional formulae, and for expression because they provide the users with models to imitate (Hanks 1987: 117). FSDs certainly account for the idiomaticity of language (see below, 8.2.6.3): they pay 'due attention to the idiomatic character of language in an excellent and unsurpassed manner' (Herbst 1996a: 336). According to Rundell (2006: 334), they work well with intransitive verbs, 'where it is critical to specify the typical range of *subjects*': 'if an agreement, offer, or official document **expires** … '; with reflexive verbs: 'if a country **allies** itself with another country … '; with transitive verbs in the passive: 'if someone is **apprenticed** to another person … '; with adjectives where the range of typical complements is narrow: '**blistering** criticism is very severe'; and with adjectives suggesting a permanent characteristic: 'someone who is **argumentative** … '. They also work with collocations and idioms (see below, 8.2.4) like *treat someone* or *something with kid gloves*, or *give them the kid glove treatment*, and generally speaking with all words whose meaning depends on the context and for which the number of possible contexts is limited. But they are not very good at defining the names of realia, and with function words they are no better than traditional definitions: 'with respect to function words, neither *Cobuild*'s lexicogrammatical definitions nor more traditional lexical definitions can be understood readily without examples' (Landau 2001: 118). And FSDs run into problems when a word is used in many contexts. If they give only one, they run the risk of what Rundell (2006: 327) calls *overspecification*: defining *innocence* by

If someone proves their **innocence**, they prove that they are not guilty of a crime

---

[32] 'One says that *a man*, that *a horse is in a sweat, all in a sweat*, to say that he or it is all wet with sweat'.
[33] 'To sabotage a thing is to destroy it so that nobody can use it'.

seems to indicate that *innocence* is used preferably, or exclusively, in a context of 'proving', which is not true: 'should the user infer that this is the only (or overwhelmingly) most frequent collocate, or simply one of many typical collocates?' (Rundell 2006: 331). But if the definition tries to pack all possible contexts into one formulation, it becomes cumbersome. Fillmore (1989: 59) compares the treatment of *rhyme v.* in *COB* and in *LDOCE2*:

LDOCE2: (with) (of words or lines of poetry) to end with the same sound, including a vowel.
COB: if one word **rhymes** with another, or if two words **rhyme**, they have a very similar sound.

Even disregarding the fact that the *COB* definition is so vague as to be almost wrong, it is clear that *LDOCE2* has more information, and that for *COB* to have the same amount of information would have required an awkward formulation. The compilers often chose the latter solution. Hausmann and Gorbahn (1989: 48) mention part of the entry *throw v.*:

11 If something **throws** a person or thing into a particular situation or state, especially an unpleasant one, it suddenly causes them to be in that situation or state.

There are many other examples, where the pronouns make the definition difficult to understand (Rundell 2006: 328):

3 If circumstances **condemn** someone to an unpleasant situation, those circumstances make it certain they will suffer in a particular way.

The use of *etc.* is not easy to interpret either: *hackles* 2 says

The **hackles** of a dog, cat, etc. are the hairs on the back of its neck, which rise when the animal is angry

Can *hackles* be used of a wolf, a horse, a hamster, a budgerigar? True, traditional definitions do not do any better, but FSDs may be more misleading, because their user is led to expect the usual context of use in the definition. On the whole, despite their shortcomings, FSDs have been very popular and have been adopted by many dictionaries, at least for some of their definitions.

7. *COB* included connotative value and usage restrictions in the definitions instead of using labels. For example:

Damn, damn you, damn it, and **dammit** are swear words which people sometimes use to express anger or annoyance

Regional varieties were indicated as in *pavement*:

In British English a path with a hard surface by the side of a street

8. *COB* arranged entries by meaning rather than by POS: for example, the entry for *conduct* had 1 verb ('conduct an activity'), 2 noun ('the conduct of an activity'), 3 noun ('someone's conduct'), 4 verb ('conduct oneself'), etc. But this is very difficult for words that have many meanings, and there were several departures from the principle: sub-entry 4 of *head* is 'head of a company' but the verb *to head* a company is only sub-entry 17.

9. *COB* used the IPA and a coding system that was 'probably the most intricate system publicly offered to foreign learners in the 101 years since the IPA was formed' (McArthur 1998: 147), with bold type and superscript numbers.

COB was very successful, like the other major learners' dictionaries, although it was distinctively different. It was not always easy to use—was this a consequence of the fact that it was the only learner's dictionary to have been compiled partly by academics (McArthur 1998: 147)?—but it was innovative and stimulating.

A second edition, called *Collins COBUILD English Dictionary* (*COB2*), still under the direction of Sinclair (with Gwyneth Fox), was published in 1995, the same year as *ALD5*, *LDOCE3*, and *CIDE1*. It had 'over 75,000 references' and was based on the BoE (see below, 9.1.7), which had about 200 million words at the time. The 100,000 odd examples were still taken from the corpus, but they were more carefully edited than in *COB1*. Like *COB1*, *COB2* had no pictures and no cultural addenda; it treated in different entries words that are identical in form but unconnected in meaning (homonyms): for example *wind* had two different entries; it grouped sub-entries by meaning; it had no precise defining vocabulary, although it said that the words used in its definitions were 'among the 2,500 commonest words of English' (xviii); it had an extra column giving syntactic patterns as well as synonyms, antonyms, and hypernyms; and it defined words in FSDs, in 'the sort of direct and informal style that teachers use when explaining words, or that friends use talking with each other' (xviii). Like *LDOCE3* but in a different way, it indicated the frequency of words: it had five filled or unfilled diamonds ♦, ◇, five black diamonds for the 700 most frequent words, four for the range 700–1,900, three for 1,900–3,400, two for 3,400–6,600 and one for 6,600–14,700.[34] The frequencies of patterns and usages were also given in the extra column: *usu* for very frequent patterns, *oft* for

---

[34] With strange results, as is inevitable in a corpus, however carefully assembled (see below, 9.1.3): Kilgarriff (1997*a*: 150) notes that '*thirteen, fourteen, seventeen* and *eighteen* have five diamonds, *fifteen* and *nineteen*, four and *sixteen*, two'.

relatively frequent, *also* for less frequent ones: for example, *lock* ('of hair') was 'usu N *of n*', *log* ('piece of wood') was 'oft N *n*' and *lock* ('something away') was 'V *n* P, Also V P *n* (not pron)'. *COB2* was offered as a CD-ROM that contained a thesaurus, a grammar, a usage manual, and a 'Wordbank' of 5 million items from the BoE, an approach that has been criticized: 'the rationale ... seems to have been roughly "Stick all the products we already have on a cd-rom and let's hope somebody can find a use for it"' (Seedhouse 1997, in Nesi 2000*b*: 841).

COB3 was published in 2001, after *ALD6* and *LDOCE4* in 2000 and the same year as *CIDE2*, under the title *Collins COBUILD English Dictionary for Advanced Learners*, acknowledging at last its main objective. It replaced the pragmatic information contained in the definitions of *COB* and *COB2* by more traditional labels, but kept the other features that had made it a success. *COB4* was published in 2003 with a title that was changed again to *Collins COBUILD Advanced Learner's English Dictionary*. *COB5* was published in 2006, with colour illustrations, and *COB6* in 2008, simply called *Collins COBUILD Advanced Dictionary*.

5.1.4 *The* Cambridge International Dictionary of English

The *Cambridge International Dictionary of English* (*CIDE*), compiled under the direction of Paul Procter, who had been the editor of *LDOCE1* in 1978, was published in 1995, the same year as *COB2*, *ALD5*, and *LDOCE3*. It had '100,000 words and phrases arranged alphabetically under 50,000 headwords'[35] and 'more than 100,000 example sentences' (Plate 21). It used the Cambridge Language Survey, at the time 100 million words (see below, 9.1.7), but did not say clearly how this affected the contents. Procter (*Foreword*) mentions collocation (see below, 8.2.4): '*Rain* is *heavy* rather than *strong*, *tea* is *strong* rather than *powerful*, *frosts* are *hard* rather than *fierce*'. But the dictionary does not list collocations explicitly or give frequencies. Examples are complete sentences, obviously more invented than authentic: at *tune*, '*That tune really brings back memories*', at *notice*, '*Mary waved at the man but he didn't seem to notice*'. *CIDE* was particularly good in its coverage of varieties of English and of idioms, following the trend of other learners' dictionaries. Like its competitors, it gave grammatical information, here in a mixture of coded symbols and complete or abbreviated labels and formulations: for example, *regard v.* had '*obj* ... [T always + adv/prep]', where *obj* and T both mean transitive (why?) and 'always + adv/prep' is self-explanatory. Like the other learners' dictionaries published in the same year except *COB2*, *CIDE* used a

---

[35] Probably only 70,000 or 75,000 according to Bogaards (1996: 232).

defining vocabulary of about 2,000 words, which are listed in an Appendix, with indications of which meanings of polysemous words are used. It had a small number of black and white pictures, including some that compared near synonyms: for example, there was a picture comparing *boil, fry, deep-fry, steam,* and *broil*. *CIDE* had a few usage notes called 'Language Portraits', for example at *get* ('"Get", "have", and other verbs used to mean "cause"'), or at *holiday* ('Holidays and special days in Britain and the US'). Like *LDOCE3*, it used short glosses for the meanings of polysemous words, here called *guidewords* (*short cuts* in *ALD6* and *signposts* in *LDOCE3*). As usual, those were criticized: Herbst (1996*a*: 350) noted that the guideword for the sense of *pit* in *orchestra pit* was HOLE: 'it is very doubtful whether a user would look for *orchestra pit* under a guide word "HOLE"'. *CIDE* had a fair number of FSDs, even for concrete nouns: for instance (Herbst 1996*a*: 326), *cream tea* was defined by

A **cream tea** is a light meal of SCONES (= a type of bread) with JAM (= a sweet soft substance made by cooking fruit with sugar) and cream

Other definitions were more traditional: *bemoan* was 'to complain about or express sadness because of'.[36] *CIDE*'s original features were:

1. An analytic macrostructure: whether etymologically related or not, mean-ings were treated in different entries: for example, *ear* had two entries, BODY PART and PLANT PART, *shock* had four, one for SURPRISE, one for OFFEND, one for DAMAGING EFFECT, and one for HAIR, etc. Within the entries, nuances of meaning were not numbered, just signalled by a bullet point, often without a definition. For example, at *gap*:

an empty space or opening in the middle of something or between two things ● *The children squeezed through a gap* **in** *the wall* ● *She has a small gap* **between** *her front teeth* ● (*fig.*) *There is a gap* (= something missing) **in** *the magazine market that needs to be filled* ● (*fig.*) *The gap* **between** *rich and poor is still widening* (= the difference between them is becoming greater). ● etc.

This, van der Meer (1999: 195–6) notes, unfortunately separates the meanings of the same word as if they were homonyms.

[*CIDE*] gives *flak* ('OPPOSITION') and *flak* ('FIRING OF GUNS') two separate 'guidewords', thus creating the impression that the two meanings are semantically unrelated. The CIDE treatment of *flak* does not differ from that of real homonyms like *bud* 'PLANT PART' and *bud* 'MAN', or homonyms like *bear* 'ANIMAL' and *bear* 'CARRY'.

---

[36] Wrong again: to 'express sadness because of' something is not always to bemoan something.

Because of its type of macrostructure, *CIDE* had only one guideword per entry.

2. An alphabetical index listing all the words (about 30,000 in tiny type fit for young eyes) used in the phrases and idioms treated in the dictionary, with a reference to the appropriate entry—it 'has perhaps gone to extremes in that it is even possible for the user to locate *make something of it* by looking up *it*, and *screw up* by looking up *up!*' (Scholfield 1999: 21).

3. Lists of 'false friends' in fourteen languages, including Japanese and Korean, taken from the Cambridge Learner Corpus (see below, 9.1.7), a feature that was 'completely new on the market' (Herbst 1996*a*: 338), hence the *International* in its title.

On the whole, *CIDE* was found to be the more demanding of the four big learners' dictionaries of the time. It was made available on a CD-ROM in 1999.

In 2001, *CIDE* was replaced by the *Cambridge Advanced Learner's Dictionary* (*CIDE2*) which had restyled pictorial illustrations, pages of colour pictures, usage notes about common mistakes and collocations, information on frequency, and numbered meanings in polysemous entries, confirming the impression that learners' dictionaries are converging towards a single model. *CIDE2* was made available online. A third edition was published in 2008, with a CD-ROM that runs on Mac (*CIDE3*).

5.1.5 *The* Macmillan English Dictionary

The *Macmillan English Dictionary for Advanced Learners* (*MEDAL*) entered the stage in 2002, after *ALD6* and *LDOCE4* (2000) and *COB3* and *CIDE2* (2001). It was compiled by a team of lexicographers headed by Rundell, who had worked on *LDOCE*, and Fox, who had worked on *COB*. It was based on the World English Corpus and a special corpus of learner productions (see below, 9.1.7), although it did not say clearly how this influenced the dictionary text. Its examples were part phrases, part full sentences, more invented than authentic: for example at *torrent*, '*They were swept away by the raging torrent*'. Meanings were ordered by frequency: *bastard* was

1 an insulting word for an unpleasant or annoying man 2 used after an adjective for talking to or about someone in a funny or sympathetic way 3 something that is very difficult or annoying 4 someone whose parents are not married to each other

It had 'over 100,000 references' drawn from the corpus. Like its predecessors, it gave its defining vocabulary, 2,500 words, but without any indication of word class, so that it was impossible to know what *record* or *smoke* stood for. It did not have short glosses for the meanings of polysemous words, but had word menus for lexical, not function, words with at least five meanings. For example *guarantee*:

1 make sth happen
2 promise sth
3 agree to repair/replace

4 pay money sb else owes
5 protect against harm

Like *LDOCE4*, it used a 'dual-track approach': the more important words, those that are needed for expression as well as for reception (*cap, capability, capable, capacity, capital, capitalism*, etc.), were printed in red, with a number of red stars indicating their frequency, and were given full treatment, with examples; the others, those that are necessary only for reception, were printed in black and treated more briefly (Plate 22). For example, *flap n.* had one red star, *flash v.* had two, *flat adj.* three but *flapjack, flashback, flask*, and *flatbed* were all black. As in *CIDE*, encoding information was given in a mixture of clear and coded language: for example, *regard v.* had [T] for transitive and *regard* 1 had '[not usually progressive]'. Some definitions were in *COB* style: *lonely* was '1 unhappy because you are alone ...'. But *grumble* was 'to complain, especially continuously ...'. Like other learners' dictionaries, *MEDAL* had several sorts of boxes on various linguistic points. Some provided encyclopedic information: for example, at the entry *babel*, the box said

From the story in the Bible of the 'tower of Babel'. When people tried to build this tower to reach heaven, God punished them by making it impossible for them to understand each other's language.

There were boxes comparing synonyms, here called 'Other ways of saying': at the entry *beautiful* the box gave *attractive, good-looking, handsome, pretty, gorgeous, striking*, and *cute*, all defined contrastively—even though the definitions were not the same as in the entries. There were boxes explaining how function words and some highly common words can be used. For example, at *because*:

Because can be used in the following ways:
as a **conjunction** (connecting two clauses): *We went by bus because it was cheaper.*
in the preposition phrase **because of** (followed by a noun): *The game was cancelled because of the snow.*

Boxes called 'Talking and writing about ... ' provided related words and phrases: for example, at *baby*, the note had *unborn child, foetus, newborn, infant, pregnancy, be having a baby, going to have a baby, be expecting, antenatal, etc.*, with definitions—although the entries for those words did not direct the reader to the boxes. 'Words that avoid giving offence', for example, at *black*, said

Use the adjective **black** (sometimes spelt **Black**) to refer to people with dark skin whose families originally came from Africa. Avoid using **black** as a noun because this is sometimes considered offensive, etc.

'Differences between British and American English', for example at *bathroom*, said

In the UK, **bathroom** usually means a room with a bath, a BASIN to wash your hands in, and sometimes a toilet. In the US, a bathroom may have a bath in it, but when American speakers ask to go to the **bathroom** they usually mean they want to use the toilet. In the UK, you would just ask to go to the toilet.

'Ways of . . . ' gave advice on pragmatic questions: for example, the box at *apologize* said

I'm sorry   the usual way of apologizing to someone you know well
I do apologize for . . .   a more polite and formal way of apologizing, etc.

'Academic writing' gave advice on how to write papers: for example, at *compare*, the box said

You often need to link two points, ideas, or situations by comparing them, and indicating that the second is similar to or different from the first . . .

MEDAL had a section called 'Language awareness', on such points of usage as Numbers, Phrasal verbs, Computer words, Spoken discourse, etc. It had illustrations, including 16 pages of pictures on House, Kitchen, Office, Car, Transport, Trees, etc.

   MEDAL's main original points were:

   1. It was published in a British and in an American edition—a first in learners' dictionaries.

   2. It was prepared with WordSketch, a software program designed to draw the 'portrait' of each word (see below, 9.1.6), a first in the compilation of a commercial dictionary.

   3. It had a few proper names: *Eastwood, Clint, Ebola, Edinburgh Festival, EFTA, Elastoplast, El Dorado, Emerald Isle, English Channel*, etc. *MEDAL* does not say how they were chosen.

4. It had minimal coding of syntactic patterns, no doubt a 'deliberate policy' (Hanks 2008: 105), confirming the evolution of all learners' dictionaries.

5. It gave detailed information on frequent collocations. It had boxes called 'Words frequently used with ... ': for example at *background*, the box gave *cultural, disadvantaged, educational, ethnic, middle-class, privileged*, etc. Collocations were also given in some entries, after a diamond: for example, *background* 2 had ◆ *background information / knowledge / reading / material*. Boxes called 'Words you can use instead of ... ' also provided collocations: they showed how the same idea can be expressed by different words according to the context. For example, the note at *bad* showed that *atrocious, awful, terrible, appalling, lousy* (informal) can be used with *meal, film, TV show, weather, behaviour*, etc., that *nasty, unpleasant, horrible, wicked* can be used with *person*, etc. This was unrivalled in other learners' dictionaries.

6. *MEDAL* had 'metaphor boxes', its most original feature. The boxes, prepared by Rosamund Moon, who had worked on *COB*, portrayed about forty families of common metaphors after the model of Lakoff and Johnson (1980), a timid introduction of cognitive linguistics into lexicography (Moon 2004*a*). For example there was a box at the entry *conversation*, headed by 'A conversation or discussion is like a **journey**, with the speakers going from one place to another'. It said:

Let's **go back** *to what you were saying earlier.* ◆ *Can we* **return** *to the previous point?* ◆ *I can't quite see where you're* **heading**. ◆ *The conversation took an unexpected* **turn/direction** ◆ *I'm listening—Go on.* ◆ *We've* **covered** *a lot of* **ground**, etc.

MEDAL2 was published in 2007. It has 'Get It Right' boxes on frequent errors, discursive sections on 'key writing functions' (Comparing and contrasting, Expressing cause and effect, Introducing a concession, etc.), exercises, personal notes, and an amazing array of extra information on usage, frequency comparisons between a corpus of academic English and a corpus of learner English, direct access to various Internet sites, etc.

To sum up, more than twenty editions of the main five learners' dictionaries have been published since 1948. Each had several editions, *ALD* being the slowest and *COB* the fastest. All have also been produced in smaller, cheaper versions for less advanced students called *elementary, intermediate, student's, essential*, or a variety of more imaginative names: the *Longman Active Study Dictionary of English* (1983; '38,000 words and phrases'), the *Oxford Wordpower Dictionary*, etc.

5.2 OTHER DICTIONARIES FOR FOREIGN LEARNERS

5.2.1 Learners' dictionaries in America and elsewhere

The first dictionaries for foreign learners to be marketed in the USA were British, but they did not sell very well. They were felt to be too British, and too much oriented towards EFL students, where the American market required dictionaries for students of English as a second language (ESL). British publishers began producing American adaptations of their dictionaries in the 1980s: the *Oxford Student's Dictionary of American English* was published in 1983, the *Oxford ESL Dictionary for Students of American English*, based on *ALD4*, was published in 1991 and the *Oxford American Wordpower Dictionary* in 1998. The *Longman Active Study Dictionary of English* had an American edition called the *Longman Dictionary of American English* (1983, 1997), described by Landau (2001: 76) as 'the first corpus-based, soundly edited ESL dictionary giving extensive coverage to American English', based on a Longman corpus (see below, 9.1.7) and employing the Longman defining vocabulary of about 2,000 words. The *Longman Interactive American Dictionary* (1997) introduced itself as 'the first interactive American dictionary', because it came with a CD-ROM containing human voice pronunciations as well as video clips and exercises with human voice responses and encouragement. Cambridge published the *Cambridge Dictionary of American English*, edited by Sydney Landau, in 2000. The *Longman Advanced American Dictionary*, adapted from *LDOCE3*, came out in 2000. Collins produced the *COBUILD Advanced Dictionary of American English* (2007).

American publishers began producing their own learners' dictionaries in the 1990s. The *Newbury House Dictionary of American English*, 1996, 'more than 40,000 entries', with a 'new edition every year' (Landau 2001: 399), was 'the first learner's dictionary developed from an American vocabulary base' (*Foreword*: vii). It was followed by the *Random House Webster's Dictionary of American English*, 1997, 'over 50,000 entries', based on the *Random House Webster's College Dictionary*, a first according to Ilson (1998: 228): 'no learners' dictionary has ever before been made by adapting a native-speaker dictionary'. The *American Heritage English as a Second Language Dictionary* (1998), was 'adapted from the *American Heritage Student Dictionary*' and *AHD*. American publishers have now become very active: in 1999, there were 'more US publishers than British ones committed to the production of learners' dictionaries! That state of affairs was unthinkable (though not unwishable) only a few short years ago' (Ilson 1999a: 236). Even Merriam-Webster has now entered the field, with the *Merriam*

Webster's Advanced Learner's English Dictionary, published in 2008. It is not particularly innovative, except that it has a dedicated website.

American learners' dictionaries have not been spared by reviewers. They came late, were smaller and less sophisticated than the Big Five, and were less innovative, tending to remain close to native-speaker dictionaries in their wordlists or defining styles. Also, because they are 'for ESL learners in America rather than for the potentially huger EFL market abroad' (Ilson 1998: 228), they tend to keep to General American and to neglect other varieties of English (Ilson 1999*a*: 225), while British learners' dictionaries have tried to capture wider markets. Ilson questions their usefulness (Ilson 1999*a*: 228 *ff.*) and concludes that some are 'pointless' and others shocking by their 'inadequacy of coverage'.

Australia and Singapore now also have their own learners' dictionaries, illustrating a localizing tendency that is contrary to the globalization seen in the market of NSDs: the *Australian Learners Dictionary* (1997); the *Times-Chambers Essential English Dictionary* (1995, 1997) for Singapore, *An Active Learning Dictionary* (2003), also sold in Japan, etc.

5.2.2 *Variations on the theme of the learner's dictionary*

5.2.2.1 The encyclopedic learner's dictionary

Some publishers have produced encyclopedic versions of learners' dictionaries, with proper names, encyclopedic information, and pages of appendices, aimed at teaching the culture of the country as well as its language. The *Oxford Advanced Learner's Dictionary of Current English, Encyclopedic Edition* (ALDE; 1992) was based on *ALD4* and had '4,500 encyclopedic entries': *Zaïre, Zambezi, Zambia, ZANU, Zanzibar, Zapata*, etc. *The Beatles* had 9 lines, *Cézanne* 5—some may disagree. The *Longman Dictionary of English Language and Culture* (*LDELC*; 1992, 1998, 2000) had the full text of *LDOCE* plus '15,000 cultural entries, covering everything from *the Spice Girls* to *Monica Lewinsky*, *Viagra* to the *Millenium Dome*'. There were interesting cross-references, for example from *Clinton* to *Lewinsky* and to *sexual relations*—but there was no entry for *sexual relations*. There were appendices listing political leaders, British monarchs, the books of the Bible, the works of Shakespeare, etc. *LDELC* is notable, and probably unique, in pointing to cultural facts associated with some names. For example, *Grey Poupon* was

a type of MUSTARD sold in the US, which is typically bought by people who eat expensive, high quality foods

Lopez, Jennifer was

a US actor, singer and dancer … She is known for being sexually attractive, and for having a sexy BOTTOM

and *Hill, Benny* was

a British COMEDIAN … His shows were often criticized for the large number of jokes about sex, and for including lots of young women wearing very little clothing, whom he was shown chasing through parks

The treatment was often more focused on detail and caricature than on serious scholarship, Stein (2002: 125 *ff.*) concluded. These encyclopedic learners' diction-aries have not been as successful as expected.

5.2.2.2 The onomasiological learner's dictionary

Dictionaries arranged onomasiologically are important for foreign learners, because they are designed to help expression (Rundell 1998). The earliest example was the *Longman Lexicon of Contemporary English* (*LLCE*), compiled by Tom McArthur and published in 1981. The dictionary was divided into fourteen broad categories, further divided so that the whole vocabulary was organized in three levels. Thus, section M52, **Sending and transporting** (verbs), had *send, transfer, transport, convey, deliver, ship* and *dispatch*, all defined and exemplified. The 15,000 headwords came from *LDOCE*—although it was compiled before *LDOCE* was finished—selected according to criteria that were not explained. In the lower-level groupings, the words were arranged by order of generality, for example *big* followed by *large, great, grand, immense, vast,* and *huge* (McArthur 1998: 183).[37] The definitions were mostly those of *LDOCE*, sometimes modified but not always, unfortunately, and therefore not always contrastive. For example:

tremble 'to shake uncontrollably as from fear, cold, excitement, etc.'
shiver 'to shake, esp. (of people) from cold or fear'
shudder 'to shake uncontrollably for a moment, as from fear, cold, or strong dislike'

The words could be accessed either via the 'List of Sets' at the beginning of the book or via the index at the end, as in a thesaurus. For example, *bed n.*[38] sent the reader to section D115 *nouns and verbs*: **beds and parts of beds** that contained entries for *bed, bedstead, mattress, blanket, quilt, (bed)sheet, bedspread, bedding, bedclothes, bedside, pillow, pillowcase,* and *bolster.* The idea was good, and one

---

[37] But McArthur says he did not have enough time to complete this organization—an interesting account of the working conditions of lexicographers.
[38] There was no *bed v.*

THE DICTIONARY FOR FOREIGN STUDENTS **193**

wishes it had been taken further, with a richer wordlist, contrastive definitions, and advice on usage. Unfortunately, it has never been updated.

The Longman Language Activator (*LLA*; 1993), based on the Longman corpora and the BNC (see below, 9.1.7), had 1,052 key terms, 23,000 meanings in all, representing basic concepts arranged in a complex system mixing alphabetical order and semantic organization. It is 'the only monolingual learners' dictionary explicitly designed for the encoding user' (Atkins and Rundell 2008: 410). 'The idea is to take the user from a basic term which he or she can be expected to know (such as **steal**) to a range of more sophisticated or specialized vocabulary items (such as **shoplift, embezzle,** or **mug**' (Rundell 1999: 49). Like *LDOCE*, *LLA* excluded proper names, and unlike *LDOCE* it excluded 'real-world' words unless they were used in linguistic expressions: for instance, *cat* was not in (no *cat out of the bag*), but *dog* was, as part of *walk the dog, dog eat dog*, etc. The definitions were inspired by those of *LDOCE*, using the same 2,000-word defining vocabulary, but they were made contrastive, so that near synonyms could be compared. For example, in *LDOCE2*, *pad* was 'walk steadily, and usu. softly ...', *creep* was 'move slowly, quietly and carefully ...', *tiptoe* was 'walk on tiptoe ...' and *sneak* was 'go quietly and secretly ...', but in *LLA* the four verbs were treated in the same paragraph and all defined by 'to walk quietly with light steps', with appropriate adverbs or phrases to distinguish each word from the others: 'steadily' for *pad*, 'carefully' for *creep*, 'on the front part of your feet' for *tiptoe* and 'trying to hide' for *sneak*. *LLA* has been highly acclaimed, and deservedly so. A second edition came out in 2002. *LDOCE3* on CD-ROM has links to *LLA*.

The *Wordfinder Dictionary* was published by Oxford University Press in 1997. It had an alphabetically arranged list of words that gave access to other related words, part semasiology and part onomasiology. For example the entry *mouth* said:

see also FACE
– the part of your face that you use for eating and speaking: **mouth**
– concerning or using the mouth: **oral** (*adverb* **orally**) ○ *oral hygiene* ○ *medicine to be taken orally*
– one of the two soft red or brown parts above and below your mouth: **lip** ○ *the upper/ lower lip* ○ *to kiss somebody on the lips*
etc.

It is not very different from the *Random House Webster's Word Menu* (1992), already mentioned, designed for native speakers but extremely useful to foreign learners: for example, the entry *skeleton* lists the bones in the human body.

Cambridge Word Routes (*CWR*) is a series of bilingual dictionaries with English words arranged in groups according to a taxonomy of concepts, which can be accessed via the foreign language, an enormous advantage over the monolingual dictionaries. *CWR* volumes also have two alphabetical indexes (one in English, one in the other language). They exist for French, Italian, Greek, Spanish, and Catalan. For the last two they are called *Cambridge Word Selector* (Bruton 1997).

All those dictionaries are admirable in their quest for new lexicographic solutions. They are perfect examples of the challenge of lexicography: how to account for the infinite subtleties and variations of linguistic usage and present them to the user in comprehensible form. The arrival of e-dictionaries offers lexicographers new solutions.

5.2.2.3 The learner's dictionary of idioms

There are many dictionaries of idioms for foreign learners: the *Longman Dictionary of English Idioms* (1979), with a second, corpus-based edition in 1998, the *Cambridge International Dictionary of Idioms*, with 7,000 entries, the *Collins Cobuild Dictionary of Idioms*, 1995, based on the BoE (211 million words at the time; see below, 9.1.7), etc.

The most ambitious was the *Oxford Dictionary of Current Idiomatic English* (*ODCIE*) in two volumes, under the direction of Cowie, with about 15,000 entries in all. Volume 1 (1975) listed 'Verbs with Prepositions and Particles', and volume 2 (1983), the larger, had 685 pages of 'Phrase, Clause and Sentence Idioms'. It gave brief definitions, frequent co-occurrents and copious examples of use.

all right for sb suitable for, acceptable to, sb; V: △ be, seem, appear □ *That sort of bike may be all right for little kids* ...

ODCIE may have been too much for the skills of some dictionary users, but it was a good dictionary. A second edition was published in 1993, under the titles *Oxford Dictionary of Phrasal Verbs* and *Oxford Dictionary of English Idioms*.

5.2.2.4 The learner's dictionary of collocations

The dictionary of collocations has recently become a genre of its own, mostly, if not uniquely, intended for language learners. All dictionaries of collocations have their own definition of *collocation*, roughly speaking either the significant co-occurrence of two lexical words in a syntactic pattern, the Hausmannian sense, or the frequent co-occurrence of two or more words, the Sinclairian sense (see below, 8.2.4).

Selected English Collocations, by H. Dzierżanowska and C. Douglas Kozłowska, published in Warsaw in 1988, was Hausmannian. At *chairman*, it had

V. appoint, become, dismiss, elect, oust ~
V. ~ give (a ruling), preside over, resign

Not much, but very useful. *Selected English Collocations* was later incorporated into J. Hill and M. Lewis' *The LTP Dictionary of Selected Collocations* (1997), 3,200 headwords and 55,000 collocations.

Cowie's *ODCIE* was to a large extent also a dictionary of collocations in the Hausmannian sense, especially the first volume for phrasal verbs. For example, the entry *catch up (with)* had

S: runner; cyclist; driver; car; student; worker. O: pack, main body (of runners); (main) party; column; rest of the class

where S stood for *subject* and O for *object*. In pre-corpus times, it had information that was not available otherwise.

The most comprehensive collection of Hausmannian collocations was the *BBI Combinatory Dictionary of English* (*BBI*, from the names of its authors, Morton Benson, Evelyn Benson, and Ilson, who had edited the *Reader's Digest Great Illustrated Dictionary*), published in 1986 (Gold 1988). It was compiled by American authors, but was sold mostly in Great Britain. It gave the collocators (see below, 8.2.4) of about 12,000 entry words, distinguishing grammatical collocations, which include a function word (for example *responsible for*), and lexical collocations, with only lexical words (for example *blind rage*). *BBI* was the first dictionary to indicate words that cannot be used without any complementation, what Fillmore calls *null instantiation*, for example *fond* (*I am fond), *base v.* (*to base something), *fare v.* (*to fare), *carry* (*to carry oneself), etc. (Atkins and Rundell 2008: 353 *ff.*). It also listed verb collocators in the entries for the noun bases, subjects or objects, something that GPDs do not normally do (see below, 8.2.4.3): for example, *trim* could be found at *sail*, or *wield* at *sword*. The second edition of *BBI*, called *The BBI Dictionary of English Word-Combinations*, published in 1997, is larger than the first by about 100 pages.

The *Oxford Collocations Dictionary* (2002), based on the 100 million word BNC (see below, 9.1.7), has 9,000 headwords, mostly nouns. Its definition of *collocation* is a compromise between Hausmann and Sinclair: any frequently occurring significant combination of two words. It has thematic sections presenting frequent collocations under sections such as 'Food and cooking', and exercises. The microstructure is rich and well organized, taking some inspiration from Mel'čuk's lexical functions (see below, 8.2.6.1).

Kjellmer's *Dictionary of English Collocations* (1994; 3 volumes, 2,000 pages), based on the Brown corpus (see below, 9.1.7) was a collection of Sinclairian collocations. It listed all sequences occurring with some frequency in the corpus, for example *a baby* (and 1,800 combinations with *a* + noun), *Benjamin Franklin* (and all proper names), *the abdomen* (and 156 pages of *the* + noun). The *Collins COBUILD English Collocations on CD-ROM* does not exist in paper form. It was published in 1995 and was also Sinclairian, of course, with a vengeance. It listed about 10,000 frequently occurring co-occurrences in the BoE (see below, 9.1.7), whatever their other characteristics, with as many as twenty citations for each, but unfortunately also included compounds (*disaster relief, schools inspector*), free combinations (*new gallery, such disaster*) and even meaningless chunks such as *nature because, religious between, advances heavy*, 'all of which reveal a regrettable lack of human intervention in the compiling process' (Siepmann 1998: np). As a consequence, it had little room for meaningful collocations. Siepmann notes that *unmitigated disaster, clear-cut distinction,* or *lag behind* are absent.

5.2.2.5 Other learners' dictionaries

There are many dictionaries of phrasal verbs besides volume 1 of *ODCIE* (1975), all for learners, by all the major publishers. There are learners' dictionaries of pronunciation: the *Longman Pronunciation Dictionary* (1990) by J. C. Wells, the *Oxford Dictionary of Pronunciation for Current English* (2003), etc. And there are bilingualized dictionaries for speakers of Japanese, Greek, Brazilian Portuguese, Arabic, Polish, Italian, Norwegian, Chinese, etc.: for example the *Oxford Student's Dictionary for Hebrew Speakers* (1985), with the text of the original English edition and Hebrew equivalents added (Reif 1987: 146), or *LDOCE* for Chinese speakers. Some bilingualized dictionaries have an index in the other language: the *Longman English Dictionary for Portuguese Speakers* (Humblé 2001: 37). Bilingualized learners' dictionaries are very popular in some countries, in Israel, where the genre was invented, in Poland, in Quebec, etc. They seem to be efficient tools for expression, although they are frowned upon by the purists of language teaching because they allow access to the foreign language via the native language.

5.2.2.6 Electronic learners' dictionaries

Most learners' dictionaries started being published in electronic form in the 1990s, usually on a CD-ROM that came out a few months, or years, after the paper edition. Since 2002 for *MEDAL*, 2003 for *LDOCE4*, 2005 for *ALD7*, etc., they have all come with a CD-ROM (Nesi 1999a: 60). Some can be also consulted on the Internet, and a number are even sold as hand-held devices (see below, 9.2.2.3):

for example the *Longman Dictionary of Contemporary English* (1987), based on *LDOCE2*, marketed by Seiko in 1995. In the late 1990s, Nesi (1996*b*) and Rundell (1998) observed that they were still at an early stage, that only a few of the innumerable possibilities offered by the computer had been exploited and that further improvements could be expected, both in the technique and in the thinking behind the contents.

5.3 LEARNERS' DICTIONARIES ARE
A NEW TRADITION

5.3.1 *Characteristic features*

Until the 1980s, learners' dictionaries were not even recognized as a category worthy of research: there was no book length study, and most dictionary typologies simply ignored them. But they have recently become the objects of several books and innumerable articles. *ALD* was the harbinger of a new genre, and now, 60 years later, we can safely say that we have all the characteristics of a distinct tradition: there are many similar dictionaries, by different publishers, they are successful and they are clearly different from the dictionaries published before (McArthur 1998: 39). Their key features are (see also Rundell 1998: 316 *ff.*):

1. A language of reference that is the usual, everyday usage, not the formal or literary.
2. An emphasis on the quality of the microstructure rather than on the quantity of the wordlist: 'a native-speaker dictionary will tell you less about more whereas a learners' dictionary will tell you more about less'.[39]
3. A focus on the more frequent words and the more frequent meanings of words.
4. The provision of information necessary for expression.
5. As much attention given to spoken as to written styles.
6. The indication of pronunciation in IPA.
7. No information that is not functional, for example no etymology.
8. Definitions written with a limited defining vocabulary.
9. The provision of many examples, authentic or fabricated.
10. Extensive front matter on 'How to use the dictionary'.

---

[39] A formula attributed by Ilson (1998: 229) to C. McGregor, but I have been unable to trace its origin.

11. Pictorial illustrations of various kinds.
12. The presence of extra sections, boxes, middle matter, etc.
13. The use of electronic format, on CD-ROM or the Internet.

These features are implemented more or less systematically in individual dictionaries, but they characterize the genre. The more recent learners' dictionaries have also exhibited new tendencies towards:

14. the use of a corpus—no one would think now of publishing a learner's dictionary that would not be 'based on' a corpus, although it is not always easy to see how this affects the contents;
15. a more user-friendly style, clearer codes, and simpler formulations;
16. a more readable format, with fonts of different sizes and colours, separated paragraphs, etc., and a complete redesign of the 'page' in e-dictionaries;
17. giving more information on the frequency of words, to be followed soon, no doubt, by the frequency of meanings;
18. giving more information on language use, particularly collocations (see below 8.2.4.3);
19. new types of illustrations, pictures, video sequences, sound, etc.

Learners' dictionaries still hesitate on a few points, usage labels, sentence definitions, coding of patterns, etc., but on the whole they are converging towards a common standard. Their features are determined to a large extent by their role as instruments for the acquisition of another language and another culture. Certainly they are important centres of innovation, and they have begun to affect NSDs to some extent (Ilson 1986b: 69; Quirk 1986: 3–4; Landau 2001: 17): at least one native speakers' dictionary, the *Longman New Generation Dictionary* (1981), meant for teenagers, was based on a learner's dictionary, *LDOCE* (Ilson 1990b: 1972), and *NODE* has some features of the learner's dictionary.

5.3.2 *The evolution of the genre*

The competition between dictionary publishers is probably even fiercer in the field of MLDs than for NSDs. The number of people learning English worldwide is huge—between 500 million and one billion—and each publisher is trying to seize the largest possible share. The 'dictionary war' 'goes on—what is more, it intensifies, to the delight of millions of advanced learners of English and their teachers worldwide' (Prćić 2004: 321). At the same time, this is a quasi-exclusively English phenomenon: no other language community has such a wealth of learners' dictionaries, because no other language community can afford to invest so much money and effort. French has only a few, and many languages have none.

After the Second World War, there was an immense effort by publishers, lexicographers, metalexicographers, and teachers of English as a foreign language to persuade the whole world that the key to success was to learn English and that the key to success in learning English was the use—and possession, of course—of a monolingual learner's dictionary. There was genuine conviction in this effort, and some serious research behind it, but there were also commercial aspirations. It is far from clear that the teaching of a foreign language has to take place, and can take place, exclusively in that language, and that a monolingual learner's dictionary is indispensable in the process (Wingate 2002: 1), 'yet this curious bridging genre flourishes like the green bay tree' (McArthur 1998: 133). The problem is that the learner's dictionary is the same for all language communities, so that the young Japanese will have the same dictionary as the young Norwegian—*CIDE* is the only dictionary that gives some thought to the difficulties of different language communities. But do they have the same needs, and the same skills (see below, 7.2)? The advocates of bilingual and of bilingualized dictionaries have a point.

Over the years, learners' dictionaries have improved, because the market is competitive, because their commercial success has brought money, and the money has been reinvested in further improvements, particularly through the constitution of corpora and lexical databases. Some thought that they were reaching perfection: one reviewer has used the phrase 'the perfect learner's dictionary', admittedly with a question mark (Herbst and Popp 1999). Others were less optimistic. They thought that the learner's dictionary had become too fat and was in danger of 'bursting the covers' (Bolinger 1990: 144): 'I'm inclined to think that the macrostructures (more technically, the nomenclatures) of EFL/ESL dictionaries are getting too large' (Ilson 1999*a*: 225). The tendency to have more may be dangerous, and Ilson was pessimistic about the future of the genre: 'Evolution teaches us that the gigantism of a species can herald its extinction' (1999*a*: 225). The solution, Ilson suggested, was to omit such technical and scientific words as *AIDS* or *penicillin*, which are 'essentially monosemous, have no variant forms, have official translations in most languages (being part of medical terminology), and present no special cultural or linguistic problems'. The space could be used for more microstructural information on more difficult words, he said.

But the times have changed. The learner's dictionary of the future comes with a CD-ROM, or as a CD-ROM, co-ordinated with a grammar, access to a corpus, pronunciation, a spellchecker, a thesaurus, a grammar checker, a set of exercises, access to websites, etc. without running the risk of 'bursting its covers'. The term

Lexical Reference Books (LRBs), recently coined as 'a convenient umbrella term for foreign learners' dictionaries, whether bilingual or monolingual, or alphabetically or semantically organized' (Bruton 1999: 1), could soon be replaced by *Lexical Reference Media* (LRM) (Bruton 1999: 3) to refer to learners' dictionaries with their accompanying static and dynamic lexical databases, all in electronic format.

6

ENGLISH DICTIONARIES OF THE TWENTIETH CENTURY: THE CULTURAL, THE FUNCTIONAL, AND THE SCIENTIFIC

WE have classified English dictionaries of the twentieth century in three groups: the scholarly dictionary of Britain, the utility dictionary of the USA, both dating back to the nineteenth century but flourishing in the twentieth, and the learner's dictionary, born in the twentieth century in Britain and adopted—and adapted—in other countries later. The three types are alive in the early years of the twenty-first century: *OED3* is being compiled in the spirit of Dean Trench's recommendations of 1857 and of *OED1*, published in 1929, *W4*, if it is produced at all, will probably look like *W3*, published in 1961 and to some extent like *W2* of 1934, and more learners' dictionaries are being prepared, with characteristics that will be close to the *ALD* published in 1942. And it seems that all three types will continue to be produced, in paper or electronic form.

6.1 CULTURAL AND FUNCTIONAL DICTIONARIES

6.1.1 *The mouthpieces of a culture*

All dictionaries are cultural in a broad sense of *culture* (Rey 2007), i.e. the 'customs, arts, social institutions, and achievements of a particular nation, people, or other social group' (*NODE*): they are part of the culture of the society in which they are produced. They are the mouthpieces of a society, texts in which it describes not only its language but also its culture and formulates its view of the world, its *Weltanschauung*. They express the knowledge, the beliefs, the values of the dominant groups of that society: 'dictionaries are a faithful reflection of the changing society that produces and consumes them' (Ilson 1990a: 1980).

A dictionary is the most alive and comprehensive of atlases. The stratigraphy, the many-layered provenance of a word, of an idiomatic phrase, encapsulates the *Lebensraum*, the memories privileged or suppressed, the laws and literature of a community and culture. Consider the *Littré* or the *Oxford English Dictionary*. Languages will conserve, with uncanny tenacity, names of trees, of fauna from lands they have long abandoned. They preserve configurations of mores and institutions long past and almost undecipherable to the present.   (Steiner 1997: 97)

In a dictionary, the worldviews of a society are apparent in the selection of words, in the wording of the definitions, in the choice of examples, and in the use of usage labels or comments. The more choice there is for the lexicographer the more revealing a feature will be. Consider examples and quotations: for every one of them the lexicographer can choose between thousands, and those that are chosen are all the more interesting. They are meant, above all, to illustrate syntactic behaviour or to provide additional semantic information, but at the same time they are often laden with cultural information: 'The examples they [i.e. the lexicographers] choose to illustrate meanings can there-fore be especially revealing of cultural expectations' (Miller and Swift 1979: 76).

Since they refer to the world, example sentences constitute a repository of the common values and interests of the society whose language is described. ... Unsigned examples reveal the society as it is seen by the lexicographer, not in a highly idiosyncratic way but in a sort of preferential description.   (Rey-Debove 1971: 272–3)

The worldviews of a society tend to strike us as odd if they are not ours, and metalexicographers have delighted in spotting the oddities. They have explored dictionaries to expose the rampant ideologies, what was valued or stigmatized

(Algeo 1990*b*: 2006–7): 'dictionaries, encyclopedias and grammars are the best examples of texts that one should read between the lines, where the conflicts, the hidden and ignored oppositions, the clichés that make up the family album of a culture can be detected more easily than anywhere else' (Meschonnic 1991: 16). Comments on old dictionaries are usually full of wonder, sometimes fondness, when the ideas that are expressed are totally outmoded. Consider the following entry for *canoe*, compiled for *OED1* and published in 1888, which is typical of the Victorian society of the time:[1]

1. A kind of boat in use among uncivilized nations: a. Originally applied to those of the West Indian aborigines, which were hollowed out of a single tree-trunk, and thence to those of other savages, or of prehistoric men, of and used generally for any rude craft in which uncivilized people go upon the water; most savages use paddles instead of oars, whence 'canoe' is sometimes this construction. b. Extended to those of other races and other construction, understood to be any vessel propelled by paddles. 2. In civilized use: A small light sort of boat or skiff propelled by paddling.

In *COD1* (1911), the entry for *subject* had the example 'The Indians are our subjects'. Thousands of similar examples can be found in all dictionaries, particularly in the larger ones, in the areas of religion, politics, sexual orientation, gender differentiation, racial and ethnic origin, disability, age, etc.

Many words are impossible to treat objectively: how could an eighteenth-century English dictionary define words like *Pope*, or *reformation*? How is the modern 'lexicographer to deal with such lexemes as *God, abortion, atheism, feminism, Scientology, moral majority, sin, after life*, and *socialism*? If all views are to be presented, the definition turns into an encyclopedia article' (Gold 1985: 233). Dictionaries never present more than one viewpoint, for reasons of space, but also because there is a way of treating those words that corresponds to what the lexicographers think that the public expects. But the worldviews are also present in other entries, in the definitions and the examples for more innocent-looking words. Only a few examples will be given here, but the interested reader will find many others in all dictionaries.

6.1.1.1 Politics and religion

Some lexicographers of the past were straightforward in the expression of their political or religious ideas: Johnson, as we have seen, Richardson, the author of *A New Dictionary of the English Language* (1836/7), who was described as 'Protestant, philosemitic and Francophobe' (Fowler 2004: 54), Littré, who occasionally

---

[1] Mentioned by Moon (1989). The wording was changed in *OED2.*

expressed his views, 'as when he observes (*république—démocratie*) that the United States may be called a democracy, but that to apply the word to France is to take it in a wrong sense' (Osselton 2000: 67). Modern dictionaries are more subtle. Dubois and Dubois (1971: 102–3) noted that the definitions of *marxisme* in twentieth-century French dictionaries were often introduced by formulae such as 'Doctrine qui prétend ... ',[2] that were not used in the definitions of words like *christianisme* or *nationalisme*—but of course the Dubois brothers were not objective either. ... In the *TLF*, *comité central*[3] is defined without any reference to the communist political system, and *bureau politique*[4] is omitted (Girardin 1979: 89). In the USA, some of the definitions of *W3* have been criticized, even though Gove made particular efforts to be objective:

One reviewer found the definitions of *democratic* and *republican* fair ... but remarked that the definition of *McCarthyism* gave only the anti-McCarthy view ... and that the definition of *Stalinism* ('the political, economic and social principles and policies associated with Stalin; *esp.*: the theory and practice of communism developed by Stalin from Marxism-Leninism') was by contrast lackluster and contained an inaccuracy: the second part of it is 'absurd, since Stalin never had a theory in his life'.   (Gold 1985: 233)

In Britain, the *Learner's Dictionary of Current English* (1948), the ancestor of *ALD*, defined *imperialism* as

the policy of maintaining the safety and protecting the welfare of the various parts of an empire (by warlike defence, close trade relations, and other lawful means).

(see Veisbergs 2002: 659)

The formulation 'carries none of the negative connotations that the word has in contemporary discourse, but even at the time when it was written, it is unlikely to have had much resonance with the liberation movements then emerging in Africa' (Atkins and Rundell 2008: 430). When *ALD* was adapted for the USSR in the early 1980s, the definitions of words such as *capitalism, censorship, democracy*, etc. had to be modified, because the original definitions were unacceptable to the Soviet authorities. For example (the original definitions in the British edition are noted GB and the definitions as they were finally adopted for the Russian edition are noted USSR) (from Moon 1989: 77–8):

capitalism (GB): economic system in which a country's trade and industry are organized and controlled by the owners of capital, the chief elements being competition, profit, supply and demand.

---

[2] 'A doctrine that claims that...'. On such formulations, see Pickett (2007).
[3] *Central committee* is in *CED* but not in *SOED4* or *NODE*.
[4] *CED* and *NODE* have *politburo, SOED4* has *politbureau*.

(USSR): an economic and social system based on private ownership of the means of production operated for private profit and on the exploitation of man by man.

communism (GB): ideology that proclaims the abolition of class oppression and exploitation, and the foundation of a society based on the common possession of the means of production and the equal distribution of goods.
(USSR): a theory revealing the historical necessity for the revolutionary replacement of capitalism by Communism.[5]

imperialism (GB): belief in the value of colonies; policy of expanding a country's empire and influence.
(USSR): the highest and last stage of capitalism.

internationalism (GB): the doctrine that the common interests of nations are greater and more important than their differences.
(USSR): the solidarity of the working people of different countries in their struggle with capitalism.

The more recent dictionaries are trying to be more objective. Atkins and Rundell (2008: 428) quote the definition of *apartheid* in *LDOCE1* (1978):

the keeping separate of races of different colours in one country, esp. of Europeans and non-Europeans in South Africa

They note that 'by failing to say anything about the motives behind apartheid, [it] implicitly endorses those who advocate the system'. This was changed in *LDOCE2* (1987) to

(in South Africa) the system established by government of keeping different races separate, esp. so as to give advantage to white people[6]

Some dictionaries are classified as progressive in politics, and others are thought of as conservative, or reactionary. In the USA, during the dictionary war that followed the publication of *W3*, *AHD* was called the 'Joe McCarthy Dictionary' (McDavid 1981: 14) or the 'George C. Wallace Dictionary' (Forgue 1981: 90), after the right-wing political leaders of the time. In France, some have distinguished between radical and conservative, if not left-wing and right-wing, dictionaries. When Guespin called *PR* a bourgeois dictionary, Rey (1977: 129) was outraged and responded acidly: 'Thus, the petit bourgeois will spontaneously turn to the Robert or to the TLF while the trade-unionist and the class-conscious intellectual will turn to the Larousse dictionaries'. Perhaps not, but dictionaries do have

---

[5] A strange example of a circular definition (see below, 8.2.5.3).

[6] For other examples of the influence of prevailing ideologies on the writing of definitions, particularly in a Chinese dictionary, see Moon (1989: 79–80). On the treatment of things Chinese in *OED2*, see Benson (2001).

public images. Moon (2002: 632) noted that in the BoE corpus (at the time 193 million words; see below, 9.1.7) British dictionary publishers tended to be associated with certain media, hence with certain social groups.

Three quarters of the occurrences of *Chambers* as collocate occurred in the broadsheet newspaper *The Independent*. The commonest sources for *Collins* as collocate were the tabloids *The Sun/News of the World* ... , and the broadsheet *The Guardian*. *Oxford*, the strongest collocate, occurred most frequently in *The Independent* and *The Guardian*—in both cases, more frequently than did *Chambers/Collins*—and in *New Scientist*.

The words of religion are as difficult as those of politics. In France, some dictionaries have been openly critical of Christianity: Lachâtre was the more violent, as we have seen, but there was also, more recently, the *Dictionnaire du Français Contemporain* (1966), where *anticléricalisme* was illustrated by 'L'anticléricalisme s'était développé en France au XIXème siècle avec l'aide que l'Eglise avait alors apportée aux pouvoirs absolus'[7] (Collignon and Glatigny 1978: 150). In the USA on the contrary, Baehr (in Landau 2001: 420–1) found that the citations of the 1952 and 1962 editions of the *Thorndike-Barnhart Beginning Dictionary*, a dictionary for children, 'reflected a disproportionate emphasis on Christianity'. Fillmore (in Atkins and Rundell 2008: 429) notes that the definition of *reincarnation* in *CED* describes it as 'a belief ... ', whereas in *AHD4* it is 'Rebirth of the soul in another body', assuming that there is such a thing. In recent American dictionaries, the definitions of *creationism* and *evolutionism* often begin, similarly, with *a belief, a doctrine*, or *a theory*, and only a few dictionaries add to their definitions of *evolutionism* comments such as 'now generally accepted'.

6.1.1.2 Ethnicity

The words used to refer to social groups as distinguished by their origins or their physical characteristics pose particular problems in lexicography: they can easily betray what Weiner calls a 'supremacist attitude' (Weiner 1997). The entry for *nègre* in the 1732 edition of the *Dictionnaire de Trévoux* explained that black Africans sell not only those of their neighbours that they can catch but also 'sometimes their wives and their children'. We have seen a few examples from the *OED* reflecting values of the late nineteenth and early twentieth century, and Mugglestone (2005: 163 *ff.*) gives more:

white man 'A man of honourable character such as one associated with a European, as distinguished from a negro'

---

[7] 'The development of anticlericalism in France in the nineteenth century had been fuelled by the help given by the Church to authoritarian regimes.'

darky 'A negro, a blacky'
hut 'A dwelling … inhabited by savages'

'Ethnonyms', the words used to refer to ethnic groups or individuals, are often omitted, to avoid offending the community and to make sure that the dictionary will sell in schools and families. Their omission is a way of denying their existence, the ultimate condemnation, while their inclusion is bound to be interpreted as a certificate of acceptability, 'unquestionably a first step towards legitimization' (Curzan 2000: 108). My study (Béjoint 1980) of the treatment of ethnonyms (*chink, coon, dago, frog, greaser,* etc.) in dictionaries of the 1970s showed that the coverage was patchy: *WNW* had none of them, no American dictionary had them all and they were better treated in British dictionaries, even though they were Americanisms. I also noted that the dictionaries were slowly becoming more generous in the inclusion of such words. Murphy (1991: 61), in the conclusion to her study of racial labels in American dictionaries, agreed that 'it is the more recent dictionaries that most accurately represent the current usage … and we can expect next year's dictionary to be even more precise than this year's'. In a study of dictionaries in South Africa published in 1998, she also noted that the treatment of race and ethnicity was often inadequate, both in imported British dictionaries such as *COD, POD,* or *CED* and in dictionaries produced in South Africa, but that there was a growing sensitivity to the problem (Murphy 1998: 24).

The inclusion of these words, like the inclusion of metaphorical phrases or words such as *go Dutch, Irish* in the sense of 'illogical', or *Jew* in the sense of 'miser', often stirs the fury of the community that feels insulted. The reactions are often extremely violent, demanding the withdrawal of the dictionary or threatening a boycott: 'toward the end of 1976, Mr. Al Grassby, Australia's commissioner for community relations, called for the withdrawal of the Australian *Pocket Oxford Dictionary* from circulation because it contained … words like *wog, wop,* and *dago*' (Burchfield 1980: 19). In 1995, 'The Robert publishing house had to withdraw 3,000 copies [of *PR*] in which *juif*[8] was proposed as a synonym of *avare.*[9] The wording was changed in 1996' (Hausmann 2003: 251).

Copies of the *Pocket [Oxford] Dictionary* were confiscated in Karachi in protest against the definition of *Pakistan*—'a separate Moslem state in India'—and a boycott by Arab countries was threatened over the definition of *Palestinian*—'(native or inhabitant) of Palestine; (person) seeking to displace Israelis from Palestine'.[10] (Morton 1994: 239–40)

---

[8] *Jew.*   [9] *miser.*
[10] Of course, the modified definition aroused the fury of 'various Jewish organizations' (Burchfield 1980: 20).

In 1997, 'the *Washington Post* reported a petition drive against Merriam-Webster to remove *nigger* from its dictionaries' (Landau 2001: 235). Even *W2* was forced to correct its entry for *chinaman*, because there was no label or usage note in the first printing (Morton 1994: 239).

For a long time, dictionaries recorded ethnonyms without any precautions: for example, *C20D* had *bogtrotter* 'an Irishman' in 1929 and the 1972 edition still had the same. Later dictionaries started using labels such as *derog(atory)*, *insult(ing)*, *off(ensive)*, etc., or more elaborate formulations, 'considered offensive by … ' or 'a rude word for … '. *COD7* (1982) had *bogtrotter* '(derog.) Irishman', *COD8* (1990) had '*sl. derog.*' and *COD10* had 'informal, offensive An Irish person'. But lexicographers have never found a satisfactory marking system. Gove, in *W3*, decided that the users could work out the usage restrictions by themselves by observing the examples, as we have seen, and that most usage labels were unnecessary (Landau 2001: 255). Burchfield (1980: 16) suggested using 'a special symbol meaning "regarded as offensive in varying degrees by the person to whom the word is applied"', and that is what *COD7* (1982) did. It had the letter **R** meaning 'racially offensive use' but it only used it for about 25 words, *coon, dago, darky, Jap, jew, Jim Crow, kike, mick, nigger*, etc., not for *bogtrotter, frog*, etc.[11] Every new dictionary has its own system, which is always different from the system of preceding dictionaries, but whatever method is used it is never enough. Labels are imprecise, different dictionaries have different labels or use the same labels in different ways (Landau 2001: 238). Atkins (1993: 27) asked for the help of linguists on that point, but I know of no research that could be useful (see Atkins and Rundell 2008: 405), which is unfortunate because usage labels are becoming more important than ever now that they can be used as sorting keys in e-dictionaries (Brewer 2004). Perhaps some future research on large corpora will come up with statistical facts that provide some guidance (Landau 2001: 228, 269). But the infinitesimal variations in the intention of the sender and the effect on the receiver are not easily reducible to a few labels. Above all, the sad truth is that a label is never as forceful as the presence or absence of a word or phrase. Labels are ignored, or disregarded, not even seen (see below, 7.2), and they do not have much influence on the reactions of the public. Lexicographers are prisoners of their descriptive *credo*, condemned to continue running around in circles trying to find an ideal solution that may not exist.

---

[11] Jean Tournier, personal communication. See also Stein (1984*b*). Perhaps the indication of differences, in cases where there is a choice between different lexical items, as in *Chambers Universal Learners' Dictionary* (1980), like *acquire* 'more formal than *get*', or *commence*, 'more formal than *begin* or *start*', could be adapted to cases of derogatory words.

6.1.1.3 The taboos of sex and excretion

There are three categories of words referring to sex and excretion, scientific words, four-letter words and euphemisms, or child words. The four-letter words are taboo in most societies (Sagarin 1963), but before the eighteenth century, they were recorded in most dictionaries:[12] 'In a polyglot dictionary published in 1548 by Pasquier Le Tellier of Paris, words are supplied for intimate functions of the human body, in eight languages' (Steiner 1980: 23–24). Florio's *A Worlde of Wordes* (1598) had the first printed mention of *fucke* in the definition for *fottere* (Landau 2001: 46, 228). Bailey's *Universal Etymological English Dictionary* (1721) also had it, as well as *cunt* and many others with definitions, sometimes in Latin, to obscure the meaning to all but the learned: *shite v.* was 'to ease nature; to discharge the belly', but *fuck* was defined by 'foeminam subagitare'. John Ash's *New and Complete Dictionary of the English Language* (1775), published after Johnson, still had 'vulgar words'.

In 1694 in France, the first edition of the *Dictionnaire de l'Académie* refused to have 'those words of passion that offend modesty',[13] and in Britain, the change came with Johnson. True to new Augustan ideals, he omitted most vulgar words, particularly the four-letter ones, keeping only those that were used in his corpus, by definition respectable texts and respectable authors: *bum, arse, piss, congress* (in the sense of 'copulation'), *fart*, and a few others were in. The latter was lavishly illustrated by two poems: the verb, defined as 'to break wind behind', had a 6-liner by Swift:

> As when we a gun discharge,
> Although the bore be ne'er so large,
> Before the flame from muzzle burst,
> Just at the breech it flashes first;
> So from my lord his passion broke,
> He *farted* first, and then he spoke.

And there was a shorter poem by Sir John Suckling for the noun: 'Love is the fart/ Of every heart;/It pains a man when 'tis kept close;/And others doth offend, when 'tis let loose'. Johnson was praised for his restraint by some of his contemporaries (Considine 1998: 580), but criticized by Webster for having too many 'low words' (Letters, to David Ramsay, 286–7). Once, the story goes, he replied with characteristic

---

[12] For Old and Middle English vocabularies, see Stein (1985: 69–71).
[13] 'ces mots d'emportement qui blessent la pudeur'.

humour to one particular lady: 'No, Madam, I hope I have not daubed my fingers. I find, however, that you have been *looking* for them.'[14]

British GPDs after Johnson were generally reluctant to admit vulgar words. *POD* (1924) listed *bumf*,[15] but this was a rare counter-example (Allen 1986: 5–6). Murray's descriptivism had to yield to Victorian prudery, as we have seen, even though the *OED* changed policy at letter N, leading to the inclusion of *shit* while *condom*, *cunt*, *fuck*, or *lesbian* had been left out (Mugglestone 2000*b*). Some were elucidated in Latin: *twat* had no definition but a quotation from Bailey's *Volume II* (1727), 'pudendum muliebre' (Mugglestone 2007: 7). Some words seem to have slipped in unnoticed: *windfucker* as another name for the kestrel and *fuckwind* for a species of hawk (Simes 2005: 10).

American dictionaries have always been even more timid in their treatment of the words of sex and excretion (Burchfield 1972: 84–9). This infuriated Walt Whitman, who, in true Whitmanian style, wanted the dictionary to reflect the vitality of the American language: 'The Real Dictionary will give all the words that exist in use, the bad words as well as any'.[16] W3 admitted *cunt* but not *fuck*, nobody seems to know why. *Fuck* was omitted from reprint after reprint, but was finally included in *9,000 Words* (1983). Desk and college dictionaries were even more cautious. Landau (2001: 229) noted in 1974 that 'none of the American college dictionaries (including *AHD*) defined *sexual intercourse*'. The words of homosexuality were never included before the 1970s (Simes 2005: 9), because '[h]omosexuals weren't then recognized as a group having independent social or political power' (Landau 2001: 233). The omission of the taboo words was due to a large extent to the fact that dictionaries need official state approval to be listed among the books recommended for use in schools. *AHD* had to print a special edition for Texas omitting the four-letter words, among which was the word *fuck*, but as one reviewer observed with amusement, it could still be found in the etymology of *snafu*,[17] where it had obviously been overlooked by the lexicographers in charge of the bowdlerization (Hoss 1974: 36). But any word remotely connected with sex or excretion could also arouse the fury of the authorities:

the educational commissioner of Texas refused to list any of the four major American college dictionaries or *The Doubleday Dictionary* for purchase. It was not just the inclusion of the four-letter words that disturbed the commissioner; *Webster's New World Dictionary* (*WNW*) did not include them but was banned anyway.

---

[14] The story is repeated in the literature (Clifford 1979: 142; Winchester 2003: 33; Hitchings 2005: 130, etc.), but it may be apocryphal (Bailey 2004: 171).

[15] *ALD4* (1989) had *bumf* among its new words.

[16] Found in Whitman's papers (*Maledicta* IV/2: 290).

[17] 's(ituation) n(ormal) a(ll) f(ucked) u(p)'.

The commissioner objected to terms like *bed*,[18] *clap, deflower, john, G-string, slut, bastard* and many others.   (Landau 2001: 230)

AHD 'was removed from school libraries and classrooms in Eldon, Mo., because of objectionable definitions it offered for such words as "bed",[19] "tail", and "nut"' (*New York Times*, in Landau 2001: 443).

Dictionaries became progressively more open after the 1960s. In Britain, *fuck* was recorded in 1965 by the *Penguin English Dictionary* (Landau 2001: 228), and the first American GPD to record it—surprisingly enough, considering the prescriptive stance of the compilers—was *AHD* in 1969, four years later. *MWC8* (1975) was the first American dictionary to admit all the taboo words freely, and their inclusion is now considered normal in all dictionaries of English except those for children: 'Striving for frankness in lexicography is now an established contemporary practice' (Steiner 1980: 23). In 1994, Rooney (1994: 254–5) berated the *Penguin Canadian Dictionary* (1990) for advertising itself as a GPD but omitting *cunt, fuck, shit*, and even *fornicate*, and she concluded that '[it] is a dictionary best aimed at school students of about 12 years of age … although the linguistic censorship of slang and swear words probably all too well known even by 12 year-olds is still to be regretted'.

In France, Feldman studied *PL* from the first edition (dated 1906) to 1980 and noted that it included more and more taboo words, although the evolution was slow in the first decades. The verb *chier*[20] appeared for the first time in 1978, and the verb *baiser*[21] was still absent in 1980 (Feldman 1981: 3, 133). *Con*[22] in its anatomical sense was recorded first in *PR* in 1970 (Girardin 1979: 93). Boulanger's study (1986: 30) of all kinds of exclusions in modern French dictionaries concluded, like Feldman, that they had become more comprehensive but that there were still traces of squeamishness. Even the scientific words were treated with restraint: *phallus* appeared in 1974, *masturbation* in 1976, and *infibulation* and *excision* were still absent from French dictionaries in 1980. The word *homophobe* appeared in 1997 in *PR* and 1998 in *PL*.

Any word that belongs to slang, to a dialect, or a technical register can be 'defined' by a synonym or a paraphrase in the prestige variety, which amounts to treating it as one would a foreign word in a bilingual dictionary (Rey and Delesalle 1979: 22). This is often done for taboo words: for example, most dictionaries define *jerk off* by 'masturbate' and *piss* by 'urinate'. The definitions

[18] Sense 5 said 'such a place regarded as the scene of sexual intercourse or procreation.'
[19] Sense 4 was 'a place for lovemaking'.   [20] 'shit'.
[21] 'screw' in the sexual sense. The noun (*un baiser*) retains its chaste meaning of kiss.
[22] 'cunt', but also 'idiot' and 'idiotic'. *Con* is now used in the etymology of *cunnilingus* in the latest editions of *PL* (Claude Boisson, personal communication).

can also be deliberately vague, or hard to understand, exactly like old dictionaries had definitions in Latin. Many definitions seem to have been designed to discourage the users from trying to learn more, leading them into a maze of confusing cross-references (Lehmann 1990). A word like *uterus* in French dictionaries sends the users to *gestation, fruit, enfant, descendant,* etc. in a spiral of diminishing usefulness and growing frustration. Frank McCourt noted the same about his English dictionary (he does not say which one).

I have to look in the dictionary to find out what a virgin is. ... The dictionary says, Virgin, woman (usually a young woman) who is and remains in a state of inviolate chastity. Now I have to look up inviolate and chastity and all I can find here is that inviolate means not violated and chastity means chaste and that means pure from unlawful sexual intercourse. Now I have to look up intercourse and that leads to intromission. ... I don't know what that means and I'm too weary going from one word to another in this heavy dictionary ... and all because the people who wrote the dictionary don't want the likes of me to know anything.[23]

Often, definitions express disapproval in non-ambiguous terms. *OED1* defined *masturbation* by 'The action or practice of self-abuse', a 'mini-sermon', Mugglestone (2007: 9) notes, embedding 'Victorian moralities'. It defined *prostitute* as:

Of women: The offering of the body to indiscrimnate lewdness for hire[24]

Sometimes the disapproval is more subtle. *AHD* defined *abortion* as:

Induced termination of pregnancy before the fetus is capable of survival as an individual

and *WBD* defined it by:

The inducing of premature delivery in order to destroy offspring

The disapproval contained in both definitions is clear if they are compared with, for example, the definitions in *C21D*:

the removal of an embryo or fetus from the uterus before it is sufficiently developed to survive independently

or in *NODE*:

The deliberate termination of a human pregnancy, most often performed during the first 28 weeks

---

[23] In *Angela's Ashes* (1996: 333), quoted in Rundell (1998: 315).
[24] It refused, however to include the definition for *condom* proposed by a contributor, 'a contrivance used by fornicators, to save themselves from a well-deserved clap'.

Moral judgements can also be conveyed by omitting some features of the definition. The word *clitoris* in *WBD* was

A small, erectile organ at the forward part of the vulva of the female of most vertebrates, homologous with the penis of the male

which omits any reference to pleasure.[25] *COB* said:

A woman's clitoris is the small sensitive lump above her vagina which, when touched, causes pleasant sexual feelings that can lead to an orgasm

which is at least clear, though excessively anthropocentric—a case of overspecification. Whether *MEDAL1*, which has

A woman's sexual organ just above her VAGINA that gives a lot of sexual pleasure when it is touched

goes too far or not is debatable. The taboo against sexual pleasure has always been strong: *orgasm* used to be defined as the 'climax of excitement' without any mention of sex, and dictionaries became explicit only recently: *LDOCE* began in 1978 ('The highest point of sexual pleasure'), *CED* in 1979, *COD* in 1999, and *ALD* in 2000.

6.1.1.4 Gender

For a long time, women were badly treated in dictionaries. Dictionaries 'usually define by antonymy the word that is perceived as semantically negative in the socio-cultural system that they describe', as in *poor* 'not rich' (Rey-Debove 1971: 244), and until a relatively recent date *woman* was defined in relation to *man*. For example, in *C20D* (1921), 'the female of man'. In France, *femme* was also defined as 'La compagne de l'homme'[26] until 1958 in *PL* and 1971 in *PR*, although of course *homme* was never defined in relation to *femme* (Lehmann and Beaujot 1978).

Men and boys are often depicted in more favourable terms than women and girls. In many American dictionaries until the early 1980s, the entries for meliorative adjectives (*brave*, *strong*, etc.) were illustrated by sentences with male subjects, while the subjects were female for pejorative adjectives like *shy*, *weak*, etc. (Gershuny 1977).

When they do not carry prejudices, dictionaries often carry stereotypes. In the *Thorndike-Barnhart Beginning Dictionary*, 'illustrative phrases consistently represented girls as good, honest, pure, truth-telling, and generally wonderful; whereas boys were represented as violent, cruel, and irremediably wicked' (Baehr, in

---

[25] On comparable words in dictionaries, see Mills (1989).   [26] 'Man's companion'.

Landau 2001: 420–1). Sometimes it is difficult to say whether we have stereotypes or prejudices, two facets of sexism. In *COD1*, the entry for *good* was illustrated by 'Give her a good beating', and the entry for *spectacle* by 'A drunken woman is a deplorable spectacle' (Allen 1986: 2). In some cases, the lexicographer was probably trying to be facetious, as in the *COD1* entry for *cure* illustrated by 'cure girls of running after officers', as we have seen, or in the *OED2* entry for *separate (or sort out) the men from the boys* illustrated by 'the Dry Martini ... is a drink that will quickly separate the men from the boys and the girls from their principles', a quotation selected by Burchfield from a 1968 copy of *House and Garden* (Brewer 2004: 21).[27] Did everybody appreciate the humour?

Dictionaries became more sensitive to gender in the course of the twentieth century, less prejudiced and less stereotypical, perhaps because more and more lexicographers are women. The 1959 edition of *C20D* defined *woman* as 'an adult female of the human race', and *COD* (1964) as 'adult human female'. Landau (2001: 422) mentions some of the changes that took place in the *Scott, Foresman Beginning Dictionary* from 1968 to 1988:

In 1968 the illustration for *check* was, 'When we finished eating, Father asked the waitress for the check.' In 1988 it is 'After we finished eating, the waiter brought the check to our table.' Not content with excising Father, who initiated the action described, the editors have been so sensitive to the relationship between Father and the waitress and about feminine-ending words in general that they have substituted *waiter* (now like most-*er* words usually defined as neutral in gender). Moreover, it is the waiter who now performs the action, apparently unsolicited by anyone.

The example sentence 'The lazy boy's parents hounded him to do his homework' (1968) was changed to 'The children hounded their parents to buy a color TV' (1988). In 1968 the illustration for *indifference* was 'The boy's indifference to his homework worried his parents' but this was changed to 'The child's indifference to food worried his parents' (Landau 2001: 423). *LDEL2* (1991) used *he/she* in its definitions. Cowie (in Norri 2000: 77) compared *ALD1* (1948) and *ALD4* (1989), and concluded 'that the editorial team of the latter decided to give greater prominence to women in the examples, and also to portray them in a wider range of professional roles than in the earlier editions'. *ALD5* (1995) had a label *sexist* applied to words that 'express an unfair or patronizing attitude towards a person of the opposite sex. They are usually used by men about women. Examples are *career girl*, *dolly-bird*, *looker*'. In *OED3*, 'care has been taken to eradicate sexist definitions' (Brewer 2004: 21), and there has been 'some systematic pruning of

---

[27] *OED1* also illustrated the entry for *woman* by, among others quotations, 'every Woman is at heart a Rake' (Pope) (Brewer 2007: 227).

sexist quotations': the 'Dry Martini' quotation is not in (Brewer 2004: 21). There is at least one dictionary that has been revised from a feminist point of view, so that the traditional roles are reversed, the *American Heritage School Dictionary* (Graham 1975). Inevitably, some have gone too far: the inclusion of *womyn* 'used as a consciously altered spelling by feminists to avoid the sequence *men* ... in *RHWC* ignited more condemnation than anything else in the dictionary' (Sheidlower 1995: 41), and it must be said that it does not give a true image of usage.

6.1.1.5 Proper names and culture

The treatment of proper names, the vehicles of culture in the stricter sense of the word, can also say something about what the lexicographers think, or what they think the users want. Some names are omitted, especially if they are not part of the 'noble' culture or if they are disapproved of: *Barbie (doll)* is not in *CED*. One of my dictionaries of French, published by a Roman Catholic priest in Lyon, Elie Blanc in 1892, *Dictionnaire alphabétique et analogique de la langue française à l'usage des écoles*, does not have an entry for Emile Zola, the scandalous author of *Nana* (1880). Some names are included, but with treatments that express disapproval or omit some features. Ilson (1997: 353) notes that *MWC10* (1993) changed the *MWC9* entry for *Marquis de Sade* from 'Fr. soldier and pervert' to 'Fr. writer of erotica'. The definition of *Côte d'Azur* in *CED* mentions that it 'forms an administrative region with Provence' but does not say a word of what the region means, or has meant, for many rich English families. The US edition of *EWED* has a photograph of Bill Gates, but not of John Kennedy. Sometimes, dictionaries treat proper names in ways that are more designed to please their readers than to reflect historical truth, giving 'credence to the idea that there may very well be an element of indoctrin- ation at play in the way the material has been devised' (Pilard 2002: 432). For example, the entry for *Dunkirk* in *LDEL* does not mention French or Belgian troops in the battle of Dunkirk in 1940, only British soldiers. *ALDE* does the same. The entry for *Joan of Arc* in *CED* manages not to mention England or the English.

6.1.1.6 What can the lexicographer do?

Lexicographers can hardly be objective, and it may not be what the users want. Dictionary users want their dictionaries to mirror the likes and dislikes of their societies: 'Although dictionary treatment of social attitudes necessarily lags behind the present, dictionaries, in choosing to recognize one set of values over other possible sets of values, give the values they select stability and authority' (Landau 2001: 423). On the other hand, should the dictionary always give the users what they want? 'Two temptations are ... always present: to pander to irrational prejudices as a merchandizing ploy and to ignore those prejudices because they are messy to deal with' (Algeo 1989a: 32). Dictionary publishers cannot afford to ignore commercial constraints, for obvious reasons, but lexicographers serve their users best by depicting reality as it is, not as some would like it to be. Like linguists, they will always insist that the dictionary should describe the language, not pass judgement on it, and describe the language as it is, not as some people would like it to be.[28] Both Murray and Gove had expressed a wish to include all the words of the language, even the more objectionable ones, Whitman-like, but their publishers forced them to omit the words that might have raised objections from the public. Hence the hesitations when a pressure group demands the withdrawal of a dictionary or of a word from a dictionary: sometimes the publishers resist, siding with the lexicographers and explaining that the job of the dictionary is only to record usage, sometimes they give in, siding with their financial advisers—usually without a comment.

6.1.2 Some dictionaries are more cultural than others

It is obvious that dictionaries reflect the values of a society through their inclusions and exclusions, definitions, examples, and usage labels. But this should be handled with care: the evidence of ideological and moral biases may delight the metalexicographer and be of some use for the sociologist but it enrages the lexicographer, who feels accused of incompetence, or carelessness, or worse, deliberate indoctrination. Any attempt at using this evidence to pass judgement on dictionaries or on lexicographers would be misguided, Landau (2001: 422) says, and alleging 'that the biases are either deliberate or the result of uncommon insensitivity [is] almost always wrongheaded and unjustified'. Objectivity in dictionaries is impossible—it is one of the unreachable ideals of lexicography— and it is unreasonable to expect lexicographers to be objective: 'All lexicographers, who are the mouthpieces of a social class, the instruments of an ideology, no doubt believe that they objectively represent a set of forms. But there is no objectivity, no picture so accurate as to eliminate the model' (Rey 1977: 88).

Yet, some dictionaries are more cultural than others. Most of the examples that we have mentioned come from native speakers' dictionaries, NSDs, not from learners' dictionaries, MLDs, and this may illustrate a basic difference between them. The arrival of the latter in the middle of the twentieth century has brought again to the fore a distinction that had disappeared in the eighteenth century: the

---

[28] The British Potato Council once 'staged a demonstration near the offices of Oxford University Press' (Abley 2009: 40) to have *couch potato* removed from the *OED*.

MLD only aims at teaching the language, while the NSD also aims at helping to integrate the user into a community; the MLD focuses on 'communication-orientated functions', i.e. teaching how to use the language, while the NSD focuses on 'cognition-orientated functions', i.e. teaching facts about the language and culture (Bergenholtz and Nielsen 2006); the NSD cannot be described without evoking the historical, social, political, ideological background against which it was compiled and published, but for the MLD the background is mostly the state of research in linguistics and in the teaching of languages; and the critical assessment of an NSD has to consider how the dictionary fits in the society in which it is published, while the critical assessment of an MLD has to focus on how well the dictionary represents the language and how useful it is in the process of language learning. NSDs, both British and American, are cultural, and MLDs are functional.

Of course, the distinction is not strictly binary. There is a scale of 'culturality' on which each individual dictionary can be placed: *COB* is close to the functional end, *CED* closer to the cultural, *NODE* somewhere in the middle, etc.

There are other reasons to consider British and American NSDs of the twentieth century as variants of the same type. They have differences, but also many features in common: a simplification of the metalanguage, the inclusion of more grammatical information, an effort to represent more varieties of English, an extension of the wordlist towards scientific and technical words, more attention to the work of linguists, a tendency to be more objective: 'The differences between British and American practice are outweighed by their similarities, and they are becoming more alike with each passing year' (Landau 2001: 381). The recent increase in the exchanges between the two sides of the Atlantic, the importation of the American tradition in Britain with *CED*, the simultaneous publication of two close versions for Britain and the USA, *NODE* and *NOAD*, and the fact that *EWED* presents itself as the first dictionary of global English support the idea that British and American NSDs are more similar than they are different: they are both what Makkai (1980: 127) calls HABIT dictionaries, for 'heterogeneous alphabetical inventories'.

6.1.3 *The common features of modern dictionaries*

6.1.3.1 Dictionaries are more user-friendly

Lexicographers have always done their best to make their texts easily accessible to their users. The pages of old dictionaries look cluttered and difficult to read for our modern eyes, although they can only be judged by the standards of their time. Each new generation of dictionaries is more readable than the preceding one.

Hausmann (2002) argues that recent dictionaries[29] are better from the point of view of visibility—how pleasant to the eye the dictionary page is—and readability—how easy it is to find information in the dictionary text—than they have ever been, and that they have reached a stage of near-perfection. This is due to an improvement of the paper, the inks and the fonts, and also to an improvement of the layout: no nesting or niching, the use of boxes, more white space—for example starting new senses on a new line—and the use of different colours to distinguish different types of information. There is also a simplification of the style. Most recent dictionaries avoid tildes, parentheses, abbreviated labels, formulae such as 'of, or pertaining to', etc.: 'it is becoming rare now to find dictionaries with hermetically sealed nuggets of information coded up to defy interpretation by all but the dogged few' (Atkins 2002: 1). At the same time, the e-dictionary is creating its own standards of 'consultablity' (see below, 9.2).

6.1.3.2 Dictionaries represent more varieties of English

In the eighteenth century, dictionaries recorded the language of the best writers of the preceding periods. Since then, they have expanded their wordlists with words of earlier times, words belonging to other social varieties or other situations of use, scientific and technical words, words of the working classes, of familiar conversation, vulgar words, and taboo words. The latest addition was words from other English-speaking areas, the words of Ireland, of America, of Australia, which accompanied the increased access of the public to the literature of those countries.

That is a recent development. At the end of a study of the treatment of Americanisms in British dictionaries (*ALD, COD, LDOCE*, and a few others) in 1981, I (Béjoint 1981*b*) came to the conclusion that it was highly unequal, often inexplicable, and that the more recent dictionaries were better than their predecessors. American dictionaries were worse: Ilson (1986*b*: 62) compared British and American dictionaries for their coverage of twelve pairs of words, one British and one American (*silencer–muffler, courgette–zucchini, nappy–diaper, torch–flashlight*, etc.), and noted that there were some Americanisms in British dictionaries but that American dictionaries had very few Briticisms:

Of the American dictionaries W9 [= *MWC9*] is the only one that comes anywhere near a respectable score: it gets seven out of the twelve … CED gets all twelve right. COD … and GID each get eleven, LDEL gets ten, *Chambers* [= *C2oD*] gets ten. Clearly, the British dictionaries are much more aware of American English than the American dictionaries are of British English.

---

[29] He discusses bilingual dictionaries but what he says also applies to monolingual dictionaries.

OED2 was more hospitable to other varieties than *OED1*, to Americanisms but also to words and phrases from South Africa, Australia, New Zealand, and Canada, and *OED3* lexicographers do not seem to consider the British variety of English as a relevant limit to their compilation (Weiner 1986). Other dictionaries have had the same evolution, especially on the British side, even though the coverage may still be uneven and the choice of words to be included and of labels to attach to them sometimes inexplicable (Norri 1996). *C21D* provides American variants: at *nappy*, it says 'N. *Amer equivalent* DIAPER' and at *pavement* 'N. *Amer* SIDEWALK'.[30] American dictionaries always leave the American variant unlabelled (Ilson 1990*b*: 1974). The evolution is partly a consequence of the commercial race to have more than the competitor and to extend the sales to new areas, but there is also a genuine need to widen the scope of the dictionary, because the national limits of yesterday no longer mean much in the global village. The ultimate step would be the compilation of a dictionary that would contain all the varieties of the English language, the 'dictionary of the English-speaking peoples' advocated by Crystal (1986: 72),[31] a huge enterprise and one which the use of computers for production and the consultation of lexical databases has made more accessible than it has ever been.

6.1.3.3 Dictionaries have more terms

The inclusion of specialized terms in dictionaries goes back to the seventeenth century with Phillips' *New World of English Words* (1658), and even further back if one considers that some of the hard words of earlier dictionaries were scientific and technical. A quick look at succeeding editions of the same dictionary in the twentieth century, *COD*, *C20D*, etc. shows that there are more and more:[32] *COD5* had sixteen entries between *chip* and *chisel*; *COD11* has twenty-eight, among which *chipboard, chiral, chi-rho, chironomid, chiropteran, chiru*, that were not in *COD5*—most of these things were unknown in 1964. Precise figures are impossible to obtain, because they rest on a shaky definition of what a specialized term is and because much depends on the organization of the macrostructure.[33] Normally, the larger a dictionary is the more terms it should have, in terms of both number and percentage. Barnhart (1978: 124) says that 'almost 40 percent of

---

[30] The recent British MLDs have all the more common Americanisms, and even label *Brit* those words or usages that are specifically British, like *nappy* or *pavement*. Some American MLDs have Briticisms, not all.

[31] See Crystal's website.

[32] On the inclusion of technical and scientific terms in French dictionaries, see Mazière (1981) and Béjoint (1988). For English dictionaries, see Landau (2001).

[33] *COD11* also has *microchip* and others in the entry *chip*.

the content of general-purpose dictionaries, such as college dictionaries, consists of scientific or technical terminology'. Landau (2001: 165) says that in *W3* 'a third or more of the terms ... are scientific and technical' but this is difficult to reconcile with Barnhart's 40 per cent. In *GR*, according to Rey, the percentage is about 50 per cent.

> In a large 'cultural' dictionary like the *Grand Robert*, the wordlist—roughly 80,000 entries—is such that, beside the 40,000 or so common or fairly common words many specific, even marginal, aspects of the lexicon are drawn upon. Among those, one finds archaisms, fairly rare literary forms, regionalisms, words specific to some circles—even the slang of criminals—and also scientific, technical, legal, professional, didactic words.
>
> (Rey 1985: 5)

Again, there is a commercial aspect, because terms are in everlasting supply and they can boost the number of words in a wordlist with little lexicographic effort. But the increase in the number of terms is also a consequence of the fact that the dictionary user is more and more interested in science and technology. Terms are included 'because the reader expects to find them' (Landau 2001: 358). This may have had an unfortunate consequence, Landau (2001: 104) says: 'modern dictionaries have a bias in favor of scientific and technical terms, and I believe the neglect of common words such as adverbs is the other side of the coin. Dictionaries have increasingly taken on an encyclopedic function that precludes full treatment of common words'. Of course, common words are more difficult to treat, and less flattering.

6.2 THE END OF A PERIOD?

6.2.1 *Lexicographers: slaves or masters?*

The work of the lexicographer, Johnson lamented, is a humble one. Culling words from texts and listing them in alphabetical order with some explanation of their meanings requires little inventiveness, let alone genius. It is menial work at the service of others: 'The work of the Lexicographer is very hard work, and very boring for the lexicographer himself, but very useful to others,' wrote the authors of the *Dictionnaire de Trévoux* (Pruvost 2002a: 123). Until the appearance of the laws on copyright, it consisted to a large extent in copying more or less openly from earlier dictionaries: the history of lexicography everywhere is a story of plagiarism (Landau 2001: 214), a 'recital of successive and often successful acts of piracy, ... little more than a record of judicious or flagrant copying from one's predecessors, sometimes with grudging acknowledgment, more often (at least in the seventeenth century) without' (Landau 2001: 43). It is hard for lexicographers to be original. They must be at least as good as their predecessors, and possibly better, but they must not copy them exactly, and the scope for improvement is limited.

Yet many lexicographers of the past were brilliant people with strong personalities, who produced highly idiosyncratic dictionaries. They were amateurs with other occupations: 'people drifted into and out of dictionary making from such diverse occupations as theology and education (Comenius), literature (the Grimm brothers, as Johnson before them), philology (Murray), medicine (Roget) and music (Grove)' (Hartmann 2001: 7). Furetière was a writer, Webster and Larousse were teachers, Littré had studied medicine, Robert was a lawyer and an orange farmer, etc. They were attracted to lexicography because of the prestige of the dictionary, because of its importance in the evolution of the language, because of its role in the teaching of the language, because of a zealous enthusiasm for the education of the people or because of a fascination for language and for capturing it and putting it in a cage to observe it. The common point between them is that they were idealists, visionaries who had learnt about life in other areas before starting in lexicography. They were witty, sceptical, scathing, recalcitrant, they used their dictionaries to scold, to preach, to mock, to condemn, to fight ignorance and pretentiousness, with little respect for the ideals of objectivity and coherence as we have come to understand them. They were unreasonable, but the paradox is that the more extravagant they were the better their dictionaries are considered by the community of lexicographers and by the public, and the more they are remembered. A dictionary compiled by a fanciful, original, independent mind may be less good but it is more attractive.

By the end of the twentieth century, dictionary making was no longer an individual enterprise, perhaps a sign that the dictionary is not as important as it had been for centuries, perhaps an illustration of what Roland Barthes was writing in 1968: The author is dead. Dictionaries are no longer compiled by identifiable authors, they are compiled by teams of lexicographers. Those teams are not new—they date back at least to Samuel Johnson—but they have become more important than their leaders. The work of modern lexicographers has become even more repetitive, and the scope for invention and imagination is narrower than ever. There is still some copying from one's predecessors, and an increasing part of the job is to extract what the corpus contains and note it on pre-formatted templates, or to adapt existing text to produce endless variations from the same database. The name game is now played differently: 'old dictionaries were named after their writers, whereas modern dictionaries are named after their publishers' (Flexner, in Algeo 1990*b*: 2004).

Modern dictionaries aim at being objective records of the language and at reflecting the values and attitudes of the public at large rather than the views of a brilliant individual. Is this a sign of progress? In a sense, yes: dictionaries must be serious. Many modern users would probably reject a highly idiosyncratic dictionary. But one cannot help thinking that modern dictionaries, although more sophisticated than ever, have also become less imaginative, less exciting. In this sense, one can regret the old days, when dictionaries were much worse, and also much better.

6.2.2 Lexicography: an art, a craft, or a science?

Until the middle of the twentieth century, there were two traditions in the lexicography of English, one British and one American, and when the learner's dictionary appeared, it created a third, but now, at the beginning of the twenty-first century, we may have two types again, cultural dictionaries, British and American NSDs, and functional dictionaries, the MLDs. Whatever their type, all recent dictionaries of English have one thing in common, their effort to be more scientific in the preparation and in the presentation of information, a trend that was begun in the mid-nineteenth century with the *OED* and continued with *W3*. Lexicography is still very much an art and a craft, as Landau (1984) said, but it is becoming more of a science.

There are three factors that have been shaping English dictionaries since the middle of the twentieth century and will probably continue to shape them as well as the dictionaries of other languages: the study of how dictionaries are used, the application of linguistics to the lexicographic description of the language, and the use of the computer in the preparation and in the consultation of the dictionary text. Linguistics can show lexicographers what should be done, at least part of it, the computer gives them better means of doing what they have decided to do, and user studies tell them how well they have done it.

7

THE STUDY OF DICTIONARY
USERS AND USES

O NE of the conclusions of the conference on lexicography that took place in
Bloomington in 1960 was that dictionaries 'should be designed with a
special set of users in mind and for their specific needs' (Householder 1962:
279). Until then, dictionaries had been shaped by the need to standardize the
language or to educate the uneducated, and by the desire of lexicographers to
exert an influence on the evolution of the language or to teach their contemporaries. Lexicographers did their best, but there was little interest in what
happened after the dictionary had been published. They never seem to have
bothered about who the users were and what they wanted: they, the lexicographers, knew what was good for the public, and the users simply had to adapt
to the dictionary as it was.

By the 1960s, some lexicographers had lost their certainties. They began to
think that the development of dictionaries should be based on a study of the
populations of dictionary users and of the different ways in which dictionaries
were used: Who are the dictionary users? What do they use the dictionary for,
and what happens when they open a dictionary? How successful are they, and
why? The results could help improve the effectivity (Swanepoel 2001) or effectiveness (Wingate 2002) of dictionaries, it was hoped, by influencing the choice
of words, of information, and of modes of presentation.

7.1 WHO USES DICTIONARIES, AND WHAT FOR?

7.1.1 *Who are dictionaries for?*

7.1.1.1 Evidence from the dictionary

The form and contents of dictionaries have always been determined by lexicographers posing as dictionary users (Rey 1977: 96), but, together with linguists, they are probably the least representative of users: both share the same peculiar interest for words that are difficult to treat, function words, polysemous words, and grammatical information, things that the average user rarely consults (see below). The difference between lexicographers and linguists is that the former will tend to excuse all weaknesses because they know how impossibly difficult it is to write a dictionary, while the latter will typically find fault with everything (see below, 8.1.1.2).

Many dictionaries of the sixteenth and seventeenth centuries explained in great detail on their title pages who their intended users were, as we have seen: foreigners, travellers, ladies, young students, and more generally people who otherwise had no access to education. Since the eighteenth century, dictionaries have been less precise: the users were those who needed a linguistic model because they were not natural users of the prestige variety, or those who needed more information on the language they used. The prefaces and publicity material always described the users in favourable terms. Furetière (1690) said that his user was 'Universal Man', defined as 'the person who has learnt several sciences and can answer with pertinence any question whatsoever' (in the entry for *universel*). Littré aimed his *Dictionnaire* (1863–73) at learned people: 'erudites, philologues, physicians and intellectuals in general'. The intended user of the *GLLF* (1978) was 'the well educated francophone'. In 1971, the *TLF* described its users:

[T]he educated person who is part of what was until fairly recently called the elite, but is now preferably referred to as the upper or middle middle class, that is to say the most active elements of the main sectors of modern life, . . . not excluding—in fact even giving some special consideration to—all those who write for work or pleasure, those who hold the pens of our culture, or the teachers of all levels who transform all their writings into didactic language so that they can be transmitted to an ever increasing number of members of the masses. (*Preface*: xviii)

Many dictionaries are vague, because it would be commercially unwise to aim at a restricted public. *W3* was compiled for 'the high school and college student, the technician, and the periodical reader, as well as the scholar and professional'

(*Preface*), obviously trying hard not to forget anyone. Smaller dictionaries can be more specific, but they still try to capture a large audience. The *Preface* of *LDOCE* (1978: viii) is typical: 'Although the dictionary is intended primarily for the foreign student, its design and the new features it contains make it particularly suitable as a small reference dictionary for any person—whether teacher, student, linguist, or writer'.

7.1.1.2 What do dictionary users need to know?

Another approach to a better understanding of dictionary users is via a study of what they need to know before opening a dictionary and what skills they need during the process of consultation. The necessary skills vary with the dictionary being used, with the dictionary type, bilingual or monolingual, electronic or paper, CD-ROM or online, etc., with the type of task, comprehension or expression, the type of word, and the type of information.

The skills needed by the user are linguistic, metalinguistic, lexicographic, and pragmatic. The users must know the writing system, the basic syntactic patterns and a fair portion of the lexis, varying with the type of dictionary: a few hundred words are enough to consult a children's dictionary, a few thousand to use a learner's dictionary, but the users of the *OED* and of many native-speaker dictionaries, British or American, need a lot more. How many words should the users master to process such definitions as 'Non-deciduous excrescence, often curved and pointed, on head of cattle, sheep, goats, and other mammals, found in pairs, single, or one in front of another' for *horn* (*COD4*), which puzzled Landau (2001: 95) when he was a child, or 'a usu. long ament densely crowded with bracts' for *catkin* in *MWC*, mentioned by Rundell (1998: 324)? Neubauer (in Hausmann 1990a: 227) estimates that the users of some 60,000-word German dictionaries need to know about 20,000 words.[1]

Dictionary users need basic metalinguistic skills: how to cut up discourse into lexical units, how to categorize words by POS, etc. The ability to understand definitions seems to be shared by all language users (Iris *et al.* 1988) because definitions are used by adults to explain words to small children, but how it helps understand dictionary definitions is not known.

Dictionary users also need some world knowledge in order to understand many definitions. If a dictionary defines *cat* as 'a domestic animal that catches mice', the users will know what animal this refers to only if they already know that in that particular society mice have to be caught, and if they know what animal is

---

[1] Around 5,000 words are needed for reading simple texts according to Ostyn and Godin (1985), but see Arnaud (2009). Of course, much depends on what 'knowing a word' means.

employed in the task. In fact, since many domestic cats do not catch mice at all, what the users have to know is that in our societies the cat is—as Wierzbicka would have it (see below, 8.2.5.7)—*thought of* as the domestic animal that catches mice, world knowledge as well as word knowledge.

Dictionary users also need to master lexicographic conventions, the use of canonical forms, or lemmas (see below, 8.2.3.1), the wording of the definitions, the use of typography, parentheses, abbreviations, etc. and they have to master the conventions of each particular dictionary.

The consultation of a dictionary is a complex process, but the difficulties should not be overestimated. The necessary skills are those of the average adult user of the language. The number of words used by dictionaries is well within the reach of any educated person, even with dictionaries using esoteric language. Also, all language users perform other complex operations everyday, without even thinking about them.

If there is a sign on a door saying 'Please knock', we do not feel compelled to knock every time we pass the door. The sign is read but not acted on—or only when there is occasion to enter the room. We are familiar with the hierarchy of linguistic functions and we know when a sign acts as a signal or as a symbol. We are also capable of reading and handling meanings dynamically. We can juggle with variations and prototypes...; we know how meanings adjust and bow to context. We understand modalities. We can use the whole/ part relationship syntactically and rhetorically. We sense what is the same, similar and dissimilar, which is a vital skill for users of a dictionary. And finally, we frequently resort to paraphrase in ordinary discourse.   (Schelbert 1988: 63)

Schelbert gives the example of the pictures of animals in dictionaries, where the flea may be as big as the elephant, or the trout as big as the whale, without posing big problems to the users, who are used to pictorial representations in other circumstances. On the whole, the skills required for dictionary use are the same as those needed to function normally in society, with the exception of the lexicographic conventions. After all, millions of people use dictionaries every day with some success.

[The] dictionary is a social artefact, no doubt with a 'prototype' of its own, whose users become familiar with its conventions unconsciously—just as lexicographers do. The 'secret language' of dictionaries is often better understood, in practice if not in theory, than sophisticated linguists claim.   (Ilson 1984: 85)

Ilson (2001: 82) observes that our societies are used to dictionaries.

Most of the French-speaking world, like much of the English-speaking world, is dictionarate: in these places dictionaries are cultural artefacts of wide diffusion and great prestige. To be fully literate in French or English requires you to be dictionarate: to have a dictionary and to use, or boast you use, it. Dictionaracy (whew!) is a characteristic of other societies too.

A study of the use of dictionaries, electronic and paper, in Aboriginal communities in Australia confirms that dictionary users must be literate. Users with a low level of literacy experience all sorts of difficulties: they fail to find the word, they do not understand the dictionary text, they find it difficult to interpret the typographical conventions, etc. (Corris *et al.* 2004).

7.1.2 *What are dictionaries for?*

For the linguist, the dictionary is a record of the lexis of a language, for the dictionary publisher it is a compendium of all the answers to all the frequently asked questions, for the politician and the lawyer it is a book that fixes the meanings of words, for the teacher it is a guide to appropriate linguistic usage, for the journalist a tool to ensure clear and persuasive prose, for mum and dad a book to settle arguments on what is proper and what is not, for grandma a book to help her do her Sunday crossword, for the teenager a book to help her do her homework, etc. The different functions of the dictionary correspond to different choices that need to be made by the lexicographer early in the process of compilation.

The decision concerning the purpose or the combination of purposes of a planned dictionary is one of the most important ones. A good part of both the scientific and the commercial success of the dictionary will be the result of how reasonably this decision was made and how adroitly it was carried out.   (Zgusta 1971: 216)

McDavid (1979: 19–20) listed four possible functions:

1. To scholars, in all probability, the most important function of a dictionary is that of a record of the language, whether a diachronic statement of the development of words and their meanings from their earliest records to the present, or the ordering of them in a contemporary context, by frequency or centrality of meaning...
2. Another function of the dictionary is that of acquainting a user with a language, or a variety of a language, other than his own...
3. A third function is to supply incidental information, linguistic or otherwise, for the casual user...
4. Finally, there is the role of a conduct book...a guide to what one should do and especially to what one should not do.

And Hartmann (1985: 5) enlarged the list to seven.

(a) the dictionary as an authority on usage;
(b) the dictionary as a store of (difficult) vocabulary;

(c) the dictionary as a tool for improving communication;
(d) the dictionary as a means of strengthening the language;
(e) the dictionary as a stimulus to reflection on language;
(f) the dictionary as an aid to foreign-language learning;
(g) the dictionary as an ideological weapon.

7.1.2.1 What the lexicographers say

Lexicographers are rarely explicit about what a dictionary is for: 'It is the function of a popular dictionary to answer the questions that the user of the dictionary asks, and dictionaries on the commercial market will be successful in proportion to the extent to which they answer these questions of the buyer' (Barnhart 1962: 161). Dubois and Dubois (1971: 15–17), having examined the front matter of French dictionaries published in the 1960s, came to the conclusion that they were either portraits of the language or instruments for its acquisition, a distinction that corresponds more or less to cultural and functional dictionaries. Typical 'portrait dictionaries' present as:

the new standard reference work for modern English and its history.
a treasury of information about every aspect of words.

while an 'instrument dictionary' says:

The...aim is to provide...a comprehensive vocabulary aid for the present-day reader, speaker and writer of English.

7.1.2.2 What the dictionary reviewers say

The reviews of dictionaries in newspapers and magazines can be expected to reflect the popular idea of what a dictionary is: they are 'at least partly reliable gauges of that opinion' (Algeo 1989a: 30). Interestingly, they are specific to the GPD: other dictionaries, bilingual dictionaries, dictionaries of synonyms, of pronunciation, etc., like grammar books and encyclopedias, are never reviewed in the popular media, only in the specialized press. The reviewer of a GPD needs no particular qualification: 'being a user of a dictionary appears to be sufficient qualification sometimes, even though the same publication would not think of asking just any reader to review a novel or a book of poetry' (Jackson 2002: 175).

Many of those reviews are not much use. Rey and Delesalle (1979: 4) noted about the review articles published in popular magazines about Littré's *Dictionary*:

When the criticism does speak out, it is primitive. If one studies how Littré's dictionary was evaluated in the press, from the day of its publication, one can easily see that, in and between the lines of hundreds of reverential articles, nondescript or pompous, virtually nothing is said.

Landau (1984: 305) noted the same about the reviews of recent American dictionaries:

The great majority of popular reviews of dictionaries serve chiefly as vehicles for displays of irrelevant learning or amusing word play. Such reviewers, however well intentioned, intelligent, and in command of the use of language, lack the basis for making informed judgments about dictionaries because they do not know why certain decisions were made (why the windows are so small). They do not even know what questions should be asked, much less how to answer them.

But the fact that review articles are published year after year in the popular press is in itself an indication of the importance of the GPD, and they can be useful from that point of view: 'The journalistic criticism of dictionaries can confront real issues, like that of the social importance of works of reference' (Rey 1982: 3).

Popular reviewers are interested in two aspects of the GPD: the words that are included or omitted and sometimes the advice on usage (Landau 2001: 204). The articles published in the French press about the annual edition of *PL* are almost exclusively about the words that have been added or those that have been left out, and nothing is ever said of the words that have been kept or deleted, of the definitions or of the methodology. Dictionaries are berated for having excluded a given word, even if the word is rare, or marginal, or ephemeral, provided the reviewer happens to think it is important. A dictionary must have the names of the latest fads, the fashionable trends, the popular neologisms, etc., however volatile. The more copious a dictionary is the better it is, however mediocre its general methodology or its microstructural treatment. This is not totally misguided—the number of words in a dictionary is important[2]—but it is only one aspect of its quality.

When the reviewers are academics, the reviews are usually better informed but they are more malicious, and on the whole not much more useful.

[Academics have a] surprising lack of interest in general principles, with incidental sniping taking the place of any real exploration of the intentions with which the works being criticized had been set up. Omissions are lamented and superfluities condemned, but the whole basis for determining the nomenclature remains largely undiscussed.   (Osselton 1989: 229; see also Atkins 1993)

---

[2] Contrary to what some linguists of the 1960s said: 'the number of words cannot be considered as a criterion to assess the quality of a dictionary' (Matoré 1968: 194).

7.1.2.3 What the users say

What people want from dictionaries is to a certain extent indicated by the sales figures. The users buy the dictionaries that they like, and the lexicographer tries to give them what they expect:

> [H]e is forced to give in to social pressures through the types of questions asked by the public and the type of answers that the public expects: he just cannot afford to disappoint his readers by not giving them what he is expected to provide.
>
> (Dubois and Dubois 1971: 100)

A dictionary that sells well is not necessarily a good dictionary, but it is certainly a dictionary that corresponds to a social need.

But the commercial success of dictionaries is not an unambiguous indicator of what the users need. Dictionary users cannot buy what they do not know or what is not on offer. If they buy a dictionary, it may be because they like it and find it useful, or it may be because they have no choice. And a dictionary that sells well creates expectations in the public, as we have seen with the *OED*. The lexicographic traditions over the centuries have created habits, however unconscious of them the users may be, and the users may mistake those habits for their real needs.

7.1.3 *How are dictionaries really used?*

7.1.3.1 The myriad ways of using a dictionary

Dictionaries can be used 'in an infinite number of ways' (W. H. Auden, in Brewer 2004: 10), some of which have little to do with what the lexicographers intended: as instruments for self-teaching; as thesauruses of literature; as first-class reading, because they are 'full of suggestion', 'raw material of possible poems', 'inexhaustible', etc.[3] (Brewer 2004: 10); as Christmas gifts, to be cherished in proportion to the feelings one has for the person who offered it; as objects on living room tables to impress the visitors; as books that sit on shelves but are never consulted; as objects of pride: Emperor Maximilian II showed his copy of Estienne's *Thesaurus Graecae Linguae* to all his visitors... but forgot all about it after two months (Considine 1998: 580); as cushions to sit children on so that they can reach the dinner-table (Hall 2001: 1), or even adults, for example W.H. Auden (Brewer 2007: 193); as thick objects to steady an old wardrobe; as heavy objects to knock

---

[3] José-Maria de Heredia, the poet, said that reading Nicot's dictionary gave him more pleasure and emotion than reading Dumas's *Three Musketeers* (Anatole France on Wikisource, article *Lexique*). Not very nice for Dumas.

on the head of unruly pupils;[4] as pillows to lay one's head on, as in Charles Dickens' *Nicholas Nickleby*: 'Dry toast and warm tea offered him every night and morning when he couldn't swallow anything—a candle in his bedroom on the very night he died—the best dictionary sent up for him to lay his head upon...'[5] (Hitchings 2005: 229); as the only book to be taken on a desert island; or as a 'cuddly toy' to be treated 'lovingly' and taken 'to bed' (Leech and Nesi 1999: 305) like a lover, 'a weighty one, but handleable' (Brewer 2007: 212).[6] In many of these roles the paper dictionary will remain forever superior to the e-dictionary.

7.1.3.2 The users buy the dictionary they have in their heads

Many users have images of the dictionary that have little to do with reality: they see it as a list of all the words of the language, as an infallible source of word meanings, as the ultimate authority on linguistic usage and on everything, etc. Those are 'misunderstandings' (Algeo 1989a: 32), dictionary myths, but they are important because the dictionary that people buy *is* that imaginary dictionary rather than the dictionary that the lexicographers produce.[7] The misunderstandings are not easy to identify, as evidence is hard to come by and to interpret when it is available: it is in everyday conversations, in fiction, in novels, plays, radio and television scripts, in letters sent to newspapers, in the proceedings of courts of justice, etc.

Dictionary myths are encapsulated in the use of the definite article and of the singular: people (present writer included) often speak of *the* dictionary, as if there was only one dictionary per language that would come in different formats and types of presentation but with the same contents (Moon 1989: 63). Many dictionaries of English have had titles with *The*—in fact the mystery is why some use the indefinite article.[8] In the BoE (see below, 9.1.7), the phrase 'according to the dictionary' occurs with great frequency (Moon 2002: 633): one says 'the dictionary' exactly as one says 'the Bible' but not *'the encyclopedia', *'the grammar' or *'the cookery book' (Ilson 1985b: 1).

---

[4] This, I am told, used to be practised in some English primary schools.   [5] Chapter 4.

[6] I have been unable to find an example of a dictionary being thrown at one's opponent's head. I have to make do with the unique episode of Becky Sharp flinging her dictionary at Miss Pinkerton. I also found on the Amazon website this ambiguous comment by a dictionary user about a new dictionary: 'I installed the CD on my computer...but I still will use the book more often...with Scrabble at the kitchen table, nothing beats having the authoritative tome at your elbow—ready for a challenge from your ignorant opponent'. I keep looking.

[7] For a discussion of dictionary myths, see also Boulanger (1986: 95–101), Collinot and Mazière (1997: 74 ff.) and Pruvost (2002a: 119–23).

[8] *COD10* had *The* on the title page, not on the dust jacket; *COD11* has it on neither. French dictionaries only have an article when the name of the author is used: 'le *Littré*', 'le *Larousse*', 'le *Robert*'.

I have met people who knew nothing about Dictionaries; they knew only that there was a book called 'The Dictionary', just as there is a book called the Bible, another called the Prayer-book, another the Koran; when they saw or heard a word that was new to them, they wondered if it was 'in the Dictionary' (Murray 1903)[9]

In some cases *the dictionary* designates a particular dictionary, seen as the paragon of its kind, Johnson's dictionary in England, or the *OED*, Webster's unabridged in the USA, *Littré* in France, but it often means *any* dictionary, big or small, old or new, good or bad, just the one that we happen to have consulted or to have in mind.

7.1.3.3 The dictionary is the Bible

The dictionary is often compared to the Bible:

In a world where men of letters were often also men of the cloth . . . it can be no surprise that wordbooks acquired (and still retain for many today) a quality of Holy Writ. Clerics and clerks, scholars and Schoolmen—there has for centuries in Europe been an interplay between the pen and the pulpit, especially when the Bible was one of the main reasons for learning to read.   (McArthur 1998: 91)

Dictionaries and Bibles have long looked the same: thick, solemn, precious books bound in leather with golden lettering that one can only open in reverence. They were also similar in contents: 'the results of the lexicographer's labours . . . is endowed with the numinous quality of Moses' tablets' (Atkins: 1985: 23). The dictionary is 'like the Bible' (Ilson 1985*b*: 1). '[P]opular opinion tends to invest the word of the lexicographer with some of the same power as the Word of God—so much so that the dictionary and the Bible are often perceived as twin (and equally incontestable) sources of authority, one secular and the other divine' (Mugglestone 2005: xvi).

Some have seen the dictionary as the *new* Bible, as if there was a chronology in history. In 1934, Aristide Quillet wrote in the preface of his splendid *Dictionnaire Encyclopédique*, with characteristic faith in the progress of a society that moves from religious belief to scientific knowledge: 'Today's Bible is the dictionary. Ancient peoples looked to the Bible in search of a revelation; modern peoples look to the dictionary in search of knowledge' (Pruvost 2000: 116).

7.1.3.4 The dictionary is a shibboleth

The dictionary is endowed with magical powers, it works wonders for its happy owners by its very presence, even if it is not used. The mere possession of a

---

[9] Lecture on dictionaries, in *OED News*, June 2003.

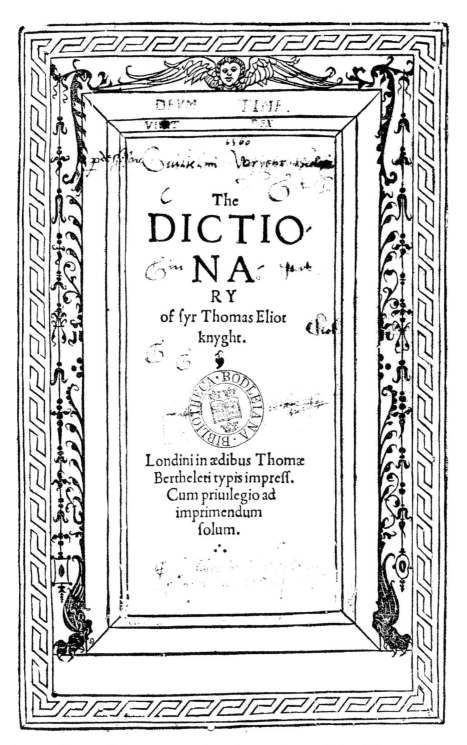

The
DICTIO
NA
RY
of ſyr Thomas Eliot
knyght.

Londini in ædibus Thomæ
Bertheleti typis impreſſ.
Cum priuilegio ad
imprimendum
ſolum.

Plate 1 Title page of *The Dictionary of Syr Thomas Eliot Knyght* (1538). [See p. 6.]

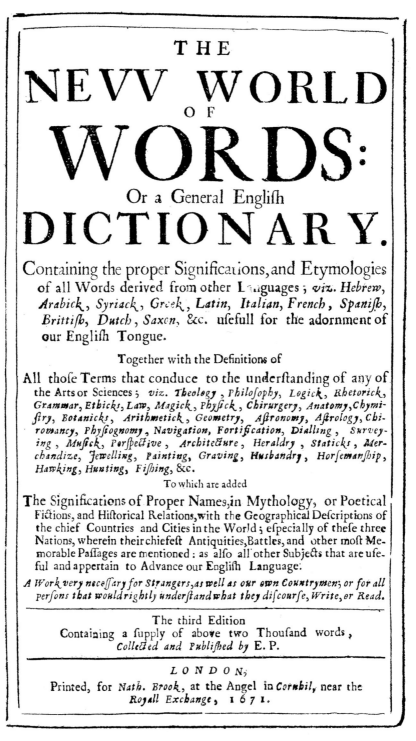

THE
NEVV WORLD
O F
WORDS:
Or a General Englifh
DICTIONARY.

Containing the proper Significations, and Etymologies of all Words derived from other Languages ; *viz. Hebrew, Arabick, Syriack, Greek, Latin, Italian, French, Spanifh, Brittifh, Dutch, Saxon,* &c. ufefull for the adornment of our Englifh Tongue.

Together with the Definitions of

All thofe Terms that conduce to the underftanding of any of the Arts or Sciences ; *viz. Theology , Philofophy, Logick, Rhetorick, Grammar, Ethicks, Law, Magick, Phyfick , Chirurgery, Anatomy, Chymiftry, Botanicks, Arithmetick , Geometry, Aftronomy, Aftrology, Chiromancy, Phyfiognomy , Navigation, Fortification, Dialling , Surveying , Mufick, Perfpective , Architecture , Heraldry , Staticks , Merchandize, Jewelling, Painting, Graving, Husbandry , Horfemanfhip, Hawking, Hunting, Fifhing,* &c.

To which are added

The Significations of Proper Names, in Mythology, or Poetical Fictions, and Hiftorical Relations, with the Geographical Defcriptions of the chief Countries and Cities in the World ; efpecially of thefe three Nations, wherein their chiefeft Antiquities, Battles, and other moft Memorable Paffages are mentioned : as alfo all other Subjects that are ufeful and appertain to Advance our Englifh Language.

A Work very neceffary for Strangers, as well as our own Countrymen; or for all perfons that would rightly underftand what they difcourfe, Write, or Read.

The third Edition
Containing a fupply of above two Thoufand words , *Collected and Publifhed by E. P.*

L O N D O N;
Printed, for *Nath. Brook,* at the Angel in *Cornbil,* near the *Royall Exchange,* 1 6 7 1.

Plate 2 Title page of *The New World of Words,* by E. P. (Edward Phillips) (1671 edition). Note that the dictionary calls itself *General* and contains specialized words and proper names. Note also the description of the intended users. [See p. 59.]

rity for the time being, both in war and peace ; he was never chosen but upon some great occasion, and his command was to last but half a year.

Dictionary, (*Lat.*) called in Greek a Lexicon; a Book wherein hard words and names are mentioned, and unfolded.

Dictum, the ancient name of a City in *Caernervonshire*, now called *Diganway*.

Dictynna, a name attributed to *Diana* : who flying from *Minos*, she cast her self into certain nets which are called Dictya.

Didapper, a kind of bird so called from the Greek word *Diadiptein*, to duck under water.

Dido, the daughter of *Belus* King of the *Tyrians* ; she was married to *Sichaeus* Priest of *Hercules*, whom *Pygmalion* slew, that he might obtain his riches ; but the gathering all the wealth she could together, fled into *Africa*, and there built a City which was first called *Byrsa*, afterwards *Carthage*, and refusing to marry *Iarbas* King of *Getulia*, because he went about to force her by war, she killed her self. Others say, it was because falling in love with *Æneas*, who was driven by tempest, on her coast, he refused to marry her.

Didram, an ancient coyn valuing fifteen pence.

Diem clausit extremum, a Writ that lyeth for the heir of him that holdeth land of the Crown, either by Knights-service, or in Soccage and dyeth. It is directed to the Escheatour, to enquire of what estate he was seized, and who is next Heir ; and this Inquisition is to be returned into the Chancery.

Dies datus, a respite given to the Tenant or Defendant before the Court.

Diennial, (*Lat.*) of two years continuance.

Diespiter, quasi diei pater, a name attributed to *Jupiter* ; he is also called *Lucetius*, from *Lux*, the light.

Diet, in Greek *diaita*, from *dais* a banquet, signifieth a general convention of the *German* Peers to consult of the affairs of the Empire.

Dieta rationabilis, a reasonable days journey; a word used in the Civil Law.

Dietetical, (*Greek*) belonging to a limited and proportionable diet.

Diezeugmenon, (*Greek*) a figure in Rhetorick in which several clauses of a sentence have reference to one verb ; as *Quorum ordo humilis, fortuna sordida, natura turpis à ratione abhorret.* It is otherwise called *Epizeugmenon*, and in Latin by *Aquila Romanus Disjunctum* and *Injunctum.*

Diffamation, (*Lat.*) a disgracing, a blemishing any one's good name.

Diffarreation, (*Lat.*) a Solemnity anciently used among the Romans, in the divorcement of man and wife.

Differences, in Heraldry are extraordinary additions, whereby bearers of the same Coat-armour, are distinguished each from others.

Difficulty, (*Lat.*) uneasiness, hardness.

Diffidence, (*Lat.*) doubtfulness, mistrustfulness.

Diffoded, (*Lat.*) digged, as a hole, or ditch is digged in the earth.

Difflation, (*Lat.*) is, when through heat, spirits arising, are with a kind of Bellows, blown in the adverse *Camera*, and they are found coagulated : a Term in Chymistry.

Diffluence, (*Lat.*) a flowing asunder, or several ways.

Diffusion, (*Lat.*) a scattering or shedding abroad. Diffusion in Philosophy, is the dilating of a substance into more parts.

Digamma, (*Greek*) the Æolic letter among the Greeks, like unto our letter F.

Digestion, (*Lat.*) a disposing : a concocting of meat in the stomack, in Caymistry its contracting and maturating of crude things by an easie and gentle heat.

Digests, in French, *Pandectes* ; a volume of the Civil Law so called, because the legal precepts therein contained, are so excellently disposed and digested.

Dight, (old word) ready, adorned.

Digit, a character which expresseth a figure in Arithmetick, as V. the figure of five : also the parts of an Eclipse.

Digitation, (*Lat.*) a pointing with the fingers, also an expressing the form of the fingers.

Digladiation, (*Lat.*) a fighting, or disputing the matter with swords.

Digne, from the Latin word *dignus*, are gentle, worthy. It is a word used by Chaucer.

Dignity, (*Lat.*) honour, reputation, advancement. Essential dignities of the Planets are when Planets are in their own houses, exaltations, triplicites, and faces. How these are assigned to every Planet, see in Mr. *Lillies* Introduct. Fo. 104.

Diguosce, (*Lat.*) to know, or discern one from another.

Digression, (*Lat.*) a wandring out of the way, a going from the matter in hand.

Dijudication, (*Lat.*) a deciding a difference between two.

Dike-grave, one that oversees the Dikes and banks of the Low-Countries, that keep the

---

Plate 3 Page showing the entries from *dictionary* to *dike-grave* in *The New World of Words*, by E. P. (Edward Phillips) (1671 edition). [See p. 8.]

A

Table Alphabeticall, con-

teyning and teaching the true
vvriting, and vnderſtanding of hard
vſuall Engliſh wordes, borrowed from
the Hebrew, Greeke, Latine,
or French. &c.

With the interpretation thereof by
plaine Engliſh words, gathered for the benefit &
helpe of Ladies, Gentlewomen, or any other
vnskilfull perſons.

Whereby they may the more eaſilie
and better vnderſtand many hard Engliſh
wordes, vvhich they ſhall heare or read in
Scriptures, Sermons, or elſwhere , and alſo
be made able to vſe the ſame aptly
themſelues.

Legere, et non intelligere , neglegere eſt.
As good not read, as not to vnderſtand.

AT LONDON,
Printed by I. R. for Edmund Wea-
uer, & are to be ſold at his ſhop at the great
North doore of Paules Church.
1 6 0 4.

Plate 4 Title page of Cawdrey's *A Table Alphabeticall* (1604). Note the copious title, with
the mention of the purpose of the dictionary and its public. [See p. 56.]

A

DICTIONARY

OF THE

ENGLISH LANGUAGE:

IN WHICH

The WORDS are deduced from their ORIGINALS,

AND

ILLUSTRATED in their DIFFERENT SIGNIFICATIONS

BY

EXAMPLES from the beſt WRITERS.

TO WHICH ARE PREFIXED,

A HISTORY of the LANGUAGE,

AND

AN ENGLISH GRAMMAR.

BY SAMUEL JOHNSON, A. M.

IN TWO VOLUMES.

VOL. I.

Cum tabulis animum cenforis fumet honeſti :
Audebit quæcunque parum fplendoris habebunt,
Et fine pondere erunt, et honore indigna ferentur.
Verba movere loco ; quamvis invita recedant,
Et verfentur adhuc intra penetralia Veſtæ :
Obſcurata diu populo bonus eruet, atque
Proferet in lucem fpeciofa vocabula rerum,
Quæ prifcis memorata Catonibus atque Cethegis,
Nunc fitus informis premit et deferta vetuſtas.   HOR.

LONDON,

Printed by W. STRAHAN,

For J. and P. KNAPTON ; T. and T. LONGMAN ; C. HITCH and L. HAWES ;
A. MILLAR ; and R. and J. DODSLEY.

MDCCLV.

Plate 5 Title page of Johnson's *A Dictionary of the English Language* (first edition 1755). [See p. 66.]

F.

FAB   FAC

F, A confonant generally reckoned by authors, and admitted by *Scaliger*, among the femi-vowels, and according to that opinion diftinguifhed in the enumeration of the alphabet by a name beginning with a vowel, yet has fo far the nature of a mute, that it is eafily pronounced before a liquid in the fame fyllable. It has in Englifh an invariable found, formed by compreffion of the whole lips and a forcible breath. Its kindred letter is V, which, in the Iflandick alphabet, is only diftinguifhed from it by a point in the body of the letter.

FABA'CEOUS. *adj.* [*fabaceus*, Latin] Having the nature of a bean. *Dict.*

FA'BLE. *n. f.* [*fable*, French; *fabula*, Latin.]
1. A feigned ftory intended to enforce fome moral precept.
> Jotham's *fable* of the bees is the oldeft extant, and as beautiful as any made fince. *Addifon's Spectator.*
2. A fiction in general.
> Triptolemus, fo fung the nine,
> Strew'd plenty from his cart divine;
> But, fpite of all thofe *fable* makers,
> He never fow'd on Almaign acres. *Dryden.*
3. A vitious or foolifh fiction.
> But refufe profane and old wives *fables.* 1 *Tim.* iv. 7.
4. The feries or contexture of events which conftitute a poem epick or dramatick.
> The moral is the firft bufinefs of the poet: this being formed, he contrives fuch a defign or *fable* as may be moft fuitable to the moral. *Dryden's Dufrefnoy.*
> The firft thing to be confidered in an epick poem is the *fable*, which is perfect or imperfect, according as the action, which it relates, is more or lefs fo. *Addifon's Spectator.*
5. A lye. This fenfe is merely familiar.

To FA'BLE. *v. n.* [from the noun.]
1. To feign; to write not truth but fiction.
> That Saturn's fons receiv'd the three-fold reign
> Of heav'n, of ocean, and deep hell beneath,
> Old poets mention, *fabling.* *Prior.*
> Vain now the tales which *fabling* poets tell,
> That wav'ring conqueft ftill defires to rove!
> In Marlbro's camp the goddefs knows to dwell. *Prior.*
2. To tell falfhoods; to lye.
> He *fables* not: I hear the enemy. *Shakefp. Henry VI.*

To FA'BLE. *v. a.* To feign; to tell of falfety.
> We mean to win,
> Or turn this heav'n itfelf into the hell
> Thou *fableft.* *Milton's Paradife Loft, b.* vi. *l.* 292.
> Ladies of th' Hefperides, that feem'd
> Fairer than feign'd of old, or *fabl'd* fince
> Of fairy damfels met in foreft wide,
> By knights. *Milton's Parad. Loft.*

FA'BLED. *adj.* [from *fable*.] Celebrated in fables.
> Hail, *fabled* grotto! hail, Elyfian foil!
> Thou faireft fpot of fair Britannia's ifle! *Tickell.*

FA'BLER. *n. f.* [from *fable*.] A dealer in fiction; a writer of feigned ftories.

To FA'BRICATE. *v. a.* [*fabricor*, Latin.]
1. To build; to conftruct.
2. To forge; to devife falfely. This fenfe is retained among the Scottifh lawyers; for when they fufpect a paper to be forged, they fay it is *fabricate.*

FABRICA'TION. *n. f.* [from *fabricate*.] The act of building; conftruction.
> This *fabrication* of the human body is the immediate work of a vital principle, that formeth the firft rudiments of the human nature. *Hale's Origin of Mankind.*

FA'BRICK. *n. f.* [*fabrica*, Latin.]
1. A building; an edifice.
> There muft be an exquifite care to place the columns, fet in feveral ftories, moft precifely one over another, that fo the folid may anfwer to the folid, and the vacuities to the vacuities, as well for beauty as ftrength of the *fabrick.* *Wotton.*
2. Any fyftem or compages of matter; any body formed by the conjunction of diffimilar parts.
> Still will ye think it ftrange,
> That all the parts of this great *fabrick* change;
> Quit their old ftation and primeval frame. *Prior.*

To FA'BRICK. *v. a.* [from the noun.] To build; to form; to conftruct.
> Shew what laws of life
> The cheefe inhabitants obferve, and how
> *Fabrick* their manfions. *Phillips.*

FA'BULIST. *n. f.* [*fabulifte*, French.] A writer of fables.
> Quitting Efop and the *fabulifts*, he copies from Boccace. *Croxal.*
> Our bard's a *fabulift*, and deals in fiction. *Ga-rick.*

FABULO'SITY. *n. f.* [*fabulofitas*, Latin.] Lyingnefs; fulnefs of ftories; fabulous invention.
> In their *fabulofity* they would report, that they had obfervations for twenty thoufand years. *Abbot's Defcription of the World.*

FA'BULOUS. *adj.* [*fabulofus*, Latin.] Feigned; full of fables, or invented tales.
> A perfon terrified with the imagination of fpectres, is more reafonable than one who thinks the appearance of fpirits *fabulous* and groundlefs. *Addifon's Spectator*, N°. 110.

FA'BULOUSLY. *adv.* [from *fabulous*.] In fiction; in a fabulous manner.
> There are many things *fabuloufly* delivered, and are not to be accepted as truths. *Brown's Vulgar Errours, b.* vi. *c.* 8.

FACE. *n. f.* [*face*, French, from *facies*, Latin.]
1. The vifage.
> The children of Ifrael faw the *face* of Mofes, that the fkin of Mofes's *face* fhone. *Exod.* xxxiv. 35.
> A man fhall fee *faces*, which, if you examine them part by part, you fhall never find good; but take them together, are not uncomely. *Bacon, Effay* 44.
> From beauty ftill to beauty ranging,
> In ev'ry *face* I found a dart. *Addifon's Spectator.*
2. Countenance; caft of the features; look; air of the face.
> Seiz'd and ty'd down to judge, how wretched I!
> Who can't be filent, and who will not lye:
> To laugh, were want of goodnefs and of grace;
> And to be grave, exceeds all pow'r of *face.* *Pope's Epiftles.*
3. The furface of any thing.
> A mift watered the whole *face* of the ground. *Gen.* ii. 6.
4. The front or forepart of any thing.
> The breadth of the *face* of the houfe, towards theEaft, was an hundred cubits. *Ezek.* xli. 14.
4. State of affairs.
> He look'd, and faw the *face* of things quite chang'd,
> The brazen throat of war had ceas'd to roar;
> All now was turn'd to jollity and game,
> To luxury and riot, feaft and dance. *Milton's Par. Loft.*
> This would produce a new *face* of things in Europe. *Addif.*
5. Appearance; refemblance.
> Keep ftill your former *face*, and mix again
> With thefe loft fpirits; run all their mazes with 'em;
> For fuch are treafons. *Ben. Johnfon.*
> At the firft fhock, with blood and powder ftain'd,
> Nor heav'n, nor fea, their former *face* retain'd;
> Fury and art produce effects fo ftrange,
> They trouble nature, and her vifage change. *Waller.*
> His dialogue has fo much the *face* of probability, that fome have miftaken it for a real conference. *Baker.*
6. Prefence; fight.
> Ye fhall give her unto Eleazar, and one fhall flay her before his *face.* *Numb.* xix. 3.
> Jove cannot fear; then tell me to my *face*,
> That I of all the gods am leaft in grace. *Dryden's Iliad.*
7. Confidence; boldnefs.
> Thinking, by this *face*,
> To faften in our thoughts that they have courage;
> But 'tis not fo. *Shakefpeare's Julius Cæfar.*
> How many things are there which a man cannot, with any *face* or comlinefs, fay or do himfelf? A man can fcarce allege his own merits with modefty, much lefs extol them: a man cannot fometimes brook to fupplicate or beg. *Bacon, Effay* 28.
> You'll find the thing will not be done
> With ignorance and *face* alone. *Hudibras, p.* ii.
> You, fays the judge to the wolf, have the *face* to challenge

8 R   that

Plate 6 Page showing the entries *F* to *face* in Johnson's *A Dictionary of the English Language* (first edition 1755). Note the careful treatment of polysemy and the extensive use of illustrative quotations, with vague references. [See p. 67.]

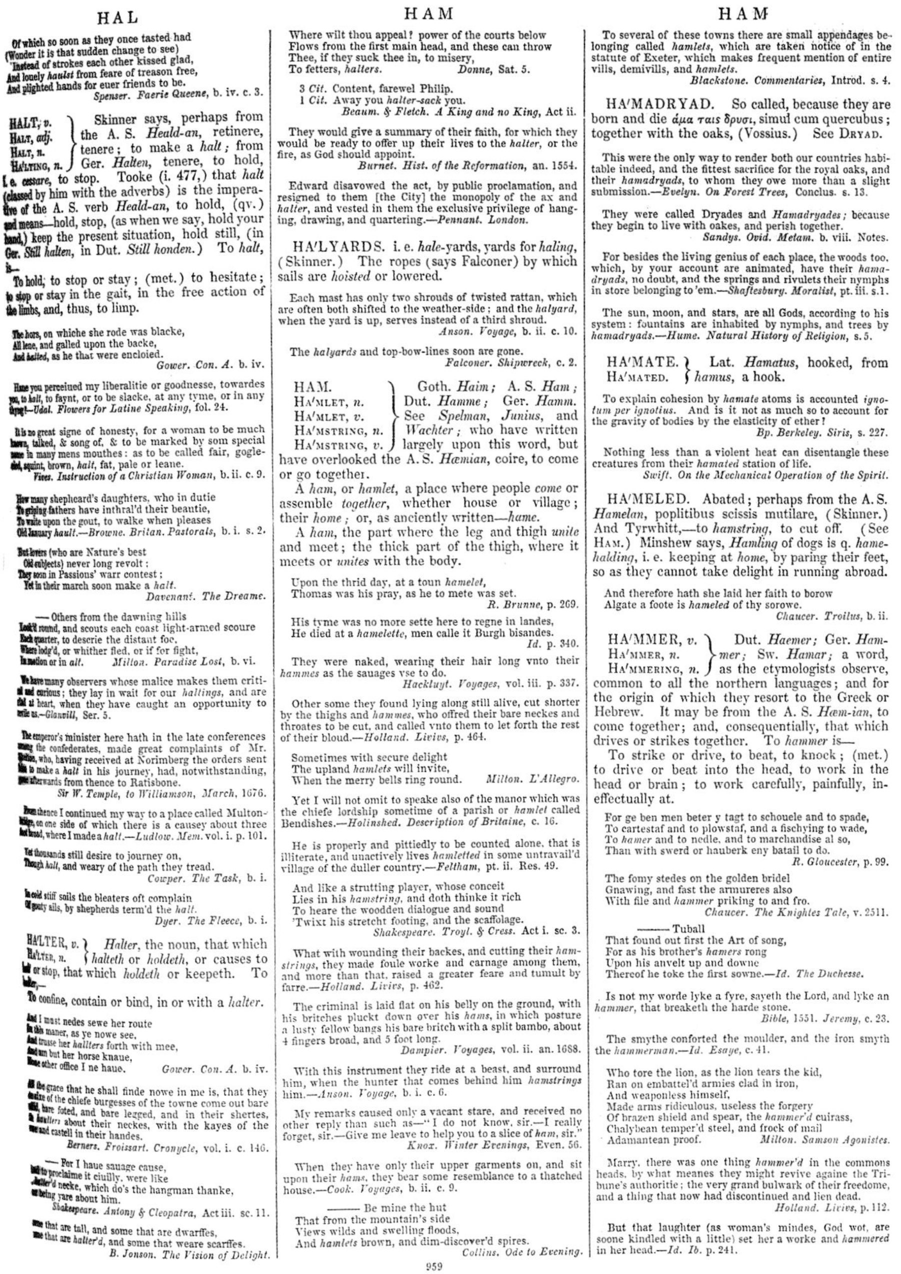

HAL | HAM | HAM

Of which so soon as they once tasted had
(Wonder it is that sudden change to see)
Instead of strokes each other kissed glad,
And louely haulst from feare of treason free,
And plighted hands for euer friends to be.
Spenser. Faerie Queene, b. iv. c. 3.

HALT, *v.* | HALT, *adj.* | HALT, *n.* | HA'LTING, *n.* } Skinner says, perhaps from the A. S. *Heald-an,* retinere, tenere; to make a *halt;* from Ger. *Halten,* tenere, to hold, i. e. cessare, to stop. Tooke (i. 477,) that *halt* (classed by him with the adverbs) is the imperative of the A. S. verb *Heald-an,* to hold, (qv.) and means—hold, stop, (as when we say, hold your hand,) keep the present situation, hold still, (in Ger. *Still halten,* in Dut. *Still honden.*) To *halt,* is—

To hold; to stop or stay; (met.) to hesitate; to stop or stay in the gait, in the free action of the limbs, and, thus, to limp.

The hors, on whiche she rode was blacke,
All lene, and galled upon the backe,
And *halted,* as he that were encloied.
Gower. Con. A. b. iv.

Haue you perceiued my liberalitie or goodnesse, towardes you, to *halt,* to faynt, or to be slacke, at any tyme, or in any thyng?—*Udal. Flowers for Latine Speaking,* fol. 24.

It is no great signe of honesty, for a woman to be much known, talked, & song of, & to be marked by som special name in many mens mouthes: as to be called fair, goggle-eied, squint, brown, *halt,* fat, pale or leane.
Vives. Instruction of a Christian Woman, b. ii. c. 9.

How many shepheard's daughters, who in dutie
To griping fathers have inthral'd their beautie,
To waite upon the gout, to walke when pleases
Old January *hault.*—*Browne. Britan. Pastorals,* b. i. s. 2.

But lovers (who are Nature's best
Old subjects) never long revolt;
They soon in Passions' warr contest;
Yet in their march soon make a *halt.*
Davenant. The Dreame.

—Others from the dawning hills
Look'd round, and scouts each coast light-armed scoure
Each quarter, to descrie the distant foe,
Where lodg'd, or whither fled, or if for fight,
In motion or in *alt.* *Milton. Paradise Lost,* b. vi.

We have many observers whose malice makes them critical and curious; they lay in wait for our *haltings,* and are glad at heart, when they have caught an opportunity to revile us.—*Glanvill,* Ser. 5.

The emperor's minister here hath in the late conferences among the confederates, made great complaints of Mr. Bethun, who, having received at Norimberg the orders sent him to make a *halt* in his journey, had, notwithstanding, gone afterwards from thence to Ratisbone.
Sir W. Temple, to Williamson, March, 1676.

From thence I continued my way to a place called Multon-bridge, on one side of which there is a causey about three foot broad, where I made a *halt.*—*Ludlow. Mem.* vol. i. p. 101.

Yet thousands still desire to journey on,
Though *halt,* and weary of the path they tread.
Cowper. The Task, b. i.

In cold stiff soils the bleaters oft complain
Of gouty ails, by shepherds term'd the *halt.*
Dyer. The Fleece, b. i.

HA'LTER, *v.* | HA'LTER, *n.* } *Halter,* the noun, that which *halteth* or *holdeth,* or causes to halt or stop, that which *holdeth* or keepeth. To halter,—

To confine, contain or bind, in or with a *halter.*

And I must nedes sewe her route
In this maner, as ye nowe see,
And trusse her *hallters* forth with mee,
And am but her horse knaue,
None other office I ne haue. *Gower. Con. A.* b. iv.

All the grace that he shall finde nowe in me is, that they desire of the chiefe burgesses of the towne come out bare headed, bare foted, and bare legged, and in their shertes, with *haulters* about their neckes, with the kayes of the towne and castell in their handes.
Berners. Froissart. Cronycle, vol. i. c. 146.

—For I haue sauage cause,
And to proclaime it ciuilly, were like
A *halter'd* necke, which do's the hangman thanke,
For being yare about him.
Shakespeare. Antony & Cleopatra, Act iii. sc. 11.

Some that are tall, and some that are dwarffes,
Some that are *halter'd,* and some that weare scarffes.
B. Jonson. The Vision of Delight.

Where wilt thou appeal? power of the courts below
Flows from the first main head, and these can throw
Thee, if they suck thee in, to misery,
To fetters, *halters.* *Donne,* Sat. 5.

3 *Cit.* Content, farewel Philip.
1 *Cit.* Away you *halter-sack* you.
Beaum. & Fletch. A King and no King, Act ii.

They would give a summary of their faith, for which they would be ready to offer up their lives to the *halter,* or the fire, as God should appoint.
Burnet. Hist. of the Reformation, an. 1554.

Edward disavowed the act, by public proclamation, and resigned to them [the City] the monopoly of the ax and *halter,* and vested in them the exclusive privilege of hanging, drawing, and quartering.—*Pennant. London.*

HA'LYARDS. i. e. *hale*-yards, yards for *haling,* (Skinner.) The ropes (says Falconer) by which sails are *hoisted* or lowered.

Each mast has only two shrouds of twisted rattan, which are often both shifted to the weather-side; and the *halyard,* when the yard is up, serves instead of a third shroud.
Anson. Voyage, b. ii. c. 10.

The *halyards* and top-bow-lines soon are gone.
Falconer. Shipwreck, c. 2.

HAM. | HA'MLET, *n.* | HA'MLET, *v.* | HA'MSTRING, *n.* | HA'MSTRING, *v.* } Goth. *Haim;* A. S. *Ham;* Dut. *Hamme;* Ger. *Hamm.* See *Spelman, Junius,* and *Wachter;* who have written largely upon this word, but have overlooked the A. S. *Hæmian,* coire, to come or go together.

A *ham,* or *hamlet,* a place where people *come* or assemble *together,* whether house or village; their *home;* or, as anciently written—*hame.*

A *ham,* the part where the leg and thigh *unite* and meet; the thick part of the thigh, where it meets or *unites* with the body.

Upon the thrid day, at a toun *hamelet,*
Thomas was his pray, as he to mete was set.
R. Brunne, p. 269.

His tyme was no more sette here to regne in landes,
He died at a *hamelette,* men calle it Burgh bisandes.
Id. p. 340.

They were naked, wearing their hair long vnto their *hammes* as the sauages vse to do.
Hackluyt. Voyages, vol. iii. p. 337.

Other some they found lying along still alive, cut shorter by the thighs and *hammes,* who offred their bare neckes and throates to be cut, and called vnto them to let forth the rest of their bloud.—*Holland. Livius,* p. 464.

Sometimes with secure delight
The upland *hamlets* will invite,
When the merry bells ring round. *Milton. L'Allegro.*

Yet I will not omit to speake also of the manor which was the chiefe lordship sometime of a parish or *hamlet* called Bendishes.—*Holinshed. Description of Britaine,* c. 16.

He is properly and pittiedly to be counted alone, that is illiterate, and unactively lives *hamletted* in some untravail'd village of the duller country.—*Feltham,* pt. ii. Res. 49.

And like a strutting player, whose conceit
Lies in his *hamstring,* and doth thinke it rich
To heare the woodden dialogue and sound
'Twixt his stretcht footing, and the scaffolage.
Shakespeare. Troyl. & Cress. Act i. sc. 3.

What with wounding their backes, and cutting their *hamstrings,* they made foule worke and carnage among them, and more than that, raised a greater feare and tumult by farre.—*Holland. Livius,* p. 462.

The criminal is laid flat on his belly on the ground, with his britches pluckt down over his *hams,* in which posture a lusty fellow bangs his bare britch with a split bambo, about 4 fingers broad, and 5 foot long.
Dampier. Voyages, vol. ii. an. 1688.

With this instrument they ride at a beast, and surround him, when the hunter that comes behind him *hamstrings* him.—*Anson. Voyage,* b. i. c. 6.

My remarks caused only a vacant stare, and received no other reply than such as—"I do not know, sir.—I really forget, sir.—Give me leave to help you to a slice of *ham,* sir."
Knox. Winter Evenings, Even. 56.

When they have only their upper garments on, and sit upon their *hams,* they bear some resemblance to a thatched house.—*Cook. Voyages,* b. ii. c. 9.

——— Be mine the hut
That from the mountain's side
Views wilds and swelling floods,
And *hamlets* brown, and dim-discover'd spires.
Collins. Ode to Evening.

To several of these towns there are small appendages belonging called *hamlets,* which are taken notice of in the statute of Exeter, which makes frequent mention of entire vills, demivills, and *hamlets.*
Blackstone. Commentaries, Introd. s. 4.

HA'MADRYAD. So called, because they are born and die ἅμα ταις δρυσι, simul cum quercubus; together with the oaks, (Vossius.) See DRYAD.

This were the only way to render both our countries habitable indeed, and the fittest sacrifice for the royal oaks, and their *hamadryads,* to whom they owe more than a slight submission.—*Evelyn. On Forest Trees,* Conclus. s. 13.

They were called Dryades and *Hamadryades;* because they begin to live with oakes, and perish together.
Sandys. Ovid. Metam. b. viii. Notes.

For besides the living genius of each place, the woods too, which, by your account are animated, have their *hamadryads,* no doubt, and the springs and rivulets their nymphs in store belonging to 'em.—*Shaftesbury. Moralist,* pt. iii. s. 1.

The sun, moon, and stars, are all Gods, according to his system: fountains are inhabited by nymphs, and trees by *hamadryads.*—*Hume. Natural History of Religion,* s. 5.

HA'MATE. | HA'MATED. } Lat. *Hamatus,* hooked, from *hamus,* a hook.

To explain cohesion by *hamate* atoms is accounted *ignotum per ignotius.* And is it not as much so to account for the gravity of bodies by the elasticity of ether?
Bp. Berkeley. Siris, s. 227.

Nothing less than a violent heat can disentangle these creatures from their *hamated* station of life.
Swift. On the Mechanical Operation of the Spirit.

HA'MELED. Abated; perhaps from the A. S. *Hamelan,* poplitibus scissis mutilare, (Skinner.) And Tyrwhitt,—to *hamstring,* to cut off. (See HAM.) Minshew says, *Hamling* of dogs is q. *hamehalding,* i. e. keeping at *home,* by paring their feet, so as they cannot take delight in running abroad.

And therefore hath she laid her faith to borow
Algate a foote is *hameled* of thy sorowe.
Chaucer. Troilus, b. ii.

HA'MMER, *v.* | HA'MMER, *n.* | HA'MMERING, *n.* } Dut. *Haemer;* Ger. *Hammer;* Sw. *Hamar;* a word, as the etymologists observe, common to all the northern languages; and for the origin of which they resort to the Greek or Hebrew. It may be from the A. S. *Hæm-ian,* to come together; and, consequentially, that which drives or strikes together. To *hammer* is—

To strike or drive, to beat, to knock; (met.) to drive or beat into the head, to work in the head or brain; to work carefully, painfully, ineffectually at.

For ge ben men beter y tagt to schouele and to spade,
To cartestaf and to plowstaf, and a fischying to wade,
To *hamer* and to nedle, and to marchandise al so,
Than with swerd or hauberk eny batail to do.
R. Gloucester, p. 99.

The fomy stedes on the golden bridel
Gnawing, and fast the armureres also
With file and *hammer* priking to and fro.
Chaucer. The Knightes Tale, v. 2511.

——— Tuball
That found out first the Art of song,
For as his brother's *hamers* rong
Upon his anvelt up and downe
Thereof he toke the first sowne.—*Id. The Duchesse.*

Is not my worde lyke a fyre, sayeth the Lord, and lyke an *hammer,* that breaketh the harde stone.
Bible, 1551. *Jeremy,* c. 23.

The smythe conforted the moulder, and the iron smyth the *hammerman.*—*Id. Esaye,* c. 41.

Who tore the lion, as the lion tears the kid,
Ran on embattel'd armies clad in iron,
And weaponless himself,
Made arms ridiculous, useless the forgery
Of brazen shield and spear, the *hammer'd* cuirass,
Chalybean temper'd steel, and frock of mail
Adamantean proof. *Milton. Samson Agonistes.*

Marry, there was one thing *hammer'd* in the commons heads, by what meanes they might revive againe the Tribune's authoritie; the very grand bulwark of their freedome, and a thing that now had discontinued and lien dead.
Holland. Livius, p. 112.

But that laughter (as woman's mindes, God wot, are soone kindled with a little) set her a worke and *hammered* in her head.—*Id. Ib.* p. 241.

959

Plate 7 Page showing the entries *hal* to *ham* in Richardson's *A New Dictionary of the English Language* (1836 edition). Note the grouping of words with a supposed common origin in a single entry. Note also the extensive use of quotations. [See p. 83.]

to peel; Arm. *delivra.* See *Liberal, Libra-ry, Librate.*]

1. To free; to release, as from restraint; to set at liberty; as, to *deliver* one from captivity.

2. To rescue, or save.
Deliver me, O my God, from the hand of the wicked. Ps. lxxi.

3. To give, or transfer; to put into another's hand or power; to commit; to pass from one to another.
Thou shalt *deliver* Pharaoh's cup into his hand. Gen. xl.
So we say, to *deliver* goods to a carrier; to *deliver* a letter; to *deliver* possession of an estate.

4. To surrender; to yield; to give up; to resign; as, to *deliver* a fortress to an enemy. It is often followed by *up*; as, to *deliver up* the city; to *deliver up* stolen goods.
Th' exalted mind
All sense of woe *delivers* to the wind. *Pope.*

5. To disburden of a child.

6. To utter; to pronounce; to speak; to send forth in words; as, to *deliver* a sermon, an address, or an oration.

7. To exert in motion. [*Not in use.*]
To deliver to the wind, to cast away; to reject.
To deliver over, to transfer; to give or pass from one to another; as, to *deliver over* goods to another.

2. To surrender or resign; to put into another's power; to commit to the discretion of; to abandon to.
Deliver me not *over* to the will of my enemies. Ps. xxvii.
To deliver up, to give up; to surrender.

DELIV'ER, *a.* [L. *liber.*] Free; nimble. *Obs.*   *Chaucer.*

DELIV'ERABLE, *a.* That may be or is to be delivered.
A bill of lading may state that the goods are *deliverable* to a particular person therein named.
Mer. Usage. Amer. Review.

DELIV'ERANCE, *n.* [Fr. *delivrance.*] Release from captivity, slavery, oppression, or any restraint.
He hath sent me to heal the broken-hearted, to preach *deliverance* to the captives. Luke iv.

2. Rescue from danger or any evil.
God sent me to save your lives by a great *deliverance.* Gen. xlv.

3. The act of bringing forth children. *Bacon.*

4. The act of giving or transferring from one to another.

5. The act of speaking or pronouncing; utterance. *Shak.*
[In the three last senses, *delivery* is now used.]

6. Acquittal of a prisoner, by the verdict of a jury. God send you a good *deliverance.*

DELIV'ERED, *pp.* Freed; released; transferred or transmitted; passed from one to another; committed; yielded; surrendered; rescued; uttered; pronounced.

DELIV'ERER, *n.* One who delivers; one who releases or rescues; a preserver.
The Lord raised up a *deliverer* to Israel. Judges iii.

2. One who relates, or communicates. *Boyle.*

DELIV'ERING, *ppr.* Releasing; setting free; rescuing; saving; surrendering; giving over; yielding; resigning.

DELIV'ERY, *n.* The act of delivering.

2. Release; rescue; as from slavery, restraint, oppression or danger.

3. Surrender; a giving up.

4. A giving or passing from one to another; as the *delivery* of goods, or of a deed.

5. Utterance; pronunciation; or manner of speaking. He has a good *delivery.* I was charmed with his graceful *delivery.*

6. Childbirth. Is. xxvi.

7. Free motion or use of the limbs. [*Obs.*] *Sidney. Wotton.*

DELL, *n.* [Qu. *dale*, or W. *dell*, a cleft or rift; or is it contracted from Sax. *degle?*] A pit, or a hollow place; a cavity or narrow opening. *Spenser. Milton.*

DELPH. [See *Delf.* No. 2.]

DELPH'IA, ⎫ *n.* A vegetable alkali lately
DELPHIN'IA, ⎭ discovered in the Delphinium staphysagria. It is crystaline when wet, but it becomes opake when exposed to air. Its taste is bitter and acrid. When heated it melts, but on cooling becomes hard and brittle like resin.
Ure. Webster's Manual.

DELPH'IAN, ⎫ *a.* [from *Delphi*, a town of
DELPH'IC, ⎭ Phocis in Greece.] Relating to Delphi, and to the celebrated oracle of that place.

DELPH'INE, *a.* [L. *delphinus.*] Pertaining to the dolphin, a genus of fishes.

2. Pertaining to the dauphin of France; as the *delphine* edition of the classics.

DELPH'INITE, *n.* A mineral called also pistacite and epidote. *Ure.*

DEL'TOID, *n.* [Gr. δελτα, the letter Δ, and ειδος, form.]

1. Resembling the Gr. Δ; triangular; an epithet applied to a muscle of the shoulder which moves the arm forwards, upwards and backwards. *Coxe.*

2. In *botany*, shaped somewhat like a delta or rhomb, having four angles, of which the lateral ones are less distant from the base than the others; as a *deltoid* leaf. *Linne. Martyn.*
Trowel-shaped, having three angles, of which the terminal one is much further from the base than the lateral ones. *Smith.*

DELU'DABLE, *a.* [See *Delude.*] That may be deluded or deceived; liable to be imposed on. *Brown.*

DELU'DE, *v. t.* [L. *deludo*; *de* and *ludo*, to play, to mock; Ch. and Heb. לוד. Class Ls. No. 3. 5. 30. 46.]

1. To deceive; to impose on; to lead from truth or into error; to mislead the mind or judgment; to beguile. *Cheat* is generally applied to deception in bargains; *delude*, to deception in opinion. An artful man *deludes* his followers. We are often *deluded* by false appearances.

2. To frustrate or disappoint.

DELU'DED, *pp.* Deceived; misled; led into error.

DELU'DER, *n.* One who deceives; a deceiver; an imposter; one who holds out false pretenses.

DELU'DING, *ppr.* Deceiving; leading astray; misleading the opinion or judgment.

DELU'DING, *n.* The act of deceiving; falsehood. *Prideaux.*

DEL'UGE, *n.* [Fr. *deluge*; Arm. *diluich*; Sp. *diluvio*; It. *id.*; L. *diluvies, diluvium,*

from *diluo, diluvio*; *di* and *luo, lavo*, to wash. If *deluge* and *diluvium* are the same word, of which there can be little doubt, the fact proves that *luo, lavo,* is contracted or changed from *lugo,* and that the primitive word was *lugo*; and it is certain that the radix of *fluo* is *flugo.* See *Flow.*]

1. Any overflowing of water; an inundation; a flood; a swell of water over the natural banks of a river or shore of the ocean, spreading over the adjacent land. But appropriately, the great flood or overflowing of the earth by water, in the days of Noah; according to the common chronology, Anno Mundi, 1656. Gen. vi.

2. A sweeping or overwhelming calamity.

DEL'UGE, *v. t.* To overflow with water; to inundate; to drown. The waters *deluged* the earth and destroyed the old world.

2. To overwhelm; to cover with any flowing or moving, spreading body. The Northern nations *deluged* the Roman empire with their armies.

3. To overwhelm; to cause to sink under the weight of a general or spreading calamity; as, the land is *deluged* with corruption.

DEL'UGED, *pp.* Overflowed; inundated; overwhelmed.

DEL'UGING, *ppr.* Overflowing; inundating; overwhelming.

DELU'SION, *n. s* as *z.* [L. *delusio.* See *Delude.*] The act of deluding; deception; a misleading of the mind. We are all liable to the *delusions* of artifice.

2. False representation; illusion; error or mistake proceeding from false views.
And fondly mourn'd the dear *delusion* gone. *Prior.*

DELU'SIVE, *a.* Apt to deceive; tending to mislead the mind; deceptive; beguiling; as *delusive* arts; *delusive* appearances.

DELU'SIVENESS, *n.* The quality of being delusive; tendency to deceive.

DELU'SORY, *a.* Apt to deceive; deceptive. *Glanville.*

DELVE, *v. t. delv.* [Sax. *delfan*; D. *delven*; Russ. *dolblyu*; to dig. Qu. Arm. *toulla*, to dig or make a hole, W. *twll*, a hole, and L. *talpa*, a mole, perhaps the *delver.*]

1. To dig; to open the ground with a spade.
Delve of convenient depth your thrashing floor. *Dryden.*

2. To fathom; to sound; to penetrate. [*Not used.*]
I cannot *delve* him to the root. *Shak.*

DELVE, *n. delv.* A place dug; a pit; a pitfall; a ditch; a den; a cave. [*Not now used.*] *Spenser.*
Delve of coals, a quantity of fossil coals dug. [*Not used or local.*]

DELV'ER, *n.* One who digs, as with a spade.

DELV'ING, *ppr.* Digging.

DEM'AGOGUE, *n. dem'agog.* [Gr. δημαγωγος, from δημος, the populace, and αγω, to lead.]

1. A leader of the people; an orator who pleases the populace and influences them to adhere to him.

2. Any leader of the populace; any factious man who has great influence with the great body of people in a city or community.

Plate 8 Page showing the entries *deliver* to *demagogue* in Webster's *An American Dictionary of the English Language* (1828). Note the etymologies, the quotations, and the use of synonyms in the definitions. [See p. 85.]

Didelphyidæ, Didelphidæ (dī-del-fī'i-dē, dī-del'fi-dē), *n. pl.* [NL., ‹ *Didelphys* + *-idæ.*] A family of marsupial animals; the opossums. They have the feet pedimanous—that is, the hind feet as well as the fore with an apposable thumb, and thus fitted for grasping; all the toes clawed excepting the hallux; the tail generally long, scaly, and prehensile; and the pouch in some forms complete, in others rudimentary or wanting. The dental formula is: 5 incisors in each upper, 4 in each lower half-jaw; 1 canine, 3 premolars, and 4 molars in each half-jaw. The vertebral formula is: cervical 7, dorsal 13, lumbar 6, sacral 2, caudal 19 or more. The family is confined to America, where it alone represents the division of marsupial mammals. The leading genera are *Didelphys*, including most of the species, and *Chironectes*, the water-opossums. See *Didelphys*, *opossum*.

Didelphys (dī-del'fis), *n.* [NL., ‹ Gr. *δι-*, two-, + *δελφύς*, womb.] The typical and leading genus of marsupial implacental mammals of the family *Didelphyidæ*, containing the American opossums which are not web-footed. The genus formerly covered nearly or quite all the marsupials. The species are terrestrial and arboreal, but not aquatic, the water-opossums being separated under the name *Chironectes*. The pouch is usually well developed, as in the best-known species, *D. virginiana*, the common opossum of the United States, but is rudimentary in some of the South American forms. See *Didelphyidæ*, *opossum*.

Didemnidæ (dī-dem'ni-dē), *n. pl.* [NL., ‹ *Didemnum* + *-idæ.*] A family of compound ascidians, typified by the genus *Didemnum*, having the body divided into thoracic and abdominal portions, and the viscera mostly situated behind the branchial cavity.

Didemnum (dī-dem'num), *n.* [NL., ‹ Gr. *δι-*, two-, + (?) *δέμνιον*, a bed.] A genus of ascidians, of the family *Botryllidæ*, or made the type of a family *Didemnidæ*. *D. candidum* is an example.

Dididæ (dī'di-dē), *n. pl.* [NL., ‹ *Didus* + *-idæ.*] A family of birds of which the dodo is the type. The leading genera are *Didus* and *Pezophaps*. See *dodo*.

didine (dī'din), *a.* [‹ NL. *didinus*, ‹ *Didus*, q. v.] Pertaining to the genus *Didus* or family *Dididæ*; being or resembling a dodo.

didn't (did'nt). A contraction of *did not*, in frequent colloquial use.

dido (dī'dō), *n.* [ME. *dido*; in allusion to the familiar tale of the trick played by *Dido*, the legendary queen of Carthage, in bargaining for as much land as could be covered by a hide, and cutting the hide into a long thin strip so as to inclose a large tract: L. *Dido*, Gr. Διδώ.] 1†. An old story.

"This is a *Dido*," quath this doctour, "a disours tale!"
Piers Plowman (C), xvi. 171.

2. A caper; a prank; a trick.—**To cut a dido**, to make mischief; play a prank; cut a caper.

Them Italian singers recitin' their jabber, showin' their teeth, and *cuttin' didoes* at a private concert.
Haliburton, Sam Slick in Eng.

didodecahedral (dī-dō"dek-a-hē'dral), *a.* [‹ *di-*[2] + *dodecahedral.*] In *crystal.*, having the form of a dodecahedral prism with hexahedral bases.

didopper (did'op-ėr), *n.* Same as *didapper*.

didrachm (dī'dram), *n.* [‹ *didrachma*, q. v.] A silver coin of ancient Greece, of the value of two drachmæ. See *drachma*.

Their [earlier coins of Corcyra's] reverse-type is, in the case of *didrachms*, two figures of square or oblong shape, whereof one has in the midst a small square and the other a small rhombus or lozenge. *Numis. Chron.*, 3d ser., I. 6.

Before the age of Solon, Aeginetan *didrachms* averaging about 194 grs. would seem to have been the only money current in Attica as in Bœotia and Peloponnesus.
B. V. Head, Historia Numorum, Int., p. xlii.

didrachma (dī-drak'mä), *n.* [LL., ‹ Gr. *δίδραχμον*, a double drachm, ‹ *δι-*, two, + *δραχμή*, a drachm: see *drachm.*] Same as *didrachm*.

didrachmon (dī-drak'mon), *n.* Same as *didrachm*.

didst (didst). The second person singular of the preterit of *do*[1], *do*[2].

diducement† (di-dūs'ment), *n.* [‹ **diduce* (‹ L. *diducere*, draw apart, separate, ‹ *di-*, *dis-*, apart, + *ducere*, draw; cf. *deduce*) + *-ment.*] A drawing apart; separation into distinct parts. *Bacon.*

diduction† (dī-duk'shon), *n.* [‹ L. *diductio(n-)*, ‹ *diducere*, pp. *diductus*, draw apart: see *diducement.*] Separation by withdrawing one part from the other.

Those [strings] that within the bladder drew so as to hinder the *diduction* of its side. *Boyle*, Works, I. 165.

diductively† (dī-duk'tiv-li), *adv.* By diduction or separation; inferentially.

There is scarce a popular error passant in our dayes which is not either directly expressed or *diductively* contained in this work [Pliny's Natural History].
Sir T. Browne, Vulg. Err., i. 8.

Didunculidæ (dī-dung-kū'li-dē), *n. pl.* [NL., ‹ *Didunculus* + *-idæ.*] A family of columbine birds, represented by the genus *Didunculus*.

Didunculinæ (dī-dung-kū-lī'nē), *n. pl.* [NL., ‹ *Didunculus* + *-inæ.*] A subfamily of *Columbidæ*, represented by the genus *Didunculus*.

Didunculus (di-dung'kū-lus), *n.* [NL., dim. of *Didus*, the generic name of the dodo. See *Didus.*] A remarkable genus of pigeons, constituting the subfamily *Didunculinæ* of the family *Columbidæ*, or made the type of a different family, *Didunculidæ*. It is considered to be the nearest living representative of the dodo, whence the name.

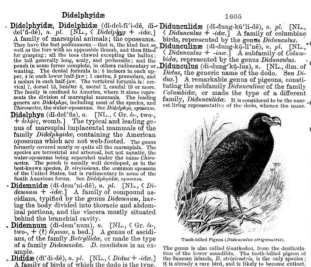

Tooth-billed Pigeon (*Didunculus strigirostris*).

The genus is also called *Gnathodon*, from the denticulation of the lower mandible. The tooth-billed pigeon of the Samoan islands, *D. strigirostris*, is the only species; it is already a rare bird, and is likely to become extinct. The color is blackish; the total length is about 14 inches; the beak, besides being toothed, is remarkably large and strong, with a very convex culmen, like that of a bird of prey.

Didus (dī'dus), *n.* [NL., Latinized form of *dodo*, altered to give it a classical look, as if after *Dido*, the mythical foundress of Carthage: see *dodo.*] The typical genus of *Dididæ*, containing the extinct dodo of Mauritius, *D. ineptus*. The general character of the genus is columbine or pigeon-like, but the size was comparatively enormous, the body massive and unwieldy, the wings unfit for flight, and the beak stout and hooked. The genus has become extinct since 1650. See *dodo*.

Didymic comma. See *comma*, 5 (*b*).

didymium (dī-dim'i-um), *n.* [NL., ‹ Gr. *δίδυμος*, double, twofold, twin: see *didymous.*] 1. Chemical symbol, D or Di. A rare metal discovered by Mosander in 1841 in the oxid of cerium, and so named from being, as it were, the twin brother of lanthanium, which was previously found in the same body, and from whose compounds those of didymium, greatly resembling them, are separated with much difficulty. Didymium never occurs free, nor even as a free salt, but always associated with cerium and lanthanium.
2. [*cap.*] A genus of fungi belonging to the *Myxomycetes*. The sporangia have a double wall, which is covered externally with crystals of lime, either scattered or compacted into a separable crust.

didymous (did'i-mus), *a.* [‹ Gr. *δίδυμος*, double, twofold, twin, ‹ *δι-*, two-, + *δύο*, = E. *two*, + suffix *-μος*.] 1. In *bot.*, twofold; twin; growing double, as the fruits of umbelliferous plants, the anthers of bedstraw, or the tubers of some orchids.—2. In *zoöl.*, twain; paired: applied to two spots, spines, tubercles, etc., when they form a pair touching each other.—**Didymous wing-cell**, in *entom.*, a wing-cell almost but not quite divided into two by a projecting short nervure.

didynam (did'i-nam), *n.* A plant of the class *Didynamia*.

Didynamia (did-i-nā'mi-ä), *n. pl.* [NL. (so named because the two larger stamens appear to dominate over the shorter), ‹ Gr. *δι-*, two-, + *δύναμις*, power: see *dynamic.*] The fourteenth class in the Linnean vegetable system, including plants with four stamens in unequal pairs. It was divided by Linnæus into two orders: *Gymnospermia*, having the fruit composed of single-seeded achenes, which he mistook for naked seeds; and *Angiospermia*, with many seeds inclosed in an obvious seed-vessel. The first included most of the *Labiatæ* and *Verbenaceæ*, the latter many *Scrophulariaceæ*, etc.

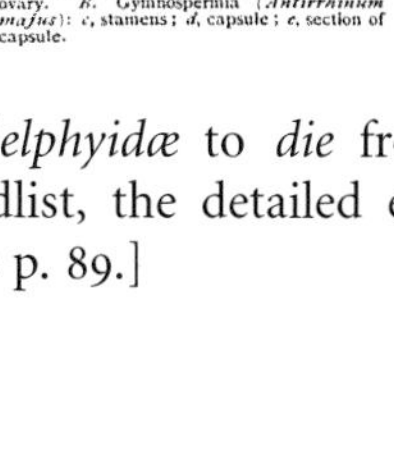

Didynamous Flowers.

A. Angiospermia (*Teucrium Scorodonia*): *c*, stamens; *d*, divided ovary; *e*, section of ovary. *B.* Gymnospermia (*Antirrhinum majus*): *c*, stamens; *d*, capsule; *e*, section of capsule.

didynamian, didynamic (did-i-nā'mi-an, -nam'ik), *a.* [‹ *Didynamia* + *-an*, *-ic.*] Same as *didynamous*.

didynamous (dī-din'a-mus), *a.* [‹ NL. **didynamus*, ‹ Gr. *δι-*, two-, + *δύναμις*, power. Cf. *Didynamia.*] In *bot.*, in two unequal pairs: applied to flowers having four stamens in two unequal pairs, as most *Labiatæ*, etc.; specifically, belonging to the class *Didynamia*.

didynamy (dī-din'a-mi), *n.* [‹ NL. **didynamia*, ‹ **didynamus*: see *didynamous.*] In *bot.*, the condition of being in two unequal pairs, as stamens.

die[1] (dī), *v. i.*; pret. and pp. *died*, ppr. *dying*. [Early mod. E. also *dye* (and dial., Sc., etc., *dee*); ‹ ME. *dien*, *dyen*, *deien*, *deyen*, *deghen*, *degen*, *digen*, etc. (not in AS., where 'die' was expressed by *sweltan* (see *swelt*) or *steorfan* (see *starve*); but the derived forms *deád*, dead, and *deáth*, death, occur), ‹ Icel. *deyja* (strong verb, pret. *dō*, pp. *dāinn*) = Goth. **diwan* (strong verb, pret. **dau*, pp. *diwans*, found only as an adj. used as a noun, *thata diwano*, the mortal, mortality, and in deriv. *undiwanei*, immortality); the other Teut. forms are weak: Norw. *döya* = Sw. *dö* = Dan. *dö* = OS. *dōian* = OHG. MHG. *touwen*, die (cf. Goth. *af-daujan*, harass, distress, OFries. *deia*, *deja*, kill), ‹ Teut. √ **dau*, whence also ult. E. *dead* and *death*, q. v. Cf. OBulg. *daviti* = Bohem. *daviti* = Russ. *daviti*, choke, = Lith. *dovīti*, plague, vex.] 1. To cease to live; lose or part with life; expire; suffer death; perish: said of sentient beings, and used absolutely (as, all must *die*), or with *of*, *by*, or *from*, to express the cause of death, or with *for* to express the object or occasion of dying: as, to *die of* smallpox, or *by* violence; to *die for* one's country.

There *dyede* Seynte Johne, and was buryed behynde the highe Awtiere, in a Toumbe. *Mandeville*, Travels, p. 22.

Christ *died for* our sins. 1 Cor. xv. 3.

And what we call to *die*, is not to appear
Or be the thing that formerly we were.
Dryden, Pythagorean Philos., l. 392.

"Whom the gods love *die* young," was said of yore.
Byron, Don Juan, iv. 12.

Every individual eventually *dies from* inability to withstand some environing action.
H. Spencer, Study of Sociol., p. 339.

2. To lose vital power or action; become devitalized or dead: said of plants or parts of plants, as a decayed tree or a withered limb or stem: as, certain plants *die* down to the ground annually, while their roots live.—3. To sink; faint.

His heart *died* within him, and he became as a stone.
1 Sam. xxv. 37.

Hence—4. To come to an end or come to nothing; cease, or cease to exist; perish; be lost.

When I look upon the tombs of the great, every emotion of envy *dies* in me.
Addison, Thoughts in Westminster Abbey.

Whatever pleasure any man may take in spreading whispers, he will find greater satisfaction by letting the secret *die* within his own breast. *Spectator.*

Nothing *died* in him
Save courtesy, good sense, and proper trust.
Browning, Ring and Book, II. 130.

5. To come to an end gradually; become extinct by degrees; vanish by or as if by death: usually with *away*, *out*, or *down*.

For 'tis much if a Ship sails a Mile before either the Wind *dyes* wholly *away*, or at least shifts about again to the South. *Dampier*, Voyages, II. iii. 6.

So gently shuts the eye of day;
So *dies* a wave along the shore.
Mrs. Barbauld, Death of the Virtuous.

There, waves that, hardly weltering, *die away*,
Tip their smooth ridges with a softer ray.
Wordsworth, Evening Walk.

The living airs of middle night
Died round the bulbul as he sung.
Tennyson, Arabian Nights.

The system of bribery did not long survive the ministry of Lord North. It may not have wholly *died out*; and has probably since been resorted to on rare and exceptional occasions. *Sir E. May*, Const. Hist. Eng., I. vi.

In the course of his ten years' attendance, all the inmates *died out* two or three times, and were replaced by new ones. *O. W. Holmes*, Old Vol. of Life, p. 2.

6. To become less and less subject to, or cease to be under the power or influence of, a thing: followed by *to* or *unto*: as, to *die to* sin.—7. To languish with affection or love.

The young men acknowledged that they *died* for Rebecca. *Tatler.*

8. To be consumed with a great yearning or desire; be very desirous; desire keenly or greatly: as, she was just *dying* to go. [Colloq.]—

Plate 9 Page showing the entries *didelphyidæ* to *die* from *The Century Dictionary* (1889–91). Note the encyclopedic wordlist, the detailed etymologies, the quotations, and the quality of the illustrations. [See p. 89.]

pursueantlye that yt belongyth to the lawe of man. 1675 J. HOWE *Living Temple* (1845) 167 We are here, pursuantly to the drift and design of the present discourse, to affirm a necessity. 1688 *Vox Cleri pro Rege* 31 Pursuantly.., 'It may be made appear, that [etc.]'. 1873 BROWNING *Red Cott. Nt.-cap* II. 872 Pursuantly, one morning—knock at door.. broke startlingly On household slumber.

Pursue (pɜsiū·, -syū), *v.* Forms: see below. [ME. a. AF. *pursiwe-r*, *pursue-r* (also *pursu-re*) = OF. *porsievre*, *porsieure*, *-sivre*, *-suire*, etc. (see SUE *v.*), mod.F. *poursuivre* = Pr. *perseguir*, *persegre*, Sp. *perseguir* and *proseguir*, It. *proseguire* and *perseguire*:—L. *prosequĕre*, *-īre*, *persequĕre*, *-īre*, popular forms of *prōsequī* and *persequī*, compounds of *sequī* to follow, which to a great extent ran together in Romanic. In ME. the L. form of the prefix, *prō-*, was sometimes, and *per-* frequently, substituted.]

A. Illustration of Forms.

α. 3 **pursiwe(n, 4–5 -suwe, -sewe, 4–6 -sew, 5 -siewe, -syewe, -sywe, -suie, -suye, -su, -swe; 4– pursue.**

c 1290 *Beket* 945 in *S. Eng. Leg.* I. 133 Ȝwane..luþere men pursiweden me: louerd, min help þov beo! 1340 HAMPOLE *Pr. Consc.* 4450 Þan sal anticrist bygyn felly To pursue men thurgh tyrauntry. *c* 1375 *Cursor M.* 19618 (Fairf.) Saule saule..qui pursewes þou me. *a* 1400 Pursywed [see B. 11 b]. *c* 1400 *Destr. Troy* 1150 Pollux with his pupull pursu on the laste. 1412–20 LYDG. *Chron. Troy* (E.E.T.S.) 506/3889 Þat with al his myȝt My deth pursuwet[h]. *c* 1430 — *Min. Poems* (Percy Soc.) 251 Heeryng this voys, after I shal purswe [*rime* remwe = remue]. 1449 *Rolls of Parlt.* V. 150/1 At the sute of him whiche in this cas will pursuye. 1470–85 MALORY *Arthur* Table II. v. 7 How Balyn was pursyewed. *a* 1533 LD. BERNERS *Huon* lix. 206 They were so hastyd and pursewyd.

β. 4 **poursuie, 4–6 -sewe, 5 -syewe, -sue, -su.**

1390 GOWER *Conf.* II. 117 Thei..lesen hope forto spede And stinten love to poursewe [*rime* hewe]. *Ibid.* [see B. 5 poursuie]. 1456 SIR G. HAYE *Law Arms* (S.T.S.) 119 To poursu bataill. 1485 CAXTON *Chas. Gt.* 150 Knowyng that he was poursyewed. 1487 HEN. VII in *Ep. Acad. Oxon.* (1898) II. 524 To be poursued unto us hereafter. 1596 SPENSER *F. Q.* IV. vii. 30 Whom seeing flie she speedily poursewed.

γ. 4–5 **porsewe, -sue.**

c 1350 *Will. Palerne* 2474 Al þe puple..þat him porsewed hadde. 1393 LANGL. *P. Pl.* C. XVIII. 167 And porsuede to haue be pope pryns of holychurche.

δ. ?4 **persywe, 5–7 persew(e, 5–8 persue, 6 -seu, -schew.**

?*a* 1400 *Trevisa's Higden* (Rolls) V. 71 (MS. γ) Persywed. *c* 1400 *Apol. Loll.* 24 Wan men schal..persew ȝow. 1414 *Rolls of Parlt.* IV. 57/1 How that I persuede diverse billes. 1526 *Pilgr. Perf.* (W. de W. 1531) 18 To resyst and persewe the kynge. 1588 in *Lib. Offic. S. Andree* (Abbotsf.) 170 Þat we nor nane..in our nayme sall perschew nor follow [etc.]. 1609 SKENE *Reg. Maj.* 22 To persew his clame. 1759 JOHNSON *Rasselas* xxx, Pekuah..entreated the princess not to persue so dreadful a purpose. *Ibid.* xxxii, Rasselas prepared to persue the robbers. 1779 Persued [see B. 10].

ε. 5 **prosew(e.**

1432–50 tr. *Higden* (Rolls) IV. 133 Anthiocus..prosewede [1387 TREVISA pursuede] Triphon.

B. Signification. I. Transitive uses.

1. To follow with hostility or enmity; to seek to injure (a person); to persecute; to harass, worry, torment. Now *rare* or *Obs.* exc. as implied in 2.

c 1290, etc. [see A. α]. 1382 WYCLIF *Matth.* v. 11 Ȝee shulen be blessid, when men shulen curse ȝou, and shulen pursue ȝou. *Ibid.*, *Acts* ix. 4, 5 'Saul, Saul, what pursuest thou me?'..'I am Jhesu of Nazareth, whom thou pursuest'. 1526 *Pilgr. Perf.* (W. de W. 1531) 97 Loue your ennemyes, ..praye for them that persueth you. 1693 PEPYS in *Lett. Lit. Men* (Camden) 212 To pursue you in the matter of the Prints soe farr beyond what in good manners I..would have done. 1750 JOHNSON *Rambler* No. 79 ⁋ 12 Those may justly be pursued as enemies to the community of nature. 1855 MILMAN *Lat. Chr.* (1864) V. IX. viii. 415 To expel, or to pursue to death, a large part..of their subjects.

†**b.** To avenge, to follow with punishment. *Obs.*

1570 *Satir. Poems Reform.* xxiii. 111 Thocht thair war nane his deith that wald persew, The michtie God he wald Reuenge his blude. 1603 SHAKS. *Meas. for M.* v. i. 109 That with such vehemency he should pursue Faults proper to himselfe. 1697 DRYDEN *Virg. Georg.* IV. 654 No vulgar God Pursues thy Crimes, nor with a common Rod.

2. To follow with intent to overtake and capture or kill; to chase, to hunt.

1377 LANGL. *P. Pl.* B. XII. 241 Þe pekok, and men pursue hym may nouȝte fleighe heighe; For þe traillyng of his taille. *c* 1400 MAUNDEV. (Roxb.) viii. 30 Kyng Pharao persued þam. 1560 BIBLE (Genev.) *Ps.* lxxi. 11 Pursue and take him, for there is none to deliuer him. 1697 DRYDEN *Virg. Georg.* III. 314 Boreas in his Race..with impetuous roar Pursues the foaming Surges to the Shoar. 1783 COWPER *Epitaph on Hare* 1 Here lies, whom hound did ne'er pursue, Nor swifter greyhound follow. 1874 GREEN *Short Hist.* VIII. vii, To rout their other wing of horse as it returned breathless from pursuing the Scots.

b. *fig.* Said of the action of things evil or hurtful.

1567 *Gude & Godlie B.* (S.T.S.) 79 Ay quhen temptatioun dois zow persew. 1613 SHAKS. *Hen. VIII*, IV. ii. 25 So went to bed; where eagerly his sicknesse Pursu'd him still. 1698 FRYER *Acc. E. India & P.* 261 The worst inconvenience that pursued us. 1842 BORROW *Bible in Spain* viii. 47 The cold still pursued me. 1895 SALMOND *Chr. Doctr. Immort.* VI. iii. 647 The penalties of a selfish life and wasted opportunity pursue one beyond death.

3. To prosecute in a court of law, to sue (a person). Chiefly *Sc.*

1580 *Rot. Scacc. Reg. Scot.* XXI. 548 Persewing the said Alexander for mair nor ten thousand pundis. 1643 *Declar. Com., Reb. Irel.* 58 The Lords of his Majesties Privy Councell have given order that Nithisdail and Aboyne be cited, and criminally pursued of high Treason. 1688 *Pennsylv. Archives* I. 102 All..such Person or Persons shall be pursued with the utmost Severities and the greatest Rigor. 1876 *World* V. 8 She cannot be pursued in Germany, for there she has committed no crime. 1893 *Dict. Nat. Biog.* XXXIII. 403 She 'pursued' him in the Scottish courts in November 1703 for the sum of 500 *l.*

4. To follow, as an attendant; to come after in order, or in time. Now *rare* or *Obs.*

c 1470 HENRY *Wallace* VI. 120 Schyr Jhon the Grayme,.. To Laynrik come, gud Wallace to persew. 1606 SHAKS. *Ant. & Cl.* III. xii. 26 Fortune pursue thee. 1658 BRAMHALL *Consecr. Bps.* iii. 74 Here we see..how al things do pursue one another. 1700 DRYDEN *Meleager & Atalanta* 339 My son requires my death, and mine shall his pursue. 1755 GRAY *Progr. Poesy* 64 Her track, where'er the Goddess roves, Glory pursue, and generous Shame. 1789 W. GILPIN *Wye* (ed. 2) 119 Grand woody promontories, pursuing each other, all rich to profusion.

b. To follow the course of (in description, etc.); to trace. *poetic.* In quot. 1883 = FOLLOW *v.* 10.

1697 DRYDEN *Virg. Georg.* IV. 1 The Gifts of Heav'n my foll'wing Song pursues. 1712 ADDISON *Hymn*, '*When all thy mercies*' xi, Through every Period of my Life Thy Goodness I'll pursue. 1883 F. M. PEARD *Contrad.* vii, Said Lady Molyneux, pursuing them with her eye-glass.

5. To sue for, to seek after; to try to obtain or accomplish, to aim at.

1390 GOWER *Conf.* III. 154 In Rome, to poursuie his riht. *c* 1400 MAUNDEV. (Roxb.) xxxiv. 152 Oþer iles þare er, wha so wald pursue þam, by þe whilk men myght ga all aboute þe erthe. *c* 1440 *Jacob's Well* v. 29 Þat he may noȝt defendyn hym þere, ne pursewyn his ryȝt. 1538 STARKEY *England* I. i. 7 For euer that wych ys best ys not of al men..to be persuyd. 1594 KYD *Cornelia* III. iii. 83 He murdred Pompey that pursu'd his death. 1611 BIBLE *Ps.* xxxiv. 14 Seeke peace and pursue it. 1712 STEELE *Spect.* No. 462 ⁋ 4 He pursued Pleasure more than Ambition. 1874 CARPENTER *Ment. Phys.* I. vii. (1879) 318 The mind instinctively pursues what is pleasurable.

†**b.** To make it one's aim or endeavour, to try (*to do* something). *Obs.*

1390 GOWER *Conf.* III. 82 Such Sorcerie..I schal eschuie, That so ne wol I noght poursuie Mi lust of love forto seche. *c* 1430 LYDG. *Min. Poems* (Percy Soc.) 67, I counsaile thow pursue all thy lyve To lyve in peas. *c* 1430 *Hymns Virg.* 62 Þi foote þou holde, And pursue for to passe þe beest. 1523 LD. BERNERS *Froiss.* I. ccxxix. 308 People and men of warre, that wolde pursue to go into Castell.

†**6.** To seek to reach or attain to, to make one's way to. *Obs.*

c 1470 HENRY *Wallace* VI. 190 Than Cartlane craggis thai persewit full fast. 1508 DUNBAR *Tua Mariit Wemen* 478 All my luffaris lele, my lugeing persewis. *a* 1520 — *Poems* ix. 84 To keipe the festuall and the fasting day, The mess on Sonday, the parroche kirk persew. 1611 HEYWOOD *Gold. Age* II. i, Dianae's Cloyster I will next pursue. 1681 DRYDEN *Abs. & Achit.* 855 Here stop, my Muse..No Pinions can pursue Immortal height.

†**b.** To attack, assail, besiege. *Sc. Obs.*

c 1470 HENRY *Wallace* VIII. 498 Sotheroun marueld giff it suld be Wallace, With out souerance come to persew that place. 1547 *Reg. Privy Council Scot.* I. 81 Our auld ynemeis intendis to cum and persew the said house..to recover the samyn furth of the said lordis handis. 1583 *Ibid.* III. 567 A greit nowmer of wickit and seditious personis..persewit the houssis of the provest and ane of the baillies.

7. To follow (a path, way, course); to proceed along; = FOLLOW *v.* 1 b. Now chiefly *fig.* In quot. 1390, to go through in reading, to peruse.

1390 GOWER *Conf.* III. 46 For full enformacioun The Scole which Honorious Wrot, he poursuieth. 1638 JUNIUS *Paint. Ancients* 120 They could not choose but chearefully pursue the same way of Art. 1697 DRYDEN *Virg. Georg.* III. 449 We too far the pleasing Path pursue. 1709 STEELE *Tatler* No. 97 ⁋ 2 To consider what Course of Life he ought to pursue. 1788 JEFFERSON *Writ.* (1859) II. 369, I..shall pursue the course of the Rhine as far as the roads will permit me. 1879 R. K. DOUGLAS *Confucianism* iii. 72 The Sage..pursues the heavenly way without the slightest deflection.

8. To proceed in compliance or accordance with; = FOLLOW *v.* 8. Now only with *method*, *plan*, *scheme*, *system*, and the like: see quots. 1817–79.

1426 LYDG. *De Guil. Pilgr.* 9039 Al hys desyrs thow pursues. ?1656 BRAMHALL *Replic.* vi. 241 This is not to alter the Institutions..of generall Councells..but..to tread in their stepps, and to pursue their grounds. 1718 POPE *Iliad* XI. 192 The king's example all his Greeks pursue. 1748 SMOLLETT *Rod. Rand.* xiv, As we were going to pursue this advice. 1817 JAS. MILL *Brit. India* II. v. i. 315 The following scheme was invented and pursued. 1879 *Techn. Drawing* in *Cassell's Techn. Educ.* IV. 69/2 The same system is now to be pursued.

9. To follow up, carry on further, proceed with, continue (a course of action, etc. begun).

1456 SIR G. HAYE *Law Arms* (S.T.S.) 119 Nocht all men that pursewis bataill is nocht cled with that vertu of force. *c* 1586 C'TESS PEMBROKE *Ps.* (1823) CXV. iv, Israel pursue Thy trust in God. 1596 DALRYMPLE tr. *Leslie's Hist. Scot.* III. xxxvi. (S.T.S.) I. 191 Thay drew to pairties, and began to pe[r]sew the mater wᵗ swordes. 1601 SHAKS. *Twel. N.* IV. ii. 76, I cannot pursue with any safety this sport [to] the vppeshot. 1668 DRYDEN *Evening's Love* IV. i, This is the Folly of a bleeding Gamester, who will obstinately pursue a losing Hand. 1736 LEDIARD *Life Marlborough* I. 99 The Earl was resolved to pursue this good Success. 1759 JOHNSON *Rasselas* xxv, The Princess persues her enquiry. 1796 JANE AUSTEN *Pride & Prej.* xxx, The subject was pursued no farther. 1802 E. FORSTER tr. *Arab. Nts.* (1815) II. 355 The brothers then pursued their journey.

b. *Law.* To carry on (an action); to lay (information); to present (a libel). Chiefly *Sc.* (Cf. 3 and 13 b.)

1478 *Acta Dom. Conc.* 3/1 Þe accioun and cause persewit be William of Cavers..on þe ta part again Andro broun.. one þe tother part. 1530–1 *Act 22 Hen. VIII*, c. 12 The moytee thereof to be to him that pursueth the informacion for the same. *c* 1750 *Interlocutor* in J. Louthian *Process* (ed. 2) 152 The Lords Justice-Clerk and Commissioners of Justiciary, having considered the Libel pursued at the Instance of *A. B.* of —— [etc.].

10. To follow as an occupation or profession; to carry on, practise; to make a pursuit of.

1523 LD. BERNERS *Froiss.* I. ccccxx. 735, I have..pursewed myne offyce, to the honoure of you and of your people. 1673 S. C. *Art of Complaisance* 25 When we enterprise any affair with hopes well conceived..we pursue it with all perseverance. 1779 *Gentl. Mag.* XLIX. 363 He persued.. his studies, or his amusements without persecution, molestation or insult. 1851 HELPS *Comp. Solit.* i. (1874) 2 Others may pursue science or art.

II. Absolute and intransitive uses.

11. To go in chase or pursuit.

c 1350 *Will. Palerne* 2196 Þe puple þanne porsewed forþ & of here prey þei missed. 1390 GOWER *Conf.* III. 236 The womman fleth and he poursuieth. 1611 BIBLE *Prov.* xxviii. 1 The wicked flee when no man pursueth. 1755 GRAY *Progr. Poesy* 32 Now pursuing, now retreating, Now in circling troops. 1853 M. ARNOLD *Scholar Gypsy* xxii, Far on the forest-skirts, where none pursue.

b. *To pursue after*, to follow in pursuit, to chase; = sense 2. Also with *indirect passive*.

1377 LANGL. *P. Pl.* B. XIX. 158 Peter..pursued after, Bothe iames & Iohan, Ihesu for to seke. ?*a* 1400 *Arthur* 574 Arthour on gret haste Pursywed after hym faste. 1560 BIBLE (Genev.) *Exod.* xiv. 9 And the Egyptians pursued after them. 1655 FULLER *Ch. Hist.* IX. vii. § 15 Left to be pursued after by hunger and cold. 1760–72 H. BROOKE *Fool of Qual.* (1809) I. 66 To take every horse he had.. and to pursue after the fugitives.

†**c.** *To pursue for*, to seek or 'hunt' after.

1412–20 LYDG. *Chron. Troy* I. 1892 Þei pursue ay for pluralite.

†**12.** To proceed with hostile intent against some one; with *on*, *upon*, *to*, to attack, assail. *Obs.*

13.. *E. E. Allit. P.* B. 1177 He pur-sued in to palastyn with proude men mony. *c* 1400 *Destr. Troy* 2773 To pursew On hom þat hir holdis, & vs harme dyd. *Ibid.* 4853 All þis wale pepull Are comyn to þis cost..And pursuyt to þis prouynse in purpos to venge Of harmys. *c* 1440 *Alphabet of Tales* 158 Þan þe Romans..wold suffre it no langer, & rase & pursewid opon hym, & drafe hym oute of þe cetie. 1480 CAXTON *Cron. Eng.* clxiv. 148 Kyng edward..ordeyned men to pursue vpon hym—and dauyd ferselich hym defended. *c* 1500 *New Not-b. Mayd* (Percy Soc.) 33 Yet yf that shrewe To hym pursue.

†**13.** To make one's suit; to sue, entreat. *Obs.*

1390 GOWER *Conf.* II. 13 For after that a man poursuieth To love, so fortune suieth. *c* 1400 *Destr. Troy* 11431 Þai ..chosyn Antenor..with the grekes to trete, And pursew for pes. 1414 BRAMPTON *Penit. Ps.* 25 To thi mercy I will pursewe, Wyth 'Ne reminiscaris, Domine!' *c* 1560 A. SCOTT *Poems* (S.T.S.) xi. 7 Ȝe may wᵗ honesty persew, Gif ȝe be constant, trest, & trew.

b. *spec.* To sue in a court of law; to make suit as plaintiff or pursuer. In later use chiefly *Sc.*

1377 LANGL. *P. Pl.* B. XVII. 302 For þere þat partye pursueth þe pele is so huge, Þat þe kynge may do no mercy. 1389 *Eng. Gilds* 71 Yei shul pursu for her Catelle in qwat cowrte yat hem liste. *c* 1440 *Jacob's Well* 29 Wherby þe man is lettyd of his ryȝt, be-cause he may noȝt pursewe in holy cherch-lawe. *c* 1470 HARDING *Chron.* clviii. ii, That al Scottes, and other that were pursuyng Might there appere, their titles claimyng. *a* 1639 SPOTTISWOOD *Hist. Ch. Scot.* II. (1677) 55 If they should happen to die intestate, it was made lawful to their nearest kinsmen to call and pursue for the same. 1756 MRS. CALDERWOOD *Journey* (1842) 226 He was bred a papist, but his mother..set on the protestant heir to pursue for his estate.

†**14.** To follow as an attendant or supporter. *Obs.*

c 1470 HENRY *Wallace* IV. 197 He thaim comandyt ay next him to persew; For he thaim kend rycht hardye, wis and trew. *c* 1470 *Gol. & Gaw.* 1292 Heir I mak yow ane grant,..Ay to your presence to persew, with al my seruice.

†**15.** To follow or come after in order. *Obs.*

1485 *Rolls of Parlt.* VI. 332/2 The Dede and Fyne, wherof the tenoure persueth. 1529 MORE *Dyaloge* IV. xvii. Wks. 284/2 Rewarde or punishement, pursuing vpon all our dooinges. 1688 HOLME *Armoury* I. i. 2 Lest..scandal do arise and effusion of blood do persue.

†**16.** To proceed continuously. In quot. *a* 1651, to go or come forth, issue. *Obs.*

1500–20 DUNBAR *Poems* lxiv. 6 In to ȝour garthe this day I did persew. *a* 1651 *Life Humphrey* in Fuller *Abel Rediv.* (1867) II. 92 Those weighty words which pleasantly pursued out of his mouth. 1652 LOVEDAY tr. *Calprenede's Cassandra* III. 189 But we pursued on our way, resigning our selves to the protection and guidance of the Gods.

17. To continue (to do or say something); to go on (speaking). Also with *on*.

1500–20 DUNBAR *Poems* xlvi. 12 Quhair did, vpone the tothair syd, persew A nychtingall, with suggurit notis new. 1583 T. WATSON *Centurie of Loue* (Arb.) 129 In the other two staffes following, the Authour pursueth on his matter. 1665 BOYLE *Occas. Refl.* IV. xi, But, (pursues Eusebius) this may supply us with another Reflection. 1718 HICKES & NELSON *J. Kettlewell* I. § 33. 58 Notwithstanding this he persued on with all the Meekness of Wisdom. 1802 MAR. EDGEWORTH *Moral T.* (1816) I. iii. 17 'And I have buried the poor cat', pursued Forester: 'and I hope [etc.]'. 1837 WHEWELL *Hist. Induct. Sc.* I. ii. § 2 'Something of this', he pursues, 'may be seen in language'.

Hence **Pursu·ed** *ppl. a.*, **Pursu·ing** *vbl. sb.* and *ppl. a.*; also **Pursu·ingly** *adv.*

1716 *Macfarlane's Geneal. Collect.* (1901) I. 136 He was

Plate 10 Page showing entries for *pursue* from *A New English Dictionary on Historical Principles* (OUP 1928). Note the extensive etymologies, the charting of the evolution of forms, the detailed polysemy with a chronological order of senses, and the dated quotations. [See p. 100.]

PURPUREAL 1625 **PURTENANCE**

E *a.* 2. -1614. **2.** *Her.* Of the colour pure; see A. 2 b. 1562.

eal (pɒɹpiūə·ɹĭăl), *a.* Chiefly *poet.* L. *purpureus* + -AL.] Of purple urple. So **Purpu·rean** *a.* (*rare*) 1615.

eo- (pɒɹpiūə·ɹio), comb. f. L. *pur-* . purple; as *p.-cobalt, -cobaltic* adj.

ic (pɒɹpiūə·rik), *a.* 1818. [f. L. URPLE + -IC.] **1.** *Chem.* Applied to etical acid ($C_8H_5N_5O_6$), the salts of purple or red. **2.** *Path.* Of, pertain- of the nature of purpura or purples; y a purple rash 1839.

in (pɒ̄·ɹpiŭrin). 1839. [f. L. *pur-* N [1].] *Chem.* A red colouring matter, OH)$_3$, used in dyeing, orig. extracted der, hence called *madder-purple*; also artificially by oxidation of alizarin.

ɒ̄ɹ), *sb.* 1601. [Cogn. w. next.] An ring; the soft murmuring sound made when pleased; also, any similar sound.

ɒ̄ɹ), *v.* 1620. [Echoic.] **1.** *intr.* Of .: To make a low continuous vibra- d expressive of satisfaction or plea- . *transf.* **a.** Of persons: To show on by low murmuring sounds, or by aviour or attitude; also, to talk on in a -satisfied way 1668. **b.** Of things: To ound suggestive of the purring of a at caused by the boiling or bubbling d, etc. 1657. **3.** *trans.* To utter or by purring 1740.

aid that the lion, jaguar, and leopard do not .

(pɒ̄ɹ). 1611. [From the voice of the A local name of the Dunlin (*Tringa is*).

e (pɒ·ri). 1852. [Hindi *peorī.*] A olouring matter, from which INDIAN s prepared.

(pɒ̄ɹs), *sb.* [OE. and ME. *purs*, app. L. *bursa* purse.] **I.** A money-bag or cle and its contents. **1.** A small pouch of leather or other flexible material, r carrying money on the person; orig. bag drawn together at the mouth with or strings. **2.** A purse with its con- ence *transf.* money, funds ME. **3.** A money collected as a present or the sum subscribed as a prize for the win- contest 1650. **4.** As tr. Arab., Pers., *kīsah, kīseh* 'purse', used in the empire for a definite sum of money **5.** A fragment of live coal starting out re with a report: regarded as a prog- of good fortune 1766.

Money in thy p. SHAKS. A heavy p. makes eart B. JONSON. **2.** Phr. *A common p.*, funds d and shared by a number of people in com- *heavy* or *long p.*, wealth. *A light p.*, poverty. *lic p.*, the national treasury or wealth. *Privy* PRIVY *a.* **3.** His Friends made a P. for him, was to travel to Ægypt BENTLEY. **4.** *The ver*) = 500 piastres. *The p. of gold* = 10,000

A bag or bag-like receptacle. †**1.** A scrip, pouch -1771. **2.** *transf. Organ- g.* A small leather bag formerly used in ion with the pull-downs which passed h the bottom board of the wind-chest, to t the escape of wind 1852. **3.** Applied ous natural receptacles (in animals or resembling a bag; e. g. a marsupium, 1528. **b.** *spec.* The scrotum 1440.

th a naturall p. vnder her belly, wherein she her young PURCHAS.

. and *Comb.*: **p.-crab,** a crab of the genus living in burrows on the E. Indian islands; bag-shaped net, the mouth of which can be together with cords **-seine,** a fishing-net or which may be pursed or drawn into the shape g, used for catching shoal-fish.

se (pɒ̄ɹs), *v.* ME. [f. prec.] **1.** *trans.* t into one's purse; to pocket. Also with Now *rare.* †**2.** *fig.* To pocket (an af- ; to withdraw or keep back (a boast); to possession of, shut up -1691. **3.** *trans.* aw together (the lips, brow, etc.) in wrin- r puckers, like the drawn-in mouth of a Often with *up.* 1604. **b.** *intr.* and To become wrinkled, to pucker 1709. *ns.* To close *up* like a purse (*rare*) 1823. o steal purses, to rob -1616. **6.** *U.S.* *trans.* To draw a purse-seine into the shape of a bag so as to close it.

1. I never p. one penny of it 1659. **2.** *Ant. & Cl.* II. ii. 192. **3.** Their Action is only to p. up the Mouth, as in whistling and blowing 1746. **5.** I'll p.; if that raise me not, I'll bet at bowling-alleys BEAUM. & FLETCHER. Hence **Pu·rsing** *vbl. sb.* (also attrib.) and *ppl. a.*, as **pursing-block, -gear, -line, -weight,** the block, etc., used in working a purse-seine.

Pu·rse-bea:rer. ME. **1.** The carrier of a purse; one who has charge of the money of another or of a company; a treasurer, bursar. **2.** *spec.* The official who carries the Great Seal in front of the Lord Chancellor in a receptacle called 'purse' or 'burse' 1688. **3.** A marsupial 1851.

Pu·rse-proud, *a.* 1681. Proud of wealth; puffed up on account of one's wealth. So **Pu·rse-pride** 1606.

Purser (pɒ̄·ɹsəɹ). ME. [f. PURSE *sb.* + -ER [1].] †**1.** A maker of purses -1638. †**2.** An officer charged with managing money matters and keeping accounts. *Obs.* in gen. sense. -1816. **b.** The officer on board a ship who keeps the accounts, and usu. has charge of the provisions 1458. **c.** In Cornwall, the treasurer of a mine, esp. one worked on the cost-book principle 1832. Hence **Pu·rsership.**

Pu·rse-string. late ME. Usu. in *pl.*: The two threaded strings by drawing which the mouth of a purse is closed; hence *fig.*

Phr. *To hold the purse-strings*, to control the expenditure of money. *To tighten* or *loosen the purse-strings*, to be sparing, or generous, in spending money.

Pursiness (pɒ̄·ɹsinės). late ME. [f. PURSY *a.*[1] + -NESS.] The state of being pursy; short-windedness.

Pursive (pɒ̄·ɹsiv), *a.* *arch.* late ME. [a. AF. *porsif*, app. var. of OF. *polsif*, mod.F. *poussif*, f. OF. *polser* to breathe with labour or difficulty:—L. *pulsare*, freq. of *pellere* to drive.] Short-winded, broken-winded, asthmatic; orig. said esp. of a horse. Hence **Pu·rsiveness** (*arch.*) = PURSINESS.

Purslane (pɒ̄·ɹslĕn). late ME. [a. OF. *porcelaine* = It. *porcellana*; altered from L. *porcil(l)aca*, used for the more usual L. *portulaca.*] **1.** A low succulent herb, *Portulaca oleracea*, used in salads, and sometimes as a pot-herb, or for pickling. Also called *Common* or *Garden P.* **2.** With qualification, denoting other species of *Portulaca* 1578.

2. **Crimson-flowered P.,** *Portulaca Thellussoni.* **Red-flowered P.,** *Portulaca splendens.* **Yellow-flowered P.,** *Portulaca aurea.* **Sea-P.,** *Atriplex portulacoides*, and *Arenaria peploides.* **Water-P.,** *Peplis Portula*, and *Isnardia palustris.*

Comb. **p.-tree,** a S. African shrub, *Portulacaria afra.*

Pursual (pɒ̆ɹsiū·ăl). *rare.* 1814. [f. PURSUE *v.* + -AL.] The action or fact of pursuing; pursuance.

Pursuance (pɒ̆ɹsiū·ăns). 1596. [f. as PURSUANT; see -ANCE.] †**1.** = PURSUIT I. 2. -1693. **2.** = PURSUIT II. 1. (Now with *end*, *object*, or the like.) 1640. **3.** The action of following out (a process); continuation, prosecution 1605. **4.** The action of proceeding in accordance with a plan, direction, or order; prosecution, following out, carrying out 1660.

2. To start in p. of that object 1878. **3.** In p. of some train of thought 1859. **4.** When they reached London in p. of their little plan DICKENS.

Pursuant (pɒ̆ɹsiū·ănt), *sb.* and *a.* [Late ME. a. OF. *por-, poursuiant*, *poursuir* to PURSUE.] †**A.** *sb.* One who prosecutes an action (at law); a suitor; a prosecutor -1657. **B.** *adj.* †**1.** Prosecuting (in a court of law) -1543. **2.** With *to*, rarely *upon*: Following upon, consequent on and conformable to; in accordance with. *Obs.* exc. as in b. 1648. **b.** quasi-*adv.* = PURSUANTLY 1675. **3.** Going in pursuit; following after, pursuing 1691.

2. If..the fine is levied p. to the deed CRUISE. **b.** P. to our method..we have concluded it necessary 1675. Hence **Pursu·antly** *adv.* in a way that is p. or consequent *to*.

Pursue (pɒ̆ɹsiū·), *v.* [ME. a. AF. *persiwer, pursuer* = OF. *porsievre, porsieure*, mod. F. *poursuivre*:—L. *prosequere, persequere*, pop. forms of *prosequi* and *persequi.*] **I.** *trans.* **1.** To follow with hostility or enmity; to seek to injure (a person); to persecute; to harass, worry, torment. Now *rare* or *Obs.* exc. as in 2. †**b.** To follow with punishment -1697. **2.** To follow with intent to capture or kill; to chase, hunt. late ME. **3.** To prosecute in a court of law, to sue (a person). Chiefly *Sc.* 1580. **4.** To follow, as an attendant; to come after in order, or in time. Now *rare* or *Obs.* 1470. **b.** To follow the course of (in description, etc.); to trace. *poet.* 1697. **5.** To sue for, to seek after; to aim at. late ME. †**6.** To seek to attain to, to make one's way to -1681. **7.** To follow (a path, way, course); to proceed along. Now chiefly *fig.* late ME. **8.** To proceed in compliance or accordance with. Now only with *method*, *plan*, and the like. late ME. **9.** To follow up (a course of action, etc. begun) 1456. **b.** *Law.* To carry on (an action); to lay (information); to present (a libel). Chiefly *Sc.* late ME. **10.** To follow as an occupation or profession; to make a pursuit of 1523.

1. Those may justly be pursued as enemies to the community of nature JOHNSON. **b.** *Meas. for M.* v. i. 109. **2.** P. and take him, for there is none to deliuer him BIBLE (Genev.) *Ps.* lxxi. 11. *fig.* The cold still pursued me BORROW. **5.** He pursued Pleasure more than Ambition STEELE. **7.** We too far the pleasing Path p. DRYDEN. **8.** As we were going to p. this advice SMOLLETT. **9.** The subject was pursued no farther JANE AUSTEN. **10.** He persued..his studies..without persecution 1779.

II. *absol.* and *intr.* **1.** To go in chase or pursuit ME. **b.** *To p. after* = sense I. 2. late ME. **2.** To sue in a court of law; to make suit as plaintiff or pursuer. In later use chiefly *Sc.* late ME. **3.** To continue (to do or say something); to go on (speaking). Also with *on.* 1500.

1. The wicked flee when no man pursueth *Prov.* xxviii. 1. Hence **Pursu·ingly** *adv.*

Pursuer (pɒ̆ɹsiū·əɹ). late ME. [f. prec. + -ER [1].] One who pursues; *spec. Civil* and *Sc. Law*, a suitor; a plaintiff, a petitioner; a prosecutor.

Pursuit (pɒ̆ɹsiū·t). late ME. [a. AF. *purs(e)ute*, OF. *por-, poursuite*, deriv. of *poursuivre*, after *suite* (:—pop.L. **sequita*) from *suivre.*] **I.** †**1.** Persecution, annoyance -1639. **2.** The action of pursuing a fleeing object, as a hunted animal or an enemy. late ME. †**3.** The action of suing or entreating; a suit, request, petition, instance -1701. **4.** *Law.* An action at law; a suit; prosecution. In later use chiefly *Sc.* late ME.

2. Each that passed that way Did join in the p. COWPER. *In p.* (*of*), said of the pursuer; *in p.* formerly sometimes of the pursued, = in flight.

II. 1. The action of seeking, or striving to obtain, attain, or accomplish something; search; †endeavour, attempt (*to do* something) 1606. **b.** *transf.* The object aimed at; aim 1592. **2.** The action of following or engaging in something, as a profession, business, recreation, etc.; that which one engages in or follows 1529. †**3.** The pursuing *of* a plan, etc. -1655. †**4.** A continuation, a sequel -1725.

1. You may hear men talk as if the p. of wealth was the business of life J. H. NEWMAN. **b.** Be love my youth's p., and science crown my Age GRAY. **2.** In our daily pursuits 1862. **4.** I return now to the p. of our voyage DE FOE.

Pursuivant (pɒ̄·ɹswivĕnt), *sb.* [Late ME. a. OF. *por-, poursivant*, pr. pple. of *pours(u)ivre*, also used subst.] **1.** Formerly, A junior heraldic officer attendant on the heralds; also one attached to a particular nobleman. Now, an officer of the College of Arms, ranking below a Herald. Also *p. at* (*of*) *arms.* †**2.** A royal or state messenger with power to execute warrants; a warrant-officer -1823. †**b.** *transf.* and *fig.* = 'messenger' -1631. **3.** A follower; an attendant 1513.

1. Pursevantes and herauldes That crien ryche folkes laudes CHAUCER. **2. b.** That great purseuaunt, Johan Baptist 1530. Hence †**Pu·rsuivant** *v. trans.* to send a p. after; to summon or arrest by a p.

Pursy (pɒ̄·ɹsi), *a.*[1] 1440. [Later form of *pursif* PURSIVE.] **1.** = PURSIVE. **2.** Fat, corpulent 1576.

2. *fig. Haml.* III. iv. 153.

Pursy (pɒ̄·ɹsi), *a.*[2] 1552. [f. PURSE *sb.* + -Y [1].] **1.** Of cloth, the skin, etc.: Having puckers, puckered; drawn together like a purse-mouth. **2.** Having a full purse; wealthy; purse-proud 1602.

Purtenance (pɒ̄·ɹtĭnăns). *arch.* [ME. a. AF. **purtinaunce*, for OF. *pertinance* PERTI-

r. Köln). ō̃ (Fr. peu). ü (Ger. Müller). ü̃ (Fr. dune). ɒ̄ (curl). ē (ēə) (there). ē̃ (ēⁱ) (rein). ɛ̃ (Fr. faire). ə̄ (fir, fern, earth).

Plate 11 Page showing the entries for *purpureal* to *purtenance* from *The Shorter Oxford English Dictionary* (1933). Note, in comparison with the *OED*, the omission of words in the wordlist, and of senses, and the reduced etymologies and quotations. [See p. 115.]

|deration for others' feelings ; shrinking from, |voidance of, the immodest or offensive ; choice |ind of food, dainty ; a nicety. [foll., -ACY] **de'licate** (-ǎt), a. Delightful (poet.) ; palatable, dainty, (of food) ; sheltered, luxurious, effeminate, (*d. living, nurture, upbringing*) ; |ne of texture, soft, slender, slight ; of exquisite |uality or workmanship ; subdued (of colour) ; |ubtle, hard to appreciate ; easily injured, liable |o illness ; requiring nice handling, critical, |cklish ; subtly sensitive (of persons or instru- |ents) ; deft (*a d. touch*) ; avoiding the offensive |r immodest ; considerate (esp. of actions). |ence **de'licate**LY[2] adv. [f. L *delicatus* cogn. |r associated w. *deliciae* delight see foll.]

deli'cious, a. Highly delightful, esp. to taste, |nell, or the sense of humour. Hence **deli'ci-** |us**LY**[2] adv., **deli'cious**NESS n. [OF, f. LL |*eliciosus* f. L *deliciae* delight f. DE(*licere* = |*icere* allure), -OSE[1]]

deli'ct, n. Violation of law, offence, (*in flag-* |*ant d.,* = IN FLAGRANTE DELICTO). [f. L *delic-* |*um* neut. p.p. of DE(*linquere* leave) come |ort]

deli'ght, v.t. & i., & n. Please highly (*shall* |*e delighted to,* in accepting invitation) ; take, |nd, great pleasure *in* (so in p.p., *the books de-* |*ghted in by the many*), be inclined and accus- |med *to* do. (N.) high pleasure, thing that |uses it ; hence **deli'ght**FUL a., **deli'ght-** |ully[2] adv., **deli'ght**SOME a. [ME *deliten* f. |F *delitier* f. L *delectare* see DELECTABLE, now |isspelt after *light*]

Deli'lah, Da-, n. Temptress, false & wily |oman. [*Judges* xvi]

deli'mit(āte), vv.t. Determine limits or ter- |torial boundary of. So **delimit**A'TION n. |it thr. F *délimiter, -itate* direct, f. L DE(*limi-* |*are* f. *limes -itis* boundary), -ATE[3]]

deli'neate, v.t. Show by drawing or descrip- |ion, portray. So **deline**A'TION, **deli'neat-** |R[2], nn. [f. L DE(*lineare* f. *linea* line), -ATE[3]]

deli'nquency, n. Neglect of duty ; guilt ; |sin of omission ; misdeed. [f. L *delinquentia* |*delinquens* part. (DELICT, -ENCY)]

deli'nquent, a. & n. Defaulting, guilty ; |n.) offender. [f. L *delinquens* (prec., -ENT)]

déli'que'sce (-ĕs), v.i. Become liquid, melt, |sg.) melt away. So **delique'scENT** a., **de-** |**lique'scENCE** n. [f. L DE(*liquescere* incept. |f *liquēre* be liquid)]

deli'rious, a. Affected with delirium, tem- |orarily or apparently mad, raving ; wildly |xcited, ecstatic ; betraying delirium or ecstasy. |Hence **deli'rious**LY[2] adv. [as foll. + -OUS]

deli'rium, n. Disordered state of mind with |ncoherent speech, hallucinations, & frenzied |xcitement ; great excitement, ecstasy ; *d.* |rēmens* (abbr. *d.t.*), special form of d. with |errifying delusions to which heavy drinkers |re liable. [L, f. DE(*lirare* (*lira* furrow)]

déli'te'scent, a., **delite'scence,** n. Latent |state). [f. L DE(*litescere* incept. of *-litēre* = *latēre* |ie hid), -ENT, -ENCE]

deli'ver, v.t. Rescue, save, set free *from* ; |disburden woman in parturition *of* child (usu. |pass. ; also fig., *was delivered of a sonnet*) ; un- |burden one*self* (*of* esp. a long - suppressed |opinion &c.) in discourse ; give *up* or *over*, |abandon, resign, hand on *to* another ; distribute |letters) to owners ; present (account) ; (Law) |hand over formally (esp. sealed deed to grantee, |so *seal & d.*) ; launch, aim, (blow, ball, attack ; |d, battle,* accept opportunity of engaging) ; re- |cite (*well-delivered sermon*). Hence **deli'ver-** |ABLE a. [f. F *délivrer* f. LL *deliberare* (DE-, L |*liberare* f. *liber* free)]

deli'verance, n. Rescue ; emphatically or

formally delivered opinion, (in jurors' oath) verdict. [f. OF *delivrance* (prec., -ANCE)]

deli'verer, n. In vbl senses : esp., saviour, rescuer. [f. OF *delivrere* nom. of *delivreor* f. LL *deliberatorem* (DELIVER, -OR[2])]

deli'very, n. Childbirth ; surrender *of* ; delivering of letters &c., a periodical performance of this (*the first, the two-o'clock, d.*) ; (Law) formal handing over of property, transfer of deed (formerly essential for validity) to grantee or third party ; sending forth of missile, esp. of cricketball in bowling, action shown in doing this (*a good, high, d.*) ; uttering of speech &c. (*its d. took two hours*), manner of doing this (*a telling d.*). [AF *delivrée* fem. part. used as n. of F *délivrer* DELIVER, -Y[4]]

dell, n. Small hollow or valley usu. with tree-clad sides. [cf. Du. *del*, G *telle*, DALE]

De'lla Cru'scan, a. & n. (Member) of the Florentine Academy della Crusca, a society for purifying the Italian language, which issued an authoritative dictionary ; following artificial literary methods ; member of a late 18thc. artificial English school of poetry. [f. It. (*Accademia*) *della Crusca* (Academy) of the bran (i. e. sifting) + -AN]

De'lphian, De'lphic, aa. (As) of the oracle of Delphi ; obscure, ambiguous. [*-ic* f. L f. Gk *Delphikos, -ian* f. L f. Gk *Delphoi* + -IAN]

De'lphin, a. The *D. classics* or *text*, in an edition prepared for the Dauphin, son of Louis XIV. [L f. Gk, =dolphin ; see DAUPHIN]

de'lphinine, n. (chem.). A poisonous alkaloid used medically. [f. bot. L f. Gk *delphinion* (dim. of *delphin* dolphin) larkspur]

de'lta, n. Fourth letter, d, of Greek alphabet (capital an equilateral triangle) ; triangular alluvial tract at mouth of river enclosed or traversed by its diverging branches, esp. that of Nile, whence **delta'**IC a. [Gk]

de'ltoid, a. & n. Triangular ; *d. muscle* or *d.,* muscle of shoulder lifting upper arm ; like a river delta. [f. Gk *deltoeidēs* (prec., -OID)]

delu'de (-ōōd, -ūd), v.t. Impose upon, deceive. [f. L DE(*ludere lus-* play)]

dé'luge (-ūj), n., & v.t. Great flood, inundation, (*the D.,* Noah's flood) ; heavy fall of rain ; flood of words &c.; (vb) flood, inundate, (lit. & fig.). [F (*dé-*), f. L *diluvium* (*diluere* DILUTE)]

delu'sion (-ōō-, -ū-), n. Imposing or being imposed upon ; false impression or opinion, esp. as symptom or form of madness, whence **delu'sion**AL a. [f. L *delusio* (DELUDE, -ION)]

delu'sive (-ōō-, -ū-), a. Deceptive, disappointing, unreal. Hence **delu'sive**LY[2] adv., **delu'sive**NESS n. [DELUDE, -IVE]

delve, v.t. & i., & n., (archaic, poet., & dial.). Dig ; make research in documents &c. ; (of road &c.) make sudden dip. (N.) cavity ; depression of surface, wrinkle. [OE *delfan*, com.-WG cf. Du. *delven*]

dema'gnetize, v.t. Deprive of magnetic quality. Hence **dema'gnetiza**'TION n. [DE-]

dé'magogue (-ŏg), n. Popular leader ; political agitator appealing to cupidity or prejudice of the masses, factious orator. Hence or cogn. **demagō'g**IC (-gĭk) a., **de'magog**ISM(2), **de'magog**Y[1] (-gĭ), nn. [f. Gk *dēmagōgos* (DEMOS, *agōgos* leading)]

dema'nd[1], n. Request made as of right or peremptorily, thing so asked, (*payable on d.,* as soon as the d. is made) ; call of would-be purchasers *for* commodity (*laws of supply and d.* in Pol. Econ. ; *in d.,* sought after) ; urgent claim (*many dd. on my time*). [f. F *demande* f. *demander* see foll.]

dema'nd[2], v.t. Ask for (thing) as right or peremptorily or urgently (*of* or *from* person ;

Plate 12a Page showing the entries *delicate* to *demand* from *The Concise Oxford Dictionary of Current English* (1911). [See p. 116.]

edly, not by accident, whence **pur'pose**LY adv.; *to the p.*, relevant, useful for one's p.; *to little, some, no, p.*, with such result or effect. Hence **pur'poseFUL**, **pur'poseLESS**, aa., **pur'posefulLY**[2], **pur'poselessLY**[2], advv., **pur'posefulNESS**, **pur'poselessNESS**, nn. [f. AF & OF *purpos*, as foll.]

pur'pose[2] (-us), v.t. Design, intend, as I *p. (arranging* or *to arrange) an interview, p. that an interview shall be arranged*; (archaic) *am purposed*, intend *(to do, doing, that)*. [f. OF PURP*oser* PROPOSE]

pur'posive, a. Having, serving, done with, a purpose; (of person or conduct) having purpose & resolution. [-IVE]

pur'pŭra, n. Disease marked by purple or livid spots on skin; genus of molluscs including some from which purple dye was derived. [L, f. Gk *porphura* (shell-fish yielding) purple]

purpūr'ic, a. Of purpura, as *p. fever*; *p. acid*, a hypothetical acid the salts of which are purple. [-IC]

pur'pŭrin, n. Red colouring matter orig. got from madder. [f. PURPURA + -IN]

purr, v.i. & t., & n. (Of cat or other feline animal, fig. of person) make low continuous vibratory sound expressing pleasure; utter, express, (words, contentment) thus; (n.) such sound. [imit.]

pŭr'ree, n. Yellow colouring matter from India & China. Hence **purre'ic** a. [f Hind. *peori*]

purse[1], n. Small pouch of leather &c. for carrying money on the person, orig. closed by drawing strings together; (fig.) money, funds, as *a common p.* (fund), *heavy* or *long p.*, wealth, *light p.*, poverty, *the public p.*, national treasury; PRIVY *p.*; sum collected, subscribed, or given, as present or as prize for contest, as *will any gentleman give* or *put up a p.?*; (in Turk. empire) *p. of silver, gold,* 500 piastres, 10,000 piastres; bag-like natural or other receptacle, pouch, cyst, &c.; *p.-bearer*, one who has charge of another's or a company's money, official carrying Great Seal before Lord Chancellor in p.; *p.-net*, bag-shaped net for catching rabbits &c., mouth of which can be closed with cords; *p.-proud*, puffed up by wealth; *p.-seine*, p.-net for fishing; *p.-strings*, strings for closing mouth of p., *hold the p.-s.*, have control of expenditure, *tighten, loosen, the p.-s.*, be sparing, generous, of money. Hence **pur'seFUL** n., **pur'seLESS** a. [OE *purs* prob. f. LL *bursa* purse f. Gk *bursa* hide]

purse[2], v.t. & i. Contract (lips, brow, often *up*) in wrinkles; become wrinkled; (rare) put (often *up*) into one's purse. [f. prec.]

pur'ser, n. Officer on ship who keeps accounts & usu. has charge of provisions. Hence **pur'serSHIP** n. [f. PURSE[1] + -ER[1]]

pur'slane (-in), n. Low succulent herb used in salads & pickled. [f. OF *porcelaine* altered f. L *porcillaca, portulaca*, on PORCELAIN]

pursu'ance, n. Carrying out, pursuing, (of plan, object, idea, &c.), esp. *in p. of*. [as foll., see -ANCE]

pursu'ant, a. & adv. Pursuing; (adv.) conformably *to (the Act* &c.), whence **pursu'antLY**[2] adv. [f. OF *porsuiant* part. as foll.]

pursue' (-ū), v.t. & i. Follow with intent to capture or kill; (fig., of consequences, penalty, disease, &c.) persistently attend, stick to; seek after, aim at, (pleasure &c., one's object); proceed in compliance with (plan &c.); proceed along, continue, (road, inquiry, conduct); follow (studies, profession); go in pursuit *(after* or abs.). Hence **pursu'ABLE** a. [f. AF *pursiwer* f. OF

porsi*evre*, f. L PRO(*sequere, -ire*, pop. varr. of *sequi* follow)]

pursu'er, n. In vbl senses, also: (Civil & Sc. Law) prosecutor. [-ER[1]]

pursui't (-ūt), n. Pursuing, esp. *in p. of* (animal, person, one's object); profession, employment, recreation, that one follows. [f. AF PUR*seute*, fem. p.p. & n. as PURSUE]

pur'suivant (-sw-), n. Officer of College of Arms below herald; (poet.) follower, attendant. [f. OF *porsivant* (as PURSUE, see -ANT)]

pur'sy[1], a. Short-winded, puffy; corpulent. Hence **pur'siNESS** n. [earlier *-ive* f. OF *polsif (polser* breathe with labour as PULSATE)]

pur'sy[2], a. Puckered. [f. PURSE[1] + -Y[2]]

pur'tenance, n. (archaic). Inwards, pluck, of animal. [earlier form of PERTINENCE]

pūr'ulent, a. Of, full of, discharging, pus. Hence or cogn. **pur'ulENCE,-ENCY**, nn., **pur'ulentLY**[2] adv. [f. L *purulentus* (PUS, see -LENT)]

purvey' (-vā), v.t. & i. Provide, supply, (articles of food) as one's business; make provision, act as purveyor, *(for* person, army, &c.). [f. AF PUR*veier* PROVIDE]

purvey'ance, n. Purveying; right of crown to provisions &c. at fixed price & to use of horses &c. [f. OF *porveance*, as PROVIDENCE]

purvey'or, n. One whose business it is to supply articles of food, esp. dinners &c. on large scale, as *P. to the Royal Household*; (Hist.) officer making purveyance for sovereign. [f. AF *purveour* (as PURVEY, see -OR[2])]

pur'view (-vū), n. Enacting clauses of statute; scope, intention, range (*of* act, document, scheme, book, occupation, &c.); range of physical or mental vision. [f. AF *purveu* provided, p.p. as PURVEY]

pŭs, n. Yellowish viscid matter produced by suppuration. [L, gen. *puris*]

Pu'seyism (-zi-), n. (Hostile term for) TRACTARIANISM. So **Pu'seyITE**[1] n. [E. B. *Pusey* d. 1882 + -ISM]

push[1] (pŏŏ-), v.t. & i. Exert upon (body) force tending to move it away; move (body *up, down, away, back,* &c.) thus; exert such pressure, as *do not p. against the fence*; (Billiards) make push-stroke; (of person in boat) *p. off*, p. against bank with oar to get boat out into stream &c.; (bibl.) butt (t. & i.) with the horns; (cause to) project, thrust *out, forth,* &c., as *plants* p. *out new roots, cape pushes out into sea*; make one's way forcibly or persistently, force (one's *way*) thus; exert oneself esp. to surpass others or succeed in one's business &c., whence **pu'shING**[2] a., **pu'shingLY**[2] adv.; urge, impel, (often *on, to do, to effort* &c.); follow up, prosecute, (claim &c., often *on*); engage actively in making (one's *fortune*); extend (one's *conquests* &c.); *p.* (matter) *through*, bring it to a conclusion; press the adoption, use, sale, &c. of (goods &c.) esp. by advertisement; press (person) hard, as *do not wish to p. him for payment*, esp. in pass., as *am pushed for* (can scarcely find) *time, money; p.-pin*, a child's game. Hence **pu'shER**[1](1, 2) n. [f. F *pousser* as PULSATE]

push[2], n. Act of pushing, shove, thrust; (Billiards) stroke in which ball is pushed, not struck; exertion of influence to promote person's advancement; thrust of weapon or of beast's horn; vigorous effort, as *must make a p. to get it done, for home*; continuous pressure of arch &c.; pressure of affairs, crisis, pinch; enterprise, determination to get on, self-assertion, whence **pu'shFUL** a.; (slang) gang of thieves, convicts, &c. [f. prec.]

pu'shtŏŏ, -tu (-ŏŏ), n. Afghan language. [f. Pers. *pashto*]

pusilla'nimous, a. Faint-hearted, mean-

Plate 12b This shows the right hand column on p. 674 and the left hand column of the facing page showing the entries from *purpose* to *pusillanimous* from the *Concise Oxford Dictionary of Current English* (1911). Note, in comparison with the *SOED*, the omission of words (for example, *pursiness*) and senses (under *pursue*, for example: *to persecute; to harass, worry, torment*), the reduction of etymologies, and the absence of quotations. [See p. 117.]

Deltaic 694 **Demembration**

del·ta′ic (dĕl·tā′ĭk), *adj.* **1**. Of, like, relating to, or characterized by a delta; also, constituting a delta.
2. [*cap.*] Specif., relating or pertaining to the delta of the Nile; having its source or chief seat in the Nile delta; as, the *Deltaic* dynasties (XXII–XXX) of Egyptian kings.
del′tal (dĕl′tăl; -t'l), *adj.* DELTAIC (sense 1).
delta plain. The level or nearly level surface of a delta.
delta plateau. A raised delta plain.
delta potential. *Elec.* The potential of a delta current.
del·ta′tion (dĕl·tā′shŭn), *n.* Deltafication.
delta winding. *Elec.* A mesh winding for armatures in which a closed figure is produced by connecting the three coils of a three-phase circuit end to end.
del·thy′ri·um (dĕl·thĭ′rĭ·ŭm), *n.; pl.* -RIA (-ȧ). [NL., fr. Gr. *dēlos* visible + *thyrion* little door.] *Zool.* The opening between the beak and the hinge through which the pedicle of certain brachiopods extends. — **del·thy′ri·al** (-ăl), *adj.*
del′tic (dĕl′tĭk), *adj.* Deltaic.
del·tid′i·um (dĕl·tĭd′ĭ·ŭm), *n.; pl.* -TIDIA (-ȧ). [NL., dim. fr. Gr. *delta*, the letter Δ.] *Zool.* **a** A plate partly or wholly closing the delthyrium of certain brachiopods; — called also *pseudodeltidium*. **b** A pair of plates (called also **deltidial plates**), not homologous with the pseudodeltidium, which performs the same function in other brachiopods. — **del·tid′i·al** (-ăl), *adj.*
del′to·he′dron (dĕl′tō·hē′drŭn), *n.; pl.* -DRA (-drȧ). [Gr. *delta*, the letter Δ + *hedra* seat, base.] *Cryst.* A solid bounded by twelve quadrilateral faces. It is a hemihedral form of the isometric system, allied to the tetrahedron.
del′toid (dĕl′toid), *adj.* [Gr. *deltoeidēs* delta-shaped, fr. *delta* (Δ) + *eidos* form. See DELTA.] **1**. Shaped like a capital delta (Δ); delta-shaped; triangular; as, a *deltoid* leaf, muscle. See LEAF, *Illust.*
2. Of the nature of, or formed like, a river delta.
del′toid, *n.* **1**. *Anat.* A large triangular muscle covering the shoulder joint and serving to raise the arm laterally. It arises from the upper anterior part of the outer third of the clavicle, and from the acromion and spine of the scapula, and is inserted into the outer side of the middle of the shaft of the humerus.
2. *Math.* **a** A plane quadrilateral symmetrical with respect to one of its diagonals. **b** Hypocycloid with three cusps.
3. *Zool.* A deltoid moth.
del·toi′dal (dĕl·toi′dăl; -d'l), *adj.* **1**. Deltoid; delta-shaped.
2. *Phys. Geog.* Pertaining to a delta.
del·toi′de·o- (dĕl·toi′dē·ō-). A combining form of NL. *deltoideus*, meaning *deltoid*.
deltoid ligament. *Anat.* The medial collateral ligament of the ankle.
deltoid moth. Any of certain moths of the family Noctuidae having a markedly triangular outline when at rest.
de·lu′brum (dē·lū′brŭm), *n.; pl.* -BRA (-brȧ). [L.] **1**. *Rom. Antiq.* A shrine or sanctuary; a sacred enclosure.
2. *Eccl.* **a** A church having a font. **b** A font.
De·luc's′ hy·grom′e·ter (dē·lüks′). [After J. A. *Deluc*, Swiss physicist.] A hygrometer on the principle of the hair hygrometer, but employing a strip of whalebone.
Deluc's pile. *Elec.* = DRY PILE.
de·lude′ (dē·lūd′), *v. t.;* DE·LUD′ED (-lūd′ĕd; -ĭd; 119); DE·LUD′ING (-lūd′ĭng). [L. *deludere, delusum*, fr. *de* + *ludere* to play, make sport of, mock. See LUDICROUS.] **1**. To lead from truth or into error; to mislead the mind or judgment of; to impose on; to deceive; trick; make a fool of.

To *delude* the nation by an airy phantom. — *Burke.*

2. *Obs.* **a** To trifle with (one) as if acting seriously; to mock. **b** To frustrate or disappoint. **c** To evade; elude. "It *deludes* thy search." *Dryden.*
Syn. — Mislead, deceive, beguile, dupe.
de·lud′er (dē·lūd′ẽr), *n.* One who deludes.
de·lu′dher (dē·lōō′thẽr), *v. t.* To delude. *Anglo-Ir.*
de·lud′ing (dē·lūd′ĭng), *adj.* That deludes. — **de·lud′ing·ly**, *adv.*
del′uge (dĕl′ūj), *n.* [OF., fr. L. *diluvium*, fr. *diluere* to wash away, fr. *di-* (= *dis-*) + *luere*; akin to L. *lavare* to wash. See LAVE; cf. DILUVIUM.] **1**. An overflowing of the land by water; an inundation; a flood; specifically, ***the Deluge***, the great flood in the days of Noah (*Gen.* vii). Among peoples in both hemispheres are found deluge traditions, considered to be based directly or indirectly on actual floods. See DEUCALION, UT-NAPISHTIM, XISUTHROS, GILGAMESH.

The geographical universality of the *Deluge* may be safely abandoned. Neither Sacred Scripture nor universal ecclesiastical tradition . . . renders it advisable to adhere to the opinion that the Flood covered the whole surface of the earth. — *Catholic Encyclopedia.*

2. An irresistible rush of anything in overwhelming numbers, quantity, or volume, etc.; as, a *deluge* of mail.
del′uge, *v. t.;* DEL′UGED (-ūjd); DEL′UG·ING (-ū·jĭng). **1**. To overflow with water; to inundate; flood.

The *deluged* earth would useless grow. — *Blackmore.*

2. To overwhelm as with a deluge; to overspread; overpower; submerge; as, the empire was *deluged* with mercenaries; he was *deluged* with letters.
de·lu′mi·nize (dē·lū′mĭ·nīz), *v. t.* To render nonluminous.
‖**de lu·na′ti·co in′qui·ren′do** (dē lū·năt′ĭ·kō ĭn′kwĭ·rĕn′dō). [Law L.] *Law.* Literally, for inquiring concerning the lunatic; — used of a writ directing an inquiry as to whether a person named in the writ is insane.
del′un·dung (dĕl′ŭn·dŭng), *n.* [Said to be Jav. name.] *Zool.* A handsomely marked East Indian carnivorous mammal (*Linsang gracilis*), related to the civets.
de·lu′sion (dē·lū′zhŭn), *n.* [L. *delusio*, fr. *deludere*. See DELUDE.] **1**. Act of deluding, or state of being deluded; esp., a misleading of the mind; as, such pleasures end in *delusion*.
2. That which is falsely or delusively believed or propagated; false belief, or a persistent error of perception occasioned by false belief or mental derangement; customary or fixed misconception; as, to cling to a *delusion*.
3. *Law.* A false conception and persistent belief, unconquerable by reason, of what has no existence in fact.
4. *Psychiatry.* A false belief regarding the self, common in paranoia, dementia praecox, and morbidly depressed states; as, *delusions* of grandeur; a *delusion* of reference, as believing all remarks and actions refer to oneself.
Syn. — DELUSION, ILLUSION, HALLUCINATION are here compared in their nontechnical connotations (for technical distinctions, see defs.); they agree in the idea of false seeming. DELUSION is, in general, a much stronger word than ILLUSION. It often carries an implication of being deceived (cf. DELUDE, *v.*), imposed on, or even consciously misled and bemocked, from which *illusion* is ordinarily free. Further, *delusion* implies a false (often harmful) impression, commonly regarding things themselves real; *illusion*, an ascription of reality (often pleasing) to that which exists only in the fancy; as, "It is all magic, poor deluded fool! She looks to every one like his first love. . . . These pleasures end in *delusion*" (*Shelley*); "The *illusions* of Chloë and Strephon have been sufficiently consecrated in poetry" (*G. Eliot*); the *delusions* of stockjobbing; to labor under a *delusion*; the *illusions* of fancy, of hope; an optical *illusion*. HALLUCINATION, as here compared, emphasizes the groundlessness of the impression; as, "Reason . . . is not swept away by the *hallucinations* of sentiment" (*R. A. Vaughan*). Cf. FALLACY, FICTION.

It had all been a voluntary, self-created *delusion*. — *Jane Austen.*

As those *illusions* [of youth] are unavoidable, and, no doubt, eminently useful to the mind as a process, what good can be gained by making observations, the tendency of which is to diminish the confidence of youth in its feelings . . . ? — *Wordsworth.*

Sight passed into vision without a trace of *hallucination*, and the landscape was my guide, my Vergil. — *Mrs. Humphry Ward.*

de·lu′sion·al (dē·lū′zhŭn·ăl; -'l), *adj.* Pertaining to, or marked by, delusions.
de·lu′sion·ist (-ĭst), *n.* One given to deluding or to having delusions.
de·lu′sive (-sĭv), *adj.* [See DELUDE.] Apt or fitted to delude; deceptive; beguiling; also, of the nature of a delusion.

Delusive and unsubstantial ideas. — *Whewell.*

— **de·lu′sive·ly**, *adv.* — **de·lu′sive·ness**, *n.*
de·lu′so·ry (dē·lū′sō·rĭ), *adj.* Delusive.
de luxe′ (dē lŏŏks′; lŭks′; *F.* dĕ lüks′). [F., lit., of luxury.] Specially elegant; sumptuous or elaborate, as in materials or workmanship; as, a *de luxe* edition of a book; accommodations *de luxe*; a *de luxe* train. — In a de luxe manner; elegantly; sumptuously; as, to travel *de luxe*.
delve (dĕlv), *v.;* DELVED (dĕlvd); DELV′ING (dĕl′vĭng). [AS. *delfan*; akin to OS. *bidelban* to bury, D. *delven* to dig, MHG. *telben*, Lith. *dalba* crowbar, handspike, *nudilbti* to cast down (the eyes). Cf. DELF, DELFT.] *Transitive:* **1**. To dig; to open or dig up (the ground) as with a spade for planting. *Now Chiefly Dial.*
2. *Archaic & Dial.* **a** To make, as a hole, by digging; to excavate. **b** To exhume. **c** To hide or bury by digging.
3. **a** *Dial. Eng.* To indent; bruise; dint. **b** To impress or inscribe deeply.
——, *Intransitive:* **1**. To dig or labor with a spade, or as with a spade; to seek laboriously (in books, records, etc.) for information; to labor as a drudge.

Delve may I not: I shame to beg. — *Wycliffe (Luke* xvi. 3).

2. To make a sudden descent; to dip; — said of a declivity.
Syn. — See DIG.
delve (dĕlv), *n.* [See DELF, 1st DELVE.] **1**. Act of delving; also, a place dug; pit; ditch; den; cave. *Rare.*
2. A surface depression; a hollow, as a wrinkle. *Rare.*
delv′er (dĕl′vẽr), *n.* One who delves; specif., *Eng.*, a barer.
dely-. For various obsolete forms in *dely-*, see those in DELI-.
-dema. [NL.] *Zool.* A combining form, from Greek *demas*, meaning *body*, in generic names in entomology.
de·mag′net·ize (dē·măg′nĕ·tīz; -măg′nĭ·tīz), *v. t.* **1**. To deprive of magnetic properties. See MAGNETIZE.
2. To free from mesmeric influence; to demesmerize. *Obs.* — **de·mag′net·i·za′tion** (-tĭ·zā′shŭn; -tī·zā′shŭn), *n.* — **de·mag′net·iz′er** (-īz′ẽr), *n.*
dem′a·gog′ic (dĕm′ȧ·gŏj′ĭk; -gŏg′ĭk), **dem′a·gog′i·cal** (-ĭ·kăl), *adj.* [Gr. *dēmagōgikos*.] Of, relating to, or like, a demagogue; factious. — **dem′a·gog′i·cal·ly**, *adv.*
dem′a·gog·ism (dĕm′ȧ·gŏg·ĭz'm), *n.* The principles or practices of demagogues; demagogic character.
dem′a·gogue (-gŏg; 185), *n.* Also **dem′a·gog**. [Gr. *dēmagōgos*, fr. *dēmos* the people + *agōgos* leading, fr. *agein* to lead. See DEMOCRAT; AGENT.] **1**. A leader or orator popular with or identified with the people. *Chiefly Hist.*
2. One skilled in arousing the prejudices and passions of the populace by rhetoric, sensational charges, specious arguments, catchwords, cajolery, etc.; esp., a political speaker or leader who seeks thus to make capital of social discontent and incite the populace, usually in the name of some popular cause, in order to gain political influence or office.
dem′a·gogue, *v. i.* Also **dem′a·gog**. To act the demagogue. *Colloq., U. S.*
dem′a·gog′uer·y (dĕm′ȧ·gŏg′ẽr·ĭ; -gŏg′rĭ), *n.* Demagogism.
dem′a·gog′y (-gŏj′ĭ; -gō·jĭ; -gŏg′ĭ; 277), *n.* [Gr. *dēmagōgia* leadership of the people.] Demagogism; demagogic character; also, rule of demagogues; demagogues collectively.
de′mal (dē′măl; dĕm′ăl), *adj.* [Appar. fr. *dm* (abbr. of *decimeter*) + *-al*.] *Physical Chem.* Having a concentration of one gram equivalent per cubic decimeter.
de·mand′ (dē·mȧnd′; *see Pron.*, § 83), *v.;* DE·MAND′ED; DE·MAND′ING. [OF. *demander*, fr. LL. *demandare* to demand, summon, send word, fr. L. *demandare* to give in charge, entrust, fr. *de* + *mandare* to commit to one's charge, commission, order, command. See MANDATE.] *Transitive:* **1**. To ask or call for with authority; to claim as due or just; as, to *demand* payment of a debt.
2. To call for urgently, peremptorily, or insistently; as, to *demand* surrender; to *demand* an apology.
3. To inquire authoritatively or earnestly; to ask, esp. in a peremptory manner; to question; as, to *demand* the password.

I did *demand* what news from Shrewsbury. — *Shak.*

4. To call for or require as necessary or useful; to be in urgent need of; as, the case *demands* care.
5. To summon; to require to appear; specif., *Law*, to summon to court.
——, *Intransitive:* To make a demand; to ask; inquire.
de·mand′, *n.* [OF. *demande*, fr. *demander*. See DEMAND, *v.*] **1**. Act of demanding; an asking with authority; a peremptory urging of a claim; a claiming or challenging as due; requisition; as, a note payable on *demand*.
2. That which is demanded, esp. by right, or as due; also, that which is urgently needed or requested; claim; as, *demands* on an estate.
3. Earnest inquiry; a question; a query.
4. A seeking or state of being sought after; an expressed desire for ownership or use, as of a commodity; as, in great *demand* socially; an increased *demand* for labor.
5. A demanding of work or of the expenditure of some resource, as time, from a source of supply; as, *demands* that overtax a piece of machinery.
6. *Card Playing.* In French boston, a proposal for another player to volunteer as one's partner, made by laying a trump face downward and saying "Je demande" (I ask).
7. *Econ.* **a** Desire to purchase a commodity, accompanied by means of payment. **b** The quantity of an article demanded at a given price. It will obviously tend to increase as the price diminishes. A graphical representation of the variations of demand as the price changes is known as a ***demand curve***. The competition of buyers and sellers tends to make such changes of price that the demand for any article in a given market will become equal to the supply. This process is known as ***equation of supply and demand***. See EQUATION, 7.
8. *Elec.* The load (in kilowatts) of an individual consumer, or power plant or the like, averaged over a period of time.
9. *Law.* **a** The asking or seeking for what is due or claimed as due. **b** The right or title in virtue of which anything may be claimed; as, to hold a *demand* against a person. **c** A thing or amount claimed to be due.
— ***on demand***. Upon presentation and request of payment; also, formerly, ***at demand***.
de·mand′ant (dē·mȧn′dănt), *n.* [F., pres. part. of *demander*.] One who demands; the plaintiff in a real action; by extension, any plaintiff.
demand bill *or* **draft**. *Finance.* A bill payable at sight. Cf. SIGHT BILL.
demand deposit. *Banking.* A deposit which may be withdrawn without notice. The United States Federal Reserve Act defines a demand deposit for reserve purposes as one payable within thirty days.
de·mand′er (dē·mȧn′dẽr), *n.* One who demands.
de·mand′ing (-dĭng), *adj.* That demands, or seeks or asks peremptorily; exacting. — **de·mand′ing·ly**, *adv.*
demand limiter. *Elec.* = CURRENT LIMITER.
de·mand′-load′ fac′tor. *Elec.* The ratio of the average load carried by a power plant or system during a given period of time to the maximum demand recorded during that period. Cf. LOAD FACTOR.
demand loan. = CALL LOAN.
demand meter. *Electrometry.* A meter used for measuring demand.
demand note. A note payable on demand; specif., *U. S. Hist.*, one of the notes composing the issues of paper money authorized by Congress early in the Civil War.
demand rate. See 3d RATE, 7.
de·man′ga·nize (dē·măng′gȧ·nīz), *v. t.* To remove manganese from. — **-ni·za′tion** (-nĭ·zā′shŭn; -nī·zā′shŭn), *n.*
de·man′toid (dē·măn′toid), *n.* [G. *demant* diamond + *-oid*.] *Mineral.* See 1st GARNET, 1.
de·mar′cate (dē·mär′kāt; dē′mär-), *v. t.;* -CAT·ED (-kāt·ĕd; -kāt′ĕd; -ĭd; 119); -CAT·ING (-ĭng). [See DEMARCATION.] To mark by bounds; delimit; hence, to separate; discriminate.
de′mar·ca′tion (dē′mär·kā′shŭn), *n.* [F. *démarcation*, fr. Sp. *demarcación*, fr. *de-* (fr. L. *de*) + *marcar* to mark, of Teut. origin. See MARK.] Act or process of demarcating; act of ascertaining and settling a limit; separation; distinction. Cf. LINE OF DEMARCATION.

The speculative line of *demarcation*, where obedience ought to end and resistance must begin, is faint. — *Burke.*

de·mar′ca·tor (dē·mär′kā·tẽr; dē′mär·kā′tẽr), *n.* One who or that which demarcates.
de′march (dē′märk), *n.* [Gr. *dēmarchos*, fr. *dēmos* people + *archein* to rule.] In classical Greece, a ruler of a deme; in modern Greece, a mayor.
‖**dé′marche′** (dā′märsh′), *n.* [F. See MARCH, *n.*] A step; course of action; esp., one involving a change of direction or policy; — used often in diplomacy.
de′march·y (dē′mär·kĭ), *n.* [Gr. *dēmarchia*.] **1**. The office of demarch or a body of demarchs; a popular government.
2. In modern Greece, a municipal body, varying in population usually from two thousand to ten thousand.
de·mar′ga·rin·ate (dē·mär′jȧ·rĭ·nāt; -gȧ·rĭ·nāt), *v. t.* [*de-* + *margarin* + 2d *-ate*, 3.] To remove the solid portion (stearin) from (an oil).
de·mark′ (dē·märk′), *v. t.;* DE·MARKED′ (-märkt′); DE·MARK′ING. To demarcate.
de′mar·ka′tion (dē′mär·kā′shŭn), *n.* Demarcation.
De′mas (dē′măs), *n.* [Gr. *Dēmas*.] *Bib.* A fellow worker who forsook Paul.
de·mast′ (dē·mȧst′), *v. t.* To remove or strip masts from.
de′ma·te′ri·al·ize (dē′mȧ·tēr′ĭ·ăl·īz), *v. t. & i.* To deprive, or become deprived, of material qualities or characteristics; esp., *Spiritualism*, to vanish, or lose material form, after having materialized; to cause to lose material form. — **de′ma·te′ri·al·i·za′tion** (-ĭ·zā′shŭn; -ī·zā′shŭn), *n.*
De·mat′i·a′ce·ae (dē·măt′ĭ·ā′sē·ē), *n. pl.* [NL., fr. Gr. *demation*, dim. of *dema* bundle; — in ref. to floccose hyphae.] *Bot.* A family of imperfect fungi (order Moniliales) comprising many genera of leaf parasites. See MONILIALES. — **de·mat′i·a′ceous** (-shŭs), *adj.*
‖**d'em′blée′** (däN′blā′), *adv.* [F.] At the first onset; hence, *Card Playing*, on the first deal; before the draw.
deme (dēm), *n.* [Gr. *dēmos* deme, in sense 1. See DEMOCRACY.] **1**. *Gr. Hist.* One of the hundred townships or administrative units (ten to each tribe) into which Cleisthenes divided Attica (about 508 B.C.). The demes in each tribe were separated by intervening demes of other tribes, the purpose being to break up local influences and jealousies. Later the number of demes was increased. Cf. PHYLE.
2. In modern Greece, a commune.
3. *Biol.* An undifferentiated aggregate of cells. *Rare.*
‖**de me** (dē mē). [L.] *Scots Law.* Of me; — said of the holding inserted in the tenenda when a subfeu is granted, this requiring no confirmation by the superior, as distinguished from a holding *a me de superiore meo*, literally, from me of my superior, where the estate is to be held of the superior, and is invalid unless confirmed by him.
de·mean′ (dē·mēn′), *v. t.;* DE·MEANED′ (-mēnd′); DE·MEAN′ING. [*de-* + *mean*, adj.] To debase; to lower; to degrade; — usually followed by the reflexive pronoun.

Her son would *demean* himself by a marriage with an artist's daughter. — *Thackeray.*

de·mean′ (dē·mēn′), *v.* [OF. *demener* to conduct, guide, manage (F. *se démener* to struggle), fr. *de-* (fr. L. *de*) + *mener* to lead, drive, carry on, conduct, fr. L. *minare* to drive animals, fr. *minari* to threaten. See MENACE.] *Transitive:* **1**. To manage; to carry on; to conduct. *Obs.*

[Our] clergy have with violence *demeaned* the matter. — *Milton.*

2. To conduct, behave, or comport (oneself).

They have *demeaned* themselves
Like men born to renown by life or death. — *Shak.*

3. *Obs. exc. Dial.* **a** To deal with; treat. **b** To maltreat.
4. To manifest by conduct; exhibit; express. *Obs.*
——, *Intransitive:* To comport oneself; behave. *Rare.*
de·mean′, *n.* [See 2d DEMEAN.] Behavior; mien. *Obs.*
de·mean′or, de·mean′our (-ẽr), *n.* [For *demeanure*, fr. *demean*. See 2d DEMEAN.] **1**. Conduct; action, or mode of action; also, management; treatment. *Obs.*
2. Outward manner or comportment; behavior; bearing; mien; as, a professional *demeanor*; a pleasing *demeanor*.
Syn. — See DEPORTMENT.
de′me·gor′ic (dē′mē·gŏr′ĭk), *adj.* [Gr. *dēmēgorikos*.] Of or pertaining to harangue.
‖**dé′mê′lé′** (dā′mĕ′lā′), *n.* [F.] A quarrel, esp. verbal.
de′mem·bra′tion (dē′mĕm·brā′shŭn), *n.* [ML. *demembratio*.] Removal of any member from the body; mutilation; dismemberment. *Chiefly Scots Law.*

del·ta′ri·um (dĕl·tā′rĭ·ŭm), *n.* = DELTIDIUM b.
del′ta-shaped′, *adj.* See -SHAPED.
de·lud′a·ble (dē·lūd′ȧ·b'l), *adj.* See -ABLE. [*Gaz.*]. *Bib.*
De′lus. Var. of DELOS (see
de·lu′siv. Delusive. *Ref. Sp.*
de·lus′ter, *v. t.* See DE-, 4.
delv, delvd. Delve; delved. *R. S.*
dem. Var. of DAMN.
de·mag′net·iz′a·ble, *adj.* See -ABLE.
dem′a·gogu·ism (dĕm′ȧ·gŏg·ĭz'm). Var. of DEMAGOGISM.
de·main′, de·maine′ (dē·mān′). Vars. of DOMAIN, DEMESNE.
demain. † DEMEAN.
‖**de mal′ en′ pis′** (dĕ mȧl′-äN′ pē′). [F.] From bad to worse.
de·mand′a·ble, *adj.* See -ABLE.
deme. † DEEM, *v. t. & i.*; DIME.
de·mean′, -meane′. † DEMESNE.
de·mean′ance, *n.* Demeanor. *Obs.*
‖**de me′di·e·ta′te lin′guae**. See JURY DE MEDIETATE LINGUAE.

āle, chāotic, câre, ădd, ăccount, ärm, ȧsk, sofȧ; ēve, hēre (116), ēvent, ĕnd, silĕnt, makẽr; īce, ĭll, charĭty; ōld, ōbey, ôrb, ŏdd, sŏft, cŏnnect; fōōd, fŏŏt;
‖ **Foreign Word.** † **Obsolete Variant of.** + **combined with.** = **equals.** **Abbreviations, Signs, etc., are explained on pages immediately preceding the Vocabulary.**

Plate 13a Page from *Webster's New International Dictionary, Second Edition* (1934). Note the many compounds given entry-word status, the paragraphs of synonyms, and the list of additional entry words at the bottom of each page. [See p. 129.]

Deluc's pile. *Elec.* = DRY PILE.

de·lude' (dē·lūd'), *v. t.; * DE·LUD'ED (-lūd'ĕd; -ĭd; 119); DE·LUD'ING (-lūd'ĭng). [L. *deludere, delusum,* fr. *de* + *ludere* to play, make sport of, mock. See LUDICROUS.] **1.** To lead from truth or into error; to mislead the mind or judgment of; to impose on; to deceive; trick; make a fool of.

To *delude* the nation by an airy phantom. *Burke.*

2. *Obs.* **a** To trifle with (one) as if acting seriously; to mock. **b** To frustrate or disappoint. **c** To evade; elude. "It *deludes* thy search." *Dryden.*

Syn. — Mislead, deceive, beguile, dupe.

de·lud'er (dē·lūd'ẽr), *n.* One who deludes.

de·lu'dher (dē·lōō'thẽr), *v. t.* To delude. *Anglo-Ir.*

de·lud'ing (dē·lūd'ĭng), *adj.* That deludes. — **de·lud'ing·ly,** *adv.*

del'uge (dĕl'ūj), *n.* [OF., fr. L. *diluvium,* fr. *diluere* to wash away, fr. *di-* (= *dis-*) + *luere;* akin to L. *lavare* to wash. See LAVE; cf. DILUVIUM.] **1.** An overflowing of the land by water; an inundation; a flood; specifically, *the Deluge,* the great flood in the days of Noah (*Gen.* vii). Among peoples in both hemispheres are found deluge traditions, considered to be based directly or indirectly on actual floods. See DEUCALION, UT-NAPISHTIM, XISUTHROS, GILGAMESH.

The geographical universality of the *Deluge* may be safely abandoned. Neither Sacred Scripture nor universal ecclesiastical tradition . . . renders it advisable to adhere to the opinion that the Flood covered the whole surface of the earth. *Catholic Encyclopedia.*

2. An irresistible rush of anything in overwhelming numbers, quantity, or volume, etc.; as, a *deluge* of mail.

del'uge, *v. t.; * DEL'UGED (-ūjd); DEL'UG·ING (-ū·jĭng). **1.** To overflow with water; to inundate; flood.

The *deluged* earth would useless grow. *Blackmore.*

2. To overwhelm as with a deluge; to overspread; overpower; submerge; as, the empire was *deluged* with mercenaries; he was *deluged* with letters.

de·lu'mi·nize (dē·lū'mĭ·nīz), *v. t.* To render nonluminous.

‖de·lu·na'ti·co in'qui·ren'do (dē lū·nǎt'ĭ·kō ĭn'kwĭ·rĕn'dō). [Law L.] *Law.* Literally, for inquiring concerning the lunatic; — used of a writ directing an inquiry as to whether a person named in the writ is insane.

del'un·dung (dĕl'ŭn·dŭng), *n.* [Said to be Jav. name.] *Zool.* A handsomely marked East Indian carnivorous mammal (*Linsang gracilis*), related to the civets.

de·lu'sion (dē·lū'zhŭn), *n.* [L. *delusio,* fr. *deludere.* See DELUDE.] **1.** Act of deluding, or state of being deluded; esp., a misleading of the mind; as, such pleasures end in *delusion.*

2. That which is falsely or delusively believed or propagated; false belief, or a persistent error of perception occasioned by false belief or mental derangement; customary or fixed misconception; as, to cling to a *delusion.*

3. *Law.* A false conception and persistent belief, unconquerable by reason, of what has no existence in fact.

4. *Psychiatry.* A false belief regarding the self, common in paranoia, dementia praecox, and morbidly depressed states; as, *delusions* of grandeur; a *delusion* of reference, as believing all remarks and actions refer to oneself.

Syn. — DELUSION, ILLUSION, HALLUCINATION are here compared in their nontechnical connotations (for technical distinctions, see defs.); they agree in the idea of false seeming. DELUSION is, in general, a much stronger word than ILLUSION. It often carries an implication of being deceived (cf. DELUDE, *v.*), imposed on, or even consciously misled and bemocked, from which *illusion* is ordinarily free. Further, *delusion* implies a false (often harmful) impression, commonly regarding things themselves real; *illusion,* an ascription of reality (often pleasing) to that which exists only in the fancy; as, "It is all magic, poor deluded fool! She looks to every one like his first love. . . . These pleas-

---

dem'a·gog'ic (dĕm'à·gŏj'ĭk; -g (-ĭ·kăl), *adj.* [Gr. *dēmagōgikó* like, a demagogue; factious. — d

dem'a·gog·ism (dĕm'à·gŏg·ĭz'm) practices of demagogues; demago

dem'a·gogue (-gŏg; 185), *n.* Also *agōgos,* fr. *dēmos* the people + to lead. See DEMOCRAT; AGENT. popular with or identified with th **2.** One skilled in arousing the p the populace by rhetoric, sensati guments, catchwords, cajolery, et or leader who seeks thus to make o and incite the populace, usually ular cause, in order to gain politic

dem'a·gogue, *v. i.* Also **dem'a·** gogue. *Colloq., U. S.*

dem'a·gog'uer·y (dĕm'à·gŏg'ẽr·ĭ;

dem'a·gog'y (-gŏj'ĭ; -gŏ·jĭ; -gŏg'ĭ; leadership of the people.] Dema acter; also, rule of demagogues; d

de'mal (dē'mǎl; dĕm'ǎl), *adj.* decimeter) + -al.] *Physical C* tration of one gram equivalent pe

de·mand' (dē·mànd'; *see Pron.,* § MAND'ING. [OF. *demander,* fr. mand, summon, send word, fr. charge, entrust, fr. *de* + *mand* charge, commission, order, com *Transitive:* **1.** To ask or call for as due or just; as, to *demand* pay **2.** To call for urgently, peremp to *demand* surrender; to *demanc* **3.** To inquire authoritatively or e peremptory manner; to question; a

I did *demand* what news fron

4. To call for or require as nece urgent need of; as, the case *demc* **5.** To summon; to require to app mon to court.

——, *Intransitive:* To make a de

de·mand', *n.* [OF. *demande,* fr. *v.*] **1.** Act of demanding; an a peremptory urging of a claim; a as due; requisition; as, a note pay **2.** That which is demanded, esp. that which is urgently needed or *mands* on an estate.

3. Earnest inquiry; a question; a **4.** A seeking or state of being so desire for ownership or use, as of a *demand* socially; an increased de **5.** A demanding of work or of the source, as time, from a source of s overtax a piece of machinery.

6. *Card Playing.* In French bo other player to volunteer as one's a trump face downward and sayin **7.** *Econ.* **a** Desire to purchase a by means of payment. **b** The q manded at a given price. It will c as the price diminishes. A graph variations of demand as the pric *demand curve.* The competit tends to make such changes of pr any article in a given market w supply. This process is known a *and demand.* See EQUATION, 7

---

del·ta'ri·um (dĕl·tā'rĭ·ŭm), *n.* = DELTIDIUM b.	See -ABLE. **De'lus.** Var. of DELOS (see | [*Gaz.*). Bib.	**delv, delvd.** Delve; delved. R. S. **dem.** Var. of DAMN. [-ABLE.	Ĭz'm **de·r**
del'ta-shaped', *adj.* See -SHAPED. **de·lud'a·ble** (dē·lūd'à·b'l), *adj.*	**de·lu'siv,** Delusive. *Ref. Sp.* **de·lus'ter,** *v. t.* See DE-, 4.		**de·mag'net·iz'a·ble,** *adj.* See **dem'a·gogu·ism** (dĕm'à·gŏg-	Vars **dem**

āle, chặotic, câre, ădd, ặccount, ärm, ặsk, sofặ; ēve, hẹre (116), ĕvent, ĕnd, silĕnt

‖ **Foreign Word.** † **Obsolete Variant of.** + **combined with.** = **equals. Abbreviation**

Plate 13b Detail of 13a showing the entries *Deluc's pile* to *delusion.* [See p. 129.]

in the defense **6 :** directive signals conveyed to a horse (as through the use of the hands, legs, shift of body weight, or voice)
aid·ance \\'ād-ᵊn(t)s\\ *n* -s [MF, fr. *aider + -ance*] *archaic* **:** a means of help **:** AID
aid·ant \\'ād·ᵊnt\\ *adj* [ME, fr. MF, pres. part. of *aider*] **:** furnishing or supplying aid
ai·da trumpet \\'ā-ᵊ-\\ *n, usu cap A* [after Aida, opera by Giuseppe Verdi 1901 Ital. composer, for which it was designed] **:** a long straight trumpet
aide \\'ād\\ *n* -s [short for *aide-de-camp*] **:** a person who acts as an assistant (as to a diplomat or a nurse); *specif* **:** a military or naval officer acting as assistant to a superior
aide-de-camp *also* **aid-de-camp** \\'ādd(ᵊ)kamp, -an(ᵊ)mp, -aimp, -ᵊñ\\ *n, pl* **aides-de-camp** *also* **aids-de-camp** \\'ādz-\\ [F *aide de camp*, lit., camp assistant] *mil* **:** AIDE
aided school *n* **:** *usu.* denominational voluntary English school receiving one half of its maintenance costs from public funds but retaining control over appointments and religious instruction — compare CONTROLLED SCHOOL
aide-mé·moire \\'ād(,)mēm'wär, -ᵊm\\\, -mem-, -wa(r\\ *n, pl* **aides-mémoirs** \\'ādz-\\ [F, fr. *aider* to aid + *mémoire* memory, fr. L *memoria* — more at MEMORY] **1 :** an aid to the memory (as a mnemonic device) **2 :** a written summary or outline of important items of a proposed agreement or diplomatic communication **:** MEMORANDUM
aid·er \\'ādə(r)\\ *n* -s [prob. fr. MF *aider* to aid] **:** an act of aiding — used esp. in pleading in the phrase *aider by verdict*
aider by verdict : the presumption after a verdict that all facts necessary to the verdict were proved
ai·dle \\'ād'l\\ *chiefly Scot var of* ADDLE
aid·less \\'ādləs\\ *adj* **:** devoid of help **:** HELPLESS (an ~ victim)
aid-major *n, obs* **:** the adjutant of a regiment
aid·man \\'ād,man, -mən\\ *n, pl* **aidmen** [*first*) *aid + man*] **:** a medical-corps enlisted man attached to a unit in the field to give first aid — compare HOSPITAL CORPSMAN
aid prayer *n, English law* **:** a defendant's appeal for aid
aids *pres 3d sing of* AID, *pl of* AID
aid station *n* [*first*) *aid*] **:** an establishment for giving emergency medical treatment; *specif* **:** a forward medical installation where wounded receive emergency treatment
aie *or* **aiee** *var of* 'AI
ai·el \\'ā(ə)l\\ *n* -s [ME, grandfather, fr. MF *ael, aiuel*, fr. (assumed) VL *aviolus*, dim. of L *avus* grandfather — more at UNCLE] **:** a writ by which an heir entered into his grandfather's estate and dispossessed the third person who had attempted to gain possession
aiery *obs var of* AIRY
ai·ga \\'ī,ga, ã'gä\\ *n* -s [Samoan *'āiga*] *Samoa* **:** FAMILY
ai·gi·a·lo·saur \\'ī'jīa(,)lō,lō,ȯ(a)r\\ *n* -s [NL *Aigialosaurus*] **:** an animal or fossil of the genus *Aigialosaurus* or family *Aigialosauridae*
ai·gi·a·lo·sau·rus \\'ī,jīa(,)lō'sȯrəs\\ *n, cap* [NL, fr. Gk *aigialos* seashore + NL *-saurus*] **:** a genus (the type of the family *Aigialosauridae*) of fossil prob. semiaquatic lizards of the Lower Cretaceous
aiglet *var of* AGLET
ai·grette \\'ā'gret, ā -\\ *n* -s [F — more at EGRET] **1 :** EGRET **1** **2 a :** a spray of feathers orig. those of the egret **b :** a spray of gems often worn on a hat or in a woman's hair **3 :** something resembling a plume or tuft (as a cluster of rays in the sun's corona seen during total eclipses) **4 :** a sharp point attached to an electrical conductor (as a lightning rod) to facilitate the formation of a corona discharge
aigue-marine *n* [F, lit., seawater] *Prov* **:** AQUAMARINE
aigues mortes *n pl* [F, lit., dead waters] *obs* **:** stagnant waters left by a river when it changes its channel — compare CUTOFF **4**
ai·guiére \\'ī'gyer(y)ē\\ *n* -s [F, fr. MF, fr. OProv *aiguiera*, fr. (assumed) VL *aquaria*, fr. L fem. of *aquarius* of water — more at EWER] **:** a decorative pitcher-shaped usu. tall and slender vessel with a handle and spout
ai·guille \\'ī,gwē, ē'gwē\\ *n* -s [F, lit., needle — more at AGLET] **1 :** a sharp-pointed pinnacle of rock commonly found in glaciated mountains **2 :** an instrument for boring holes in stone or other masonry materials or holes used in blasting
ai·guille-esque \\'ī(,)gwēl'esk\\ *adj* **:** having the shape of an aiguille
ai·guil·lette \\'ī,gwə'let\\ *n* -s [F — more at AGLET] **1 :** AGLET; *specif* **:** a shoulder cord worn by a military aide to the president of the U.S. and to high-ranking officers — compare FOURRAGERE **2 :** long narrow strips of cooked food (as meat or fowl)
ai·ka·ne \\'ī'känē\\ *n* -s [Hawaiian *aikāne*] *Hawaii* **:** a good friend **:** CHUM

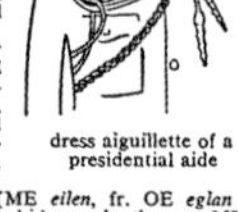

ai·kin·ite \\'īkə,nīt\\ *n* -s [Arthur *Aikin* †1854 Eng. chemist + E *-ite*] **:** a mineral PbCuBiS₃ consisting of lead, copper, bismuth, and sulfur occurring massive and in lead-gray needle-shaped orthorhombic crystals (hardness 2, sp. gr. 7.07)

dress aiguillette of a presidential aide
'ail \\'il\\ *vb* **ailed; ailed; ailing; ails** [ME, fr. OE *eglan* to trouble, afflict; akin to OE *egle* hideous, troublesome, MLG *egelen* to annoy, Goth *usagljan* to oppress and perh. to Mir *ālad* wound, Skt *agha* evil and perh. to OE *ege* fear, OHG *egī, egiso*, Goth *agis* fear, Gk *achos* pain, OIr *ad-āgor* I fear; basic meaning: fearing] *vt* **:** to affect with an unnamed disease or physical or emotional pain or discomfort : trouble or interfere with **:** to be matter with — used only of unspecified causes (can the doctor tell what ~ the patient) (he will not concede that anything ~s his business) (what ~s that naughty boy) *~vi* **:** to become affected with pain or discomfort : have something the matter (he ~ed throughout his childhood) (the business is ~ing) (was ~ing from a cold)
²ail \\'il\\ *n* -s [ME *eil*, fr. *eilen*, v.] **:** INDISPOSITION, AILMENT, TROUBLE
³ail \\'il(ə)l\\ *n* -s [ME *aile*, fr. OE *egl*; akin to OE *ecg* edge, sword — more at EDGE] *now dial Eng* **:** the beard of grain — usu. used in pl.
ai·lan·thus \\ī'lan(t)thəs, ī'-\\ *n* [NL, fr. Amboinese *al lanto*, lit., tree (of) heaven] **1** *cap* **:** a small genus of East Indian and Chinese trees (family Simaroubaceae) with odd-pinnate leaves and terminal panicles of greenish flowers succeeded by oblong twisted samaras **2** -es **:** a tree of the genus *Ailanthus* (esp. *A. altissima*) — see TREE OF HEAVEN
ailanthus silkworm *n* **:** a large green silkworm (*Samia cynthia* or *S. walkeri*) native to eastern Asia but introduced into the U.S. that feeds on ailanthus leaves and has been used experimentally for the commercial production of silk — compare CYNTHIA MOTH
ai·lan·to \\ī'lantō, -tə\\ *n* [Amboinese *al lanto*] **:** AILANTHUS **2**
ai·lao \\'ī,laȯ\\ *n, pl* **ailao** *or* **ai-laos** *usu cap* **A** [a West Yunnan people of the Tⁱai group who formed the Nan-chao kingdom in southwestern China from the 8th to 13th centuries but were absorbed into the Ai-lao people
ai·la·vo·tor *or* **ai·le·va·tor** \\'ī'āla,vād-ə(r)\\ *n* -s [blend of *aileron* and *elevator*] **:** ELEVON
aile *obs var of* AISLE
ai·le·ron \\'īlə,rän\\ *n* -s [F, bird's pinion, aileron, dim. of *aile* wing, fr. L *ala* — more at AISLE] **1 :** a half gable or wing wall (as at the end of the aisle of a church) **2 :** a movable portion of an airplane wing or a movable airfoil external to the wing that is usu. located at the trailing edge near the wing tips and whose function is to impart a rolling motion to the airplane and thus provide lateral control
aileron roll *n* **:** a flight maneuver in which an airplane is rotated about its longitudinal axis through a full 360 degrees by means of the ailerons without altering its flight path
ailes de pi·geon \\eldapēzhōⁿ\\ *n pl* [F, lit., pigeon wings] **:** PIGEONWING 3

ai·lette \\a'let\\ *n* -s [F, fr. OF *ailette, alette, elette* small wing, dim. of *ele* wing — more at AISLE] **:** a plate of forged iron or steel worn over a coat of mail to protect the shoulder
ail·ing *adj* **:** having or suffering from an ailment
ailt \\'īlt\\ *n* -s [W] **:** one of a semi-servile class among the early Cymry; *also* **:** TENANT FARMER
ail·ment \\'īlmant\\ *n* -s **1 :** a bodily sickness, disorder, or chronic disease (always complaining of some ~ or other) **2 :** UNREST, UNEASINESS (symptomatic of the nation's ~)
ails *pres 3d sing of* AIL, *pl of* AIL
ail·sy·te \\'ā,sīt\\ *n* -s [*Ailsa* Craig, island off the coast of Scotland, its locality + E *-yte* (var. of *-ite*)] **:** a rock composed of an alkalic microgranite containing considerable riebeckite
ailu- *or* **ailuro-** *or* **aeluro-** *or* **aeluro-** *comb form* [NL, fr. Gk *ailouros, fr. ailouros*] **:** cat (ailurodon) (ailurophobia)
ai·lu·roi·dea \\,īlyu'ròidēa, ,āl-\\ *syn of* AELUROIDEA
ai·lu·ro·phile \\ī'lūrə,fīl, ā'-\\ *or* **ae·lu·ro·phile** \\-s [*ailur-, aelur- + -phile*] **:** a cat fancier **:** a lover of cats
ai·lu·ro·phobe *or* **ae·lu·ro·phobe** \\,-'fōb\\ *n* -s [*ailur-, aelur- + -phobe*] **:** one that hates or fears cats **:** one suffering from ailurophobia
ai·lu·ro·pho·bia *or* **ae·lu·ro·pho·bia** \\,·ʌ-'fōbēa\\ *n* -s [NL, fr. *ailur-, aelur- + -phobia*] **:** abnormal fear of cats
ai·lu·rop·o·da \\,īlyu'räpədə, ,āl-\\ *n, cap* [NL, fr. *ailur- + -poda*] **:** a genus of Procyonidae including only the giant panda
ai·lu·ro·pus \\ī'lūrəpəs, ā'-\\ *n* [NL, fr. *ailur- + -pus*] *syn of* AILUROPODA
ai·lu·rus \\ī'lūrəs, ā'-\\ *n, cap* [NL, fr. Gk *ailouros* cat] **:** a genus of mammals (family Procyonidae) comprising the panda and formerly regarded as the type of a separate family
'aim \\'īm\\ *vb* **-ED/-ING/-S** [ME *aimen, amen* to guess, estimate, aim, fr. MF *aesmer & esmer*; MF *aesmer* fr. OF, fr. *a-* (fr. L *ad-*) + *esmer*, fr. L *aestimare* to estimate — more at ESTEEM] *vi* **1 a :** to direct a course (point a weapon at an object : direct a missile so as to try to hit an object — usu. used with *at*, sometimes with *for* or *toward* (scientific knowledge ~ed at being wholly impersonal —Bertrand Russell) (that gun is ~ing straight at me —V.C Aldrich) (this fact will give you something to ~ for —S.L.Payne) (officer-candidate schools toward which men . . . can ~ —J.J.O'Donnell) **b :** ASPIRE — often used with *high* (the monastic scholars did not ~ high —R.W.Southern) **2** *obs* **:** to guess with intent to discover meaning or truth (~ at another man's speech) (~ at suspected enmity) **3 :** to have as a purpose : PLAN, INTEND — used only with infinitive (he ~ to encourage mutual understanding —*Saturday Rev.*) (this book ~*s to* effect a partial remedy of this situation —E.A.Mazarz) (I ~ to finish up this job —S.S. Cobb) *~vt* **1** *obs* **:** GUESS, CONJECTURE **2 a :** to direct or point (as a weapon or a missile) at or so as to hit an object (on the lawn a small cannon was ~*ed* into space) (a camera was ~*ed* at the scene) (he ~*ed* the duck at the dog) **b :** to direct (as an act or proceeding) at or toward a specified object or attainment (the study was ~*ed* at developing a comparative picture —*N. Y. Times*) (the haphazard transcription inevitable in work ~*ed* solely at vocabulary collecting —Stanley Newman) c : to intend for (a new printing press ~*ed* at medium and small-sized newspapers —*Wall Street Jour.*) (radio and TV shows ~*ed* at juvenile audiences —*Current Mag.*)
²aim \\'\\ *n* -s [ME *aime, acne, fr. aimen, amen*, v.] **1** *obs* **:** the point intended to be hit (as by an arrow) : MARK, TARGET **2 :** the pointing of a weapon (as a gun) at an object intended to be hit (to take ~ at the target) : the ability to hit a target (his ~ was deadly) **3 :** effectiveness of a weapon (the ~ is accurate up to 75 feet) **3** *obs* **a :** CONJECTURE, GUESS (man's ~ at the divine will) **b :** the directing of effort toward an object in order to affect it (ambitious ~ against the monarchy) c : direction or guidance as to a course or procedure to be followed (to give ~ to travelers on the road) **4 :** the object intended to be attained : PURPOSE, DESIGN (his ~ being the translation of certain religious and devotional writings —Edward Clodd) (the ~ of the Elizabethans was to attain complete realism —T.S.Eliot) (the only fault I find in the book is a certain lack of ~ —Geoffrey Boumphrey) (such exaggeration is purely impressionistic in ~ —R.M.Weaver) *syn* see INTENTION
ai·mak \\'ī,mäk, 'ī,-\\ *n* -s [ON *aymag*, clan] **1 :** a clan or tribal band among Mongolian peoples **2 a :** a province or administrative district of Outer Mongolia
aimara *syn cap, var of* AYMARA
aiming circle *n* **:** an instrument for measuring horizontal and vertical angles and magnetic azimuths in determining gunnery data and laying guns and in artillery surveying
aiming point *n* **:** the point at which the line of sight is directed when sighting (as for the dropping of bombs) or when a firing piece is being laid for direction
aiming stake *also* **aiming post** *n* **:** a stake used as an aiming point for laying mortars and artillery pieces for direction
aim·less \\'īmlə̃s\\ *adj* [*aim* **1** + *-less*] **:** without aim or purpose (an ~ existence) — **aim·less·ly** *adv* — **aim·less·ness** *n* -ES
ai·mo·re \\'īmə'rā\\ *n, pl* **aimore** *or* **aimores** *usu cap* [Pg & Sp *aimoré*, of AmerInd origin] **:** BOTOCUDO
'ain \\'īn\\ *adj or n* [ME (northern dial.) *an*, fr. OE *ān* — more at ONE] *chiefly Scot* **:** ONE
²ain \\'\\ *adj or n* [prob. fr. ON *eigin* — more at OWN] *dial Brit* **:** OWN
³ain *var of* AYIN
⁴ain *or* **ain** *var of* 'AYN
aince \\'ēn(t)s\\ *adv* [ME (northern dial.) *anes* — more at ONCE] *chiefly Scot* **:** ONCE
ai·nhum \\'ī'nyūm, -ū̃\\ *n* -s [Pg, fr. Yoruba *ayun¹*] **:** a tropical disease of unknown cause that results in increasing fibrous constriction and ultimately in spontaneous amputation of the toes, esp. the little toes
ai·ni \\'īnī\\ *n* -s [Quechua *dyni*, lit., recompense] **:** a Quechuan system of exchange of assistance usu. in the form of labor; *also* **:** a group that lends such assistance
ai·noi \\'īnoi\\ *n, pl* [MGk, fr. Gk, pl. of *ainos* praise, tale — more at ENIGMA] **:** a part of the divine office concluding the orthros in the service of the Eastern Church
ai·noid \\'ī,noid\\ *adj, usu cap* [*Ainu + -oid*] **:** resembling the Ainu
ain't \\'ānt\\ *also* **an't** \\'\\ *also* **'ant** *or like* AREN'T\\ [prob. contr. of *are not, is not, am not, & have not*] **1 a :** are not (you ~ going) (they ~ here) (things ~ what they used to be) **b :** is not (it ~ raining) (he's here, ~ he) c : am not (I so ready) — though disapproved by many and more common in less educated speech, used orally in most parts of the U.S. by many cultivated speakers esp. in the phrase *ain't I* **2** *substand* **a :** have not (I ~ seen him) (you ~ told us) **b :** has not (he ~ got the time) (~ the doctor come yet)
ai·nu \\'ī,nū *sometimes* ,-nyū\\ *also* **ai·no** \\,-nō, n, pl* **ainu** *also* **ainus** *or* **ainos** *usu cap* [Ainu, lit., man] **1 a :** an indigenous Caucasoid people of Japan formerly occupying all or most of the archipelago but now confined to part of Hokkaido, Sakhalin, and parts of the Kurile islands **1 b :** a member of such people **2 :** the language of the Ainu people
²ain \\'īn\\ *var of* 'IRE
²air \\'\\ *n, pl* **airs** *or* **air·s** *n* -s often attrib [ME, fr. OF, fr. L *aer*, fr. Gk *aēr* air, mist; prob. akin to Gk *aētēs* wind, *gale* — more at WIND] **1 a :** the element described by early natural philosophers as having the qualities of moisture and heat **b :** a mixture of invisible odorless tasteless compressible elastic sound-transmitting and liquefiable gases composed chiefly of nitrogen and oxygen nearly in the ratio of four volumes to one together with 0.9 percent argon, about 0.03 percent carbon dioxide, varying amounts of water vapor, and minute quantities of helium, krypton, neon, and xenon, that surrounds the earth, half its mass being within four miles of the earth's surface, its pressure at sea level being about 14.7 pounds per square inch, and its weight being 1.293 grams per

ailettes, A

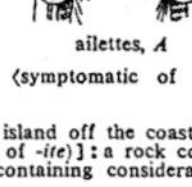

liter at 0°C and 760 mm. pressure c : the portion of the earth's atmosphere that immediately surrounds us and affects the senses (the tang of wood smoke is in the ~ —Corey Ford) (the open ~) (the ~ was not so stale and sultry in the room as it was downstairs —Carson McCullers) d : out-scent given off by exhalation into the atmosphere : ODOR (the ~ of rotting vegetation) e : ATMOSPHERE 8 (canvases with much light and color with 2) f : air in motion 2 a gentle breeze (we moved onward in light ~s to the Narrows and dropped anchor —Kenneth Roberts) g *archaic* **:** soft or faint breathing : BREATH (the least ~ of suspicion) *h archaic* : GAS (the generation of ~d by explosions) **1 (1) :** empty space (needle in ~) I stopped what I was making —Eudora Welty) (the victim of the hanging danced on ~) **(2) :** NOWHERE (the figure of 10 billion dollars . . . was a nice round amount taken out of the ~ —J.P. Warburg) **(3)** *slang* **:** an obvious snub or a sudden severance of relations — usu. used with *the* (give me the ~ —last night —Gwethalyn Graham) (she threatened to give me the ~ —Robert Graves) j : air as a working fluid (as in ventilation systems, measuring and testing, fuel combustion, and pressure-operated devices) **2 COMPRESSED AIR** (mine ~ shafts) (~ barometer) (~ adapters located between the compressor outlets and the combustion chambers) (borings made with an ~ drill) **k (1) :** air as a field of operation for aircraft (the battle of the ~); *also* **:** travel or transportation by aircraft (European editions which reached me by ~ —Marcia Davenport) (~ parcel post) (bus and ~ terminals) **(2) :** AIR FORCE **1** : the medium of transmission of radio waves; *also* **:** RADIO, TELEVISION (advertisers who use the ~ as a means for reaching —C.A.Siepmann) (at the studio an hour before —time —Newsweek) — often used in the phrase *on the air* (he went on the ~ with the first of a series of Saturday-night broadcasts —*Atlantic*) **2 :** public utterance usu. oral : PUBLICITY (he gave to his opinion) **3 [F, fr. OF] a (1) :** the look, appearance, or bearing of a person : attitude or action peculiar to or expressive of some personal quality or emotion : DEMEANOR (an rigidly erect with the ~ of a man accustomed to brief parleys —L.C.Douglas) **(2) :** an artificial or affected manner : show of style or vanity : HAUGHTINESS (to put on ~s) (to give oneself ~s) **(3) :** the artificial motion or carriage of a horse **b :** outward appearance of a thing : apparent character : MANNER, STYLE (my work may have an ~ of fiction —Van Wyck Brooks) (a pioneer town with broad dusty streets, that has not yet acquired an ~ of decadence —Ivor Jones) **c :** a surrounding or pervading influence or condition 2 ATMOSPHERE (the controversy which has been troubling the ~ about us —Victor Riesel) (the place had a little of the ~ of a college dormitory after the final exams —John Dos Passos) (simple it could take to clear the ~ considerably and give evidence before the world of its good intentions —*N.Y.Times*) **4 [prob. trans. of It *aria*] a** *Elizabethan and Jacobean music* **:** an accompanied song or melody in strophic form **b :** the chief voice part or melody in choral or other part music d : TUNE, MELODY **d :** a separate instrumental composition or one of the optional movements of the classical suite typically of a lyric character **5** [trans. of NGk *aēr*] **:** not protected by some substantial obstacle (as a river, mountain, or fortification) against flank attacks or turning movements — **on air** *adv* — **in the air** **1 :** in an uncertain or undecided state : BUOYANTLY (walking *on air*) (treading *on air*) — **up in the air :** in a state of confusion, perturbation, or disorder : not yet settled or decided : in suspense (the question was still *up in the air* —*Time*)
²air \\'\\ *vb* **-ED/-ING/-S** *vt* **1a (1) :** to expose to the air for the purpose of drying or purifying : VENTILATE (~ damp clothing) (stench of whiskey and of things that were never ~*ed* —Ellen Glasgow) (~ the house) **(2)** *archaic* **:** to expose to heat so as to expel dampness or to warm (a brisk fire will soon ~ the room) **b :** to expose to the air for the purpose of cooling or refreshing (exercise in the open air (she left the overheated room to ~ herself) (take the dog out and ~ him) **2 a :** to display ostentatiously (expose to public view (~ the latest fashions) (he constantly ~s his stupidity) **b :** to expose for the sake of public notice : make open to the public (he did not ~ his politics in the pulpit —K.B. Murdock) (the text will be thoroughly ~*ed* —*Newsweek*) **3 :** to transmit by radio or television : BROADCAST (programs which will be ~*ed* in the future —*Musical Digest*) *~vi* **1 :** to become exposed to the open air (your suit is ~*ing* on the line **2 :** to become broadcast (the program ~s daily) *syn* see EXPRESS
³air *n* -s [ME (northern dial.) *aire*, ar, fr. OE & ON of EARLY — more at OAR] *Scot* : OAR
⁴air *Scot var of* EYRE
⁵air *var of* ARY
ai·ra \\'īra\\ *n, cap* [NL, fr. Gk, darnel] **:** a genus of delicate annual grasses with 2-flowered spikelets
air alert *n* **1 :** the period during which military and civilian agencies are required to be in readiness for an enemy air attack; *also* **:** the warning signal that begins such a period **2 :** combat or standby status of the aircraft, aircrew, and ground communications system that may have to repel the enemy air attack
ai·ram·po \\ī'rämpō\\ *n, pl* \\-'rām(,)pōz\\ *n* -s [Sp, fr. Quechua *ayrampú*] **:** a prostrate cactus (*Opuntia soehrensii*) whose dried seeds yield a substance used in the Andes for coloring jellies red
ai·ran \\'ī'rān\\ *n* -s [Turk *ayran*] **:** an Alaic and Turkish drink prepared from fermented milk
air base *n* **:** a base of operations for military aircraft and for the housing and repairing of the craft, the storage of munitions, the housing of aviation personnel, and the administrative center of control over the operations of the aircraft
air bath *n* **1 :** a hygienic exposure of the body to the open air **2 :** a bath (of air) or a receptacle (as a small oven heated from below) containing such a bath
air bell *n* **1 :** an air bubble **2 :** an undeveloped spot on a negative or print caused by the adherence of an air bubble to the film surface during development
air bladder *n* **1 :** AEROEMBOLISM
airbill *var of* AIRWAYBILL
air billow *n* **:** a wave at the interface of two horizontal layers or air caused by their difference in velocity
air bladder *n* **:** a bladder containing gas, esp. air : as **a :** a hydrostatic organ present in most fishes that consists of a gas-filled sac lying dorsal to the alimentary canal and sometimes being connected with the organ of hearing and that serves also as an accessory respiratory organ in dipnoans and some ganoids — called *also* **swim bladder**; compare LUNG **b :** FLOAT **4b**
air bleed *n* **:** a slow escape or admission of air provided for in a mechanical system (as for equalizing pressure)
air blue *n* **:** AZURITE BLUE
airboat \\,-\\ *n* **1 :** SEAPLANE **2 :** a shallow-draft boat driven by an airplane propeller and steered by an airplane rudder
airborne \\,·,-\\ *adj* **1 :** supported wholly by aerodynamic and aerostatic forces (an airplane is ~ after attaining flying speed in takeoff) **2 :** transported or designed to be transported by air (~ infantry) (~ bacteria) **3 :** employing forces other than paratroops that are transported by air (an ~ attack)
air brake *n* **1 :** a brake operated by a piston driven by compressed air from reservoirs connected to brake cylinders by triple valves which upon reduction of air pressure in the brake pipe automatically admit air from the reservoirs into the brake cylinder **2 :** a surface (as an aileron) that may be projected into the airstream for increasing the resistance and lowering the speed of an airplane
air brush \\,-\\ *n, brksiv, -ziv\\ *adj* [*³air + abrasive*] **:** relating to the grinding of tooth surfaces by means of a stream of abrasive particles under air or gas pressure (the ~ method of preparing cavities for filling)
air-break switch *n* **:** an electrical switch that breaks the circuit in air — compare OIL-BREAK SWITCH
air brick *n* **:** a hollowed or perforated brick or a metal box of brick size with grated sides used for ventilation

---

Plate 14a   Page from *Webster's Third New International Dictionary* (1961) showing the entries *aidance* to *air brick*. Note the few illustrations and the absence of capitalized entries. [See p. 130.]

point for laying mortars and artillery pieces for direction

aim·less \'āmləs\ *adj* [²*aim* + -*less*] **:** without aim or purpose ⟨an ~ existence⟩ — **aim·less·ly** *adv* — **aim·less·ness** *n* -ES

ai·mo·re \ˌīməˌrā\ *n, pl* **aimore** *or* **aimores** *usu cap* [Pg & Sp *aimoré; of AmerInd origin] **:** BOTOCUDO

¹ain \'ān\ *adj or n* [ME (northern dial.) *an,* fr. OE *ān* — more at ONE] *chiefly Scot* **:** ONE

²ain \"\ *adj or n* [prob. fr. ON *eiginn* — more at OWN] *dial Brit* **:** OWN

³ain *var of* AYIN

'ain *or* **ain** *var of* 'AYN

aince \'ān(t)s\ *adv* [ME (northern dial.) *anes* — more at ONCE] *chiefly Scot* **:** ONCE

ai·nhum \ī'nyüm, -ü\ⁿ\ *n* -S [Pg, fr. Yoruba *e¹yun³*] **:** a tropical disease of unknown cause that results in increasing fibrous constriction and ultimately in spontaneous amputation of the toes, esp. the little toes

ai·ni \'īnē\ *n* -S [Quechua *áyni,* lit., recompense] **:** a Quechuan system of exchange of assistance usu. in the form of labor; *also* **:** a group that lends such assistance

ai·noi \'ānē\ *n pl* [MGk, fr. Gk, pl. of *ainos* praise, tale — more at ENIGMA] **:** a part of the divine office concluding the orthros in the service of the Eastern Church

ai·noid \'ī,nȯid\ *adj, usu cap* [*Ainu* + -*oid*] **:** resembling the Ainu

ain't \'ānt\ *also* **an't** \"\ *also* 'ant *or like* AREN'T\ [prob. contr. of *are not, is not, am not,* & *have not*] **1 a :** are not ⟨you ~ going⟩ ⟨they ~ here⟩ ⟨things ~ what they used to be⟩ **b :** is not ⟨it ~ raining⟩ ⟨he's here, ~ he⟩ **c :** am not ⟨I ~ ready⟩ — though disapproved by many and more common in less educated speech, used orally in most parts of the U. S. by many cultivated speakers esp. in the phrase *ain't I* **2** *substand* **a :** have not ⟨I ~ seen him⟩ ⟨you ~ told us⟩ **b :** has not ⟨he ~ got the time⟩ ⟨~ the doctor come yet⟩

ai·nu \'ī,nü *sometimes* -,nyü\ *also* **ai·no** \-,nō\ *n, pl* **ainu** *also* **ainus** *or* **ainos** *usu cap* [Ainu, lit., man] **1 a :** an indigenous Caucasoid people of Japan formerly occupying all or most of the archipelago but now confined to part of Hokkaido, Sakhalin, and parts of the Kurile islands **b :** a member of such people **2 :** the language of the Ainu people

¹air \'ār\ *var of* ¹ERE

²air \"\ *adj* -ER/-EST [ME (northern dial.) *ar, are* — more at ERE] *Scot* **:** EARLY

³air \a(a)(ə)r, 'e(ə)r, 'a(a)ə, 'eə\ *n* -S *often attrib* [ME, fr. OF, fr. L *aer,* fr. Gk *aēr* air, mist; prob. akin to Gk *aētēs* wind, gale — more at WIND] **1 a :** the element described by early natural philosophers as having the qualities of moisture and heat **b :** a mixture of invisible odorless tasteless compressible elastic sound-transmitting and liquefiable gases composed chiefly of nitrogen and oxygen nearly in the ratio of four volumes to one together with 0.9 percent argon, about 0.03 percent carbon dioxide, varying amounts of water vapor, and minute quantities of helium, krypton, neon, and xenon, that surrounds the earth, half its mass being within four miles of the earth's surface, its pressure at sea level being about 14.7 pounds per square inch, and its weight being 1.293 grams per

Plate 14b Detail of 14a showing the entries *aimless* to *³air*. In the entry for *ain't* note the discursive treatment of usage and the absence of a label for sense 1. [See p. 153.]

WOF (in New Zealand) *abbrev. for* Warrant of Fitness.
wog[1] (wɒg) *n. Brit. slang, derogatory.* a foreigner, esp. one who is not White. [probably from GOLLIWOG]
wog[2] (wɒg) *n. Slang, chiefly Austral.* influenza or any similar illness. [C20: of unknown origin]
woggle (ˈwɒgᵊl) *n.* the ring of leather through which a Scout neckerchief is threaded. [C20: of unknown origin]
wok (wɒk) *n.* a large metal Chinese cooking pot having a curved base like a bowl and traditionally with a wooden handle. [from Chinese (Cantonese)]
woke (wəʊk) *vb.* a past tense of **wake.**
woken (ˈwəʊkən) *vb.* a past participle of **wake.**
Woking (ˈwəʊkɪŋ) *n.* a town in S England, in central Surrey: mainly residential. Pop.: 81 358 (1981).
wold[1] (wəʊld) *n. Chiefly literary.* a tract of open rolling country, esp. upland. [Old English *weald* bush; related to Old Saxon *wald,* German *Wald* forest, Old Norse *vollr* ground; see WILD]
wold[2] (wəʊld) *n.* another name for **weld**[2].
Wolds (wəʊldz) *pl. n.* **the.** a range of chalk hills in NE England: consists of the **Yorkshire Wolds** to the north, separated from the **Lincolnshire Wolds** by the Humber estuary.
wolf (wʊlf) *n., pl.* **wolves** (wʊlvz). **1.** a predatory canine mammal, *Canis lupus,* which hunts in packs and was formerly widespread in North America and Eurasia but is now less common. See also **timber wolf.** Related adj.: **lupine. 2.** any of several similar and related canines, such as the red wolf and the coyote (**prairie wolf**). **3.** the fur of any such animal. **4. Tasmanian wolf.** another name for the **thylacine. 5.** a voracious, grabbing, or fiercely cruel person or thing. **6.** *Informal.* a man who habitually tries to seduce women. **7.** *Informal.* the destructive larva of any of various moths and beetles. **8.** Also called: **wolf note.** *Music.* **a.** an unpleasant sound produced in some notes played on the violin, cello, etc., owing to resonant vibrations of the belly. **b.** an out-of-tune effect produced on keyboard instruments accommodated esp. to the system of mean-tone temperament. See **temperament** (sense 4). **9. cry wolf.** to give a false alarm. **10. have** *or* **hold a wolf by the ears.** to be in a desperate situation. **11. keep the wolf from the door.** to ward off starvation or privation. **12. lone wolf.** a person or animal who prefers to be alone. **13. throw to the wolves.** to abandon or deliver to destruction. **14. wolf in sheep's clothing.** a malicious person in a harmless or benevolent disguise. ~*vb.* **15.** (*tr.;* often foll. by *down*) to gulp (down). **16.** (*intr.*) to hunt wolves. [Old English *wulf;* related to Old High German *wolf,* Old Norse *ulfr,* Gothic *wulfs,* Latin *lupus* and *vulpēs* fox] —ˈ**wolfish** *adj.* —ˈ**wolf,like** *adj.*
Wolf (*German* vɔlf) *n.* **1. Friedrich August** (ˈfriːdrɪç ˈaugʊst). 1759–1824, German classical scholar, who suggested that the Homeric poems, esp. the *Iliad,* are products of an oral tradition. **2. Hugo** (ˈhuːgo). 1860–1903, Austrian composer, esp. of songs, including the *Italienisches Liederbuch* and the *Spanisches Liederbuch.* **3.** (wʊlf). **Howlin'.** See **Howlin' Wolf.**
Wolf Cub *n. Brit.* the former name for **Cub Scout.**
Wolfe (wʊlf) *n.* **1. James.** 1727–59, English soldier, who commanded the British capture of Quebec, in which he was killed. **2. Thomas (Clayton).** 1900–38, U.S. novelist, noted for his autobiographical fiction, esp. *Look Homeward, Angel* (1929).
Wolfenden Report (ˈwʊlfəndən) *n.* a study produced in 1957 by the Committee on Homosexual Offences and Prostitution in Britain, which recommended that homosexual relations between consenting adults be legalized. [C20: named after Baron John Frederick *Wolfenden* (1906–85), who chaired the Committee]
wolfer (ˈwʊlfə) *n.* a less common spelling of **wolver.**
Wolf-Ferrari (*Italian* ˈvɔlfferˈraːri) *n.* **Ermanno** (erˈmanno). 1867–1948, Italian composer born of a German father, in Germany from 1909. His works, mainly in a lyrical style, include operas, such as *The Jewels of the Madonna* (1911) and *Susanna's Secret* (1909).
Wolffian body (ˈvɒlfɪən) *n. Embryol.* another name for **mesonephros.** [C19: named after K. F. *Wolff* (1733–94), German embryologist]
wolffish (ˈwʊlf,fɪʃ) *n., pl.* **-fish** *or* **-fishes.** any large northern deep-sea blennioid fish of the family *Anarhichadidae,* such as *Anarhichas lupus.* They have large sharp teeth and no pelvic fins and are used as food fishes. Also called: **catfish.**
wolfhound (ˈwʊlf,haʊnd) *n.* the largest breed of dog, used formerly to hunt wolves.
Wolfit (ˈwʊlfɪt) *n.* Sir **Donald.** 1902–68, English stage actor and manager.
wolfram (ˈwʊlfrəm) *n.* another name for **tungsten.** [C18: from German, originally perhaps from the proper name, *Wolfram,* used pejoratively of tungsten because it was thought inferior to tin]
wolframite (ˈwʊlfrə,maɪt) *n.* a black to reddish-brown mineral consisting of tungstates of iron and manganese in monoclinic crystalline form: it occurs mainly in quartz veins and is the chief ore of tungsten. Formula: $(Fe,Mn)WO_4$.
Wolfram von Eschenbach (*German* ˈvɔlfram fɔn ˈɛʃənbax) *n.* died ?1220, German poet: author of the epic *Parzival,* incorporating the story of the Grail.
Wolf-Rayet star (ˈwʊlfˈreɪət) *n.* any of over 100 very hot intensely luminous stars surrounded by a rapidly expanding envelope of gas. Sometimes shortened to **W star.** [C19: named after Charles *Wolf* (1827–1918) and Georges *Rayet* (1839–1906), French astronomers]
wolfsbane *or* **wolf's-bane** (ˈwʊlfs,beɪn) *n.* any of several poisonous N temperate plants of the ranunculaceous genus *Aconitum,* esp. *A. lycoctonum,* which has yellow hoodlike flowers.
Wolfsburg (*German* ˈvɔlfsbʊrk) *n.* a city in NE West Germany, in Lower Saxony: founded in 1938; motor-vehicle industry. Pop.: 125 935 (1980 est.).
wolf spider *n.* any spider of the family *Lycosidae,* which chase their prey to catch it. Also called: **hunting spider.**
wolf whistle *n.* **1.** a whistle made by a man to express admiration of a woman's appearance. ~*vb.* **wolf-whistle. 2.** (when *intr.,* sometimes foll. by *at*) to make such a whistle (at someone).
wollastonite (ˈwʊləstə,naɪt) *n.* a white or grey mineral consisting of calcium silicate in triclinic crystalline form: occurs in metamorphosed limestones. Formula: $CaSiO_3$. [C19: named after W. H. *Wollaston* (1766–1828), English physicist]
Wollongong (ˈwʊləŋ,gɒŋ) *n.* a city in E Australia, in E New South Wales on the Pacific: an early centre of dairy farming; now a coal-mining and heavy industrial centre. Pop.: 230 950 (1981 est.).
Wollstonecraft (ˈwʊlstən,krɑːft) *n.* See (Mary Wollstonecraft) **Godwin.**
wolly (ˈwɒlɪ) *n., pl.* **-lies.** *East London dialect.* a pickled cucumber or olive. [perhaps from OLIVE]
Wolof (ˈwɒlɒf) *n.* **1.** (*pl.* **-of** *or* **-ofs**) a member of a Negroid people of W Africa living chiefly in Senegal. **2.** the language of this people, belonging to the West Atlantic branch of the Niger-Congo family.
Wolsey (ˈwʊlzɪ) *n.* **Thomas.** ?1475–1530, English cardinal and statesman; archbishop of York (1514–30); lord chancellor (1515–29). He dominated Henry VIII's foreign and domestic policies but his failure to obtain papal consent for the king's divorce from Catherine of Aragon led to his arrest for high treason (1530); he died on the journey to face trial.
wolver (ˈwʊlvə) *or* **wolfer** *n.* a person who hunts wolves.
Wolverhampton (,wʊlvəˈhæmptən) *n.* a town in W central England, in the West Midlands: iron and steel foundries. Pop.: 252 447 (1981).
wolverine (ˈwʊlvə,riːn) *n.* a large musteline mammal, *Gulo gulo,* of northern forests of Eurasia and North America having dark very thick water-resistant fur. Also called: **glutton.** [C16 *wolvering,* from WOLF + -ING[3] (later altered to *-ine*)]
wolves (wʊlvz) *n.* the plural of **wolf.**
woman (ˈwʊmən) *n., pl.* **women** (ˈwɪmɪn). **1.** an adult female human being. **2.** (*modifier*) female or feminine: *a woman politician; woman talk.* **3.** women collectively; womankind. **4.** (usually preceded by *the*) feminine nature or feelings: *babies bring out the woman in her.* **5.** a female servant or domestic help. **6.** a man considered as having female characteristics, such as meekness or cowardliness. **7.** *Informal.* a wife, mistress, or girlfriend. **8. the little woman.** *Informal.* one's wife. **9. woman of the streets.** a prostitute. ~*vb.* (*tr.*) **10.** *Rare.* to provide with women. **11.** *Obsolete.* to make effeminate. [Old English *wīfmann, wimman;* from WIFE + MAN (human being)] —ˈ**womanless** *adj.* —ˈ**woman-,like** *adj.*
womanhood (ˈwʊmən,hʊd) *n.* **1.** the state or quality of being a woman or being womanly. **2.** women collectively.
womanish (ˈwʊmənɪʃ) *adj.* **1.** having qualities or characteristics regarded as unsuitable to a strong character of either sex, esp. a man. **2.** characteristic of or suitable for a woman. —ˈ**womanishly** *adv.* —ˈ**womanishness** *n.*
womanize *or* **womanise** (ˈwʊmə,naɪz) *vb.* **1.** (*intr.*) (of a man) to indulge in many casual affairs with women; philander. **2.** (*tr.*) to make effeminate. —ˈ**woman,izer** *or* ˈ**woman,iser** *n.*
womankind (ˈwʊmən,kaɪnd) *n.* the female members of the human race; women collectively.
womanly (ˈwʊmənlɪ) *adj.* **1.** possessing qualities, such as warmth, attractiveness, etc., generally regarded as typical of a woman, esp. a mature woman. **2.** characteristic of or belonging to a woman. —ˈ**womanliness** *n.*
womb (wuːm) *n.* **1.** the nontechnical name for **uterus. 2.** a hollow space enclosing something, esp. when dark, warm, or sheltering. **3.** a place where something is conceived: *the Near East is the womb of western civilization.* **4.** *Obsolete.* the belly. [Old English *wamb;* related to Old Norse *vomb,* Gothic *wamba,* Middle Low German *wamme,* Swedish *våmm*] —**wombed** *adj.* —ˈ**womblike** *adj.*
wombat (ˈwɒmbæt) *n.* either of two burrowing herbivorous Australian marsupials, *Vombatus ursinus* or *Lasiorhinus latifrons,* constituting the family *Vombatidae* (or *Phascolomidae*) and having short limbs, a heavy body, and coarse dense fur. [C18: from a native Australian language]
women (ˈwɪmɪn) *n.* the plural of **woman.**
womenfolk (ˈwɪmɪn,fəʊk) *or U.S. (sometimes)* **womenfolks** *pl. n.* **1.** women collectively. **2.** a group of women, esp. the female members of one's family.
Women's Institute *n.* (in Britain and Commonwealth countries) a society for women interested in the problems of the home and in engaging in social activities.
Women's Liberation *n.* a movement directed towards the removal of attitudes and practices that preserve inequalities based upon the assumption that men are superior to women. Also called: **women's lib.**
Women's Movement *n.* a grassroots movement of women concerned with women's liberation. See **Women's Liberation.**
women's refuge *n. Social welfare.* a house where battered women and their children can go for protection from their oppressors.
Women's Royal Voluntary Service *n.* a British auxiliary service organized in 1938 as the Women's Voluntary Service for work in air raids and civil defence: active throughout World War II and since 1945 in providing support services for those in need: became the Women's Royal Voluntary Service in 1966. Abbrev.: **WRVS.**
women's studies *pl. n.* courses in history, literature, psychology, etc., that are particularly concerned with women's roles, experiences, and achievements.

Plate 15 Page showing the entries from *WOF* to *women's studies* in *Collins Dictionary of the English Language* (second edition 1986). Note the presence of proper names in the wordlist and the absence of pictorial illustrations. Note also, in the entry for *wolf,* the encyclopedic definition. [See p. 156.]

etc.) ; *recognition of danger.*

rec-og-niz-a-ble [rékəgnàizəbl] *adj.* that can be recognized.

re-cog-ni-zance [rikɔ́(g)nizəns] *n.* Ⓒ ❶ a bond by which a person is bound to appear before a court of law at a certain time, or to keep certain conditions, and to ·pay a certain sum if he fails to appear, etc., as *to enter into recognizances* (i. e. enter into such an agreement). ❷ the sum which must be paid if the bond is not kept.

rec-og-nize [rékəgnaiz] *vt.* ❶ (P 1) know again; realize to be identical with something previously known, as *to recognize an old acquaintance; to recognize a tune.* ❷ (P 1) acknowledge as known or as a friend, etc. *The Browns no longer recognize the Smiths.* ❸ (P 1, 10) admit as genuine. *They recognized him as the lawful heir.* ❹ (P 1, 11) be prepared to admit; acknowledge. *He recognized the danger.* ❺ (P 1) acknowledge and notice by some favour or reward. *His services to the cause have been recognized.* ❻ (P 1) give formal acknowledgment of; admit the lawful existence of.

re-coil [rikɔ́il] *vi.* (P 21, 24) ❶ draw back; shrink from. ❷ rebound after striking something; (of a gun) kick. ❸ (fig.) come back upon; react upon. *His meanness recoiled upon his own head.* —*n.* ❶ rebound; springing back, as *the recoil of a gun.* ❷ a feeling of disgust; a shrinking from.

rec-ol-lect [rèkəlékt] *vt. & i.* (P 1, 11, 13, 15, 21) remember; call to mind again, as *to recollect old scenes. As far as I recollect . . .* (i. e. if I remember aright . . .).

re=col-lect [rìːkəlékt] *vt.* (P 1) collect or gather together again. *The shepherd re-collected his flock.* **recollect oneself,** regain calmness of mind.

rec-ol-lec-tion [rèkəlékʃən] *n.* ❶ Ⓤ the act or power of recalling to the mind, as *scenes which arise in quiet recollection of the past.* **to the best of my recollection,** if I remember aright. ❷ Ⓤ the time over which one's memory goes

back. ❸ (often pl.) that which is remembered or recalled to the mind; memories.

rec-om-mend [rèkəménd] *vt.* ❶ (P 1, 10, 18, 19) speak favourably of to another; give a good report of as fitted for use or employment. *I can recommend this soap. Can you recommend her as a good cook?* ❷ (P 1, 3, 11) give advice (to) as to a course of action, etc. *I recommend you on do what he says.* ❸ (P 18) give into the charge of; entrust; commend, as *to recommend oneself [one's soul] to God.* ❹ (P 1) cause to create a good impression; make others think well of.

rec-om-men-da-tion [rèkəmendéiʃən] *n.* ❶ Ⓤ the act of recommending or speaking well of to another, as *to speak in recommendation of (a person or thing).* ❷ Ⓒ a statement or document recommending a person or thing. ❸ Ⓒ those qualities, etc. which cause a person to be well thought of.

rec-om-pense [rékəmpens] *vt.* (P 1, 18) ❶ reward or punish; give an equal return for, as *to recompense a man for his trouble; to recompense good with evil.* ❷ give an adequate compensation for loss, injury, etc. —*n.* Ⓒ & Ⓤ that which is given to recompense a person; a a reward; an atonement; satisfaction, as *to receive a recompense for one's services [the loss of one's time, etc.]; to work without recompense.*

rec-on-cile [rékənsail] *vt.* ❶ (P 1, 18) cause to be friendly again after disagreement. ❷ (P 1) settle or arrange (a quarrel, etc.). ❸ (P 1, 18) bring (facts, etc.) into agreement; harmonize; make consistent. *I can't reconcile these figures with the statement you prepared.* ❹ (P 18, reflexive or passive) resign oneself to; be content with. *I must reconcile myself to a life of poverty.*

rec-on-cil-i-a-tion [rèkənsiliéiʃən] *n.* Ⓤ reconciling or being reconciled; Ⓒ a renewing of friendship; an agreement; a bringing into harmony, as *to live in reconciliation with one's enemies.*

rec-on-dite [rékəndait, rikɔ́ndait] *adj.* obscure to the ordinary under-

Plate 16 Page showing the entries *recognizable* to *recondite* in *Idiomatic and Syntactic English Dictionary* (1942). Note in the entry for *reconcile* the simple definitions, the syntactic patterns for each meaning, and the invented examples. [See p. 165.]

current verb sense (from the notion of drawing purse strings) dates from the early 17th cent.

purser ▶ **noun** an officer on a ship who keeps the accounts, especially the head steward on a passenger vessel.

purse seine /seɪn/ ▶ **noun** [usu. as modifier] a fishing net or seine which may be drawn into the shape of a bag, used for catching shoal fish.
– DERIVATIVES **purse-seiner** noun.

purslane /ˈpəːslən/ ▶ **noun** any of a number of small, typically fleshy-leaved plants which grow in damp or marshy habitats, in particular:
• (also **sea purslane**) an edible plant which grows in salt marshes (*Atriplex portulacoides*, family Chenopodiaceae).
• (also **pink purslane**) a small pink-flowered North American plant of damp places (genus *Claytonia*, family Portulacaceae).
– ORIGIN late Middle English: from Old French *porcelaine*, probably from Latin *porcil(l)aca*, variant of *portulaca*, influenced by French *porcelaine* 'porcelain'.

pursuance ▶ **noun** [mass noun] formal the carrying out of a plan or action: *you have a right to use public areas in the* ***pursuance*** *of your lawful hobby.*
■ the action of trying to achieve something: *staff took industrial action in pursuance of a better deal.*

pursuant /pəˈsjuːənt/ ▶ **adverb** (**pursuant to**) formal in accordance with (a law or a legal document or resolution): *the local authority applied for care orders pursuant to section 31 of the Children Act 1989.*
▶ **adjective** archaic following; going in pursuit: *the pursuant lady.*
– DERIVATIVES **pursuantly** adverb.
– ORIGIN late Middle English *poursuiant* (as a noun in the sense 'prosecutor'): from Old French, 'pursuing', from the verb *poursuir*; later influenced in spelling by **PURSUE**.

pursue ▶ **verb** (**pursues, pursued, pursuing**) [with obj.] **1** follow (someone or something) in order to catch or attack them: *the officer pursued the van* | figurative *a heavily indebted businessman was being pursued by creditors.*
■ seek to form a sexual relationship with (someone) in a persistent or predatory way: *Sophie was being pursued by a number of men.* ■ seek to attain or accomplish (a goal), especially over a long period: *should people pursue their own happiness at the expense of others?* ■ archaic or poetic/literary (of something unpleasant) persistently afflict (someone): *mercy lasts as long as sin pursues man.*
2 (of a person or way) continue or proceed along (a path or route): *the road pursued a straight course over the scrubland.*
■ engage in (an activity or course of action): *Andrew was determined to pursue a computer career* | *the council decided not to pursue an appeal.* ■ continue to investigate, explore, or discuss (a topic, idea, or argument): *we shall not pursue the matter any further.*
– DERIVATIVES **pursuable** adjective.
– ORIGIN Middle English (originally in the sense 'follow with enmity'): from Anglo-Norman French *pursuer*, from an alteration of Latin *prosequi* 'prosecute'.

pursuer ▶ **noun** a person or thing that pursues another.
■ Scots Law a person who brings a case against another into court; a plaintiff.

pursuit ▶ **noun 1** [mass noun] the action of following or pursuing someone or something: *the cat crouched in the grass* ***in pursuit*** *of a bird* | *those whose business is the pursuit of knowledge.*
■ [count noun] a cycling race in which competitors set off from different parts of a track and attempt to overtake one another. ■ Physiology the action of the eye in following a moving object.
2 [with adj. or noun modifier] (often **pursuits**) an activity of a specified kind, especially a recreational or sporting one: *a whole range of leisure pursuits.*
– PHRASES **give pursuit** (of a person, animal, or vehicle) start to chase another.
– ORIGIN late Middle English: from Anglo-Norman French *purseute* 'following after', from *pursuer* (see **PURSUE**). Early senses included 'persecution, annoyance' and in legal contexts 'petition, prosecution'.

pursuivant /ˈpəːsɪv(ə)nt/ ▶ **noun 1** Brit. an officer of the College of Arms ranking below a herald. The four ordinary pursuivants are Rouge Croix, Bluemantle, Rouge Dragon, and Portcullis.
2 archaic a follower or attendant.
– ORIGIN late Middle English (denoting a junior heraldic officer): from Old French *pursivant*, present participle (used as a noun) of *pursivre* 'follow after'.

pursy ▶ **adjective** archaic **1** (especially of a horse) short of breath; asthmatic.
2 (of a person) fat.
– DERIVATIVES **pursiness** noun.
– ORIGIN late Middle English: reduction of Anglo-Norman French *porsif*, alteration of Old French *polsif*, from *polser* 'breathe with difficulty', from Latin *pulsare* 'set in violent motion'.

purulent /ˈpjʊərʊl(ə)nt/ ▶ **adjective** Medicine consisting of, containing, or discharging pus.
– ORIGIN late Middle English: from Latin *purulentus* 'festering', from *pus, pur-* (see **PUS**).

purvey ▶ **verb** [with obj.] provide or supply (food, drink, or other goods) as one's business: *shops purveying cooked food* | figurative *the majority of newspapers purvey a range of right-wing attitudes.*
– DERIVATIVES **purveyor** noun.
– ORIGIN Middle English: from Anglo-Norman French *purveier*, from Latin *providere* 'foresee, attend to' (see **PROVIDE**). Early senses included 'foresee', 'attend to in advance', and 'equip'.

purveyance ▶ **noun** [mass noun] the action of purveying something.
■ Brit. historical the right of the sovereign to buy provisions and use horses and vehicles for a fixed price lower than the market value.
– ORIGIN Middle English (in the senses 'foresight' and 'pre-arrangement'): from Old French *porveance*, from Latin *providentia* 'foresight' (see **PROVIDENCE**).

purview ▶ **noun** [in sing.] the scope of the influence or concerns of something: *such a case might be within the purview of the legislation.*
■ a range of experience or thought: *social taboos meant that little information was likely to come within the purview of women generally.*
– ORIGIN late Middle English: from Anglo-Norman French *purveu* 'foreseen', past participle of *purveier* (see **PURVEY**). Early use was as a legal term specifying the body of a statute following the words 'be it enacted …'.

pus ▶ **noun** [mass noun] a thick yellowish or greenish opaque liquid produced in infected tissue, consisting of dead white blood cells and bacteria with tissue debris and serum.
– ORIGIN late Middle English: from Latin.

Pusan /puːˈsan/ an industrial city and seaport on the SE coast of South Korea; pop. 3,797,570 (1990).

Pusey /ˈpjuːzi/, Edward Bouverie (1800–82), English theologian. In 1833, while professor of Hebrew at Oxford, he founded the Oxford Movement, and became its leader after the withdrawal of John Henry Newman (1841). His many writings include a series of *Tracts for the Times*.
– DERIVATIVES **Puseyism** noun, **Puseyite** noun.

push ▶ **verb 1** [with obj. and adverbial] exert force on (someone or something), typically by setting one's hand against them, in order to move them away from oneself or the origin of the force: *she pushed her glass towards him* | *he pushed a card under the door* | [no obj.] *he* ***pushed at*** *the skylight, but it wouldn't budge.*
■ [with obj.] hold and exert force on (something) so as to cause it to move in front of one: *a woman was pushing a pram.* ■ move one's body or a part of it into a specified position, especially forcefully or with effort: *she pushed her hands into her pockets.* ■ [with obj.] press (a part of a machine or other device): *the lift boy pushed the button for the twentieth floor.* ■ figurative affect (something) so that it reaches a specified level or state: *they expect that the huge crop will push down prices.*
2 [no obj., with adverbial] move forward by using force to pass people or cause them to move aside: *she pushed her way through the crowded streets* | *he pushed past an old woman in his haste.*
■ (of an army) advance over territory: *the guerrillas have pushed south to within 100 miles of the capital.* ■ exert oneself to attain something or surpass others: *I was pushing hard until about 10 laps from the finish.* ■ (**push for**) demand persistently: *the council continued to push for the better management of water resources.* ■ [with obj.] compel or urge (someone) to do something, especially to work hard: *she believed he was pushing their daughter too hard.* ■ (**be pushed**) informal have very little of something, especially time: *I'm a bit* ***pushed*** *for time at the moment.* ■ (**be pushed to do something**) informal find it difficult to achieve something: *he will be pushed to retain the title as his form this season has been below par.* ■ (**be pushing**) informal be nearly (a particular age): *she must be pushing forty, but she's still a good looker.*
3 [with obj.] informal promote the use, sale, or acceptance of: *the company is pushing a £500 asking price.*
■ put forward (an argument or demand) with undue force or in too extreme a form: *he thought that the belief in individualism had been pushed too far.* ■ sell (a narcotic drug) illegally.
4 [with obj.] Computing prepare (a stack) to receive a piece of data on the top.
■ transfer (data) to the top of a stack.
5 [with obj.] Photography develop (a film) so as to compensate for deliberate underexposure.
▶ **noun 1** an act of exerting force on someone or something in order to move them away from oneself: *he closed the door with a push.*
■ an act of pressing a part of a machine or device: *the door locks at the push of a button.* ■ figurative something which encourages or assists something else: *the fall in prices was given a push by official policy.*
2 a vigorous effort to do or obtain something: *many clubs are joining in the fund-raising push* | *he determined to make one last push for success.*
■ a military attack in force: *the army was engaged in a push against guerrilla strongholds.* ■ an advertising or promotional campaign: *TV ads will be accompanied by a colour press push.* ■ [mass noun] forcefulness and enterprise: *an investor with the necessary money and push.* ■ (**a push**) informal something that is hard to achieve: *we're managing on our own but it's a push.*
– PHRASES **at a push** Brit. informal if absolutely necessary; only with a certain degree of difficulty: *there's room for four people, or five at a push.* **get** (or **give someone**) **the push** (or **shove**) Brit. informal be dismissed (or dismiss someone) from a job. ■ be rejected in (or end) a relationship. **push at** (or **against**) **an open door** have no difficulty in accomplishing a task. **push the boat out** see **BOAT**. **push someone's buttons** see **BUTTON**. **pushing up the daisies** see **DAISY**. **push one's luck** informal take a risk on the assumption that one will continue to be successful or in favour. **when push comes to shove** informal when one must commit oneself to an action or decision: *when push came to shove, I always stood up for him.*
▶ **push ahead** proceed with or continue a course of action or policy: *he promised to* ***push ahead*** *with economic reform.*
push along Brit. informal go away; depart.
push someone around (or **about**) informal treat someone roughly or inconsiderately.
push in go in front of people who are already queuing.
push off 1 use an oar, boathook, etc. to exert pressure so as to move a boat out from a bank. **2** informal go away.
push on continue on a journey: *the light was already fading, but she pushed on.*
push something through get a proposed measure completed or accepted quickly.
– ORIGIN Middle English (as a verb): from Old French *pousser*, from Latin *pulsare* 'to push, beat, pulse' (see **PULSE**[1]). The early sense was 'exert force on', giving rise later to 'make a strenuous effort, endeavour'.

pushbike ▶ **noun** Brit. informal a bicycle.

push-button ▶ **noun** [usu. as modifier] a button that is pushed to operate an electrical device: *a push-button telephone.*

pushcart ▶ **noun** a small handcart or barrow.

pushchair ▶ **noun** Brit. a folding chair on wheels, in which a baby or young child can be pushed along.

pusher ▶ **noun 1** informal a person who sells illegal drugs.
2 a person or thing that pushes something: *the checkout trolley-pushers.*
■ informal a forceful or pushy person: *she got things moving, she was a tremendous pusher.*

push fit ▶ **noun** a fit between two parts in which one is connected to the other by manually pushing or sliding them together:

pushful ▶ **adjective** arrogantly self-assertive; pushy.
– DERIVATIVES **pushfully** adverb, **pushfulness** noun.

Pushkin /ˈpʊʃkɪn/, Aleksandr (Sergeevich) (1799–1837), Russian poet, novelist, and dramatist. He wrote prolifically in many genres; his first success was the romantic narrative poem *Ruslan and Ludmilla* (1820). Other notable works include the verse novel *Eugene Onegin* (1833) and the blank-verse historical drama *Boris Godunov* (1831).

pushover ▶ **noun 1** informal a person who is easy to

a **cat** | ɑː **arm** | ɛ **bed** | ɛː **hair** | ə **ago** | əː **her** | ɪ **sit** | i **cosy** | iː **see** | ɒ **hot** | ɔː **saw** | ʌ **run** | ʊ **put** | uː **too** | ʌɪ **my** | aʊ **how** | eɪ **day** | əʊ **no** | ɪə **near** | ɔɪ **boy** | ʊə **poor** | ʌɪə **fire** | aʊə **sour**

Plate 17a Page showing the entries *purser* to *pushover* in *The New Oxford Dictionary of English* (1998). Note the presence of a few proper names in the wordlist, the treatment of polysemy and the treatment of phrases in special paragraphs. [See p. 158.]

– DERIVATIVES **pursuantly** adverb.

– ORIGIN late Middle English *poursuiant* (as a noun in the sense 'prosecutor'): from Old French, 'pursuing', from the verb *poursuir*; later influenced in spelling by **PURSUE**.

pursue ▶ verb (**pursues, pursued, pursuing**) [with obj.] **1** follow (someone or something) in order to catch or attack them: *the officer pursued the van* | figurative *a heavily indebted businessman was being pursued by creditors.*

   ■ seek to form a sexual relationship with (someone) in a persistent or predatory way: *Sophie was being pursued by a number of men.* ■ seek to attain or accomplish (a goal), especially over a long period: *should people pursue their own happiness at the expense of others?* ■ archaic or poetic/literary (of something unpleasant) persistently afflict (someone): *mercy lasts as long as sin pursues man.*

2 (of a person or way) continue or proceed along (a path or route): *the road pursued a straight course over the scrubland.*

   ■ engage in (an activity or course of action): *Andrew was determined to pursue a computer career* | *the council decided not to pursue an appeal.* ■ continue to investigate, explore, or discuss (a topic, idea, or argument): *we shall not pursue the matter any further.*

– DERIVATIVES **pursuable** adjective.

– ORIGIN Middle English (originally in the sense 'follow with enmity'): from Anglo-Norman French *pursuer*, from an alteration of Latin *prosequi* 'prosecute'.

pursuer ▶ noun a person or thing that pursues another.

   ■ Scots Law a person who brings a case against another into court; a plaintiff.

Plate 17b Detail of 17a. In the entry *pursue*, note the treatment of polysemy, with 'main' and 'secondary' senses. [See p. 158.]

■ freedom from immorality, esp. of a sexual nature: *white is meant to represent purity and innocence.*

–ORIGIN Middle English: from Old French *purete*, later assimilated to late Latin *puritas*, from Latin *purus* 'pure.'

Pur•kin•je cell |pərˈkinjē| ▸n. Anatomy a nerve cell of a large, branched type found in the cortex of the cerebellum.

–ORIGIN mid 19th cent.: named after Jan E. *Purkinje* (1787–1869), Bohemian physiologist.

purl[1] |pərl| ▸adj. [attrib.] denoting or relating to a knitting stitch made by putting the needle through the front of the stitch from right to left. Compare with KNIT.

▸n. a purl stitch.

▸v. [trans.] knit with a purl stitch: *knit one, purl one.*

–ORIGIN mid 17th cent. (as a noun): of uncertain origin.

purl[2] ▸v. [intrans.] (of a stream or river) flow with a swirling motion and babbling sound.

▸n. [in sing.] a motion or sound of this kind.

–ORIGIN early 16th cent. (denoting a small swirling stream): probably imitative; compare with Norwegian *purla* 'bubble up.'

pur•lieu |ˈpərl(y)o͞o| ▸n. (pl. **purlieus** or **purlieux** |-l(y)o͞o(z)|) the area near or surrounding a place: *the photogenic* ***purlieus of*** *Princeton.*

■ figurative a person's usual haunts. ■ Brit., historical a tract on the border of a forest, esp. one earlier included in it and still partly subject to forest laws.

–ORIGIN late 15th cent. (denoting a tract on the border of a forest): probably an alteration (suggested by French *lieu* 'place') of Anglo-Norman French *puralee* 'a going around to settle the boundaries.'

pur•lin |ˈpərlən| ▸n. a horizontal beam along the length of a roof, resting on a main rafter and supporting the common rafters or boards.

–ORIGIN late Middle English: perhaps of French origin.

pur•loin |pərˈloin| ▸v. [trans.] steal (something): *he must have managed to purloin a copy of the key.*

–DERIVATIVES **pur•loin•er** n.

–ORIGIN Middle English (in the sense 'put at a distance'): from Anglo-Norman French *purloigner* 'put away,' from *pur-* 'forth' + *loign* 'far.'

pu•ro |ˈpo͝orō| ▸n. (pl. **-os**) (in Spanish-speaking regions) a cigar.

–ORIGIN Spanish, literally 'pure.'

pu•ro•my•cin |ˌpyo͝orəˈmīsin| ▸n. Medicine an antibiotic used to treat sleeping sickness and amoebic dysentery.

•This antibiotic is produced by the bacterium *Streptomyces alboniger.*

–ORIGIN 1950s: from PURINE + -MYCIN.

pur•ple |ˈpərpəl| ▸n. a color intermediate between red and blue: *the painting was mostly in shades of blue and purple.*

■ purple clothing or material. ■ (also **Tyrian purple**) a crimson dye obtained from some mollusks, formerly used for fabric worn by an emperor or senior magistrate in ancient Rome or Byzantium. ■ (**the purple**) (in ancient Rome or Byzantium) clothing of this color. ■ (**the purple**) (in ancient Rome) a position of rank, authority, or privilege: *he was too young to assume the purple.* ■ (**the purple**) the scarlet official dress of a cardinal.

▸adj. of a color intermediate between red and blue: *a faded purple T-shirt.*

▸v. become or make purple in color: [intrans.] *Ed's cheeks purpled.* | [trans.] *the neon was purpling the horizon above the highway.*

–PHRASES **born in** (or **to**) **the purple** born into a reigning family or privileged class.

–DERIVATIVES **pur•ple•ness** n.; **pur•plish** |ˈpərp(ə)lisн| adj.; **pur•ply** |ˈpərp(ə)lē| adj.

–ORIGIN Old English (describing the clothing of an emperor), alteration of *purpre*, from Latin *purpura* 'purple,' from Greek *porphura*, denoting mollusks that yielded a crimson dye, also cloth dyed with this.

pur•ple gal•li•nule ▸n. **1** another term for GALLINULE.

2 a marsh bird of the rail family, with a purplish-blue head and breast and a large red bill, found throughout the Old World.

•*Porphyrio porphyrio*, family Rallidae.

pur•ple heart ▸n. **1** (**Purple Heart**) (in the US) a military decoration for those wounded or killed in action, established in 1782 and reestablished in 1932.

2 a large tree of the rain forests of Central and South America, with dark purplish-brown timber that blackens on contact with water.

•Genus *Peltogyne*, family Leguminosae: several species, in particular *P. paniculata.*

3 Brit., informal a mauve-colored heart-shaped stimulant tablet, esp. of amphetamine.

pur•ple leaf plum ▸n. a shrub or small tree with white flowers and small red and yellow edible fruit. Native to southwestern Asia, it is used as stock for commercial varieties of plum. Also called FLOWERING PLUM, MYROBALAN.

•*Prunus cerasifera*, family Rosaceae.

■ the fruit of this tree.

pur•ple mar•tin ▸n. a martin with purplish-blue plumage. It is the largest North American swallow, and the male is the only swallow with uniform dark plumage on its belly.

•*Progne subis*, family Hirundinidae.

pur•ple pas•sage ▸n. an elaborate or excessively ornate passage in a literary composition.

pur•ple patch ▸n. **1** informal, chiefly Brit. a run of success or good luck.

2 another term for PURPLE PASSAGE.

pur•ple prose ▸n. prose that is too elaborate or ornate.

pur•port ▸v. |pərˈpôrt| [with infinitive] appear or claim to be or do something, esp. falsely; profess: *she is not the person she purports to be.*

▸n. |ˈpərˌpôrt| the meaning or substance of something, typically a document or speech: *I do not understand the purport of your remarks.*

■ the purpose of a person or thing: *the purport of existence.*

–DERIVATIVES **pur•port•ed•ly** adv.

–ORIGIN late Middle English (in the sense 'express, signify'): from Old French *purporter*, from medieval Latin *proportare*, from Latin *pro-* 'forth' + *portare* 'carry, bear.' The sense 'appear to be' dates from the late 18th cent.

pur•pose |ˈpərpəs| ▸n. the reason for which something is done or created or for which something exists: *the purpose of the meeting is to appoint a trustee* | *the building is no longer needed for its original purpose.*

■ a person's sense of resolve or determination: *there was a new* ***sense of purpose*** *in her step as she set off.* ■ (usu. **purposes**) a particular requirement or consideration, typically one that is temporary or restricted in scope or extent: *pensions are considered as earned income for tax purposes.*

▸v. [trans.] formal have as one's intention or objective: *God has allowed suffering, even purposed it.*

–PHRASES **on purpose** intentionally. **to no purpose** with no result or effect; pointlessly. **to the purpose** relevant or useful: *you may have heard something from them that is to the purpose.*

–ORIGIN Middle English: from Old French *porpos*, from the verb *porposer*, variant of *proposer* (see PROPOSE).

pur•pose-built ▸adj. chiefly Brit. built for a particular purpose: *purpose-built accommodations for the elderly.*

pur•pose•ful |ˈpərpəsfəl| ▸adj. having or showing determination or resolve: *the purposeful stride of a great lawyer.*

■ having a useful purpose: *purposeful activities.* ■ intentional: *if his sudden death was not accidental, it must have been purposeful.*

–DERIVATIVES **pur•pose•ful•ly** adv.; **pur•pose•ful•ness** n.

pur•pose•less |ˈpərpəsləs| ▸adj. done or made with no discernible point or purpose: *purposeless vandalism.*

■ having no aim or plan: *his purposeless life.*

–DERIVATIVES **pur•pose•less•ly** adv.; **pur•pose•less•ness** n.

pur•pose•ly |ˈpərpəslē| ▸adv. on purpose; intentionally: *she had purposely made it difficult.*

pur•pos•ive |ˈpərpəsiv; pərˈpō-| ▸adj. having, serving, or done with a purpose: *teaching is a purposive activity.*

–DERIVATIVES **pur•pos•ive•ly** adv.; **pur•pos•ive•ness** n.

pur•pu•ra |ˈpərp(y)ərə| ▸n. Medicine a rash of purple spots on the skin caused by internal bleeding from small blood vessels.

■ [with adj.] any of a number of diseases characterized by such a rash: *psychogenic purpura.*

–DERIVATIVES **pur•pu•ric** |pərˈpyo͝orik| adj.

–ORIGIN mid 18th cent.: from Latin, from Greek *porphura* 'purple.'

pur•pure |ˈpərpyər| ▸n. purple, as a heraldic tincture.

–ORIGIN Old English (in the sense 'purple garment'), from Latin *purpura* (see PURPURA), reinforced by Old French *purpre* and influenced by words ending in *-ure*.

pur•pu•rin |ˈpərpyərin| ▸n. Chemistry a red dye originally extracted from madder and also prepared artificially by the oxidation of alizarin.

•An anthraquinone derivative; chem. formula: $C_{14}H_8O_5$.

–ORIGIN mid 19th cent.: from Latin *purpura* 'purple' + -IN[1].

purr |pər| ▸v. [intrans.] (of a cat) make a low continuous vibratory sound usually expressing contentment.

■ (of a vehicle or machine) make such a sound when running smoothly at low speed. ■ [no obj., with adverbial of direction] (of a vehicle or engine) move smoothly while making such a sound: *a sleek blue BMW purred past him.* ■ speak in a low soft voice, esp. when expressing contentment or acting seductively: [with direct speech] *"Would you like coffee?" she purred* | [trans.] *she purred her lines seductively.*

▸n. a low continuous vibratory sound, typically that made by a cat or vehicle.

–ORIGIN early 17th cent.: imitative.

purse |pərs| ▸n. a small bag used esp. by a woman to carry everyday personal items.

■ a small pouch of leather or plastic used for carrying money, typically by a woman. ■ the money possessed or available to a person or country: *institutions are funded from the same general purse.* ■ a sum of money given as a prize in a sporting contest, esp. a boxing match.

▸v. (with reference to the lips) pucker or contract, typically to express disapproval or irritation: [trans.] *Marianne took a glance at her reflection and pursed her lips disgustedly* | [intrans.] *under stress his lips would purse slightly.*

–PHRASES **hold the purse strings** have control of expenditure. **tighten** (or **loosen**) **the purse strings** restrict (or increase) the amount of money available to be spent.

–ORIGIN late Old English, altèration of late Latin *bursa* 'purse,' from Greek *bursa* 'hide, leather.' The current verb sense (from the notion of drawing purse strings) dates from the early 17th cent.

purs•er |ˈpərsər| ▸n. an officer on a ship who keeps the accounts, esp. the head steward on a passenger vessel.

purse seine ▸n. [usu. as adj.] a fishing net or seine that can be drawn into the shape of a bag, used for catching shoal fish.

–DERIVATIVES **purse sein•er** n.

purs•lane |ˈpərslən; -ˌslān| ▸n. any of a number of small, typically fleshy-leaved plants that grow in damp habitats or waste places, in particular:

• *Portulaca oleracea*, a prostrate North American plant with tiny yellow flowers. • *Sesuvium maritimum* (**sea-purslane**), an edible plant that grows in damp sand along coastal shores.

–ORIGIN late Middle English: from Old French *porcelaine*, probably from Latin *porcil(l)aca*, variant of *portulaca*, influenced by French *porcelaine* 'porcelain.'

pur•su•ance |pərˈso͞oəns| ▸n. formal the carrying out of a plan or action: *you have a right to use public areas* ***in the pursuance of*** *your lawful hobby.*

■ the action of trying to achieve something: *they are considering a walkout in pursuance of a better deal.*

pur•su•ant |pərˈso͞oənt| ▸adv. (**pursuant to**) formal in accordance with (a law or a legal document or resolution): *conversations that they wiretap pursuant to court order.*

▸adj. archaic following; going in pursuit: *the pursuant lady.*

–DERIVATIVES **pur•su•ant•ly** adv.

–ORIGIN late Middle English *poursuiant* (as a noun in the sense 'prosecutor'): from Old French, 'pursuing,' from the verb *poursuir*; later influenced in spelling by PURSUE.

pur•sue |pərˈso͞o| ▸v. (**pursues, pursued, pursuing**) [trans.] **1** follow (someone or something) in order to catch or attack them: *the officer pursued the van* | figurative *a heavily indebted businessman was being pursued by creditors.*

■ seek to form a sexual relationship with (someone) in a persistent way: *Sophie was being pursued by a number of men.* ■ seek to attain or accomplish (a goal), esp. over a long period: *should people pursue their own happiness at the expense of others?* ■ archaic poetic/literary (of something unpleasant) persistently afflict (someone): *mercy lasts as long as sin pursues man.*

2 (of a person or way) continue or proceed along (a path or route): *the road pursued a straight course over the scrubland.*

■ engage in (an activity or course of action): *Andrew was determined to pursue a computer career* | *the council decided not to pursue an appeal.* ■ continue to investigate, explore, or discuss (a topic, idea, or argument): *we shall not pursue the matter any further.*

–DERIVATIVES **pur•su•a•ble** adj.; **pur•su•er** n.

–ORIGIN Middle English (originally in the sense 'follow with enmity'): from Anglo-Norman French *pursuer*, from an alteration of Latin *prosequi* 'prosecute.'

pur•suit |pərˈso͞ot| ▸n. **1** the action of following or pursuing someone or something: *the cat crouched in the grass* ***in pursuit of*** *a bird* | *those whose business is the pursuit of knowledge.*

■ a bicycle race in which competitors start from different parts of a track and attempt to overtake one another. ■ Physiology the action of the eye in following a moving object.

2 [with adj.] (often **pursuits**) an activity of a specified kind, esp. a recreational or athletic one: *a whole range of leisure pursuits.*

Plate 18 Page showing the entries *Purkinje cell* to *pursuit* in *The New Oxford American Dictionary* (2001). [See p. 159.]

layabout /leɪəbaʊt/, **layabouts**. If you say that someone is a **layabout**, you mean they are idle and lazy. EG *He's just a drunken layabout.*   N COUNT = loafer

lay-by, lay-bys. A **lay-by** is a short strip of road by the side of a main road, where cars can stop for a while. EG *Pull into the next lay-by.*   N COUNT ≈ area

layer /leɪə/, **layers**. **1** A **layer** of a material or substance is a quantity or piece of it that covers something or that exists in a flat, thin strip underneath or on top of other similar strips. EG *Rocks lie in layers... A fine layer of dust covers everything... He wrapped each component in several layers of foam rubber... ...the electrically charged layer in the atmosphere.*   N COUNT : USU + SUPP

2 If you refer to **layers** when you are talking about ideas, systems, people's personalities, etc, you are referring to the different parts of them and the way that they are added together or hide each other. EG *There are many layers of meaning... The ritual was buried beneath layer after layer of civilization... ...another layer of government.*   N COUNT : USU N IN PL + SUPP ≈ level

layered /leɪəd/. Something that is **layered** is made or exists in layers. EG *Put the potatoes in the dish layered with the onion and parsley mixture... ...the layered nature of certain rocks.*   ADJ CLASSIF

layette /leɪet/, **layettes**. A **layette** is a set of the things that you need for a baby, such as clothes and nappies. People usually buy a layette before the baby is born; a formal word.   N COUNT : USU SING ≈ equipment

layman /leɪmən/, **laymen**. A **layman** is **1** a person who is not trained, qualified, or experienced in a particular subject or activity. EG *To the layman, the questions which a doctor puts to the patient may seem irrelevant... ...a task for industrial experts rather than for laymen.* **2** a man who is involved with the Christian church but is not a member of the clergy or a monk. EG *...a prominent Catholic layman.*   N COUNT   N COUNT

layoff /leɪɒf/, **layoffs**; also spelled with a hyphen. A **layoff** is **1** the act of an employer telling people to leave their jobs, usually because there is no more work for them to do. EG *Is a layoff in prospect?... In defense industries, sudden layoffs are common... Textile companies announced 2,000 fresh layoffs last week.* **2** a period of time in which people do not work or take part in their normal activities, often because they are resting or are injured. EG *He was bowling badly after his long lay-off.*   N COUNT = redundancy   N COUNT = break

layout /leɪaʊt/, **layouts**. The **layout** of a garden, building, piece of writing, etc is the way in which the parts of it are arranged. EG *...the general layout of the farm... He knew the airport layout intimately... ...a full-page layout in tomorrow's paper... ...the poor layout and organization of the report.*   N UNCOUNT + SUPP ≈ design = arrangement

laze /leɪz/, **lazes, lazing, lazed**. If you **laze** or **laze about** in a place or for a period of time, you relax and enjoy yourself, not doing any work or anything else that requires effort. EG *They can laze in the sun without a care... ...cleaning and washing up while the other women laze about... ...lazing by the hotel pool.*   V, OR PHRASAL VB : V + ADV ≈ rest = lounge

lazy /leɪzɪ/, **lazier, laziest**. **1** Someone who is **lazy** does not want to work or make any effort to do anything; used showing disapproval. EG *He became remarkably lazy... ...a lazy fellow... His teacher thought he was lazy.* EG *Only laziness prevented him from doing it.*   ADJ QUALIT = idle   ◇ N UNCOUNT = idleness

2 Lazy actions or ways of behaving are done gently or easily without making very much effort. EG *She gave a lazy smile... He had a lazy, drawling way of talking.* ◇ **lazily.** EG *Thomas looked at it lazily... ...lazily combing his hair.*   ADJ QUALIT : ATTRIB ≈ casual   ◇ ADV WITH VB ≈ casually

3 If you describe the movement of something as **lazy**, you mean that it moves slowly and gently. EG *The current is lazy and meandering... ...going at the same lazy pace.* ◇ **lazily.** EG *The clouds passed lazily across the sky... The Mercedes drove lazily past.*   ADJ QUALIT   ◇ ADV WITH VB

4 Lazy ideas, excuses, etc are unsatisfactory because they have not been thought about carefully enough; used showing disapproval. EG *The generation gap is a lazy excuse for the age-old problems between parents and children... ...the lazy assumption that he was past the worst of his problems.*   ADJ QUALIT : ATTRIB

lazybones /leɪzɪbəʊnz/. If you say that someone is a **lazybones**, you mean that they are very lazy indeed.   N COUNT

lb, lbs. lb is an abbreviation for a pound in weight; used in written English, usually after a number. EG *...a 2lb bag of sugar... ...from 1000 lbs to 11 tons... I even gained 3lb.*

lead, leads, leading, led. The word is pronounced /liːd/ in all paragraphs except paragraphs 26 to 28, where it is pronounced /led/. **1** If a person or vehicle **is leading** a moving group, they are in front of the other people or vehicles. EG *Jenny was leading and I was at the back... ...two tanks leading, the remainder of the force in two parties behind.* ● If you are **in the lead**, you are in front of a moving group. EG *I now had Sheila in the lead and Bob at the rear.*   V OR V + O ≈ head   ● PHR : USED AS AN A

2 If you **lead** a group of moving people, you walk or ride in front of them, because you are in charge of them. EG *...a general leading an army into battle... He led a demonstration through the City.*   V + O : USU + A ≈ head

3 If you **lead** someone to a particular place or object, you go with them to show them where it is. EG *'This way.' Morris led Ellen to a cabinet in the store... Mrs Kaul was leading him to his seat... Captain Imrie led me round the crew's quarters.* ● If you **lead the way** along a particular route, you go along it in front of someone in order to show them where to go. EG *Jack led the way down the rock... I led the way to Andrew's cabin.*   V + O + A ≈ take = escort, guide   ● PHR : VB INFLECTS

4 If you **lead** a person or animal, you hold the person's arm, hold the animal by a rope, etc in order to keep control over them, in case they fail or try to run away. EG *My mother takes me by the hand and leads me downstairs... I was led into the prisoner's dock... I let them lead the camels.*   V + O ≈ take

5 If something such as a road, pipe, or wire **leads** to a particular place or in a particular direction, it goes to that place or follows that direction. EG *...a path leading straight to Stonehenge... The steps lead down to his basement... ...a road leading away from the town... ...two wires leading to an amplifier.* ● If a road or route **leads** someone to a particular place or in a particular direction, they get to that place or go in that direction by using it. EG *He went where the path led him.*   V + A   ● V + O + A ≈ send = direct

6 If a door or other entrance **leads** to or into a place, you can get to that place by going through it. EG *There was a gate on our left leading into a field... ...the entrance that leads to the House of Commons.*   V + A (to/into)

7 If you **lead** at a particular point in a race or competition, you are winning at that point. EG *Who is leading?... Becker leads by five games to four.* ● If you have **the lead** at a particular point in a race or competition, you are winning at that point, for example by being in front of your opponents, or by having more points or goals than they have. EG *They share the first round lead... This win gave him the overall lead... New Zealand went into an early lead.*   V   ● N SING WITH DET ≈ position

8 The **lead** that someone has at a particular point in a race or competition is the distance, amount of time, etc by which they are winning. EG *A recount gave McClellan a lead of only 3,472 over Hearst... The Australian yacht's lead looked unbeatable.*   N SING WITH DET : USU + SUPP

9 If one company or country **leads** others in a particular activity such as scientific research or business, it is more successful or advanced than they are in that activity. EG *Britain briefly led the world in computing science... In 1950-73 Japan led the industrial growth league.*   V + O, OR V : USU + A

10 If you **lead** a group of people, organization, or activity, you are officially in control or in charge of them. EG *The Labour Party was led by Wilson... His brother was about to lead an expedition into Arctic Canada... He lacked any desire to lead.*   V OR V + O

11 If you **lead** an activity such as a political campaign or a riot, you start it or are very involved or active in it. EG *The rioting was led by students... The educated middle class led the move towards independence.*   V + O ≈ initiate

12 If you **take the lead** or **take a lead** in a particular situation or group, **12.1** you put yourself in a position of authority in it and start making decisions and organizing people. EG *He always takes the lead in any group... Other feminists won't mind us taking a lead.* **12.2** you develop new ideas or methods that other people consider to be a good example or model to follow; used showing approval. EG *Other firms are now following the company's lead in the integration of research and development... The European Community should give a lead in respect of disarmament*   PHR : VB INFLECTS   N COUNT

Plate 19 Page showing the first part of the entry for *lead* in *Collins COBUILD English Language Dictionary* (1987). Note the treatment of all homographs in the same entry, the full-sentence definitions, the authentic examples from the corpus, and the side column with syntactic patterns and semantic relations. [See p. 177.]

about people, etc.) being told; getting around **5** out of debt: *Please lend me some money to keep me afloat*

a·foot /ə'fʊt/ *adv, adj* [Wa5;F] **1** *often derog* being prepared, made ready, or in operation: *There is a plan afoot to pull down the old building.|There is some strange business afoot* **2** *old use* on the move, esp. on foot

a·fore·said /ə'fɔːsed‖ə'for-/ also **a·fore·men·tioned** /ə,fɔː'menʃənd‖ə,for-/— *adj* [Wa5;A;GU] *fml* said or named before or above: *The aforesaid (person/people) was/were present at the trial*

a·fore·thought /ə'fɔːθɔːt‖ə'for-/ *adj law* see MAL-ICE

a for·ti·o·ri /,eɪ fɔːti'ɔːraɪ, -ri‖-fɔrti'or-/ *adv* [Wa5] *Lat* for a still stronger reason; with greater respect: *A man with a quick temper is, a fortiori, not a patient man*

a·fraid /ə'freɪd/ *adj* **1** [F (*of*,3,5a)] full of fear; FRIGHTENED: *Don't be afraid of dogs.|She was afraid to excite him in case he became dangerous.|She was afraid that it would bite* **2** [F (*of*,3,5a)] worried or anxious about possible results: *Don't be afraid of asking for help* **3** [F5a,b] *polite* sorry for something that has happened or is likely to happen: *I am afraid I've broken your pen.|"Are we late?" "I'm afraid so."|"Are we on time?" "I'm afraid not."*

a·fresh /ə'freʃ/ *adv* [Wa5] *fml* once more; again: *I've spoiled the painting and must do it afresh*

Af·ri·can[1] /'æfrɪkən/ *n* a person from Africa

African[2] *adj* of, from, or about Africa

Af·ri·kaans /,æfrɪ'kɑːns/ *n* [R;U] a language of South Africa very much like Dutch

Af·ri·ka·ner /,æfrɪ'kɑːnə/ *n* a South African whose native language is Afrikaans, esp. a descendant of the Dutch settlers of the 17th century

Af·ro /'æfrəʊ/ *n* **Afros** a hairstyle for men and women in which the hair is shaped into a large round bushy mass

Afro- *comb. form* **1** African; of Africa: *an Afro-American* **2** African and: *Afro-Asiatic*

aft /ɑːft‖æft/ *adv* [Wa5;F] *tech* in, near, or towards the back part (STERN) of a boat —opposite **fore**

af·ter[1] /'ɑːftə‖'æf-/ *adv* [Wa5;F;E] following in time or place; later; afterwards: *We arrived soon after.|"They lived happily ever after"* (phrase used in children's stories)

after[2] *prep* **1** following in time or order; later than; next: *We shall leave after breakfast.|They will return the day after tomorrow.|"after dark"* (SEU S.) **2** following continuously: *Year after year went by without hearing of him* **3** following in place or order: *He entered the room after his father.|Your name comes after mine in the list* **4** behind: *Shut the door after you* **5** as a result of; because of: *After the way he treated me I shall never want to see him again* **6** in spite of: *After all my care in packing it the clock arrived broken* **7** in the manner or style of: *It was a painting after the great master* **8** in accordance with: *You are a man after my own heart; we think and act alike in nearly all things* **9** in search of (esp. in order to punish); with a desire for: *The policeman ran after the thief.|They are after me.|"He's probably after you* (= with sexual intentions), *not that I blame him"* (SEU W.) **10** concerning; about: *Somebody asked after you today* **11** with the name of: *The boy was named after his uncle*

USAGE 1 **After** is properly used as a PREPOSITION (**after** *dinner*) or as a CONJUNCTION (**after** *he left*). In very informal English it is also used as an adverb with the same meaning as **afterwards** or **later**: *We had dinner and went home* **after.** Teachers and examiners do not like this use of after in an expression of time, though **after** (*adv*) can correctly be used when speaking of space or direction: *to*

follow **after.** 2 **Later** can be followed by **than**: *He stayed later than I did.* Note: *just* **after/afterwards|** IMMEDIATELY **after/afterwards|***a little/much* **later.**

after[3] *conj* at a later time than (when): *I found your coat after you had left the house*

after[4] *adj* [Wa5;A] **1** later in time: *He grew weak in after years* **2** in the back part, esp. of a boat: *the after DECK*

after- *prefix* [n→n] something that comes or happens after: AFTERBIRTH|*aftercare*

after all /,·· '·/ *conj, adv* **1** in spite of everything: *So you see I was right after all!* **2** it must be remembered (that): *I know he hasn't finished the work, but, after all, he is a very busy man*

af·ter·birth /'ɑːftəbɜːθ‖'æftərbɜrθ/ *n* [U] the material that comes out of a woman just after she has given birth to a child

af·ter·care /'ɑːftəkeə‖'æftər-/ *n* [U] the care or treatment given to someone after a period in hospital, prison, etc.

af·ter·ef·fect /'ɑːftərᵻfekt‖'æf-/ *n* [often *pl.*] an effect (usu. unpleasant) that follows some time after the cause or after the main effect

af·ter·glow /'ɑːftəgləʊ‖'æftər-/ *n* [usu. *sing.*] **1** the light that remains in the western sky after the sun has set **2** a pleasant feeling that remains after the main feeling

af·ter·life /'ɑːftəlaɪf‖'æftər-/ *n* **-lives** /laɪvz/ [usu. *sing.*] **1** the life that is thought by some people to follow death **2** the later part of one's life, esp. after a particular event

af·ter·math /'ɑːftəmæθ‖'æftər-/ *n* [usu. *sing.*] the result or period following a bad event such as an accident, storm, war, etc.: *Life was much harder in the aftermath of the war*

af·ter·noon /,ɑːftə'nuːn‖,æftər-/ *adj, n* **1** (of) the period between midday and sunset: *I shall sleep in the afternoon.|I shall have an afternoon sleep* **2** a rather late period (as of time or life): *She spent the afternoon of her life in the South of France*

af·ter·noons /,ɑːftə'nuːnz‖,æftər-/ *adv AmE* in the afternoon repeatedly; on any afternoon

af·ters /'ɑːftəz‖'æftərz/ *n* [P] *BrE infml* the part of a meal that comes after the main dish, usu. something sweet

af·ter·shave /'ɑːftəʃeɪv‖'æftər-/ also (*fml*) **after-shave lo·tion** /'·· · ,··/— *n* [U;C] a liquid with a pleasant smell for use on the face after shaving (SHAVE (1, 2))

af·ter·taste /'ɑːftəteɪst‖'æftər-/ *n* a taste that stays in the mouth after the food that caused it is no longer there

af·ter·thought /'ɑːftəθɔːt‖'æftər-/ *n* **1** an idea that comes later **2** something added later: *Surprisingly, the best part of the palace was an afterthought put on more than 20 years after the main part had been finished!*

af·ter·wards /'ɑːftəwədz‖'æftərwərdz/ *AmE* also **af·ter·ward** /'ɑːftəwəd‖'æftərwərd/— *adv* later; after that

a·gain /ə'gen, ə'geɪn‖ə'gen/ *adv* [Wa5] **1** once more; another time: *Please say that again.|You must never do that again* **2** back to the place, condition, position, etc., that one was in before: *She was ill but now she is well again* **3** besides; further: *That wasn't much; I could eat as much again* **4** in addition: *Then again, do not forget you have no experience of travelling.|Again, there is another matter to consider* **5** **again and again** also **time and time again**— very often; repeatedly **6 now and again** sometimes (but not very often); from time to time **7 once/yet again** one more time

a·gainst /ə'genst, ə'geɪnst‖ə'genst/ *prep* **1** in an opposite direction to: *We sailed against the wind* **2** in opposition to: *We will fight against the enemy.|*

Plate 20a Page showing the entries *afoot* to *against* in *Longman Dictionary of Contemporary English* (1978). Note the definitions in simple words, the treatment of polysemy, and the patterns for nouns and adjectives as well as verbs. [See p. 171.]

said or named before or above: *The aforesaid (person/people) was/were present at the trial*

a·fore·thought /əˈfɔːθɔːt‖əˈfor-/ *adj law* see MAL-ICE

a for·ti·o·ri /ˌeɪ fɔːtiˈɔːraɪ, -riˈ‖-fɔrtiˈor-/ *adv* [Wa5] *Lat* for a still stronger reason; with greater reason: *A man with a quick temper is, a fortiori, not a patient man*

a·fraid /əˈfreɪd/ *adj* **1** [F (*of*,3,5a)] full of fear; FRIGHTENED: *Don't be afraid of dogs.|She was afraid to excite him in case he became dangerous.|She was afraid that it would bite* **2** [F (*of*,3,5a)] worried or anxious about possible results: *Don't be afraid of asking for help* **3** [F5a,b] *polite* sorry for something that has happened or is likely to happen: *I am afraid I've broken your pen.|"Are we late?" "I'm afraid so."|"Are we on time?" "I'm afraid not."*

a·fresh /əˈfreʃ/ *adv* [Wa5] *fml* once more; again: *I've spoiled the painting and must do it afresh*

Af·ri·can¹ /ˈæfrɪkən/ *n* a person from Africa

African² *adj* of, from, or about Africa

Af·ri·kaans /ˌæfrɪˈkɑːns/ *n* [R;U] a language of South Africa very much like Dutch

Af·ri·ka·ner /ˌæfrɪˈkɑːnər/ *n* a South African whose native language is Afrikaans, esp. a descendant of the Dutch settlers of the 17th century

Af·ro /ˈæfrəʊ/ *n* **Afros** a hairstyle for men and women in which the hair is shaped into a large round bushy mass

Afro- *comb. form* **1** African; of Africa: *an Afro-American* **2** African and: *Afro-Asiatic*

aft /ɑːft‖æft/ *adv* [Wa5;F] *tech* in, near, or towards the back part (STERN) of a boat —opposite **fore**

af·ter¹ /ˈɑːftər‖ˈæf-/ *adv* [Wa5;F;E] following in time or place; later; afterwards: *We arrived soon after.|"They lived happily ever after"* (phrase used in children's stories)

after² *prep* **1** following in time or order; later than; next: *We shall leave after breakfast.|They will return the day after tomorrow.|"after dark"* (SEU S.) **2** following continuously: *Year after year went by without hearing of him* **3** following in place or order: *He entered the room after his father.|Your name comes after mine in the list* **4** behind: *Shut the door after you* **5** as a result of; because of: *After the*

bawl *(obj)* /£bɔːl, $baːl/ *v* to shout or sing in a very loud rough voice, or to cry loudly • *She bawled* **at** *me to sit down at once.* [I] • *The hall was full of schoolchildren bawling the school song.* [T] • *The two girls were now bawling* (= crying loudly) *in unison.* [I] • *Lindy came into the room, bawling* **her eyes out** (= crying loudly). [T]

bay COAST /beɪ/ *n* [C] a part of the coast where the land curves inwards so that the sea is surrounded by land on three sides • *We sailed into a beautiful, secluded bay.* • *Dublin Bay* • *the Bay of Naples*

bay SPACE /beɪ/ *n* [C] a partly enclosed or marked space • *Visitors must park their cars in the marked bays.* • *The books you need are in bay number five.* • A **bay window** is a window that sticks out from the outer wall of a house and usually has three sides. • See also SICKBAY. • PIC⟩ **Window**

bay CALL /beɪ/ *v* [I] (of dogs and WOLVES) to make a low and long deep cry repeatedly • *The* **hounds** *were baying as they drew closer to the fox.* • *(fig. disapproving) By now the crowd was* **baying for blood** (= wishing to see violence).

bay TREE /beɪ/ *n* [C] a small evergreen tree, the leaves of which are dried and used in cooking to add flavour • PIC⟩ **Herbs and spices**

bay HORSE /beɪ/ *n* [C] a reddish brown horse

bay PREVENT HARM /beɪ/ *n* [U] **hold/keep at bay** to prevent (someone or something unpleasant) from harming you • *She left the light on at night to keep her fears at bay.* • *Exercise can help keep fat at bay.*

bay CAUGHT /beɪ/ *n* [U] **at bay** (of an animal) about to be caught or attacked • *A frightened animal at bay can turn violent.*

bay·o·net /ˈbeɪ·ə·nət/ *n* [C] a long sharp blade fixed on to a RIFLE (= gun) • *Fix bayonets!* • *The soldiers were ordered to do bayonet practice.* • PIC⟩ **Knife**

bay·o·net *obj* /ˈbeɪ·nət/ *v* [T] **-t-** or **-tt-** • *He viciously bayoneted the straw dummy.*

bay·ou /ˈbaɪ·uː/ *n* [C] (in the southern US) an area of slowly moving water away from the main river

bazaar /£bəˈzaːr, $-ˈzaːr/ *n* [C] an area of small shops and people selling things esp. in the Middle East and India, or any group of small shops or people selling goods of the same type • *The tourists were bargaining/haggling for cheap consumer goods in the covered bazaar.* • *The wide pavement on one side of the street has become an open-air bazaar with stalls and street traders.* • *These weapons are available in international arms bazaars.* • *We spent the morning happily exploring an antiques bazaar.* • A **bazaar** is also an event where people sell things to raise money esp. for an organization which helps other people: *a Christmas bazaar* ○ *A group of friends organized bazaars and jumble sales to raise money for medical treatment for the children injured in the war.*

Plate 21 Detail showing the entries *bawl* to *bazaar* in the *Cambridge International Dictionary of English* (1995). Note the treatment of homographs in separate entries and the use of guidewords for each sense. [See p. 184.]

FCO, the /ˌef siː ˈəʊ/ noun the Foreign and Commonwealth Office: the official name for the British Foreign Office

FDA, the /ˌef diː ˈeɪ/ noun the Food and Drug Administration: a US government department that controls the food and drugs that are allowed to be sold

fealty /ˈfiːəlti/ noun [U] mainly literary loyalty that someone promised to a king or queen in the past

fear¹ /fɪə/ noun ★★★
1 [U] the feeling you have when you are frightened: *Edward knew it was dangerous, but he felt no fear.* ♦ **+of** *She eventually managed to overcome her fear of the dark.* ♦ **live in fear (of)** (=be afraid all the time) *Many people live in fear of violence.* ♦ **in fear** *Martin screamed in fear.* ♦ **be filled with fear** *I was suddenly filled with fear.* ♦ **shake/tremble with fear** *She was shaking with fear.*
2 [C] something bad or unpleasant that you are afraid might happen: *A meeting was set up to try to allay workers' fears.* ♦ **+about** *There are fears about the safety of the nuclear plant.* ♦ **+of** *This latest case has raised fears of an epidemic.* ♦ **+for** *He expressed fears for his missing wife's safety.* ♦ **+that** *Sandbags were placed along the shore amid fears that the lake would overflow.*
3 [C/U] the possibility that something bad will happen: **+of** *There's no fear of becoming bored in a place like this.* ♦ **+(that)** *I don't think there's any fear that that will happen.*

for fear of (doing) sth/for fear (that) in case you make something bad happen: *I didn't tell Susan about our meeting for fear of upsetting her.* ♦ *Scientists reject a total ban for fear it will undermine efforts to stop the spread of malaria.*

no fear *Br E informal* used for saying that you definitely do not intend to do something

put the fear of God into sb *informal* to make someone feel very frightened
→ STRIKE¹

Words frequently used with **fear**		
verbs	conquer, dismiss, overcome	1
	allay, alleviate, assuage, calm, dispel, ease, soothe	2

fear² /fɪə/ verb [T] ★★★
1 to feel worried and afraid that something bad will happen or has already happened: *The refugees fear persecution if they return to their own country.* ♦ *One person is still missing, feared dead.* ♦ **+(that)** *Health experts fear that a flu epidemic will hit Britain this winter.*
2 to feel afraid of someone or something because they might harm you: *He was hated and feared by his colleagues.* ♦ **fear to do sth** *neighbourhoods where police feared to go*

fear not *old-fashioned* used for telling someone not to worry

fear the worst (for) to feel worried that something very bad will happen or has already happened: *They were very late, and I was beginning to fear the worst.* ♦ *Local shopkeepers fear the worst if the new supermarket is built.*

I fear (that)/so/not *spoken formal* used for saying that you believe something bad has happened or might happen and that you are sad about it: *I fear that we may never know what really happened.* ♦ *'Will he help us?' 'I fear not.'*
→ NEVER

fear for phrasal vb [T] [**fear for sb/sth**] to feel worried about someone or something because you think something bad may happen to them or has happened to them: *Police now fear for the children, who have not yet been found.* ♦ *He fears for the future of the restaurant if customer numbers continue to fall.* ♦ **fear for sb's life** *Hundreds of innocent civilians fear for their lives.* ♦ **fear for sb's safety** *I fear greatly for their safety.*

fearful /ˈfɪəfl/ adj **1** frightened: *Fearful parents kept their children indoors.* ♦ **+(that)** *We're fearful that fighting will start up again.* ♦ **+of** *Fearful of another attack, civilians are fleeing the capital.* **2** *informal old-fashioned* used for emphasizing how bad someone or something is: *She's a fearful gossip.* ♦ *a fearful mess/muddle* **3** *old-fashioned* frightening —**fearfulness** noun [U]

fearfully /ˈfɪəfli/ adv **1** in a way that shows you are frightened: *She kept looking fearfully over her shoulder.*

2 *informal old-fashioned* extremely: *I'm fearfully busy at the moment.*

fearless /ˈfɪələs/ adj not afraid of anyone or anything. This word shows that you admire people like this. —**fearlessly** adv, **fearlessness** noun [U]

fearsome /ˈfɪəs(ə)m/ adj *mainly literary* very frightening

feasibility /ˌfiːzəˈbɪləti/ noun [U] the chances that something has of happening or being successful: **+of** *an investigation into the feasibility of building a new bridge* ♦ **a feasibility study** *A feasibility study found the site unsuitable for development.*

feasible /ˈfiːzəbl/ adj ★ possible or likely to succeed: *There seems to be only one feasible solution.* ♦ **it is feasible to do sth** *It is financially feasible to use coal as an energy source.* —**feasibly** adv

feast¹ /fiːst/ noun [C] **1** a large meal **1a.** a large meal for a lot of people, usually in order to celebrate something **1b.** a large amount of a particular food that you enjoy eating: *a feast of wild raspberries* **2** a large number of good, enjoyable, or interesting things to do or see: *a feast of football* **3** a religious festival such as Christmas or Passover: *the Feast of St Nicholas*

a feast for the eyes/ears something that is impressive and enjoyable to look at or hear

feast or famine a situation in which there is either far too much of something or not nearly enough

feast² /fiːst/ verb [I] to eat and drink a lot on a special occasion

feast your eyes on to take great pleasure in looking at someone or something

feast on phrasal vb [T] [**feast on sth**] to eat a lot of a particular food with enjoyment: *We feasted on strawberries and cream.*

feat /fiːt/ noun [C] something impressive that someone does: *feats of strength/endurance/skill* ♦ **be no mean feat** (=not be easy to achieve) *We've remained profitable for 27 years, and that's no mean feat.*

feather¹ /ˈfeðə/ noun [C] ★ one of the narrow tubes with thin soft hairs on each side that cover a bird's body **a.** [only before noun] filled with feathers: *a feather bed/pillow/duvet*

a feather in your cap an achievement that you can feel pleased and satisfied about

feather

feather² /ˈfeðə/ verb **feather your nest** to obtain money for yourself, usually by doing something dishonest

feather-bedding noun [U] the practice of employing more workers than you need in order to avoid making people unemployed

feather 'boa noun [C] a long thin piece of clothing made from feathers that women wear round their neck

feather-brained /ˈfeðə ˌbreɪnd/ adj *informal* very silly

feather 'duster noun [C] a stick with feathers at one end used for removing dust from things

feathered /ˈfeðəd/ adj covered with feathers or made from feathers

our feathered friends *humorous* birds

featherweight /ˈfeðəˌweɪt/ noun [C] a BOXER who weighs between 53.5 and 57 kilograms

feathery /ˈfeðəri/ adj **1** like a feather: *a feathery leaf/tail* **2** soft and delicate: *Light feathery snowflakes were falling.*

feature¹ /ˈfiːtʃə/ noun [C] ★★★
1 an important part or aspect of something: *Each room has its own distinctive features.* ♦ **safety features** *The latest model has a lot of new safety features.* ♦ **+of** *the natural features of the landscape*
2 [usually plural] a part of your face such as your eyes, nose, or mouth: *Her large blue eyes were her best feature.* ♦ *his handsome rugged features*
3 a newspaper or magazine article that concentrates on a particular subject: **+on** *a special feature on new children's books* ♦ **a feature writer/editor/article** *He now works as a freelance feature writer.* **3a.** a part of a

---

Plate 22 Page showing the entries *FCO, the* to *feature*, including *fear* noun and verb, in *Macmillan English Dictionary for Advanced Learners* (2002). Note that (in the published text) the most common words in the wordlist are printed in a different colour, the indication of frequency by little stars, and the box with frequent collocations. [See p. 187.]

Macmillan English Dictionary

Advanced Search

Search For :	dictionary
Category :	Selected categories
Part of speech :	Any part of speech
Grammar :	Any grammar
Region :	Any region
Style :	Any style
Frequency :	Any frequency
Subject :	Any subject

Clear Go

Search Result (32)

dictionary noun
walking dictionary
example noun
gazetteer noun
headword noun
intransitive adjective
italics noun
lemma noun
lexicography noun
lexicon noun
the OED
primary stress noun
reference book noun
rhotic adjective

You need a dictionary.
A really good French dictionary, that's what I'm after.
a dictionary with a list of irregular verbs at the back
a bilingual dictionary
the compilation of a dictionary
a dictionary of the English language
a German-English dictionary
a dictionary of art/music
the dictionary entry for the word 'play'
There was the usual rush to get the dictionary out on time.
a medical dictionary for the layman
I didn't know what 'loquacious' meant and had to look it up in a dictionary.
a monolingual dictionary
a pocket dictionary
The purpose of this dictionary is to help students of English.
It isn't really a dictionary – it's a sort of phrase book.
a Russian dictionary
a dictionary that is a touchstone for legal definitions

Plate 23 Screen showing search options from the CD-ROM version of *Macmillan English Dictionary for Advanced Learners* (2007). Note the indication of compounds, frequent collocations, phrases, etc. [See p. 372.]

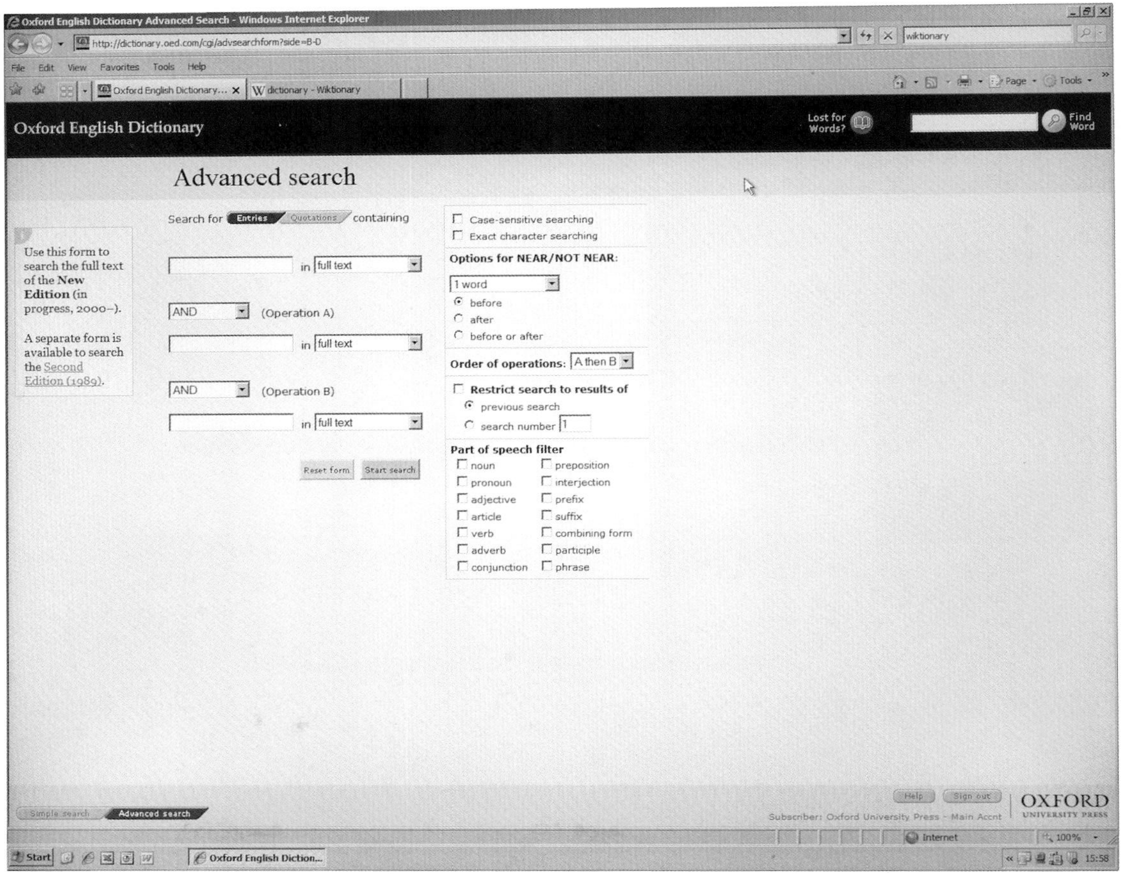

Plate 24 Screen showing search options from *The Oxford English Dictionary Online* (May 2009). There are so many options that it takes time and training to realize their full potential. [See p. 372.]

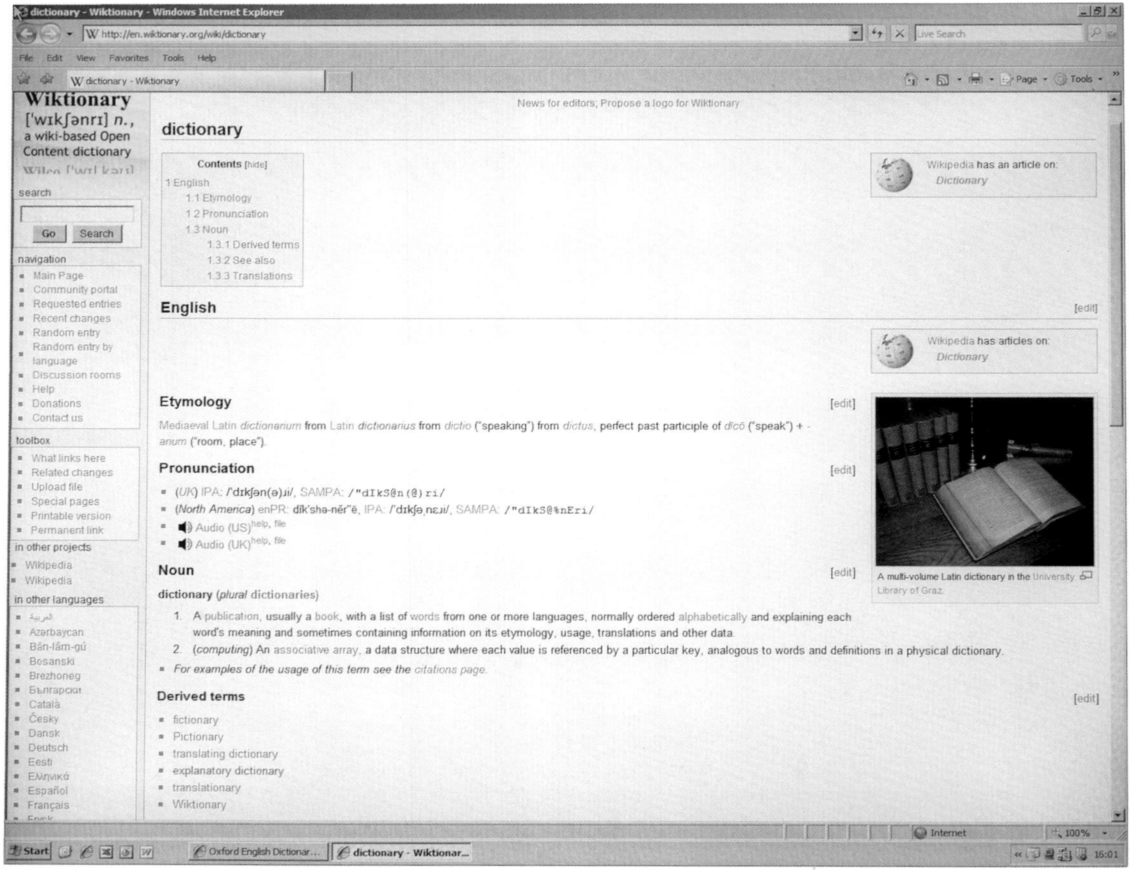

Plate 25 Entry *dictionary* from *Wiktionary* (June 2009). [See p. 374.]

Plate 26 The first OED Scriptorium was, from 1880 to 1885, at Mill Hill School in London, where James Murray was a schoolmaster. The picture shows Murray in the prime of life getting to grips with a batch of quotation slips, with the help of two unidentified assistants and one of his sons. [See p. 98.]

Plate 27 Murray built a new and more spacious Scriptorium in the garden of the house at 78 Banbury Road, Oxford where he and his family moved in 1885. This housed the vast and ever accumulating number of quotation slips and was where Murray worked on the OED until practically the day of his death in July 1915. [See p. 98.]

Plate 28 The 'Dictionary Room' in the Old Ashmolean (now the Museum of the History of Science), where Murray's fellow Editors and their staffs worked after 1901. Henry Bradley and William Craigie (both bearded) can be seen to the right of the picture; Charles Onions, the fourth Editor, is seated behind and between them. [See p. 99.]

Plate 29 The north-west corner of the OED office showing John Simpson, the editor of the *OED*, to the right and Edmund Weiner, the deputy editor, on the left. The contrast between the working environment in 2009 and Murray's a century earlier could hardly be greater. [See p. 113.]

dictionary is enough to make one feel that one belongs to the more prestigious social group: 'The dictionary is an emblematic object that testifies to the fact that one belongs to the class of those who possess knowledge' (Galisson 1983: 85).

> The dictionary ... acts as a rallying signal, a sign of recognition: by owning a large 'dictionnaire de langue' or consulting one I can—through a relation that is almost amorous and quasi-narcissistic (I recognize myself in the eyes of somebody else)—perceive that I belong to a certain circle, to a certain élite.   (Buzon 1979: 44)

The dictionary, Galisson (1983: 19) says in lyrical terms, is 'a locus where fantasies originate, a refuge for the imagination, a mythical bulwark against the hard realities of a world that is there to be conquered'.

7.1.3.5 The dictionary is an arbiter

The dictionary is often used to settle arguments, 'its authority is invoked, rightly or wrongly, to settle disputes' (Ilson 1985b: 1). It is, Pruvost (2002a: 119) says, an 'oracle', 'raised to the rank of unchallengeable reference'—with, however, a caveat: 'the oracle-dictionary' leaves its readers blind, as they cannot verify what it says. The dictionary does not bear contradiction or doubt, as word games on the radio or television demonstrate everyday. Dictionary entries 'are or ought to be statements of truth' (Pickett 2007: 53), which explains the violence of the reactions of the users when the dictionary does not say what they expect. Most dictionary users, Landau (1994a: 317) writes, 'are likely to believe that whatever they read in a dictionary is absolutely true'. Coleman Silk, a hero of Philip Roth's[10] says, talking about his father, a saloonkeeper: 'Back of the bar, he kept two things to help settle arguments among his patrons, a blackjack and a dictionary'.

This trust explains the role played by the dictionary in courts of justice, the 'dictionary as law' (Pruvost 2002a: 120–1). In 1893, in the USA Supreme Court, a dictionary was used to determine whether a tomato was a fruit or a vegetable 'in order to determine tariff' (Robinson 1982: 112).[11] Moon (1989: 60–1) mentions a case in Britain in 1988 when a tenant sued his landlord who had promised 'board and lodging'. *SOED* was used to determine the meaning of *board and lodging*: does a continental breakfast count as *board*? In another case the word to define was *souvenir*: is a tee shirt a souvenir? If so, it can be sold on Sundays (Harris 1981: 190–1). An *OED* lexicographer was recently asked to give evidence on the

---

[10] (2001), *The Human Stain* (London: Vintage): 84.
[11] The judgement can be found on the Internet at http://caselaw.lp.findlaw.com: Nix v. Hedden, 149 U.S. 304 (1893).

meaning of *foil*—for which the *OED* definition had been written in 1897![12] Other
words have been the object of court proceedings: *oleomargarine, vaccine, snuff,
rags, junk,* etc., often nouns for things that can be sold, exchanged, or rented, but
sometimes also more interesting words, as in the case of the gentleman sued by a
lady who accused him of having called her *chicken*: 'The man claimed no wrong
and called as his witness "Webster's dictionary".[13] The judge then consulted
"an antiquated copy of Webster", found the word did refer to a young woman,
and subsequently released the defendant' (Robinson 1982: 110). Pruvost (2002*a*:
120–1) mentions similar cases in France where the dictionary was used in law-
courts to determine the meaning of words like *jambe, empoisonnement,* or
Clochemerlesque.[14]

In all those cases, only one dictionary was used, probably a dictionary with a
prestigious name, perhaps an outdated copy, but the exact title was relatively
unimportant. In every case, it was what Moon (1989: 63) calls 'the UAD: the
Unidentified Authorizing Dictionary', a unique, mythical object that nobody has
ever seen but that everybody uses.[15]

Lexicographers do not relish the role of supreme authority. *OED* staff normally
decline invitations to take part in law cases.

If an enquirer writes to the *OED* in a legal argument, our most typical response is a
regretful refusal to comment, on the grounds that we claim no authority in matters of
law or legal interpretation. The courts do use our dictionaries in support of arguments
about the commonly accepted meaning of words, but the legal authority comes from the
court's decision, not from the dictionary's definition.[16]

7.1.3.6 The dictionary is eternal

The paper dictionary ages in proportion to its use: the binding tires, pages get
ruffled or torn or are found missing, marginal jottings are added, and coffee
spots ... and above all it soon ceases to be representative of the language of the
day. Yet many people think that what the dictionary says is timeless, that it will

---

[12] *OED News,* September 2004.

[13] The available documents do not say which 'Webster's dictionary' it was.

[14] 'leg', 'poisoning', 'Clochemerlesque' (typical of Clochemerle, from *Clochemerle,* 1934, a novel by
Gabriel Chevallier depicting petty struggles about the construction of a public toilet in a small French
village).

[15] In a study of the use of dictionaries by the American Supreme Court the dictionaries most often
used were *W3* (135 times), the *OED* (47 times), Webster's *American Dictionary* (27 times), and Samuel
Johnson's *Dictionary* (12 times)—the last two were authorities when the American constitution was
written (*DSNA Newsletter* (2005, 29/1: 5). On the use of Johnson's *Dictionary* in courts of justice, see
Hitchings (2005: 230).

[16] *OED News,* September 2004.

eternally be true. Pruvost (2002*a*: 121) calls this 'the atemporal dictionary'. 'For a large number of people the dictionary is a book that does not age, that has no right to age, whose words and definitions remain unchanged for ever' (Boulanger 1986: 96). Hence the tendency in many families to keep the same dictionary for decades, usually the one that was bought in one's adolescence, when one started secondary school. People tend to have one dictionary, once in their lives, once and for all. Hence also the fact that old dictionaries are sometimes offered for sale as if they were new. Littré's *Dictionnaire* is still sold, with minor adjustments, and many people are still impressed, and convinced that they are buying *the* dictionary.

Dictionary producers often do their best to hide the date of publication to encourage the users in their belief that the dictionary they are buying is eternal. But of course at the same time they have to persuade people to buy new dictionaries . . .

7.1.3.7 The dictionary is infallible on the meanings of words

Most people believe that there is, for every word, a 'true' meaning, that is stored somewhere, and that the job of the lexicographer is to find it and copy it in the dictionary.

It is commonly believed that there is one exact meaning for each word (hence questions like *What exactly does that word mean?*). This is paralleled by the social corollary of the *division of labour* (Putnam, 1975): if you do not know exactly what a word means, then somebody else, who is better educated and whose social role it is to do so, can tell you (hence the total confidence in dictionaries).   (Kleiber 1988: 5; see also 1990*a*: 27)

7.1.3.8 The dictionary has all the words of the language

Many people think that the dictionary has 'all the words of the language' (Urdang 1997: 77), and this is encouraged by the publishers and the publicity documents that they produce. When it appeared in 1961, W3 was advertised in a booklet entitled 'Hold the English language in your two hands'. Thus, if a word or phrase is not in the dictionary, the users think that it does not belong to the language, or even that, somehow, 'there is no such word' (Algeo 1989*a*: 32). For many people, the work of the lexicographer is to pick up the words that are there, somewhere, ready to be harvested: 'The lexicographer has nothing to do but arrange what he reads and hears in alphabetical order. . . . This idea is deeply rooted, even among the educated classes and the teaching professions' (Rey-Debove 1971: 39).

7.1.3.9 The dictionary has all the answers to all questions

'They that take a dictionary into their hands,' Johnson wrote in his *Preface*, 'have been accustomed to expect from it a solution of almost every difficulty.' The dictionary is seen as a repository of all knowledge—hence the phrase 'a walking dictionary', used of someone who knows everything. The main role of the dictionary is to sit somewhere within easy reach in every home, ready to answer any sort of question about anything, as Barnhart (1962: 61) said. 'The dictionary is the universe in alphabetical order' (Anatole France, in Matoré 1968: 36). The word *universal* was used in the titles of many dictionaries: by Bailey for the *Universal Etymological English Dictionary* (1721), by Dyche for the *Universal Dictionary of Arts and Sciences* (1753–54), by Scott for the *New Universal English Etymological Dictionary* (1755), by Barlow for *A Complete and Universal English Dictionary* (1772), by Barclay for his *Complete and Universal English Dictionary* (1774), by Worcester for the *Universal and Critical Dictionary of the English Language* (1846), by Wyld for the *Universal Dictionary of the English Language* (1932), for the *Chambers Universal Learners' Dictionary* (1980), for the *Longman New Universal Dictionary* (1982), etc. Some lexicographers may have believed it, as if they were 'enchanted by the idea of putting world and words in order or of revealing the hidden order of nature' (see Marello 1990: 1084), but it is only an illusion: 'the dictionary represents an illusion of totality, of an immobile order of things, of harmony. It seems to exhaust the universe and the lexis' (Rey 1970c: 14).

An interesting study by Galisson (1983) of a population of students in France and the USA illustrates the illusions of some users: he found that there was a gap between what the subjects imagined their dictionaries to be, the 'image', and what they actually did with them, the 'usage', and he noted that the one was only vaguely related to the other:

'Image' and 'usage' are not linked by a cause and effect relation . . . , they are not related by any logical link, in the sense that the interest of the subjects for their dictionaries (they buy dictionaries, take them along with them, keep them around and deem them indispensable to the learning of a foreign language, etc.) is as obvious as the fact that they do not know them very well, and do not use them as well as they could.   (Galisson 1983: 84)

In other words, the dictionary is useful because it *can* be used as much as by the fact that it *is* used. It is thought to contain the answers, and that is reassuring enough.

The dictionary . . . exerts . . . a kind of attraction/fascination to which the users are submitted but which they do not explain. This underlines the fact that the dictionary is different from all other books, that it is a 'charm' which is thought to possess almost magical powers that protect against the disturbing opacity of the world, quasi-mysterious powers that enable the users to understand other people and to be understood by them.

(Galisson 1983: 25)

One of the consequences of these naive ideas about the dictionary is that for many people all dictionaries, old or new, linguistic or encyclopedic, good or bad, are the same. Most dictionary users have no idea of the different kinds of dictionaries available on the market or what each kind has to offer (Kirkpatrick 1985: 7). Users 'will look for the encyclopedic definition of *hyperthyroidism* in *Petit Robert* and the uses of the verb *voir*[17] in *Petit Larousse*' (Pruvost 2002a: 122).

My students—indeed my friends, family and some of my colleagues—will refer to the *Oxford Dictionary* with no sense of the number and range of dictionaries that might be described by that title. They all possess desk dictionaries but cannot tell you the publishers or the date. They have no sense of how a *Webster's* compares with a *Collins*, or with a *Chambers*. Getting them to discriminate between dictionaries, let alone evaluate their respective characteristics and quality, is like trying to teach someone with no sense of taste the difference between claret and blackcurrant juice.   (Brewer 2006: 141)

However at odds with reality they may be, dictionary myths are evidence that the dictionary is a valued object. It is respected because it is a big book, because it is full of information, because it is beautiful, because it is expensive, because it is handy, because it is useful, because it has all the answers, because it materializes the language and the culture, because everybody has one and because it procures a feeling of belonging to the best part of a linguistic community.

The faith of the users in their dictionaries varies from country to country: it may be extreme in the USA, where it verges on 'lexicographicolatry', Algeo (1989a: 29) writes. It also varies according to social class: the more educated users are less likely to treat their dictionary as the 'UAD': 'The working classes tend to trust the dictionary more than the middle or lower middle classes and more than the teaching professions' (Descamps and Vaunaize 1983: 99–100). And it varies with time. Murray himself thought as early as 1903 that the 'people who knew nothing about Dictionaries' were disappearing:

That there are dictionaries *and* dictionaries, or that, sad to say, dictionaries differ, had not yet dawned upon their apprehension. But of late years the merits and excellencies of rival dictionaries have been thundered upon us by daily papers from *The Times* downward, so loudly and so long, that the number of these ingenuous people must be greatly diminished.[18]

---

[17] 'see'.   [18] Lecture on dictionaries, *OED News*, June 2003.

Modern societies are probably less naive, more realistic, about many things, including dictionaries. Hausmann (1984: 37) saw 'an overall awakening to the phenomenon of the dictionary', a gradual realization of what the dictionary really is, and Quemada (1987: 242) agreed:

The image of the dictionary is now clearly being debunked among the general public—through the language games that use it as an arbiter for the learners of French and through the generalization of its use in schools, where it has become a sort of manual of vocabulary. Having become the object of daily discussion, if not of critical assessment, the dictionary is no longer thought to be infallible, as it was not so long ago. More and more dictionary users now know that there is no such thing as an all-purpose dictionary and that it is important to use dictionaries properly in order to make the most of them.

Hausmann (1986: 109) takes this new awareness as a good sign. He thinks that the more enlightened the public is the better dictionaries will be: 'Only when the public knows as much—if not more—about dictionaries as the publishers will the market be able to exert pressure on the publishers to improve dictionary quality'. But this is debatable. It is clear that the image of the dictionary has changed over the last decades, but this may be a sign of an increased wariness, a general distrust of authority, and it may be destructive for the very existence of the dictionary.

7.2 THE SCIENTIFIC STUDY OF DICTIONARY USE

In the late 1960s, the need was felt to go beyond empirical observations and to study in a more rigorous fashion the populations of dictionary users and the processes of dictionary consultation.

A preparatory sociological study, carried out jointly with a 'market' study, would make it possible to determine more precisely the nature of the public and to cater to their needs more adequately: thus the arrangement of entries, the choice of words, the type of definition, etc. could be adapted to a certain social class, or rather to a certain techno-logical category.   (Matoré 1968: 19)

Some were not impressed, thinking that this was a wild-goose chase, 'a fine exercise in ESP, wishful thinking, and ethnocentric projection' (Forgue 1981: 93), a huge enterprise that would turn out not to have been worth the effort. Landau (1999: 252) denied 'that there is any prototypical "user" of NSD's, and the assertion that there is, or that...dictionary editors know what "the user" knows or doesn't know is pure hubris'.

The study of who uses dictionaries, what for and how began in the 1970s, and there are now so many studies that they cannot all be mentioned: Tono (1998) and Dolezal and McCreary (1999) mention more than a hundred.[19] Only the more meaningful results will be mentioned here.

7.2.1 Questions of method

Most studies of dictionary use have been about dictionaries of English. The dictionaries under scrutiny have been monolingual or bilingual or bilingualized, in various combinations. Sometimes they were real dictionaries, sometimes just dictionary entries compiled for the purpose of the experiment. The subjects were adults, adolescents, or children, native or non-native speakers, often students of various levels and specializations, sometimes teachers or translators. Much of the research has been carried out by academics and has been concerned with the use of dictionaries in the context of learning English, and the researchers have tended to use their students, a captive audience.

The early studies of dictionary use were carried out by means of questionnaires, either distributed to the subjects *in presentia* or sent to them or to their teachers by post. The advantages of questionnaire studies are well known: the researcher can study a large number of subjects and keep a record of the study that can be analysed at length, with results that can be added up and shown in statistical form. But the method has been criticized, as it had been in dialectology a few decades before, particularly if the questionnaire is not filled in in the presence of the researcher. It was pointed out that the more subjects there are the less the researcher knows about them and that one can never be sure how much the subjects understand of the questions. Also, more generally, it was said that the results are more representative of what the subjects think they should answer in the circumstances than of what they really think or do.

Are subjects saying here what they do, or what they think they do, or what they think they ought to do, or indeed a mixture of all three?...Do we not, on this basis, arrive at a consensus on how subjects are likely to behave when faced with a particular questionnaire, rather than authentic data on what they use the dictionary for?   (Hatherall 1984: 184)

Hatherall is right, but this does not invalidate studies based on questionnaires (Lew 2002*a*): in linguistics as in biology, anthropology, archaeology, or paleontology, one knows that the thing being observed is modified by the act of observation, the Observer's Paradox (Labov 1972: 90), and questionnaires can

---

[19] See also Tono (2001) and Wingate (2002).

be designed to expose the differences between reality and opinion, image and usage, as they were in sociolinguistics.

There are alternative ways of studying dictionary use. One is, using the model of dialectologists and sociolinguists, direct observation, where the behaviour of the subjects is observed, typically when they are performing a task—'the only reliable method of collecting data on dictionary user behaviour' according to Hatherall (1984: 184). Another is the 'think-aloud' procedure (Wingate 2002: 20), where the subjects are asked to verbalize what they do at the same time as they do it. The price to pay in both of these methods is a far smaller number of subjects, sometimes only two or three per researcher.

Most of the later studies have used a combination of different methods, and some have allowed a comparison of what the subjects say they do and what they actually do. A recent development is the use of the Internet to collect information (Nesi 1999*b*), as Macmillan has recently done for the preparation of *MEDAL2*.

It is difficult to arrange existing studies in neat stacks, as most use more than one method and deal with more than one issue (McCreary and Dolezal 1999: 110). The following review will first look at studies of the reference needs of the users, then at studies of their skills, or what happens during the consultation process, and finally at studies of how useful dictionaries are for reading and for learning the language. In each group the studies will be arranged chronologically. Some studies may be mentioned more than once.

7.2.2   Studies of reference needs

7.2.2.1   What do the users look up?

The study of reference needs aims at answering a very simple question: What do the users look up in a dictionary, what sort of entries, and what sort of information? In 1979, Tomaszczyk (1979: 103) deplored the absence of such studies: 'Of the main factors determining the shape of popular commercial dictionaries the needs of the audience they are designed for have thus far received very little attention'. But there have been many since then, of course, all studies of what the users do look up rather than of what the users need to look up.

Barnhart's study (1962) was the first. He sent a questionnaire to 108 teachers in 99 higher education establishments in 27 American states, representing 56,000 native English-speaking students in freshman year. He sums up his conclusions in a few lines:

The teachers were asked to rate six types of information commonly given in college dictionaries according to their importance to the college freshman. Their replies indicate that the college freshman uses his dictionary most frequently for meaning and almost as frequently for spelling. Pronunciation is third with synonym studies and lists, usage notes, and etymologies far behind.   (Barnhart 1962: 162–3)

Quirk (1973) questioned a population of 220 British university students. They declared that they used their monolingual dictionaries above all for meaning (67 per cent), occasionally for spelling (26 per cent), other uses such as etymology, pronunciation, etc. accounting for only 13 per cent and games 7 per cent (1973: 80).[20] Their families, the students said, used dictionaries for meaning (37 per cent), spelling (26 per cent), and games (17 per cent).

Greenbaum *et al.* (1984) emulated Quirk's study in the USA with a population of 240 university students. They owned or consulted more dictionaries than the British students, more than one dictionary each, they used their dictionaries more frequently, and they were more interested in spelling. Also, there were fewer differences between the use of dictionaries by the students and by their families, oddly enough in the country where there are family dictionaries. But on the whole, the results were very similar to Quirk's.

Tomaszczyk's study (1979) was the first to investigate the needs of foreign learners of English. It was carried out in Poland and the USA with university students of foreign languages, teachers, and professional translators, in all 449 persons of sixteen different language backgrounds. The subjects used their dictionaries, bilingual and monolingual, for meaning (85.4 per cent), synonyms (74 per cent), spelling (72 per cent), pronunciation (65 per cent), grammar for expression (59 per cent), and etymology (19 per cent). The types of lexical item most often consulted were idioms (72 per cent) and taboo words (45 per cent). The subjects preferred their bilingual dictionaries when they needed information for expression, whatever their level of competence in the foreign language, although the more advanced subjects also used monolingual dictionaries for that purpose. All deplored the absence of proper names, of pictorial illustrations, and of specialized terms. The more advanced learners were more satisfied with their monolingual than with their bilingual dictionaries (Tomaszczyk 1979: 116).

I (Béjoint 1981*a*) investigated the use of dictionaries in a population of 122 French university students of English. Almost all owned and used their monolingual dictionaries, although they only bought those that were recommended by their teachers; in fact, they hardly knew any others. The subjects were generally more satisfied with their monolingual than with their bilingual dictionaries, as in Tomaszczyk's study. However, they did not use all the information that the dictionaries contained, and many were not even aware that it was there. The front matter

---

[20] The percentages have been calculated from Quirk's figures.

was hardly ever read, and less than half of the subjects declared that they used the coding of syntactic patterns. The monolingual dictionaries were used for translating from English to French (86 per cent), reading (60 per cent), and translating from French to English (58 per cent). The percentages by type of information were: meaning (87 per cent),[21] syntactic patterns (53 per cent), synonyms (52 per cent), spelling (25 per cent), pronunciation (25 per cent), language varieties (19 per cent), and etymology (5 per cent). The lexical elements that were most often looked up were idioms (68 per cent looked them up very often), encyclopedic words (55 per cent sometimes), culture-specific words[22] (53 per cent sometimes), abbreviations (49 per cent sometimes), and slang words (40 per cent sometimes). In contrast, 66 per cent never looked up common words, 47 per cent never looked up function words, 45 per cent never looked up taboo words, perhaps because the students were reluctant to admit—especially to their teachers—that they looked up such words in their dictionaries. The subjects deplored the absence of technical and scientific words, slang words, and Americanisms (in British dictionaries), probably to read modern literature. They found the entries for the more frequent words too long, too complex, and divided up according to criteria that they did not understand. Finally, the students did not feel the need for other microstructural information such as word frequency, collocations, or pictures.

Herbst and Stein (1987) noted that most of their 160 first-year German university students of English and 60 teachers of English did not even know that syntactic patterns were coded in their dictionaries.

A study of dictionary use by native speakers in Britain carried out by Longman was reported on by Summers (1988: 113–14). The conclusions were:

[L]ooking up meaning was actually the most frequent use for the dictionary in most households, with checking for correct spelling coming second. Reference to the dictionary for word meanings was not for common words, but 'hard words':

1. words commonly confused or misused (e.g. *aggravate* being used to mean *annoy*, instead of *make worse*; *infer* being used instead of *imply*);
2. encyclopedic words—from science and technology, politics, economics, etc.;
3. new words (e.g. *rate-capping*, *spreadsheet*);
4. rare or obsolete words (*abigail*, *pellucid*).

The dictionary, in our research project at least, was more commonly referred to for word games and to settle family arguments than for schoolwork or individual interest. Clarification about word meaning appears to be the main native-speaker requirement.

---

[21] The figures represent the numbers of students who placed the information among the first three when asked which information they looked up most often.

[22] I provided examples, but could not be sure that the subjects understood the question.

The use of dictionaries in households for word games is consistent with the findings of Barnhart and Quirk, and it was confirmed later: 'A recent survey for the Oxford University Press suggests that "a third of all dictionary use today is by people seeking help in word games"' (Augarde 1999: 352).

Bareggi (1989) found that her subjects, 70 Italian students of English, were interested in the information on expression provided by learners' dictionaries: 'students look up not only meaning and spelling but also information on the usage and collocations of words' (1989: 176). Nuccorini (1992) later produced similar results.

The study by Atkins *et al.* (Atkins and Varantola 1997, 1998) was the largest study of dictionary use ever. It took several years and questioned about 1,100 students of English in seven countries of Europe, with four native languages, Spanish, Italian, French, and German, in decreasing order of the number of subjects. The results showed that more than half the subjects owned at least one dictionary, that 60 per cent had never had any instruction on how to use it (the worst being the French), that bilingual dictionaries were used much more often than monolingual dictionaries, and that monolinguals were mostly used for reception.

7.2.2.2 Dictionaries are for meaning and spelling

The results of studies of the needs of dictionary users are difficult to compare, but the conclusions are clear.

1. Monolingual dictionaries are mostly used for meaning, particularly of rare words, and secondly for spelling.
2. Monolingual dictionaries are often used in families for word games.
3. The entries for frequent words, especially function words, are hardly ever consulted, even by foreign students.
4. Information on expression in monolingual dictionaries is not used much, particularly when it is in coded form. Foreign students, who need it most, prefer using their bilingual dictionaries for that purpose. In fact, information on expression is probably even less used than the results indicate, because some subjects probably feel guilty about not using the dictionary as they were instructed to. As a consequence, foreign learners do not find learners' dictionaries more useful than dictionaries for native speakers.
5. The front matter on how to use the dictionary is rarely consulted.
6. The subjects are not clear about what other types of information they would like their dictionaries to carry.

These conclusions may disappoint both lexicographers and teachers, but they are not really surprising: the dictionary is used as a tool for quick and easy reference, for simple answers to simple questions.

7.2.2.3 The lexicographer's paradox

The studies of reference needs show that information on frequent, polysemous words and information for encoding are hardly ever consulted. Frequent words are almost never looked up, perhaps because the users think they know them and probably also because the entries are too long and complex; encoding information is rarely sought, because it is too difficult to understand and perhaps also because people are not always conscious of gaps in their knowledge: a gap in syntax can exist for a long time without being detected or hampering communication, as it is always possible to choose an alternative formulation. Thus lexicographers are faced with a paradox: dictionaries are used almost exclusively as collections of difficult words with their definitions, while the information that takes most time to prepare is the least consulted. 'Users are apparently not much concerned about the things to which lexicographers devote their attention' (Algeo 1989*a*: 31). One may therefore wonder whether the efforts to compile complex entries are justified. Some metalexicographers think they are not:

> [L]exicographers consistently, or perhaps persistently, put into dictionaries certain kinds of information for which the vast majority of users have no need and would not miss if they were not included in dictionaries. Into this category would come grammatical information including part-of-speech labels, etymology, and perhaps pronunciation.
>
> (Jackson 1988: 198–9)

The solutions are obvious: either omit from dictionaries the entries and kinds of information that are never consulted, or find ways to make the users consult them. But both are difficult to carry out: the former goes against the deep-rooted opinion that a dictionary should contain 'all' the words of a language and as much information as possible on each word, and the latter may be unrealistic.

Further research is needed on the reasons why some items of information are consulted and others are not. The Internet provides publishers and lexicographers with a means of collecting huge amounts of data. With online dictionaries, it is even possible to keep a log of all look-ups, who consults the dictionary, when, on what, how long the consultation takes, and with what results (De Schryver and Joffe 2004). De Schryver *et al.* (2006) addressed the correlation between the frequency of a word in a corpus and the number of times the word is looked up. In an English-Swahili dictionary, the article *the*, the most frequent form in the English corpus, was ranked twelfth in the number of look-ups, *of*, second in frequency was ranked 41st, *was*, tenth, was 258th in look-ups, etc. The authors concluded that it was 'impossible to "predict" which words will be of interest to the dictionary user' (2006: 78), at least on the basis of frequency.

It would also be interesting to determine what the users need when they look up particular categories of lexical items, and even particular words: intuitively, one can say that most users looking up *inexhaustible* or *focused* will be interested in spelling, that for *Canutism* it will be etymology, for *serendipity* meaning, for *different* syntax, etc. Subjects asked to write sentences after having consulted dictionary definitions (see below) tend to make the same errors on the same words (Maingay and Rundell 1987: 133–4). For *reminisce*, most of the errors are syntactic: 'We stayed all morning reminiscing our childhood'; for *debris*, the errors are semantic: 'He always gives the debris of the meal to the dog'; and for *new-fangled*, the errors are connotative: 'My brother is crazy about new-fangled machines'.

[M]any of the pitfalls are in fact highly predictable and to some extent preventable, and . . . some progress can be made towards dealing with them if the defining process is informed by an analysis of each headword on the basis of its semantic, stylistic, syntactic, and collocational features. . . . This in turn argues for considerable flexibility and diversity, both in the way the various features of a word are distributed throughout the entry, and in the degree to which individual features may be singled out for special emphasis.

(Maingay and Rundell 1987: 135)

More research is needed with dictionaries that are different from those that are on offer. The users tend to think that the dictionaries they know are the only ones that exist or even that can be produced, as if there was a direct implication between the linguistic facts and their lexicographic representation, and researchers should imagine new types of dictionaries to test whether the users like them: without definitions, with only corpus lines, with discursive explanations, with information in tabular form, etc. Lastly, more research is also needed on what type of reference tool is best for a given type of information: dictionary (bilingual, monolingual, paper, electronic), grammar, encyclopedia, or search engine on the Internet.

7.2.3 *Studies of how dictionaries are used*

7.2.3.1 The look-up process

The prototypical situation of dictionary use is when the user is reading and needs to find out the meaning of a word.

Recall what happens when you interrupt your reading to look up a word. The continuity of your thought is broken, but the context in which the unfamiliar word occurred must be kept in mind while you search: first you search for the dictionary itself, then you search through the dictionary alphabetically for the word you want. Then, once you have found your word, you may still have to make several decisions: first, you may have to choose among two or three different entries on the basis of part of speech; next, within the chosen entry, you may have to decide among several alternative senses. And, finally, the context of your original passage must be compared with a succession of contexts in the dictionary until a best guess can be made about the intended sense. Context-matching is a high-level cognitive skill. It is hardly surprising that children have trouble finding and understanding the information that they need.   (Miller and Gildea 1985: np; see also 1987: 97)

The different operations of dictionary consultation can be listed as follows, in chronological order (see also Scholfield 1982: 186–93; Tono 2001: 97–115):

1. identifying the problem;
2. deciding whether to use a dictionary or another reference tool;
3. choosing the appropriate dictionary;
4. determining where in the dictionary the problem is most likely to be treated (A–Z section, back matter, etc.);
5. guessing what form the word will be listed under;
6. finding the word as a headword or in an entry, choosing among homographs if necessary;
7. choosing among the different meanings of a polysemous word if necessary;
8. finding the part of the entry or sub-entry that answers the question;
9. interpreting the information that has been found;
10. integrating the information into the text being read.

Experimental studies of the look-up process have addressed such questions as: What happens when a user opens a dictionary? How does the user manage to find what is needed in the macrostructure and in the microstructure? Is there anything in dictionary design or in the contents that slows down the consultation process or makes the users go astray?

How do they interpret what they find? Do they read the whole entry or only the parts in roman type? Do they skip definitions ..., and subconsciously try to extract information from the examples? Do they skip all the words and abbreviations that they do not understand? ... How good are they at knowing when they should be turning to their dictionary? Does being taught 'dictionary skills' improve their chances of successful dictionary use?   (Atkins 1998: 1)

This is a difficult area for research, because the details of the look-up process vary according to the type of information being sought, the type of dictionary, the particular dictionary, the user, the circumstances, etc.: 'Nobody knows how a

Latin–French dictionary is read by a class which is sweating over Tacitus, in what way the *Littré* was useful to the writer around 1900, nor how a peasant family can decipher the dog-eared pages of an old copy of *Larousse*' (Rey 1977: 95).

7.2.3.2 General look-up strategies

Mitchell (1983) observed 94 schoolchildren using monolingual English dictionaries when reading a text. She found that they did not use context very well, they did not understand POS distinctions, they often chose the wrong homonym, they chose a dictionary entry or sub-entry too rapidly and as a consequence they often hit upon the wrong answer. An interesting observation was that the children often adopted a 'negative choice strategy': they proceeded by elimination, eventually choosing what was not explicitly rejected by the dictionary.

Tono (1984) noticed that his 402 Japanese students tended to avoid reading whole entries, especially long ones, if they could, and to stop reading as soon as they saw something that looked vaguely like what they were looking for. As a consequence, they often chose the first solution that their dictionary proposed, as long as it was not too obviously wrong, as in Mitchell's study. This led Rundell (1999: 39) to evoke 'the depressing yet plausible notion that less skilled users typically search no further than the first part of an entry'. Alphonse Allais[23] would have said: If they read only the first part, the solution is to write entries with only first parts . . . The qualities of a dictionary that the subjects seemed to value most were clarity and brevity—meaning, of course, giving the answer they needed and only the answer they needed. However, Tono showed that English majors were better dictionary users than non-specialists and that those who had been taught how to use dictionaries obtained better results than those who had not. This was confirmed in his later study (2001) and by Kipfer (1985) with American students.

The Hebrew students in Neubach and Cohen (1988) also tended not to go beyond the first part of the entry, they found the definitions difficult and often failed to find the answers they were looking for. The subjects in Müllich (1990) found their French dictionary too difficult, particularly the definitions. They also tended to choose what they could understand rather than what was appropriate and they read only the beginning of the entry.

Wingate (2002) also found that her students read only the beginning of an entry, did not know where to look up multiword items and tended to take a vaguely familiar word in a definition for a synonym of the word that they were

---

[23] Who may be the author of the well-known aphorism: 'Cities should be built in the country, where the air is so much purer'.

looking for, a source of errors first pointed out by Miller and Gildea (1987; see below) that has come to be known as the 'kidrule' strategy.

Atkins *et al.* (Atkins and Varantola 1997, 1998) tried to determine the rate of success of dictionary look-ups. They noted that each problem required an average of almost two look-ups ('1000 look-ups in trying to solve 574 problems'), with only 57 per cent of all searches being followed by only one look-up, 25 per cent requiring two look-ups, etc. And yet, 'there were no naive dictionary users' among the group, which was 'very unrepresentative' (Atkins and Varantola 1997: 3). Some studies have suggested that success in look-up might be correlated with how close the native language of the subjects was to the language being learnt (Ard 1982; Nesi 1994), but this has not been confirmed.

7.2.3.3 Understanding the definitions

In many studies, the subjects said that they found the definitions hard to understand: native-speaker students in England (Quirk 1973) or in the USA (Greenbaum *et al.* 1984), foreign students and teachers in Poland (Tomaszczyk 1979), Japanese students (Baxter 1980), German high-school students of English and French (Müllich 1990).

Miller and Gildea (1985) carried out a study of dictionary use in which young American children were given words that they did not know, together with their dictionary definitions, and were then asked to use the words in sentences of their own. One of the words was *chaste*, with the entry:

1. innocent of unlawful sexual intercourse 2. celibate 3. pure in thought and act, modest 4. severely simple in design or execution, austere

The 7-year-old subjects produced sentences such as 'The amoeba is a chaste animal', probably after reading definition 1, and 'The plates were still chaste after much use', after reading definition 3 or 4. Another example was *repudiate*:

1. cast off; disown: 'to repudiate a son' 2. refuse to accept; 'to repudiate a doctrine' 3 . refuse to acknowledge or pay: 'to repudiate a debt'

One child wrote 'The rocket repudiate [*sic*] into the sky', probably as a result of reading only the beginning of definition 1. Another example was 'Mrs Morrow stimulated the soup', because *stir up* was in the definition of *stimulate* (Miller and Gildea 1987: 97). The experimenters explained that the subjects in such a situation will seize any word that they know in a definition, decide that it is what they are looking for, and thus bring the consultation process to an end. The children 'repeatedly assume that some familiar word in a definition can be substituted for the unfamiliar word it defines' (Miller 1984: 462). The main cause was that the dictionary did not provide enough context, Miller said. A later example of this 'kidrule strategy' is 'My mother's plummet is 130 pounds' because *plummet* was defined as '1 a plumb, 2 a weight' (Bogaards 2003a: 32). It has also been observed in older subjects (Nesi 2000a: 92; Wingate 2002).

Yet, Miller and Gildea's experiment was unfair: the dictionaries they used were for adults, not children, and the definitions used difficult words such as *celibate*, *austere*, *disown*, *doctrine*, or *acknowledge* and even concepts that are not normally known to a child. The results would have been different with other words, and probably better with the same words illustrated by definitions drawn from children's or learners' dictionaries. Above all, the task was not representative of any real situation of dictionary use: looking up an unknown word in a dictionary does not normally mean that one will be able to use it. No definition, no dictionary contains all the information that is necessary for appropriate expression (see below, 8.2.6.1).[24] The study only confirms that reading a dictionary definition is not enough for anyone to grasp the full meaning of a word, let alone be able to use it appropriately. It may be enough for the word to begin to enter the passive vocabulary, but certainly not the active vocabulary.

7.2.3.4 Where do the users look for multiword items?

In my 1981 study (Béjoint 1981a), one of the questions was aimed at determining where the users looked for multiword items, compounds, phrasal verbs, and idioms. The results, in decreasing order of number of responses, were that *artificial insemination* would be sought at *insemination* by 93 per cent of the subjects, *boil down to* at *boil* (81 per cent), *false alarm* at *alarm* (80 per cent), *magnetic tape* at *tape* (79 per cent), *come down with* at *come* (71 per cent), *lose sight of* at *sight* (65 per cent), *rid of* at *rid* (58 per cent), and *fountain pen* at *pen* (58 per cent) (1981a: 218). Clearly, the subjects tended to expect nominal compounds to be treated in the entry for the head[25] of the compound. This means that they are aware of the existence of a head, when there is one: the users know, for example, that *magnetic tape* is a 'kind of tape'. Two results indicate that the strategies may depend on the native language of the users: for *ice cream*, the answers were about

---

[24] Fillmore (in Atkins and Rundell 2008: 409) gives the example of a definition of *carrion* as 'the rotting meat of a dead animal': it is enough for decoding but for encoding one needs to know that it is 'the word used for the food of scavengers'.

[25] The head of a multiword item is the word that governs its relation with the other elements of the sentence. It is the same part of speech as the multiword item and often its hypernym: for example, the head of *magnetic tape* is *tape*, of *ice cream* is *cream*, etc. But many multiword items do not have heads, and there are many unclear cases.

50 per cent for *ice* and 50 per cent for *cream*, because for French speakers *ice cream* is a kind of *glace* ('ice', but also 'ice cream'), and also a kind of *crème* ('cream'); in the case of *living room*, more students said they would look it up under *living* than under *room*, probably because in French a living room is referred to as *le living*. For verbal compounds, the results were not clear, and for all items the function words were ignored. The intuition of the relative frequency and polysemy of the elements may also play a part in the decision: the more frequent and polysemous a word is the longer the entry will be, and consequently the more difficult to consult.

Tono (1987) had different results with his Japanese students: in some cases such as *ministering angel* or *disorderly house* they tended to go for the unfamiliar word. In Bogaards (1990) the French students tended to go for the least frequent word and the Dutch students seemed to prefer to use the noun wherever possible— perhaps a consequence of the differences in the lexicographic traditions (see Rey-Debove 1989c: 933). Bogaards (1990: 101) himself recommends caution: 'Given that this is a new area for research, and that the surveys described in the present article are only valid up to a point, the preceding conclusions can only be provisional. Many questions remain, that await an answer'.

Atkins and Varantola (1998) did not find any correlation between native language and look-up tendencies for multiword items. Tono (2001: 116–42) concluded that the users go for the word with restricted combinability and for the word that is most unfamiliar to them.

7.2.3.5 Conclusions: are dictionaries used competently?

The main conclusion that emerges from the studies of how dictionaries are used is that look-ups often fail, roughly 50 per cent of the time. There are several possible reasons: the appropriate information is not in the dictionary, or the users cannot find it, or they do not recognize it, or they misinterpret it, or they misuse it, extending or restricting it beyond what the dictionary allows (Thumb 2004: 32). The studies showed that the users often try to read as little as they can of the entry. Also, many users find the definitions difficult to understand, even in their native language. On the brighter side, dictionaries are used more competently by the more competent users, and by those who have been taught how to use them.

The general conclusion is, again, that dictionary users do not make full use of the wealth of information in dictionaries. When they consult a dictionary, they are typically engaged in some linguistic activity, usually reading a text, and they do not want this activity to be interrupted for too long. The dictionary may be a useful tool but it must also be a book that can be consulted quickly. Nielsen (2008) proposes the notion of 'lexicographical costs' for the ratio between the time and effort to retrieve information from the dictionary and the benefit gained from that piece of information. Clearly, a dictionary will succeed if the lexicographical costs of consulting it are kept to a minimum.

7.2.4 Studies of how dictionaries help

7.2.4.1 Is there a better definition style?

Some studies of dictionary use have aimed at determining what type of dictionary, what type of technique for the arrangement of the macrostructure, for the definitions, etc. the users prefer. Another aim is to determine whether these preferences coincide with what the lexicographers and the linguists think is preferable. And yet another is to see whether the preferred solutions are also the more effective.

There have been many studies of the preferences of the users in defining style. They all concluded that the users preferred the definitions in learners' dictionaries to the definitions in native speakers' dictionaries. MacFarquhar and Richards' (1983) study of non-native speakers of English in Hawaii, for example, showed a strong preference for the definitions of *LDOCE* and judged the definitions in *WNW* least satisfactory, those of *ALD* being in between. The study, however, did not investigate whether this preference led to better performance. Among the definitions in learners' dictionaries, some studies showed that FSDs were preferred by foreign learners and native speakers alike (Tickoo 1989; McKeown 1993; Cumming *et al.* 1994) but again it was not clear that those definitions helped the users produce better text. Nesi and Meara's (1994) subjects performed equally well with the definitions of *LDOCE2* and *COB1* while *ALD4* led to more semantic errors. Nesi (1998) compared the definitions of some concrete nouns (*colander, insole, plunger, shoehorn,* and *spout*) in *ALD5, LDOCE3, COB2, CIDE,* and *COD8* with 158 students from different countries, all taking English as a foreign language. She concluded (1998: 167) that 'LDOCE and CIDE were judged most helpful, and COD was judged least helpful', and that 'LDOCE and CIDE entries were slightly more effective than the others, while COD entries were the least effective' (1998: 169). In all, it was *CIDE* that 'appeared to help users complete tasks more successfully' (1998: 170), but FSDs did not seem to improve the effectiveness of the entry. Nesi (2000a: 92) concluded that there is little difference in intelligibility between *ALD4, LDOCE2,* and *COB*: 'Apparently neither the restricted LDOCE defining vocabulary nor COBUILD definitions make dictionary reading quicker or more successful'. Wingate (2002) found that FSDs were more effective for her intermediate students. McCreary and Amacker (2006) concluded that the definitions were more effective in *MEDAL* than in *MWC11* for their 350 American students. Especially counter-productive in *MWC11* were the length of the definitions and the use of difficult words—as well as the chronological ordering of meanings. Dziemianko (2006) showed that for her Polish students FSDs were better than traditional definitions for providing syntactic information, and Lew and Dziemianko (2006) found that traditional definitions were better than *when*-definitions as found in *LDOCE4*. But they noted that the results might have been different with speakers of other languages, and with non-student users. They suggested (2006: 231), interestingly, that Polish speakers might be less accessible to FSDs than other communities because in Poland one does not spontaneously define words in FSD-type definitions.

7.2.4.2 How should information for expression be conveyed?

Early studies showed that language learners prefer to use bilingual dictionaries when they need information for expression and that monolingual dictionaries are not much used for that purpose, except by the more advanced students.

Black's (1985) study has not been published, but it is described in Maingay and Rundell (1987: 132–3) and in Summers (1988: 118–23). It compared the efficacy of definition, or example, or definition + example for the production of sentences. The conclusion was that 'the mix of definition plus example would be seen as the most successful, being equal to the examples-only entry style in producing correct . . . sentences, but producing fewer incorrect sentences . . . than examples only' (Summers 1988: 122). Bogaards (1996) discussed the quality and user-friendliness of information for expression in the four major learners' dictionaries published in 1995: *ALD5*, *LDOCE3*, *COB2*, and *CIDE*. He concluded that all were good but that *COB2* was marginally better. Nesi (1996a: 201), studying the effectiveness of *LDOCE* entries with and without examples for production, came to the conclusion that there was 'no statistical evidence that subjects were more productively competent when they were provided with illustrative examples', an unexpected conclusion that was later confirmed in Nesi (2000a: 116), where 'dictionary examples were not found to significantly affect the success of productive dictionary use'. Harvey and Yuill (1997) observed that their subjects did not use the extra column in *COB* but used the example sentences and the definitions when they needed information for expression.

Bogaards and van der Kloot (2001) came to the conclusion that it is impossible to say which of the different methods used by learners' dictionaries to give

grammatical information (abstract codes, more transparent codes, explicit information, information built into the definition) is more effective for Dutch students. Bogaards and van der Kloot (2002) concluded that 'traditional grammar
codes in terms of word classes seem to be only very rarely used', even by the more
advanced students, that 'the implicit information that is given in Cobuild-style
definitions does not seem to be used as it could be' but that 'examples are widely
used' and that the users prefer to use both definitions and examples (2002: 755).
Dziemianko (2004) concluded that the most user-friendly piece of information
on syntax for her Polish students was the examples, followed by pattern illustrations, and that FSDs were better for expression than traditional definitions.

7.2.4.3 Does the dictionary help users understand words?

Some studies have tried to assess whether the use of a dictionary helps users
understand words. Miller and Gildea (1985) asked 12-year-olds to guess the
meanings of words for which they were given dictionary definitions or example
sentences drawn from dictionaries, or again sentences drawn from the *New York
Times*. Their conclusion (1985: 8) was that definitions were the least efficient
means of conveying meaning and examples were the best. However, the experimenters wisely observed that dictionaries are meant to help remember meanings
rather than to acquire new meanings from scratch (see also Miller *et al.* 1990: 240).
    Another issue is the type of example, authentic or invented. Laufer (1992)
found that for students learning English in Israel invented examples were significantly better than authentic corpus examples for reception and comprehension, whether the users had only examples or examples with definitions. This was
later confirmed in Laufer (1993), but Potter (1998: 358) found 'overwhelming
approval among teachers and learners of English for real examples taken directly
from a corpus'. 'Despite a certain amount of research into this issue (e.g. Laufer
1992, Humblé 1998), the jury is still out on the relative merits of corpus-based and
lexicographer-produced examples' (Rundell 1998: 334).

7.2.4.4 Dictionaries and understanding a text

Some studies have compared the performance on a given comprehension task of
users with a dictionary and users without one. In most studies, dictionary users
had better results than non-dictionary users (Tono 1987, 1998; Summers 1988;
Luppescu and Day 1993; Knight 1994; Scholfield 1999, etc.). Tono (2001: 81–2),
using a sophisticated method, came to the conclusion that for his Japanese
students 'a significant difference in performance exists between reading comprehension with dictionaries and that without dictionaries' and that 'there are

positive effects from continuous dictionary use on overall reading comprehension'. In some studies, however, subjects with a dictionary did not do better than those without one, sometimes even worse (Bensoussan *et al.* 1984; Neubach and Cohen 1988; Padron and Waxman 1988; Nesi and Meara 1991; Hulstijn *et al.* 1996; McCreary and Dolezal 1999; Nesi 2000*a*, etc.). Several reasons have been mentioned. Perhaps, for the less proficient subjects, the dictionary is useless because it is too difficult to consult and they waste time trying to find answers to their questions. Some even have difficulties with the alphabetical ordering of entries: 'Bogaards (1994) hinted at the deleterious effect on comprehension scores caused by the drudgery of looking up words alphabetically. We might be led by these studies to question basic ideas, or "conventional wisdom", such as the primacy of and the efficiency of alphabetical order' (McCreary and Dolezal 1998: 614). Perhaps the dictionary can also be useless for the more proficient subjects because it does not have any of the answers that they need. Perhaps other variables are not adequately controlled for (Tono 2001: 29, 75). Perhaps the reading comprehension tests are 'made up of items which were not likely to be affected by the availability of a dictionary' (Nesi 2000*a*: 69–70). The concept of reading comprehension is not a simple one, and it is not clear how it could be measured (Wingate 2002: 18).

7.2.4.5 Conclusions: does the dictionary help?

It is difficult to draw clear conclusions from the studies of how helpful a dictionary can be. It seems that most users prefer the definitions in MLDs to the definitions in NSDs, probably because of the restricted defining vocabulary. Full-sentence formulations are generally rated highly, but it is not clear that they are more effective. For expression, coding systems are rarely used, and examples seem to be used by many users, but they are less effective in the absence of definitions. Examples are also useful for understanding words.

Laufer (2000: 849) managed to draw optimistic conclusions from all those studies:

[P]eople who use a dictionary almost always acquire more words than people who read without a dictionary.... [W]hen words [are] looked up in a dictionary, some of them are retained (Luppescu and Day 1993, Knight 1994). Looked up words were shown to be remembered better than words inferred from context (Mondria 1993), or words whose meaning is given by the teacher (Hulstijn [*et al.*] 1996).

Not everybody will share her optimism, but it is reasonable, and preferable for lexicography, to think that dictionaries are useful, in some cases, at least, and to some people.

7.2.5 Different types of dictionaries

7.2.5.1 Bilingual, bilingualized, or monolingual?

Some studies of dictionary use have compared monolingual and bilingual dictionaries and, more recently, bilingualized dictionaries. The hypothesis, a doxa in foreign language teaching, was that monolingual dictionaries are more effective. The main argument is well known and makes sense: only the monolingual dictionary allows the acquisition of a lexical item in the context of other words of the same language, with the definition, the syntagmatic relations (in the examples) and the paradigmatic relations (synonym, hypernym, etc.), in contrast with the bilingual dictionary and the wordlist, where lexical items are learned either with their equivalents in the other language or in isolation. But the superiority of the monolingual has never been convincingly demonstrated. There is also another line of thought, what some call the 'involvement hypothesis', that the harder the effort to learn a word the more effective the learning process will be: a word is better remembered if it is associated with the effort of the acquisition (Laufer 2000: 853). This, however, may favour either the bilingual or the monolingual dictionary, and it is dangerous, as it might prompt the production of dictionaries that are made deliberately difficult to use.

In some studies, the monolingual dictionary is given higher general ratings than the bilingual (Baxter 1980; Béjoint 1981a; Lew 2004), but in others it is the reverse (Bensoussan *et al.* 1984; Atkins and Varantola 1997: 32), particularly for expression. The bilingual dictionary is consistently found easier to use and some studies (Luppescu and Day 1993; Laufer and Melamed 1994; Wingate 2002: 106; Lew 2002b) even found that it led to better performance than the monolingual. But this seems to vary with the competence of the users: the skilled users obtain better results in comprehension and in production with monolingual dictionaries than the less skilled users. Laufer and Melamed (1994: 575), however, noted that the bilingualized dictionary was always the best of the three:

The highest scores were almost always obtained when the bilingualized dictionary was used. This was true for all learners in the case of comprehension, and for the good and average users in the case of production. Only the unskilled user did better on production with a bilingual dictionary.

The conclusions are that dictionary users generally admire their monolinguals but often prefer using their bilingual, or their bilingualized, dictionary, particularly for expression. All the results are undoubtedly influenced, to an extent that is difficult to measure, by the familiarity of the subjects with particular types of dictionaries and with particular dictionaries.

7.2.5.2 Paper or electronic?

The skills required to consult e-dictionaries are not the same as those required to use paper dictionaries. Some (Geeraerts 2000; Nesi 2000*b*) have even argued that most of the skills required of the users of paper dictionaries are not necessary with e-dictionaries. In some studies, e-dictionaries have been shown to be used more readily than paper dictionaries when the users had a choice, possibly because they cause less disruption in the reading process (Aust *et al.* 1993; Laufer and Hill 2000; Siegel 2007), although it is not clear that they lead to better performance. Nesi (2000*b*) reviews the literature and reports that 'the subjects who used online glossing achieved significantly higher vocabulary quiz scores than those using glosses on paper' and that 'the ED [electronic dictionary] users looked up more words, found the process easier, and were more satisfied with their dictionary consultations' (2000*b*: 845). Similarly, Laufer (2000: 851) concluded that her 'computer group achieved significantly higher retention scores than the paper gloss group'.

The e-dictionary is rated highly in all available studies, and it is perhaps more effective than the paper dictionary. But some of its superiority, particularly with younger users, may be due to a 'novelty effect', i.e. to 'the tendency for performance to initially improve when new technology is instituted, not because of any actual improvement in learning or achievement, but in response to increased interest in the new technology' (*Wikipedia*).

7.2.6 How useful are the studies of dictionary use?

The studies of dictionary use have used different research methods to investigate populations of users that differ in native language, in age, in language proficiency, in culture, in interests, using different dictionaries for different tasks and in different situations of use. They have tried to evaluate highly complex notions such as the knowledge of a lexical item or the understanding of a text. No wonder it is difficult to draw clear conclusions. They are, according to Nesi (2000*a*: 54) 'ultimately inconclusive, either because they report on the beliefs and perceptions of dictionary users, rather than on the observed consequences of dictionary use, or because different studies of similar phenomena have resulted in contradictory findings'. Hartmann (2001: 94–5) listed seven reasons why the results should be considered with caution:

1. The number and scale of user studies is still too small...
2. The target populations observed are still extremely limited...
3. The types of reference works whose use is observed are still restricted mostly to general dictionaries...

4. The various studies that have been carried out are difficult to evaluate and compare because the methods employed and the settings in which they take place are so diverse...

5. The results of various studies are of limited generalisability...

6. Many factors and variables have hardly been studied at all, e.g. differences in personality, attitudes, learning styles...

7. Finally, most user studies are 'ex-post', i.e. they are carried out with existing products.

One might add that the statistical treatment has often been basic: 'Not a single reliable measurement of dictionary using skills has become available so far' (Tono 2001: 84).

The conclusions that do emerge are mostly predictable: dictionary users use their monolingual dictionaries for meaning and spelling and they are often not competent enough to make full use of all the resources that their dictionaries contain. They are also very impatient: anything sophisticated, or abstract, or too long, or expressed in codes will be neglected, because the amount of time and energy necessary to find and understand the information is too much compared with the benefit derived from the consultation: the lexicographical costs are too high. It is still not known how and how much dictionary use enhances vocabulary learning and facilitates reading and in what circumstances a monolingual, or a bilingual, or a bilingualized dictionary should be recommended. What type of definition is best for whom and when, what types of macrostructural and microstructural arrangements, etc. also remain to be established.

What is clear is that dictionaries run the risk of becoming too sophisticated for their users, 'in danger with each innovation of outstripping the often rudimentary reference skills of those it is designed to serve' (Cowie 1983a: 136). The challenge facing the e-dictionary is to include more information and at the same time improve the accessibility of this information.

What is the future of the studies of dictionary use? They need to continue refining their methodologies. They need to focus on the difficulties of clearly identified language communities: what do the Koreans, what do the Peruvians, need? Studies also need to make use of specialized techniques used in the investigation of social phenomena by neighbouring disciplines (Tono 2001: 54 *ff.*). They need to focus on why we use dictionaries at all. And they need to enlarge their scope and consider other sources of reference, encyclopedias, corpora, the web, etc. (for a pioneering study see Frankenberg-Garcia 2005).

It seems that most of the research into dictionary use has been carried out by academics, not by lexicographers, although there is probably some research carried out in publishing houses that is not made available to the general public.

If that is correct, it is rather worrying. Clearly the study of the needs and skills of a group of dictionary users is a good subject for an MA or a doctoral dissertation, but the neglect of the lexicographers might also mean that they doubt that studies of dictionary use can really help them. Potential researchers, however, should not be discouraged: there is still plenty of room for improvement in methodology as well as scope for further research. Studies of dictionary use are indispensable, even though they may not be as fruitful as some expected them to be.

7.3 BETTER DICTIONARIES, OR BETTER USERS?

There are two possible explanations for the failure of users to use their dictionaries optimally: 'learner-related' reasons or 'dictionary-related' reasons (Wingate 2002: 221 *ff.*), and there are two solutions: try to produce dictionaries that are better and easier to use, or train the users so that they become more competent (Rundell 1988: 127, 1999: 48).

There are two direct routes to more effective dictionary use: the first is to radically improve the dictionary; the second is to radically improve the users. If we are to do either of these things—and obviously we should try to do both—the sine qua non of any action is a very detailed knowledge of how people use dictionaries.

(Atkins and Varantola 1997: 1)

7.3.1 Better dictionaries

Improving dictionaries means two things: making them more complete and accurate, and for this the lexicographers need the help of the linguists (see below, Chapter 8); and making them more user-friendly by reducing the lexicographical costs, for which dictionary use studies and the help of specialists in dictionary design are important. The two can easily be contradictory: the more information a dictionary carries the more it runs the risks of outwitting its users.

The studies of dictionary use have already had some influence on dictionaries. There are several examples of small improvements in individual entries that may have been prompted by particular studies: two example sentences in *LDOCE2*, 'The two ideas interact' for *interact* and 'It was the managing director who perpetrated that frightful statue in the reception area' for *perpetrate*, that had been shown to be useless or misleading, were changed in *LDOCE3* to 'Vanessa interacts well with other children in the class' and 'crimes that have been perpetrated in the name of religion' (Nesi 2000*a*). More generally, recent evolutions such as the adoption of more user-friendly styles for definitions, for usage labels, and for the indication of syntactic patterns (Atkins and Rundell 2008: 401), the use of FSDs for some words, the use of signposts in polysemous entries, etc. may have been prompted by the findings of studies of dictionary use.

Interestingly, some metalexicographers do not think that dictionaries should be made more user-friendly:

[I]t is not at all clear to me why we ought to make dictionaries more user friendly by changing them to be more in accord with users' needs. No other book caters to its users in such a way—least of all a reference book—and I am not yet convinced that such changes will increase the 'usability': for instance, one of the most difficult, but interesting and useful, dictionaries to read is the *Oxford-Duden Pictorial English Dictionary*, one whose format is arguably the way it is because it is 'user-friendlier' since it is entirely visual.   (Frawley 1988: 208)

The idea is that a dictionary should above all be good, and that if it is good enough the users will make the necessary efforts to use it—an opinion reminiscent of that of Dr Johnson.

7.3.2 *Educate the dictionary users*

There is certainly a lot to be done to improve users' skills:

Like most lexicographers, I meet many serious and dedicated users who have not discovered half of what the dictionary entry contains for them. This is a chastening experience for both them and me. They go off to read the Introduction (but they won't), and I go off to cut down the content and improve the accessibility of the next dictionary (but regularly gang agley at the proof stage).   (Atkins 1985: 23)

But what can one do? Lexicographers have added detailed 'How to use this dictionary' documents in the front matter of learners' dictionaries, but user studies show that they are hardly ever read. Probably because of this, the front matter of learners' dictionaries increased at first, 28 pages in *ALD2*, 33 pages in *ALD3*, 45 pages in *LDOCE2* but has now been reduced, 4 pages for *ALD6* and *ALD7* and 3 pages in *MEDAL1* and *MEDAL2*. Lexicographers have also compiled separate booklets of explanations and exercises, either for dictionaries in general or for a particular dictionary, but they are more likely to be used by teachers or even potential lexicographers than by the average user, unless they are used in class. The most efficient way to improve the skills of dictionary users is no doubt through the educational system, in class, as part of the normal curriculum (Béjoint 1989*b*). This is not practised everywhere, although experimental results indicate that it works. Crystal (1986: 79), tongue in cheek, portrays the ideal dictionary users that would result:

Such users have been taught to understand dictionary conventions...in junior school, where they were given a nice-looking dictionary,...and not...a book which looks boring, is falling apart, and which is written in a language well above what would be expected of them in other aspects of the curriculum. During school, they have taken part in several of the national dictionary-using competitions which have been sponsored by national academic bodies and publishers.... As adults, they have continued to go in for such competitions, and have probably subscribed to *English Today*.

The task of improving the skills of the dictionary user is difficult, because it requires the cooperation of teachers, teaching systems, and governments in many cases, provided the users themselves are ready to be educated. Crystal (1986: 78–9) suggests an 'attempt to educate the consumer into new ways of behaving— at the very least, a national campaign to persuade dictionary users to read their prefaces', obviously a joke.

7.3.3 *Learn more about language and its acquisition*

The acquisition of a lexical item is an extremely complex process. Where does the information come from? How is it processed? When is the process completed? Do we acquire all types of word in the same way? Are some words, concrete words for example, more easily and quickly acquired and remembered than others? How do we integrate the newly acquired information into the pre-existing lexicon? Do we go first for a general meaning and then only distinguish the features, or do we 'accumulate' features to form concepts? How are words connected in our brains? By form or by meaning? Are derivatives stored as independent units or are they made up every time we use them? (see Aitchison 1994). Are multiword items acquired and stored as wholes? (see Wray 2002: 262 *ff*.). Is the difficulty encountered in the process of learning a new word associated with a better quality of learning?[26] All these questions are of course relevant to lexicography.

It is not clear what part the dictionary can play in these processes. The role of the dictionary in the acquisition of a native language is almost nil, and in the acquisition of a foreign language it is only slightly more important. In both cases

---

[26] For handy guides to the different aspects of word knowledge (form, derivations, conjugations, variations in syntax, syntactic behaviour, collocability, frequency, appropriateness in discourse, meaning, meaning relations, etc.) see Richards (1976: 83) and Nation (1990: 31).

the dictionary can only provide additional information, essentially associated with 'incidental' word learning, i.e. with knowledge which is not deliberately learnt but acquired while doing something else. But dictionaries could do better in this—admittedly minor—role if they were compiled with a better awareness of how their information will be used: a 'psycholexicography' could emerge out of a better knowledge of 'psycholexicology' (Miller *et al.* 1990: 236).

LEXICOGRAPHY AND LINGUISTICS

8.1 LINGUISTS AND LINGUISTICS IN ENGLISH AND AMERICAN DICTIONARIES

THE first lexicographers were not linguists, because being a linguist was not a recognized profession. There have always been people who thought, wrote, and taught about language, but it was not until the late nineteenth century that they began to constitute a community with its rituals, publications, meetings, conferences, university courses, associations, networks, and eventually its traditions. Even after that, linguists and lexicographers lived side by side for some time, ignoring each other, with occasional forays of the ones into the domain of the others. Yet the two conditions are clearly related. Much of the research done by linguists has potential applications in dictionaries, and every dictionary conveys ideas about what language is and how it can be described: 'Each lexicographic work reflects a linguistic theory which the author more or less consciously applies' (Quemada 1972: 427). The two communities work on the same object, language. All lexicographers handle linguistic concepts, and all linguists use dictionaries for their research. Some linguists have compiled dictionaries, usually specialized dictionaries, of etymology, of pronunciation, of synonyms, of regional dialects, or of lesser-known languages. Yet, many lexicographers have little formal training in linguistics and many linguists have little idea how dictionaries are compiled. Linguists are interested in theory, and are judged by their peers; lexicographers have to produce an artefact that must please its users; linguists can choose their objects of study, while lexicographers have to treat a language from A to Z; linguists can afford to be wrong, and start again, lexicographers cannot (but they often are); linguists have time to think and try out solutions; lexicographers are 'lexicologist[s] with a deadline'.[1]

8.1.1 Linguists and dictionaries in the USA

8.1.1.1 Linguists to boost the sales

As early as the second half of the nineteenth century, linguists were invited to contribute to the compilation of American GPDs. William Dwight Whitney, a philologist who was much admired by Saussure,[2] was the editor of the *Century Dictionary* (1891), but most contributions were more superficial. Thomas A. Knott,[3] a phonetician, took part in the compilation of *W2* (1934), Leonard Bloomfield, Charles C. Fries,[4] and Kemp Malone[5] were on the editorial team of *ACD* (1947), which also used the work of Thorndike, the psychologist who specialized in the acquisition of language.[6] The *Funk and Wagnalls College Dictionary* (1963) had a committee of experts with Albert H. Marckwardt,[7] a dialectologist and Samuel Hayakawa,[8] a semanticist, *AHD* had Calvert Watkins,[9] a specialist of Indo-European and Henry Kučera,[10] perhaps the first corpus linguist ever, in its first edition (1969) and Lee Pederson, a dialectologist, Dwight Bolinger,[11] and Geoffrey Nunberg[12] in the second (1982). The latest edition (2000) has Nunberg and Watkins.

The presence of those linguists whose names and affiliations were proudly displayed in the first pages is surprising, because American dictionaries have not been characterized by their zeal in the application of the latest advances in linguistics. In fact, the role of the linguists was mostly marginal, ornamental, cosmetic: they were asked to express their views in essays on the history of the

[1] Attributed to Fillmore (reference unknown).
[2] Claude Boisson (personal communication). Whitney wrote *The Life and Growth of Language: An Outline of Linguistic Science* (1875), *Sanskrit Grammar* (1879), etc.
[3] Author of *A Pronouncing Dictionary of the American Language* (1944).
[4] Author of *American English Grammar* (1940), *The Structure of English* (1952).
[5] *Wikipedia* mentions 'his hundreds of publications'.
[6] Who wrote more than 500 (!) books, among which *The Teacher's Word Book* (1921), *A Semantic Count of English Words* (1938; with Irving Lorge), *The Teacher's Word Book of 30,000 Words* (1944; also with Irving Lorge), etc.
[7] Who wrote *American English* (1958).
[8] Whose main books were *Language in Action* (1941) and *Language in Thought and Action* (1949).
[9] He wrote *Indo-European Origins of the Celtic Verb* (1962), etc.
[10] The author, with Nelson Francis, of *Computational Analysis of Present-Day American English* (1967), known as the Brown Corpus (see below, 9.1.7.3).
[11] Who wrote *Aspects of Language* (1970), *Language: the Loaded Weapon* (1980), etc.
[12] Author of *The Way We Talk Now* (2001), *Talking Right* (2006).

English language, on etymology, on grammar, or on dialects to be placed in the front matter, where their competence was undisputable, but their influence on the dictionary text was negligible. They were enrolled to pander to the taste of the American public for science, to boost the sales, but they were not allowed to interfere with the dictionary text because any interference would have met with the hostility of the public, who wanted their dictionaries to be familiar, unpretentious, easy-to-use everyday tools, not mouthpieces for the complex and vaguely dangerous theories of academics.

8.1.1.2 The influence of structuralism

The linguistic schools that were influential in America in the twentieth century did not have much to say about lexicography. The lexicon, after being the prime object of investigation of the philologists in the nineteenth century trying to trace the relations between Sanskrit and many of the languages of Europe, had been neglected because it was thought to be less important than syntax or phonology and also because it was more difficult to describe and encapsulate in rules. This was clearly expressed by the structuralists: 'Certainly we descriptive linguists tend to be contemptuous of vocabulary. It is almost a dogma among us that vocabulary is the least significant part of language (save for a group among us who even doubt that vocabulary is really a part of language after all)' (Gleason 1962: 86). The semantics of the first three-quarters of the twentieth century was mostly formal, and lexicology was hardly recognized as a branch of linguistics (Ullmann 1962: 29).[13]

American linguists seldom discussed dictionaries but when they did, they were severe. Dictionary definitions, for example, were incoherent (Gleason 1962: 100), used ill-defined terms (Gleason 1962: 100), failed to see the difference between meaning and context-bound applications (Weinreich 1962: 29), were entangled in old traditions (Weinreich 1962: 30), failed to distinguish between word knowledge and world knowledge (Weinreich 1964), did not account for connotation (Lakoff 1973: 151), etc. On the whole, dictionaries, they said, were badly contrived, with no scientific rigour, inaccurate and incomplete, indifferent to the advances of linguistics, with no redeeming features.

W3 was described as a structuralist dictionary by many people, particularly its enemies. Popular reviewers denounced 'the influence of structuralist linguists,

---

[13] The word *lexicology* was first used at the end of the eighteenth century according to Considine (2007: viii). The *OED* has 1828, in Webster's *Dictionary*. But before the late twentieth century, few books used it in their titles, and they were translations: Doroszewski, W. (1973), *Elements of Lexicology and Semiotics* (Mouton: The Hague).

who were accused of being in favour of descriptivism' (Marckwardt 1963/1967: 37). Gove himself was a good linguist, an admirer of the linguists of his time, he thought that dictionaries could only benefit from more knowledge on language and he even tried to recruit linguists for the compilation of *W3*. But he had to be cautious in the expression of his beliefs, for fear of frightening the publishers and the potential buyers, and he failed to convince the linguists he had approached (Gates 1986: 84). The list of outside consultants has several specialists of etymology and particular languages but only one for linguistics, W. Freeman Twaddell, Professor of German and linguistics.

Mitterand (1963: 111–12) outlined what lexicographers under the influence of the French structuralist school[14] would do:

They refuse to mix up diachrony and synchrony and tend to give less importance to the definition. Instead of the latter, or at least in addition to it, they give a reasoned—and exhaustive, whenever possible—list of the networks of opposition and fundamental contrasts which the word enters into, for a particular state of the language. They use literary citations only cautiously, preferring extracts from conversations, the press or didactic texts, and they exclude citations from a language variety that is not the language of reference. They do their best to rigorously distinguish the various systems of distribution that those contextual networks constitute, and that coincide either with homonymic oppositions, or with socio-professional distinctions. . . . Lastly, they give primary importance to the syntactic constructions of each word, using them as the governing principle for the internal organization of the entry.

This was implemented in the *Dictionnaire du Français Contemporain* (1966), compiled by Jean Dubois and published only five years after *W3*, which described the use of words in their networks of lexical relations and in their contexts. Does *W3* resemble this? Take the entry for *nice* in Figure 8.1.[15] We see that:

1. the entry provides morphological information;
2. definitions are mostly by synonyms;
3. there are a few contexts, not quotations (there are some in other entries);
4. the contexts are ordinary usage, not literary (some are, in other entries);
5. there are cross-references to other entries.

Those features could be called structuralist: the word is described in its paradigmatic relations and to some extent in its syntagmatic relations as well. Other features, not present in this extract, that do not depart from structuralist ideals,

---

[14] This was not exactly the same as the American variety.
[15] This is an extract from the Internet edition, which differs from the paper edition only in small details.

Inflected Form(s): nic·er; nic·est

Etymology: Middle English, foolish, wanton, from Anglo-French, silly, simple, from Latin *nescius* ignorant, from *nescire* not to know—more at NESCIENCE

1 *obsolete* **a** : WANTON, DISSOLUTE **b** : COY, RETICENT

2 a : showing fastidious or finicky tastes : PARTICULAR <too *nice* a palate to enjoy junk food> **b** : exacting in requirements or standards : PUNCTILIOUS <a *nice* code of honor>

3 : possessing, marked by, or demanding great or excessive precision and delicacy <*nice* measurements>

4 *obsolete* : TRIVIAL

5 a : PLEASING, AGREEABLE <a *nice* time> <a *nice* person> **b** : well-executed <*nice* shot> **c** : APPROPRIATE, FITTING <not a *nice* word for a formal occasion>

6 a : socially acceptable : WELL-BRED <from a *nice* family> **b** : VIRTUOUS, RESPECTABLE <was taught that *nice* girls don't do that>

7 : POLITE, KIND <that's *nice* of you to say>

synonym see CORRECT

- **nice** *adverb*
- **nice·ly** *adverb*
- **nice·ness** *noun*

Figure 8.1 Entry for *nice* in W3

are W3's descriptivism, its interest in the spoken language and the indication of pronunciation, including the pronunciation of words in context and with their dialectal variations, its lists of synonyms and its notes on usage. Otherwise, W3 was traditional in its treatment of syntax and of meaning. Meanings were ordered chronologically, the entry began with etymology and the synonyms in the definitions and in the special paragraph were just listed, with no attempt at showing any organization, any structure. Hanks (1979: 33) argues that the definitions of W3 are bad because they rest on theory, 'and when theory comes into lexicography, all too often common sense goes out', but he is referring to the dogma of the definition according to Gove, not to linguistic theory. On the whole, it is 'difficult to find even a hint of structuralism in the handling of the definitions' (Marckwardt 1963/1967: 37).

The conclusion is clear: there was not much structuralism in W3. Weinreich agreed with Gove that W3 owed virtually nothing to linguistics, and he regretted it: 'It is disconcerting that a mountain of lexicographic practice such as an unabridged dictionary of English should yield no more than a paragraph-sized molehill of lexicological theory' (1964: 408). Of course, his condemnation could have been reversed: any lexicographer could be disconcerted that so many mountains of linguistic theory should have yielded so little that was applicable to lexicography.

8.1.1.3 Can a dictionary be generative?

Transformational generative linguists were as little interested in the lexicon as the structuralists, at least in the beginning: 'In the very earliest version of the Chomskyan model the lexicon was not recognized as an autonomous component at all; words were considered to be merely the observable elements through which syntax manifested itself' (Singleton 2000: 23).[16] Not surprisingly, generative linguistics had no influence on dictionaries: 'The Chomskyan revolution... passed by pretty well unnoticed, at least as far as lexicography in English is concerned' (Hanks 1990: 31). A generative dictionary would have had to be a record of the potentialities of the language, providing the building blocks, the morphemes, and the rules to be used to assemble them to produce discourse. A huge task, if at all possible: 'I think that if we imagine 100 tomes of the size of the unabridged *Oxford English Dictionary*, we may get through a third of the English alphabet in that kind of a notation. I consequently rather doubt if a fully specified TG [transformational generative] dictionary of any natural language will ever be written' (Makkai 1976: 53).

8.1.1.4 A renewed interest in the lexicon

American linguists began showing an interest in the lexicon, and even, for some, in lexicography, in the 1950s, at the same time as in France:

Over the past few decades—particularly after 1950—an explicit interest for the dictionary as an object has become manifest. First, it was the lexicographers themselves, but they found it difficult to evaluate a practice that absorbed them in its multiple daily difficulties. Sometimes, though not as often, linguists envisaged with some condescension the procedures and processes of description, which they evaluated from the point of view of the most up-to-date, often the most fragile and the least well-assimilated theories of linguistics. (Rey and Delesalle 1979: 4–5)

In 1958, one year after the publication of Chomsky's *Syntactic Structures*, Knudsen and Sommerfelt (1958: 98) were writing: 'I [*sic*] think it is time to take up a systematic study of the lexicological principles which ought to be followed.... Curiously enough, this question seems to have interested few linguists'. A new semantics, called *lexical semantics*,[17] appeared alongside formal compositional semantics, first in Britain (see below) and then in the USA. It was a 'bottom-up'

---

[16] On the history of the lexicon in generative grammar, see Zaenen and Engdahl (1994: 182 *ff*.).

[17] I have been unable to trace the origin of the term *lexical semantics*. The earliest occurrence I found is 1974 in the title of a book in the Soviet Union. The term has different definitions by different authors.

approach focused on the study of the formal and semantic properties of individual words, their role in discourse and their relations with other words (Cruse 1986). This was more promising for lexicography: 'In the mid-eighties formal linguistic theory had close to nothing to say about the most important problems of lexical semantics, but the last fifteen years have seen a great change in this situation' (Zaenen 2002: 231).

The interest of American linguists for dictionaries materialized in the organization of the first conference on lexicography in 1960 at the University of Indiana. The title, 'Problems of lexicography', was broad by today's standards but it showed that the relations between linguistics and lexicography had changed. The conference welcomed lexicographers, but it was meant for academics: the proceedings have papers by Weinreich, Gleason, Hoenigswald, Malone, etc. A more recent sign was the publication of a special issue of *Dictionaries*, the journal of the Dictionary Society of North America, dated 1993–4, on what linguistics could contribute to lexicography, with papers by linguists (Aitchison, Apresjan, Cruse, Frawley, McCawley, Wierzbicka, Zgusta) and by lexicographers (Atkins, Hanks, Landau)—although it was difficult by then to distinguish the two groups. The publication is all the more notable as the journal had been more interested in questions of practical lexicography and in the history of dictionaries than in theoretical issues.

8.1.2 Lexicographers and linguists in Britain

8.1.2.1 Linguists-cum-lexicographers

In Britain, dictionary publishers never listed the names of linguists to impress the potential buyers, but good linguists have been recruited to edit dictionaries since the end of the nineteenth century. Murray was a philologist before he took over the compilation of the *OED*, although his career as a linguist slowed afterwards. Wyld, the editor of the *Universal Dictionary of the English Language* (1932), was also a specialist of the history of English.[18] Hornby, the main compiler of *ALD* (1941), was a linguist specializing in the teaching of languages,[19] and he continued his career as a linguist after the publication of the dictionary.

In Britain, linguists have always been more interested in the lexicon than in the USA. In the 1930s, J. R. Firth[20] was teaching in London a linguistic theory known as *polysystemicism* (Crystal 1985), whose object was the study of meaning in all its

[18] He wrote *A Short History of English* (1914), *A History of Modern Colloquial English* (1920), etc.
[19] He published *A Guide to English Patterns and Usage* (1954).
[20] Who wrote relatively little but has been immensely influential, particularly in Britain. He is the author of *Papers in Linguistics 1934–1951*.

forms, including the lexicon. This influenced his contemporaries and students, M. A. K. Halliday[21] and, to a lesser extent, Randolph Quirk[22] and Geoffrey Leech,[23] who all had brilliant careers as linguists as well as a sustained interest in dictionaries. Some linguists took part in the compilation of dictionaries, sometimes superficially, like Crystal for the *Penguin Wordmaster Dictionary* (1987), but also as chief editors, like Cowie for *ODCIE* (1975–83) and Sinclair for *COB* (1987), and their dictionaries naturally had traces of modern linguistics in their indication of syntactic patterns, their focus on the everyday language, including the spoken varieties, and their description of the lexicon as a system, a functional code. The use of a corpus in *COB* and its FSDs are all applications of Sinclair's work. *LDOCE*'s first page acknowledges the contributions of Quirk, Crystal, Leech, A. C. Gimson,[24] Arthur Bronstein,[25] etc. for 'advice and suggestions'. The listing of all the elements of multiword items in *CIDE* and the treatment of metaphors in special paragraphs in *MEDAL* are applications of the recent interest of linguistics for phraseology (see below) and for metaphor.

Some British lexicographers became active in linguistics in the 1980s: Sue Atkins, Patrick Hanks, Rosamund Moon, and others began as lexicographers but eventually gained recognition as linguists. They believe that lexicography can only progress if it takes into account the work of linguists, their methods, their questions and their answers. The first lexicography conference in Britain was organized by Reinhard Hartmann in 1979 at Exeter, almost 20 years after the Indiana conference. It brought together lexicographers (Hanks, Urdang) and linguists (Cowie, Osselton).

8.1.2.2 *The case of the* OED

The *OED* was influenced by the project of the Grimm brothers to write a dictionary of the German language as a logical sequel to their research on the evolution of languages. Of course the circumstances were different—in Britain, the aim was not to fix a language for a newly created nation—but the British Philological Society was impressed by the method, particularly the decision to trace the earliest occurrences of every word so as to show its evolution.

The *OED* was not a totally original dictionary. It had been preceded by Johnson, Richardson, and a few others, from whom it had taken its interest in the isolated

---

[21] Author of *Cohesion in English* (1976) with R. Hasan, etc.
[22] Who edited the monumental *Comprehensive Grammar of the English Language* (1985) with G. Leech and J. Svartvik, etc.
[23] Author of *Meaning and the English Verb* (1971), *Semantics* (1974), etc.
[24] A student and colleague of Daniel Jones, he took over the compilation of Jones's *English Pronouncing Dictionary* in 1962.
[25] Author of *Pronunciation of American English* (1960).

...Forms: ME **necy, nesy, nyci, nys, nysse**, ME, 16 **nece**,... [< Anglo-Norman *nice, nis, nise* and Old French *nice* (*c*1160; *c*1250 as *niche*; now French regional) < classical Latin *nescius* (see NESCIOUS *a.*). Cf. Old Occitan *nesci* (*c*1150; also attested as *neci, nesi, nessi*; Occitan *neci*), Spanish *necio* (1220–50), Catalan *neci, nici* (both fourteenth cent.), Portuguese *necio* (fourteenth cent.; fifteenth cent. as *néscio*), Italian *nescio* (1321), all in sense 'foolish, simple, ignorant'.

The semantic development of this word from 'foolish, silly' to 'pleasing' is unparalleled in Latin or in the Romance languages. The precise sense development in English is unclear. *N.E.D.* (1906) s.v. notes that 'in many examples from the sixteenth and seventeenth cent. it is difficult to say in what particular sense the writer intended it to be taken'.]

A. *adj.* I. General uses.

1. a. Of a person: foolish, silly, simple; ignorant. *Obs.*

*c*1300 *St. Mary Magdalen* (Laud) 493 in C. Horstmann *Early S.-Eng. Legendary* (1887) 476 Bote ich e [seide] hou heo heold mi lif, for-soe ich were nice.... *c*1400 (?*a*1300) *King Alexander* (Laud) 652 He dude e childe habbe noryce, Gentil leuedyes and nouth nyce.

b. Of an action, utterance, etc.: displaying foolishness or silliness; absurd, senseless. *Obs.*

*c*1390 CHAUCER *Reeve's Tale* 4282 Hys wyfe..wiste nothyng of this nyce [*v.rr.* nyse, nesy] stryf.... *c*1400 (?*c*1390) *Sir Gawain and Green Knight* 323 yn askyng is nys..ou foly hatz frayst. of suche

2. a. Of conduct, behaviour, etc.: characterized by or encouraging wantonness or lasciviousness. *Obs.*

*a*1387 J. TREVISA tr. R. Higden *Polychron.* (St. John's Cambr.) IV. 67 It was i-doo wi foule songes and gestes and iapes and nyse menstralcie.... *a*1450 (*a*1425) J. MIRK *Instr. Parish Priests* (Claud.) 61 From nyse iapes and rybawdye, Thow moste turne a-way yn ye.

Figure 8.2 Entry for *nice* in *OED3*

word considered as a distinct entity with characteristics that are independent of the contexts in which it is used, its focus on literary language and on quotations, etc. What was new in the *OED* was the detailed, scientific description of the evolution of meaning, in accordance with the research of the philologists of the time. Take the example of the adjective *nice* in Figure 8.2 (here part of the entry in *OED3*).

We see that:

1. the entry begins with a detailed etymology, part of which is in a discursive style;
2. the meanings are ordered chronologically;
3. the date of the first recorded occurrence of each meaning is given in the quotations;
4. each meaning is illustrated by at least one quotation, often more;
5. most quotations are literary;
6. there is no systematic and visible treatment of morphology, of synonymy, or of phraseology;
7. there are no cross-references to other entries.

The *OED* was undoubtedly a modern dictionary—some would say revolution-ary—when it was first published, but it was closer to the philology of the period when compilation began than to the linguistics of the time when the last volume was published. It was a pre-Saussurean dictionary, in which words were treated as independent from each other and from their contexts.

On the whole the main theories of twentieth-century linguistics have had little influence on the compilation of the two monuments of modern English lexicog-raphy, *W3* and the *OED*. Of course, it is particularly difficult for large dictionaries to experiment with new solutions, but the smaller native speakers' dictionaries of the same periods were equally unaffected.

Strange delays can be observed: just when linguistics, after de Saussure, was leaving comparativism and historicism and taking up the immediate description of the functions of the language—classical philology remaining alive and active in itself—dictionaries developed their own tradition out of the reach of doctrines, or with the help of those of the past.   (Rey 1970c: 22)

In 1989, Hausmann and Wiegand (1989: 342) could still write about NSDs: 'we are far from having attained a (truly) Saussurean lexicography. Too many dictionar-ies make do with definitions and neglect verb patterns, collocations, synonyms, and antonyms, not to mention morphosemantic paradigms'.

8.1.3 Where are we?

8.1.3.1 Things are better than ever, but...

There are reasons to be optimistic. The number of lexicographers interested in linguistics and of linguists interested in dictionaries has increased dramatically over the last decades. Many linguists in English-speaking countries and elsewhere have produced work that is important for lexicography. Of course, they do not envisage all the problems of the preparation of a dictionary, but their approaches are more or less directly relevant to the work of the lexicographer. Learned journals and books abound in notes on words, what Apresjan (2002: 99) calls *lexicographic portraits*, mentioning semantic and syntactic characteristics that could be included in dictionaries.[26] All those linguists agree that dictionaries are important and that 'sound lexicography

---

[26] Examples are *alone* (Apresjan 2002), *bake* (Atkins *et al.* 1988), *cook* (Atkins 2002), *cup, mug*, etc. (Wierzbicka 1985), *crawl* (Fillmore and Atkins 2000), *lean* and *tank* (Hanks 2002), *over* (Tyler and Evans 2001), *risk* (Fillmore and Atkins 1992, 1994), *seem, try, believe*, and *persuade* (Zaenen and Engdahl 1994), the 'shake verbs' (*quake, quiver, shake, shiver, shudder, tremble*, and *vibrate*) (Atkins and Levin 1995), *take* (Norvig and Lakoff 1987), etc.

can only be based on sound linguistic theory and...recent theoretical developments are of paramount importance for practical dictionary making' (Apresjan 2002: 91). Atkins (2002: 25), looking back to her career, begun in the 1970s, was satisfied that her work had been changed by linguistics: 'The most significant difference, I believe, between the 1967 lexicography and that of today is that in the interval my approach to lexicography has benefited from the insights of linguistics....Linguistic theory, particularly recent work in lexical semantics, can light the way to better lexicography'.

8.1.3.2 ...they are not ideal

All this is a significant improvement over the preceding decades, but we are still far from the ideal. In the USA, as in many other countries, the role of linguists in dictionaries has not changed since the early twentieth century: they are still welcome in the blurbs and first pages but they have no real influence on the dictionary text: 'although more theoreticians would be a welcome addition to the field, they must remember that their theories should be interpretable above all in terms of practicality' (Urdang 1963: 594). The number of American lexicographers who are active in linguistics and aware of what it can contribute to dictionaries is still small, and there are no signs that it is on the increase. Many lexicographers are still unconvinced that linguists can be any help, because their writings are too complex to be taken into account in any but the most sophisticated dictionaries, because they illustrate different theories that are difficult to reconcile, and because they address only a tiny portion of the lexicographer's problems. Typically, the number of words studied by linguists is negligible compared to the immensity of the lexicon, and some are not even those that are problematic in dictionary making:

> Cups and mugs, bikes and cars, cats and dogs, and names of fruits and vegetables are not the words that cause us intractable problems as do most of the polysemous verbs (e.g. *taste*) or nouns whose usage swings between countability and uncountability (e.g. *taste* again), or 'relational' words like *sister* or *bride* or *enemy*—the list is endless.
>
> (Atkins 1993: 23)

Wierzbicka herself (1996: 246), who wrote extensively on cups and mugs, bikes and cars, and cats and dogs, agrees: 'The problem with the semanticists,' she writes, is that none of them 'has attempted to test their ideas, original and fruitful as they may be, in large-scale lexicographic studies, involving hundreds of lexical items and hundred of definitions.'

Many lexicographers think that the courses offered in universities are not much use, and that the only way lexicographers can be trained is hands on: 'I have not found that people with a sound theoretical understanding of current linguistic theory make good definition writers. It is a literary, not a scientific activity,' Hanks (1979: 37) writes. Lexicographers need not be university graduates, Landau says: 'There is no evidence that lexicographers now are better trained or more competent than they were in the past' (Landau 2001: 323). Many lexicographers are in fact trying to keep away from linguistics as much as they are allowed to:

Many people in contemporary lexicography deal with theoretical linguistics by keeping their heads down below the barricades and getting on with writing dictionary entries. Sometimes an academic title whistles past, like 'What linguists might contribute to dictionary-making if they could get their act together' (McCawley 1986); or a plaintive sentence crashes onto one's desk, such as 'Lexicography has no theoretical foundations, and even the best lexicographers, when pressed, can never explain what they are doing, or why' (Wierzbicka 1985: 5).   (Atkins 1993: 5)

On the other hand, many linguists have continued to be wary of commercial lexicography.

Although commercial works of reference have inevitably benefited in terms of quality from their academic connections, and although academics have also benefited financially from their commercial connections, a certain (sometimes incompletely stated) resentment is still detectable on the part of scholars, in that they seem to wish they did not have to sully themselves in this way.   (McArthur 1986b: 137)

The criticism of dictionaries has never ceased: dictionaries are 'anecdotal, circular, and devoid of any scholarly value' (Raskin 1985: 99), 'impoverished and inconsistent' (Pustejovsky and Boguraev 1994: 295), a commercial artefact, 'a purely practical enterprise unworthy of scholarly interest' (Apresjan 2002: 91), etc.

[T]he interplay and tension between ivory-tower academic lexicography and clearcut commercial lexicography (as for example in Oxford) has tended to sustain a kind of scholarly suspicion of the commercial, whether in terms of dictionaries or encyclopedias. Something that might be sold in a dimestore or hawked from door to door did not necessarily appeal to the cultural aesthetics of university men. Although such men might be capitalists, they did not want to be seen as hucksters, and often their academic susceptibilities and principles were at odds with the marketplace interests of the publishers.   (McArthur 1986b: 137)

The criticism may be justified but unfair to the lexicographers: 'Linguists who inveigh against lexicographers for not noticing or not recording this or that nice distinction often do not realize that lexicographers have strong incentives to work fast, even if working at home as free-lancers: namely, to earn enough money to make working worthwhile' (Landau 2001: 323).

As a consequence, dictionaries have not improved as much as could have been expected. Dictionaries do not change easily: lexicographers 'simply do not feel the need to improve in the ways that recent research would make possible' (Zaenen 2002: 239). The production of a dictionary involves many people in a highly complex chain, and '[c]hanging these highly labour-intensive products is not to be undertaken lightly' (Atkins 2002: 1).

British dictionaries have changed over the last decades, and some of these changes are due to the influence of linguistics, but in the USA, as well as in other countries, '[m]ost dictionaries are sublimely unaffected by the highly relevant work currently being done by linguists, especially in lexical semantics' (Atkins 2002: 1). It is probably not a coincidence that American observers of lexicography have always been, and still are, pessimistic: 'Nothing significantly new has happened in lexicography since the first printed dictionaries after Gutenberg invented the printing of books' (Makkai 1976: 55).

Zgusta's (1971) handbook remains a seminal work in lexicography not only because it is well done in and of itself and therefore deserves praise, but also because little has changed over the years in lexicographic practice: for example, current definitional practice is not that different from Aristotle's. Similar comments may be made about Landau's (1984) book, which is an excellent, synoptic study of dictionaries, but which is also an affirmation of distinguished PAST practice rather than a book of new ideas. It is therefore understandable that Bailey (1986) should remark that it is difficult to find a 'new idea' in lexicography since what evolution there has been in lexicographic practice has been slow indeed: '...we will agree, I think, that there is no abrupt or revolutionary change in the more than 250 years of English lexicography' (p. 124).... As a consequence, when lexicographic practice is raised for scrutiny, the very deeply foundational questions are rarely asked, and if such questions are asked, the answers infrequently conflict with established, conservative practice.   (Frawley 1988: 189–90)

For Landau (2001: 17), 'dictionaries for native speakers... for the entire latter half of the twentieth century remained, with one or two exceptions, completely impervious to meaningful innovation'. Hanks (2008: 106) even blames Merriam-Webster for paralysing the market:

The corpus revolution and the grammatical analyses of Quirk and other empirically minded grammarians, which have led to so many improvements in British monolingual dictionaries, have up to now been passed by in American lexicography, suffering as it does under the stranglehold of a market leader that has made little or no investment in serious lexicographical research or innovation for over 40 years.

8.2 LINGUISTIC QUESTIONS IN LEXICOGRAPHY

There is a large amount of linguistic knowledge in dictionaries, but there is little linguistic theory. Yet there are many lexicographic questions whose solutions can, or could, or should, be based on what the linguists know about language and its use.

> [A] large proportion of the decisions made by the lexicographer are linguistic decisions, and so we should consider particularly, but not exclusively, the contribution of theoretical linguistics to theoretical lexicography, and hence the role of the theoretical linguist in dictionary-making.   (Atkins 1993: 5)

They are the decisions for which the lexicographer has a choice, as opposed to those for which the choices are made by the publishers and imposed on the lexicographer (Atkins 1993: 7). All the branches of linguistics have something to contribute: etymology, phonetics, morphology, syntax, semantics, dialectology, sociolinguistics, pragmatics, corpus linguistics, etc.[27] What the linguists can provide is accuracy in individual entries and consistency across different entries, in what Weiner (1994: 415) calls the 'vertical arrangement of lexical data into major and minor categories'. In some cases, the contribution of linguists is relatively unproblematic: a phonetician can be asked to provide phonetic transcriptions and an etymologist to write word histories. In others the linguist can only provide information that will be processed by the lexicographer: what can be considered as a lexical item, what is an idiom, how to define and describe polysemy, how word meaning can best be captured and accounted for, what are the syntactic patterns in which the word is used, how to note the obligatory, preferred or possible contextual environments of words, etc. Those are the most difficult parts of a lexicographer's job: Kilgarriff (1998b: 54) asked lexicographers working on *LDOCE3* to rate the different aspects of their work in terms of difficulty, and the top of the list was: '1 Finding right wording 2 Splitting: identifying the senses 3 Priority... meaning and use 4 Multi-word items', etc. They are the questions that take time and the kind of expertise that typically the linguist possesses.

---

[27] Hartmann and Smith (2003) and Fontenelle (2008a) are anthologies of texts written mostly by linguists about lexicographic questions.

8.2.1 Questions of nomenclature

8.2.1.1 Choosing the lexical items for the wordlist: nature

The substance of dictionaries comes from discourse, whether in the form of a corpus or not. Every graphic word in a text, defined as 'any string of characters separated by blanks or punctuation' (Kilgarriff 1997a: 144), is a potential candidate for inclusion as an entry. 'Discourse can be cut up in segments that will be used as the entry words of dictionaries and . . . to each of these segments corresponds a content which is the object of the dictionary article' (Guilbert 1969: 4–5). Some forms can be discarded, immediately or at a later stage: errors, of course, aberrant usages, symbols, signs, numbers as well as abbreviations, rare onomatopoeia, trademarks,[28] proper names,[29] children's words, foreign words, etc., according to the policy of each dictionary.

But dictionaries list words, or lexical items, not forms, and that is where the difficulties begin. Some forms are identical in discourse but are different lexical items. If they are partial homonyms, like *light* noun and *light* adjective, they can be recorded as different items. But in other cases it is more difficult to decide whether they are the same item or not. Possible criteria can be pronunciation, as in *row*, *bow*, etc. It can be etymology: for example, '*page* = "sheet of paper" has a different history from that of *page* = "retainer"; so too with *lock* = "device for fastening something securely" and *lock* = "tress of hair"' (Moon 1987b: 88). But linguists know that an etymon may evolve into two distinct lexical items in synchrony, for example *ear* (Lyons 1977: 552). It can also be syntactic patterns, for example 'a bar' vs. 'the bar', but different patterns of use do not prove that there are two lexical items. The problem is that all of the criteria can only be applied *a posteriori*, when one already knows, or supposes, that there are two distinct items, or just one. In fact, linguistics does not have much to say, and the first selection of the items for the wordlist is done intuitively, leaving the more difficult questions for the later stage of the organization of the macrostructure (see below).

Some forms are different in discourse but are the same lexical item. Spelling variants are treated according to the policy of each particular dictionary: only one spelling retained, or both, with a preference for one of them. Cases like *umbrella*

---

[28] On regulations on the use of trademarks in dictionaries, see Landau (2001: 409).

[29] Proper names are not the names of categories, they cannot be used with an indefinite article, they are not synonymous with a definition, etc. (but see Kleiber 1996). Many lexicographers seem to be so keen on excluding them that they forget to mention their uses as common nouns, for example *a Picasso* 'a promising painter', *a true Rockefeller* 'a rich person', etc. (Urdang 1979). *SOED* has *Rockefeller* 'an immensely rich person; a millionaire', *COD11* has *Einstein* 'a genius', *Hitler* 'an authoritarian or tyrannical person', but most dictionaries ignore those uses.

and *umbrellas* must be lemmatized, i.e. grouped under a canonical form, or lemma, which stands for all the different forms that the lexical item can take in discourse, *go* for *go, goes, going, gone,* and *went.* In English, nouns are lemmatized in the masculine singular form and verbs in the infinitive without *to,* but other languages have different rules. In some cases, plural forms are different words, as in *clothes, customs, means,* etc., and have to be listed separately. Some inflected forms, for example *damned,* should also be listed separately, because they have meanings that are more than the meaning of the base form. The irregular inflected forms, *went, better, best,* are usually included in the list, not because they are different lexical items but because some users may need them.

Some forms in a text are only part of a larger lexical item, and it is the whole item that must be collected for the wordlist: compounds, phrasal verbs, and all sorts of phrases (see below). Again, it is often difficult to decide whether a string of words in a text is a multiword lexical item or just a free combination of words happening to be used together in a particular text, a feature of 'parole' or of 'langue': what are *friendly fire* or *weapons of mass destruction* (Teubert and Čermakova 2004), *railway director,*[30] or *molecular biologist* (Nida 1997: 268)? There are traces of this difficulty in dictionaries: some include *high-pitched* but not *low-pitched, long range* but not *short range, knee-high* but not *waist-high, more and more* but not *less and less,* etc. (Gates 1988: 100–2). The smaller dictionaries exclude the more transparent combinations, whose meanings are predictable because of their forms,[31] and the less frequent (see below), but the choices are often difficult to explain (Teubert and Čermakova 2004: 86): 'Why do dictionaries have some syntagms as entry-forms, and why those particular ones rather than others?' Rey-Debove (1971: 113) wonders. Mackintosh (2006: 55) suspects that some choices may be ideological: '[I]f *green peach aphid* makes the [*NCD10*] list, then surely *child abuse* should'.

Linguists say that a word combination can be considered as a lexical item if the words cannot be exchanged for a synonym (*house broken,* not **home broken*) or moved around (*spick and span,* not **span and spick*); if they do not accept another word between them (**shaving smooth cream*); if they designate a concept that has a place in a conceptual organization, a taxonomy, partonomy, etc. (*German measles,* not *severe measles*), etc. Corpus linguists have recently added frequency: lexical items are typically more frequent than other strings. But these work only in some cases, not all, and there are no simple criteria that lexicographers can use to choose the lexical items and leave out the free chunks: 'theoretical writings

---

[30] Included by Craigie in *OED1* against the advice of Murray and kept by Burchfield in *OEDS*.

[31] On the transparency of word combinations, see Gove (1966).

have so far offered no solution' (Atkins 1993: 28). In the absence of criteria, dictionaries cast their nets far and wide: *fellow traveller, guided missile, investment company, senatorial district,* etc. are entries in *MWC8, ALD7* has *herbaceous border, hiding place, home improvements,* etc.

Finally, some parts of words, morphemes, may be considered for inclusion in the wordlist: prefixes and suffixes, combining forms,[32] generally speaking all forms used productively in the language. *COD11* has entries for *-ist, -ista, -ite, -itic, -ition, -itious, -itis, -itive,* etc.

8.2.1.2　Choosing the lexical items for the wordlist: importance

As dictionaries increased their wordlists and aimed at representing the language, it became necessary to use a criterion of centrality, or importance in the language, for choosing the lexical items of the wordlist. The idea was to select the most important words first, and then continue the selection by including less and less important words in accordance with the size of the projected dictionary.

The lexis of a language has been pictured in poetic terms, for want of a more rigorous definition, as 'a spot of colour on a damp surface, which shades away imperceptibly into surrounding colourlessness', as 'an illuminated area in a midnight landscape, whose beams practically end somewhere, but no eye hath beheld the vanishing line' (Brewer 2007: 117), or less poetically as a circle that becomes increasingly indistinct as one moves from the centre to the outer edges.

The English vocabulary contains a nucleus or central mass of many thousand words whose 'Anglicity' is unquestioned; some of them only literary, some of them only colloquial, the great majority at once literary and colloquial,—they are the *Common Words* of the language. But they are linked on every side with other words which are less and less entitled to this appellation, and which pertain ever more and more distinctly to the domain of local dialect, of the slang and cant of 'sets' and classes, of the peculiar technicalities of trades and processes, of the scientific terminology common to all civilized nations, of the actual languages of other lands and peoples.　(*OED*: xxvii)

---

[32] The term *combining form* is used in many dictionaries but inconsistently, and rarely defined (Stein 2002: 51 *ff.*). *OED2* labels *-athon* a combining form but *-thon* a suffix; *NODE* labels *hypo-* and *supra-* prefixes but *hyp-* and *super-* combining forms, and the *-in* of *sit-in* is a combining form in one entry and an adverb in another! (Thanks to Jean Tournier, n.p., n.d.). *W3* says 'a linguistic form that occurs only in compounds or derivatives and can be distinguished descriptively from an affix by its ability to occur as one immediate constituent of a form whose only other immediate constituent is an affix (as *cephal-* in *cephalic*) or by its being an allomorph of a morpheme that has another allomorph that may occur alone (as *electro-* representing *electric* in *electromagnet* ....'. For Atkins and Rundell (2008: 166), combining forms are forms used in combinations such as *-covered, -leafed, -legged, -topped,* etc.

In such a system, the lexicographer can easily select the more common words in the centre and then move away in concentric circles as the size of the intended dictionary increases. But reality is not so simple: 'there is absolutely no defining line in any direction: the circle of the English language has a well-defined centre but no discernible circumference' (*OED*: xxvii). The truth is that even the centre is ill defined, and it is often difficult to decide whether a word belongs to the centre of the system or to the outer edges. The lexis of a language is 'a conglomerate of several entities' (Ducháček 1959: 98).

It is easy to show that dictionaries come to different conclusions in their choice of words. Finkenstaedt and Wolff (1973) found that *ALD* had proportionally more words of music than *SOED* and that *SOED* had more words of mineralogy.[33] The compilers of *W3* confessed several years after publication that the dictionary was particularly poor in words of mathematics, simply because the 'marking and reading program was fairly weak' (*Preface to 6,000 Words*: 17a). *SOED*'s 'intensive coverage of the vocabulary of surfing reflects the special interests of an individual reader' (Brewer 2004: 15). Rey-Debove (1971: 79–80) compared the wordlists of three French dictionaries of different dimensions (*PL, PR,* and *DFC*) and noted that 'no wordlist is totally contained in another'. Each dictionary, even the smaller one, had entries that neither of the others had.

8.2.1.3 Choosing the lexical items for the wordlist: frequency

Even before electronic corpora became available, the importance of a word was chiefly determined by its frequency: 'the notion of importance ... is essentially based on frequency of occurrence in discourse.... Roughly, the words that are pronounced and written most often are the most important' (Rey-Debove 1971: 30). In pre-corpus lexicography, frequency was evaluated intuitively, with results that naturally differed in different dictionaries, as we have seen, because lexicographers can agree on a large proportion of what words are the more frequent but they differ more and more as frequency decreases.

The selection of the wordlist by frequency was revolutionized by the arrival of electronic corpora. The computer can count forms, and to some extent words (see below, 9.1.5), list them, and order them by frequency. For the first time lexicographers had quantitative data to support or invalidate their hypotheses.

---

[33] They say (1973: 105) that 'W. Whewell, one of the scientists who played a part in the launching of the *OED*, was a mineralogist himself', but Whewell—who, incidentally, proposed the word *scientist* in its modern sense in 1840—died in 1866 and did not play any significant part in the *OED*. The amateur mineralogist was Murray himself (Richard Bailey, personal communication).

Table 8.1 Frequency of occurrence of words in the Birmingham
Corpus

Ranking	Frequency of occurrence	Number of types[a]
1	100,000 or more	19
2	99,999 to 10,000	156
3	9999 to 1000	1,550
4	999 to 100	8,796
5	99 to 10	33,058
6	9 to 4	29,389
7	3	13,964
8	2	28,838
9	1	131,298[b]

Notes: [a] A type here is a form. Every occurrence of a type in a text is a token: *boys will be boys* has 4 tokens but only 3 types. The 18 million-word Birmingham corpus had 247,068 types.
[b] This is about half the total number of types.
Source: Adapted from Hanks (1989: 9).

Table 8.1 shows what an analysis of the 18 million-word Birmingham corpus used for the compilation of *COB* (see below, 9.1.7) looked like in 1989.

This means that an average-sized dictionary of 75,000 types would have to list types from ranks 1 to 7, but not all the types in rank 7. To list all types with at least 3 occurrences, a dictionary would have to have 86,932 types. A dictionary listing all types in ranks 1 to 5, i.e. with frequencies of 10 and more, would have 43,579 types.

Frequency lists have confirmed the lexicographers' intuitions to a large extent. The most frequent words are the function words: the article *the* is the most frequent word in the English language, 'accounting for one word in fifteen, with a count of 6.2 million in the British National Corpus' (Kilgarriff 1997a: 136; see below, 9.1.7). In his corpus of 1 million words containing written and spoken documents (ICE-GB; see below, 9.1.7.4), Nelson (1997: 114) found that *the*, with 59,471 occurrences, was almost twice as frequent as *of*, the next word on the list, with 29,895 occurrences. The next words, in decreasing order, were also function words: *and, to, a, in, that, it, you, is.* The results are almost the same in all corpora, at least for the most frequent words (Kilgarriff 1997a: 148). The words of a corpus exhibit a 'Zipfian'[34] distribution: the most common word has about twice as many occurrences as the second most common, three times as many as the third, a hundred times as many as the hundredth, etc. (Kilgarriff 1997a: 136).

[34] Zipf, G. K. (1935), *The Psychobiology of Language* (Boston: Houghton Mifflin).

As a consequence, '[t]he 100 most frequent words in English make up around 45 per cent of the BNC's 100 million words' (Atkins and Rundell 2008: 60).

Of course, frequency lists are not enough to select the words for the wordlist. In small corpora, it was found that some important words had relatively low frequencies, so that two other criteria were considered: *répartition*, roughly the number of people who use the word and *disponibilité*, how easily the word comes to mind (Rey-Debove 1971: 67–8). In all corpora, there are always many forms with low frequencies, one, two, or three occurrences. The lexicographers cannot take all of them in the wordlist and they have to use criteria that are not quantitative to sort out the unwanted items. Some items can be eliminated even though they are as frequent as others: for example, those that are transparent: *amazingly, fairness, indistinct, irritating, surprised*, all the *anti-*, the *be-*, the *un-*, the *non-* words, etc.[35] Not something that 'lexicographers cherish but [that] they are compelled to adopt to save space' (Landau 2001: 162). On the other hand, some items must be included even though they may not be frequent in the corpus, for example the members of closed lexical sets, such as days of the week: *Thursday* cannot be omitted even if it is less frequent than *Sunday*.

The selection of the more frequent words and the omission of the highly infrequent in all except dictionaries of rare words rest on the assumption that the more frequent words are the more important and that the more important words in the language are also the more important in a dictionary. But surveys of dictionary use indicate that the more frequent words are hardly ever consulted, as we have seen. How can an entry be useful if it is never used? From the point of view of information theory, the rarer an item is the more information it carries, and the more useful it is. Perhaps the more useful words in a dictionary are in fact the least frequent ones. Perhaps dictionaries should pack in as many obscure words as possible, coming back to the tradition of the dictionary of hard words, and make space for them by ignoring the more frequent words, or treating them cursorily as in some dictionaries of the eighteenth century. The idea is discussed in the entry *dictionary* of the *Encyclopaedia Britannica*, 1877 edition, and it surfaces from time to time. Weinreich (1962: 26–7), for example: 'The fact that in our peculiar culture there is great demand for monolingual defining dictionaries, which include definitions of words so common that no one would conceivably want to look them up, is itself an interesting ethnographic datum'; or Quine (1973: 249): 'It has long seemed odd to me to clutter a popular domestic dictionary with idly compulsive definitions of words that all speakers of the language know'. But a GPD that would not have the frequent words is difficult to

---

[35] Murray complained that there were too many for the *OED* to record them (Burchfield 1993: 93).

imagine today. It would use many words in the microstructure that are not explained (see below), and above all it would forsake its role as a portrait of the language. Perhaps the hard word tradition will be back one day, with online dictionaries (see below, 9.2).

The appropriate criteria for the choice of the elements of the wordlist will differ with each dictionary project, but the basic criterion remains frequency: no lexical item is recorded unless it is used by a certain number of people over a reasonably long period, what Leech (1981: 205) calls 'corporate lexical competence'—the only exception being the *hapax legomena* of famous authors in dictionaries such as the *OED*. In the age of corpus lexicography, frequency is the easiest criterion to use and the more representative of a lexicography that aims as representing the language.

8.2.2 Questions of macrostructure

8.2.2.1 The different types of macrostructure

Some of the words of the wordlist can be included in special sections, in the back matter, in lists of proper names, of irregular verbs, of currencies, of ranks in the Army, etc. The others are left to the main A–Z list, where they have to be organized in a macrostructure. There are two sorts of macrostructure, at least in theory. One is a list of forms that are all different, so that each entry groups all the meanings that the form can have, even if there are no semantic links between them: for example, there will be only one entry *wind* for the verb and the noun, one entry *light*, etc. Atkins (1993: 16) calls this organization *non-homographic*.[36] The other type is a list of items that have only one meaning each, so that many entries will have the same form: for example, there will be several entries for *host* or *light*, each with one meaning. This is what Atkins calls a *totally homographic* macrostructure.

No dictionary has a totally homographic macrostructure, and few are non-homographic: most dictionaries are partly homographic, with some grouping of related meanings in complex entries and also different entries with the same form: *COD11*, for example, has one entry *market* with (at least) four meanings for the noun and three meanings for the verb, but three entries for *light n.*, *light adj.*, and *light v.* Of course, different dictionaries have different solutions: *CIDE* has one entry for *marquee* 'large tent' and another for *marquee* 'roof-like structure', while *COD11* treats both in the same entry; *bay*, 'part of the coast' and *bay*,

---

[36] Some say that the organization of the mental lexicon might be 'non-homographic' (Altmann 1997: 77 *ff.*).

'marked space' are treated in the same entry in *MEDAL* but in two different entries in *NODE*; ' "cricket bat", "baseball bat", and "ping-pong bat" are assigned to a single lexeme of *bat* by CED, to two lexemes ("cricket or baseball bat"; "ping-pong bat") by W9 [= *MWC9*], and to three lexemes by GID [= *Reader's Digest Great Illustrated Dictionary*]' (Ilson 1993: 25).

Dictionary entries are often determined by etymology. In some cases, the decisions are linguistically sound but lexicographically debatable. For example, the meanings of *game* are usually treated in the same entry because they have the same origin, but in the minds of most language users the meaning 'activity, sport' is one item and the meaning 'wild animals' another,[37] so that the word can reasonably be treated in two entries. Rundell (1988: 129–30) argues that in many cases the use of etymology to group meanings in a single entry or on the contrary to have different entries is counter-intuitive.

Most learners, for example, would probably see some connection between *bay*, in its meaning of 'an indentation in the coastline', and *bay*, when it means 'a recess' (as in *a loading bay* or *a bay window*); conversely, few learners would see any connection whatever between the two main meanings of *club* ('a society that people join' and 'a heavy stick used as a weapon'). Nevertheless, the historically-motivated (but counter-intuitive) organization of the native-speaker tradition has in general been carried over into the MLDs, so that *bay* appears in LDOCE and ALD as five separate noun homographs, while *club* appears as just one. Even more confusingly, *drill* ('a tool for making holes') and *drill* ('a form of instruction based on repetition') are grouped together in one homograph, while *drill* ('an agricultural tool for planting seeds') is shown as a separate entry.

The organization of a macrostructure is a lexicographic decision, in which linguistics only has a minor role. The question is to a large extent practical and psycholexicographic: what type of organization best allows the users to find what they are looking for and to benefit from the consultation of the dictionary?

8.2.2.2 Entries, sub-entries, and run-ons

Among the items in the main A–Z list, some are treated as if they were of lesser importance, because they can easily be accessed via other words. They are derived forms, i.e. forms with a prefix or a suffix or a combining form (*incompetent, disharmonious, pricewise, crust-like*, etc.), deverbal nouns in *-ing* (*hunting*), adjectives in *-ed* or *-ing* (*closed, interesting*), adverbs in *-ly* (*properly*), or multiword items of all kinds (see below). They can be deleted from the list, or treated as sub-headwords or run-ons.

---

[37] From an Old Saxon word meaning 'fellowship', and the use of the word for amusements, and hunting as an amusement, and a metonymy. Even the learners' dictionaries have only one entry *game*.

Prefixed forms (*anticyclone, non-committal*, etc.) usually have their own entries, because otherwise the users would not find them. Suffixed forms can be run-ons if their meanings can be deduced from the base word: in *COD11* nouns in -*ence*, -*ency*, -*er*, -*ion*, -*ience*, -*ing*, -*ism*, -*ness*, etc., adjectives in -*able*, -*al*, -*ary*, -*ful*, etc. and adverbs in -*ly* are run-ons. If their meanings cannot be easily inferred they can have their entries or sub-entries in the entry for the base word. Dictionaries vary: *COD8* had run-ons for *inclusion, managerial, resourceful*, etc.; *COD11* has separate entries for *inclusion, inclusive, jingoism, jobber, jobbery*, etc.; *AHD, C20D*, and *CED* do not mention *irritating* (in *AHD irritatingly* is a run-on in the entry for *irritate*), *COD11* and *C21D* have it as a run-on at the end of *irritate, CIDE* has a sub-entry in *irritate*, and the *Penguin All English Dictionary* (1970) has a short, and *LDOCE4* a long, entry *irritating*.

Naturally, considerations of space are important, and there are often more run-ons than there should be: *significantly* is 'almost never defined in dictionaries', although it is common and one of its main meanings is not 'in a significant way' (Landau 2001: 297);[38] 'in all the American college dictionaries except for *Merriam-Webster's Collegiate Dictionary*, Tenth Edition..., as well as in *CED*, *obviously* is run on to *obvious*, without a definition' (Landau 2001: 102). The feminine forms of some nouns, for example *manageress*, are sometimes treated as run-ons even though they have specific meanings. Even when there is a definition it is often minimal: 'Almost all dictionaries simply define adverbs ending in -*ly* like "oddly" and "obviously" formulaically with the definition "in a (such-and-such) manner", without specifying which of the many adjectival senses the adverb might apply to' (Landau 1991: 95; see also Atkins and Rundell 2008: 237). In *NODE* and *COD11, manageress* has an entry but it is only defined as 'a female manager'.

Multiword items can be either headwords or sub-headwords in the entry for one of their constituents: *hop, skip and jump* at *hop*, at *skip*, or at *jump*, or at all three, or at two of the three. If they are sub-headwords, they can be in the entry for the first word, for example *easy chair* at *easy*, or in the entry for the head of the compound, i.e. at *chair*. Some user studies suggest that the users are aware of the existence of a head, when there is one, in which case *easy chair* should be at *chair*. The problem is when the head is a well-known word and the other element is not: for example *forage fish*. In that case, the users will go to the unknown word (*forage*), especially if they do not realize that the two constitute a compound.

---

[38] In the *Cambridge Dictionary of American English* (2000), edited by Landau, it is defined as 'by a noticeably large amount'. In the *Oxford American Wordpower Dictionary* (1998), it has two meanings: '1. in a noticeable way', and '2. in a way that shows a particular meaning'.

The use of sub-entries and run-ons is mostly dictated by space constraints, but the resulting organization can be interpreted by the users as a reflection of the organization of the lexis, with words and meanings that are more or less close, and it is therefore important.

8.2.3 Questions of polysemy

8.2.3.1 The two sorts of lexical item

There are two sorts of lexical item in dictionaries: one is the association of one meaning with one form, which can be a simple entry with a simple definition or a section of a complex entry with a simple definition; the other is a grouping of related meanings sharing form and etymology treated in a complex entry. In linguistics, the distinction is between what Cruse (1986: 77) calls a *lexical unit* (LU), the association of a form and a single sense, a *lexie* for the Mel'čukians (Polguère 2003: 50), and what Cruse calls a *lexeme*, a *vocable* for Mel'čuk, which is a group of LUs, traditionally called a *word*. Both are hard to define: in order to define an LU one has to determine what constitutes a single meaning, a difficult task to say the least; and to define a lexeme one has to decide how close two meanings are, and what are the criteria to decide that they belong to the same unit (see below).

As language users, we are conscious of the two levels. We know what an LU is, because we know that meanings differ by their definitions, their paradigmatic relations, and their syntax: *table* 'piece of furniture' is related to *chair*, to *house*, to *sit*, etc., none of which applies to *table* 'set of facts or figures'; you *win a game of chess*, but you *shoot game*. But we also know what a lexeme is. We know that the same word can have different meanings. We can answer such questions as 'What is the meaning of *bay*?' (Iris *et al.* 1988: 249) using what Cruse (2000a: 108) calls the *default reading* of words, the meaning that comes to mind 'in the absence of any contextual information', or we can hesitate and ask which *bay* is meant.

What use is the distinction between LUs and lexemes in dictionary making? Is it 'good sound common sense dressed up in pompous verbiage'?[39] No it is not. For some of their tasks, pronunciation, POS, etymology, etc., lexicographers deal with lexemes, and for the others, definition, syntactic information, semantic relations, etc., they deal with LUs, and it is important to keep the two clearly separated. The distinction has now become part of the tool kit of many lexicographers (see Atkins and Rundell 2008).

---

[39] As 'one senior and respected dictionary editor' said to Atkins 'on hearing Cruse's definition of a lexical unit' (Atkins 1993: 30).

8.2.3.2 The identification of word meanings: tradition ...

Some words are monosemous:[40] they have only one meaning; others are polysemous. Polysemy is present in all languages, and polysemous words tend to be the same everywhere: names for body parts, for example, have multiple meanings in many languages. Polysemy has often been described as an unfortunate phenomenon, because it can create ambiguity in discourse, but it is indispensable, if the limited resources of a language are to account for the unlimited variations of reality. 'If [languages] had as many different forms as there are notions, objects or relations among them in the world outside the language, they would be impossible to use, because of the enormous burden they would impose on our memories' (Hagège 1985: 126). It is impossible to know how many English words are polysemous, because there is no easy test to determine whether a word has only one meaning or more than one, as we shall see. *LDOCE* has 46 per cent of its entries with more than one meaning (Stevenson and Wilks 2000: 166). *CED* has an average of 1.74 meanings for nouns and 2.11 for verbs (Fellbaum 2000: 53).

The distinction between polysemy and homonymy rests on the evaluation of the degree of semantic proximity. Some lexicographers have argued that it can be ignored: 'In the day-to-day practice of lexicography, especially commercial lexicography, no one is concerned about the theoretical imperatives of distinguishing between homonymy and polysemy' (Landau 2001: 101). But of course the lexicographer 'cannot avoid making definite decisions, which will determine the number and the structure of his entries' (Robins 1987: 54). Polysemous words are normally treated in complex entries and homonyms in different entries.[41]

The lexicographer has two problems with polysemous words: deciding how many meanings they have, and presenting those meanings in a way that is accessible to the users. The main problem is the identification of meanings. To the average language user, things are simple: if the dictionary one happens to consult says that a word has six meanings it does. But 'it is not as easy to say how many meanings a word has as casual reflection might suggest' (Lyons 1981: 22), and lexicographers do not have ready-made solutions.

What set of procedures do lexicographers have available to them to pin down those protean entities, 'meanings'? Faced with the almost unimaginable diversity of the

---

[40] The word *monosémie* seems to have been invented by Bréal (1897), as the antonym of *polysémie*. In English, *monosemous* is the more common form for the adjective, although some use *monosemic* (see Ruhl 1979; Cruse 2000*a*).

[41] In which case homonymous entries must also be ordered, at least in paper dictionaries, by frequency (the more frequent homonym first), by POS (verbs before nouns, or vice versa), or by some other criterion.

language they are trying to describe, with the knowledge that what for the sake of convenience we are pleased to call a language is in many ways a synthesis of shifting patterns that change from year to year, from locality to locality, from idiolect to idiolect, how do they arrive at those masterpieces of consensus, dictionaries? How do they decide what, for the purpose of a dictionary, constitutes the meaning of a word, and where, in the case of polysemous words, one meaning ends and the next begins?   (Ayto 1983: 89)

Different dictionaries have different numbers of meanings for the same word, and this is not always correlated with the dimensions of the dictionary: *fasten* has only one meaning in *LDOCE1* and seven in *CED*; *expire* has five meanings in *COD7*, only three in *CED*; *LDOCE* has only one meaning for *knife n.*, *COB2* has two: 'cutlery' and 'weapon'; *bake* 'to affect by cooking' and *bake* 'to create by cooking' are one meaning in *NODE* but two in *MEDAL1* (Ilson 1993: 22); *NODE* has 'five numbered senses, by comparison with CED4's fourteen' for *horse* (Jackson 2002: 89), etc. Sometimes the number of meanings is counter-intuitive.

Ask an English speaker what *perfect* means, and they will probably give you a simple definition like 'when something is as good as it could possibly be'. But if you ask them what a *party* is, they are likely to say 'well, that depends which sense you mean'. Yet the entry for *party* in *OALD-7* has just four numbered senses..., while *perfect* has seven.
(Atkins and Rundell 2008: 263)

Sometimes it is even difficult to see how many meanings the dictionary distinguishes because meanings can be separated in different ways: numbers, but also letters, sometimes semi-colons and even wordings in definitions: *line n.* has five meanings in *COD5* and 33 in *COD6*, no doubt in part because the semi-colons signalling sense divisions in *COD5* were replaced by numbers in *COD6*. One dictionary starts the entry for *pray* by '1a. to entreat earnestly; esp. to call devoutly on (God or a god) b. to wish or hope fervently' (Wierzbicka 1996: 268): how many meanings do we have here? One, two, three, four, more? And even when the number of meanings is similar in two dictionaries the meanings are not always the same: *length* has twelve meanings in *COD9* and eleven in *Collins Concise 4*, but only six of the twelve and seven of the eleven match with the other dictionary (Jackson 2002: 90); *COD8*, *CED3*, *MWC9*, and *AHD2* have significantly different meanings for *taste* (Atkins 1993: 19 *ff.*).

The problem is in what one calls a meaning.

Lexicographers are masters of the unsubstantiated assertion.... There is no way of mapping the sense divisions of one dictionary onto another. This implies that there is no simple, 'correct' way of analysing and defining the meaning of any given word. It is all a matter of literary taste and judgement.   (Hanks 1998: 151)

The identification of word meanings is one of the most difficult tasks of lexicography. It was what Murray complained most of in the preparation of the *OED* (Silva 2000: 90): ' "The terrible word *Black* and its derivatives" took one of the volunteer helpers...three months to arrange; even then it required a further three weeks' work from one of the Scriptorium assistants, and another week from Murray himself' (Mugglestone 2000*b*: 17). And lexicographers are rarely explicit about how they came to their conclusions: 'It is rare for a dictionary style guide to give the lexicographers criteria for identifying a valid dictionary sense' (Atkins 1993: 19).

Once the lexicographer has identified the homonyms, the remaining forms are either monosemous or polysemous. The need to divide a meaning into two or more may appear in the definition: for example, *cup* 'to drink from' and *cup* 'trophy' are obviously related but if you try to provide a definition covering both meanings you note that they require different elements; the conclusion is that they are best considered as different meanings (Ayto 1983). Or it may appear in syntactic behaviour: *blanket* is almost always *blanket of + n* when it does not mean 'bed covering'; or in their lexical environments: *turkey* 'bird' goes with *gobble* and *turkey* 'meat' with *roast* (Fillmore and Atkins 2000: 101), *pursue someone* can take a human object and *pursue a career* takes a non-human object; or in semantic relations: *mouse* 'computer accessory' is linked to *mouse* 'animal' by metonymy; or in lexical relations: *knife* 'table knife' has *cutlery* as hypernym and *fork, spoon* as co-hyponyms, but *knife* 'weapon' has *weapon, gun*, or *grenade* and *knife* 'garden knife' has *tool, secateurs, shears*, etc. (Cruse 2000*b*: 36);[42] or in derived forms: *act, action, active, activity*, and *act, actor, actress* are different acts (Moon 1987*b*: 94). Unfortunately, none of these criteria is completely foolproof.

8.2.3.3 Word meanings: contributions from semantics

Research that is potentially helpful for lexicographers in the identification of word meanings comes mostly from lexical semantics and from computational linguistics.[43] Many linguists have worked on what they call *ambiguity*, i.e. the fact that an utterance may be interpreted in different ways, and its relation to polysemy, a source of potential ambiguities. For example *bank* may mean 'slope of land alongside a river' or 'financial institution' and sentences using *bank* are potentially ambiguous. Humans usually have no problem identifying

---

[42] There is also *knife* 'in kitchen'. Is it a different meaning of *knife*? *Garden knife* has 17,300 returns on Google (22 September 2008), *kitchen knife* has 1,230,000!

[43] There is also research in psycholinguistics (Aitchison 1994), but it is less immediately relevant to lexicography.

the appropriate meaning. Hanks (2000*b*: 126) claims that *I went to the bank* is never ambiguous in context, despite what many semanticists have said: it is always clear whether *bank* refers to one or the other meaning, unless the context has been invented by a linguist to make it deliberately ambiguous.[44] But how do we do it? The complexity of the operation is apparent when linguists try to teach a machine to disambiguate automatically (see below, 9.1.5). 'How do human language-users effortlessly perform a task which computers find so difficult?' (Atkins and Rundell 2008: 270).

Cruse (1986) proposed a range of tests that aim to determine whether two uses of the same form are different lexemes or whether they are different meanings of the same lexeme. They are tests of acceptability in which a word is inserted in a context, a sentence, a text, or a dialogue and the linguist, if necessary with the help of informants, decides whether the sentence is acceptable or not. There are several types, one of which is the zeugma test,[45] designed to measure the compatibility of two uses. For example (Cruse 1986: 62), it is possible to say

My cousin, who is pregnant, was born on the same day as Arthur's, who is the father

But you can't say

*John and his driving licence expired last Thursday

because *expire* has (at least) two different meanings (Cruse 1986: 61). There are many other tests, but unfortunately for lexicographers, they suggest that meaning can be even more complex than they thought: some words have different aspects that can be highlighted, brought to the fore in some contexts and kept in the background in others even though the word is not polysemous. He calls these aspects *facets* (Cruse 2000*a*: 114). Take *book* in

1. Put this book back on the shelf
2. I find this book unreadable

In 1, the facet 'tome' is foregrounded and in 2 it is the facet 'text'. Yet the two, the 'text' facet and the 'tome' facet, 'co-ordinate quite happily, without producing a sense of punning' (Cruse 2000*a*: 114), as in

Put this book back on the shelf: it's quite unreadable

---

[44] Asher and Lascarides (1996: 70) give the following example: 'The judge asked where the defendant was. The barrister apologized, and said he was at the pub across the street. The court bailiff found him slumped underneath the bar'.

[45] Zeugma is the strange effect caused by the use of two words in the same context inappropriately, as in 'He was wearing a scarf, a pair of boots, and a look of considerable embarrassment' (Cruse 1986: 13).

So that one would hesitate to say that *book* has a 'text' meaning and a 'tome' meaning. Another example is 'Sam picked up and finished his beer', where beer is both 'liquid' and 'container'. When two uses cannot co-exist, as in (Kilgarriff 1997*b*: 141; see also Copestake and Briscoe 1996: 55)

*The newspaper costs 25p and sacked all its staff

we have two different meanings, not two facets.

Facets are everywhere, even in proper names: *Shakespeare* means 'the writings' in 'I have all Shakespeare on this shelf' or 'the man' in 'Shakespeare died in 1616', although no lexicographer would ever think of treating *Shakespeare* as having two meanings. In some cases there are default facets, as in 'John ordered a pizza' as opposed to 'The pizza doesn't look too happy with what he's been given'.

Cruse's tests have been criticized. They require appropriate contexts, they use contexts that are tiny compared to real-life language use, they rest on an evaluation of acceptability by the linguist and different tests sometimes give contradictory results.[46] But the idea that some meanings have facets suggests that there may be a middle ground between monosemy and polysemy. Lexicographers can try Cruse's tests when they have doubts, but the result may be a highly complex entry, not suitable for all dictionaries.

[A] full Cruse lexical entry would contain: a specification of polysemous senses; their lexical relations including their relations to each other; whether they were antagonistic or not; the facets, shared or otherwise, of each, and the extent to which distinct facets of meaning could operate autonomously, so approach the status of senses on their own.

(Kilgarriff 1997*b*: 138)

Frame semantics, introduced by Charles Fillmore in the early 1980s,[47] posits that word meaning should be described in terms of the elements of the situation in which the word is used. Words do not only belong to static systems, typically taxonomic, as in traditional semantics, they also belong to dynamic systems, typically frames or scenarios.

A word's meaning can be understood only with reference to a structured background of experience, beliefs, or practices, constituting a kind of conceptual prerequisite for understanding the meaning. Speakers can be said to know the meaning of a word only by first understanding the background frames that motivate the concept that the word encodes. Within such an approach, words or word senses are not related to each other directly, word to word, but only by way of their links to common background frames and

---

[46] On the deficiencies of tests of acceptability, see Zwicky and Sadock (1975).
[47] Based on Minsky (1975).

indications of the manner in which their meanings highlight particular elements of such frames.   (Fillmore and Atkins 1992: 76–7)

For example, an act of purchasing involves four elements: a seller, a buyer, the thing being sold/bought, and the price, and all four elements correspond to words (*sell, buy, charge, charge, cost,* etc.) that are used in different positions and roles in different syntactic constructions. Similarly for *risk*, which has a protagonist, an outcome, a decision, a goal, a setting, a possession, and a source (Fillmore and Atkins 1994: 367). The objective of frame semantics 'is to describe all possible constellations of frame elements and how these can be realized, syntactically and lexically, at the surface level' (Fontenelle 2002: 225). Frame semantics can help sort out meanings more quickly, more easily and with more precision, as has been shown by Hanks (1994) or Atkins *et al.* (2003*b*). For example, it shows that *argue* has three meanings because it is used in three different frames that Atkins *et al.* (2003*b*: 337) call evidence (*argue* = 'constitute evidence in support of something'), conversation (*argue* = 'exchange diverging or opposite views'), and reasoning (*argue* = 'give reasons or cite evidence in support of something'). *COD10* had obviously not seen the 'constitute evidence' meaning, and had only two:[48]

1 exchange diverging or opposite views heatedly. 2 give reasons or cite evidence in support of something

Wierzbicka always starts by assuming that a word is monosemous, then checks her definition against the different uses of the word and posits the existence of another meaning only if necessary. If the analysis is carried out thoroughly, she says, many words that are often considered polysemous will be shown to be monosemous: 'in ordinary English the word *plant* is not even polysemous, as has sometimes been suggested (Casson 1981: 78). Linguistic evidence shows that in ordinary English it has only one meaning' (Wierzbicka 1985: 155).

Many other semanticists, Mel'čuk and his Meaning → Text Theory (1988*a*), Hoey[49] and his Lexical Priming (2005), Hanks and his Theory of Norms and Exploitations (2004*b*), Sinclair and others have contributed usefully to research on the identification of meanings. They are all very different, working with corpora or not, but they all claim that the different meanings of a polysemous word correspond to different patterns of use and that a thorough analysis of contexts can identify them. On the whole, most of the recent work of corpus

---

[48] *COB2* has seven meanings for argue, but not 'constitute evidence' either. On the use of frame semantics in dictionaries, see Atkins and Rundell (2008: 144 *ff.*).

[49] Who was 'Chief Adviser' for *MEDAL*.

linguists, of cognitive linguists, and of more traditional semanticists argues that meanings are flexible, that there is an infinity of sub-senses and sub-sub-senses in discourse and that meaning is 'embodied', i.e. meanings are best described not in terms of features as in traditional semantics but in terms of contexts, situations, scenarios, scenes, frames, schemata, etc. that represent the interaction of humans with the world around them.

8.2.3.4 Word meanings: contributions from corpus linguistics

Modern semantics is dominated by cognitive linguistics and corpus linguistics. The (irreducible?) difference between the two is that for the former meaning is in the minds of the language users whereas for the latter meaning is in the contexts (Teubert 2005). Linguists working with corpora argue that contexts are normally enough to separate meanings. The reason why sentences are rarely ambiguous for human readers is that humans analyse the context in ways that are still out of reach for even the most sophisticated machines.

One of the aims of corpus linguistics is to identify word meanings automatically by an analysis of context (see below). This is important in information retrieval, in text interpretation, in machine translation, and many other applications. The first attempts at identifying meanings automatically in a corpus were in the 1970s, but at the time the programs involved a large amount of human intervention, and since then the focus has been towards a greater automatization of the task and an improvement in the accuracy of the results. A vast multi-language project of word sense disambiguation (WSD) called SENSEVAL, with regular workshops[50] (Kilgarriff (1997b), aimed at comparing the performances of different disambiguating systems (Kilgarriff and Palmer 2000) against an identification of word meanings in context by three experienced lexicographers. The results are only half convincing, the best systems reaching a ceiling of about 70 per cent accuracy. Some specialists (Ide and Wilks 2006: 48) think that the operation has been aiming too high, at the level of fine nuances of meaning whereas the level of homonymy or clear polysemy, for example *bank* 'institution' and *bank* 'side of river' or *crane* 'bird' and *crane* 'machine', is enough for most applications. But it is precisely the finer nuances that are interesting for the lexicographer, as the grosser differences are reachable intuitively. The big problem of SENSEVAL is that it works backwards, from pre-established meanings in a lexical database or in a machine-readable dictionary (see below, 9.3.1), tying in the results to the imperfections of the source that is used. The attempts to extract meanings directly from textual evidence, a data-driven approach, have so far

---

[50] Senseval 1 was in 1997, Senseval 2 in 2001, and Senseval 3 in 2004. See http://www.senseval.org.

failed (Ide and Wilks 2006: 54): 'The trouble with word sense disambiguation', Kilgarriff (2006: 29) concludes, 'is word senses'. There is no pre-packaged product that lexicographers can use for the automatic identification of meanings.

Pending full automation of the task, Kilgarriff (1997b: 144) claims that the only way to identify word meanings is to work humbly and empirically from the corpus, group the citation lines with appropriate criteria in clusters according to their most obvious features, and refine the distinctions progressively, until one reaches the stage that is appropriate to each dictionary project—a good way not to repeat what other dictionaries have done. This is not easy, because of the avalanche of infinitely variable contexts for some words (see below, 9.1.6), but it ensures that no important meaning or use will be overlooked. An additional advantage is that it will eventually establish the frequency of the different meanings, although that is not yet possible (Atkins and Rundell 2008: 207). The results might not be impeccable, but they are the best that can be done.

The identification of meanings is a process of decontextualization and general-ization: each individual use of a lexeme is stripped of its idiosyncrasies in discourse, in what Atkins (1993: 7) calls 'the analysis process' of lexicography, and only the more general features are kept, to create groups of occurrences. The final decisions will depend on the intended size of the dictionary, the intended users, etc. It is an impossibly difficult task for which there are no simple answers, but lexicographers can take solace in the fact that after all, here again, there is no such thing as perfection and what counts is how useful the results of their efforts are for the dictionary user.

8.2.3.5 Splitting or lumping senses?

At some stage in the identification of word meanings, the lexicographer will be faced with a choice: either lump uses or meanings together or distinguish as many meanings as possible: lumping or splitting. A word in a dictionary 'can have about as many senses as the lexicographer cares to perceive' (Hanks 2002: 159). Both extreme solutions make things difficult for the user: too much grouping means vague meanings and definitions, and too many fine distinctions means excessively complex entries.

Most lexicographers have tended to be splitters rather than lumpers (Moon 1987a: 177), 'meaning-finders' rather than 'meaning-losers' (Gove in Morton 1994: 81), in England and in France (Rey-Debove 1971: 255–6), perhaps because of a desire to be exhaustive, perhaps because it is easier to split than to lump, or because of a desire to produce definitions that are substitutable (see below).

[T]here is ample evidence, from lexicographic theory and practice to publishers' pro-motional literature, to suggest that the provision of the maximum possible number of word-meanings is—whether implicitly or explicitly—the central aim of lexicographers working in the NSD tradition.   (Rundell 1988: 128)

Johnson had five pages and 88 sections for *set*. Murray disapproved of Craigie:

[He] divided senses to a degree [Murray] saw as excessive [and] demanded 'reduction of the number of senses and sub-senses, esp. by making definitions broad enough to cover the latter, and abandonment as far as possible of the contextual distinctions introduced by "Of persons" "Of animals" "Of qualities", etc., etc.'   (Silva 2000: 86)

But with 341 different meanings for *take* (Moon 1987*a*: 177), 28 divisions of senses for the adjective *black*, 18 pages for *set*, 'fifty-four divisions of sense' and 'seventeen columns of text' for *do* (Mugglestone 2005: 43), the *OED* was the archsplitter. *OED2* continued the tradition: it had 260 senses for *make*, and this was increased to 267 in *OED Online*.[51] *MWC7* has 125 meanings for *run*; *RHD2* has 97 meanings for *run* as a verb, plus 25 idioms, 49 meanings for the noun, with 5 idioms, and 2 meanings for the adjective. This, Nida (1997: 268) says, is unreasonable: 'all of these "meanings" are primarily different contexts in which *run* occurs in English'. Rundell (1988: 132) also thinks that lexicographers split too much: 'An expression like *sing the baby to sleep* is used to generate a separate "meaning" of *sing* along the lines of "bring someone into the specified state by singing" (e.g. W9 [= *MCW9*], CED, LDOCE1)'. As we have seen, *LDOCE1* had different meanings of *walk* according to the number of legs of the walker. The *Oxford Paperback Dictionary* has a separate meaning for *friend* 'a helpful thing or quality, e.g. *darkness was our friend*'. *ALD7* at *propose* has a meaning 'suggest plan' and another 'suggest explanation': 'Consider the phrase "propose a hypothesis". Is this sense 1 or sense 5 of *propose*?' (Hanks 2008: 101). *EWED* has a meaning *fly v.* 'to travel with a particular airline or in a particular class in an aircraft: *She always flies with the same airline*' that is difficult to distinguish from another meaning 'to travel in an aircraft'. Landau (2000: 119) did not like it at all: 'you can also say "She always flies with her husband" or "She always flies with a full stomach." Should we add definitions like "to travel with one's spouse" and "to travel after eating"? With whom or in what condition she flies is adventitious and has nothing to do with the sense here'. Goddard (2000: 149) blames the 'faulty methodology' of lexicographers for 'a wholesale proliferation of "false polysemy"'. And the use of a corpus 'exacerbates the problem' (Atkins and Rundell 2008: 313), because it multiplies the occurrences that the lexicographer processes and the occasions to see new 'meanings'.

---

[51] *OED News*, July 2000.

Even before cognitivism and corpus linguistics, there were linguists who thought that dictionaries distinguished too many meanings: words like *take*, *give, come, go, break, hit*, and even *thing*, or *be*, Catford (1983) wrote, are basically monosemous. And so are *expire, recognise, realise* (Bäcklund 1981: 410), *break, cut, tear* (Ruhl 1980), etc. They are polysemous in dictionaries 'because their essential, general meanings are confused with contextual, inferential meanings' (Ruhl 1979: 93). Those linguists were brushed aside as an 'aberrant branch of linguistic research' by Landau (2001: 433), but their views were eventually supported by linguists such as Wierzbicka, by corpus linguists, and by some lexicographers. Moon (1987*a*: 173) argued that *mouth* had several aspects, probably the same as Cruse's facets,

He took the cigarette out of his mouth [OPENING]
She had a wide and smiling mouth [LIPS]
He put the meat into his mouth [CAVITY]

but was monosemous.

The most recent linguistic theories of meaning, whether corpus-inspired or not, contend that there is more coherence in the meanings of polysemous words than was once thought. Perhaps because of this research, and perhaps also because of a desire to adapt the dictionary text to the skills of the users, there is a tendency in modern lexicography towards lumping, or at least less splitting: 'After years of corpus lexicography, I am inclined to believe, with Moon (1987*a*, 1988) and others, that many words are basically monosemous, and it does the user a disservice to suggest otherwise by dividing them into "senses"' (Atkins 1993: 31). Seeing different meanings of *bank* in *river bank, sand bank, grassy bank*, etc. is unwise, Hanks (2000*b*: 127) says, and he recommends the use of Ockham's razor to 'avoid a needless multiplicity of entities'.

Of course, the more you lump the more general the definition will have to be, and the more difficult to write, as lexicographers have known for a long time (Zgusta 1989*c*: 204). The formulation runs the risk of being so vague as to be of no practical utility, like the first of *C2oD*'s definitions of *game*: 'sport of any kind'. For a word like *bank*, a definition capturing such uses as *data bank, blood bank, seed bank*, and *sperm bank*, Hanks (2000*b*: 126) argues, would be something like 'any of various other institutions for storing and safeguarding any of various other things', a 'catch-all' definition, a 'lexicographer's copout'.[52] Even in a simple case like *empress*, it is difficult to think of a definition that would encompass the

---

[52] But Hanks managed quite well in *NODE*: 'a stock of something available for use when required: *a blood bank* | figurative *Britain has a bank of highly exportable skills*.'

two meanings: 'woman *who is connected to* an emperor'?[53] As always in lexicography, the optimal position is somewhere in between: not too much splitting but not too much lumping either.

8.2.3.6 Different sorts of polysemy

The meanings of a polysemous word are related in different ways: there can be semantic restriction, from a meaning to a narrower one (from *drink* 'absorb a liquid' to *drink* 'consume too much alcohol') or extension, from a meaning to a broader one (from *sacrifice* 'kill for religious motives' to *sacrifice* 'give up something important'). There can be a metaphor (from *mouse* 'animal' to *mouse* 'computer accessory') or a metonymy (from *mouth* 'opening in human face' to *mouth* 'child to be fed'). These relations are usually indicated in dictionaries by labels such as *partic., by ext., meton., by anal., Hence*, etc. Many British (and French) dictionaries have also used *fig.* for *figurative*, to indicate a new meaning, usually abstract from concrete. For example *NODE*:

deluge ■ figurative a great quantity of something arriving at the same time[54]

But Ayto (1988) has convincingly argued that the meaning of *figurative* is not clear. It has never been used in American dictionaries and is hardly ever used now even in Britain.

Polysemous lexemes differ by the way their meanings are organized. The simplest organization is the kind that the *OED* looked for: a meaning B develops from a meaning A, then a meaning C from meaning B, etc. This is called *linear polysemy*. Another kind is *radial polysemy*, where all meanings are connected to a central meaning. Yet another is what Wittgenstein (1953: 31–2) in his well-known discussion of *game* known as *family resemblances*: B is connected to A and C is connected to B but not to A, etc., so that C and A may have nothing in common. This was later used by many linguists, particularly in prototype theory (see below), and has had enormous influence.[55] The idea that a new meaning has at least one feature in common with another, existing, meaning is unproblematic, but the idea that there is not a single feature that is common to all the meanings of a polysemous word is more debatable. Wierzbicka (1996: 245) argues that family

---

[53] *C20D* has 'see *emperor*', where *empress* is a run-on.

[54] *NODE* does not use *figurative* for *cascade, torrent*, etc.

[55] Wittgenstein was also a lexicographer. He 'compiled an innovative dictionary for primary-school children' the *Wörterbuch für Volksschulen*, with 5,700 words (1925): 'using the dialects of the Austrian countryside and respecting its culture, [it] was well within the spirit of the reforms [of the Pedagogic Institute]' 'seeking children's active engagement through self-discovery and problem-solving' (Edmonds and Eidinow 2001: 19, 61, 237).

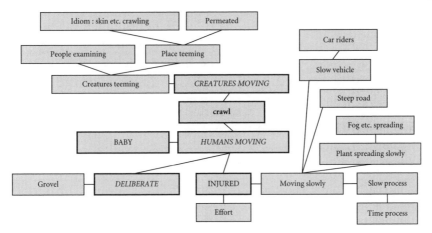

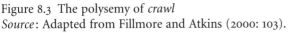

Figure 8.3 The polysemy of *crawl*
Source: Adapted from Fillmore and Atkins (2000: 103).

resemblances 'never had any empirical basis', that they are 'the speculative idea of a philosopher' and that they have been 'particularly damaging' because they have been used as an 'excuse for lexicographic laziness or as a justification for lexicographic despair' (Wierzbicka 1996: 269). It does seem reasonable, and clearly preferable for lexicography, to posit that there is a semantic invariant, a hard 'nodule' shared by all the meanings of a polysemous word, as suggested by Wierzbicka in her definition of *game* (1996: 159; adapted):

many kinds of things that people do, for some time, 'for pleasure', they want some things to happen, they don't know what will happen, they know what they can and cannot do[56]

Most polysemous words, unfortunately for the lexicographer, are neither clearly linear nor radial but exhibit complex patterns of relations between their meanings. Fillmore and Atkins (2000: 103) propose to represent the polysemy of *crawl* as in Figure 8.3 (here slightly adapted). Such patterns are obviously difficult to represent in a dictionary.

8.2.3.7 Regularities in the lexicon and the dictionary
Some of the uses of polysemous words are predictable, because they implement rules that apply to all, or almost all, words in similar cases. For example, in English, the word used to refer to an animal, say *rabbit*, can also be used to refer to its flesh, a phenomenon sometimes called *animal grinding*. There are many other types: 'a representation of a thing can be called by the same term as the

---

[56] On Wierzbicka's definitions, see below.

thing depicted' (Lehrer 1990: 238); the name of an institution can refer to the building (*bank, school*); the name of a musical instrument can be used to refer to the person who plays it (*violin*); the name of a text can refer to the contents or to the object, as we have seen (*book*); the name of a periodical can refer to the text, the object or the institution (*newspaper, magazine*).

The newspapers attacked the president for raising taxes
Mary spilled coffee on the newspaper
John got angry at the newspaper   (Pustejovsky 1995: 91)

Those are well known. There are other cases, in which the use depends on the context and seems somehow less clearly lexicalized.[57] The name of an object can be used to refer to the section of a department store where the object is sold: 'She moved from handbags through gifts to the flower shop' (Kilgarriff 1997*b*); the name of a dish can be used to refer to the person who orders it in a restaurant: 'The ham sandwich is getting restless'; the name of a piece of clothing, or of a physical characteristic can be used to refer to the person wearing or having it: 'the red beret in the corner/the nose wart/pink specs/etc. is getting impatient'.[58]

These uses are what Cruse called *facets*. Dictionaries have always recorded some of them: *COD5* had

book 1. Portable written or printed treatise filling a number of sheets fastened together (forming roll, or usu. with sheets sewn or pasted hingewise and enclosed in cover); literary composition that would fill such a set of sheets (or several) if printed;

But the treatment is rarely consistent. *COB* has a contents meaning for *carafe* ('the amount of liquid that it contains'), for *bottle, bucket, glass*, and *pail* but not for *pitcher*; *ALD7* has a 'glass of' meaning for *whisky*, but not for *Calvados, crème de menthe*, or *grappa* (Atkins and Rundell 2008: 313); *C20D* and *COD11* have a definition 'one who carries a gun' for *gun*, not *COB*; most dictionaries distinguish *door* 'the opening' from *door* 'the thing that closes up that opening' (Schelbert 1988: 65) and sometimes even *door* 'the door of a public building', but the distinction is more rarely applied to *window*; 'virtually every standard American dictionary lists a "meat" sense for the words *chicken* and *tuna*, whereas we have found only one that gives an equivalent sense for *turkey* and none that lists this

---

[57] *Lexicalization* is not a clear concept. It is variously defined as the creation of a lexical item to refer to a concept that has just appeared or that has never been named before; or as the integration of a neologism into the lexicon; or as the creation of a lexical item from a phrase.

[58] But there are restrictions: can a teacher refer to one of his students as 'The big tits is very smart'? (Claude Boisson, personal communication). Is there any research on that? Such cases are hard to distinguish from the inventive use of words as in 'Three Martinis later …'. Clearly 'the time necessary to drink a Martini' cannot be considered as a meaning of *Martini*. Is it a facet?

use of *salmon*' (Nunberg and Zaenen 1992: 395). *COD11* has none of these, except for *salmon*! *COD11* has a definition for *white* 'the player of the white pieces in chess or draughts', not *ALD7*; *COD8*, like *COD7* before it, had a *horse* meaning 'representation of horse' but no such meaning for *cow*, *dog*, etc.; *SOED* has a 'player' meaning for *drum*, *flute*, and *violin* but not for *guitar*. Of course no dictionary has a 'department' meaning for *handbag* or a 'person' meaning for *ham sandwich*, *pizza*, or *beret*. Some of the omissions can be justified if the meanings are not frequent enough, but not all.

Linguists have written extensively about regular meaning extensions recently, as part of a general realization that there are regularities in the lexicon (Lehrer 1990). They were first described by Apresjan (1973*b*), who called them *regular polysemy* and then by others under various names: *systematic polysemy* (Nunberg 1978), *semantic transfer rules* (Leech 1981), *lexical implications rules* (Ostler and Atkins 1992), *logical polysemy* (Pustejovsky and Boguraev 1996: 1), etc. Ostler and Atkins (1992) list about 130 regularities in English, not all cases of polysemy because they include changes of form and/or of POS: the name of a dance can be used as a verb to refer to the action of doing the dance (*waltz* ↔ *to waltz*); the name of an artefact can be used as a verb to refer to the action of using the artefact: *button* ↔ *to button*, *hammer* ↔ *to hammer*; the name of a substance allows an N + -*en* adjective meaning 'made of': *gold* ↔ *golden*, *wood* ↔ *wooden*, etc. There are exceptions, cases of 'lexical blocking' (Peters and Kilgarriff 2000: 308). Some are established in the language: *cow*, *bull*, *calf*, *ox*, *pig*, and *sheep* cannot be used to refer to their meat because the role was taken up by other words.[59] Some -*er* deverbal nouns have not been realized: **stealer*, for example, is blocked by *thief* (Copestake and Briscoe 1996: 56); *cooker* is the name of the piece of equipment, not of the person who cooks. Some names of artefacts cannot be used as verbs: *to pen* but **to computer*. Some names of animals cannot be used to refer to their skins used as fur because the sellers invented posher words: one does not wear *rat*. Some fish have different names when they are alive and when they are sold as food. Other blockings are only in discourse. The 'food' reading of *hedgehog* is not normally activated because we do not normally eat hedgehog, but it could be: the LOB corpus (see below, 9.1.7) has 'Badger hams are a delicacy in China while mole is eaten in many parts of Africa' (Copestake and Briscoe 1996: 37).

The linguists are interested in listing these relations, in trying to understand the exceptions and in determining how much the regularities cover in a particular

---

[59] There are exceptions to the exceptions, always stylistically marked: 'Hot sausages, two for a dollar, made of genuine pig...', 'There were five thousand extremely loud people on the floor eager to tear into roast cow...' (Copestake and Briscoe 1996: 38).

language and across languages. Ostler and Atkins note that regular polysemy exists in many languages, perhaps in all, but that the rules differ,[60] so that they must be part of the description of the lexicon. They are neither arbitrary nor predictable, but motivated (Lakoff 1987: 379): they cannot be predicted, but they are not totally arbitrary either, the link between a new meaning and another meaning can always be explained, often by metaphor or metonymy.

> Two attitudes are equally untenable: choosing arbitrariness, and choosing total predict-ability.... The shift from *veau* (the animal) to *veau* (the meat) is motivated by the relation of metonymy that links the two. If there were total predictability, all animals would give rise to such metonymies, which is not the case. If it was only an arbitrary convention, there would be no link between the two. Thus, polysemy is fundamentally seen as a phenomenon of motivated convention.   (Kleiber 1988: 53)

Kleiber's example may not be the best one, but the point is clear: some meanings or uses are motivated, if not totally predictable.

For the lexicographer, the question is whether those regular meaning exten-sions should be listed or whether they can be left for the users to infer from their knowledge of the lexicon and its rules. This is partly a practical problem. If space is at a premium, as in all paper dictionaries, is it reasonable to indicate predict-able meaning extensions such as *glass* 'contents'? '[T]he complete representation of all such regularities would swell real dictionaries to an unmanageable size, with material much of which would be of doubtful practical use' (Ilson 1990*a*: 130). Do I need to be told that I can bolero to my heart's content? But it is also a linguistic problem: what is a meaning and what is only inventive discourse? The answer lies in the assessment of the frequency and the regularity of each use: how many times does it occur in the corpus, how many different sources use it, how many similar cases does the rule apply to and are there exceptions? Kilgarriff (1997*b*: 148), studying the occurrences of *handbag* in his corpus, noted that it had a 'weapon' meaning ('determined women armed with heavy handbags') and a 'music genre' meaning ('Handbag Djs will love it'), and decided that the former was frequent enough to warrant inclusion, not the latter.

8.2.3.8 Do word meanings exist?

The idea that word meanings can be identified and listed is popular with the language users and handy for lexicographers, because it produces neat entries suited to punctual consultation. We tend to view words as a set of fixed separate

---

[60] Russian uses the names of body organs to refer to diseases: *'She has a kidneys'. Eskimo does not use the name of an animal to refer to its meat (Nunberg and Zaenen 1992).

meanings, and it is difficult to know which came first: do dictionaries copy popular views of the lexicon, or do we have such views because of dictionaries? Van der Meer (2000*b*: 420) thinks the latter is true: 'the notion of various *separate* senses for one word is . . . to a large extent inculcated by the numbering found in many dictionaries'.

But what Fillmore (1975) called the 'checklist theories of meaning', Pustejovsky and Boguraev (1994: 296) a 'canonical' view of word meaning, and Atkins and Rundell (2008: 272) a 'Platonic inventory of senses "out there"', the idea that there is a fixed number of senses per word has been challenged recently by linguists and lexicographers working with corpora. 'Lexicographers who have . . . examined hundreds of individual citations minutely in an attempt to find objective evidence for the existence of dictionary senses, report that in many cases such objective evidence simply is not there' (Atkins 1991: 168). Atkins (1993: 19 *ff.*) extracted 43 contexts of *taste* from the Oxford Pilot Corpus (see below, 9.1.7.5) and noted that it was difficult to decide how many different meanings there were. There were too many slight variations in context, and meanings did not divide up neatly. 'Dictionary makers and dictionary users persist in speaking as if word meanings are entities with a real existence which can be captured scientifically', Hanks (1998: 151) said, but 'the notion that a given word has five or ten or twenty "senses" is simply a useful working convention without any objective truth-value: in reality, word meaning is a far more elusive phenomenon' (Rundell 1999: 40). Hanks (2000*b*: 125) concluded:

[C]hecklist theories in their current form are at best superficial and at worst misleading. If word meanings do exist, they do not exist as a checklist. The numbered lists of definitions found in dictionaries have helped to create a false picture of what really happens when language is used.

Many words, Hanks (2000*b*: 128) says, are vague,[61] they admit variations according to the contexts in which they are used. There are contexts, he says, in which more than one dictionary meaning is activated, so that the word means something close to two of the meanings but not quite the one or the other. The meaning of a word should be seen as a set of semantic components that are 'possible rather than necessary contributors to the meaning of texts'. When the word is used, one at least of these components is evoked, but 'no one of them is a necessary condition' (2000*b*: 129). This is intriguing, because it implies that meanings are 'events, not entities' (2000*b*: 130). They are perpetually in the

---

[61] *Vagueness* should be distinguished from *generality*: *vertebrate* is general (there are many kinds of vertebrates) but not vague (it can be defined precisely); *cousin* is vague (it can be male or female), not general (Cruse 1986: 81).

making. Such a view is supported by the diachronic dimension of polysemy: meanings develop over time, with each new use of a word, and there are an infinite number of stages before a meaning has enough autonomy and frequency to be recognized as established, or lexicalized, and stored by the members of the community.

This has far-reaching consequences. One is that WSD may be misguided, since much of it 'proceeds on the basis of there being a computationally relevant, or useful, or interesting, set of word senses in the language, approximating to those stated in a dictionary' (Kilgarriff 1997*b*: 138). What use is it to judge how close a disambiguating system comes to dictionary senses if dictionary senses misrepresent reality? Another consequence is that the basic unit of language use may not be the LU with its meaning but the individual instance of use of an LU. In every new use there is something new, something different from any other use: 'a lexical unit may justifiably be said to have a different meaning in every distinct context in which it occurs' (Cruse 1986: 53). As Heraclitus said, one cannot step into the same river twice.[62] This is a dangerous line for lexicography: the dictionary must decontextualize and generalize if it is to be useful, it must 'impose some order on this babel' (Atkins and Rundell 2008: 311), it cannot record individual instances of use.

The format of the traditional dictionary does not accurately represent usage. It 'fails to account for the creative use of words in novel contexts' (Pustejovsky and Boguraev 1994: 297). Word meaning 'cannot be sliced up into distinct bundles, labelled (however carefully) and packaged into a dictionary entry' (Atkins 1991: 180). 'Faced now with the overwhelming richness and subtlety of the language in a computerized corpus, I no longer believe that it is possible to give a faithful, far less true, account of the "meaning" of a word within the constraints of the traditional entry structure' (Atkins 1993: 20). The dictionary creates 'a false picture of what really happens when language is used' (Hanks 2000*b*: 205). Sad news for the lexicographer. And if word meanings do not exist, the dictionary cannot be the authority on language that its users want it to be: 'a dictionary which presents... meaning as context-dependent or variable or flexible, will be of little use for purposes of settling arguments' (Kilgarriff 1997*b*: 143).

Some linguists are less pessimistic. First of all, this flexibility of meaning may be less true of some words: Atkins and Rundell (2008: 266) note that *party* 'is described in identical terms in *LDOCE*-4, *OALD*-7, *MED*-2, and *COBUILD*-5. Each of these dictionaries identifies five lexical units (LUs)—four main senses and one multiword expression', which means, perhaps, that those meanings are

---

[62] 'As they step into the same rivers, different and still different waters flow...'.

clearly distinct. Secondly, there may be a difference between what happens in texts and what the language users have in their minds. Wierzbicka, the 'reliable contrarian' of Atkins and Rundell (2008: 434), argues (1996: 269) that meanings do exist in the minds of the language users, even if the uses of words in corpora are hard to sort out, that there are no shades of meaning in our minds even though there may be in texts, and that the fuzziness described by some linguists and lexicographers may be the result of their failure to identify meanings clearly, for want of time, energy, competence, and a clear theory (Wierzbicka 1996: 242). She disagrees with those who argue that 'the number of usable senses for any lexical item is limitless' (Murphy 2003: 18) and claims that what counts is not the endless variability of the uses of a lexical item but the fact that it contributes something to discourse. What a lexical item contributes is what the language users have in their minds, its 'meaning potential' (Copestake and Briscoe 1996: 53). The idea that word meanings do not exist is a perverse idea of linguists who believe in prototype theory (PT) based on a shallow analysis of a short and obscure passage by Wittgenstein, Wierzbicka says, and it can only discourage lexicographers: 'How can a lexicographer be expected to undertake the necessary effort if he or she does not believe that the task is feasible at all?' (Wierzbicka 1996: 267). The only way to allow lexicographers to plod on is indeed to posit that meanings may vary endlessly in contexts but that there is a hard, fixed, nodule of meaning for every lexical unit in the language users' minds, and that that nodule is what the dictionary should describe.

8.2.3.9 New ways of presenting polysemous entries

The aim of lexicographers is clear: they must recognize the existence of different meanings, because that is what the users need and what will be most useful to them, but they should also 'devise some way to represent meanings that have reached a transitional stage when the context in which the literal sense is used still has force, even while it is applied to novel situations unrelated to the original sense' (Landau 2001: 202). Fortunately, the idea that there is some flexibility in meaning is not totally new (Geeraerts 2006a: 333 *ff.*) and dictionaries have always had ways of encoding 'a variety of relations in the grey area between "same sense" and "different sense"' (Kilgarriff 1997b: 143). Definitions can be written in such a way that some scope is left for variation: parentheses, open-ended enumerations, words like *etc.*, *especially*, etc.

Prototype theory (PT) appeared in the 1970s in cognitive psychology (Rosch 1977, 1978), to explore linguistic categories (Taylor 1995). It was a reaction against the classical, Aristotelian, theory of necessary and sufficient conditions (NSCs) in which categories are rigid and a concept belongs or does not belong to it. The problem is that if you say that dog must be +FOUR LEGS +CARNIVOROUS +DOMESTIC +KEEPS HOUSE you may have a perfect definition but then you do not know what to do with a three-legged dog. PT claims that categories do *not* have clear boundaries, that they are fuzzy, and that some members are better members than others, more representative, more typical, more central. Rosch's demonstration is well known: the category 'bird' can be shown experimentally to have members that are more 'birdy' than others, the robin more than the eagle, the eagle more than the chicken, the chicken more than the penguin, etc. PT was eagerly adopted by many, particularly cognitive, linguists and has had an enormous influence on modern semantics. But others have been less impressed. Kleiber (1990*a*) showed that the theory was less clear than its early adepts said. Wierzbicka has repeatedly warned against the dangers of PT: it 'has tended to be uncritically welcomed as a panacea by people dissatisfied with earlier approaches.... Everything that does not fit into a "classical" semantic straitjacket tends to be thrown into this black hole' (in Aitchison 1993: 215). PT has been used to justify shallow analyses of meaning, she says, and it has tended to become 'an excuse for intellectual laziness and sloppiness', a 'thoughtsaving device'.

Some lexicographers have been influenced by PT. Hanks (2000*a*: 9) thinks it is 'of immense importance to lexicography', and in *NODE* the treatment of complex words was PT-inspired, as we have seen: words are depicted as having central meanings, with secondary meanings related to a central meaning. Here is (part) of the entry *climb*:

climb ▸ verb 1 [with obj.] go or come up a (slope, incline, or staircase); ascend: *we began to climb the hill* | [no obj.] *the air became colder as they climbed higher* | *he **climbed up** the steps slowly.* ∎ [no obj.] (of an aircraft or the sun) go upwards: *we decided to climb to 6,000 feet.* ∎ [no obj.] (of a road or track) slope upwards or up: *the track climbed steeply up a narrow, twisting valley.* ∎ (of a plant) go up (a wall, tree or trellis) by clinging with tendrils or by twining: *when ivy climbs a wall it infiltrates any crack* | [no obj.] *there were roses climbing up the walls* ∎ [no obj.] increase in scale, value, or power: *deer numbers have been climbing steadily* | *the stock market climbed 23.9 points.* ∎ move to a higher position in (a chart or table): *Wrexham's bid to climb the second division table.* ∎ [no obj.] informal (in sports journalism) leap into the air to reach or deliver the ball: *Kernaghan climbed to head in Putney's corner.*
2 [no obj., with adverbial of direction] move with effort, especially into or out of a confined space; clamber: *Howard started to climb out of the front seat.*

The two central meanings are 'going upwards' and 'moving with effort', and secondary meanings that differ by their subjects, objects, or other features are attached to the first. This 'makes no claim to account for all possible textual instantiations of the word, but it is loose enough to accommodate considerable variation at the level of individual language events' (Atkins and Rundell 2008: 279). Landau (2001: 371) was impressed:

I am encouraged by *NODE's* innovative defining system, as I believe that, except in the largest of dictionaries, the separate enumeration of very closely allied senses serves no useful purpose. Dictionaries are generally too timid to cut anything that gives the appearance of full coverage, because they fear (correctly) that reviewers who compare the numbered definitions for a word in two dictionaries will conclude that the book with more definitions is the better book.

Rundell (2002: 148) says that *MEDAL* distinguishes those meanings that are clear and 'conform quite well to the conventional dictionary model' from 'other much fuzzier *meaning-clusters*, where a basic semantic core is elaborated, in real text, in a variety of ways'. The objective was 'to show the underlying relatedness among the "meanings" of essentially monosemous (or at least oligosemous) words...', and also make it easier to account for semantic nuance, speaker attitude, and metaphor'. *MEDAL* gives the main meaning first and then lists the less important ones: *escape* has five meanings, with a first 'to get away from sth bad' followed by 'avoid sth unpleasant', 'not remember/notice', 'come out by accident', etc. Both *NODE* and *MEDAL*, Rundell (2002: 148) says, 'recognize "fuzziness" and attempt to create lexicographic structures to reflect it'. Both are 'an effort to achieve a more linguistically plausible and (for dictionary users) more intuitively satisfying account of word meaning'.

But even the more inventive dictionaries have to make do with the linearity of the dictionary text (Geeraerts 2007: 1168), and only the e-dictionary opens up new possibilities for the presentation of facts of such complexity. The only limit is what the dictionary users are prepared to put up with, and they are conservative: they want their meanings clearly separated and ordered in a list.

8.2.3.10 Ordering meanings

The different meanings of polysemous words can be organized in different ways. The organization should be clear and accessible, and give a faithful image of the semantic structure of the word as much as possible. Since Martin's *Lingua Britannica Reformata* (1749), meanings have been numbered (Osselton 1988: 246) and ordered. The structures of complex entries can be either flat (1, 2, 3, etc.) or tiered in various ways (I, 1, 1a, 1b, 2, 2a, 2b, 2c, II, etc.) to account for the semantic distances between the different meanings: a flat structure means that every meaning is 'equally distinct' (Atkins and Rundell 2008: 249), while in tiered structures some meanings are closer than others.

Johnson discussed the ordering of meanings in his *Preface*, and he decided to use a 'logical' ordering: most important, central, pivotal, etc. sense first, followed by derived senses and finally specialized senses. For example, for *mash* he had

1. The space between the threads of a net..., 2. Anything mingled or beaten together...
3. A mixture for a horse

The compilers of the *OED* aimed at arranging meanings by chronological order of their first occurrences, older meaning first, as we have seen, although they often positioned meanings not in their right chronological place so to show semantic links (Zgusta 1989c: 200). Chronological ordering is ideal for tracing the history of words, but forces the users of long entries to plod through old, often obsolete meanings before finding the more current meanings. Some dictionaries have used chronological order in reverse, most recent meaning first: the first was the *Funk and Wagnalls Standard* in 1893, and the solution was adopted later by *RHD* (1966), *AHD* (1969), and *CED* (1979).

Arrangement by frequency appeared in the early twentieth century and is now used in dictionaries. The appreciation of the frequency of each meaning was impressionistic at first, but can now be substantiated to some extent by the use of a corpus, even though meanings cannot be sorted out automatically. For example, *MEDAL2* has (adapted)

pursue 1 to follow a course of activity 2 to try to achieve something 3 to chase someone or something in order to catch them 4 to keep trying to persuade someone to start a sexual relationship with you

This type of ordering is more representative of the language in synchrony, as a functional code, but some have wondered 'whether advanced learners are really helped if they have to go through a number of familiar meanings in order to get to the unknown ones they need' (Bogaards 1996: 288). No solution is ideal.

Arrangement by frequency poses another problem: the most frequent meaning is usually not the most salient, i.e. the meaning that comes to mind most spontaneously.[63] In fact, it is usually a meaning that is context-bound rather than independent (Sinclair 1991: 112), synsemantic rather than autosemantic:[64] for instance, the most frequent use of *instance* is in the phrase *for instance* (Moon

---

[63] *Salience* is used in cognitive linguistics to refer to the presence of a concept in the language user's mind. Concepts that come to mind most quickly and effortlessly are said to be *salient*.

[64] The distinction between *autosemantic*, applied to words that have meaning out of context, and *synsemantic*, applied to words that do not, or only partly, comes from Anton Marty, the German philosopher, who applied it to concepts in 1908. I have not found it in any dictionary of linguistics.

1988: 110); 'the commonest use of *take* in English is delexical' (Hanks 1990: 35);[65] the most frequent meaning of the verb *run* is 'manage', as in *run a business* (Barlow, in Murphy 2003: 23); *time* is relatively infrequent in its 'central' sense in the Birmingham corpus (see below, 9.1.7), and most uses are in phrases (Moon 1988: 114).

The problem is that no lexicographer wants to have a context-bound meaning first. In *CED*, the most frequent meaning of *back* ('in, to, or towards the original starting point, place, or condition') is no. 47, while the first meaning ('the posterior part of the human body') is rare; the most frequent meaning of *pursue*, 'to apply oneself to (one's studies, hobbies, interests, etc.)' is no. 5, and the first meaning, 'to follow (a fugitive) in order to capture or overtake', is much less frequent. Yet there is nothing special about *CED*: for *pursue*, ALD, LDOCE2, and COD have the same ordering, and C20D has a first meaning 'harass, persecute, persist in opposing or seeking to injure' and the meaning 'to follow in order to overtake and capture or kill' is no. 3.

Putting the most salient meaning first is probably the most satisfying solution for the dictionary users (Atkins and Rundell 2008: 251) and it is, after all, what many lexicographers have done, including Johnson. But it is not easy to identify the appropriate meaning. Sinclair (1991: 113) hypothesizes that it could be 'the most frequent independent' meaning. It is the one from which the other meanings can be explained (van der Meer 2000b). Cruse (1986: 69) has tests that show that, for example, a *novel* is above all a text, and secondarily an object.

1. I'm not interested in the cover design, or binding—I'm interested in the novel
2. ?I'm not interested in the plot, or the characterisation, or anything of that nature—I'm interested in the novel

There are also psycholinguistic experiments showing that meanings are not equally important in our minds: for example the adjective *firm* has a central reading [SOLID] and a non-central reading [STRICT] (Kilgarriff 1997b: 142). Unfortunately, these tests or experiments cannot be used with all polysemous words, and the appreciation of the salience of a meaning is still very much intuitive. Many dictionaries continue to use a rule-of-thumb ordering, frequent before rare, current before obsolete, general before specific, concrete before abstract, 'original' before metaphoric, etc., just like Johnson did. Even *NODE* has

pursue 1 follow (someone or something) in order to catch or attack them

[65] A *delexical* verb, or *support verb*, *light verb*, or *empty verb*, is a verb that is only a support for the accompanying noun, and that has virtually no meaning in itself: for example *have* in *have an influence*, *take* in *take a look*, *take control*, *give* in *give a lecture*, *do* in *do a dance*, etc.

E-dictionaries as we know them are not better than paper dictionaries on the ordering of meanings in entries, since they return an entry, or part of an entry from which the users must choose the part that contains what they are looking for. The revolution will be when the dictionary returns only the relevant meaning and nothing else. This can be achieved if the computer can analyse the context and deduce which meaning is used, provided the user is reading a text on the screen.

8.2.4 Multiword items

8.2.4.1 The different sorts of multiword items

In discourse, words tend to occur in groups in which the choice of a word entails the obligatory or preferential choice of another, or others. When these combinations are well identified, when they are used often enough, when they are stored as wholes in our memories and chosen at one go by the language user, when they are 'the significant co-occurrence of two or more words' (Atkins 1993: 28), they are called *phrases*,[66] or *multiword units* or *items*, or *pre-fabs* (Bolinger 1976), *composites* (Cowie 1998a), *phrasemes* (Mel'čuk 1998: 24), *collocations* (Siepmann 2005), etc. (see Wray 2002: 8 *ff.*). There are many sorts: *of course, kick the bucket, An apple a day keeps the doctor away, When all is said and done, Read my lips, It never rains but it pours, Ladies and gentlemen, Good morning, spick and span, take the bull by the horns, as cool as a cucumber, red herring,* etc. Unfortunately different authors use different terms for the same sort, or the same term for different sorts. Phrases can be listed by introspection or collected in dictionaries, or they can be identified automatically in a corpus by the frequency of the co-occurrence of their constituents (see below) or other criteria (Moon 1998a: 28), and the different methods of collection probably explain some of the differences in definition. Research in the area is particularly difficult, and the following is only a brief overview.

Some phrases are lexical, i.e. behave like lexical items, like *shoot the breeze,* some are clauses, or sentences, like *You reap what you sow.* They are numerous in all languages. Estimates vary, however, no doubt because they are based on different definitions. 'Pawley and Syder (1983) suggest that such familiar expressions as *I think a lot of X* and *Come to think of it...* probably amount to several hundred thousand' (Cowie 1994: 167), but Kilgarriff (1997a: 144) says that

---

[66] Some say *expressions*, but I prefer to keep this as a general term for any linguistic usage. The word *phrase* is also used in many theories of syntax, notably structuralism and transformationalism, to refer to sentence constituents (Crystal 1985).

English has 'around 600' everyday expressions like *as well as, at least, by all means, no doubt, not at all, see you soon, pleased to meet you,* etc. (see also Wray 2002: 15, 28). Phrases are not only numerous; they are important in the acquisition of a language: mastering a language means, among other things, storing its prefabricated chunks and being able to use them adequately.[67] And phrases are interesting for the linguist because they have peculiar semantic and syntactic characteristics.

Phrases are defined by two features: frozenness, or petrification (Cowie (1983*b*: xii), and non-compositionality. A frozen expression is an expression that is always composed of the same words in all its occurrences, always in the same form, and in the same order, as in *spick and span, Ladies and gentlemen,* etc. Expressions become frozen over time if they are used with enough frequency by enough people.

Frozenness is both lexical and syntactic. Typically, phrases do not admit lexical changes: you cannot have **He kicked the pail yesterday.* However, Moon (1998*a*), after examining the Birmingham corpus (see below, 9.1.7.5), noted that many phrases admit some variations: of verb (*throw/toss in the towel*), of noun (*a skeleton in the closet/cupboard*), of adjective (*a bad/rotten apple*), of preposition (*on/along the right lines*), or of conjunction (*when/while the cat is away*). She found the following variants of the same phrase (Moon 1999: 269):

wash	*one's*	*dirty linen/laundry*	*in public*
air	*one's*	*dirty laundry/linen*	*in public*
do	*one's*	*dirty washing*	*in public*
wash/air	*one's*	*dirty linen/laundry*	
wash/air	*one's*	*linen/laundry*	*in public*
launder	*one's*	*dirty washing*	

Such variability can even give rise to playful uses: *shake/quake/quiver in their boots/shoes/Doc Martens* (Atkins 2002: 7). Corpus studies show that in many cases there are preferred choices: *in fine fettle* rather than *?in splendid fettle* (Moon 1998*a*: 103), *take something with a pinch of salt* rather than *with a fistful of salt* (Rundell 1998: 326). Frozenness is also syntactic: phrases typically resist insertions (**He kicked the big bucket yesterday*), passivization (**His bucket was kicked yesterday*), pronominalization (**He kicked it yesterday*), etc. Cruse (1986: 47)

---

[67] Wray (2002) argues that children start using formulas, in which they distinguish words only if necessary, in the same way, perhaps, as prehistoric humans started using undifferentiated sounds before discovering that distinguishing smaller meaningful units made the system much more flexible. Foreign language learners are usually taught words, and therefore need to be shown how those words are used in formulaic language.

mentions exceptions, *He kicked the proverbial bucket, His goose was well and truly cooked,* or *He has a large chip on his shoulder,*[68] but argues that the insertions are metalinguistic comments on the whole phrase and do not change the nature of the phrase. Phrases sometimes exhibit aberrant syntactic behaviour: *dog eat dog,* etc. Lexically and syntactically, there is a scale of frozenness: phrases are more or less frozen according to the lexical variations that they admit in discourse and to the syntactic manipulations that they allow. The fact that they can function in discourse even though there are variants shows that the language users have stored them in their minds in a flexible form.

A non-compositional expression is an expression whose meaning is not the sum of the meanings of its elements (Leech 1974: 226): the meaning of *spick and span* is not the meaning of *spick* and the meaning of *span*—neither has any meaning anyway—just as the meaning of *cupboard* is not the sum of the meanings of *cup* and *board*. Phrases are typically non-compositional: *kick the bucket* does not normally mean 'hit the pail with one's foot'. The lexical words in the phrase, *kick* and *bucket,* are semantically empty (Cruse 1986: 39), and the whole phrase is opaque. Compositionality, like frozenness, is not a clear dichotomy: phrases are more or less compositional, and consequently more or less transparent. Phrases like *kick the bucket* are totally non-compositional, but *let off steam* is partly compositional (Cruse 1986: 39). The different words of a phrase may be more or less transparent: in *spill the beans, spill* is more transparent than *beans.*

Maximum non-compositionality and frozenness are two defining features of a particular sort of phrase called *idioms,*[69] many of which are also characterized by their picturesque nature, the fact that they use words that would be bizarre if they were interpreted literally: *rake over the coals, blow away the cobwebs, hot under the collar, keep your hair on,* etc. Defining them by their non-compositionality, by saying that their 'meaning cannot be accounted for as a compositional function of the meanings its parts have when they are not parts of idioms' (Cruse 1986: 37) has 'a curious element of circularity' in it, Cruse shows: it implies that one already knows what an idiom is before defining it. He proposes to change the formulation slightly and to call *idioms* those phrases that are impossible to analyse semantically into smaller semantic elements: in 'This will cook Arthur's goose', *this, will,* and *Arthur* are semantic constituents, but not *cook* and *goose.*

Another type of expression must be mentioned here because it is important for lexicography: *collocations.* The term, unfortunately, has more than one meaning, as we have seen. In its broad, statistical, sense, as used by Sinclair (1991), a

---

[68] And there is the inevitable *He kicked the fucking bucket yesterday.*

[69] French does not have a ready equivalent: French authors say *idiotisme, expression idiomatique, locution,* etc.

collocation is any frequent co-occurrence of two or more words, whatever the relation between them. In its narrow, semantic, sense, as used by Hausmann (1979), a collocation is the significant co-occurrence of two lexical words in a meaningful syntactic pattern: N +Adj (*redeeming feature*), V +(obj) +Adv (*take sth hard*), V +(art) +N (*face the music*) or Adv +(prep) +Adj (*bitterly cold*). One word is the base: it is the word that has its full meaning and the one that is chosen first by the language user, for example *rain* in *heavy rain* or *cold* in *bitterly cold*; the other is the collocator:[70] it can only be chosen once the base has been chosen.

> In verb +noun collocations…the noun is the base, and the verb is the collocator. In adjective +noun collocations…the noun is once again the base, and the adjective is the collocator. In adverb +verb collocations…the verb is the base, and the adverb is the collocator. In adverb +adjective collocations the adjective is the base, and the adverb is the collocator.   (Benson 1989: 6)

In *sleep soundly, trim sails, heavy drinker, sound asleep, confirmed bachelor, make the bed*, etc. the bases (*sleep, sails, drinker, asleep, bachelor, bed*) can be defined out of context, they are 'semiotactically "autonomous"' (Hausmann 1999: 205), or autosemantic, while the collocators cannot: they are synsemantic.[71] The two words of a lexical collocation typically illustrate what Mel'čuk calls a *lexical function* (see below): for example, *cancel an agreement, lift a ban, raise an embargo, abolish a penalty*, etc. illustrate the same function, called LIQU by Mel'čuk, meaning 'putting an end to'.

Collocations are typically less frozen than idioms syntactically. The two words can be separated by other words: 'It had been raining all night, so heavily that …'. Hence the notion of *span*, the number of words separating the two words of a collocation in discourse (Ooi 1998: 76), an important notion in the exploration of an electronic corpus. Most collocations occur in a four-word span (Jones and Sinclair 1974: 21). The words can be used in a different order and even surface as different POS: *trim the sails, the sails were trimmed, heavy rain, raining heavily*. But the lexical choices are always restricted: the collocator cannot be exchanged for a synonym in, for example, **break one's voyage*. The choice of the collocator is arbitrary.

Why do we say a *heavy* smoker or drinker rather than a *big* smoker or drinker? Why does a building *fall* into disrepair rather than *go* into disrepair? Why do we say we are *a little*

---

[70] For Atkins and Rundell (2008: 218), a collocator is a word used in an entry to point to a category of words: for example *region* is a collocator of *develop* to indicate that other similar words can also be used, in that case *area, province, state, country*, names of countries, etc.

[71] Benson *et al.* (1986) also have what they call *grammatical collocations*, with only one lexical item, like *responsible for* (*patterns* for Hunston and Francis 2000; see below), to be distinguished from *lexical collocations*.

tired or we were *a little* late or we have *a little* time left but not "We are a little sorry"? Why can two people eat *in silence* but not *in quiet*? Why does one sometimes get a *busy signal* when making a telephone call? (Landau 2001: 316)

The categories free combination, collocation, and idiom are hard to distinguish. Cowie (1978: 133) proposes the following cline:

run   a machine/car/army/team/business/scheme
explode   a theory/claim/fallacy/case
foot   the bill
fill   the bill

The first line is a group of free combinations with the verb *run*. The second is a group of collocations, with a particular use of *explode* and a restricted set of possible objects, all semantically related. The third is a partly compositional idiom, with only one possible object of the verb *foot* but a transparent element, *bill*. The last line is a full idiom: only *bill* can collocate with *fill* in that sense of *fill*, and the whole is non-compositional.

Some collocations are also hard to distinguish from compound nouns and adjectives. Different criteria have been proposed. The two normally have different stress patterns: one stress on the first element only for compounds and one on each word for collocations and free strings, but this is difficult to verify. They also differ semantically: *heavy rain* is a collocation because it adds up the meanings of the two words, but *guinea pig* is a lexical item, because it is non-compositional and stands for a single concept. But what is a single concept? How can one demonstrate that *heavy rain* is not a 'permanent' category in the minds of the language users? Sometimes it is possible to show that a concept has a place in a structure, and to conclude that the expression that refers to it is a lexical item, not a collocation: for example *guinea pig* is in a taxonomy of rodents with *rat, rabbit,* etc., *scarlet fever* is in a taxonomy of diseases with *German measles*, etc. (Landau 2001: 358). I recently discovered that *brisk walking* refers to a precise concept for doctors in relation to other types of walking, and is therefore a lexical item, not a collocation. But there are many doubtful cases: *school board, safety glass, tea service, marriage service, heavily retarded*, etc.

The first studies of phraseology were carried out in Russia in the late 1940s (Cowie 1998*a*). In France, the first mention is in Bally's *Traité de stylistique française* (1909: 66), where the author calls *phraseological series* such strings as *gravement malade* and *grièvement blessé*,[72] noting that though *gravement* and *grièvement* have the same meaning, ?*gravement blessé* is dubious and *grièvement

---

[72] 'seriously ill' and 'seriously injured'.

malade is impossible. But the great impetus in the study of idiomaticity came from Britain under the influence of Firth, who proposed the word *collocation* (1957*b*: 194) and argued that words should be studied in their contexts. American linguists were less interested, because of the strong influence of structuralism and of generative grammar, in which idiomaticity was seen as an unwelcome disruption of the neat distinction between syntax and lexis. 'Neo-Bloomfieldian structuralism, Transformational-Generative Grammar and Tagmemics have had little to say about the place of idiomaticity in language structure' (Makkai 1992: 265).

There is now a huge body of work on phraseology in general and idiomaticity in particular in many languages.[73] In English, most studies have been focused on idioms and collocations. The most studied type of idiom has been the metaphorical *kick-the-bucket* type, because it is typical, and also perhaps because it is important in the study of style, particularly literary style. Moon (1988: 109) showed that many of those idioms, *kick the bucket, red herring*, etc. are actually infrequent in usage and that they are used in truncated or distorted form more frequently than in their canonical forms: 'For example, the saying *you can't have your cake and eat it* typically occurs in a positive form' (Moon 1988: 109).

Idioms have 'received considerable attention from Cognitive Linguistics' (Geeraerts 2006*a*: 198), because their creation, storage, and use say something of the way our minds work. Psycholinguists have also been interested in what happens when an idiom is used (Gibbs 2007). The receiver of the message can choose between an idiomatic interpretation and a literal interpretation. Moon (1988: 107) quotes from Tom Stoppard's play *Rosencrantz and Guildernstern are Dead*:

Guildernstern: How do you know?
Player: I keep my ear to the ground
Guildernstern: One day someone will step on your head.[74]

Another example is in an obituary that J. R. R. Tolkien, once a lexicographer working for the *OED*, wrote for Henry Bradley in 1923: 'occasional visitors, or workers, in that great dusty workshop, that brownest of brown studies' (Gilliver *et al.* 2006: 38). Some misunderstandings may occur if the receiver of the message

---

[73] For a bibliography, see Cowie and Howarth (1996)—an updated version can be found on the EURALEX website; see also Wray (2002). There is a European society of phraseology, Europhras, founded in 1999.

[74] Even compound nouns can be given literal interpretations, typically jocularly. When the writer and wit Tristan Bernard was at the Drancy concentration camp, he received a letter from his friend Sacha Guitry asking him 'Qu'est-ce que je peux vous envoyer ?' ('What can I send you?'). 'Un cache-nez' ('A scarf'), he answered. 'Cache-nez' is literally 'hide-nose'.

opts for the wrong interpretation, as is possible with such expressions as *out of patience* and *out of sympathy* (Ruhl 1978: 375).

Recently, corpus linguists have also been interested in collocations in the Sinclairian sense. The computer can identify frequent co-occurrences in a corpus by methods that Kilgarriff and Tugwell (2002: 126) have called *collocation statistics*, 'a sub-field of computational linguistics'. Interesting co-occurrences can be extracted by various techniques: Mutual Information (MI; see Church and Mercer 1993), t-score (Church and Hanks 1989), z-score, etc. MI calculates the probability of any given word appearing next to another word within a given span, typically four words to the left and four words to the right. 'A high MI score is evidence that the association of two words is greater than chance' (Landau 2001: 309). The problems with MI are that it does not work for expressions made of more than two words, and it does not take corpus size into account. T-score does: a t-score has to be at least 2 to be considered significant. 'T-score favours high-frequency function words' while 'MI favours the less common content words' (Hanks 2002: 181). Whatever the method, the collocations that are returned are not all relevant and may have to be sorted out by hand.

All linguists recognize the two broad categories of idioms and collocations, but many other types and sub-types are also mentioned in the literature: bound collocations, dead metaphors (Cruse 1986), semi-idioms, figurative idioms, restricted collocations (Cowie 1983*b*), defective collocations, anomalous collocations (Moon 1998*a*), phrasemes and half-phrasemes (Mel'čuk here and there), etc. The distinctions between the different types are not clear (Wray 2002: 47). The tests invented by linguists work sometimes, but not always, and different tests yield different results, so that we have clusters of phrases that are similar and many outliers. Many linguists now seem to accept that the distinction between collocations and idioms 'is actually a cline, a continuum rather than a clear-cut dichotomy' (Fontenelle 2008*b*: 6).

8.2.4.2 The treatment of phrases in dictionaries

Phrases are not predictable, they are not totally transparent, they cannot be made up with grammatical rules and they have to be learnt: therefore they should be treated in dictionaries. But they are difficult, a 'quagmire' for the lexicographer (Atkins 1993: 6).

Nothing is more difficult in a monolingual dictionary than to give an adequate description of phraseology: proper attention must be given to legitimate collocations (those that are in 'langue') rather than to stylistic ones (those that are in 'parole'), and the phenomenon of lexicalization (the free syntagm becoming frozen little by little) must be accounted for.   (Gorcy 1989: 909)

The list of phrases treated in a dictionary and the way they are treated can always be challenged: 'no one has yet produced a set of watertight criteria to apply as a means of identifying the various types and handling them systematically' (Atkins and Rundell 2008: 360). Figurative idioms are usually listed, because they are easily spotted, but other phrases, collocations, everyday expressions, etc. are listed according to criteria that are never completely clear, and cannot be. Take the example of *fish and chips*. It is undoubtedly a phrase: 'not any kind of fish, nor any method of cooking and presentation, will qualify for the description' (Cruse 1986: 39). It is listed in some learners' dictionaries, *ALD7, LDOCE4, CIDE, MEDAL1*,[75] as well as in *C21D, CED, SOED*, etc., but not in *C20D* or *COD11*. Gates (1988: 100) notes that *come what may, as best one can, lo and behold, that is to say*, etc. are not included in *AHD2, C20D, CED, LDEL, MW9*, and *WNW2*.

The lexicographer must also decide in what form the phrase will be listed. Landau (2001: 316) found *move/push/relegate/ something to the back/front burner, the back/front burner*, and *back/front burner* in his corpus. He finally decided to cite the phrase as *the back burner* and *the front burner*, arguing that the verb is 'part of the idiom semantically but not morphologically'. *CED* has *dirty linen, C21D wash one's dirty linen in public, COD11 wash one's dirty linen* (or *laundry*) *in public; ALD7* has *shake in your shoes, LDOCE4 quake in your boots, COB2 you are quaking in your boots/shoes, C20D shake/shiver in one's shoes; ALD7* has *make sb's hackles rise/raise sb's hackles, LDOCE4* has *raise sb's hackles, COB2* has *something raises your hackles* or *makes your hackles rise, CIDE* has *something makes someone's hackles rise, gets their hackles up*, or *raises hackles, MEDAL2* has *your hackles rise* or *something raises your hackles, C21D* and *COD11* have *make someone's hackles rise*. Some dictionaries use parentheses to include more variants, but the result may be difficult to read: *COD11* has (*as*) *thick as two* (*short*) *planks* (or *as a plank*). The choice of the citation form should reflect the frequency of the variants in the corpus, but that may not be enough if the most frequent form is truncated.

The next step is to decide which word will be used to place the phrase in the macrostructure, whether as a headword or in the entry for another headword. The 'dirty linen' phrase is at *dirty* in *CED* and *MEDAL2*, at *linen* in *C21D*, at *wash* in *COD11*; the 'shake in shoes' phrase is at *shake* in *ALD7, C20D*, and *NODE*, at *quake* in *LDOCE4* and *COB2*; 'money burns a hole in sb's pocket is explained under **money** in OALD, under **burn** in LDOCE and CIDE, and under **pocket** in COBUILD [= *COB2*]' (Bogaards 1996: 285–6). Sometimes the word used for classification is the first lexical word, as for compounds, *storm* for *storm in a teacup, shoot* for *shoot one's mouth off*, as in *LDOCE3* (Bogaards 1996: 286). Highly

---

[75] *COB* has *fish and chips shop*, but not *fish and chips*.

frequent and semantically vague words can be ignored: *bull* rather than *take* for *take a bull by the horns*. Sometimes the chosen word is the least frequent word of the phrase, *linen* for *wash your dirty linen in public*, etc., a clever solution if the phrase is placed within an entry, because the least frequent word will have the shortest entry, but can the users be expected to understand it? Sometimes dictionaries have precise policies, for example by POS: the first noun, or the first verb if there is no noun, or the first adjective if there is no noun or verb (Jackson 2002: 100). All solutions have their advantages and disadvantages. The simpler systems, the more predictable, and the more consistently applied are best. A network of cross-references, as in most British and in some American dictionaries, is a great help. The 'Phrase Index' of *CIDE*, which contains all the words used in all the multiword items treated in the dictionary, is also handy. Of course, none of this applies to the e-dictionary, where the user can always type in any element of a phrase and be directed to it, wherever it has been stored.

The next step is to decide whether the item will be a main entry or a sub-entry. Foreign phrases like *ad hoc* and *raison d'être* usually have their own entries (Gates 1988: 102), simply because there is no entry that they can be attached to. Hyphenated forms and phrasal verbs can be main entries, but most phrases are included in another entry. Within the entry, some dictionaries attach phrases to a particular meaning, but this is problematic for totally non-compositional idioms. Many recent dictionaries list phrases in a special paragraph at the end of the entry, as Furetière did in 1690, in alphabetical order of their main word: for example *COD10* has, at the end of the entry *hand*, a paragraph entitled PHRASES with *all hands on deck, at hand, at* (or *by*) *the hands* (or *hand*) *of, by hand, get* (or *keep*) *one's hand in, give* (or *lend*) *a hand, hand in glove*, etc. This is convenient, though it obscures any semantic relations between the phrase and one of the meanings of the headword.

8.2.4.3 The treatment of collocations in dictionaries

Early dictionaries were full of chunks of discourse that were glossed, explained, or defined. The tradition continued, in French dictionaries through the *Dictionnaire de l'Académie*, but collocations then disappeared from most dictionaries after the eighteenth century in England and in France, when dictionaries were formalized and focused on the lexical item, only to reappear recently. *PR* has *crise d'asthme* in the entry *asthme*, for example, and the *TLF* has special paragraphs containing collocations, which it calls *syntagmes*. For example, at the entry *angoisse*

SYNT. une sueur d'angoisse, un frisson d'~, crier, suer, frissonner d'~, être saisi d'~

This was only equalled recently in English lexicography, and only by learners' dictionaries (see below).

The first step in the treatment of collocations is to identify them, not an easy task. Dictionaries of collocations can help, and now the software tools used in the exploration of corpora. The next step is to decide what to do with them. Traditional GPDs have no precise policy, leaving the mention of occasional collocations to the definitions or the examples. Many verb +object collocations are given in the definitions for the verbs (the collocator), often between parentheses, simply because the verbs cannot be defined otherwise: for example, *claim* 'demand as one's due or property (recognition, etc., to be, that one should be, recognized, etc.)', *meet* 'fulfil (a demand etc.), *refute* 'prove falsity or error of (statement, opinion, argument, person advancing it)', *throw* 'to be subjected to (a fit), *trim* 'set (sails) to suit the wind'. The preposition *of* is often used in the definitions of adjectives: *ample* 'said of people or parts of the body: very large or fat', *bijou* '(especially of a house or flat) small and elegant', *buxom* '(of women) plump and healthy-looking; having a large bosom', *convoluted* '(especially of an argument, story, or sentence) extremely complex and difficult to follow'. In FSDs, the base is included in the first part of the definition: for example, *kinky* 'Behaviour that is **kinky** is considered to be strange...', and what is defined is the collocation, not the word (Hausmann 1999: 207). But GPDs never give collocations in the entry for the base, although that is what the users start from: *trim* is never mentioned in the entry for *sail*.

Sometimes collocations are presented as examples: *hackneyed* 'used too often and therefore boring: *a hackneyed phrase/subject*'. But the user cannot know whether the expression is a phrase or a free combination: *?a hackneyed word/text/book*. 'While it is undoubtedly better to include collocations in example sentences than to leave them out altogether, the value for the learner is much greater if the special character of these combinations is pointed out by giving them typographical prominence of some sort' (Herbst 1996*a*: 336).

The dictionaries of collocations are more helpful. They list collocations at the entry for the base, for example *meet* at *requirement*, as in the *BBI*, and they order them alphabetically, by POS, by meaning, or by syntactic pattern. *BBI2* has

statement 1. to issue, make a ∼ 2. to confirm, sign a ∼ 3. to deny; refute; retract; withdraw a ∼ 4. a brief, short; preliminary; succinct; terse ∼.

ODCIE has a still more sophisticated version, with a definition (here simplified):

cast up throw, deposit. **S:** sea, wave, tide. **O:** flotsam and jetsam; dead fish; body; seaweed. **o:** shore, beach; reef, rock.

where **S** is for subject, **O** for direct object and **o** for prepositional object. Whatever the presentation, the main problem with collocations is their degree of openness.

The user never knows how to interpret the collocates: are they the only possibility, or are there others (Svensén 1993: 102)?

Collocations are now better treated in GPDs than they have ever been, no doubt because there is a general tendency for dictionaries to be less word-centred and more phrase-centred, to give more prominence to the environments in which words produce their semantic effect (see below). Learners' dictionaries 'show great awareness of the importance of prefabricated elements in language' (Herbst 1996a: 335). The big breakthrough was in the early years of the twenty-first century when they began having special boxes on frequent collocates as observed in their corpora: at *role*, *LDOCE3* (2003) has a box

have/play a role in (doing) sth
an important/key/vital/crucial role
a leading/major/central role
an active role
a dual role
take a role

MEDAL2 (2008) has a box 'Adjectives frequently used with *role* 1':

■ central, crucial, decisive, dominant, important, key, leading, major, positive, prominent, significant, vital

This certainly beats the best pre-corpus dictionaries, including the *TLF*, in the sense that only the more frequent collocations are given. But it does not beat an ECD, where collocates are classified by their semantics (see below). And an ideal treatment should also have some indication of relative frequency, a central (or is it crucial, decisive, dominant, etc.?) role of the dictionary.

All dictionaries can still be found wanting in their treatment of phrases, in exhaustiveness, in accuracy or both. They still include items whose status is at best debatable but sometimes miss important ones.

The absence of *strike a deal* from larger dictionaries and specialized idiom dictionaries illustrates that the recognized lists of idioms, those we are aware of as part of our cultural heritage, represent no more than the tip of an iceberg. Time and again, corpus evidence suggests that there are many more semantically relevant collocations than dictionaries tell us.   (Teubert 2004: 87)

The task is immense, and it is important:

It is comparatively easy, if there are no insuperable space constraints, for a lexicographer to make sure that the grammatical information in a dictionary entry is fairly comprehensive. It is much less easy, and requires much more space, to make the collocation information even remotely adequate. The fact that many more users are seeking the latter type of information than the former is a challenge to lexicographers and language teachers alike.   (Atkins and Varantola 1997: 15)

On the whole, linguists have made progress in the comprehension of idiomaticity but the more they publish the more complex the whole area appears to be for lexicographers. The temptation is to conclude that no dictionary will ever succeed in conveying all the complexities of the use of every phrase and in doing justice to every category of phrase, and to decide that it is no use trying. If the chances of success are so slim, why bother?

8.2.5 *Definition*

8.2.5.1 Different types of definition

The main function of the monolingual dictionary is to explain the meanings of the lexical items of a language: 'a dictionary is a text that describes the meanings of words' (Landau 2001: 6). The ability to do this rests on three assumptions. The first is obvious: human language, unlike the languages of animals, can describe itself; it has a metalinguistic function. The meaning of a word, we all know, is other words.[76] The second assumption is that any meaning can be expressed in at least two different ways.

The **definition of the word** is a paraphrase which is **semantically equivalent** to it: this means that, the content being considered as an invariant and being, so to speak, put between parentheses, there are at least two ways of expressing the content. In other words, the lexicographic definition of a word presupposes the existence of a semantic universal: there is always at least **one synonym for each term** of the language, word or sentence. It is always possible to replace a word or a sentence by another without modifying the meaning.   (Dubois and Dubois 1971: 85)

The synonymy of definitions, like all synonymies, works in both directions: 'dog = common, four-legged, flesh-eating domestic animal used for hunting' and 'common, four-legged, flesh-eating domestic animal used for hunting = dog'; if it does not, the statement is not a definition: 'dog = well-known animal'. The third assumption is that the definition, sometimes called the *definiens*, is easier to understand than the word being defined, or *definiendum*—just like an equivalent in a bilingual dictionary is easier to understand than the word in the foreign

---

[76] Unless one thinks, like the inhabitants of Laputa, that words are 'only names for things', and that consequently 'it would be more convenient for all Men to carry about them, such *Things* as were necessary to express the particular Business they are to discourse on' (Swift, *Gullivers' Travels*, Part III, Chapter V).

language. Expressing the meaning of a word in different words in such a way that it is easier to understand is what the art of defining is all about.

The definition of a word is not its meaning: it is an attempt at describing its meaning in such a way that it will clarify it. It is a deliberate construction; it is an artefact. Writing a definition is difficult, one of the most difficult tasks of the lexicographer. Words are 'hourly shifting their relations, and can no more be ascertained in a dictionary, than a grove, in the agitation of a storm, can be accurately delineated from its picture in the water,' Johnson wrote in his *Preface*. Present-day lexicographers can take inspiration from preceding dictionaries, but when they have to define a word that has never been defined, they are 'truly in uncharted waters. The intellectual effort is analogous to that employed in deciphering a message in code, except that, unlike cryptographers, definers never know whether they have the message right' (Landau 2001: 215). The art of defining is the hallmark of the trade, what distinguishes the good lexicographer.

Philosophers and logicians have written extensively on definition, but not much has been written since Aristotle that has proved useful in lexicography. Since the eighteenth century, lexicographers have used a few definition types that have become familiar to the users.[77]

> What seems to have happened is that a whole range of conventional defining formulae has become 'ossified' in the almost liturgical domain of the dictionary: users accept such formulae, even expect them, in dictionary definitions, even though they would be considered deviant in most other environments.   (Rundell 1988: 131)

The most prestigious type of definition, the type that has been most often discussed in the literature, is the Aristotelian, or intensional, definition, sometimes called *logical*. It is a formula that gives the necessary and sufficient conditions (NSCs) for a concept to belong to a category. It has a *genus* word, the hypernym, which is the name of the category to which the concept belongs, and *differentiae*, the characteristics that distinguish the concept from the other concepts in the same category. For example,

snail 'gastropod with spiral shell able to enclose whole body'

This type of definition assumes that meaning can be described as a set of semantic constituents, those atoms of meaning that have been recognized for a long time and that modern semanticists have called *semantic features*, sometimes *semantic constituents, traits, characteristics*, or *semes*.[78] It also assumes a hierarchy,

---

[77] On definition, see Robinson (1954); on dictionary definitions, see Rey-Debove (1971), Landau (1984/2001), Atkins and Rundell (2008).
[78] Crystal (1985) attributes the invention of the word *seme* to Coseriu.

an 'is-a' type structure of the field to which the category belongs. This is usually traced back to Aristotle but it is much older, probably a universal in the organization of concepts in the human mind: each word is placed under its hypernym, at the place where the corresponding concept is (X is-a Y), and horizontally next to its co-hyponyms (X differs from A, B, C, etc.). The model for lexicographers is the classification of animals and plants, as scientifically established by Linnaeus in a taxonomy, but there are also folk hierarchies for all sorts of concepts.

In the definitions of living creatures, for which there are scientific taxonomies, the most obvious choice for the genus word is the name of the species, or of the genus, family, order, or class: *duck* is 'an *Anatidae*...'. But these are scientific words that are difficult for the non-specialist, and many dictionaries use more common words that are easier to understand though scientifically less precise: *water bird, fowl, swimming fowl*. In theory, it could also be *bird* or even *creature* or *animal*, but the choice of the genus word has consequences on the rest of the definition (see below). In defining artefacts, there is no scientific classification to resort to, and the genus word can only be the name of a category in which the language users place the concept: *device, implement, vehicle*, etc. Extremely vague words or formulae such as *thing* or *something* are of little use. A bad genus word is one that does not correspond to common sense, like *biped* or *animal* in the famous definitions of *man* by Plato as 'a featherless biped' or by Aristotle as 'a reasonable animal': we do not normally classify humans as a category of bipeds or of animals. The appropriateness of the genus word can be assessed by tests such as the anaphora test: 'What a delicious fruit, the strawberry!' but '*What a convenient vehicle, the lift!' (Collinot and Mazière 1997: 180 *ff.*). But there are words for which no genus word comes to mind spontaneously: *lift* is one of them, it does not belong to a recognized category; it is 'an apparatus' (*SOED*), 'a platform or compartment' (*NODE*), 'a machine' (*ALD7*), 'a device' (*COB*), etc. Of course, co-hyponyms should have the same genus word, at least in the same dictionary, but that is not always the case: '*NODE* relates *fork* and *spoon* to the genus term *implement*, but *knife* is related to *instrument*' (Jackson 2002: 98).

The *differentiae* of an intensional definition vary with the genus word that has been chosen, because they have to supply information not given by the genus word: the more general the genus word the more information will have to be carried by the *differentiae*. If *duck* is a 'water bird', a few *differentiae* will be enough to distinguish it from other water birds; if it is a 'bird', more *differentiae* will be needed. In some cases, the same word or concept can be used as the genus word or among the *differentiae*: *hedge* can be 'a fence formed by shrubs or low trees' or 'a row of bushes or low trees forming a boundary' (Landau 1994*a*: 320).

Differentiae, like genus words, can be more or less scientific: *peach* can be defined by 'lanceolate leaves', 'sessile', etc. or by 'edible', 'sweet', etc.

Some *differentiae* are criterial,[79] i.e. they are indispensable to distinguish the concept from all neighbouring concepts, others are not. It was the aim of componential analysis to identify criterial features, those that are necessary and sufficient, so that definitions did not have to say more than what was strictly necessary and were real 'définitions de mot'. For example, *man* was +HUMAN + ADULT +MALE, *woman* was +HUMAN +ADULT−MALE, *boy* +HUMAN−ADULT + MALE, etc. (Leech 1974: 96). Those features could be listed and used for more than one word, possibly across languages. This works well with words that belong to small groups with easily identified differences, with *chair*, and *tremble*, and *shimmer*, but less well with *chalice*, *trick*, or *shipwreck*. Some dictionaries have definitions that look like componential analyses: for example, LDOCE1 had *girl* 'a young female person'.[80] But most dictionary definitions are less minimal: *triangle* could be 'a figure with three angles', but real definitions are 'a flat shape with three straight sides and three angles' in almost all British dictionaries and 'the plane figure formed by connecting three points not in a straight line by straight line segments' or 'a figure that has three sides and three angles, the sum of which is 180°' (Weinreich 1962: 32) in some American dictionaries. These definitions are Aristotelian in structure but encyclopedic in content. The definition of *sugar* by 'a sweet substance that consists wholly of *sucrose*, is colourless or white when pure, tending to brown when less refined, is usually obtained commercially from sugarcane or sugar beet...' is also clearly a 'définition de chose' (Wierzbicka 1996: 262). The order in which the *differentiae* are given is important, since dictionary users often stop reading definitions before the end (Atkins and Rundell 2008: 440): criterial differentiae should be given first.

The intensional definition defines the referent of a lexical item, or its concept, or its *signifié*. As a consequence it works best with concrete nouns, names of artefacts or living creatures, less well with general nouns and adjectives, adverbs and verbs, and not at all with function words. Nobody has ever reckoned how many definitions in a given dictionary are intensional: 'Perhaps some on-line dictionary-cruncher can tell me how many meanings of how many nouns and verbs in our general vocabulary are in fact treated this way in dictionaries—not all, by any means, and certainly very few adjectives and adverbs, and probably no conjunctions, prepositions, or interjections' (Atkins 1993: 32). The intensional definition says nothing of the 'emotional, connotative, attitudinal, pragmatic

---

[79] Some say *diagnostic* instead of *criterial*.
[80] Thanks to Gilles-Maurice de Schryver (personal communication) for pointing this out.

kind of meaning' (Sinclair 2004*a*: 8), what Galisson (2001) calls *lexiculture*: for example, French dictionaries define *accordéon* without mentioning the role of the instrument in French popular culture, *muguet* (*lily of the valley*) without mentioning the tradition of offering the flowers on the first of May (Pruvost 2002*b*: 82) or *champagne* without saying that it is expensive and used to celebrate (Bullon 1988; Stock 1992).

Another type of definition is the extensional definition, which lists the names of the concepts that belong to a category: for example *colour* 'red, blue, yellow, etc.', *ocean* 'any of the Atlantic, Pacific, Indian, Arctic and Antarctic' or *parent* 'father or mother'. This is not much used, because it only works for a limited number of words, typically words that have a few well-identified hyponyms. Also, some definitions are *operational*, on the model of the definitions used by some scientists, that define a word by the operation that brings the object or concept into existence: for example, *metre* was defined in 1799 as the length of a particular platinum bar. The definition of *triangle* as 'the plane figure formed by connecting three points...' (*AHD*) is operational, as is the definition of *cake* as 'sweet baked mixture of flour, liquid, eggs, and other ingredients in loaf or rounded layer form'. The similarity with when-definitions is obvious: a cake is 'when you bake ...', a bizarre formulation for a logician, but perhaps good enough to convey the meaning of *cake*.

Dictionaries also have 'definitions' by synonyms or antonyms, sometimes called *synthetic definitions* (Geeraerts 2003: 89). They are used mostly for adjectives (*wealthy* 'rich, prosperous', *rich* 'wealthy', *courageous* 'brave, bold', *shallow* 'not deep', *dead* 'not alive', etc.), sometimes for verbs (*astonish* 'amaze'). In American dictionaries, they are very common: *reply n.* 'an answer; response; counter-attack'; *resign* 'to yield to another; surrender formally; withdraw from; submit calmly', etc. They save space, but their defining power is limited if the synonyms used as defining words are polysemous, and they may be difficult to understand if several synonyms are listed (Weinreich 1962: 40), as in

collect 5 'to call for : pick up : escort' (*MCW7*)

Such definitions may be circular if A is defined by B and B by A (see below). They only work well for words belonging to sub-codes, which can be explained by their synonyms in the standard dialect or in more common terms, as in *dough* 'money' or *patella* 'kneecap', provided the synonyms are properly defined.

There have been few innovations in defining techniques since the beginnings of lexicography. The FSDs of *COB* are one of the rare examples. Many people would agree with Landau (2001: 164) that they have 'improved the quality of definition', and some would agree with Rundell (2006: 335) that they 'junk[ed] the whole repertoire of traditional defining practices'. It is a fact that they were adopted in many other dictionaries, particularly learners' dictionaries, although not as widely as Sinclair had hoped (Sinclair 2004*a*). The only other recent innovation is the 'when' definition, also invented to imitate folk definitions, as we have seen, but it has not had much success (Atkins and Rundell 2008: 444).

8.2.5.2 The rules of definition: 1. simplicity

The definition of a word should clarify its meaning, it should be easier to understand. This is easy for difficult words, but difficult for easy words, as noted by the French 'académiciens', who wrote in the *Preface* of the first edition of their dictionary (1694): 'The word Idée is among those that are so clear that they cannot be explained by others, because there are none that are clearer and simpler'. Fortunately, the more common words are those that are the less in need of a definition, not because they are simple—they are not—but because they are usually acquired by the child or the language learner through ostension or examples rather than through a definition.

Even when simpler definitions are possible, some lexicographers choose definitions that are difficult. 'It is customary, if not obligatory, when citing the rule [of simplicity] to quote with great glee Samuel Johnson's definition of *network*' (Landau 2001: 167). Gove's policy in *W3*, as we have seen with *door*, was to explore all the limits of the concept, and the resulting definitions were not simple. Modern American dictionaries, particularly the Merriam-Webster dictionaries, generally use scientific terms. Mackintosh (2006: 50) found the following for *glass* in *MWC9*:

an amorphous inorganic usu. transparent or translucent substance consisting of a mixture of silicates or sometimes borates or phosphates formed by fusion of silica or of oxides of boron or phosphorus with a flux and a stabilizer into a mass that cools to a rigid condition without crystallization

Landau (2001: 167) mentions the definition of *feather* in *MWC10*:

any of the light horny epidermal outgrowths that form the external covering of the body of birds and that consist of a shaft bearing on each side a series of barbs which bear barbules which in turn bear barbices commonly ending in hooked hamuli and interlocking with the barbules of an adjacent barb to link the barbs into a continuous vane

Bloomfield himself (1933: 139) thought that the names of plants or animals should be defined by terms of botany or zoology, and that even such a common word as *salt* should be defined by 'sodium chloride (NaCl)' (Urdang 2000: 41).

Scientific words in definitions are accurate. They can initiate a process of acquisition if the users look them up: the word *Anatidae* in the definition for *duck* may start them on a chain of look-ups, and they will learn something—if they are prepared to spend the time. Perhaps scientific words also give dictionaries an extra aura of respectability that the users like. But there is clearly a danger of being obscure: 'Many things can misrepresent a meaning, including an excess of erudition' (Bolinger 1985: 73).

Some learners' dictionaries provide glosses of the more difficult words in definitions: for example

shrimp 'any of numerous decapod (10-legged) crustacean animals'
elephant 'a very large grey animal with four legs, two TUSKS (=long curved teeth) and a TRUNK (=long nose) that it can use to pick things up'

It is a good idea to provide more than one definition for different levels of users, as e-dictionaries can easily do. For example, *flea* can be

Any of various small wingless parasitic insects of the order Siphonaptera, which live on the skin of mammals and birds, feeding on blood, and are noted for their agility in jumping (*SOED*)

or it can be

A small wingless jumping insect of the order Siphonaptera, feeding on human and other blood (*COD8*)

or

A small jumping insect that feeds on blood (*The Progressive English Dictionary*)

With e-dictionaries, the users can choose the level of definition that they need, for every word that they look up or more generally (Atkins and Rundell 2008: 445).

Lexicographers have to determine what type of definition they need for each dictionary, and how far they are ready to sacrifice scientific accuracy for the sake of user-friendliness, or to sacrifice user-friendliness for the sake of scientific accuracy (Ilson 1993: 29). Children's dictionaries naturally tend towards simplicity and technical dictionaries towards accuracy. College dictionaries 'fall between the two extremes' (Landau 2001: 169). Landau (2001: 169) thinks that *OED3* tends more towards accuracy than *OED1*, but learners' dictionaries tend towards simplicity.

8.2.5.3 The rules of definition: 2. non-circularity

Two definitions are said to be *circular* when A is defined by B and B by A. The rule of non-circularity was adopted by lexicographers in the eighteenth century (see Auroux 1990: 37),[81] and it makes good sense: one cannot discover the meaning of A through B if B is explained by A. There are different types of circularity. The simplest is 'the hypothetical "*gorse n*: furze" and "*furze n*: gorse"'(Ilson 1999*a*: 234) or the real *bobcat* 'lynx' and *lynx* 'bobcat' (Landau 2001: 157). Sometimes, the definition of A contains B and the definition of B contains A: *pain n.* 'the feeling you have when part of your body hurts' and *hurt v.* 'if a part of your body hurts, you feel pain in it' (*LDOCE3*; Ilson 1999*a*: 233–4) or *device* 'a machine or tool used for a specific task' and *machine* 'any mechanical or electrical device that automatically performs tasks' (*CED*). Sometimes the definition of A contains a word B that is related to A morphologically: *poet* 'a writer of poems' and *poem* 'the work of a poet' in Johnson's *Dictionary* (Hitchings 2005: 161); *glaze v.* 'cover (pottery, etc.) with glaze' and *glaze n.* 'substance used to glaze pottery' (*COD7*); *think* 'be capable of conscious thought' and *thought* 'an act of thinking' (Wierzbicka 1996: 48); *beauty* 'the state of being beautiful' and *beautiful* 'full of beauty' (Landau 2001: 157). The *Robert méthodique* has an entry *fraise* defined as 'fruit du fraisier' in which there is a sub-entry *fraisier* 'plante qui produit des fraises'.[82]

Pascal (1667/1963: 350) thought that circular definitions, like 'la lumière est le mouvement luminaire des corps lumineux',[83] were ridiculous. Littré was also indignant about *chaleur* defined by 'qualité de ce qui est chaud'[84] (Rey 1970*c*: 310). More recently, Wierzbicka has insisted that circularity must be avoided (see below). But there are many cases of circular definitions in all dictionaries, because they save space, and also because in some cases they can hardly be avoided: *feather* cannot be defined without *bird* and *bird* is difficult to define without *feather*; *honey* cannot be defined without *bee*, and it is difficult to define *bee* without *honey*; the definition of *parent* cannot avoid *father* or *mother* and many definitions of *father* or *mother* mention *parent*. Circular definitions are also often used for noun–verb pairs such as *dream n.* and *dream v.* Lexicographers know that this is 'bad lexicographic practice', especially if one of the two words is not properly defined, as in *fear* 'the state of being fearful', 'where *fearful* is nowhere defined' (Landau 2001: 158), but they cannot always do better. Rey (1970*c*: 310) notes that circular definitions are never totally useless:

Littré does not see that the equivalence between the contents of the *-eur* morpheme and the phrase *qualité de ce qui est…*, linking the form of the former and the 'intelligible'

---

[81] Rey (1973: 80) says that it goes back to Avicenna.
[82] *strawberry* 'fruit of the strawberry plant'; *strawberry* 'plant that produces strawberries'.
[83] 'light is the luminary movement of luminous bodies'.
[84] *heat* 'the state of being hot'.

concept expressed by the latter, may be the most fundamental piece of information provided by monolingual dictionaries.

And in many cases they may be enough for the dictionary users to understand: 'it is hard to imagine the average user even being aware of the problem, still less being as fazed by it as Wierzbicka appears to be' (Atkins and Rundell 2008: 435).

There is also circularity between more than two definitions, if A is explained by B, B is explained by C, C is explained by N, and N by A. In fact, as has often been noted, there is a fundamental circularity in the lexicon of natural languages, 'infinite regress' (Wilks *et al.* 1996: 33) as well as in the dictionary text. One can only define a word by using other words, and any word used in a definition must also be defined, until there is no word left unless one comes back to a word that has already been used. A fascinating consequence of the metalinguistic function of human language that has preoccupied philosophers and linguists for a long time (see below).

8.2.5.4 The rules of definition: 3. closedness

The dictionary is closed, as we have seen, if all the lexical items used in the dictionary text are also in the macrostructure. The rule of closedness, the *WNI* (*Word Not In*) *rule* (Landau 2001: 160), applies particularly to definitions: all the words used to define other words must be treated in their own entries or sub-entries. Even the specialized words used in the definitions of the names of animals or plants should be listed, even though they would not qualify for inclusion by any other criteria.

The WNI rule was not strictly observed in the past, because before the age of the computer it was just too time consuming to check the text before publication. Even in modern dictionaries there are exceptions: scientific words, if they are too specialized, for example *loxodonta* in the definition of *elephant*, words using well known morphemes (*treelike*, *eyeless*, etc.), which presumably the user will understand even if they are not defined, proper names or words derived from proper names, for example *Greece* in the definition of *Greek*, if the dictionary does not have proper names, etc. Some omissions are simply errors, particularly because the wordlist is modified until the last minute of the preparation stage. Landau (1994*a*: 336) notes that *RHWC* uses *bull's eye*, 'a commendable way to avoid the technical *annular*' in its definition of *Lyme disease*, but does not 'include a definition for *bull's eye* in this sense'; the definition of *arrest* in *LDOCE* is 'to seize by the power of the law', but this 'meaning of *seize* is not any of those given in the same dictionary' (Sinclair 2004*a*: 6). Also, no computer can sort out meanings, so that a word used in a definition may be included in the wordlist but with a different meaning, especially since dictionaries never specify in what sense they use a polysemous word in a definition.

8.2.5.5 The rules of definition: 4. substitutability

A good definition should be 'written in such a way that it can be substituted for the definiendum in any context in which it appears' (Atkins and Rundell 2008: 435). The rule dates back to at least Leibniz in the eighteenth century (Rey 1973: 135; Hanks 1987: 119), and it makes sense, since the *definiendum* is a synonym of the *definiens*. But it does not work in practice, because in most contexts a phrase cannot be used in place of a word without losing some naturalness. Landau (2001: 164) playfully takes the example of *MWC10*'s definition of *rose*: 'How sweet of you to give me a rose!' he notes, would become 'How sweet of you to give me any of a genus (*Rosa* of the family Rosacea, the rose family) of usu. prickly shrubs with pinnate leaves and showy flowers having five petals in the wild state but being often double or partly double under cultivation.' In fact, few dictionary definitions are substitutable, apart from definitions by synonyms: most of Johnson's definitions were not (Hanks 1987: 120) and many modern definitions are not either. In the case of function words and of highly common nouns and verbs, substitution is totally impossible. 'The substitution principle is not appropriate or even practical in writing accounts of the meaning of all words and lexemes— for example, it is inappropriate for *be, damn, in, it, ought, phew, sock it to me, the, to, tut tut, what?*, and *yes*' (Hanks 1979: 36). Substitution is also impossible for full-sentence definitions and for when-definitions.

The conclusion is clear: 'a claim of interchangeability between the term and its definition...is preposterous for natural languages' (Weinreich 1962: 39). The only thing that lexicographers can implement is that the definition must be the same POS as the word. In the case of intensional definitions, this means that the genus word must be the same POS as the word: the definition of a noun must be nominal, etc.

The problem is whether a substitutable definition is a better definition. Sometimes, one feels that a definition is unnatural because the lexicographer was trying to make it substitutable, as when an adjective is defined by *of, or pertaining to*, etc.: *ocular* 'of, or relating to the eye' (*MWC8*). Also, the effort to produce substitutable definitions may be one of the causes of the multiplication of meanings: 'in the interests of strict substitutability, a word like *shy* is given separate definitions to cover, on the one hand, *a shy person* and, on the other hand *a shy smile* ("showing the quality of shyness")' (Rundell 1988: 132). It is interesting to note that children often define words in formulae that are not substitutable. An (untraceable) example in French is

– C'est quoi, un dictionnaire ?
– C'est quand la maîtresse elle sait pas ce que ça veut dire un mot.[85]

One can imagine that the 'deep structure' of the definition contains a genus word, something like 'A book that the teacher uses when she...', but the definition is clearly not substitutable. Many spontaneous definitions by adults are not either. Here are two English examples (from Manes 1980):

A:...warped...   B: It's when wood gets bent out of shape
A: What's a coup?   B: When the military takes over

The style reminds one of the *when*-definitions used in some recent learners' dictionaries. If these spontaneous definitions work, then perhaps dictionary definitions can work as well, even if they are not substitutable.

8.2.5.6 Different definitions for different types of word
All words cannot be defined in the same way. In terms of POS, nouns are 'the easiest of all words to define' (Landau 2001: 171), mostly with intensional definitions. Verbs, Landau (2001: 173) says, are 'the most difficult', because their meanings depend to a large extent on their subjects and objects. Adjectives are also difficult, for the same reasons (Gove 1968a, 1968b; Ayto 1986). Function words can hardly be defined at all: dictionaries 'have not quite known how to handle them.... all end up trying to assign traditional definitions to them' (Landau 2001: 118), for example *not* 'in no manner; to no degree' (*WNW*), *because* 'for the reason that' (*MCW8*), etc. But there are also dictionaries that only describe their function in discourse: *not* 'a word expressing denial, negation, or refusal' (*C2oD*). For Sinclair, they can be clarified by showing the contexts in which they are used.

In a study of the function word *of*, John Sinclair shows that with the use of a corpus, function words can be defined lexicogrammatically, that is, by showing their grammatical functions and lexical contexts in which they occur, as in *a piece of wood, a cup of tea*, etc.
(Landau 2001: 117)

Words differ by their degree of specialization, from common words to the most esoteric terms. The definitions of common words have to be extracted from their contexts while the definitions of scientific terms can only be written by the specialists of the domain (Landau 2001: 165). Common words are difficult because they have multiple and flexible meanings, scientific words are difficult because their meanings are not easily couched in simple terms. Barnhart (1949: 37)

---

[85] '– What is a dictionary? – It is when the teacher doesn't know what a word means.'

had a scale of complexity with a different method for each level in a dictionary for children.

For very simple, axiomatic words he [the lexicographer] gives only a picture (e.g. *spoon*) or only illustrative sentences (e.g. *be*); for more advanced words he combines a definition and a picture (e.g. *spur*) or uses a definition plus a sentence (e.g. *sputter*); for harder words that only more mature pupils will look up (e.g. *spell-bound, specification*), he is often content with a definition.

Words can also be grouped by subject. The definitions for the names of animals or plants, often referred to in semantics as natural kinds,[86] always contain a more or less encyclopedic description of the referent. The definitions of artefacts indicate their functions. The definitions of parts of artefacts must mention the name of the whole, which is a sort of frame, but the definition of the whole need not mention the name of all parts. For example all definitions of *bicycle* mention *pedal*, but not *saddle*. The definitions of animals have to say wild or domestic, carnivorous or herbivorous, etc. The definitions of diseases mention their symptoms and the definitions of microbes mention the diseases that they carry. The compilers of thesauruses or onomasiological dictionaries have to write definitions that allow comparisons between the members of a group.

Colour nouns and adjectives are particularly difficult to define (Wierzbicka 1996: 287 *ff.*). They can be defined in scientific terms. For *W3*, Gove asked a specialist to provide definitions in terms of '*hue, lightness* (light, medium, dark), and *saturation* (dull, strong, vivid)' (Morton 1994: 92). The definition of *orange* in *MWC7* reads

any of a group of colors that ... are of medium lightness and moderate to high saturation ... that lie midway between red and yellow in hue

Another strategy is to define them through a prototypical referent: *blue* is the colour of the sky on a nice day, *white* is the colour of snow—of limited use in some countries—or of milk, *red* the colour of blood, *green* the colour of grass or leaves, *yellow* the colour of a lemon or of egg yolk,[87] *brown* the colour of earth, wood, or coffee, etc. These definitions are easy to understand but they give no idea of the range of the word: there are more blues than the blue of the sky. Some dictionaries can afford to do both: in the *OED*, the definitions for the colours of the rainbow '(except for *Indigo*) gave examples of objects from nature in which

---

[86] Natural kinds are categories determined by nature, for example animals or plants. There is considerable debate on whether such natural categories exist, for example on the notion of species.

[87] Other referents are gold, butter, the buttercup, 'the sun' (*CIDE*), 'ripe lemons or sunflowers' (*MWC8*), 'sulphur or the primrose' (*C20D*), etc. Some French dictionaries mention saffron.

the colours might be observed', but '(except for *Violet*) also mentioned their place in the spectrum' (Silva 2000: 85). That is obviously the best solution, no problem in an e-dictionary.

Linguists can help lexicographers categorize words: 'One of the biggest challenges to the theoretical lexicographer is to devise a typology of vocabulary items and a parallel typology of defining strategies suited to each' (Atkins 1993: 26).[88] User studies could also help identify categories according to the types of difficulties encountered by the users. Lexicographers can prepare a style guide with templates for each category, to make sure that their definitions are both complete and consistent with the definitions of the other words of the same category (Atkins and Rundell 2008: 125).

8.2.5.7 Linguistics and dictionary definitions

The work of philosophers and logicians on definition is of little practical use for lexicographers, because they have been more interested in the logic of the definitions of concepts than in defining words, and in definitions that are impeccable rather than understandable. Linguists are interested in the definition of words, but they have not produced much. Componential analysis has helped lexicographers identify criterial differentiae, as we have seen, and has facilitated the writing of 'définitions de mots', if that is what the lexicographers want. More recently, prototype theory has helped identify the more important features via the prototype of each category to produce definitions that are 'définitions de choses'. A PT-inspired definition lists the most important features of the prototype, not of the best exemplar of the category—or the definition of *bird* would be the same as the definition of *robin*. Its advocates claim that it breaks free from the constraints of the traditional model: 'Instead of definitions that rigidly take the form of separately general and mutually distinctive features, we expect the intrusion of unorthodox definitional methods such as enumerations, disjunctions, and the accumulation of near-synonyms' (Geeraerts 2006*a*: 354). Not very clear, and Kleiber (1990*a*: 74) was not, either: 'the point is not to say what distinguishes a dog from a cat but to describe what a dog is and what a cat is'. Let us take the definition of *door* in *AHD*:

Any movable structure used to close off the entrance to a room, building, vehicle or covered enclosure, typically consisting of a panel of wood, glass or metal, that swings on hinges

---

[88] But Atkins and Rundell (2008: 4) do not even believe any more that there is such a thing as theoretical lexicography (see below, Chapter 10).

This, in PT, could begin by

A movable panel of wood used to close off the entrance to a room

to be followed by definitions of less central kinds of door.[89] In that particular case, the definition in *NODE* is not PT-inspired:

a hinged, sliding, or revolving barrier at the entrance to a building, room, or vehicle, or in the framework of a cupboard

The most PT-like definition might be in *CIDE*:

A flat, usually rectangular, object, often fixed at one edge, that is used to close the entrance of something such as a room or building

Not all words can be explained by PT-inspired definitions, but general words like *bird* can, as well as names of complex artefacts like *nature morte* (Ilson 1999*b*), *detective story, concerto*, or *dictionary*. Such definitions are interesting but perhaps not as original as their authors say. Geeraerts (2007: 1163) argues that traditional definitions have always indicated prototypicality by using adverbs such as *especially, typically, usually, often*, etc. to 'introduce descriptive features that are not general but … typical (prototypical, if one likes)', as in

empire 'a group of nations or states under the control of a single ruler or ruling power, especially an emperor or empress' (*C21D*)

He notes that these adverbs are used extensively: in *SOED*, for example, they are used '28,335 times in 18,274 entries'. Also, the PT-inspired definitions in *NODE* are not always spectacularly different. For example, the first core meaning of *pedal* is

a foot-operated lever or control for a vehicle, musical instrument or other mechanism

and the first sub-meaning is

each of a pair of levers used for powering a bicycle

But the more traditional *COD11* has a numbered list of meanings in which the first is

each of a pair of foot-operated levers for powering a bicycle

NODE may be more successful in its representation of the polysemy of *pedal*, but *COD* is probably equally useful.

---

[89] Non-prototypical uses can be expressed by more specific words, *car door, cupboard door*, etc., but **house door* is impossible.

Wierzbicka is not a fan of PT, as we have seen. It has provided lexicographers with justification for vagueness in definitions, she says (1996: 267). She maintains that meanings can be described accurately in definitions that use natural meta-language rather than abstruse formalisms, hence the name of her theory, natural semantic metalanguage (NSM). She claims that dictionary definitions can be improved[90] by a careful, in-depth, time- and effort-consuming analysis of syntagmatic and paradigmatic associations, rather than by linguistic tests, and (1996: 10) that all words can be defined by easy words: 'A definition which attempts to explain the simple word *if* via the complex word *implication* flies in the face of the basic principle of sound semantic analysis put forward more than two millennia ago by Aristotle'. In order to avoid circularity, she proposes, after Leibniz and other philosophers, a set of 'primitives' or 'logical atoms', which can be used to define other words but cannot be defined.[91] Her first list had 13 primitives: *want, don't want, think of, imagine, say, become, be part of, something, someone, I, you, world,* and *this,* which according to her were enough to define all other words.[92] This was later expanded to 37 in 1993, 55 in 1996, and currently stands at 61.

One of Wierzbicka's earliest definitions produced on those principles (Wierzbicka 1985) was *cup,* after Labov (1973). She argued that the differences between *cup* and *mug* lie in the function of the objects, i.e. in the nature of human interaction with them. She proposed (1985: 33–4) a two-page definition beginning

CUPS

A KIND OF THING THAT PEOPLE MAKE

IMAGINING THINGS OF THIS KIND PEOPLE WOULD SAY THESE THINGS ABOUT THEM:

they are made for people to use repeatedly for drinking hot   PURPOSE

liquids such as tea or coffee

one person from one thing of this kind

being able to put them down on something else

[etc.]

where PURPOSE in the right-hand column is a label for a semantic category of features. Wierzbicka has by now produced hundreds of such definitions, an unusual achievement for a semanticist. They aim at describing what the language users have in their minds, or what every one of us assumes that the other members of the same linguistic community think of when they think of the

---

[90] She often draws her examples from mediocre dictionaries, but she would probably justify this by the fact that they are the dictionaries that most people use.

[91] The defining vocabulary of some dictionaries is a toned-down version of the same idea.

[92] On primitives, see Wilks *et al.* (1996) and Hudson and Holmes (2000). Two questions are: Are they words or concepts? and Are they universal?

word, what Putnam (1975) calls *stereotypes*.[93] Wierzbicka's definitions are logically impeccable, although much too long and too original to be used in commercial lexicography. Also, they assume that the users need to acquire a lexical item from scratch, which is not the most frequent situation of use of a dictionary. This has led Geeraerts (2006a: 331) to speculate that Wierzbicka 'tends to underestimate the distinction between practical lexicography and theoretical semantics'. As they are, however, her definitions are good examples of the kind of thorough analysis that a definition should be based on and therefore food for thought for the lexicographer (Atkins 1993: 23). The ideas that a definition must define what the language users have in their minds and that the meaning of a word must always be considered in relation to the humans who use the concept are important. Why do the definitions of fruit so sparingly evoke the eating of the fruit, the size, the taste, the juiciness, etc.?

Corpus linguistics has not had much to say on definition so far, but a possible avenue for research would be to identify and collect spontaneous definitions, paraphrases, and explanations of all kinds in texts. Those can also be expected to reflect what the language users 'have in their minds' (see Teubert 2005) and could be adapted for the dictionary.

8.2.5.8 Do dictionary definitions define?

Many linguists find dictionary definitions unsatisfactory, incomplete, obscure, or inaccurate. No wonder: writing a definition is an effort to reach objectives that are either unreachable or contradictory. A definition should be precise and simple, it should be substitutable and it should not be circular, but it cannot be all of that at the same time. Some definitions are bad simply because lexicographers work in conditions that do not leave them much time for thought, because they are badly trained, or because their work is not checked carefully enough, but there are more interesting explanations. One is that there is no way a definition can be shown to be accurate. 'Is there any reason—other than tradition or pious optimism—to believe that a dictionary entry gives a true account of what a native speaker knows about the semantic properties of a word?' (Atkins 1991: 169). Wierzbicka would say that this can be deduced from an observation of what people know and say about language, but how do we know if the conclusions are right? In the absence of clear criteria, anyone can say that a definition is bad.

Another possible reason why definitions are often unsatisfactory is that some meanings might be impossible to describe in linguistic terms. That is what Saint

---

[93] As distinguished by Putnam from *extensional concepts*, which represent the knowledge of the expert.

Augustine said about time: 'What, then, is time? If no one asks me, I know what it is. If I wish to explain it to him who asks me, I do not know'[94] (Landau 2001: 167). To paraphrase Johnson, no words can express the meaning, 'though the mind easily perceives it'.[95]

Many critical semantic components may be perceptual and consequently may not be expressible in a spoken language. The general shape of a dog, for example, must be important in defining (in the wide sense) the concept [dog]. However, this shape cannot be described in English to any degree of satisfaction.   (McNamara and Miller 1989: 358)

Many user studies have also found dictionary definitions unsatisfactory, which raises the biggest problem: what are dictionary definitions supposed to do? What do the users expect when they read a definition? Is the main objective of the lexicographer to reach the 'essence' of the concept or to say what the language users need to know? Dictionary definitions are not generally used to learn a lexical item, as we have seen, but to find the information one needs in particular circumstances, because one has forgotten, etc.: 'for a very large part of the vocabulary of our languages, the only form a definition can take is that of pointing to...things and actions and institutions and indicating the words used for naming and describing parts and aspects of them' (Fillmore 1977: 133). Eventually, one could say that dictionary definitions can only hope to give what the users might need: 'their main task is to supply a series of hints and associations that will relate the unknown to something known' (Bolinger 1965: 572).

Definitions should above all be adapted to the needs and skills of the users.

If usefulness and usability of definitions are always in the forefront of the lexicographer's mind, as I believe they should be, he must be able to...transcend, or even break, the rules, in order to compose definitions that communicate, and are not merely dumb monuments to arcane speculations.   (Ayto 1983: 98)

A useful definition, in Hanks's (1973: 252) deliberately vague terms, is 'a short statement about some features of the word or the object denoted by it, chosen by the lexicographer on the basis of his guess as to what a user might be doing when he is looking at that word for the definition'. A useful definition of *second* would be something like 'the shortest unit of time', of *dog* 'a domestic animal that barks', etc. 'Dictionaries do not exist to define, but to help people grasp meanings' (Bolinger 1965: 572).

---

[94] *Confessions*, XI, xiv.
[95] What he actually wrote, about near synonyms, was: 'Ideas of the same race, though not exactly alike, are sometimes so little different, that no words can express the dissimilitude, though the mind easily perceives it' (*Preface*).

Defining words in a way that is satisfactory both for the linguists and for the dictionary users may well be impossible. Hanks (1979: 34) argues that the term *definition* has been 'appropriated by logicians to describe the process of drawing a line between what is included in a class or set and what is excluded', and that what lexicographers write should not be called *definition*. Johnson proposed to call them *explanations* and Wiegand (1999) proposes *paraphrases*.

8.2.5.9 Can dictionaries do without definitions?

There are many ways of explaining meaning. Bilingual dictionaries do it with equivalents, some monolingual dictionaries, such as the *Deutsches Wörterbuch* of the Grimm brothers, have used Latin (Osselton 2000: 62), others have relied on examples or quotations, like Richardson's *Dictionary* (1836/7) and many children's dictionaries (Ilson 1986*b*: 70). Sub-entries often have only examples, as in *CIDE* for *laterally* (at *lateral*):

To solve this puzzle you'll need to **think** *about it laterally*

Murray disapproved of the technique, but used it in some cases where a quotation seemed to be clear enough.[96] Hausmann (1990*a*) wondered whether a definition was really necessary, and recently some corpus linguists have argued that providing the user with corpus lines might be enough to clarify meaning. But this is doubtful: the dictionary user cannot be expected to carry out an analysis of meaning on the basis of contexts, however rich or numerous; that is the job of the lexicographer.

The use of pictorial illustrations,[97] called *ostensive definition* if it is the only method of explaining meaning (Robinson 1954), has a long history, dating back to the *Dictionary of Syr T. Eliot Knyght* in 1538 (Stein 1991*a*: 101). Illustrations were used in many early dictionaries, particularly for technical terms, but they then virtually disappeared from British dictionaries. They have been used in almost all American GPDs since 1828 and in most learners' dictionaries. The advantages are obvious. For concrete nouns, *capybara* or *onager*, *delphinium* or *marigold*, *blunderbuss* or *kayak*, a picture provides features, shape, colour, dimensions, elements of the real world context, that cannot be provided by the definition. Abstract nouns, general nouns like *animal* or *plant*, many adjectives, verbs, and function words are difficult to illustrate, but one can illustrate most prepositions, for

---

[96] '*OED3* has discarded this convention, but retains the *OED*'s practice of referring to quotations in order to supplement the definition' (Silva 2000: 90).

[97] On pictorial illustrations in dictionaries, see Ilson (1987*b*), Hupka (1989), Stein (1991*a*), Bogaards (1996).

example, and even some idioms. Pictorial illustrations can be used onomasiologically to find the unknown word corresponding to a known thing. They also make the dictionary page attractive, and the dictionary users like them (Tomaszczyk 1979: 114). How many of us have fond childhood memories of hours spent browsing through an illustrated dictionary?

Yet some have been against their use. Larousse thought that they were frivolous: in the *Preface* to the *Grand Dictionnaire universel du XIXe siècle*, he wrote indignantly about a rival dictionary: 'Engravings! Engravings! ...' (Pruvost 2000: 28), although pictures were introduced in Larousse dictionaries by his successors and have remained a constant feature. Indeed, illustrations are often chosen for aesthetic reasons, to embellish the dictionary, rather than to explain meaning (van der Meer and Sansome 2001: 286). The most serious argument is that no illustration can show the limits of the concept (Weinreich 1962: 31) if the word is common and polysemous, and no illustration can replace a definition:

> A picture is at best a representative example of the type of thing defined, yet it does not encompass anything approaching the full range of possibilities defined by the term it is supposed to illustrate.... To say that a picture obviates the need for definition makes the mistake of substituting an example representing a class of things... for the qualities that define the object.... [T]he idea that simple words like *dog* and *cat* need no definition [is] primitive, ill-conceived and vacuous.   (Landau 2001: 144; see also Sinclair 2004a: 10)

Recent dictionaries have invented new types of illustrations. *LDOCE4* has a double page on environmental problems, with pictures for 'fossil fuels and global warming', 'waste', 'air pollution', 'intensive farming', etc., a commercial gimmick. Some illustrations show the differences between words that could be confused, or strings of events constituting a 'situation' or 'script'. E-dictionaries also have video and sound illustrations (see below, 9.2.1).

8.2.6 Words in contexts

8.2.6.1 Information for expression

GPDs have always been designed more for comprehension than for expression. Syntagmatic rules are not absent: there are POS labels, the examples and quotations provide models, many dictionaries have usage notes and learners' dictionaries have lists of syntactic patterns which give the obligatory, preferential, or possible patterns in which each LU is used. But these are never enough: 'Statements are made about what the words mean, but very little is said about how they are used' (Hanks 1987: 121). Grammatical notations and classifications are neither complete nor reliable: for example, most dictionaries distinguish transitive and intransitive verbs, but they have different definitions, and many do not specify the necessity of a third argument. *MWC* 'focuses obsessively, repetitively, and often inaccurately on the transitive/intransitive distinction, while saying nothing at all about the third argument, seemingly being unaware of it' (Hanks 2008: 106). Even the indication of syntactic patterns in learners' dictionaries has proved so difficult that most lexicographers have given up and now rely on examples to show how words can be used.

Contextual information has been treated 'haphazardly by dictionary-makers' (Frawley 1988: 197): *COD11* does not give *for* in the entry *responsible*, or *against* in the entry *revolt*; most dictionaries do not say that *I don't like him much* is all right but not **I like him much* (McCarthy 1988*b*: 54); *AHD3* fails to specify that *averse*, *loath*, etc. can only be used as predicates, *galore* only after the noun, *for love or money* only in a negative context (Urdang 1993: 136–9); most dictionary definitions of *budge* fail to say that it can only be used in the negative (McCawley 1986: 4–5); *AHD* does not indicate that *rice* is an uncountable and *bean* a countable (McCawley 1986: 4); the sixth definition of *place* in *CED* is 'a house or living quarters', failing to indicate that this meaning of *place* must be preceded by a possessive, thus authorizing sentences such as ***'There are five places on that street'; 'MW [= *MWC*] implies... that **I put the cup* is a well-formed sentence of English' (Hanks 2008: 106), etc. The entry for *strong* may contain *strongly*, but it never mentions *strength* and *strengthen*, which are different entries. The definition of *thief* often mentions *steal* (it can hardly avoid it) but rarely mentions *theft* (Scholfield 1979). *MEDAL* is an exception:

Someone who steals something. An instance of stealing something is called a **theft**

The circular definitions of the type *think* 'be capable of conscious thought' and *thought* 'an act of thinking' do have virtues after all. Also, the meanings of polysemous words are never linked: for example in *LDOCE4*, *head n.* 'PERSON IN CHARGE a leader or person in charge of a group or organization' has no link to *head v.* 'BE IN CHARGE to be in charge of a team, government, organization, etc.'. Atkins (1993: 8) argues that the absence of information for expression is logical in dictionaries that are not designed for expression, so that it was 'precluded at the dictionary design stage by the defining style chosen by the editor for such words as these'.

The best examples of dictionaries for expression are Mel'čuk's ECDs, compiled according to the principles of the Meaning → Text theory: 'An ECD is PRODUCTION-ORIENTED. It is intended to supply all the information which is conveyed by individual lexical units and which is necessary to express a given meaning in a completely idiomatic way' (Mel'čuk 1988*a*: 167). An ECD entry has a syntactic zone, with 'skeleton' sentences, as in teach I.1 'X teaches Y to Z = X, having knowledge of, or skills in, Y, causes Z intentionally and methodically to learn Y'

and another zone containing the syntagmatic and paradigmatic associations of the headword, the *lexical functions*, as in the entry for *control, n.*

MAGN: strict / rigid
ANTIMAGN: lax
OPER1: have
INCEPOPER1: establish / set up
FINOPER1: lose
etc.

There are about sixty lexical functions in the present state of research, although of course for any given word only some functions are relevant, not all. Unfortunately, the data is obtained by introspection, not in a corpus, and therefore allows correct but not always natural expression. Also, the resulting text is too complex for commercial lexicography. But even as it is it provides 'an invaluable checklist for lexicographers' (Atkins and Rundell 2008: 151).

LLA provides a different sort of help: it leads the users from a word that they know to its near synonyms and shows how they differ. Also, with its many example sentences, it shows how each can be used. *Control* occupies 5.5 pages, with 21 groups, no. 2 compares *control, regulate,* and *govern* and the examples show that you can control 'temperatures', 'the electricity supply', 'the flow of immigrants', 'how quickly blood is pumped round the body', you can regulate 'the food supply', 'wages and working hours', 'the body's temperature' (some in the passive) and you can govern 'cigarette advertisements', 'the price of a metal', and 'people's lives' (mostly passive).

Recent dictionaries have included more information for expression (Nida 1997: 265), and not only learners' dictionaries, as part of a general evolution of lexicography, also illustrated by the dictionaries of collocations, of idioms, of phrasal verbs, etc. Linguists can help lexicographers collect and classify information for expression, 'syntactic behaviour, collocational preferences and selectional restrictions, sociolinguistic features (including register and regional variety), semantic features, contextual effects' (Rundell 1999: 37), and there is a lot of work. Zaenen and Engdahl (1994: 206) end their study on a pessimistic note: 'That linguistic theory in actual fact gives little guidance when one has to decide how to encode (syntactically relevant) lexical information [is] abundantly clear'. And the more the linguists progress in their discoveries the more difficult it is for the lexicographers to include the new information: 'the effort involved seems to exceed what any dictionary publisher would be willing to invest' (Zaenen 2002: 233).

Jackson (2002: 182) mentions a review of *ALD* by Bolinger (1990), 'which took the dictionary to task for not representing accurately some very subtle syntactic peculiarities of verbs, which, had they been so treated, would have probably baffled most users of the dictionary'.

Progress in the indication of information for expression means a corpus containing the information, linguists to discover and organize it, lexicographers to prepare it for the dictionary, 'space in which to set out the conclusions of the research' (Fillmore and Atkins 1994: 375), and publishers to produce dictionaries that contain it. It also means time for the innovations to be accepted by the users. The e-dictionary will no doubt make all this easier.

8.2.6.2 Extended units of meaning

In the compilation of a dictionary, every word is transported out of its milieu and put under a microscope for examination.

> The necessities and traditions of the trade force [the lexicographer] to extract a word from its context and thus to cut through the rich, multi-layered tissues which connect it with other words and keep it alive. For the sake of analysis he is obliged . . . to examine this lifeless thing out of its natural environment—discourse.   (Moulin 1981: 180–1)

The first step is when the lexicographer ' "atomizes" connected discourse into individual "words" ' (Rundell 1999: 40)—in lexicography as elsewhere, 'we murder to dissect' (Wordsworth).[98] 'Discourse is seen as a concatenation of elements that have an existence of their own. They are in the language system, but they live independently and can be isolated from it' (Guilbert 1969: 4–5). This may give a false idea of usage, 'misleadingly giv[ing] the impression that words exist independently of each other, in isolation of their co-texts' (Moon 2000: 507). The semantics of lexicography is a semantics of the word.

> Tradition, whose object is only to preserve the most useful means to satisfy a social need, gives to the semantics of dictionaries a certain number of characteristics which have no theoretical value but which one must be well aware of if one is to appreciate the characters of the 'fait dictionnaire' (Marcel Cohen). It is above all, in a very obvious way, a *semantics of the lexical unit*, whether word or phrase.   (Rey 1977: 15)

This focus on the isolated word appeared in the history of lexicography when glossaries became dictionaries. Glossaries were meant to clarify any expression that was difficult to understand in a text, but in dictionaries the information had

---

[98] In 'The Tables Turned'.

to be applicable to all contexts, and the word was the smallest unit that was easily generalizable and transferable from one context to another. Words are easier to treat and easier to classify.

All the major linguistic schools of the twentieth century have also tended to look at words. The philologists were interested in comparing the lexical stocks of languages. For structuralism and generative grammar in their many varieties, syntax came first and words were then inserted in their place in the syntagmatic chain of discourse. But some linguists began to think differently towards the middle of the twentieth century. In the 1950s, Firth proposed the word *collocation* and created the concept of *colligation*, i.e. the 'syntagmatic grammatical relations' that a word or a set of words enters into (Crystal 1985; see also Siepmann 2005):[99] the preference of a verb for the passive, of a noun for the plural, of an adjective for predicative position, of a word for initial position in a clause or sentence, for a negative context, etc. The two concepts looked like handy additions to the study of language, but they turned out to be more than that: they changed the focus of lexical studies. The word in its traditional sense appeared more and more as too narrow for linguistic study.

The advocates of the word-in-context position, particularly cognitive linguists, found support, if not inspiration, in one of the sayings of Wittgenstein, again, that 'the meaning of a term is its use in the language'. Some interpreted this as meaning that words do not have meanings out of context, but this is untenable: it 'may offer an escape from certain lexicographic impasses in connection with polysemy, but as a general theory it would require us to renounce dictionaries and to be satisfied, at most, with concordances' (Weinreich 1962: 29; see also Kleiber 1990b). It is more reasonable to say that words do have meanings but that their meanings are to some extent determined by the contexts in which they are used, no big discovery.

The choice of any word at any point in a discourse raises the question, what is the special contribution of that word to the discourse? Much of what is contributed will depend on the context into which the term is introduced, among other matters. But at core, each term in a language has a particular set of potentials for contributing meaning to discourse. (Hanks 1988: 45)

Naturally, corpus linguists are particularly interested in contexts. Sinclair proposed the concept of *idiom principle* in discourse (see below) and some of his followers took up Palmer's and Hornby's concept of *pattern* in the description of each word: the pattern of a word is all the words and structures that are associated

---

[99] The definition is borrowed from Hoey.

with it, Hornby and Palmer had said, but corpus linguists added 'frequently and normally' and 'that contribute to its meaning' (Hunston and Francis 2000). *Pattern* is a general word: it includes collocations, syntactic patterns à-la-Hornby and also co-occurrences over larger spans. Patterns are at work in many expressions: 'much of language comes in pre-packaged strings which display a limited number of patterns, as opposed to . . . the classical linguistic notion that language consists of a series of syntactic "slots" into which lexical items may be deposited' (McCarthy 1988*b*: 56). They suppose the existence of lexical sets (see below), the groups of LUs that can be used in the same environment, and they determine meaning to some extent: all the LUs that are used in a certain pattern have semantic features in common or, to look at the same phenomenon from the other end, a certain meaning tends be used in certain patterns.

The study of the frequent and normal contexts of an LU reveals its *semantic prosody* (Louw 1993; Stubbs 1996, 2001), i.e. its positive or negative associations, what would probably have been called *connotation*[100] in other schools. For example, the verb *cause* has a negative semantic prosody, because it tends to collocate with words like *grievous, bodily,* etc., and with objects that denote something negative, for example *confusion, consternation, disease, disruption, furore, havoc, uproar, inconvenience,* etc. So do *consequence, happen,* or *set in.* The verb *build up* can be positive or negative (Louw 1993: 171): 'things which *build up* (intransitive) are overwhelmingly negative and undesirable, whereas things that people *build up* (transitive) are almost always positive' (Atkins and Rundell 2008: 304): 'people build up a business, confidence, etc.' but 'inflation, tension, cholesterol, etc. builds up'. Most of the eighty-seven instances of *speck(s) of* in the BNC (see below, 9.1.7) 'are used in a context that implies that the speck of mud or dirt etc. was not welcome' (Atkins and Rundell 2008: 375). The language users may not be conscious of the semantic prosody of words, but the fact that words are repeatedly used in the same environments shows that somehow it is part of language competence.

The focus on words in context is a challenge for lexicography. It invites lexicographers to deal not with words but with 'extended units of meaning' (Tognini-Bonelli 2001: 106 *ff.*), the 'prefabs' of Bolinger (1976: 1) or the 'formulaic language' of Wray (2002). Hanks (2008: 103 *ff.*) argues that dictionaries are still too much 'meaning-driven', including *COB*, and that they should be 'pattern-driven': instead of asking the question 'How many senses does each word have,

---

[100] Except that semantic prosody is defined via the co-occurrent words. It is difficult to find a clear definition of *connotation* in the literature. It is defined as anything that is not the denotation, or referential meaning; or as what the use of the word makes the language users think of. See Kerbrat-Orecchioni (1977).

and what is the definition of each sense?', they should ask 'How many patterns does each word participate in, and what is the sense of each pattern?' This solves part of the problem of polysemy, because words are not ambiguous when they are considered together with their contexts: 'The ambiguity we had to deal with in traditional linguistics will disappear once we replace the medieval concept of the single word by the new concept of a collocation or a unit of meaning' (Teubert and Čermakova 2004: 151). But it is not easy for lexicographers used to dealing with individual words to start dealing with word patterns, which are more difficult to identify, to classify, and to generalize.

Dictionaries have always mentioned groups of words in examples, in quotations and in definitions. Function words, highly frequent lexical words, most adjectives, some transitive verbs, etc. cannot be defined otherwise. But it is easy to find examples of words that are defined out of the pattern to which they belong: *LDOCE1* has a definition 'an area of mind or feeling' for *spot*, which only makes sense in the phrase *have a soft spot for*; *CED* has a meaning 'dislodge' for *throw*, but does not say that this requires HORSE as a subject and HORSEMAN as an object (Hanks 1988: 44). McCawley (1973: 167) mentions a definition of *egg* in *WBD* as 'a person *a bad egg*', that allows sentences like *'Yesterday an egg tried to sell me a stolen watch'.

Lexicographers have become increasingly aware of the existence of word patterns (Nida 1997: 265), and corpora have provided them with huge amounts of information that was not available before. *COB* first, and then all learners' dictionaries have begun to define words in their typical patterns in FSDs, and native speakers' dictionaries have also improved: 'most MLDs now describe the lexical unit **have a think** as a single item, rather than perpetuating the pretence that **think** is in any useful sense a noun (traditionally defined as "an act of thinking")' (Rundell 1998: 326).

8.2.6.3 The idiom principle

The study of corpora has given substance to the notions of colligation and of word patterns. It has also shown that the choice of a word in a particular sense often entails the obligatory or preferential choice of other words or constructions in much larger spans sometimes implying more than one sentence (Tognini-Bonelli 2001: 18 *ff.*). For example, the form *set eyes on* tends to be associated with the auxiliary *has*, with a pronoun as subject of the verb, and with an indication of time, typically an adverb like *never* or a phrase like *the moment, the first time* (Sinclair 1991: 111); the verb *set about* is generally preceded by *to*, and followed by a transitive verb in the *-ing* form, *how* is often in the immediate vicinity of the word, generally to the left, and the context is generally that of 'problem-solving'

(Sinclair 1991: 75–6); in the BNC (see below, 9.1.7), 'there are 125 occurrences [of the verb *strike* in the sense of "appear to"]. Of these 125, no less than 109 have a pronoun as the direct object. *Me* is overwhelmingly the most frequent' (McCarthy 1988a: 55). These phenomena account for much of what goes on in discourse, Sinclair (1991: 110) says. They illustrate what he calls the *idiom principle*, using *idiom* in an extended sense, of a chunk of language of any length that has some petrification, in which the choice of a word entails the choice of other words. He contrasts it with the *open-choice principle*, in which words are strung one after the other without any constraints other than grammar and semantics.

The lexical choices in such expressions are not only grammatical; they are *acceptable*, Sinclair says, or *natural* (McCarthy 1988b), or *appropriate* or *typical* (Hanks 1988). Sinclair argues that their relative regularity makes them predictable and facilitates communication: the linguistic expressions that are associated with recurrent situations can be acquired and stored more easily. Literary and journalistic styles tend to favour non-idiomatic strings, to avoid 'pre-packaged' chunks or use them in an unexpected form. Scientific and didactic languages prefer idiomatic sequences so as not to distract the receiver.

This type of idiomaticity cannot be properly treated in dictionaries. The only thing lexicographers can do is give the users access to large extracts from the corpus and let them observe how discourse works. That is what some have begun doing.

8.2.6.4 Lexical sets

There are many words in the lexis of a language that can be grouped in sets according to their meanings: the names of animals, of the days of the week, of musical instruments, of flowers, abstract nouns, verbs of movement, adjectives of colour, etc. Some groups are open (diseases, birds, etc.), others are closed (months, military ranks, etc.) and some are a bit of both (numbers, etc.). Language teachers have always grouped words by domain (the human body, agricultural implements, etc.), by situation (at the market, in the railway station, etc.) or by function (apologizing, arguing, etc.), and linguists keep discovering new possible groupings.

Words can also be grouped according to the patterns in which they are typically used. The nouns that can be used as objects of, say, *govern*, obviously have something in common. Hanks (2008: 122 *ff.*), noticing that a word can belong to several groups, proposed the notion of *shimmering lexical sets* to refer to sets of words appearing in the same role in a given pattern and that vary slightly with each individual pattern. For example, *sparrow, finch, osprey, hawk,* and *penguin* can all be the subjects of *lay eggs*; the subjects of *fly* can be *sparrow, finch*, *osprey*, and *hawk* but not *penguin; penguin* however is part of the set of words that can be the subjects of *swim*, together with new companions, including other birds. 'In this sense, a lexical set may be said to "shimmer". Its membership is not constant, but changeable' (Hanks 2008: 124).

The words that belong to a group must be given a similar microstructural treatment: lexicography should both unify and individuate (Apresjan 2002: 100). Apresjan calls this *systematic lexicography*, searching for 'systematicity in lexicon as manifested in various classes of lexemes' (Apresjan 2002: 91), and Mel'čuk calls it the *principle of uniformity* (Mel'čuk *et al.* 1995: 40). Some dictionaries, for example *W3* (Morton 1994: 91), have tried defining words in groups, to ensure uniformity. Recently, lexicographers have begun to use templates with ready-made fields for each category of words, to ensure that no important semantic and syntactic information is missed. But there are limits to the treatment of words in groups. Atkins (1993: 22), after having called for the help of linguists on the creation of lexical sets, eventually doubted whether group defining was advisable, because words tend to belong to more than one category and because most (all?) lexicographic projects progress basically by alphabetical order. The problem is that it is not words that belong to a set but LUs.

Compiling entries for words in semantic sets entails an additional pass through the wordlist, greatly increasing the time and expense of dictionary production. For instance, the adjective *civil* would require to be compiled in the 'Military', and the 'Social Behaviour' sets... when all such uses had been compiled individually, the final version of the entry would have to be assembled. Reducing this to the correct length might then have a knock-on effect on the various sets involved. Editors have nightmares of an infinite loop.   (Atkins 2002: 25)

8.3 DO DICTIONARIES INFLUENCE LINGUISTICS?

The exploration of what linguistics has given to lexicography is frustrating. One feels that linguistics is indispensable and that it has contributed to the improvement of dictionaries, but the most important questions of lexicography have not been solved: what is *a* meaning and how many different meanings does a word have? What is a lexical item, a collocation, an idiom, etc.? On some of these points, it is not even certain that we can expect answers in the future, and lexicography may remain for ever an art more than a science. Also, the more information the linguists come up with the more difficult it is to include it in a dictionary: 'it certainly seems that we have now reached the stage when the amount of information that lexicographers wish to convey, and that learners wish to acquire, far outweighs the space available in a single-volume book' (Nesi 2000*a*: 138). Even the acquisition of more space, as in e-dictionaries, does not solve all the lexicographer's problems. Any idea put forward by linguists risks being rejected if the effect on the dictionary is not spectacular and easy to implement: 'the user is as much entitled as the linguist to his vision of what a good English dictionary should be' (Osselton 1983: 13). The dictionary must be understandable as well as scientifically impeccable. And it must be acceptable to the publishers.

> Publishers expect to publish, bookshops expect to sell, and buyers expect to buy and use dictionaries which, for each word, provide a (possibly nested) list of possible meanings and uses. Large sums of money are invested in lexicographic projects, on the basis that a dictionary has the potential to sell hundreds of thousands of copies. Investors will not likely adopt policies which make their product radically different to the one known to sell. However inappropriate the nested list might be as a representation of the facts about a word, for all but the most adventurous lexicographic projects, nothing else is possible.
>
> (Kilgarriff 1997*b*: 143).

Perhaps lexicographers are condemned to be shallow linguists.

The reason why linguistics does not have all the answers might be that it relies too much on dictionaries. Some of the accepted principles of 'mainstream linguistics',[101] Hudson (1988: 287–8) argues, have been imposed by our lexicographic traditions.

> The basic problem is that any of us linguists is also a citizen, with the same experiences as any other typical citizen. We all have dictionaries on our shelves, and have grown up in a society where dictionaries are standard items of furniture. These dictionaries are of course the traditional commercial ones, which have various structural characteristics.... What I am suggesting, then, is that folk linguistics contains various ideas about the lexicon, alias dictionary, which are at least in part founded on the traditional practice of lexicographers. Any linguist brought up in a culture where these folk ideas are prevalent is likely to be infected by them in early life and must beware of building them, without critical examination, into their professional thinking.

If Hudson is right, then the lexicographers who turn to linguistics for help may actually get ideas that originated in dictionaries.

And forward-looking lexicographers must be even more careful not to mistake ideas which originated in traditional lexicography for carefully considered and researched tenets of scientific linguistics. I applaud any attempt by a lexicographer to learn from

---

[101] Hudson (1988: 290) means 'the theories which are heavily influenced by Chomsky'.

linguistics (or from any other relevant discipline), in the hope of being able to move towards radically new and better kinds of dictionary; but it would be tragic if the effect of this contact with linguistics was just to tie lexicographers even more firmly to their own tradition.   (Hudson 1988: 288)

Of course the lexicographers will accept these ideas all the more readily as they confirm age-old practices and they have acquired the additional aura of science in the process. If that is true, then dictionaries are what they are partly because of linguistics, and linguistics is what it is partly because of dictionaries.

It is clear that modern linguistics and modern lexicography have been moving in the same direction, towards more interest in common, everyday language and in the syntagmatic and paradigmatic environments of words. Whether we have a case of influence of the one on the other, or simply parallel courses, the future of the dictionary is obviously in a closer collaboration between them, on an equal footing: 'one should definitely not assume that theoreticians in principle have the answers and that lexicographers simply have to follow' (Geeraerts 2007: 1172).

9

COMPUTERS AND CORPORA IN LEXICOGRAPHY

THE third factor that has been shaping dictionaries in the past decades, besides linguistics and the study of dictionary use, is the computer. It has become so important in the preparation and in the consultation of dictionaries that it is now almost ridiculous to write a chapter on its role in lexicography. Indeed, it has been mentioned abundantly in this book. The following chapter collects information that has not been given so far.

The invention of the computer is comparable in magnitude to the invention of a writing system: it multiplies the possibilities of storing and treating information, thus relieving us of the effort of memorizing. In *Phaedrus*, Plato has Socrates declare:

O most ingenious Theuth, the parent or inventor of an art is not always the best judge of the utility or inutility of his own inventions to the users of them. And in this instance, you who are the father of letters, from a paternal love of your own children have been led to attribute to them a quality which they cannot have; for this discovery of yours will create forgetfulness in the learners' souls, because they will not use their memories; they will trust to the external written characters and not remember of themselves. The specific which you have discovered is an aid not to memory, but to reminiscence, and you give your disciples not truth, but only the semblance of truth; they will be hearers of many things and will have learned nothing; they will appear to be omniscient and will generally know nothing; they will be tiresome company, having the show of wisdom without the reality.   (275A)

Computational lexicography (CL) appeared in the 1960s with the use of the computer to transfer the dictionary text onto perforated tape (Ooi 1998: 32). Larousse was among the first to use punch cards for the preparation of the *Grand Larousse encyclopédique* in the late 1950s (Pruvost 2002a: 67), and Urdang (1993: 132) used computers in the early 1960s 'in the classification of data into the several categories required for the structure of an entry' for the preparation of *RHD*, with machines that could convert the text into 'punched tape'. By 1984, Landau (2001: 285) writes, 'we were able to edit on screen, but we still had to send our tapes to St. Louis to be processed'. In those early days, the computer was also used to 'automate the arduous (formerly manual) process of checking cross-references' and to check that definitions used only the words of the defining vocabulary (Atkins and Rundell 2008: 112).

Important dates in the history of CL are 1978, the publication of *LDOCE*, the first dictionary to become available on tape for research (see below), and 1987, the publication of *COB1*, the first dictionary to be derived from a corpus. The computer is now used in all dictionary projects, sometimes for very simple tasks but sometimes in highly sophisticated ways. Its advantages are well known: it can treat huge quantities of information in much less time than humans, it is perfectly accurate, consistent, and free from the bias that humans often introduce. With e-mail and the Internet, it also allows lexicographers to work from their homes: *EWED* (1999) was 'one of the first major dictionary projects to be run in this way, with a small in-house staff managing a large team of home-based editors on three continents' (Atkins and Rundell 2008: 113).

9.1 CORPORA FOR DICTIONARIES

The study of linguistic questions with the help of a corpus, a collection of texts assembled for given purposes, began in the late nineteenth century.[1]

Even as early as the end of the nineteenth century large corpora were used to develop the first frequency lists. F.W. Kaeding's study, for instance, entitled *Haufigkeitswörterbuch der deutschen Sprache* (published in 1898) was based on a corpus of eleven million words manually analysed to establish the frequencies of graphemes, syllables, and words. Using this data, J.B. Estoup, in his *Gammes sténographiques* (published in Paris in 1907), noted the statistical regularities in the list of the word forms in a text, ranked in order of

---

[1] For an introduction to corpus linguistics, see Biber *et al.* (1998), Kennedy (1998), Tognini-Bonelli (2001), Meyer (2002), McEnery *et al.* (2006).

decreasing frequency, and this became the starting-point of the well-known work of G.K. Zipf (1935). (Atkins *et al.* 1994: 20)

In the USA, the first corpora appeared in the 1920s.

The first, modern, large-scale corpus of English compiled for lexical study, as distinguished from literary analysis, was Edward L. Thorndike's word count of 4.5 million words, published as the *Teacher's Word Book* in 1921 and subsequently enlarged over the following decades in several stages to a corpus of 18 million words, which produced *The Teacher's Word Book of 30,000 Words*, by Thorndike and Irving Lorge.... Another early corpus of considerable size is Ernest Horn's *A Basic Writing Vocabulary: 10,000 Words Most Commonly Used in Writing*... published in 1926. (Landau 2001: 273)

Others followed (Landau 2001: 273 *ff.*). After the Second World War, the corpus was readily adopted in Britain by linguists for whom, after Firth, the object of linguistics was the study of observable, attested discourse, *parole* in Saussure's terms. The corpus gave them access to huge quantities of information hitherto impossible to assemble and treat. It showed real, or ordinary, use as opposed to imagined, or exemplary, use, and also how frequent a word, a phrase, or a pattern was, paving the way for a new focus on what is common, normal usage.

Early corpus studies in Britain and France were aimed at establishing word frequencies: Fries' *American English Grammar* (1940), based on a corpus of several thousand letters, showed that less than 5,000 words 'account for 95% of most written texts, that 1,000 types account for 85%', etc. (Landau 2001: 275). Or they were for the study of syntax: the Survey of English Usage, 'the first large-scale project to collect language data for empirical grammatical research' (Teubert 2004: 107), assembled by Quirk at University College London in the 1950s was used for the compilation of the huge *Grammar of Contemporary English* (1972) by Quirk *et al.* and again for the *Comprehensive Grammar of the English Language* (1985) by the same authors. It started as a collection of 200 samples of 5,000 words each including a fair portion of speech (about 500,000 words), all on paper slips, and was later converted into a computer database under the supervision of Jan Svartvik.

In the late 1950s, corpus studies became less popular in the USA and elsewhere, because of the influence of Chomsky and his followers, who have always maintained that corpus linguistic studies are misguided (Hanks 2000*a*: 3 *ff.*): 'The standard method of the sciences is not to accumulate huge masses of unanalyzed data and to try to draw some generalizations from them,' Chomsky said (Andor 2004: 97). The corpus tells us what people have said, not what they could have said; in other words, it does not give access to the code. It illustrates performance, while linguists should study competence. But corpus studies regained popularity everywhere with the generalized availability of the computer in the humanities in the 1970s. The corpus was then given its current definition of a large collection of texts assembled in electronic form according to a set of criteria to be used for a specific purpose. The term *corpus linguistics* was used for the first time in the early 1980s (McEnery *et al.* 2006: 3).[2]

9.1.1 *The history of corpus lexicography*

Kilgarriff and Tugwell (2002: 125) distinguish four ages in the history of corpus lexicography.[3] The first, before the arrival of the computer, was when the lexicographer collected quotations, as in Johnson's dictionary or in the *OED*. The second age started with the compilation of the first edition of *COB* in the early 1980s, for which the lexicographers collected all their data from their corpus. The third age was in the late 1990s when corpora became so big that their users needed to summarize the thousands of lines that they obtained for some words:

[T]he focus in corpus lexicography has begun to move away from issues such as the size and composition of corpora (which preoccupied us in the 1980s and 1990s) towards the newer challenges of how best to extract lexicographically relevant information from very large text databases.   (Rundell 2002: 140)

The fourth age was when lexicographers could use profiling software (see below) to obtain a summary of the evidence for every word.

Many dictionaries now use electronic corpora in many languages. But many are still produced either with small corpora assembled expressly for the purpose or with no corpus at all, either because there are none, or because existing corpora are unsuitable, or because the financial returns expected from the dictionary sales are too meagre for publishers to invest in corpus building or in the exploitation of an existing corpus. The English language community is rich, because it sells more dictionaries than any other language, but it is the exception rather than the rule. Even in the English-speaking world, some publishers have been more enthusiastic than others, British lexicographers more than American ones, and learners' dictionaries more than NSDs.

9.1.2 *Different sorts of corpora*

A corpus can be compiled for a variety of purposes, language teaching, translation, the writing of grammars, the preparation of teaching material, sociolinguistic

---

[2] A Corpora Discussion List is at http://www.hit.uib.no/corpora/welcome.txt.
[3] On corpus lexicography, see Atkins and Zampolli (1994), Ooi (1998).

studies, even forensic enquiries. If a corpus is to be used for lexical studies, it must be large, larger than for the study of pronunciation and even larger than for the study of grammar: 'In corpus lexicography, size matters a lot' (Rundell 1998: 320). It must also be representative of a language, or of a variety of a language (McEnery *et al.* 2006: 13 *ff.*; see below).

A lexicographic corpus can be closed or open, specialized or general, written or spoken, synchronic or diachronic. Specialists also distinguish monitor corpora, designed to monitor the evolution of the language; reference (or general-purpose) corpora, recording the standard variety of the language; opportunistic (or canni- balistic) corpora, collecting as much data as possible with minimal selection criteria; full text corpora, with only full texts; sample corpora, with text samples, useful for comparing varieties; learner corpora, with texts produced by learners of a language; development corpora, with texts produced by children, etc. Bilingual lexicographers can use parallel corpora, with the same texts translated in different languages or comparable corpora, with texts on the same subjects in different languages.

The choice for lexicographers preparing monolingual dictionaries is between monitor corpora and sample corpora. Monitor corpora are large and all-inclusive, sample corpora are smaller and selective. Monitor corpora are useful for studying the evolution of the language, but their compilation is a permanent operation and is therefore costly, and one can never be sure how representative they are. Also, when you use them you have to specify what version you are using, because they keep changing (McEnery *et al.* 2006: 68–9). That is why most lexicographers prefer to use sample corpora, which are easier to compile and use.

9.1.3 Corpus design

Corpus design is vital, because it has a direct influence on the quality of the information that will be collected (Meyer 2002: 30 *ff.*). To compile a corpus, one must define precise criteria for inclusion and exclusion, which specify what type of discourse the corpus contains and in what form. Those criteria vary with the nature of the corpus, its size, what it is designed for, and for what users the end product is prepared. They will allow comparisons between corpora, of two periods of the same language, of two regional varieties, of two languages, etc.[4]

Before compiling a corpus, many practical decisions have to be made: How to obtain the right to use texts that are protected by copyright? Where will the

---

[4] Guidelines for the creation of corpora are on the site of EAGLES: http://www.cs.vassar.edu/CES/.

corpus be stored? In what form will the texts be? Who will have access to it? How?, etc.[5]

Corpora have become bigger and bigger since the 1980s, and their dimensions have begun to pose problems. The current trend seems to be towards both large corpora used for reference and smaller corpora used for particular projects. Even for lexicography, a smallish corpus is enough for a majority of the decisions made by the lexicographer: for 'practical purposes, samples smaller than 500 lines can often be sufficient to give an overview for... structuring a dictionary entry' (Hanks 2002: 165). Atkins and Rundell (2008: 60) show that 121 lines are enough to 'underpin a useful description' of *adjudicate*.

The most difficult problem of corpus design is representativeness (Biber 1993). Representativeness is determined by balance, i.e. 'the range of genres included in a corpus' and sampling, i.e. 'how the text chunks for each genre are selected' (McEnery *et al.* 2006: 13 *ff.*). The corpus compiler needs a typology of texts, not an easy thing to produce because there is an infinite variety of criteria and no two specialists agree on what is important. Most would agree that there are two types: internal criteria, which are the linguistic characteristics of the text, and external criteria, which are features imposed on the text, i.e. date, the identity of the writer, age, education, gender, etc. If the texts are selected according to internal criteria, the corpus will contain the linguistic features that have been introduced into it. Therefore external criteria are preferable, but they are the ones for which typological features are especially difficult to identify (McEnery *et al.* 2006: 14).

The representativeness of a corpus encounters the same difficulties as the representativeness of the wordlist of a dictionary. Rundell and Stock (1992: 49) distinguish language that is produced, for which a representative corpus should contain 'a very high proportion of spoken language, a reasonable amount of newspaper text, and a tiny percentage of everything else', and language that is consumed, for which 'the corpus would be dominated by popular newspapers and lowbrow fiction—other forms of text such as literary fiction or academic discourse would be only thinly represented'. The proportions of spoken text and written text are determined by what the corpus is for, but the inclusion of spoken text is always costly, in spite of the software that can convert speech into electronic text (Meyer 2002: 32). 'One corpus linguist estimates that it takes ten hours to transcribe one hour's worth of recorded speech (usually 7,000–9,000 words) with minimal prosodic markup,' Landau (2001: 324) wrote in 2001. Wray (2002: 27) argues that no corpus is 'likely to be representative of the rather

---

[5] On all these questions, see Meyer (2002), Bowker and Pearson (2002), Atkins and Rundell (2008: 53 *ff.*).

narrower linguistic experience of any one individual...presumably only relatively few people regularly read both tabloid and broadsheet newspapers and
listen to both pop quizzes and heavy current affairs programmes on the radio—
the sorts of data that are thrown together in a corpus'.

A corpus can have full texts, in which case some texts will be much longer than
others and some linguistic characteristics will be over- or under-represented: the
corpus will be skewed; or it can contain only texts of a pre-defined size, which is
another misrepresentation of the real use of language. In the latter case, the corpus
compiler must determine a standard size and locate the samples in their respective
original sources: always the same part, the beginning, the end, the middle, etc. The
BNC takes its samples systematically from the middle of documents. The place of
the samples can be determined by random techniques (McEnery *et al.* 2006: 20).
For a given corpus size, 'it is better to include more texts from many different
speakers and writers than fewer texts from a smaller number of speakers and
writers' (Meyer 2002: 39). Here again cost is a factor: it can be expensive to acquire
the right to use full texts in the case of novels, plays, etc., but the cost also rises with
the number of texts that are used. The Brown corpus contains only 2,000-word
samples, the Survey of English Usage and the London-Lund Corpus 5,000; the
BNC has texts between 25 and 40,000 words; the Lampeter Corpus of Early
Modern English Tracts has only full texts (Meyer 2002: 38).

It is impossible to be sure that a corpus is representative, however refined the
techniques are, because there is no reliable scientific measure of corpus balance
(McEnery *et al.* 2006: 16). For practical purposes, a representative corpus is a
corpus that honestly attempts to represent the diversity of the language, but this
is largely an act of faith rather than a statement of fact. In the Brown corpus,
words like *abysmal, checkup, landslide*, and *rap* occur only twice; *ballistics, gnaw,
invert*, and *radiate* occur only once (Landau 2001: 279). The BNC, generally
recognized as a balanced corpus, has only 73 occurrences of *temerity*, 45 of
exasperating, 31 of *inattentive*, and 20 of *barnstorming* (Atkins and Rundell
2008: 60); *mucosa* has the same frequency as *unfortunate* (Atkins and Rundell
2008: 69, 88); the fourth most statistically significant combination noun *adult* +
noun is *adult worm*, from a single source on parasitology (Atkins and Rundell
2008: 93); subjects such as making cakes, taking care of dogs, hotel management,
village life in Nepal are covered but not badminton, heavy-metal music, or
carpentry (Atkins and Rundell 2008: 74). Fortunately, as with a wordlist, the
question is not whether a corpus is good, it is whether it is good enough for the
use for which it was compiled.

This has led some to recommend that the building of corpora be left to
specialists: 'It would be preferable in the long run if descriptive linguists played

no part in the way corpora are created, but just accepted what they were given by experts in the use of language in society' (Sinclair 2003*a*: 171), and this may become the rule in the future. In the meantime, lexicographers should continue to use existing corpora, or produce their own, in spite of their recognized or supposed shortcomings: 'It would be short-sighted indeed to wait until one can scientifically balance a corpus before starting to use one, and hasty to dismiss the results of corpus analysis as "unreliable" or "irrelevant" because the corpus used cannot be proved to be "balanced"' (Atkins *et al.* 1992: 6).

The advocates of monitor corpora argue that representativeness can be ensured by sheer size (Sinclair 1991: 24 *ff.*), because size annihilates potential bias, but this is not widely accepted. The BoE at 450 million words had words 'nobody has ever heard of...', for example *abelch, airpad, eurocrisis* and *keyphone*' (Teubert and Čermakova 2004: 115). Is there a threshold beyond which a corpus can be considered as representative? Some think that this is impossible:

> The main limitation of a corpus is that no matter how large it is and how carefully it has been assembled, it cannot possibly represent truly the myriad ways in which language is used spontaneously in speech and deliberately in writing. A corpus is always a selection and can only represent the speech and writing of those transcriptions and texts that are selected.   (Landau 2001: 321)

True, modern dictionaries are not supposed to account for 'the myriad ways in which language is used'; they aim at describing normal, typical, natural usage.

9.1.4 *The uses of a corpus in dictionary making*

In lexicography, a corpus is distinguished from a *citation file*, which is 'a selection of potential lexical units in the context of actual usage' (Landau 2001: 190).[6] Because of its size, the corpus provides what Rundell and Stock (1992: 22) call 'inescapable' evidence: 'If you are confronted with not two or three but dozens or even hundreds of instances of a word being used in a particular way, there is really no arguing with what the corpus is telling you'. This is uncertain in theory, as no doubt the Chomskyans would argue, but it makes sense in practice.

Corpora can be used for a variety of purposes: they provide evidence on 'the associated syntactic structures, phraseological patterns, and collocations; contexts of use; frequencies and distributions in terms of variety, genre, and register; and, where diachronic corpora are available, evidence of changes in currency and usage' (Moon 1998*b*: 347). They can also help decide which words, phrases and

---

[6] Some use *archive*, 'a repository of available language materials' (Leech 1990: 5).

meanings ought to be included, distinguish between synonyms (Tognini-Bonelli 2001: 35 *ff.*), determine what spellings or forms are the most frequent in a given variety or genre, etc. (Rundell 1998: 321 *ff.*), distribute usage labels, etc.

9.1.4.1 Corpus evidence vs. introspection

In traditional lexicography as well as in linguistics, usage is described intuitively. Chomsky has always relied on introspection to decide what was acceptable and what was not, even though his teacher, Zellig Harris, used statistics in the study of language. Many modern linguists, Cruse, Mel'čuk, Wierzbicka, maintain that introspection, complemented if necessary by the use of informants—'introspection...at one remove' (Atkins 2002: 24)—can give access to usage. But corpus linguists have challenged this view: there are many facts of usage that turn up in corpora but are not accessible to introspection, and many of those that introspection proposes turn out to be rare or nonexistent in corpora. Introspection 'is a very flawed technique,' Hanks (2000a: 4) concludes. 'We have no access through introspection to how the language really behaves out there in the linguistic community' (Atkins 2002: 24).

Corpus studies indicate that there is an inverse relationship between cognitive salience (what we can come up with by means of introspection) and social salience (what we find in corpora). We human beings are wired to register the unusual in our minds...But we fail to pay any attention to the commonplace patterns of usage on which we rely so heavily in our everyday communications.   (Hanks 2000a: 4)

There are many examples of differences between cognitive salience and frequency. Intuitions of polysemy may be wrong, as in the case of *party* and *perfect* seen above (Atkins and Rundell 2008: 263). The most salient meanings are not the most frequent, as we have seen: 'ordinary English speakers asked to list the most common meanings of **take** never include expressions of time in their lists ("How long will it take?", "It only took a few minutes"), although general English corpora show this to be extremely common' (Hanks 2000a: 4; see also Wray 2002: 277). Even skilled linguists and lexicographers make mistakes: Malone's study of 500 citations for the word *mahogany* revealed that the chief meaning was not mentioned in *MWC2* (Malone 1940, in Landau 2001: 206). Svartvik (1999: 291) compared a study of collocations (*good*, *strong*, and *high* with *likelihood*, *probability*, *possibility*, and *chance*) by Bolinger (1975) with what the BNC says, and noticed that some of the collocations that Bolinger found acceptable were rarely used (for example *good likelihood*, one occurrence) and that some collocations that he thought were unacceptable were in fact used (for example *strong chance*, 13 occurrences). No wonder dictionaries that do not use a corpus sometimes misrepresent current usage. Rundell and Stock (1992: 22–3) found evidence of uses of the verb *represent* as a copula meaning 'be' that were not recorded in the dictionaries they used. 'Corpus lexicography has taught us that packing an entry with cognitively salient items does not produce a good description of naturally occurring language' (Atkins 2002: 24).

9.1.4.2 Corpus-based or corpus-driven lexicography?

Corpus linguists distinguish between corpus-based and corpus-driven studies (Tognini-Bonelli 2001: 65 *ff.*), and the distinction applies to lexicography. In corpus-based lexicography, the corpus is used to test and exemplify the lexicographer's hypotheses; in corpus-driven lexicography, every piece of information is drawn from the corpus without pre-conceived ideas. The two are not mutually exclusive, as McEnery *et al.* (2006: 8 *ff.*) show, but constitute a cline according to the relative importance given to the facts of the corpus and to the pre-conceived ideas brought to its preparation and exploitation. But the opposition has far-reaching consequences. Corpus-based lexicography is like boxing oneself into a corner, say Atkins and Rundell (2008: 92), because the corpus can only return what the lexicographer introduced. A corpus-driven approach seems more attractive, but it requires a huge non-annotated corpus so as to reduce bias and increase the chances of identifying all the linguistic features of interest, and it is effort- and time-consuming. Because of those problems, many linguists prefer corpus-based studies, and corpus lexicography is generally corpus-based.

9.1.5 *The annotation of the corpus*

Lexicography studies individual words but it must also keep track of the position and role of each word in its environment. In order to do this, all except the staunchest defenders of corpus-driven lexicography agree that a corpus should be annotated, or enriched. If it is not, certain types of searches that can only be performed with pre-defined categories, all nouns, all intransitive verbs, all subjects, all concrete nouns, all verbs of movement, etc. (McEnery *et al.* 2006: 11) will be impossible, and the corpus will be difficult to use again for similar or different purposes (McEnery *et al.* 2006: 30).

There are two sorts of corpus annotation: *mark-up*, which is the marking of the external, apparent characteristics of the text, its title, its formal features, its use of font, its author, etc., and *annotation* proper, which is the marking of its internal, linguistic features, syntax, POS, meaning, etc. Software tools have been developed, or are being developed, for all those operations, some of which can now be carried out automatically. This saves a lot of time and money, but the results are not totally reliable, depending on the tool used and on the nature of the operation, on the corpus and on the language, and they must often be completed or corrected manually. The whole field is moving at a mind-boggling pace, and up-to-date information can be obtained on specialized websites.[7]

9.1.5.1 Mark-up

Mark-up marks external features of the text that may be necessary in an analysis of the contents of the corpus. A particularly important point is the header of the text, which classifies it in its relevant categories, genre, date, author, etc. The more precise the categorization the finer the results that will be available, but also the more labour-intensive and time-consuming the process will be.

The best-known mark-up scheme is the Text Encoding Initiative (TEI), launched in the 1980s (Ide and Veronis 1995).

The TEI has as its task the production of a set of guidelines to facilitate both the interchange of existing encoded texts and the creation of newly encoded texts. The guidelines are meant to specify both the types of features that should be encoded and also the way these features should be encoded, as well as to suggest ways of describing the resulting encoding scheme and its relationship with pre-existing schemes.   (Ooi 1998: 39)

The TEI used SGML at the beginning but the later versions use XML, a coding system that is compatible with the web.[8] Some linguists find the TEI cumbersome, and Sinclair (2003b: 192) even thinks it should not be used:

TEI, the Text Encoding Initiative, is a way of analysing documents, which adds immensely to the effort of building a corpus, and requires lengthy, verbose and illegible insertions at the beginning of each document. It is vigorously promoted for corpus work by archivists, but cannot be recommended for a number of reasons.

A simpler scheme, the Corpus Encoding Standard (CES) is designed specifically for corpora in linguistic studies (McEnery *et al.* 2006: 26).

The TEI system can also be used to structure the dictionary text in preparation. It allows the drafting of a Document Type Definition (DTD) for each new dictionary, which specifies the formal features and the organization of the dictionary text to ensure consistency (Atkins and Rundell 2008: 113 *ff.*). In a

---

[7] On corpus annotation tools, see http://personal.cityu.edu.hk/~davidlee/devotedtocorpora.

[8] SGML seems to have been abandoned. A good indication of the speed at which the domain evolves is this, published in 2002: 'At this point, it is not clear how widely used XML will become in the corpus linguistics community' (Meyer 2002: 84).

DTD, each piece of information has a precise position indicated by a specific sign, for example < where the information begins and /> where it ends. Many dictionary writing systems (DWS) have been developed on this basis, and they are used by many dictionary projects.

[DWS systems] lead to a more rational approach to compiling (say, in lexical sets); they reduce the potential for errors and inconsistency by automating some routine tasks, removing a good deal of the drudgery along the way; they allow the lexicographers to look at already compiled text and to benefit from previous work by the team; they give the managing editors the opportunity of tailoring work packages to the skills and needs of the team members; they facilitate the editing process, reducing the steps in the text flow from initial editor to printed entry; and they monitor the timing and text length according to the project schedule.   (Atkins 2002: 3)

9.1.5.2 Annotation

The segmentation of the text into graphic words, or *tokenization*, is necessary for all further operations, from the most basic to the most sophisticated. It is a complex operation in some languages, and even in English there are problems with hyphens in words (*lily livered* or *lily-livered*) or at the end of lines, and with apostrophes *(isn't, the family's home, she's back)*. Concordancers can arrange forms by frequency or in KWIC (Key Word in Context) lists, for example in the order of the form to the right of the word:

1922 and 1988 PP. The study's main	**measure** of an acquisition's success
of Prester John. But the price was a	**measure** of autonomy granted to what
in no doubt whatsoever that a	**measure** of change in your life is
embarrassment" that finally led to a	**measure** of change. With them, she
PP. As Taff poured me a good	**measure** of cider and handed me a
said they should not be used as a	**measure** of comparative living
of calculations. PP The common	**measure** of computer performance,

The lines can also be ordered by the word to the left, etc., by lemma (for example, the forms *go, gone, going*, and *went* for *go*), by word-class, etc. for the whole corpus or for specific sections. Each concordance line has a coded reference, usually in a left-hand column, to the source text. If more information is needed on an occurrence, a click gives access to a larger extract from the text. Several concordancers are available, usually within multi-purpose tools: WordSmith (Scott 1999), MonoConc, Tact, ICECUP, which was used to extract information from ICE-GB, etc. The concordancers used by lexicographers are usually 'custom-built and proprietary' (Landau 2001: 335), like WordCruncher, developed at Brigham Young University (Hofland 1991).

Lemmatization, the grouping of forms under a lemma, can be performed automatically in many languages. It is important for highly inflectional languages but less important for English, which is why 'few English corpora are lemmatized' (McEnery *et al.* 2006: 36).[9] If you ask for *measure*, the system can return the occurrences *measure, measures, measured,* and *measuring,* and it can distinguish between *measure n.* (*measure, measures*) and *measure v.* (*measure, measures, measured,* and *measuring*). The concordancer can then be asked to select only the occurrences of *measure* preceded by an adjective, or followed by a preposition, etc. The first POS tagger was developed in the 1970s to tag the Brown Corpus. There are different systems, using either a statistical (probabilistic) or a rule-based approach, or a bit of both (Meyer 2002: 86 *ff.*). The probabilistic approach is more promising, because the tagger can be trained and improved progressively. CLAWS (Constituent Likelihood Automatic Word Tagging System), a hybrid system developed at Lancaster University which was used to tag the BNC, is said to have an average precision rate of 97 per cent on written English (McEnery *et al.* 2006: 34). The Brill tagger is a flexible system that can use various tagsets and treat texts in any language. The number of tags used by the different systems is extremely variable: the ICE tagger has more than 250, with 8 tags for *do* for example (Meyer 2002: 90).

Parsing, the breaking down of the sentences of the corpus into their constituents, is almost as common as POS tagging, and many systems do parsing as well as tagging. Parsers are also probabilistic or rule-based and again the probabilistic approach is more interesting, because it can cope with ungrammatical formulations, which are frequent in speech. Their precision rates are not as good as those of POS taggers, and the results typically have to be checked by hand. Atkins and Rundell (2008: 92) note that, for example, parsers have difficulties distinguishing phrases like

guidelines for treating patients with AIDS
guidelines for treating patients with antibiotics

No large corpus of English is parsed, but some small ones are, and parts of the larger ones (Meyer 2002: 96).

Semantic parsing, or word-sense tagging, marks the meanings of words. It typically relies on external sources, a dictionary or a lexical-knowledge base, and suffers from the difficulties of word-sense disambiguation, whether manual or

---

[9] Corpus studies have shown that lemmatization is not as straightforward as it looks, as different forms of the same lemma (for example *decline, declines,* and *declining*) may have different patterns (Sinclair 1991: 46).

automatic. It therefore involves a lot of human judgement in the creation of the
categories and the assignment of the tags. Once tokens have been tagged, it
becomes possible to navigate in the corpus, or in the dictionary, from word to
word using the feature(s) they have in common: for example from *cancel* to *lift*,
raise, *abolish*, etc., if they have all been tagged PUTTING AN END TO. But semantic
tagging is still very imperfect: it cannot 'give a reliable account of sense frequency'
(Atkins and Rundell 2008: 251).

A number of other annotating programmes have been developed: coreference
annotation, which identifies anaphora and cataphora, important in text cohesion
(Halliday and Hasan 1976); pragmatic annotation, which marks texts in terms of
speech acts; stylistic annotation, which marks figures of speech, etc.; error
tagging, which marks errors in learner corpora by category, etc. (on all of these,
see McEnery *et al.* 2006: 38 *ff.*).

Corpus annotations can be either *embedded* or *standalone*: embedded annotations are mixed in with the text of the corpus and are inseparable from it, while
standalone annotations are in a separate document linked to the corpus. Because
of the quantity of tags, and because those tags tend to be obscure to anyone but
the specialist, a corpus with embedded annotations is virtually unreadable.
Standalone annotations are less aggressive, but the operation is more complex
(McEnery *et al.* 2006: 44). Some programs can display mark-up or turn it off
(Meyer 2002: 86).

The advocates of corpus-driven studies are committed 'to the integrity of the
data as a whole' (Tognini-Bonelli 2001: 84), and they prefer to carry out their
explorations on a corpus that is not annotated, so as to create their own
hypotheses based only on the contents of the corpus. They say that if the corpus
is annotated the linguists then process 'the tags rather than the raw data'
(Tognini-Bonelli 2001: 73). That is true, but most corpus linguists and lexicographers would say that a hypothesis can always be modified if it is not borne out
by the available evidence, and that exploring a non-annotated corpus is a waste of
precious time.

9.1.6 *Corpus query systems*

For a long time the concordancer was the main tool of the lexicographer, but
corpora are now so big that in many cases it returns too many lines. Since the
1990s tools have been created for the exploration of large corpora, corpus-query
systems (CQS), 'a new generation of "lexical profiling" software that would
analyze large corpora and produce statistical summaries of considerable delicacy'
(Rundell 2002: 140) to 'allow the lexicographer to see what words co-occur with a

given word, to examine what syntactic structures the word occurs in, what other words enter into what syntactic relations with the word and how often, and to retrieve all the corpus lines corresponding to any of these configurations' (Grefenstette 1998: 28).[10]

WordSketch (Kilgarriff and Rundell 2002) can produce a 'portrait' of every word in a corpus, in which the most frequent collocates are arranged by syntactic pattern with two scores, one for absolute frequency and the other for salience[11] (Kilgarriff and Tugwell 2002: 131). Table 9.1 shows the beginning of the portrait of *bank*, illustrating the two basic meanings, where the collocates in each pattern are ordered by salience:

Table 9.1 WordSketch portrait of *bank*

		num	sal
subject of	lend	95	21.2
	issue	60	11.8
	etc.		
object of	burst	27	16.4
	rob	31	15.3
	overflow	7	10.2
	etc.		
modifier	central	755	25.5
	Swiss	87	18.7
	commercial	231	18.6
	grassy	42	18.5
	etc.		
with preposition	governor of	108	26.2
	balance at	25	20.2
	borrow from	42	19.1
	account with	30	18.4
	etc.		
modifies	holiday	404	32.6
	account	503	32.0
	loan	108	27.5
	lending	68	26.1
	etc.		

[10] On CQS, see Atkins and Rundell (2008: 103 *ff.*).

[11] *Salience* is defined by Kilgarriff (in Atkins and Rundell 2008: 370) as 'the product of the MI (mutual information score) and the log of joint frequency'.

WordSketch also gives access to the corpus lines that contain the word under investigation in a given pattern. It can arrange words by sets according to the combinations each word enters into, their patterns, and thus help distinguish meanings: 'a WordSketch for nouns occurring as objects of the verb *forge* can separate words like *relationship, connection,* and *alliance* from words like *passport, signature,* and *letter*' (Atkins and Rundell 2008: 111). Unfortunately it works with words, not with LUs or multiword items, and cannot handle categories. The system has been used for the compilation of *MEDAL,* providing the editors with

a compact and revealing snapshot which contributes powerfully to the identification of word meanings (one of the hardest of all lexicographic tasks). Recent experience suggests, therefore, that lexical profiling software of this type may have quite significant methodological implications for the practice of lexicography.
(Rundell 2002: 141)

Some corpus-query systems have built-in statistical capabilities 'so that as corpus linguists study particular linguistic constructions (e.g. collocations) they can perform statistical analyses to see whether the results they obtain are significant' (Meyer 2002: 120). The word portraits do not replace the lexicographers, who still have to decide what they want, but they are extremely helpful.

Lexicographers also need help to reduce the available evidence to manageable size: 'The 20-million general language corpus that offers 2,000 instances of the lemma *list, extra,* or *save,* will swamp compilers with 10,000 for *pay, same,* or *again*' (Atkins 1993: 15). A 200-million word corpus would have about 1,500 lines for *forge,* 3,500 lines for *forgive,* and 25,000 lines for *forget* (Rundell 2002: 140), so that the 'lexicographer is like a person standing underneath Niagara Falls holding a rainwater gauge, while the evidence sweeps by in immeasurable torrents' (Church *et al.* 1994: 153). The craft of lexicography demands, more than ever before, 'not only the ability to collect data, but also the ability to make sense of it' (Atkins 2002: 25). Because of this, specialists have developed software that can extract samples for frequent words, for example by selecting every *n*th occurrence up to 250 or 500 lines, with exclusion criteria if necessary.

No annotation system, no corpus-query system is perfect, but this does not matter much for lexicography, because the lexicographer is only interested in the features that appear frequently: 'the technology is tolerant of the occasional glitch' (Atkins and Rundell 2008: 92).

9.1.7 Corpora for dictionaries of English

The following review lists only the most important corpora for English dictionaries. The order is based on Xiao (2007).[12]

9.1.7.1 National corpora

The British National Corpus (BNC) is a closed, general, balanced, annotated
corpus developed by a consortium of publishers, the University of Lancaster, the
University of Oxford, and the British Library, with government funding (Landau
2001: 288). It was begun in 1991 and published in 1995, with about 100 million
words[13] in 4,124 texts representing British English speech (10 million) and writing
(90 million), fiction and non-fiction. Texts are classified by domain (Imaginative,
Commerce/Finance, Applied science, etc.), by date (1960–74, 1975–93, etc.), and by
medium (Book, Periodical, etc.). Spoken documents are classified by region
(South, Midlands, etc.), by interaction type (Dialogue, etc.), and by context
(Business, Leisure, etc.). The BNC is annotated according to the TEI guidelines
and it can be explored with WordSmith. It is publicly owned and is widely
available in various versions, including a CD-ROM (BNC Baby), a free sample
available on the Internet, etc. The BNC was used for the compilation of a number
of dictionaries, among which *COD* after the tenth edition and *ALD* after the fifth.

The American National Corpus was started in 1998 along the same lines as the
BNC but it contains only texts produced after 1990. The first version, released in
2003, had 10 million words, and it has now reached 22 million. It is encoded in
XML, with standalone annotation.

9.1.7.2 Monitor corpora

The Bank of English (BoE) was started in 1991 in Birmingham on the basis of an
earlier corpus compiled by Sinclair. It is now a monitor corpus containing about
75 per cent written texts (textbooks, novels, newspapers, guides, magazines,
ephemera) and 25 per cent speech (television, radio, meetings, conversations,
etc.), about 70 per cent British English, 20 per cent American English, and 10 per
cent other varieties. It currently has about 550 million words. It has been
automatically tagged using probabilistic tagging software developed at Collins
with the University of Helsinki, and part of it has been parsed. It is used by the

---

[12] Other listings of available corpora are in Meyer (2002: 142 *ff.*), Agirre and Edmonds (2006:
339 *ff.*). Interesting sites are: http://personal.cityu.edu.hk/-davidlee/devotedtocorpora; http://www.
ruf.rice.edu/-barlow; http://www.ldc.upenn.edu (the Linguistic Data Consortium).

[13] Numbers given for corpora are always tokens.

Collins dictionaries. A 56 million word sampler is available online free of charge but the main corpus is not widely available. It has been included in the Collins World Web, which has French, German, and Spanish corpora.

The Global English Monitor Corpus, begun in 2001, collects texts from leading newspapers in Britain, the USA, Australia, Pakistan, and South Africa. The latest information on the Internet is dated 2001.

9.1.7.3 The Brown corpus and its family

The corpus that came to be known as the Brown Corpus (actually the Brown University Standard Corpus of Present-Day American English) was assembled in 1963–64 at Brown University (Kučera and Francis 1967). It has 500 texts of 2,000 words each from American sources published in 1961 and is categorized in 15 genres, 1 million words representing about 50,000 types. It has inspired several other similar corpora, among which the LOB Corpus (for Lancaster, Oslo, Bergen), a collection of British English texts undertaken at the University of Lancaster and completed in 1978. It also used 500 texts of 2,000 words each, all published in 1961 to ensure comparability with the Brown corpus.[14]

9.1.7.4 Synchronic and diachronic corpora, spoken corpora, etc.

The International Corpus of English (ICE) is a follow-up from the Survey of English Usage designed for the comparison of different varieties of English. It contains twenty corpora of 1 million words each of the English of Britain, Australia, Canada, the Caribbean, East Africa, India, Singapore, South Africa, Hong Kong, etc. (Nelson 1997: 112), with written (40 per cent) and spoken (60 per cent) sources produced in the early 1990s. Some of those corpora are annotated, and the British part is tagged and parsed. The Helsinki Corpus of English Texts has about 1.5 million words in 400 samples from the eighth to the eighteenth centuries, and another section on regional varieties of English. The ARCHER corpus (A Representative Corpus of Historical English Register) has 1.7 million words covering the period 1650–1990 in Britain and the USA (Biber *et al.* 1994). It is not available. The London-Lund Corpus (LLC), a corpus of spoken English started in the mid-1970s and completed in 1980, is also derived from the Survey of English Usage and the Survey of Spoken English at Lund University (Svartvik 1990).

---

[14] See the website of ICAME.

There are also innumerable specialized corpora, of correspondence, of various domains, periods, language varieties, of academic English, teenager English, of telephone conversations, etc. Lately, treebanks have also been created: they are corpora of sentences that are already half annotated, to be used as training and testing material by the designers of annotation systems. For English, ICE is usable as a treebank.

9.1.7.5 Publisher corpora

Dictionary publishers have played a part in the compilation of the BNC (Oxford University Press, Longman, and Chambers Harrap) and the BoE (Collins). They have also developed their own corpora, of written and/or spoken English, of native or learner English, etc. that are not available to the public. For example, the COBUILD Corpus began as English Lexical Studies in Edinburgh in 1963, a corpus compiled by Sinclair for the study of words and their environments (Krishnamurthy 2003). It was then moved to Birmingham, where it was developed jointly by the University of Birmingham and Collins (Sinclair 1987*a*) to become the BoE. In 1982, it had 7.3 million words of British, American, and other Englishes; in 1987, when *COB* was published, it had grown to 20 million (Renouf 1987). American Heritage compiled a corpus of school textbooks for their *School Dictionary* in 1971 (Landau 2001: 284). The Longman Lancaster English Language Corpus was developed in the late 1980s under the direction of Leech and Della Summers (Summers 1993). It has about 30 million words, 50 per cent British, 40 per cent American and 10 per cent other. The Longman Written American Corpus, modelled on it and on the BNC, has about 100 million words. Longman also has a Corpus of Spoken American English, 5 million words, a Longman British Spoken Corpus, 10 million words and

[a] Learner Corpus...drawing on material from students' examination scripts, compositions, and other written assignments, and this database now runs to over 10 million words of text. More recently, the International Corpus of Learner English (ICLE), a major research enterprise, has begun to accumulate learner text produced by students from 14 different first-language backgrounds.   (Rundell 1999: 47)

The first version of ICLE, about 2.5 million words, was published on a CD-ROM in 2002 (Granger 2003). The Louvain Corpus of Native English Essays (LOC-NESS) is a corpus of essays written by schoolchildren and university students, for a total of about 320,000 words (De Cock and Granger 2004). Those corpora were used in the preparation of the Longman dictionaries, particularly *LDOCE* after the third edition.

Cambridge University Press has the Cambridge International Corpus (CIC), which used to be called the Cambridge Language Survey, 'a computerized database of contemporary spoken and written English which currently [i.e. 2001] stands at over 300 million words. It includes British English, American English, and other varieties of English' (Landau 2001: xiii–xiv). It was used for the compilation of *CIDE* in 1995, when it had 100 million words. CANCODE is a corpus of spoken text used by the Cambridge lexicographers (Carter and McCarthy 1995). Cambridge also developed its own Learner Corpus (CLC), which is error-tagged. Microsoft claims that *EWED* was based on the Bloomsbury Corpus of Words, a corpus of 50 million words of world English.

Oxford University Press has the Oxford English Corpus, begun in 2006, which 'broke the one-billion word (10^9) barrier, and is still growing' (Atkins and Rundell 2008: 58).

9.1.7.6 Corpora for other languages

Many other language communities have corpora.[15] Czech has the Czech National Corpus, 100 million words. Danish has a 40-million word corpus of general language for the period 1983–92 to serve as a source for a six-volume dictionary of contemporary Danish (Norling-Christensen and Asmussen 1998). Dutch has the Twente Nieuws Corpus, 300 million words of newspaper texts. German has the Institut für Deutsche Sprache corpus, 'more than a billion words', an 'opportunistic corpus' (Teubert and Čermakova 2004: 118, 121) and the DWDS (for *Digitales Wörterbuch der Deutschen Sprache*) Kerncorpus (100 million words), etc. Swedish has the Språkbanken, 75 million words. French lags behind with FRANTEXT, which has only about 3,000 texts from the sixteenth to the twentieth century, almost all literature.

9.1.8 *The web as a corpus*

The web contains a wealth of information that is relevant for lexicography: 'when one doesn't know the meaning of a word, the Web gives, even without special tools, a quick and dirty concordance that in many cases is sufficient for one's needs' (Zaenen 2002: 237). Grefenstette (2002: 202) showed that the number of occurrences of a given word on the web was huge compared to the BNC of the time (Table 9.2). I have added a column with the results of searches via Google on 10 March 2009 (in M occurrences):

---

[15] See the ELRA (European Language Resources Association) website.

Table 9.2 Comparison between the web and the BNC of occurrences of a given word (Grefenstette 2002)

Phrase	BNC count	Altavista	Google
medical treatment	414	627522	13.9
prostate cancer	39	518393	19.3
deep breath	732	170921	6.5
acrylic paint	30	43181	1.0
perfect balance	38	35494	2.6
electromagnetic radiation	39	69286	5.5
powerful force	71	52710	1.0
concrete pipe	10	21477	0.4
upholstery fabric	6	8019	0.7
vital organ	46	28829	0.1

Software such as WebBootCaT, a part of the Sketch Engine (Atkins and Rundell 2008: 74), has been produced to help linguists use the web as a corpus.[16] The Oxford English Corpus contains only texts taken from the web, as does the UKWAC (United Kingdom Web Archiving Consortium), more than 2 billion words.

Compiling a corpus from the web is especially useful for languages that do not have corpora: for example, a corpus was compiled from the web in 1999 for Swahili (De Schryver 2002, *in* De Schryver 2008: 437). Of course, the quality of the documents is extremely variable: the texts are of varying quality, there is no representativeness and the web is extremely time sensitive (Zaenen 2002: 237). But frequency helps sort out what is valid, at least for errors in spelling, grammar, conjugation, etc., which are much less frequent than the correct corresponding forms (Grefenstette 2002: 207). Researchers have noted that frequencies on the web are in fact 'highly correlated with the counts obtained from the BNC' (Atkins and Rundell 2008: 80).

Kilgarriff and Grefenstette (2003) think that the corpus of the future might be a set of URLs that can be renewed periodically, thus circumventing any problems of copyright. If they are right, corpora as we know them might already be passé!

9.1.9 Lexicographers and corpora: ... yes of course

All lexicographers agree: 'The advent of large corpora has brought fundamental and irreversible changes to the process of dictionary-making' (Rundell 1998: 323); 'the corpus is a tool that has breathed new life into the art of lexicography'

---

[16] See the Sketch Engine website.

(Landau 2001: 305); 'the use of computerized corpora has transformed lexicography' (Kilgarriff and Tugwell 2002: 125). Atkins (2002: 24) calls it a 'transfiguration'. The corpus has become part and parcel of all dictionary projects, or soon will: 'In the past, the existence of an ongoing citation file is what distinguished reputable general dictionaries from purely derivative works; in the future, it will be the existence of sound electronic corpora' (Landau 2001: 193); 'no new major dictionary, whether for native speakers or foreign learners, can hope to be taken seriously if it is not based on corpus research, and I have no doubt that soon enough every new dictionary will claim, whether truly or not, that it is based on a huge corpus of texts' (Landau 2001: 287).

The corpus revolution has not solved all the problems of lexicography. Some lexicographers were unimpressed for a long time by the 'frenzy' (Rey 1995: 105) of British lexicographers: the corpus provides (more than) abundant evidence for those facts that are already known, the sceptics say, and is useless for the less frequent features. De Schryver *et al.* (2006: 78) argue that 'if one needs to prepare a large dictionary... with several thousands of entries, then the use of a corpus as an arbiter on what to include and what to exclude from the dictionary makes little sense for all low-frequency lemmas.' Also, compiling a corpus is a Sisyphean task, which has to be maintained forever or renewed for every dictionary project and every new edition. A corpus ages rapidly, if it aims at representing current usage. Some even think that the electronic corpus is dangerous, because it encourages the publishers to think that dictionaries can be produced automatically, from a lexical database, without the expertise of the lexicographer (Landau 2001: 323).

From a theoretical point of view, Chomsky's objections have already been mentioned. The corpus shows what is used, not what is not used but is part of the language. It does not distinguish what is possible but not attested from what is impossible. It provides data, but cannot give explanations. It provides plenty of examples of the use of the code, discourse, but says nothing on the code itself, the language. It is about performance, not competence. Corpus studies are like describing the fall of an apple instead of formulating the law of gravity. The advocates of corpus-driven linguistics admit that 'each concordance line is clearly an instance of *parole*', but they believe that 'When many such instances are gathered together and sorted, new patterns emerge, this time on the vertical axis', and they are 'patterns of *langue*' (Tognini-Bonelli 2001: 98). Not everybody will agree.

The corpus has changed the lexicographer's job, but it has not reduced the quantity of work. The lexicographer still has to interpret what the corpus returns and select what is relevant: 'the arrival of corpus data has not in fact significantly diminished the role of human skill and human judgement in the dictionary-making process' (Rundell 1998: 325).

Although the use of an electronically stored collection of texts...has replaced many of the functions of the old paper citation files and dramatically improved the capacity of the lexicographer to examine and analyze words in their contexts, it has not lessened the amount of work to be done in defining words like *set* in a large dictionary. The lexicographer, facing a computer display of thousands of uses of *set* (or *art*), will have no easier time than Murray, and may find it even harder to limit the extent of his search than Murray did, since the corpus evidence for such a word will be potentially huge and easily accessible.   (Landau 2001: 44)

Not everything in a corpus is directly usable, as the example sentences in *COB* have shown, and 'fundamentalist' approaches (Rundell 1998: 323) may be unwise. The concepts of *normalcy* (Tognini-Bonelli 2001) and of *lexicological* and *lexicographical relevance* (Atkins *et al.* 2003a) have become important, and will become even more important as corpora become bigger. A normal feature of language is a feature that is frequently used and is acceptable to a large number of users; relevant data is data that is not only present in the corpus but also worth retaining for further study (lexicological relevance) or for inclusion in the dictionary (lexicographical relevance) because it is used often enough by enough people and because it may be needed by the users (Atkins and Rundell 2008: 150). Rundell sees the need to use these concepts as a good sign for the profession: 'the growing contribution of computers to the lexicographic process will entail not the progressive "de-skilling" of lexicographers but—paradoxically, perhaps—an even greater need for skilled human editors with a good grounding in relevant linguistic disciplines *and* highly developed intuitions about language' (Rundell 2002: 139). His optimism is not shared by all lexicographers.

   On the whole, there is no doubt that all lexicographers want, or will want, to base their dictionaries on a corpus. The corpus has even had an influence on linguistics: corpus linguistics, unlike virtually all the linguistic schools that preceded it, sees usage not as a matter of right or wrong but as an interaction in which the sender of the message selects a preferred form from among several possibilities which are more or less expected, normal, natural, so that any formulation can be more or less right, or wrong. 'Grammaticality, according to corpus linguistics, is a gradable', Hanks (2000a: 4) writes, and 'some sentences are more grammatical than others'. Maybe after all corpus linguistics is not just a methodology but a theory of language, or at least part of one.

9.2 ELECTRONIC DICTIONARIES

9.2.1 *The advantages of electronic dictionaries*

There are three sorts of e-dictionaries: dictionaries on CD-ROM, online dictionaries, and pocket dictionaries. All are characterized by the fact that their contents are accessible via a computer, or an electronic system, and are displayed on a screen.

The electronic medium has many well-known advantages. It can store huge quantities of information, which is why encyclopedias became electronic as soon as the technology allowed them to. One CD-ROM is enough for the 24 volumes of the *Encyclopedia Universalis* or the 44 million words of the *Encyclopedia Britannica*. The nine volumes of *GR*, the seventeen volumes of *TLF* and the twenty volumes of *OED2* are each on a single CD-ROM, and the publishers of smaller dictionaries often add extra documents, grammars, thesauruses, encyclopedias, tips for teachers, student activities, games, etc. to which the contents of the dictionary can be linked (Nesi 1999a: 59). Online dictionaries can also have ongoing information, new words, links to websites, etc., and their capacity is literally unlimited. There is so much to be given that lexicographers have to be selective, so that the users will not be swamped by unwanted information: 'we need to be clear about the difference between doing things just because we can, and doing them because they will be of real value to the user' (Atkins and Rundell 2008: 239), a new challenge for lexicographers.

The units for the display of information in an e-dictionary are the screen and the window, where the paper dictionary had the entry and the page. The screen has explicit information, and a certain number of tabs that give access to extra information in extra windows. A request returns only one entry on the screen, and each window can be designed to be easily readable, with spaces between the lines, the use of different colours, etc. E-dictionaries can also use a more user-friendly style, with all abbreviations and elliptic formulations given in full, and they can give information that could not be given before: complete inflections for every word, etymologies, synonyms, corpus lines, etc.

The e-dictionary frees the user from the constraints of alphabetical order. The contents can be accessed via a form, word, phrase, morpheme, abbreviation, etc., and even incomplete or incorrect queries can be treated. Finding an idiom such as *talk the hind legs off a donkey*, a difficult process with a paper dictionary, is easy in an e-dictionary (Rundell 1998: 328). Cross-references are, literally, at the tip of one's fingers. The user can also, for example, request all the occurrences of a given word in the entries, or all the definitions containing a particular word, or two words, etc., according to how the text of the dictionary has been annotated (Nesi 1999*a*: 62) (Plate 23).

The e-dictionary has sound and visual facilities. It can provide the pronunciation of words, sometimes even of sentences, with a choice of accents, perhaps its main advantage: 'hearing the pronunciation is the only unarguable improvement of a CD over a book' (Landau 2001: 97). It has sound illustrations for musical instruments, verbs of sound, the cries of animals, the songs of birds, thunder, speech defects, or music genres: 'The best way to understand reggae is to hear some. Bob Marley singing "No Woman No Cry" will do the trick better than any definition' (Ilson 1999*b*: 73). It also has video clips. The *Longman Interactive English Dictionary* and the *Longman Interactive American Dictionary* have 'minidramas', *ALD* on CD-ROM (2000) and *MEDAL2* have video sequences to illustrate the meaning of some verbs, for example *argue*. These are useful: 'Defining a cicada or a trill without sound, an eclipse or a lock on a canal without an animated picture already looks insufficient' (Pruvost 2002*a*: 88). In some recent dictionaries, the users can even record and play back their own pronunciations, and surely there will be new developments: their potential 'has not yet been fully exploited' (Leech and Nesi 1999: 297).

The latest electronic dictionaries exhibit a dazzling array of choices for the user, and there is more to come (Plate 24). 'Key features of the electronic dictionary of the future will be "customizability" and "personalizability": in this model, the "dictionary" is essentially a collection of lexical resources..., which users can select from and configure according to their needs' (Atkins and Rundell 2008: 239). Another avenue for future developments is the intelligent dictionary that returns only the exact piece of information that is needed, after an evaluation of the context, provided the text is read on screen. Yet another is the interrogation of the dictionary database in natural language, possibly leading to interaction between the user and the dictionary.

There are so many possibilities that some think that the e-dictionary might tend to replace good old lexicographic work with displays of technical wizardry:

[A]dvocacy of electric dictionaries threatens to be less an advance than a retreat into vagueness from the hard work of investigating what information should be offered in LORWs [Lexically Oriented Reference Works] and how to display it best. It is an answer to please those people who would like to believe that the combination of hardware and software will eliminate the need for fleshware: the human mind of the human lexicographer. (Ilson 2001: 82)

And there are those who think that the e-dictionary is just too good to be any good for the users, that the ease with which information can be extracted from it is counter-productive, because 'information so easily extracted may be just as easily forgotten' (Leech and Nesi 1999: 298), the 'involvement hypothesis'. Are the users spoilt?

The e-dictionary is part of a change of attitude to information, which is no longer something that is hard to come by and has to be stored like a treasure but something that is easily found when needed and does not have to be memorized—the disposable society extended to knowledge. The most important thing for the language users is no longer the ability to accumulate knowledge but the ability to retrieve and use it (Ilson 1985*b*: 4). We are moving from an age of information storage to an age of information retrieval. Food for thought for teachers and lexicographers.

9.2.2 *Electronic dictionaries of English*

9.2.2.1 Dictionaries on CD-ROM

The first dictionaries on CD-ROM were published in the 1980s. Their contents were identical with the paper editions, which were still published. In France, the first was the *Dictionnaire Hachette* in 1988, and the first large dictionary was *GR*, in 1989. The smaller *PR* appeared on CD-ROM in 1996, with a text that had been prepared specially for the electronic edition; the competitor *PL* also appeared on CD-ROM in 1996. In Britain, *CED3* (1991) was first made available on floppy disks, before adopting the CD-ROM in 1994, and it may well have been the first dictionary in electronic form. The first learners' dictionaries on CD-ROMs were also published in the 1990s, and the simultaneous production of the paper dictionary with a CD-ROM began in 2002 for *MEDAL1*, 2003 for *LDOCE4*, and 2005 for *ALD7*. The *Oxford Phrasebuilder Genie* (2003) has the text of *ALD6* and of the *Oxford Collocations Dictionary*.

9.2.2.2 Online dictionaries

There is a literally infinite number of online dictionaries, either free of charge or against payment, of various qualities and dimensions. Typing a non-existent word or phrase on Google may return dozens of offers of definition. Among the dictionaries produced by professional lexicographers, some are just the text of an existing dictionary, and others are special texts in constant evolution, like *OED3* or the *Longman Web Dictionary*. The free site yourdictionary.com gives access to the definitions of *WNW4*. The updating of online dictionaries may in the near future be adapted to the look-ups.

Updating a dictionary is not a new operation, but what is revolutionary is that the users can follow the updating, day after day, that the articles indicate the date when they were written as well as perhaps the name of the author. The resulting dictionary is no longer the sovereign reference, just a tool for momentary consultation. Like the modern encyclopedia, the dictionary 'is no longer a sacred text', no longer 'a monument but a faithful, modest, reliable and learned travelling companion' (Pruvost 2000: 164).

The final step in online dictionaries is interactive lexicography, where the dictionary is being constantly produced by its users—an illustration, perhaps, of Putnam's division of knowledge, except that the end user has no guarantee on the quality of the experts. An example is the *Wiktionary* project, a relative of *Wikipedia*, in which *elephant* is

A mammal of the order *Proboscidea*, having a trunk, and two large ivory tusks jutting from the upper jaw. (*figuratively*) Anything huge and ponderous.

Entries have etymology, pronunciation, scientific names, derived terms, related terms, translations, references, and multiple invitations to edit the contents—which in some cases seems urgently necessary (Plate 25). In the *Collins Living Dictionary*, the users even propose words that they have invented, but apparently the project has been discontinued.

9.2.2.3 Pocket electronic dictionaries

Pocket electronic dictionaries (PEDs) are hand-held devices with a screen and a keyboard that have become popular in some countries, particularly Japan and Singapore, where they have replaced pocket paper dictionaries. They are published not by the traditional dictionary publishers but by companies selling electronic products. They are no bigger than a matchbox or even a credit card, but they contain enormous quantities of information (Nesi 1999*a*: 59). Coupled with other facilities, they can work technical wonders: for example, 'the Seiko *Quicktionary*..., sometimes called "the reading pen", translates and pronounces words scanned in directly from the printed page' (Nesi 2000*b*: 843). Some are basic in terms of contents, only random compilations of existing, sometimes outdated, dictionaries:

[R]elatively little seems to have been spent on lexicographic input as opposed to software design, and they...have tended to reproduce old hard-copy dictionary text....Interest in the lexicographical aspect of some electronic dictionary projects is so weak that the provenance of the dictionary is downplayed or even ignored.

(Nesi 2000b: 840)

Doubtless they will improve and become popular in other countries, and the contents will become (perhaps already are) available on mobile phones.

9.2.3 The end of the paper dictionary?

The e-dictionary has so many advantages that the question is whether paper dictionaries will survive. Their death has often been announced, but the announcements have been grossly exaggerated. In 1992, Meijs (1992: 152) predicted 'the imminent demise of the dictionary as a book. In a decade or so, online dictionaries on disk or CD-ROM will no doubt be the norm rather than the exception.' Lexicographers were more cautious: Atkins (1993: 4), for example, observed in 1993 that 'the whole of the dictionary production still consists of books—and I know no publisher who sees an imminent profitable market for custom-built electronic dictionaries. The electronic dictionaries that exist today all started life as books.' Leech and Nesi (1999: 295), six years later, thought that 'the paper dictionary no doubt has a long and worthwhile future ahead of it—although it is unclear how far forces of inertia will serve to prolong its vitality in the next millennium.'

The paper dictionary still has advantages. It is cheap, it may be quicker to consult than the e-dictionary for just one search, it allows the user to compare two entries or two pages, side by side. It does not depend on the computer system and on the provision of energy: one may wonder whether the e-dictionaries of today will still be easily consulted in the year 2413, which is the same distance from us as Cawdrey's *Table*. Also, paper dictionaries are a treat for those who find pleasure in handling books, in smelling paper and ink, in holding those beautiful objects in their hands. E-dictionaries do not have the appearance, the binding, the thickness, the weight, the leather of the Bible, and they do not have the respectability either: anybody can produce an electronic document and change it immediately—literally—without anybody noticing.

However, there is no doubt that more and more e-dictionaries will appear, for students and young people first, and then will also be found in families, slowly replacing paper dictionaries. The question is how long the process will take. It might take longer than was once thought if publishers start using websites to complement their paper dictionaries, to provide extra information, regular updatings, etc.

9.3 DICTIONARIES AND LINGUISTIC RESEARCH

9.3.1. Machine-readable dictionaries

Dictionaries have always been the only available repositories of the words of a language with (some of) their semantic and syntactic properties that linguists could use for research. The electronic format has enhanced their potential for that purpose, especially if they can be read by a computer. Machine-readable dictionaries (MRDs) have been developed since the 1980s.

The exploitation of machine-readable commercial dictionaries can be traced back to two doctoral dissertations which exerted a profound influence on the field of computational lexicography. Amsler's seminal work on the structure of the Merriam-Webster Pocket Dictionary (Amsler 1980)[17] [and] Michiels's dissertation explored the elaborate grammatical coding system of LDOCE (Fontenelle 1997b: 276).

The first dictionary to be produced on magnetic tape was *MWC7* in the 1960s, but it was not widely available. The most heavily used dictionary has been *LDOCE* (1978), which was made available on tape for researchers—for the public it was only published on paper—with extra information (semantic marking, etc.) not in the paper edition. It has been found to be 'eminently suitable for the automatic acquisition of lexical-semantic information' (see Michiels 1982; Fontenelle 1997c). The dictionaries used in NLP (Natural Language Processing) have tended to be dictionaries for foreign learners, because the information that they contain is more explicit than in dictionaries for native speakers.[18]

MRDs can be used for many applications of NLP: machine translation, parsing programs, systems that summarize articles or extract bits of important information, etc. Unfortunately, they have not had 'a central place in word-based NLP' (Zaenen 2002: 240), and as a consequence the NLP specialists have had little impact on dictionaries, probably because the publishers thought that their work was incompatible with the constraints of commercial lexicography: 'While NLP groups have made innumerable corrections, improvements, additions and extensions to the dictionary databases they have licensed from publishers, these changes have never been used by the publisher to improve the next printing or the next edition of the dictionary' (Kilgarriff 2000: 107).

---

[17] Amsler (1980) extracted the genus words from the definitions of the *Pocket Merriam-Webster Dictionary* in order to place each word in 'IS-A' relations, in a taxonomy that is important in information retrieval (Fontenelle 2002: 217).

[18] Guidelines for the evaluation of dictionaries from an NLP perspective are available from ELRA.

9.3.2 *Lexical databases*

The idea of a lexical database, or lexical knowledge base, was contained in Quemada's distinction (1987: 235) between *lexicography* and *dictionarics*:[19] for him, lexicography is

the collection and analysis of the forms and meanings of the lexical units; its main objective is the construction of lexicographical databases, whose role is to provide the richest possible range of data on words and their uses, without necessarily being directly linked to the making of a specific dictionary. The users of such databases would be not only dictionary-makers, but all those—linguists and non-linguists—who process, analyse, and study words as they exist both in the mental lexicon and in texts. The role of 'dictionarics' is to address the development and distribution of language dictionaries of various types, including possibly the customised extraction and editing of the data from lexicographical databases.   (Zampolli 1994: 4)

A lexical database is an electronic document storing information on the lexical items of a language, which can be used by linguists.[20] They are huge projects, but their advantage over a machine-readable dictionary is that they can be designed to include whatever information the linguists think will be useful to their project.

9.3.2.1 WordNet and EuroWordNet

The first lexical databases were compiled in the early 1980s (Ooi 1998: 41). The most famous is WordNet, started at Princeton University in 1985 by Miller as a research tool for psychologists interested in the acquisition of lexical knowledge by children, not for linguists.[21] It currently has more than 150,000 words organized by POS and in semantic networks. Each node of the network corresponds to a word or to a set of 'synonyms', a synset. There are about a dozen types of relations, hypernymy, hyponymy, antonymy, meronymy, etc., between the nodes. Because WordNet is organized by POS, there are nearly no relations between, say, nouns and verbs, as in most dictionaries. Here is the entry for *accent* (simplified) where each synonym is linked to its own entry:

---

[19] In French *lexicographie* and *dictionnairique*. *Dictionnairique* 'was used by Charles Fourier in the nineteenth century but ... had been forgotten until Bernard Quemada brought it forth again' (Pruvost 2002*b*: 56).
[20] Atkins and Rundell (2008: 100 *ff.*) also call *lexical database* the electronic database produced in some dictionary projects in which all the available information on words is stored prior to the compilation of any given dictionary.
[21] See *IJL* 3/4 (1990), Special issue, 'WordNet: An On-Line Lexical Database'.

Noun

(n) accent, speech pattern (distinctive manner of oral expression) *'he couldn't suppress his contemptuous accent'*

(n) emphasis, accent (special importance or significance) *'the red light gave the central figure increased emphasis'*

(n) dialect, idiom, accent (the usage or vocabulary that is characteristic of a specific group of people) *'the immigrants spoke an odd dialect of English'*

(n) stress, emphasis, accent (the relative prominence of a syllable or musical note (especially with regard to stress or pitch)) *'he put the stress on the wrong syllable'*

(n) accent, accent mark (a diacritical mark used to indicate stress or placed above a vowel to indicate a special pronunciation)

Verb

(v) stress, emphasize, emphasise, punctuate, accent, accentuate (to stress, single out as important) *'Dr. Jones emphasizes exercise in addition to a change in diet'*

(v) stress, accent, accentuate (put stress on; utter with an accent) *'In Farsi, you accent the last syllable of each word'*

WordNet is far from being perfect. The words have very little context: 'although originally Miller's dissatisfaction with traditional dictionaries was that they did not provide context to allow children to understand what the definitions meant, WordNet doesn't represent context anymore than a traditional dictionary' (Zaenen 2002: 234). Also, lexical knowledge and encyclopedic knowledge are inextricably mixed, which may suit some linguists but not all: WordNet is a structure of concepts as much as of words, and the purely lexical differences between different words referring to the same concept (the synonyms) are vastly ignored. Yet, because it has been freely accessible on the web since the early 1990s, WordNet has become the most often used source of lexical knowledge for many applications, the standard for NLP (Zaenen 2002: 234). It was used for SENSE-VAL (see Fellbaum 1998*a*).

EuroWordNet, modelled on WordNet, is a lexical database for eight European languages: English, Dutch, Italian, Spanish, French, German, Czech, and Estonian (Vossen 2004).

9.3.2.2 FrameNet

FrameNet was begun by Fillmore at the University of Berkeley in the 1990s (Fillmore 2008).[22]

Its aim is to analyse and record, for each sense of a word or phrase, the full range of its semantic and syntactic relations. To do this, they have devised a suite of codes denoting

---

[22] See *IJL* 16/3 (2003), Special issue, 'FrameNet and Frame Semantics'.

semantic roles ('frame elements') and grammatical relationships, which allow them to document in detail the corpus contexts in which a word is found.

(Atkins and Rundell 2008: 145)

FrameNet has 'developed descriptions of over 800 frames, and nobody is ready to estimate how many there are altogether' (Fillmore 2008: 50). It provides lexicographers with the means to identify meanings, analyse the meaning of an LU, disambiguate synonyms, and describe the valence of a unit, i.e. the words that appear next to it in a frame (Atkins *et al.* 2003*b*). The database continues to grow. Similar projects are under way for German, Spanish, Japanese, etc.

9.3.2.3 Other lexical databases

ACQUILEX was a project funded by the European Union, aimed at exploring the issues of the acquisition of lexical data from machine-readable dictionaries. It was finished in 1995 (Ooi 1998: 100 *ff.*). Hanks's Pattern Dictionary is an ongoing database of the normal patterns of the 8,000 most common English verbs obtained by *corpus pattern analysis* (CPA) (Hanks and Pustejovsky 2005), that will be usable in lexicography (Hanks 2004*b*).

9.4 WILL THERE BE LEXICOGRAPHERS IN 3000?

In 1998, Grefenstette published a paper entitled 'Will there be lexicographers in the year 3000?' The question is worth asking. It is obvious that the use of the computer and of corpora has changed dictionaries, but it has also had unfortunate consequences on the working conditions of the lexicographers.

It sometimes seems to me that as technology has improved the speed and power with which we can examine the language, the pressures to produce quickly and with fewer staff have kept pace, so that on balance nothing is accomplished faster or better. The expectations of management seem to rise at the same rate as the speed and power of the computer increase. (Landau 2001: 323)

Landau (1994*a*: 349) argues that the dictionary publishing houses only see the computer revolution as a good opportunity to press the lexicographers to produce more with less investment.

I am afraid that the claim of electronic revision of electronic databases will be used as a smokescreen for not making the enormous investment of revising a work from A to Z, reexamining each and every entry in the light of new evidence. It is easy to maintain a skeleton staff to insert neologisms and update biographical entries, but this will inevitably result in a deteroriation of quality over time.

The human contribution, Rundell (2002: 139) agrees, 'may indeed become rather marginal—hardly an encouraging outlook for the professional (human) linguist or lexicographer.' Computer technology 'has given new currency to the idea that the machinery of dictionary production is more central to successful lexicography than people. Believers in this idea underestimate the human effort and skill involved in dictionary making' (Landau 2001: 401). Is this excessive pessimism from lexicographers seeing that their job is changing too fast? Grefenstette (1998: 39) himself was more optimistic: we will continue to need, he said, 'the reasoned condensations that only lexicographers provide.'

10

A THEORY OF
LEXICOGRAPHY?

T HE chapter on the theory of lexicography will be as short as a chapter on snakes in Ireland. I simply do not believe that there exists a theory of lexicography, and I very much doubt that there can be one. Those who have proposed a general theory have not been found convincing by the community, and for good reasons. A theory is a system of ideas put forward to explain phenomena that are not otherwise explainable. A science has a theory, a craft does not. All natural phenomena need a theory, but how can there be a theory of the production of artefacts? There are theories of language, there may be theories of lexicology, but there is no theory of lexicography. Lexicography is above all a craft, the craft of preparing dictionaries, as well as an art, as Landau (2001) says. It may be becoming more scientific, but it has not become a science. It does not try to explain phenomena. In 1993, Atkins (1993: 5) was wondering 'Does theoretical lexicography exist?', and Atkins and Rundell (2008: 4) answered her question: it makes sense 'to think in terms of the *principles* that guide lexicographers in their work' but there is no such thing as theoretical lexicography, and 'it is no use looking for it.'

CONCLUSION

A LL dictionaries in all languages and all countries have some features in common, because they are the result of the interplay of forces that are the same everywhere: what the users want, what the lexicographers can offer and what the publishers are ready to finance. All dictionaries have common origins and have followed a similar historical evolution, from the Renaissance to the present day through the eighteenth century, with copious mutual influences. Dictionaries are bought because they satisfy the popular idea of what a dictionary should be, and in all societies the users have wanted dictionaries to solve similar problems of knowledge and communication.

The essential form of presentation; the identity of the lexical units (with emphasis still on the discrete word form, and with a hierarchy of valuation, with derived forms at the bottom of the heap) deemed worthy of definition, pronunciation and etymology; the analysis of meaning; the preeminence (in spite of all public-relations blather to the contrary) given the written word over the spoken: all of these have indeed changed very little in the last two centuries.   (Landau 1994a: 348)

Yet there are differences between different language communities. The dictionaries of the same language share features that distinguish them from the dictionaries of other countries.

A comparative study of the monolingual dictionaries of several languages would reveal similarities in the naive metalinguistic approach of the linguistic systems, as well as—probably—points of view that vary according to the society and are independent of the system itself. The metalinguistics of societies should be studied by sociolinguists.

(Rey-Debove 1971: 316)

Johnson was inspired by Martin, Webster by Johnson, Murray by Webster and Johnson, Gove by Murray, most lexicographers by Murray and Gove, and more recently Hornby and Sinclair, creating a complex criss-cross of influences that has brought all their dictionaries closer, and kept them apart from those of other language communities.

The decades since the 1950s have been a period of intense activity for lexicography in general and for the lexicography of English in particular. The dictionaries have continued the old traditions: a tradition of scholarly dictionaries begun by the *OED* in Britain and a tradition of utility dictionaries illustrated by *W2* and others in the USA. Yet there have also been a number of changes. The first is a rapprochement between traditions and communities: dictionary publishers now have headquarters and activities in many English-speaking countries, some dictionaries aim at more than one market and the tastes of the public are less different than they used to be. Another change was the creation of a new tradition, the dictionaries for foreign learners, with their defining vocabulary, their defining techniques, their insistence on encoding information and on words in their contexts, their use of electronic supports, their reliance on linguistics, etc., and their use of corpora. In their wake, and with the arrival of the computer, the dictionaries for native speakers have also improved the quality both of their contents and of their presentation, pulling the whole lexicographic production towards a more scientific approach, although there is still a large amount of subjective judgement in the lexicographer's job. There have been new types of dictionaries, dictionaries of idioms, of phrasal verbs, of new words, mostly aimed at foreign learners and designed to help expression. Some dictionaries have been produced by new publishers, even by some that had never published a book before.

In spite of all this activity, there were still types of dictionaries that English-speaking countries had *not* produced by the late twentieth century.

There is now no British *dictionnaire analogique* like the French *Petit Robert*, with its panoply of cross-references from a given lexeme to other lexemes in its semantic field; but analogical information was given sporadically by the *Pocket Oxford Dictionary* (POD) until its Sixth Edition.... Neither is there a British dictionary with a morpheme-based macro-structure like that of *Le Robert Méthodique*. Nor is there a family of dictionaries from Britain that includes (as does the Van Dale series) a monolingual dictionary and bilingual dictionaries with the same basic format, allowing users to investigate their own language or learn others with minimal change in the dictionary skills required.

(Ilson 1990*b*: 1972)

And this is still true twenty years later.

The intense activity of lexicography has been accompanied by intense competition between dictionary publishers, particularly in Britain among the publishers of learners' dictionaries, as is natural when a market is profitable. This competition may be a sign that people are interested in dictionaries, but it is essentially a commercial affair. Many publishers have succeeded in selling dictionaries in huge numbers not only because their dictionaries were good but also, perhaps mainly, because they managed to convince millions of people that they needed them.

Lexicography is booming, but not all lexicographers are happy. The publishers have increased their pressure to get more for less, more dictionaries for less money, less time spent by less qualified lexicographers, and often less investment in research. They have been encouraged by the computer and corpus revolution: there is no need to hire a brilliant lexicographer if the work can be done by a machine. As a result, the great lexicographers of the second half of the twentieth century are not being replaced, and the new lexicographers are not recruited to star in lexicography conferences (but some do, and others will). All academics teaching lexicography courses have had to present lexicography to their students more as a job than as a career: 'What a shame, then, that (at least in Britain) lexicography is a dying profession!', especially so soon after having become an 'emerging' profession! 'There are more and more dictionaries, fewer and fewer lexicographers' (Ilson 1999*b*: 77).

Dictionaries are now produced by teams of people with different and complementary skills, to which were recently added the computer scientist, the corpus expert, the XML specialist, and the DTD builder. The computer could have meant a return to the lexicographer compiling a dictionary on his own, and it certainly has, in some cases, but the corpus and the need to reduce the time spent in compilation have in fact reinforced the tendency to work with large groups of collaborators, only confirming the idea that lexicography is an objective occupation.

What can be predicted for the near future? The larger dictionaries will disappear in paper form, as Quemada (1983: 119) foresaw long ago: 'The larger dictionaries are almost certainly doomed to disappear':

[T]he unabridged dictionary as a genre is obsolete, whether in print or in electronic form. It may survive in name only as an electronic database, but I doubt that it will have the same quality of content. A century after the creation of the genre, the unabridged dictionary is doomed by the staggering costs of a thorough revision of the general lexicon..., the proliferation and growing importance of scientific vocabulary, and—the final nail in the coffin—the emergence of a cheaper and more flexible alternative to print, an alternative in which it is easy to fake improvement.

(Landau 2001: 89–90)

Historical dictionaries, dictionaries of regionalisms, dictionaries of new words may never be produced again. GPDs will continue to be marginally influenced by the results of the studies of dictionary users and uses, by the work of theoretical linguists and more importantly by the technical development of computers and by the evolution in the compilation and exploitation of corpora, and they will become more and more similar across cultures.

In 1971, Rey-Debove defined *dictionary* as a list of separate graphic statements, designed for consultation, with two structures, in which items are classified by form or content, in which the information is linguistic in nature and explicitly didactic, giving information about signs and corresponding to a predetermined set, structured if not exhaustive. Thirty-five years later, this is no longer enough. It is clear that we are on the way to a dramatic reassessment of the nature and the role of the dictionary: it used to be focused on the meanings of individual words, it is now focused on words in groups and in syntactic patterns; it was dedicated to decoding, it is now, to a large extent, for encoding as well; it was an attempt at describing the language, it now describes discourse; it was a book and it is now an electronic document; it was a prestigious repository of knowledge, it is now an undistinguished instrument for quick reference. The dictionary is no longer an instrument of authority; it is a pure and simple tool. In 1994, dictionaries were in the process of improving; in the future they may begin to change; it was then a matter of degree, it is now a matter of kind.

The challenge facing lexicographers is clear: dictionaries have to improve the quality of their description of language while maintaining a reasonable accessibility of the information that they provide. They have to refine their evaluation of the dictionary user's needs and skills, and at the same time refuse to be guided exclusively by the desire to be accessible. The dictionary of the future will be the result of what the users need and are able to process, what the linguists can contribute and what the specialists of the computer are able to design. The dictionary of the future will use more computers and larger electronic corpora, will have a more utilitarian inclination but less pretention to faultlessness, to prestige, and to eternity.

For the more distant future, it is difficult to predict what will happen. The dictionaries of the English language may be the forerunners of the evolution of lexicography in all countries.

As broad-band cables take over the market and Internet access becomes a feature of television programming instead of one's computer, access to on-line dictionaries and other reference books may become part of the cable-television package. That's as far as I care to look in my crystal ball.   (Landau 2001: 395)

Probably the dictionary as we know it is on its way out, and we will see the emergence of new kinds of tools, reference tools encompassing more than the dictionary, containing other kinds of information and providing a better treatment of the more traditional information. There will be online thesauruses with huge quantities of data and specialized dictionaries for expression, for translation, etc. As a means of access to superficial, factual, simple, quick, and easy information, the old monopoly of the dictionary is being challenged by spell-checkers and by search engines. The paper dictionary, and perhaps even the dictionary on CD-ROM, may already have become too complex, too forbidding for the Internet generations. We are entering a period where knowledge cannot be further than a click away.

Yet, reference tools might become more important than they have ever been. The need for linguistic guides and records is bound to increase at a time of international and intercultural communication, when more people work with languages that are not their native languages, when speed is at a premium, where more and more of the relations between people are regulated by texts, and where competition between individuals becomes more intense.

The twentieth century might have been the century of dictionaries, but its end certainly was the end of an era as well. The early twenty-first is a beginning, in which there is ample room for work to imagine the new reference tools, and neither the lexicographer nor the metalexicographer are in any danger of being idle.

BIBLIOGRAPHY

IJL = International Journal of Lexicography
U = University, UP = University Press, OUP = Oxford UP, CUP = Cambridge UP, etc.

DICTIONARIES

6,000 Words (1976) (Springfield, MA: G. & C. Merriam CO.).

9,000 Words (1983) (Springfield, MA: G. & C. Merriam CO.).

12,000 Words (1986) (Springfield, MA: G. & C. Merriam CO.).

Abecedarium Anglo-Latinum (1552) (London), Richard Huloet; New edition (1572), John Higgins.

An Active Learning Dictionary (2003) (Singapore: Learners Pub.).

The Advanced Learner's Dictionary of Current English (1963) (London: OUP), A. S. Hornby, E. V. Gatenby, and H. Wakefield.

An Alphabetical Dictionary (1668) (London: S. Gellibrand and J. Martin), John Wilkins [and William Lloyd].

An Alvearie or Triple Dictionarie, in Englishe, Latin, and French (1573) (London), John Baret.

An Alvearie or Quadruple Dictionarie (1580) (London), John Baret.

American College Dictionary (1947) (New York: Harper & Brothers), Clarence L. Barnhart.

An American Dictionary of the English Language (1828) (New York: S. Converse), Noah Webster; New and revised edition (1847), Chauncey A. Goodrich; Revised and enlarged, 'Pictorial' edition (1859), Chauncey A. Goodrich; 'Unabridged' or 'Webster–Mahn' edition (1864) (Yale UP), Noah Porter and C. A. Mahn.

The American Heritage College Dictionary, Third edition (1993) (Boston: Houghton Mifflin); Fourth edition (2004).

The American Heritage Dictionary of Idioms (1997) (Boston: Houghton Mifflin).

The American Heritage Dictionary of the English Language (1969) (Boston: Houghton Mifflin), William Morris; Third edition (1992); Fourth edition (2000).

The American Heritage Dictionary, Second College Edition (1982) (Boston: Houghton Mifflin).

The American Heritage English as a Second Language Dictionary (1998) (Boston: Houghton Mifflin).

The American Heritage School Dictionary (1972) (Boston: Houghton Mifflin).

The American Thesaurus of Slang (1942) (New York: Crowell), Lester Berrey and Melvin van den Bark.

Austral English: A Dictionary of Australian Words, Phrases and Usages (1898) (London: Macmillan & Co.), Edward E. Morris.

The Australian Concise Oxford Dictionary (1986) (Melbourne: OUP); Second edition (1992); Third edition (2000); Fourth edition (2004).

The Australian Learners Dictionary (1997) (National Centre for Language Teaching and Research).

The Australian National Dictionary, A Dictionary of Australianisms on Historical Principles (1989) (Melbourne: OUP).

The Australian Pocket Oxford Dictionary (1976) (Melbourne: OUP); Fifth edition (2002).

The BBI Combinatory Dictionary of English (1986) (Amsterdam / Philadelphia: John Benjamins), Morton Benson, Evelyn Benson, and Robert Ilson.

The BBI Dictionary of English Word-Combinations (1997) (Amsterdam / Philadelphia: John Benjamins), Morton Benson, Evelyn Benson, and Robert Ilson.

Biblioteca Eliotaea (1548) (London), Thomas Cooper.

Biblioteca Scholastica (1589) (Oxford), John Rider; New edition (1606), Francis Holyoke.

British Synonymy: or an Attempt to regulate the Choice of Words in Familiar Conversation (1794), Hester Lynch Piozzi (Thrale).

The Cambridge Advanced Learner's Dictionary (2001) (Cambridge: CUP); Third edition (2008).

Cambridge Dictionary of American English (2000) (New York: CUP), Sydney Landau.

Cambridge International Dictionary of English (1995) (Cambridge: CUP), Paul Procter.

The Canadian Oxford Dictionary (1998) (Don Mills, Ontario: OUP).

The Cassell Dictionary of Slang (1998) (London: Cassell), Jonathon Green; Second edition 2005.

The Century Dictionary: An encyclopedic lexicon of the English language (1889–91) (New York: The Century Co.), William Dwight Whitney. Revised edition (1895).

Chambers Dictionary of Etymology (1999) (Chambers), Robert K. Barnhart.

Chambers's Encyclopedia, A Dictionary of Universal Knowledge for the People (1860–68) (Edinburgh: W. & R. Chambers), Robert and William Chambers.

Chambers' English Dictionary (1872) (Edinburgh). Editions called *Chambers's Twentieth Century Dictionary* since 1901.

Chambers' Twentieth Century Dictionary of the English Language (1901) (Edinburgh: W. & R. Chambers). Editions called *The Chambers Dictionary of the English Language* since 1993; Eleventh edition (2008).

Chambers 21st Century Dictionary (1996) (Edinburgh: Chambers), Robert Allen; Revised edition (2000).

Chambers Universal Learners' Dictionary (1980) (Edinburgh: W. & R. Chambers), E. M. Kirkpatrick.

A Classical Dictionary of the Vulgar Tongue (1785) (London), Francis Grose; Third edition (1796).

Cocker's English Dictionary (1704) (London: John Hawkins), Edward Cocker.

Collins COBUILD Advanced Dictionary (2008) (London: Harper Collins), Sixth edition.

Collins COBUILD Advanced Dictionary of American English (2007) (HarperCollins).

Collins COBUILD Advanced Learner's English Dictionary (2003) (London: HarperCollins) Fourth edition, John Sinclair; Fifth edition (2006).

Collins COBUILD Dictionary of Idioms (1995) (London: HarperCollins), John Sinclair.

Collins COBUILD English Collocations on CD-ROM (1995) (London: HarperCollins), John Sinclair.

Collins COBUILD English Dictionary (1995) (London: HarperCollins), John Sinclair; Third edition (2001).

Collins COBUILD English Language Dictionary (1987) (London and Glasgow: Collins), John Sinclair, Patrick Hanks, Gwyneth Fox, Rosamund Moon, and Penny Stock.

The Collins Dictionary of the English Language (1986) (London and Glasgow: Collins), Patrick Hanks and Laurence Urdang.

The Collins English Dictionary (1979) (London and Glasgow: Collins), Patrick Hanks and Laurence Urdang. Third edition (1991); Ninth edition (2007).

Collins New Zealand Compact English Dictionary (1984) (HarperCollins).

The Columbian Dictionary of the English Language (1800) (Boston: E. Thomas & E. T. Andrews), Caleb Alexander.

The Compact Oxford Dictionary of Current English (Oxford: OUP), Second edition (2002); Third edition (2005).

A Compendious Dictionary of the English Language (1806) (Hartford and New-Haven), Noah Webster.

A Compleat English Dictionary (1735), B. N. Defoe.

A Complete and Universal English Dictionary on a new plan (1774) (London), James Barclay.

A Complete Dictionary of the English Language (1780) (London: C. Dilly), Thomas Sheridan.

The Complete English Dictionary (1753) (London), John Wesley.

Complete English Dictionary, or General Repository of the English Language (1772) (London: T. Evans *et al.*), Frederick Barlow.

A Comprehensive Pronouncing and Explanatory Dictionary of the English Language (1830) (Boston: Hilliard *et al.*), Joseph Worcester.

The Concise Oxford Dictionary (1995) (Oxford: OUP) Ninth edition; Tenth edition (1999).

The Concise Oxford Dictionary of Current English (1911) (Oxford: Clarendon Press), H. W. and F. G. Fowler; Second edition (1929), H. W. Fowler; Third edition (1934) and H. G. Le Mesurier; Fourth edition (1951); Fifth edition (1964); Sixth edition (1976); Seventh edition (1982).

The Concise Oxford Dictionary of Proverbs (1998) (Oxford: OUP), Third edition.

Concise Oxford English Dictionary (2004) (Oxford: OUP), Eleventh edition.

The Concise Oxford Thesaurus: A Dictionary of Synonyms (1995) (Oxford: OUP), E. M. Kirkpatrick.

A Critical Pronouncing Dictionary of the English Language (1791) (London), John Walker.

Cyclopaedia, or an Universal Dictionary of Arts and Sciences (1728) (London: D. Midwinter *et al.*), Ephraim Chambers.

A dictionarie French and English (1567–68) (London: Lucas Harrison), Thomas Chaloner or Claude de Sainliens.

Dictionarium Anglo-Britannicum, or A General English Dictionary (1708) (London: J. Phillips), John Kersey.

Dictionarium Britannicum (1730) (London: T. Cox), Nathan Bailey.

Dictionarium decem Linguarum (1585) (Lugdunum: E. Michel), Ambrogio Calepino.

Dictionarium Linguae Latinae et Anglicae (1587) (Cambridge), Thomas Thomas.

A Dictionary of Africanisms (1982) (Connecticut: Greenwood Press), Gerard Dalgish.

A Dictionary of American English on Historical Principles (1938–44) (Chicago: U of Chicago P), William Craigie, James R. Hulbert *et al.*

A Dictionary of American Idioms (1975) (Woodbury, New York: Barron), Maxine Boatner, Edward Gates, and Adam Makkai.

A Dictionary of Americanisms on Historical Principles (1951) (Chicago UP), Mitford M. Mathews.

Dictionary of American Regional English (1985–2002) (Cambridge, MA: Belknap P), Frederic Cassidy.

Dictionary of American Slang (1960) (New York: Thomas Y. Crowell), Harold Wentworth and Stuart B. Flexner.

A Dictionary of Bahamian English (1982) (Cold Spring, NY: Lexik House).

A Dictionary of Canadianisms on Historical Principles (1967) (Toronto: W.J. Gage), Walter S. Avis.

Dictionary of Caribbean English Usage (1996) (Oxford: OUP), Richard Allsopp.

Dictionary of Contemporary Slang (1997) (London: Bloomsbury), Tony Thorne.

A Dictionary of English Collocations (1994) (Oxford: OUP), Goran Kjellmer.

Dictionary of Jamaican English (1967) (Cambridge: CUP), Frederic G. Cassidy and R. B. Le Page.

A Dictionary of Modern English Usage (1926) (Oxford: Clarendon Press), H. W. Fowler.

A Dictionary of New English (1973) (London: Longman), Clarence L. Barnhart; Volume 2 (1980); Volume 3 (1990).

Dictionary of Newfoundland English (1982) (Toronto: U of Toronto P).

The Dictionary of New Zealand English: A Dictionary of New Zealandisms on Historical Principles (1997) (Oxford: OUP), H. W. Orsman.

Dictionary of Old English (1986–) (Toronto), Angus Cameron *et al.*

Dictionary of Prince Edward Island English (1988) (Toronto: U of Toronto P).

Dictionary of Pronunciation (1965) (Cranbury, NJ: A. S. Barnes), S. Noory.

A Dictionary of Slang and Unconventional English (1937), Eric Partridge; Eighth edition 1984.

A Dictionary of South African English on Historical Principles (1996) (Oxford: OUP), Penny Silva.

The Dictionary of Syr Thomas Eliot knyght (1538) (London: Thomas Berthelet).

A Dictionary of the English Language (1755) (London: J. & P. Knapton), Samuel Johnson.

A Dictionary of the English Language (1815) (London: Longmans *et al.*), Samuel Johnson and H. J. Todd.

A Dictionary of the English Language (1860) (Boston: Swan, Brewer and Tileson), Joseph Worcester.

A Dictionary of the English Language (1866–70) (London: Longmans, Green & Co.), Samuel Johnson, H. J. Todd, and R. G. Latham.

A Dictionarie of the French and English Tongues (1611) (London: Adam Islip), Randle Cotgrave.

Dictionary of the Older Scottish Tongue from the Twelfth Century to the End of the Seventeenth (1931–2001) (Chicago: U of Chicago P), William Craigie, A. J. Aitken *et al.*

Difference between Words Esteemed Synonymous in the English Language (1766) (London: J. Dodsley), John Trusler.

Encarta World English Dictionary (1999) (New York: St. Martins Press), American edition.

Encarta World English Dictionary (1999) (Pan Macmillan), Australian edition.

Encarta World English Dictionary (1999) (London: Bloomsbury), British edition.

Encarta Webster's Dictionary of the English Language (2004) (Bloomsbury, USA), Anne Soukhanov.

Encyclopaedic Dictionary (1879–88) (London: Cassell), Robert Hunter.

The English Dialect Dictionary (1898–1905) (London: H. Frowde), Joseph Wright.

The English Dictionarie: or, An Interpreter of Hard English Words (1623) (London: Nathaniel Butter), H. C., Henry Cocker(r)am.

An English Dictionary (1676) (London: Samuel Crouch), Elisha Coles.

An English Expositor, Teaching the Interpretation of the Hardest Words Used in Our Language (1616) (London: John Legatt), John Bullokar.

An English Pronouncing Dictionary (1917) (London: J.M. Dent), Daniel Jones; Seventeenth edition 2006.

English Synonyms Discriminated (1813) (London), William Taylor.

English Synonyms Explained (1816) (London: Baldwin *et al.*), George Crabb.

Funk & Wagnall's Modern Guide to Synonyms and Related Words (1968) (New York: Funk & Wagnalls), S. I. Hayakawa; reprinted as *Use the Right Word: The Reader's Digest Modern Guide to Synonyms* (1987) (New York: Harper and Row), with Paul Fletcher; published as *Cassell's Modern Guide to Synonyms* (1971) (London: Cassell); as *The Penguin Modern Guide to Synonyms and Related Words* (1987) (London: Penguin). Second edition, revised by Eugene Ehrlich, published as *Choose the Right Word* (1994) (New York: Harper).

Funk & Wagnalls New College Standard Dictionary (1947) (New York: Funk & Wagnalls).

Funk and Wagnalls New Standard Dictionary of the English Language (1913) (New York: Funk & Wagnalls).

Funk and Wagnalls Standard Dictionary of the English Language (*International edition*) (1958) (New York: Funk & Wagnalls).

Gage Canadian Dictionary (1983).

Gazophylacium Anglicanum (1689) (London: E. H and W. H.), anonymous. Reprinted (1691) as *A New English Dictionary*, anonymous.

Geiriadur Prifysgol Cymru (1967–2002) (Aberystwyth, Wales: U of Wales P).

The General Basic English Dictionary (1940) (London: Evans Brothers), C. K. Ogden.

A General Dictionary of the English Language (1784) (London), Thomas Sheridan.

A General Service List of English Words (1953) (London: Longmans, Green), Michael West.

Glossographia Anglicana Nova (1707) (London: Dan Brown *et al.*), anonymous.

Glossographia: or, A Dictionary Interpreting all such Hard Words … as are now used in our refined English Tongue (1656) (London: Th. Newcombe), T. B. (Thomas Blount).

The Grand Repository of the English Language (1775) (Newcastle upon Tyne: T. Saint), Thomas Spence.

A Greek-English Lexicon: Based on the German Work of Franz Passow (1845) (Oxford: OUP), H. G. Liddell, R. Scott, and Franz Passow.

Hamlyn's Encyclopedic World Dictionary (1971) (London: Hamlyn), Patrick Hanks.

Heinemann Australian Dictionary (1976) (South Yarra, Vic.: Heinemann).

Heinemann New Zealand Dictionary (1979) (Auckland: Heinemann), H. W. Orsman; Second edition 1982.

Historical Dictionary of American Slang (1994–) (New York: Random House and Oxford: OUP).

Idiomatic and Syntactic English Dictionary (1942) (Tokyo: Kaitakusha), A. S. Hornby, E. V. Gatenby, and H. Wakefield.

The Imperial Dictionary English, technological, and scientific (1850) (Glasgow: Blackie and Son), John Ogilvie.

The Imperial Dictionary of the English Language (1882) (Glasgow: Blackie and Son), John Ogilvie and Charles Annandale.

The Introductory to Wryte and to Pronounce French (1521) (London: Robert Coplande), Alexander Barclay.

Janua Linguarum Reserata (1631) (Prague), Comenius.

Kenkyusha Dictionary of Current English Idioms (1964) (Tokyo: Kenkyusha).

A Large Dictionary in Three Parts (1677) (London: Rawlins), Thomas Holyoke.

A Learner's Dictionary of Current English (1948) (Oxford: OUP), A. S. Hornby, E. V. Gatenby, and H. Wakefield.

Lesclarcissement de la langue françoyse (1530) (London), John Palsgrave.

Lexicon Technicum: or, an universal English dictionary of arts and sciences (1704) (London: Dan Brown *et al.*), John Harris.

Lingua Britannicae (1757) (London: A. Millar), James Buchanan.

Lingua Britannica Reformata, or, A New English Dictionary (1749) (London: J. Hodges *et al.*), Benjamin Martin.

The Little Oxford Dictionary (1930) (Oxford: OUP); Eighth edition (2002).

Longman Active Study Dictionary of English (1983) (London: Longman), Della Summers.

Longman Advanced American Dictionary (2000) (London: Longman).

Longman American Idioms Dictionary (1999) (London: Longman).

Longman Dictionary of American English (1983) (London: Longman); Second edition (1997).

Longman Dictionary of Contemporary English (1978) (London: Longman), Paul Procter; Second edition (1987), Della Summers and Michael Rundell; Third edition (1995), Della Summers; Fourth edition (2000), Della Summers.

Longman Dictionary of English Idioms (1979) (London: Longman), T. H. Long and Della Summers; Second edition (1998).

Longman Dictionary of English Language and Culture (1992) (London: Longman), Della Summers.

Longman Dictionary of the English Language (1984) (London: Longman).

Longman English Larousse (1968) (London: Longman).

Longman Interactive American Dictionary (1997) (London: Addison Wesley Longman).

Longman Language Activator (1993) (London: Longman), Della Summers and Michael Rundell.

Longman Lexicon of Contemporary English (1981) (London: Longman), Tom McArthur.

Longman Modern English Dictionary (1976) (London: Longman).

Longman New Generation Dictionary (1981) (Harlow: Longman).

Longman New Universal Dictionary (1982) (Harlow: Longman).

Longman Pronunciation Dictionary (1990) (Harlow: Longman), J. C. Wells; Second edition (2000).

LTP Dictionary of Selected Collocations (1997) (Various publishers), Jimmie Hill and Michael Lewis.

Macmillan English Dictionary for Advanced Learners (2002) (Oxford: Macmillan), Michael Rundell; Second edition (2007).

The Macquarie Dictionary (1981) (Sydney: The Macquarie Library), Arthur Delbridge.

The Macquarie Dictionary of New Words (1990) (Sydney: The Macquarie Library).

Merriam-Webster's Collegiate Dictionary (1993) (Springfield, MA: Merriam-Webster) Tenth edition; Eleventh edition (2003).

Merriam-Webster's Collegiate Thesaurus (1988) (Springfield, MA: Merriam-Webster).

Merriam-Webster's Dictionary of Synonyms (1993) (Springfield, MA: Merriam-Webster).

Middle English Dictionary (1952–2001) (Ann Arbor: U of Michigan P), Hans Kurath *et al.*

NBC Handbook of Pronunciation (1943) (New York: Thomas Y. Crowell Co.); Third edition (1964); Fourth edition (1984).

The New American Roget's College Thesaurus in Dictionary Form (1962) (New York: New American Library).

The New and Complete Dictionary of the English Language (1775) (London: E. and C. Dilly), John Ash.

The Newbury House Dictionary of American English (1996) (Boston: Heinle & Heinle).

The New Collins Concise Dictionary of the English Language, New Zealand Edition (1982) (Auckland: Collins).

New Dictionary of American Slang (1986) (New York: HarperCollins), Robert L. Chapman.

A New Dictionary of the English Language (1773) (London), William Kenrick.

A New Dictionary of the English Language (1837) (London: William Pickering), Charles Richardson.

A New English Dictionary (1702) (London: Henry Bonwicke *et al.*), J. K. (John Kersey).

A New English Dictionary on Historical Principles (1928) (Oxford: Clarendon Press).

A New English Dictionary Showing the Etymological Derivation of the English Tongue (1691), anonymous. Reprint of *Gazophylacium Anglicanum* (1689).

A New General English Dictionary (1735) (London: Richard Ware), Thomas Dyche and William Pardon.

The New Method English Dictionary (1935) (London: Longmans, Green), Michael P. West and James G. Endicott.

The New Oxford American Dictionary (2001) (Oxford: OUP), Elizabeth J. Jewell, Frank Abate *et al.*; Second edition (2005), Erin McKean.

The New Oxford Dictionary of English (1998) (Oxford: OUP), Judy Pearsall and Patrick Hanks.

The New Penguin Dictionary of Abbreviations (2000) (Penguin).

The New Shorter Oxford English Dictionary (1993) (Oxford: Clarendon Press), Lesley Brown.

The New Spelling Dictionary (1764) (London: Dilly), John Entick.

A New Universal Etymological English Dictionary (1755) (London: T. Osborne *et al.*), Joseph N. Scott; Revision of the fifteenth edition (1753) of Bailey (1721).

The New World of English Words, or a General English Dictionary (1658) (London: Nath. Brooke), E. P. (Edward Phillips).

The New World of Words, or Universal English Dictionary (1706), J. K. (John Kersey).

The New Zealand Oxford Dictionary (2005) (Melbourne: OUP).

The New Zealand Pocket Oxford Dictionary (1986) (Auckland: OUP), Robert Burchfield.

The Nomenclator omnium rerum (1567) (London), Hadrianus Junius.

NTC's American English Learner's Dictionary (1998) (Chicago: NTC Publishing), Richard A. Spears.

NTC's American Idioms Dictionary (1987) (Lincolnwood, IL: NTC), Richard A. Spears.

NTC's Dictionary of Phrasal Verbs and Other Idiomatic Verbal Phrases (1993) (Lincolnwood, IL: NTC), Richard A. Spears.

Orbis Sensualium Pictus (1658) (Nuremberg), Comenius.

Ortus Vocabulorum (*c.*1500), Galfridus Grammaticus.

Oxford Advanced Learner's Dictionary of Current English (1974) (Oxford: OUP), Third edition, A. S. Hornby, A. P. Cowie, and J. Windsor Lewis; Third edition revised (1980), A. S. Hornby, A. P. Cowie, and A. C. Gimson; Fourth edition (1989), Anthony P. Cowie; Fifth edition (1995), Jonathan Crowther; Sixth edition (2000), Sally Wehmeier; Seventh edition (2005), Sally Wehmeier.

Oxford Advanced Learner's Dictionary of Current English, Encyclopedic Edition (1992) (Oxford: OUP), Jonathan Crowther.

Oxford American Dictionary (1980) (New York: HarperCollins), Stuart B. Flexner, Joyce M. Hawkins, and Eugene Ehrlich.

Oxford American Wordpower Dictionary (1998) (Oxford: OUP).

Oxford Collocations Dictionary for Students of English (2002) (Oxford: OUP).

Oxford Dictionary of Abbreviations (1998) (Oxford: OUP).

Oxford Dictionary of Current Idiomatic English (1975) (Oxford: OUP) Volume 1: Verbs with Prepositions and Particles, Anthony P. Cowie and Ronald Mackin. Second edition (1993), *Oxford Dictionary of Phrasal Verbs*.

Oxford Dictionary of Current Idiomatic English (1983) (Oxford: OUP) Volume 2: Phrase, Clause & Sentence Idioms, Anthony P. Cowie, Ronald Mackin, and I. R. McCaig. Second edition (1993), *Oxford Dictionary of English Idioms*.

Oxford Dictionary of English (2003) (Oxford: OUP), Catherine Soanes and Angus Stevenson; second edition of *New Oxford Dictionary of English*.

Oxford Dictionary of English Etymology (1966) (Oxford: OUP), Charles T. Onions *et al.*

Oxford Dictionary of English Idioms (1993) (Oxford: OUP); second edition of *Oxford Dictionary of Current Idiomatic English*, Vol. 2.

The Oxford Dictionary of New Words (1997) (Oxford: OUP), Elizabeth Knowles and Julia Elliott.

The Oxford Dictionary of New Words: A Popular Guide to Words in the News (1991) (Oxford: OUP), Sara Tulloch.

Oxford Dictionary of Phrasal Verbs (1993) (Oxford: OUP); second edition of *Oxford Dictionary of Current Idiomatic English*, Vol. 1.

The Oxford Dictionary of Pronunciation for Current English (2003) (Oxford: OUP).

Oxford Dictionary of Slang (1998) (Oxford: OUP), John Ayto.

The Oxford Encyclopedic English Dictionary (1991) (Oxford: OUP), Joyce M. Hawkins and Robert Allen.

The Oxford English Dictionary (1989) (Oxford: Clarendon Press), Second edition, John Simpson.

Oxford English Dictionary Additions Series (1993) (Oxford: Clarendon Press) Volume 1, John Simpson and Edmund Weiner.

Oxford English Dictionary Additions Series (1993) (Oxford: Clarendon Press) Volume 2, John Simpson and Edmund Weiner.

Oxford English Dictionary Additions Series (1997) (Oxford: Clarendon Press) Volume 3, John Simpson.

The Oxford English Dictionary Supplement (1933) (Oxford: Clarendon Press), Charles Onions and William Craigie.

The Oxford English Reference Dictionary (1996) (Oxford: OUP).

Oxford ESL Dictionary for Students of American English (1991) (Oxford: OUP), Christina Ruse.

Oxford Illustrated Dictionary (1962) (Oxford: Clarendon Press).

Oxford Learner's Wordfinder Dictionary (1997) (Oxford: OUP).

The Oxford Paperback Dictionary (1979) (Oxford: OUP).

Oxford Phrasebuilder Genie (2003) (Oxford: OUP).

The Oxford Senior Dictionary (1982) (Oxford: OUP).

Oxford Student's Dictionary for Hebrew Speakers (1985) (Tel Aviv: Kernerman Publishing), A. S. Hornby and Jo Reif.

Oxford Student's Dictionary of American English (1983) (Oxford: OUP).

The Oxford Thesaurus. An A–Z Dictionary of Synonyms (1991) (Oxford: Clarendon Press), Laurence Urdang; Second edition (1997).

The Oxford Thesaurus, American Edition (1992) (Oxford: Clarendon Press), Laurence Urdang.

Oxford Wordpower Dictionary (2000) (Oxford: OUP), Second edition; Third edition (2006).

The Penguin Canadian Dictionary (1990) (Canada: Penguin Books), Thomas M. Paikeday.

The Penguin Dictionary of Proverbs (1983) (London: Allen Lane); Second edition (2001).

The Penguin English Dictionary (1965) (Harmondsworth, Middlesex: Penguin Books).

The Penguin Thesaurus (2004) (Harmondsworth, Middlesex: Penguin Books).

The Penguin Wordmaster Dictionary (1987) (Harmondsworth, Middlesex: Penguin Books).

The Pocket Oxford Dictionary of Current English (1924); Second edition (1934); Third edition (1939); Ninth edition, 2002.

A Popular and Complete English Dictionary (1848) (London: William Collins), John Boag.

The Progressive English Dictionary (1952) (London: OUP), A. S. Hornby and E. C. Parnwell.

Promptorium Parvulorum, sive Clericorum (c.1440) (London 1499), Anonymous (Galfridus Grammaticus?).

Pronouncing and Spelling Dictionary (1764) (London), William Johnston.

A Pronouncing Dictionary of American English (1944) (Springfield, MA: G. & C. Merriam Co.), John S. Kenyon and Thomas A. Knott.

A Pronouncing, Explanatory, and Synonymous Dictionary of the English Language (1855) (Boston), Joseph Worcester.

The Random House College Dictionary (1968) (New York: Random House), Laurence Urdang.

The Random House College Thesaurus (1984) (New York: Random House).

The Random House Dictionary of the English Language Unabridged (1966) (New York: Random House); Second edition (1987).

The Random House Webster's College Dictionary (1991) (New York: Random House).

The Random House Webster's Dictionary of American English (1997) (New York: Random House).

Random House Webster's Unabridged Dictionary (1996) (New York: Random House).

The Random House Webster's Word Menu (1992) (New York: Random House).

The Reader's Digest Great Encyclopedic Dictionary (1966) (Pleasantville, New York: Reader's Digest Association), Sidney I. Landau.

The Reader's Digest Great Illustrated Dictionary (1984) (Reader's Digest), Robert Ilson.

The Reader's Digest Oxford Wordfinder (1993) (Oxford: Clarendon Press).

The Royal Standard English Dictionary (1778) (London), William Perry.

School Dictionary (1798) (New Haven: O'Brien), Samuel Johnson Jr.

Scott, Foresman Beginning Dictionary (1968) (Glenview: IL: Scott, Foresman), Clarence L. Barnhart and Edward L. Thorndike.

Scottish National Dictionary (1931–76).

Selected English Collocations (1982) (Warsaw: Panstwowe Wydawnictwo Naukowe), Halina Dzierzanowska and Christian Douglas Kozlowska.

The Senior Dictionary (1979); Successive editions called *The Gage Canadian Dictionary* or *The Canadian Senior Dictionary*.

A Shorte Dictionarie of English and Latin for Yonge Beginners (1553) (London: Lewis Evans), John Withals.

The Shorter Oxford English Dictionary (1933) (Oxford: Clarendon Press), W. Little, H. W. Fowler, and J. Coulson; Fifth edition (2002).

Slang and its Analogues, Past and Present (1890–1904) (London), J. S. Farmer and W. E. Henley.

South African Concise Oxford Dictionary (2002) (OUP).

South African Pocket Oxford Dictionary (1987) (OUP), William Branford.

A Standard Dictionary of the English Language (1893–95) (New York: Funk & Wagnalls), Isaac Funk.

A Supplement to the Oxford English Dictionary (1972–86), Volumes I–IV (Oxford: Clarendon Press), Robert Burchfield.

The Synonymous, Etymological, And Pronouncing Dictionary (1805) (London), William Perry.

A Table Alphabeticall, conteyning and teaching the true writing and vnderstanding of hard vsuall English wordes (1604) (London: Edmund Weaver), Robert Cawdrey.

A Thesaurus Dictionary of the English Language (1903) (Philadelphia: Historical Publishing Co.), Francis March and Francis March Jr.

Thesaurus Linguae Latinae Compendiarius (1736) (London: J. J. & P. Knapton), R. Ainsworth.

Thesaurus Linguae Romanae et Britannicae (1565) (London), Thomas Cooper.

Thesaurus of English Words and Phrases (1852) (London), Peter Mark Roget.

Times-Chambers Essential English Dictionary (1995) (Singapore: Federal Publications).

The Treasurie of the French tong (1580) (London: Bynneman), Claudius Hollyband.

A Universal and Critical Dictionary of the English Language (1846) (Boston: Wilkins, Carter & Co.), Joseph E. Worcester.

The Universal Dictionary of the English Language (1932) (London: Routledge & Kegan Paul), Henry C. Wyld.

An Universal Etymological English Dictionary (1721) (London), Nathan Bailey.

An Universal Etymological English Dictionary containing an additional collection of words (not in the first volume) … Volume II (1727) (London), Nathan Bailey.

Webster's Collegiate Dictionary (1898) (Springfield, MA: G. & C. Merriam).

Webster's Collegiate Thesaurus (1976) (Springfield, MA: G. & C. Merriam).

Webster's Dictionary of Synonyms (1942), (Springfield, MA: G. & C. Merriam); Second edition (1951).

Webster's International Dictionary (1890) (Springfield, MA: G. & C. Merriam).

Webster's New Collegiate Dictionary (1975) (Springfield, MA: G. & C. Merriam) Eighth edition.

Webster's New Dictionary of Synonyms (1968) (Springfield, MA: G. & C. Merriam).

Webster's New International Dictionary of the English Language (1909) (Springfield, MA: G. & C. Merriam); Second edition (1934).

Webster's New World Dictionary of Synonyms (1984) (New York: Macmillan).

Webster's New World Dictionary of the American Language (1951) (Cleveland, OH: World Publishing Company); Second edition (1970).

Webster's New World Dictionary of the American Language, College Edition (1953) (Cleveland: World), David Guralnik; Second edition (1970), David Guralnik; Third edition (1988), Victoria Neufeldt; Fourth edition (1998).

Webster's New World Thesaurus (1971) (New York: World), Charlton G. Laird.

Webster's Ninth New Collegiate Dictionary (1983) (Springfield, MA: G. & C. Merriam).

Webster's Seventh New Collegiate Dictionary (1965) (Springfield, MA: G. & C. Merriam).

Webster's Third New International Dictionary (1961) (Springfield, MA: G. & C. Merriam), Philip B. Gove.

The Word Finder (1947) (Allentown, PA: Rodale Books).

The Wordtree (1984), Henry G. Burger.

The World Book Dictionary (1963) (Chicago: Doubleday & Co.), Clarence L. Barnhart and Robert K. Barnhart.

A Worlde of Wordes, or Most Copious, and exact Dictionarie in Italian and English (1598) (London: Hatfield), John Florio.

OTHER WORKS

AARTS, F. (1999), 'Syntactic information in OALD5, LDOCE3, COBUILD2 and CIDE', *in* Herbst and Popp (eds): 15–32.

—— and MEIJS, W. (eds) (1986), *Corpus linguistics II* (Amsterdam: Rodopi).

ABATE, F. (1991), 'Review of *Random House Webster's College Dictionary*', *Dictionaries* 13: 153–72.

—— (1994), 'Review of *Merriam-Webster's Collegiate Dictionary, Tenth Edition*', *Dictionaries* 15: 175–88.

ABLEY, M. (2009), *The Prodigal Tongue* (London: Arrow Books).

AGIRRE, E. and EDMONDS, P. (eds) (2006), *Word Sense Disambiguation* (Dordrecht: Springer).

AITCHISON, J. (1993), 'Review of Tsohatzidis, *Meanings and Prototypes: Studies in Linguistic Categorization*', *IJL* 6/3: 215–21.

—— (1994), *Words in the Mind, An Introduction to the Mental Lexicon* (Oxford: Blackwell). First edition 1987.

—— (2005), 'Review of Murphy, *Semantic Relations and the Lexicon: Antonymy, Synonymy and Other Paradigms*', *IJL* 18/1: 106–9.

AITKEN, A. J. (1987), 'The period dictionaries', *in* Burchfield (ed.): 94–116.

ALGEO, J. (1987), 'A dictionary of Briticisms', *Dictionaries* 9: 164–78.

—— (1989*a*), 'Dictionaries as seen by the educated public in Great Britain and the USA', *in* Hausmann *et al.* (eds): 28–34.

—— (1989*b*), 'The image of the dictionary in the mass media: USA', *in* Hausmann *et al.* (eds): 34–7.

—— (1990*a*), 'Review of *The Longman Register of New Words*', *IJL* 3/3: 211–18.

—— (1990*b*), 'American lexicography', *in* Hausmann *et al.* (eds): 1987–2009.

—— (1994), 'Problems in new-word lexicography', *Dictionaries* 15: 39–46.

—— (1995), 'A short history of new-word study', *Dictionaries* 16: 3–15.

—— (2003), 'Review of *The New Oxford American Dictionary*', *Dictionaries* 24: 236–52.

ALLEN, R. E. (1986), 'A concise history of the *COD*', *in* Hartmann (ed.): 1–11.

—— (1999), 'Lumping and splitting', *English Today* 16/4: 61–3.

ALLERTON, D. J., NESSELHAUF, N., and SKANDERA, P. (eds) (2004), *Phraseological Units: Basic Concepts and their Applications* (Basel: Schwabe).

ALLSOPP, R. (1987), ' "Like if say you see a jumbie or a duppy": Problems of definitional differentiae in a complex of anglophone cultures', *in* Bailey (ed.): 75–98.

ALTMANN, G. M. (1997), *The Ascent of Babel* (Oxford: OUP).

ALVAR EZQUERRA, M. (ed.) (1992), *EURALEX '90 Proceedings* (Barcelona: Biblograf/VOX).

AMSLER, R. A. (1980), 'The Structure of the *Merriam-Webster Pocket Dictionary*', Ph.D., Austin: U of Texas.

ANDOR, J. (2004), 'The master and his performance: An interview with Noam Chomsky', *Intercultural Pragmatics* 1/1: 93–111.

APRESJAN, I. A. (1973*a*), 'Synonymy and synonyms', *in* Kiefer, F. (ed.), *Trends in Soviet Theoretical Linguistics* (Dordrecht: Reidel): 173–90.

—— (1973*b*), 'Regular polysemy', *Linguistics* 142: 5–32.

—— (2000), *Systematic Lexicography* (Oxford: OUP).

—— (2002), 'Principles of systematic lexicography', *in* Corréard (ed.): 91–104. Also in Fontenelle 2008*a*.

——, MEL'ČUK, I., and ZOLKOVSKIJ, A. K. (1969), 'Semantics and lexicography: towards a new type of unilingual dictionary', *in* Kiefer, F. (ed.), *Studies in Syntax and Semantics* (Dordrecht: Reidel): 1–33.

ARD, J. (1982), 'The use of bilingual dictionaries by ESL students while writing', *ITL Review of Applied Linguistics* 58: 1–27.

ARNAUD, P. J. L. (2008), 'Noun modifiers', Paper delivered at a meeting of CRTT, Université Lyon 2.

—— (2009), 'Aspects quantitatifs de l'acquisition / apprentissage du lexique d'une langue étrangère', *in* Maniez, F. (ed.), *Lexicologie et terminologie, histoire de mots* (Lyon: Presses Universitaires de Lyon).

ASHER, N. and LASCARIDES, A. (1996), 'Lexical disambiguation in a discourse context', *in* Pustejovsky and Boguraev (eds): 69–108.

ATKINS, B. T. S. (1985), 'Monolingual and bilingual learners' dictionaries: a comparison', *in* Ilson (ed.) 1985*b*: 15–24.

—— (1987), 'Semantic ID tags: Corpus evidence for dictionary senses', *in The Uses of Large Texts Databases, Proceedings of the Second Annual Conference of the UW Centre for the New OED* (Waterloo, Canada).

—— (1991), 'Building a lexicon: The contribution of lexicography', *IJL* 4/3: 167–204.

—— (1993), 'Theoretical lexicography and its relation to dictionary-making', *Dictionaries* 1992/93/14: 4–43. Also in Fontenelle 2008*a*: 247–72.

—— (1995), 'Analyzing the verbs of seeing: a frame semantics approach to corpus lexicography', *in* Gahl, S. *et al.* (eds), *Proceedings of the Twentieth Annual Meeting of the Berkeley Linguistic Society*, 1994 (Berkeley, CA: U of California).

—— (1996), 'Bilingual dictionaries. Past, present and future', *in* Gellerstam *et al.* (eds), 515–46; also *in* Corréard (ed.) 2002: 1–29.

—— (ed.) (1998), *Using Dictionaries, Studies of Dictionary Use by Language Learners and Translators* (Tübingen: Niemeyer).

—— (2002), 'Then and now: Competence and performance in 35 years of lexicography', *in* Braasch and Povlsen (eds): 1–28. Also in Fontenelle 2008*a*.

—— and KNOWLES, F. E. (1990), 'Interim report on the EURALEX AILA research project into dictionary use', *in* Magay and Zigány (eds): 381–92.

—— and LEVIN, B. (1995), 'Building on a corpus: A linguistic and lexicographical look at some near-synonyms', *IJL* 8/2: 85–114.

—— and RUNDELL, M. (2008), *The Oxford Guide to Practical Lexicography* (Oxford: OUP).

—— and VARANTOLA, K. (1997), 'Monitoring Dictionary Use', *IJL* 10/1: 1–45. In a slightly modified version *in* Atkins (ed.) 1998: 83–122. Also in Fontenelle 2008*a*: 337–75.

—— and VARANTOLA, K. (1998), 'Language Learners Using Dictionaries: The Final Report on the EURALEX / AILA Research Project on Dictionary Use', *in* Atkins (ed.) 1998: 21–81.

—— and ZAMPOLLI, A. (eds) (1994), *Computational Approaches to the Lexicon* (Oxford: OUP).

——, CLEAR, J., and OSTLER, N. (1992), 'Corpus design criteria', *Literary and Linguistic Computing* 7/1: 1–16.

——, FILLMORE, C., and JOHNSON, C. (2003a), 'Lexicographic relevance: Selecting information from corpus evidence', *IJL* 16/3: 251–80.

——, KEGL, J., and LEVIN, B. (1988), 'Anatomy of a verb entry: from linguistic theory to lexicographic practice', *IJL* 1/2: 84–126.

——, LEVIN, B., and ZAMPOLLI, A. (1994), 'Computational Approaches to the Lexicon: An Overview', *in* Atkins and Zampolli (eds): 17–45.

——, RUNDELL, M., and SATO, H. (2003*b*), 'The contribution of FrameNet to practical lexicography', *IJL* 16/3: 333–57.

AUGARDE, T. (1999), 'Review of *The Oxford Crossword Dictionary*', *IJL* 12/4: 352–4.

AUROUX, S. (1990), 'La Définition et la théorie des idées', *in* Centre d'Etudes du Lexique (1990): 30–9.

—— (1994), *La Révolution technologique de la grammatisation* (Liège: Pierre Mardaga).

AUST, R., KELLEY, M. J., and ROBY, W. (1993), 'The use of hyper-reference and conventional dictionaries', *Educational Technology Research and Development* 41/4: 63–73.

AYTO, J. (1983), 'On specifying meaning: semantic analysis and dictionary definitions', *in* Hartmann (ed.) 1983c: 89–98.

—— (1986), 'Of or pertaining to dictionaries', *English Today* 6: 39–40.

—— (1988), 'Fig. leaves. Metaphor in dictionaries', *in* Snell-Hornby (ed.): 49–54.

—— (1992), 'Review of *The Macquarie Dictionary of New Words*', *IJL* 5/3: 239–41.

—— (1999), 'Lexical evolution and learners' dictionaries', *in* Herbst and Popp (eds): 151–9.

—— (2000), 'Review of *The Oxford Dictionary of New Words*', *IJL* 13/1: 46–50.

BABINI, M. (2000), 'Proposition de modèle de dictionnaire terminologique onomasiologique', Ph.D., Lyon: Université Lumière Lyon 2.

BÄCKLUND, U. (1981), 'Pregnant and specific objects: A collocational investigation of *Recognize* and *Realize*', *in* Copeland, J. E. and Davis, P. W. (eds), *The Seventh LACUS Forum* (Columbia, SC: Hornbeam Press): 399–411.

BAHNS, J. (1996), *Kollokationen als lexikographisches Problem* (Tübingen: Niemeyer).

BAILEY, R. W. (1986), 'Dictionaries of the next century', in Ilson (ed.) (1986e): 123–37.

—— (ed.) (1987), *Dictionaries of English. Prospects for the Record of our Language* (Ann Arbor: U of Michigan Press).

—— (1996), '*The Century Dictionary*: Origins', *Dictionaries* 17: 1–16.

—— (2000), '"This Unique and Peerless Specimen": The Reputation of the *OED*', *in* Mugglestone (ed.) 2000a: 207–27.

—— (2004), 'Review of Winchester, *The Meaning of Everything: The Story of the* Oxford English Dictionary', *Dictionaries* 2004: 169–74.

BAKER, M., FRANCIS, G., and TOGNINI-BONELLI, E. (eds) (1993), *Text and Technology: In Honour of John Sinclair* (Amsterdam: Benjamins).

BALLY, C. (1909), *Traité de stylistique française*. 2nd edn (1930) (Paris: Klincksieck).

BAREGGI, C. (1989), 'Gli studenti e il dizionario: un'inchiesta presso gli studenti di inglese del Corso di Laurea in Lingue e Letterature Straniere della Facoltà di Lettere di Torino', *in* Prat Zagrebelsky (ed.): 155–90.

BARNBROOK, G. (2002), *Defining Language: A Local Grammar of Definition Sentences* (Amsterdam: Benjamins).

—— (2005), 'Usage notes in Johnson's *Dictionary*', *IJL* 18/2, 189–201.

BARNHART, C. L. (1949), 'Contributions of Dr. Thorndike to lexicography', *Teachers College Record* 51/1: 35–42.

—— (1962), 'Problems in editing commercial monolingual dictionaries', *in* Householder and Saporta (eds): 161–81. Reprint 1975.

—— (1978), 'American lexicography, 1947–1973', *American Speech* 53/2: 83–140.

BARNHART, R. K. (1996), '*The Century Dictionary*: Aftermath', *Dictionaries* 17: 116–25.

—— and BARNHART, C. L. (1990), 'The dictionary of neologisms', *in* Hausmann *et al.* (eds) (1989/91): 1159–66.

BATTENBURG, J. D. (1989), 'A Study of English Monolingual Learners' Dictionaries and their Users', Ph.D., Purdue U.

—— (1991), *English Monolingual Learners' Dictionaries, A User-oriented Study* (Tübingen: Niemeyer).

BAXTER, J. (1980), 'The dictionary and vocabulary behavior: a single word or a handful?', *TESOL Quarterly* 14/3: 325–36.

BEAL, J. (2004), 'An autodidact's lexicon: Thomas Spence's *Grand Repository of the English Language* (1755)', *in* Coleman and McDermott (eds): 63–70.

BEAUJOT, J.P. (1989), 'Dictionnaire et idéologie', *in* Hausmann *et al.* (eds) (1989/91): 79–88.

BÉJOINT, H. (1980), 'La représentation de l'étranger dans le lexique américain', *Revue Française d'Etudes Américaines* 9: 107–16.

—— (1981*a*), 'The foreign student's use of monolingual English dictionaries. A study of language needs and reference skills', *Applied Linguistics* 2/3: 207–22.

—— (1981*b*), 'Les américanismes dans les dictionnaires britanniques récents', *Trema* 7: 19–34.

—— (1981*c*), 'Les marques d'usage dans les dictionnaires de langue anglaise', *Trema* 7: 69–74.

—— (1988), 'Scientific and technical words in general dictionaries', *IJL* 1/4: 354–68.

—— (1989*a*), ' "Codedness" and lexicography', *in* James, G. C. (ed.), *Lexicographers and their Works* (Exeter: U of Exeter), 1–4.

—— (1989*b*), 'The teaching of dictionary use', *in* Hausmann *et al.* (eds) (1989/91): 208–15.

—— (1999), 'Compound nouns in learner's dictionaries', *in* Herbst and Popp (eds): 81–99.

BENBOW, T., CARRINGTON, P., JOHANESSEN, G., TOMPA F., and WEINER, E. (1990), 'Report on the New *Oxford English Dictionary* User Survey', *IJL* 3/3: 155–203.

BENSON, M. (1989), 'The structure of the collocational dictionary', *IJL* 2/1: 1–14.

——, BENSON, Y., and ILSON, R. (1986), 'Introduction', *in The BBI Combinatory Dictionary of English, A Guide to Word Combinations* (Amsterdam: Benjamins): ix–xxvi.

BENSON, P. (2001), *Ethnocentrism and the English Dictionary* (London: Routledge).

BENSOUSSAN, M., SIM, D., and WEISS, R. (1981), 'The effect of dictionary usage on EFL test performance compared with student and teacher attitudes and expectations', *in* Sigurd, B. and Svartvik, J. (eds), *AILA 81, Proceedings I* (Lund University). Later published in (1984), *Reading in a Foreign Language* 2: 262–76.

BERGENHOLTZ, H. and NIELSEN, S. (2006), 'Subject-field components as integrated parts of LSP dictionaries', *Terminology* 12/2: 281–303.

BERNAL, E. and DeCESARIS, J. (eds) (2008), *Proceedings of the XIII EURALEX International Congress* (Barcelona: IULA).

BESTERMAN, T. (1943), 'On a bibliography of dictionaries', *Proceedings of the British Society for International Bibliography IV*: 63–73.

BIBER, D. (1993), 'Representativeness in Corpus Design', *Linguistic and Literary Computing* 8/4: 243–57. Also in Fontenelle 2008*a*.

——, FINEGAN, E., and ATKINSON, D. (1994), 'ARCHER and its challenges: Compiling and exploring a representative corpus of historical English registers', in Fries, U., Tottie, G., and Schneider, P. (eds), *Creating and Using English Language Corpora* (Cambridge: CUP): 1–14.

——, CONRAD, S., and REPPEN, R. (1998), *Corpus Linguistics: Investigating Language Structure and Use* (Cambridge: CUP).

BLACK, A. (1985), 'The effects on comprehension and memory of providing different types of defining information for new vocabulary' (Cambridge: MRC Applied Psychology Unit).

BLOOMFIELD, L. (1933), *Language* (New York: Holt, Rinehart and Winston).

BOGAARDS, P. (1990), 'Où cherche-t-on dans le dictionnaire ?', *IJL* 3/2: 79–102.

—— (1996), 'Dictionaries for learners of English', *IJL* 9/4: 277–320.

—— (1997), 'Les informations collocationnelles dans les dictionnaires', *Revue Française de Linguistique Appliquée*, special issue: 'Dictionnaires: nouvelles technologies, nouveaux produits ?', II/1: 31–42.

—— (1998a), 'Scanning long entries in learners' dictionaries', *in* Fontenelle *et al.* (eds): 565–2.

—— (1998b), 'Des dictionnaires au service de l'apprentissage du français langue étrangère', *Cahiers de lexicologie* 72: 127–67.

—— (1998c), 'What type of words do language learners look up?', *in* Atkins (ed.): 151–7.

—— (2003a), 'Uses and users of dictionaries', *in* van Sterkenburg (ed.): 26–33.

—— (2003b), 'MEDAL: A fifth dictionary for learners of English', *IJL* 16/1: 43–55.

—— and VAN DER KLOOT, W. A. (2001), 'The use of grammatical information in learners' dictionaries', *IJL* 14/2: 97–121.

—— and VAN DER KLOOT, W. A. (2002), 'Verb constructions in learners' dictionaries', *in* Braasch and Povlsen (eds): 747–57.

BOGURAEV, B. and BRISCOE, T. (eds) (1989), *Computational Lexicography for Natural Language Processing* (London and New York: Longman).

BOISSON, C., KIRTCHUK, P., and BÉJOINT, H. (1991), 'Aux origines de la lexicographie: les premiers dictionnaires monolingues et bilingues', *IJL* 4/4: 261–315.

BOLINGER, D. (1965), 'The atomization of meaning', *Language* 41: 555–73.

—— (1975), *Aspects of Language*, 2nd edn (New York: Harcourt Brace Jovanovich).

—— (1976), 'Meaning and memory', *Forum Linguisticum* 1/1: 1–14.

—— (1980), *Language, the Loaded Weapon, The Use and Abuse of Language Today* (London: Longman).

—— (1985), 'Defining the undefinable', *in* Ilson (ed.) (1985b): 69–73. Also in Fontenelle (2008a).

—— (1990), 'Review of *Oxford Advanced Learner's Dictionary of Current English*', *IJL* 3/2: 133–45.

BOULANGER, J.-C. (1986), *Aspects de l'interdiction dans la lexicographie française contemporaine* (Tübingen: Niemeyer).

—— (2002), 'Petite histoire de la conquête de l'ordre alphabétique dans les dictionnaires médiévaux', *Cahiers de lexicologie* 80: 9–24.

—— (2003), *Les Inventeurs du dictionnaire. De l'eduba des scribes mésopotamiens au scriptorium des moines médiévaux* (Ottawa: Presses de l'Université d'Ottawa).

BOWKER, L. and PEARSON, J. (2002), *Working with Specialized Language, A Practical Guide to Using Corpora* (London: Routledge).

BRAASCH, A. and POVLSEN, C. (eds) (2002), *Proceedings of the Tenth EURALEX International Congress* (Copenhagen: U of Copenhagen).

BRÉAL, M. (1897), *Essai de sémantique* (Paris: Hachette).

BREWER, C. (2000), 'OED Sources', *in* Mugglestone (ed.): 40–58.

—— (2004), 'The "Electronification" of the *Oxford English Dictionary*', *Dictionaries* 25: 1–43.

—— (2006), 'Educating the dictionary user', *Dictionaries* 27: 139–42.

—— (2007), *Treasure-House of the Language* (New Haven and London: Yale UP).

BROOKES, I., NATHAN, J., and NORRIS, H. (2001), *Words, Wit and Wisdom: A Hundred Years of the Chambers Dictionary* (Edinburgh: Chambers).

BRUNET, E. (1992), 'Le mot *dictionnaire*', *Études de Linguistique Appliquée* 85–6: 33–51.

—— (1997), 'Les dictionnaires électroniques', *Revue Française de Linguistique Appliquée* II/1, special issue: 'Dictionnaires: nouvelles technologies, nouveaux produits ?': 7–30.

BRUTON, A. (1997), 'Review of *Cambridge Word Selector*', *IJL* 10/4: 339–42.

—— (1999), 'Introduction', *IJL* 12/1: 1–4. Special issue: Lexical reference books.

BULLON, S. (1988), 'The treatment of connotation in learners' dictionaries', *in* Magay and Zigány (eds) (1990): 27–34.

BURCHFIELD, R. (1972), 'Four-letter words and the *Oxford English Dictionary*', *Times Literary Supplement* 13 Oct. 1972: 1233. Also in Scholler and Reidy (eds) (1973): 84–9.

—— (1980), 'Dictionaries and ethnic sensibilities', *in* Michaels, L. and Ricks, C. (eds), *The State of the Language* (Berkeley): 15–23.

—— (1986), '*The Oxford English Dictionary*', *in* Ilson (ed.) (1986e): 17–27.

—— (ed.) (1987), *Studies in Lexicography* (Oxford: Clarendon Press).

—— (1989), *Unlocking the English Language* (London: Faber and Faber).

—— (1992), 'BudaLEX Presidential Debate 1988: Part 1', *IJL* 5/4: 246–51.

—— (1993), 'The evolution of English lexicography. By James A. H. Murray. The Romanes Lecture, 1900', *IJL* 6/2: 89–122.

BURKETT, E. M. (1979), *American Dictionaries of the English Language before 1861* (Metuchen, NJ: Scarecrow Press).

BURNETT, L. (1988), 'Making it short: the *Shorter Oxford English Dictionary*', *in* Snell-Hornby (ed.): 229–33.

—— (1989), 'A Number of problems for the *New Shorter Oxford English Dictionary*', *Dictionaries* 11: 139–47.

BUZON, C. (1979), 'Dictionnaire, langue, discours, idéologie', *Langue Française* 43: 27–44.

CANDEL, D. and GAUDIN, F. (eds) (2006), *Aspects diachroniques du vocabulaire* (Mont-Saint-Aignan: Publications des universités de Rouen et du Havre).

CARNEY, F. (1988), 'Review of *The Penguin Wordmaster Dictionary*', *IJL* 1/1: 61–2.

CARTER, R.A. (1989), 'Review of LDOCE and *COBUILD Dictionary of the English Language*', *IJL* 2/1: 30–43.

—— and MCCARTHY, M. (eds) (1988), *Vocabulary and Language Teaching* (London: Longman).

—— and McCarthy, M. (1995), 'Grammar and the spoken language', *Applied Linguistics* 16/2: 141–58.

Cassidy, F. G. (1987*a*), 'The *Dictionary of American Regional English* as a resource for language study', *in* Burchfield (ed.): 117–35.

—— (1987*b*), 'The *Oxford English Dictionary* and the *Dictionary of American Regional English*: Some differences of practice', *in* Bailey (ed.): 22–9.

—— (1997), 'The rise and development of modern labels in English dictionaries', *Dictionaries* 18: 97–112.

Casson, R. W. (1981), *Language, Culture and Cognition, Anthropological Perspectives* (New York: Macmillan).

Catford, J. C. (1983), 'Insects are free; reflections on meaning in linguistics', *Language Learning* 33/5: 13–32.

Channell, J. (1990), 'Vocabulary acquisition and the mental lexicon', *in* Tomaszczyk and Lewandowska-Tomaszczyk (eds): 21–30.

Chapman, R. L. (1996), 'Review of Morton, *The Story of Webster's Third*', *IJL* 9/4: 367–71.

Chaurand, J. and Mazière, F. (eds) (1990), *La Définition* (Paris: Larousse).

Chi, Man Lai A. (1998), 'Teaching dictionary skills in the classroom', *in* Fontenelle *et al.* (eds): 565–77.

Chomsky, N. (1995), 'Categories and transformations' *in* The Minimalist Program (Cambridge MA: MIT Press): 219–394.

Church, K. W. and Hanks, P. (1989), 'Word Association Norms, Mutual Information and Lexicography', *in Proceedings of the 27th Annual Meeting of the Association for Computational Linguistics* (Vancouver): 76–83. Reprinted in (1990), *Computational Linguistics* 16/1, and in Fontenelle 2008*a*.

—— and Mercer, R. L. (1993), Introduction to the special issue on computational linguistics using large corpora, *Computational Linguistics* 19/1: 1–24.

—— Gale, W., Hanks, P., Hindle, D., and Moon, R. (1994), 'Lexical Substitutability', *in* Atkins and Zampolli (eds): 153–77.

Clifford, J. (1979), *Dictionary Johnson: Samuel Johnson's Middle Years* (New York: McGraw-Hill).

Coleman, J. (2004), 'The third edition of Grose's *Classical Dictionary of the Vulgar Tongue*: Bookseller's hackwork or posthumous masterpiece?', *in* Coleman and McDermott (eds), 71–81.

—— and Kay, C. J. (eds) (2000), *Lexicology, Semantics and Lexicography* (Amsterdam: Benjamins).

—— and McDermott, A. (eds) (2004), *Historical Dictionaries and Historical Dictionary Research* (Tübingen: Niemeyer).

Collignon, L. and Glatigny, M. (1978), *Les Dictionnaires—initiation à la lexicographie* (Paris: Cedic).

Collinot, A. and Mazière, F. (1997), *Un prêt à parler: le dictionnaire* (Paris: PUF).

Collison, R. L. (1982), *A History of Foreign-Language Dictionaries* (London: Andre Deutsch).

CONGLETON, J. and CONGLETON, E. C. (1984), *Johnson's Dictionary, Bibliographical Survey 1746–1984* (Terre Haute: Indiana State U and Dictionary Society of North America).

CONGLETON, J., GATES, J. E., and HOBAR, D. (eds) (1979), *Papers on Lexicography* (Indiana State U and Dictionary Society of North America).

CONSIDINE, J. (1997), 'Discussion 2: Etymology and the *Oxford English Dictionary*: a response', *IJL* 10/3: 234–6.

—— (1998), 'Why do large historical dictionaries give so much pleasure to their owners and users?', *in* Fontenelle *et al.* (eds): 579–87.

—— (2003), 'Dictionaries of Canadian English', *Lexikos* 13, 250–70.

—— (2007), 'Introduction', *in* Considine and Iamartino (eds): vii–xvii.

—— and IAMARTINO, G. (eds) (2007), *Words and Dictionaries from the British Isles in Historical Perspective* (Newcastle: Cambridge Scholars Publishing).

COPESTAKE, A. A. and BRISCOE, E. J. (1995), 'Regular polysemy and semi-productive sense extension', *Journal of Semantics* 12: 15–67.

—— and BRISCOE, E. J. (1996), 'Semi-productive polysemy and sense extension', *in* Pustejovsky and Boguraev (eds): 15–67.

CORBIN, P. (1998), 'La lexicographie française est-elle en panne ?', *Circle de Conferències 96–97: Lèxic, corpus i diccionaris* (Barcelona: Universitat Pompeu Fabra, Institut Universitari de Lingüística Aplicada).

—— (2001), 'Des imagiers aux dictionnaires: cadrage d'un champ de recherche', *in* Pruvost (ed.): 15–66.

CORINO, E, MARELLO, C., and ONESTI, C. (eds) (2006), *Atti del XII Congresso Internazionale di Lessicografia* (Alessandria: Edizioni dell'Orso).

CORMIER, M., FRANCOEUR, A., and BOULANGER, J. C. (eds) (2003), *Les dictionnaires Le Robert* (Montréal: Les Presses de L'Université de Montréal).

CORNERI, A. (1990), 'Il *Dictionnaire* di P. Richelet (1680): un secolo e un autore', *in* Deslex (ed.): 13–52.

CORRÉARD, M.-H. (ed.) (2002), *Lexicography and Natural Language Processing, A Festschrift in Honour of B. T. S. Atkins* (EURALEX, Göteborg University).

CORRIS, M., MANNING, C., POETSCH, S., and SIMPSON, J. (2004), 'How useful and usable are dictionaries for speakers of Australian indigenous languages?', *IJL* 17/1: 33–68.

COWIE, A. P. (1978), 'The place of illustrative material and collocations in the design of a learner's dictionary', *in* Strevens (ed.): 127–39.

—— (1979), 'The treatment of polysemy in the design of a learner's dictionary', *in* Hartmann (ed.): 82–8.

—— (1980), 'English dictionaries for the foreign learner', Paper read at the Exeter Summer School on Lexicography, printed as Cowie (1983a).

—— (1983a), 'The pedagogical/learner's dictionary. English dictionaries for the foreign learner', *in* Hartmann (ed.): 135–44.

—— (1983b), Introduction to the *Oxford Dictionary of Current Idiomatic English* (Oxford: OUP): vi–lvii.

—— (ed.) (1987a), *The Dictionary and the Language Learner* (Tübingen: Niemeyer).

—— (1987b), 'Syntax, the dictionary and the learner's communicative needs', *in* Cowie (ed.): 183–92.

—— (1994), 'Phraseology', *in* Asher, R. E. and Simpson, J. M. Y. (eds), *The Encyclopedia of Language and Linguistics*, Vol. 6 (Oxford: Pergamon Press): 168–71. Also in Fontenelle 2008a: 163–7.

—— (ed.) (1998a), *Phraseology: Theory, Analysis and Applications* (Oxford: Clarendon Press).

—— (1998b), 'A.S. Hornby: a Centenary Tribute', *in* Fontenelle *et al.* (eds), 3–16. Revised and extended version in *IJL* 11/4: 251–68.

—— (1999a), *English Dictionaries for Foreign Learners: A History* (Oxford: Clarendon Press).

—— (1999b), 'Phraseology and corpora: some implications for dictionary-making; a review of Moon, *Fixed Expressions and Idioms in English*', *IJL* 12/4: 307–23.

—— (2002), 'Examples and collocations in the French "Dictionnaire de langue"', *in* Corréard (ed.): 73–90.

—— (ed.) (2008), *The Oxford History of English Lexicography* (Oxford: OUP).

—— and HOWARTH, P. (1996), 'Phraseology—A Select Bibliography', *IJL* 9/1: 38–51.

CRESSWELL, T. J. and MCDAVID, V. (1986), 'The Usage Panel in *The American Heritage Dictionary, Second College Edition*', *in* Frawley and Steiner (eds): 83–96.

CROFT, W. and CRUSE, D. A. (2004). *Cognitive Linguistics* (Cambridge: CUP).

CROWTHER, J. (1999), 'Encyclopedic learners' dictionaries', *in* Herbst and Popp (eds): 213–19.

CRUSE, D. A. (1986), *Lexical Semantics* (Cambridge: CUP).

—— (2000a), *Meaning in Language* (Oxford: OUP).

—— (2000b), 'Aspects of the micro-structure of word meanings', *in* Ravin and Leacock (eds): 30–51.

CRYSTAL, D. (1985), *A Dictionary of Linguistics and Phonetics* (London: Andre Deutsch). First edition 1980.

—— (1986), 'The ideal dictionary, lexicographer and user', *in* Ilson (ed.) (1986e): 72–81.

—— (1988), *The English Language* (Harmondsworth: Penguin Books).

—— (ed.) (2005), *Samuel Johnson, A Dictionary of the English Language* (Harmondsworth: Penguin Books).

CUMMING, G., CROPP, S., and SUSSEX, R. (1994), 'On-line lexical resources for language learners: assessment of some approaches to word definition', *System* 22/3: 369–77.

CURZAN, A. (2000), 'The Compass of the Vocabulary', *in* Mugglestone (ed.) (2000a): 96–109.

D'ALEMBERT, J. LE ROND (1763), *Discours Préliminaire de l'Encyclopédie*. 1965 edition (Paris: Gonthier).

DARNTON, R. (1979), *The Business of Enlightenment, A Publishing History of the Encyclopédie 1775–1800* (Cambridge, MA: Harvard UP).

DAVIES, A. M. (1998), 'Nineteenth-century linguistics' *in* Lepschy, G. (ed.), *History of Linguistics*, vol. 4 (London: Longman).

DE COCK, S. and GRANGER, S. (2004), 'Computer learner corpora and monolingual learners' dictionaries: the perfect match', *Lexicographica* 20: 72–86.

DELBRIDGE, A. (1983), 'On national variants of the English dictionary. The English dictionary in different parts of the world', *in* Hartmann (ed.) (1983c): 23–40.

DEMARIA, R. (1986), *Johnson's Dictionary and the Language of Learning* (Chapel Hill, NC: U of North Carolina Press).

DESCAMPS, J.-L. and VAUNAIZE, R. (1983), 'Le dictionnaire au jour le jour en milieu adulte. Une pré-enquête', *Etudes de Linguistique Appliquée* 49: 89–109.

DE SCHRYVER, G. M. (2008), 'An analysis of *The Oxford Guide to Practical Lexicography* (Atkins and Rundell 2008)', *Lexikos* 18: 423–45.

DE SCHRYVER, G. M. and JOFFE, D. (2004), 'On how electronic dictionaries are really used', *in* Williams and Vessier (eds): 187–96.

DE SCHRYVER, G. M. and PRINSLOO, D. J. (2003), 'Compiling a lemma-sign list for a specific target user group: The Junior Dictionary as a case in point', *Dictionaries* 24: 29–58.

DE SCHRYVER, G. M., JOFFE, D., JOFFE, P., and HILLEWAERT, S. (2006), 'Do dictionary users really look up frequent words?—On the overestimation of the value of corpus-based lexicography', *Lexikos* 16: 67–83.

DESLEX, M. G. (ed.) (1990), *Società alla specchio: Ideologie nei dizionari francesi* (Turin: Tirrenia Stampatori).

DE VRIES, C. M. (1994), *In the Tracks of a Lexicographer: Secondary Documentation in Samuel Johnson's* Dictionary of the English Language (Leiden: LED).

DIAB, T. (1990), *Pedagogical Lexicography* (Tübingen: Niemeyer).

DIDIER, B. (1996), *Alphabet et raison. Le paradoxe des dictionnaires au XVIIIe siècle* (Paris: PUF).

DI SCIULLO, A.-M. and WILLIAMS, E. S. (1987), *On the Definition of Word* (Cambridge MA: MIT Press).

DOCHERTY, V., (2000), 'Dictionaries on the Internet: an Overview', *in* Heid *et al.* (eds): 67–74.

DOLEZAL, F. T. (1985), *Forgotten but Important Lexicographers, John Wilkins and William Lloyd: A Modern Approach to Lexicography Before Johnson* (Tübingen: Niemeyer).

—— (1986), 'How abstract is the English dictionary?', *in* Hartmann (ed.): 47–55.

—— (2007), 'Writing the history of English lexicography: Is there a history of English lexicography after Starnes and Noyes', *in* Considine and Iamartino (eds): 1–13.

—— and MCCREARY, D. R. (1996), 'Language learners and dictionary users: Commentary and an annotated bibliography', *Lexicographica International Annual* 12: 125–65.

—— and MCCREARY, D. R. (1999), *Pedagogical Lexicography Today. A Critical Bibliography on Learners' Dictionaries with Special emphasis on Language Learners and Dictionary Users* (Tübingen: Niemeyer).

DOWNIE, J. (1918), Macaulay's *Life of Johnson* (London: Blackie and Son).

DRYSDALE, P. D. (1979), 'Aspects of Canadian lexicography', *in* Congleton *et al.* (eds): 37–45.

—— (1987), 'The role of examples in a learner's dictionary', *in* Cowie (ed.) (1987*a*): 213–23.

DUBOIS, J. (1970), 'Dictionnaire et discours didactique', *Langages* 19: 35–47.

—— and DUBOIS, C. (1971), *Introduction à la lexicographie: le dictionnaire* (Paris: Larousse).

DUCHAČEK, O. (1959), 'Sur le problème de la structure du lexique et de son évolution', *Cahiers de lexicologie* 1: 89–98.

DZIEMIANKO, A. (2004), 'Verb syntax in monolingual English learners' dictionaries: A study of user-friendliness', *in* Williams and Vessier (eds): 683–91.

—— (2006), *User-friendliness of Verb Syntax in Pedagogical Dictionaries of English* (Tübingen: Niemeyer).

ECCLES, M. (1986), 'Claudius Hollyband and the earliest French–English dictionaries', *Studies in Philology* 83: 51–61.

ECO, U. (1984), *Semiotics and the Philosophy of Language*, (London: Macmillan).

EDMONDS, D. and EIDINOW, J. (2001), *Wittgenstein's Poker* (London: Faber and Faber).

ENCKELL, P. (2005), *Comment asphyxier un éléphant?* (Paris: Tallandier).

EVANS, V. (2007), *A Glossary of Cognitive Linguistics* (Edinburgh: Edinburgh U Press).

—— and GREEN, M. (2006), *Cognitive Linguistics: An Introduction.* (Edinburgh: Edinburgh U Press).

——, BERGEN, B., and ZINKEN, J. (2007), *The Cognitive Linguistics Reader* (London: Equinox).

FELDMAN, J. (1981), *La Sexualité du Petit Larousse ou Le Jeu du dictionnaire* (Paris: Editions Tierce).

FELLBAUM, C. (ed.) (1998*a*), *WordNet: An Electronic Lexical Database and Some of its Applications* (Cambridge, MA: MIT Press).

—— (1998*b*), 'Review of Wilks, Slator and Guthrie, *Electric Words*', *IJL* 11/3: 238–42.

—— (2000), 'Autotroponomy', *in* Ravin and Leacock (eds): 52–67.

FERRARIO, E. and PULCINI, V. (2002), *La Lessicografia Bilingue tra presente e avvenire* (Vercelli: Mercurio).

FILLMORE, C. J. (1969), 'Types of lexical information', *in* Kiefer (ed.), *Studies in Syntax and Semantics* (Reidel: Dordrecht): 109–37.

—— (1975), 'An alternative to checklist theories of meaning', *in* Cogen, C. *et al.* (eds), *Proceedings of the First Annual Meeting of the Berkeley Linguistic Society* (Berkeley, CA: UC Press): 123–31.

—— (1977), 'Topics in lexical semantics', *in* Cole, R. W. (ed.), *Current Issues in Linguistic Theory* (Bloomington: Indiana U Press): 76–138.

—— (1989), 'Two dictionaries', *IJL* 2/1: 57–83.

—— (1992), ' "Corpus linguistics" or "Computer-aided armchair linguistics" ', *in* Svartvik, J. (ed.), *Directions in Corpus Linguistics* (Berlin: Mouton de Gruyter): 35–66. Also in Fontenelle 2008*a*.

FILLMORE, C. J. (2008), 'Border conflicts: FrameNet meets construction grammar', *in* Bernal and DeCesaris (eds): 49–68.

——and ATKINS, B. T. S. (1992), 'Towards a frame-based lexicon: The semantics of RISK and its neighbors', *in* Lehrer, A. and Kittay, E. (eds), *Frames, Fields, and Contrasts: New Essays in Semantics and Lexical Organization* (Hillsdale, NJ: Lawrence Erlbaum): 75–102.

——and ATKINS, B. T. S. (1994), 'Starting where the dictionaries stop: the challenge of corpus lexicography', *in* Atkins and Zampolli (eds): 349–93.

——and ATKINS, B. T. S. (1998), 'FrameNet and lexicographic relevance', *in* Rubio, A. et al. (eds), *Proceedings of the First International Conference on Language Resources and Evaluation* (Paris: ELRA): 417–23.

——and ATKINS, B. T. S. (2000), 'Describing polysemy: The case of "crawl"', *in* Ravin and Leacock (eds): 91–110.

FINKENSTAEDT, T. and WOLFF, D. (1973), *Ordered Profusion. Studies in Dictionaries and the English Lexicon* (Heidelberg: Carl Winter, Universitätsverlag).

FIRTH, J. R. (1957*a*), 'A synopsis of linguistic theory, 1930–1955', *Studies in Linguistic Analysis*, Philological Society: 1–32.

——(1957*b*), *Papers in Linguistics 1934–1951* (Oxford: OUP).

FOLLETT, W. (1962), 'Sabotage in Springfield: Webster's third edition', *The Atlantic* 209: 73–7. Also in Sleds and Ebbitt (eds) (1962): 111–19.

FONTENELLE, T. (1997*a*), 'Dictionnaires électroniques et relations lexicales : une comparaison entre quelques programmes européens', *Revue Française de Linguistique Appliquée* II/1: 65–78. Special issue: 'Dictionnaires : nouvelles technologies, nouveaux produits ?'.

——(1997*b*), 'Using a bilingual dictionary to create semantic networks', *IJL* 10/4: 275–303. Also in Fontenelle 2008*a*.

——(1997*c*), *Turning a Bilingual Dictionary into a Lexical-Semantic Database* (Tübingen: Niemeyer).

——(2002), 'Lexical knowledge and natural language processing', *in* Corréard (ed.): 216–29.

——(ed.) (2008*a*), *Practical Lexicography, A Reader* (Oxford: OUP).

——(2008*b*), 'Introduction', *in* Fontenelle (ed.) (2008*a*): 1–15.

——(2008*c*), 'Lexicon Creator: A tool for building lexicons for proofing tools and search technologies', *in* Bernal and DeCesaris (eds): 359–70.

——, HILIGSMANN, P., MICHIELS, A., MOULIN, A., and THEISSEN, S. (eds) (1998), *Actes EURALEX '98 Proceedings* (Liège: Université de Liège).

FORD, J. (1996), 'Language mavens learn cybernetics: general use electronic dictionaries', *Dictionaries* 17: 207–24.

FORGUE, G. J. (1981), 'Postwar americanisms and cultural change', *Trema* 7: 89–97.

FOWLER, R. (2004), 'Text and meaning in Richardson's *Dictionary*', *in* Coleman and McDermott (eds), 53–62.

Fox, G. (1987), 'The case for examples', *in* Sinclair (ed.) (1987*a*): 137–49.

FRANKENBERG-GARCIA, A. (2005), 'A peek into what today's language learners as researchers actually do', *IJL* 18/3: 335–55.

FRAWLEY, W. (1988), 'New forms of specialized dictionaries', *IJL* 1/3: 189–213.

——and STEINER, R. (eds) (1986), *Advances in Lexicography* (Edmonton, Alberta: Boreal).

FRIEND, J. H. (1967), *The Development of American Lexicography 1798–1864* (The Hague: Mouton).

GALISSON, R. (1983), 'Image et usage du dictionnaire chez les étudiants (en langue) de niveau avancé', *Etudes de Linguistique Appliquée* 49: 5–88.

——(2001), 'Une dictionnairique à géométrie variable au service de la lexiculture', *in* Pruvost (ed.) (2001*a*): 115–38.

GATES, E. (1986), 'Preparation for lexicography as a career in the United States', *in* Ilson (ed.) (1986*e*): 82–8.

——(1988), 'The treatment of multiword lexemes in some current dictionaries of English', *in* Snell-Hornby (ed.): 99–106.

GAUDIN, F. (2002), 'Lettres à André Clas à propos du *Nouveau Dictionnaire Universel* de Maurice Lachâtre', *Cahiers de lexicologie* 80: 43–54.

——(2006), 'Le monde perdu des dictionnaires de Maurice Lachâtre (2): le *Dictionnaire La Châtre* (1898–1907), *in* Candel and Gaudin (eds), 241–67.

GEERAERTS, D. (1985*a*), 'Les données stéréotypiques, prototypiques et encyclopédiques dans le dictionnaire', *Cahiers de lexicologie* 46: 27–43.

——(1985*b*), 'Polysemization and Humboldt's principle', *Cahiers de l'Institut de Linguistique de Louvain* 11/3–4: 29–50.

——(1987), 'Types of semantic information in dictionaries', *in* Ilson (ed.) (1987*c*): 1–10.

——(1989), 'Principles of monolingual lexicography', *in* Hausmann *et al.* (eds) (1989/91): 287–96.

——(1990), 'The lexicographical treatment of prototypical polysemy, *in* Tsohatzidis, S. L. (ed.), *Meanings and Prototypes: Studies in Linguistic Categorization* (London: Routledge).

——(2000), 'Adding electronic value. The electronic version of the grote van Dale', *in* Heid *et al.* (eds): 75–84.

——(2003), 'Meaning and definition', *in* van Sterkenburg (ed.): 83–93.

——(2006*a*), *Words and Other Wonders, Papers on Lexical and Semantic Topics* (Berlin: Mouton de Gruyter).

——(ed.) (2006*b*), *Cognitive Linguistics: Basic Readings* (Berlin: Mouton de Gruyter).

——(2007), 'Lexicography', in Geeraerts and Cuyckens (eds), 1160–74.

——and CUYCKENS, H. (eds) (2007), *The Oxford Handbook of Cognitive Linguistics* (New York: OUP).

GELLERSTAM, M., *et al.* (eds) (1996), *EURALEX '96 Proceedings* (Göteborg: Göteborg University).

GERSHUNY, L. H. (1977), 'Sexism in dictionaries and texts: omissions and commissions', *in* Nielsen, A. P. *et al.* (eds), *Sexism and Language* (Urbana, IL: NCTE): 143–59.

GIBBS, R. W., Jr. (2007), 'Idioms and formulaic language', *in* Geeraerts and Cuyckens (eds): 697–725.

GILLIVER, P. (2000), 'Review of Winchester, *The Professor and the Madman*', *Dictionaries* 21: 160–8.

—— (2004), '"That brownest of brown studies": The work of the editors and in-house staff of the *Oxford English Dictionary* in 1903', *Dictionaries* 24: 44–64.

——, MARSHALL, J., and WEINER, E. (2006), *Tolkien and the* Oxford English Dictionary (Oxford: OUP).

GIRARDIN, C. (1979), 'Contenu, usage social et interdits dans le dictionnaire', *Langue Française* 43: 84–99.

GLEASON, H. A. (1962), 'The relation of lexicon and grammar', *in* Householder and Saporta (eds): 85–102.

GODDARD, C. (2000), 'Polysemy: A problem of definition', *in* Ravin and Leacock (eds): 129–151.

GOETSCHALCKX, J. and ROLLING, L. (eds) (1982), *Lexicography in the Electronic Age* (Amsterdam: North Holland).

GOLD, D. L. ((1985), 'The debate over *Webster's Third* twenty-five years later: Winnowing the chaff from the grain', *Dictionaries* 7: 225–36.

—— (1988), 'Review of *The BBI Combinatory Dictionary of English, A Guide to Word Combinations*', *IJL* 1/1: 56–9.

—— (1989), 'Review of *A Dictionary of South African English*, 3rd edition 1987', *Dictionaries* 11: 242–60.

GOLDSTEIN, M. C. (1991), 'Tibetan Lexicography', *in* Hausmann *et al.* (eds) (1989/91): 2548–50.

GORCY, G. (1989), 'Différenciation des significations dans le dictionnaire monolingue: problèmes et méthodes', *in* Hausmann *et al.* (eds) (1989/91): 905–17.

GÖRLACH, M. (1990), 'The dictionary of transplanted varieties of languages: English', *in* Hausmann *et al.* (eds) (1989/91): 1475–99.

—— (2004), 'Review of *Shorter Oxford English Dictionary*, Fifth edition', *IJL* 17/1: 88.

GOUWS, R. H. and PRINSLOO, D. J. (1998), 'Cross-referencing as a lexicographic device', *Lexikos* 8: 17–36.

GOVE, P. B. (1964) '"Noun often attributive" and "adjective"', *American Speech* 39: 163–75.

—— (1966), 'Self-explanatory words', *American Speech* 41: 182–98.

—— (1967a), 'The dictionary's function', *in* Gove (ed.): 5–8.

—— (ed.) (1967b), *The Role of the Dictionary* (Indianapolis: Bobbs-Merrill).

—— (1968a), 'On defining adjectives, part I', *American Speech* 43: 5–32.

—— (1968b), 'On defining adjectives, part II', *American Speech* 43: 243–67.

GRAHAM, A. (1975), 'The making of a non-sexist dictionary', *ETC. Review of General Semantics* 31: 57–64. Also in Thorne, B. and Henley, N. (eds), *Language and Sex: Difference and Dominance* (Rowley, MA: Newbury House): 57–63.

GRANGER, S. (2003), 'The International Corpus of Learner English: A new resource for foreign language learning and teaching and second language acquisition research', *TESOL Quarterly* 37/3: 538–46.

GREEN, J. (1996), *Chasing the Sun: Dictionary Makers and the Dictionaries They Made* (New York: Henry Holt and Co. / London: Jonathan Cape).

GREENBAUM, S. (1977), 'The linguist as experimenter', *in* Eckman, R. (ed.), *Current Trends in Linguistics* (Washington: Hemisphere Publishing Corp.).

——, MEYER, C. F. and TAYLOR, J. (1984), 'The image of the dictionary for American college students', *Dictionaries* 6: 31–52.

GREFENSTETTE, G. (1998), 'The future of linguistics and lexicographers: Will there be lexicographers in the year 3000?', *in* Fontenelle *et al.* (eds): 25–42. Also in Fontenelle 2008*a*.

—— (2002), 'The WWW as a resource for lexicography', *in* Corréard (ed.): 199–215.

—— and TAPPANAINEN, P. (1994), 'What is a word, what is a sentence? Problems of tokenization', *in* Kiefer *et al.* (eds): 79–87.

GRIFFIN, P. J. (1985), 'Dictionaries in the ESL classroom', Master of Arts Thesis, Carbondale, IL: Southern Illinois University.

GUILBERT, L. (1969), 'Dictionnaires et linguistique: essai d'une typologie des diction-naires monolingues français contemporains', *Langue Française* 2: 4–28.

HAEBLER, T. (1989), 'The reception of the *Third New International Dictionary*', *Diction-aries* 11: 165–218.

HAGÈGE, C. (1985), *L'Homme de paroles* (Paris: Fayard).

HAIMAN, J. (1980), 'Dictionaries and Encyclopedias', *Lingua* 50: 329–57.

—— (1982), 'Dictionaries and Encyclopedias again', *Lingua* 56: 353–5.

HALE, J. (1994), *The Civilization of Europe in the Renaissance* (New York: Atheneum).

HALL, J. H. (2001), 'Frederic Gomes Cassidy, October 10, 1907–June 14, 2000', *Dictionaries* 22: 1–13.

HALLIDAY, M. A. K. (1992), 'Language as system and language as instance: The corpus as a theoretical construct', *in* Svartvik (ed.): 61–77.

—— (1993), 'Quantitative studies and probabilities in grammar', *in* Hoey, M. (ed.), *Data, Description, Discourse. Papers on the English Language in Honour of John McH. Sinclair* (London: HarperCollins): 1–25.

—— (2004), 'Lexicology', *in* Halliday *et al.* (eds.): 1–22.

—— and HASAN, R. (1976), *Cohesion in English* (London: Longman).

——, TEUBERT, W., YALLOP, C., and Čermakova, A. (eds) (2004), *Lexicology and Corpus Linguistics* (London: Continuum).

HALLIG, R. and VON WARTBURG, W. (1952), *Begriffssystem als Grundlage für die Lexico-graphie* (Berlin: Akademie). 2nd edn: 1963.

HANCHER, M. (1996), 'Illustrations', *Dictionaries* 17: 79–115.

HANKS, P. (1973), 'Discussion', *in* McDavid and Duckert (eds): 251–2.

——(1979), 'To what extent does a dictionary definition define?', *in* Hartmann (ed.): 32–8.

——(1987), 'Definitions and explanations', *in* Sinclair (ed.) (1987a): 116–36.

——(1988), 'Typicality and meaning potentials', in Snell-Hornby (ed.): 37–47.

——(1989), 'How common is "common"?', *The Collins Dictionary Diary* 1989: 2–12.

——(1990), 'Evidence and intuition in lexicography', *in* Tomaszczyk and Lewandowska-Tomaszczyk (eds): 31–41.

——(1994), 'Linguistic norms and pragmatic exploitations, or why lexicographers need prototype theory, and vice versa', *in* Kiefer *et al.* (eds): 89–113.

——(1998), 'Enthusiasm and Condescension', *in* Fontenelle *et al.* (eds): 151–66.

——(2000a), 'Contributions of lexicography and corpus linguistics to a theory of language performance', *in* Heid *et al.* (eds): 3–13.

——(2000b), 'Do word meanings exist?', *Computers and the Humanities* 34: 205–15. Also in Fontenelle 2008a: 123–34.

——(2002), 'Mapping meaning onto use', *in* Corréard (ed.): 156–98.

——(2004a), 'Corpus pattern analysis', *in* Williams and Vessier (eds): 87–97.

——(2004b), 'The syntagmatics of metaphor and idiom', *IJL* 17/3: 245–74.

——(2005), 'Johnson and modern lexicography', *IJL* 18/2: 243–66.

——(2008), 'Lexical patterns: From Hornby to Hunston and beyond', *in* Bernal and DeCesaris (eds): 89–129.

——and PUSTEJOVSKY, J. (2005), 'A pattern dictionary for natural language processing', *Revue Française de Linguistique Appliquée* X/2: 63–82.

HANON, S. (1990), 'La concordance', *in* Hausmann *et al.* (eds) (1989/91): 1562–7.

HARLEY, A. (2000), 'Cambridge Dictionaries Online', *in* Heid *et al.* (eds): 85–8.

HARRIS, R. (1981), *The Language Myth* (London: Duckworth).

HARTMANN, R. R. K. (ed.) (1979), *Dictionaries and their Users* (Exeter: U of Exeter).

——(1983a), 'On theory and practice. Theory and practice in dictionary-making', *in* Hartmann (ed.) (1983c): 3–11.

——(1983b), 'The bilingual learner's dictionary and its uses', *Multilingua* 2/4: 195–201.

——(ed.) (1983c), *Lexicography: Principles and Practice* (London: Academic Press).

——(ed.) (1984), *LEXeter '83 Proceedings* (Tübingen: Niemeyer).

——(1985), 'Dictionaries of English: The user's perspective', manuscript.

——(ed.) (1986), *The History of Lexicography: Papers from the Dictionary Research Centre Seminar at Exeter, March 1986* (Amsterdam: Benjamins).

——(1987), 'Four perspectives on dictionary use: a critical review of research methods', *in* Cowie (ed.) (1987a): 11–28.

——(2001), *Teaching and Researching Lexicography* (Harlow: Longman).

——and JAMES, G. (1998), *Dictionary of Lexicography* (London: Routledge).

——and SMITH, M. R. K. (2003), *Lexicography, Critical Concepts* (London: Routledge).

HARVEY, K. and YUILL, D. (1997), 'A study of the use of a monolingual pedagogical dictionary by learners of English engaged in writing', *Applied Linguistics* 18: 253–78.

HATHERALL, G. (1984), 'Studying dictionary use: some findings and proposals', *in* Hartmann (ed.): 183–9.

HAUSMANN, F. J. (1979), 'Un dictionnaire de collocations est-il possible ?', *Travaux de Linguistique et de Littérature* 17/1: 187–95.

—— (1984), 'Trois paysages dictionnairiques: la Grande-Bretagne, la France et l'Allemagne. Comparaisons et connexions', *Lexicographica* 1: 24–50.

—— (1986), 'The training and professional development of lexicographers in Germany', *in* Ilson (ed.) (1986*e*): 101–10.

—— (1988), 'L'essor d'une discipline: la métalexicographie à l'échelle mondiale', *Verba, Anuario galego de filoloxía* 29: 79–109.

—— (1989*a*), 'Dictionary criminality', *in* Hausmann *et al.* (eds) (1989/91): 97–101.

—— (1989*b*), 'Pour une histoire de la métalexicographie', *in* Hausmann *et al.* (eds) (1989/ 91): 216–24.

—— (1989*c*), 'Wörterbuchtypologie', *in* Hausmann *et al.* (eds) (1989/91): 968–81.

—— (1989*d*), 'Le dictionnaire de collocations', *in* Hausmann *et al.* (eds) (1989/91): 1010–19.

—— (1990*a*), 'La définition est-elle utile ?', *in* Chaurand and Mazière (eds): 225–35.

—— (1990*b*), 'Le dictionnaire analogique', *in* Hausmann *et al.* (eds) (1989/91): 1094–9.

—— (1990*c*), 'Das Kinderwörterbuch', *in* Hausmann *et al.* (eds) (1989/91): 1365–8.

—— (1990*d*), 'The dictionary of synonyms: discriminating synonymy', *in* Hausmann *et al.* (eds) (1989/91): 1067–75.

—— (1999), 'Semiotaxis and learners' dictionaries', *in* Herbst and Popp (eds): 205–11.

—— (2002), 'La lexicographie bilingue en Europe: Peut-on l'améliorer?', *in* Ferrario and Pulcini (eds): 11–31.

—— (2003), 'Beaucoup de splendeurs, peu de misères: bilan sur les dictionnaires Le Robert', *in* Cormier *et al.* (eds), 246–62.

—— and BLUMENTHAL, P. (2006), 'Présentation: collocations, corpus, dictionnaires', *Langue française* 150: 3–13.

—— and GORBAHN, A. (1989), '*COBUILD* and *LDOCE II*: A comparative review', *IJL* 2/1: 44–56.

—— and WIEGAND, H. E. (1989), 'Component parts and structures of general monolingual dictionaries: A survey', *in* Hausmann *et al.* (eds) (1989/91): 328–60.

——, REICHMANN, O, WIEGAND, H. E., and ZGUSTA, L. (eds) (1989/91), *Wörterbücher/ Dictionaries/Dictionnaires: An International Encyclopedia of Lexicography* (volume 1: 1989, volume 2: 1990, volume 3: 1991), (Berlin: de Gruyter).

HAYWOOD, J. A. (1986), 'The Entry in Medieval Arabic Monolingual Dictionaries: Some Aspect of Arrangement and Content', *in* Hartmann (ed.): 107–13.

HEID, U. and FREIBOTT, G. (1991), 'Collocations dans une base de données terminologiques et lexicales', *Méta* 36/1: 77–91.

HEID, U., EVERT, S., LEHMANN, E. and ROHRER, C. (eds) (2000), *Proceedings of the 9th EURALEX International Congress* (Stuttgart: Universität Stuttgart).

HEINZ, M. (ed.) (2005), *L'Exemple lexicographique dans les dictionnaires français contemporains* (Tübingen: Niemeyer).

HERBST, T. (1990), 'Dictionaries for foreign language teaching', *in* Hausmann *et al.* (eds) (1989/91): 1379–85.

—— (1996*a*), 'On the way to the perfect learner's dictionary; a first comparison of *OALD5, LDOCE3, COBUILD2* and *CIDE*', *IJL* 9/4: 321–57.

—— (1996*b*), 'What are collocations?—Sandy beaches or false teeth', *English Studies* 77/4: 379–93.

—— and POPP, K. (eds) (1999), *The Perfect Learners' Dictionary(?)* (Tübingen: Niemeyer).

—— and STEIN, G. (1987), 'Dictionary-using skills: a plea for a new orientation in language teaching', *in* Cowie (ed.) (1987*a*): 115–27.

HIGASHI, N., TAKEBAYASHI, S., NAKAO, K., SAKURAI, M., YAMAMOTO, F., MASUDA, H., and YAWATA, S. (1992), 'Review of the *Concise Oxford Dictionary of Current English*, Eighth edition', *IJL* 5/2: 129–60.

HITCHINGS, H. (2005), *Dr Johnson's Dictionary* (London: John Murray).

HOBAR, D. (ed.) (1982), *Papers of the Dictionary Society of North America 1977* (Terre Haute, IN: Indiana State University).

HOEY, M. (1991), *Patterns of Lexis in Text* (Oxford: OUP).

—— (2005), *Lexical Priming* (London: Routledge).

HOFLAND, K. (1991), 'Concordancing Programs for Personal Computers', *in* Johanson and Stentström (eds): 284–306.

HOLLANDER, M. and GREIDANUS, T. (1996), 'Incidental vocabulary learning for advanced foreign language students: The influence of marginal glosses, dictionary use, and reoccurrence of unknown words', *The Modern Language Journal* 80: 327–39.

HOSS, N. (1974), 'Words. Lexicography in America or why Texans don't shit', *Penthouse* January 1974: 36–8.

HOUSEHOLDER, F. W. (1962), 'Summary report', *in* Householder and Saporta (eds): 279–82.

—— and SAPORTA, S. (eds) (1962/1975), *Problems in Lexicography* (Bloomington: Indiana University).

HOWARTH, P. A. (1996), *Phraseology in English Academic Writing. Some Implications for Language Learning and Dictionary Making* (Tübingen: Niemeyer).

HUDSON, R. A. (1984), *Word Grammar* (Oxford: Blackwell).

—— (1988), 'The linguistic foundations for lexical research and dictionary design', *IJL* 1/4: 287–312.

—— and HOLMES, J. (2000), 'Re-cycling in the encyclopedia', *in* Peeters (ed.): 259–90.

HULBERT, J. R. (1955/1968), *Dictionaries: British and American* (London: Andre Deutsch).

HÜLLEN, W. (ed.) (1994), *The World in a List of Words* (Tübingen: Niemeyer).

—— (1999), *English Dictionaries 800–1700. The Topical Tradition* (Oxford: Clarendon Press); paperback edn 2006.

—— (2004*a*), *A History of Roget's Thesaurus* (Oxford: OUP). 2nd edn paperback: 2005.

—— (2004*b*), 'Roget's Thesaurus, deconstructed', *in* Coleman and McDermott (eds), 83–93.

HULSTIJN, J., HOLLANDER, M., and GREIDANUS, T. (1996), 'Incidental vocabulary learning by advanced foreign language students: the influence of marginal glosses, dictionary use, and reoccurrence of unknown words', *Modern Language Journal* 80/3: 327–39.

HUMBLÉ, P. (1998), 'The use of authentic, made-up and "controlled" examples in foreign language dictionaries', *in* Fontenelle *et al.* (eds): 593–99.

—— (2001), *Dictionaries and Language Learners* (Frankfurt am Main: Haag + Herchen).

HUNSTON, S. and FRANCIS, G. (2000), *Pattern Grammar, A Corpus-Driven Approach to the Lexical Grammar of English* (Amsterdam: Benjamins).

HUPKA, W. (1989), 'Die Bebilderung und sonstige Formen der Veranschaulichung im allgemeinen einsprachigen Wörterbuch', *in* Hausmann *et al.* (eds) (1989/91): 704–26.

HYLDGAARD-JENSEN, K. and ZETTERSTEN, A. (eds) (1985), *Symposium on Lexicography II* (Tübingen: Niemeyer).

—— and ZETTERSTEN, A. (1988*a*), *Symposium on Lexicography III* (Tübingen: Niemeyer).

—— and ZETTERSTEN, A. (1988*b*), *Symposium on Lexicography IV* (Tübingen: Niemeyer).

—— and ZETTERSTEN, A. (1992), *Symposium on Lexicography V* (Tübingen: Niemeyer),

IDE, N. and VERONIS, J. (1995), 'Encoding dictionaries', *in* Ide and Veronis (eds), *The Text Encoding Initiative: Background and Context* (Dordrecht: Kluwer): 167–80.

—— and VERONIS, J. (1998), 'Introduction to the special issue on word sense disambiguation: the state of the art', *Computational Linguistics* 24/1: 1–40.

—— and WILKS, Y. (2006), 'Making sense about sense', *in* Agirre and Edmonds (eds): 47–73.

ILSON, R. F. (1984), 'The communicative significance of some lexicographic conventions', *in* Hartman (ed.): 80–6.

—— (1985*a*), 'The linguistic significance of some lexicographic conventions', *Applied Linguistics* 6/2: 162–72.

—— (ed.) (1985*b*), *Dictionaries, Lexicography and Language Learning* (Oxford: Pergamon Press).

—— (1986*a*), 'Introduction', *in* Ilson (ed.) (1986*e*): xii–xiv.

—— (1986*b*), 'British and American Lexicography', *in* Ilson (ed.) (1986*e*): 51–71.

—— (1986*c*), 'General English dictionaries for foreign learners: Explanatory techniques in dictionaries', *Lexicographica* 2: 214–22.

—— (1986*d*), 'Lexicographic archaeology: Comparing dictionaries of the same family', *in* Hartmann (ed.): 127–36.

—— (ed.) (1986*e*), *Lexicography: An Emerging International Profession* (Manchester: Manchester U Press).

ILSON, R. F. (1987a), 'Towards a taxonomy of dictionary definitions', *in* Ilson (ed.) (1987c): 61–73.

—— (1987b), 'Illustrations in dictionaries', *in* Cowie (ed.) (1987a): 193–212.

—— (ed.) (1987c), *A Spectrum of Lexicography, Papers from AILA Brussels 1984* (Amsterdam: Benjamins).

—— (1990a), 'Semantic regularities in dictionaries', *in* Tomaszczyk and Lewandowska-Tomaszczyk (eds): 123–32.

—— (1990b), 'Present-day British lexicography', *in* Hausmann *et al.* (eds) (1989/91): 1967–83.

—— (1992), 'BudaLEX Presidential Debate 1988: Part 4', *IJL* 5/4: 275–7.

—— (1993), 'OCELang: background articles', *IJL* 6/1: 19–29.

—— (1997), 'Review of *Wörterbücher/Dictionaries/Dictionnaires: An International Encyclopedia of Lexicography*', *IJL* 10/4: 348–57.

—— (1998), 'Review of *The Newbury House Dictionary of American English*, and *Random House Webster's Dictionary of American English*', *IJL* 11/3: 227–37.

—— (1999a), 'Nine learners' dictionaries', *IJL* 12/3: 223–37.

—— (1999b), 'The treatment of meaning in learners' dictionaries—and others', *in* Herbst and Popp (eds): 71–9.

—— (2000), 'Review of *Encarta World English Dictionary*', *IJL* 13/4: 326–36.

—— (2001), 'Review of Atkins, *Using Dictionaries*', *IJL* 14/1: 80–3.

IRIS, M. A., LITOWITZ, B. E., and EVENS, M. W. (1988), 'Moving towards literacy by making definitions', *IJL* 1/3: 238–52.

JACKENDOFF, R. (1983), *Semantics and Cognition* (Cambridge, MA: MIT Press).

—— (1997), *The Architecture of the Language Faculty* (Cambridge, MA: MIT Press).

JACKSON, H. (1988), *Words and their Meaning* (London: Longman).

—— (1998), 'How many words in YOUR dictionary?', *English Today* 14/3: 27–8.

—— (2002), *Lexicography: An Introduction* (London: Routledge/Taylor and Francis).

—— and ZÉ AMVELA, E. (2000), *Words, Meaning and Vocabulary* (London: Continuum).

—— (ed.) (1989), *Lexicographers and Their Works* (Exeter: U of Exeter).

JAMES, G. (1994), 'Towards a typology of bilingualised dictionaries', *in* James, G. (ed.), *Meeting Points in Language Studies: A Festschrift for Ma Talai* (Hong Kong: HKUST Language Centre): 184–96.

JANSEN, J., MERGEAI, J. P., and VANANDROYE, J. (1987), 'Controlling LDOCE's controlled vocabulary', *in* Cowie (ed.) (1987a): 78–94.

JOHANSSON, S. and STRENTSTRÖM, A. (eds) (1991), *English Computer Corpora: Selected Papers and Research Guide* (Berlin: Mouton de Gruyter).

JONES, S. and SINCLAIR, J. (1974), 'English lexical collocations', *Cahiers de lexicologie* 24/1: 15–61.

JOOS, M. (1961), *The Five Clocks* (New York: Harcourt, Brace and World).

KACHRU, B. B. and KAHANE, H. (eds) (1995), *Cultures, Ideologies, and the Dictionary: Studies in Honor of Ladislav Zgusta* (Tübingen: Niemeyer).

KATRE, S. (1965), *Lexicography* (Annamalainagar: Annamalai University).

KAYE, G. (1989), 'The Oxford English Dictionary on CD-ROM', IJL 2/1: 84–7.

KEGL, J. (1987), 'The boundary between word knowledge and world knowledge', in Proceedings of the Third Workshop on Theoretical Issues in Natural Language Processing (Las Cruces, New Mexico: Association fror Computational Linguistics), 26–31.

KENNEDY, G. (1998), An Introduction to Corpus Linguistics (London: Longman).

KERBRAT-ORECCHIONI, C. (1977), La Connotation (Lyon: Presses Universitaires de Lyon).

KIEFER, F., KISS, G., and PAJS, J. (eds) (1994), Papers in Computational Lexicography COMPLEX '94 (Budapest: Research Institute for, Hungarian Academy of Sciences).

—— et al. (1996), COMPLEX '94: Papers in Computational Lexicography COMPLEX '96 (Budapest: Linguistics Institute, Hungarian Academy of Sciences).

KILGARRIFF, A. (1993), 'Dictionary word sense distinctions: an enquiry into their nature', Computers and the Humanities 26/1–2: 365–87.

—— (1997a), 'Putting frequencies in the dictionary', IJL 10/2: 135–55.

—— (1997b), 'I don't believe in word senses', Computers and the Humanities 31/2: 91–113. Also in Fontenelle 2008a: 135–51.

—— (1998a), 'SENSEVAL: An exercise in evaluating word sense disambiguation programs', in Fontenelle et al. (eds): 167–74.

—— (1998b), 'The hard parts of lexicography', IJL 11/1: 51–4.

—— (2000), 'Business models for dictionaries and NLP', IJL 13/2: 107–18.

—— (2006), 'Word sense', in Agirre, E. and Edmonds, P. (eds): 29–45.

—— and GREFENSTETTE, G. (eds) (2003), Web as Corpus, Special issue of Computational Linguistics 29/3.

—— and PALMER, M. (eds) (2000), 'Special issue on SENSEVAL: Evaluating word sense disambiguation programs', Computers and the Humanities 34/1–2.

—— and RUNDELL, M. (2002), 'Lexical profiling software and its lexicographic applications: a case study', in Braasch and Povlsen (eds): 807–18.

—— and TUGWELL, D. (2001), 'WORD SKETCH: Extraction and display of significant collocations for lexicography', Proceedings of the Workshop COLLOCATION: Computational Extraction, Analysis and Exploitation (Toulouse: ACL and EACL): 32–38.

—— and TUGWELL, D. (2002), 'Sketching words', in Corréard (ed.): 125–37.

—— RYCHLY, P, SMRZ, P., and TUGWELL, D. (2004), 'The sketch engine', in Williams and Vessier (eds): 105–15. Also in Fontenelle 2008a.

KIPFER, B. (1985), 'Dictionaries and the intermediate student: Communicative needs and the development of user reference skills', M.Phil., U of Exeter.

KIRKPATRICK, B. (1985), 'A lexicographical dilemma: monolingual dictionaries for the native speaker and for the learner', in Ilson (ed.) (1985b): 7–13.

—— (1989), 'User's guides in dictionaries', in Hausmann et al. (eds) (1989/91): 754–61.

KISTER, K. F. (1977), Dictionary Buying Guide, A Consumer Guide to General English-Language Wordbooks in Print (New York: R.R. Bowker).

KLEIBER, G. (1988), 'Prototype, stéréotype: un air de famille?', DRLAV 38: 1–61.

KLEIBER, G. (1990*a*), *La Sémantique du prototype* (Paris: P.U.F).

—— (1990*b*), 'Sur la définition sémantique d'un mot—Les sens uniques conduisent-ils à des impasses ?', *in Centre d'études du lexique*, 125–48.

—— (1996), 'Noms propres et noms communs: un problème de dénomination', *Méta* 41/4: 567–89.

KLOTZ, M. (2003), 'Review of *Oxford Collocations Dictionary for Students of English*', *IJL* 16/1: 57–61.

KNIGHT, S. (1994), 'Dictionary use while reading: The effects on comprehension and vocabulary acquisition for students of different verbal abilities', *The Modern Language Journal* 78: 285–98.

KNOWLES, E. M. (1990), 'Dr Minor and the *Oxford English Dictionary*', *Dictionaries* 12: 27–42.

KNUDSEN, T. and SOMMERFELT, A. (1958), 'Principles of unilingual dictionary definitions', *in* Sivertsen (ed.): 92–8.

KOLB, G. J. and DEMARIA, R. (2005), *Johnson on the English Language* (New Haven: Yale U Press).

—— and KOLB, R. A. (1972), 'The selection and use of illustrative quotations in Dr. Johnson's *Dictionary*', *in* Weinbrot (ed.) (1972*b*): 61–72.

KRAPP, G. P. (1925), *The English Language in America* (New York: The Century Co.). Facsimile edition 1966, New York: Frederic Ungar).

KRISHNAMURTHY, R. (1987), 'The process of compilation', *in* Sinclair (ed.) (1987*a*): 62–85.

—— (ed.) (2003), *English Collocation Studies: The OSTI Report* (Birmingham: U of Birmingham Press).

KRUISINGA, E. (1931) 'Grammar and the Dictionary', *English Studies* 13: 7–14.

KUČERA, H. and FRANCIS, W. (1967), *Computational Analysis of Present-Day English* (Providence: Brown UP).

KÜHN, P. (1999), 'Positionen und Perspektiven der Wörterbuchdidaktik und Wörterbucharbeit im Deutschen', *Lexicographica* 14: 1–13.

LABOV, W. (1972), *Sociolinguistic Patterns* (Philadelphia: U of Pennsylvania Press).

—— (1973), 'The boundaries of words and their meanings', *in* Bailey, C. J. and Shuy, R. (eds), *New Ways of Analyzing Variation in English* (Washington: Georgetown U Press): 340–73.

LAIRD, C. G. (1970), *Language in America* (New York: World Publishing Company).

LAKOFF, G. (1973), 'Lexicography and generative grammar I: Hedges and meaning criteria', *in* McDavid and Duckert (eds): 144–53.

—— (1987), *Women, Fire and Dangerous Things* (Chicago: U of Chicago Press).

—— and JOHNSON, M. (1980), *Metaphors we Live By* (Chicago: U of Chicago Press).

LAMB, S. (1973), 'Linguistic and cognitive networks', *in* Makkai, A. and Lockwood, D. (eds), *Readings in Stratificational Linguistics* (U of Alabama Press): 60–83.

LANCASHIRE, I. (2004), 'Lexicography in the early modern English period: the manuscript record', *in* Coleman and McDermott (eds), 19–30.

—— (2005), 'Johnson and seventeenth-century English glossographers', *IJL* 18/2: 157–71.

LANDAU, S. (1964), 'Dictionary entry count', *RQ* 4/1: 13–15.

—— (1984), *Dictionaries. The Art and Craft of Lexicography* (New York: Charles Scribner's Sons). 2nd edn (2001) (Cambridge: CUP).

—— (1985), 'The expression of changing social values in dictionaries', *Dictionaries* 7: 261–9.

—— (1991), 'Approaches to meaning and their uses in lexicography', *Dictionaries* 13: 91–114.

—— (1994*a*), 'The American college dictionaries', *IJL* 7/4: 311–351.

—— (1994*b*), 'The expression of changing social values in dictionaries: Focus on family relationships', *in* Little, G. D. and Montgomery, M. (eds), *Centennial Usage Studies* (Tuscaloosa: U of Alabama Press): 32–9.

—— (1999), 'Review of *The New Oxford Dictionary of English*', *IJL* 12/3: 250–7.

—— (2000), 'Review of *Encarta World English Dictionary*', *Dictionaries* 21: 112–24.

—— (2001), *Dictionaries. The Art and Craft of Lexicography*, 2nd edn (Cambridge: CUP).

—— (2005), 'Johnson's influence on Webster and Worcester in early American lexicography', *IJL* 18/2: 217–29.

LAUFER, B. (1992), 'Corpus-based versus Lexicographer Examples in Comprehension and Production of New Words', *in* Tommola *et al.* (eds): 71–6. Also in Fontenelle 2008*a*.

—— (1993), 'The effect of dictionary definitions and examples on the use and comprehension of new L2 words', *Cahiers de lexicologie* 63: 131–42.

—— (2000), 'Electronic dictionaries and incidental vocabulary acquisition: does technology make a difference?', *in* Heid *et al.* (eds): 849–54.

—— and HADAR, L. (1997), 'Assessing the effectiveness of monolingual, bilingual, and "bilingualised" dictionaries in the comprehension and production of new words', *The Modern Language Journal* 81/2: 189–96.

—— and HILL, M. (2000), 'What lexical information do L2 learners select in a CALL dictionary and how does it affect word retention?', *Language Learning and Technology* 3/2: 58–76.

—— and MELAMED, L. (1994), 'Monolingual, bilingual and "bilingualized" dictionaries: Which are more effective, for what, and for whom?', *in* Martin *et al.* (eds): 565–76.

LEA, D. and RUNCIE, M. (2002), 'Instruments and fine distinctions: a collocations dictionary for students of English', *in* Braasch and Povlsen (eds): 819–29.

LEECH, G. (1974), *Semantics* (London: Pelican Books).

—— (1981), *Semantics: The Study of Meaning* (London: Penguin).

—— (1990), *Proceedings of a Workshop on Corpus Resources* (Oxford: DTI/Speech and Language Technology Club).

—— and NESI, H. (1999), 'Moving towards perfection: The learners' (electronic) dictionary of the future', *in* Herbst and Popp (eds): 295–306.

LE GUERN, M. (2003), *Les Deux logiques du langage* (Paris: Champion).

LEHMANN, A. (1981), Analyse du discours lexicographique: le corps sexué dans le *Petit Larousse Illustré* de 1906 à 1980, Thèse de 3e cycle, Université Paris 8.

——(1990), 'De définition à définition—L'interprétation dans le dictionnaire par le jeu des renvois', *in* Chaurand and Mazière (eds): 208–24.

——(2002), 'Constantes et innovations dans la lexicographie du français destinée aux enfants (1970–2001)', *IJL* 15/1: 74–88.

——(2005), 'L'exemple lexicographique dans les dictionnaires français contemporains', *in* Heinz (ed.): 315–30.

——(2006), 'Josette Rey-Debove: du dictionnaire à la sémiotique, une oeuvre à plusieurs dimensions', *Cahiers de lexicologie* 88/1: 201–10.

——and BEAUJOT, J.-P. (1978), 'Dictionnaire, langue, idéologie: le discours tenu sur *femme* et *fille* dans le *Petit Larousse Illustré* de 1906 à 1978', *Bulletin du Centre d'Analyse du Discours 3*, Université de Lille III: 1–175.

LEHRER, A. (1974*a*), 'Homonymy and polysemy: Measuring similarity in meaning', *Language Sciences* 3: 33–9.

——(1974*b*), *Semantic Fields and Lexical Structure* (Amsterdam: North Holland).

——(1990), 'Polysemy, conventionality, and the structure of the lexicon', *Cognitive Linguistics* 1/2: 207–46.

LEROY-TURCAN, I. (1996), 'Modalités de mise en oeuvre de l'informatisation de la première edition du *Dictionnaire de l'Académie françoise* (1694), *in* Wooldridge, T. (ed.), *Actes du colloque Les dictionnaires électroniques du français des XVIè et XVIIè siècles* (Toronto: SIEHLDA).

LESCHIERA, S. (1990), 'Le lessie "homme" e "femme" nelle microstrutture dei dizionari francesi dal Cinquecento all'epoca contemporanea', *in* Deslex (ed.): 53–109.

LEVI, J. N. (1983), 'Complex nominals: New discoveries, new questions', *in* Hattori, S. and Inoue, K. (eds), *Proceedings of the XIIIth International Congress of Linguists* (Tokyo): 183–97.

LEVIN, B. (1991), 'Building a lexicon: The contribution of linguistics', *IJL* 4/3: 205–26.

——(1993), *English Verb Classes and Alternations: A Preliminary Investigation* (Chicago: U of Chicago Press).

LEW, R. (2002*a*), 'Questionnaires in dictionary use research: A reexamination', *in* Braasch and Povlsen (eds): 267–71.

——(2002*b*), 'A study in the use of bilingual and monolingual dictionaries by Polish learners of English: A preliminary report', *in* Braasch and Povlsen (eds): 759–63.

——(2004), 'How do Polish learners of English rate bilingual and monolingual dictionaries?', *in* Williams and Vessier (eds): 697–706.

——and DZIEMIANKO, A. (2006), 'A new type of folk-inspired definition in English monolingual learners' dictionaries and its usefulness for conveying syntactic information', *IJL* 19/3: 225–42.

LI, L. (1998), 'Dictionaries and their users at Chinese universities: with special reference to ESP learners', *in* McArthur and Kernerman (eds): 61–79.

LIBERMAN, A. (1998), 'An annotated survey of English etymological dictionaries and glossaries', *Dictionaries* 19: 21–96.

LIPKA, L. (1990), *An Outline of English Lexicology* (Tübingen: Niemeyer).

LOUW, B. (1993), 'Irony in the text or insincerity in the writer? The diagnostic potential of semantic prosodies', *in* Baker, M. *et al.* (eds), *Text and Technology* (Amsterdam: Benjamins): 157–76.

LUNA, P. (2004), 'Not just a pretty face: The contribution of typography to lexicography', *in* Williams and Vessier (eds): 847–57.

—— (2005), 'The typographic design of Johnson's *Dictionary*', *in* Lynch, J. and McDermott, A. (eds), *Anniversary Essays on Johnson's Dictionary* (Cambridge: CUP): 175–97.

LUPPESCU, S. and DAY, R. R. (1993), 'Reading dictionaries, and vocabulary learning', *Language Learning* 43/2: 263–87.

LURQUIN, G. (1982), 'The orthophonic dictionary', *in* Goetschalckx and Rolling (eds): 99–107.

LYNCH, J. (2004), *Samuel Johnson's Dictionary* (New York: Walker and Company).

—— (2005), 'Johnson's Encyclopedia', *in* Lynch, J. and McDermott, A. (eds), *Anniversary Essays on Johnson's Dictionary* (Cambridge: CUP): 129–46.

LYONS, J. (1977), *Semantics* (London: CUP).

—— (1981), *Language, Meaning and Context* (London: Fontana).

McADAM, E. L. and MILNE, G. (eds) (1963), *Johnson's Dictionary: A Modern Selection* (London: Victor Gollancz). 2nd edn (1982) (London: Papermac).

McARTHUR, T. (1986a), 'Thematic lexicography', *in* Hartmann (ed.): 125–7.

—— (1986b), *Worlds of Reference* (Cambridge: CUP).

—— (ed.) (1992), *The Oxford Companion to the English Language* (Oxford: OUP).

—— (1998), *Living Words: Language, Lexicography and the Knowledge Revolution* (Exeter: Exeter U Press).

McARTHUR, T. and KERNERMAN, I. (eds) (1998), *Lexicography in Asia* (Tel Aviv: Password Publishers).

McCARTHY, M. (1988a), 'Questions of naturalness in language', *in* McCarthy (ed.) (1988b): 47–60.

—— (ed.) (1988b), *Naturalness in Language*, *ELR Journal* 2.

McCAWLEY, J. D. (1973), 'Discussion paper', *in* McDavid and Duckert (eds): 165–8.

—— (1986), 'What linguists might contribute to dictionary making if they could get their act together', *in* Bjarman, P. and Raskin, V. (eds), *The Real-World Linguist* (Norwood, NJ: Ablex): 1–18.

McCLUSKEY, J. (1989), 'Dictionaries and labeling of words offensive to groups, with particular attention to the second edition of the *OED*', *Dictionaries* 11: 111–23.

McCONCHIE, R.W. (1997), *Lexicography and Physicke: The Record of Sixteenth-Century English Medical Terminology* (Oxford: Clarendon Press).

McCorduck, E. (1995), 'Review of the *Longman Dictionary of American English for Microsoft Windows*^{TM}', IJL 8/1: 55–64.

McCreary, D. R. and Amacker, E. (2006), 'Experimental research on college students' usage of two dictionaries: A comparison of the *Merriam-Webster Collegiate Dictionary* and the *Macmillan English Dictionary for Advanced Learners*', in Corino *et al.* (eds): 871–85.

—— and Dolezal, F. T. (1998), 'Language learners and dictionary users', in Fontenelle *et al.* (eds): 611–18.

—— and Dolezal, F. T. (1999), 'A study of dictionary use by ESL students in an American university', IJL 12/2: 107–45.

McCrum, R., Cran, W., and MacNeil, R. (2002), *The Story of English*, 3rd edn (London: Faber and Faber).

McDavid, R. I. Jr. (1973*a*) 'Opening remarks', in McDavid and Duckert (eds): 5–7.

—— (1973*b*), 'Go slow in ethnic attributions: Geographical mobility and dialect prejudices', in Bailey, R. W. and Robinson, J. L. (eds), *Varieties of Present-Day English* (New York: The Macmillan Company): 258–73.

—— (1979) 'The social role of the dictionary', in Congleton *et al.* (eds): 17–28. Also in McDavid, R. I. Jr. (ed.) (1980), *Varieties of American English* (Stanford, CA: Stanford U Press): 296–309.

—— (1981), 'The American linguistic chastity since H.L. Mencken', *Trema* 7: 5–18.

—— and Duckert, A. R. (eds) (1973), *Lexicography in English* (New York: New York Academy of Sciences).

McDermott, A. (2005), 'Johnson's definitions of technical terms and the absence of illustrations', IJL 18/2: 173–87.

—— and Moon, R. (2005), 'Introduction: Johnson in Context', IJL 18/2: 153–5.

McEnery, T., Xiao, R., and Tono, Y. (2006), *Corpus-Based Language Studies* (London: Routledge).

MacFarquhar, P. D. and Richards, J. C. (1983), 'On dictionaries and definitions', *RELC Journal* 14/1: 111–24.

Mackenzie, I. and Mel'čuk, I. (1988), 'Crossroads of obstetrics and lexicography: A case study', IJL 1/2: 71–83.

McKeown, M. (1993), 'Creating effective definitions for young word learners', *Reading Research Quarterly* 28/1: 16–31.

Mackintosh, K. (1998), 'An empirical study of dictionary use in L2–L1 translation', in Atkins (ed.) (1998*b*): 123–49.

—— (2006), 'Biased books by harmless drudges: How dictionaries are influenced by social values', in Bowker, L. (ed.), *Lexicography, Terminology and Translation* (Ottawa: U of Ottawa Press), 45–63.

McNamara, T. P. and Miller, D. L. (1989), 'Attributes of theories of meaning', *Psychological Bulletin* 102/1: 355–76.

Magay, T. and Zigny, J. (eds) (1990), *BudaLEX '88. Proceedings of the Third EURALEX Congress* (Budapest: Akadémiai Kiadó).

MAINGAY, S. and RUNDELL, M. (1987), 'Anticipating learners' errors—implications for dictionary writers', *in* Cowie (ed.) (1987*a*): 128–35.

MAKKAI (1976), 'Toward an ecological dictionary of English', *in* Reich, P. A. (ed.), *The Second LACUS Forum* (Columbia, SC: Hornbeam Press): 52–9.

—— (1980), 'Theoretical and practical aspects of an associative lexicon for 20th-century English', *in* Zgusta (ed.): 125–46.

—— (1992), 'BudaLEX Presidential debate 1988: Part 2', *IJL* 5/4: 252–69.

MALKIEL, Y. (1962), 'A typological classification of dictionaries on the basis of distinctive features', *in* Householder and Saporta (eds): 3–24.

MALONE, K. (1962), 'Structural linguistics and bilingual dictionaries', *in* Householder and Saporta (eds): 111–18.

MANES, J. (1980), 'Ways of defining: folk definitions and the study of semantics', *Forum Linguisticum* 5/2: 122–38.

MARCKWARDT, A. H. (1963), 'Dictionaries and the English language', *English Journal* 12: 336–45. Also in Gove (ed.) (1967*b*): 31–8.

MARELLO, C. (1990), 'The thesaurus', *in* Hausmann *et al.* (eds) (1989/91): 1083–94.

—— (1996*a*), 'Les différents types de dictionnaires bilingues', *in* Béjoint and Thoiron (eds), *Les Dictionnaires bilingues* (Louvain-la-Neuve: Duculot): 31–52.

—— (1996*b*), *Le parole dell'italiano, lessico e dizionari* (Bologna: Zanichelli).

—— (1998), 'Hornby's bilingualized dictionaries', *IJL* 11/4: 292–314.

MARKOWITZ, J. and FRANZ, S. K. (1988), 'The development of defining style', *IJL* 1/3: 253–67.

MARTIN, W. (1990), 'The frequency dictionary', *in* Hausmann *et al.* (eds) (1989/91): 1314–22.

—— *et al.* (eds) (1994), *EURALEX '94 Proceedings* (Amsterdam: Vrije Universiteit).

MATHIOT, M. (1979), 'Folk definitions as a tool for the analysis of lexical meaning', *in* Mathiot, M. (ed.), *Ethnolinguistics: Boas, Sapir and Whorf Revisited* (The Hague: Mouton): 121–260.

MATORÉ, G. (1968), *Histoire des dictionnaires français* (Paris: Larousse).

MAZIÈRE, F. (1981), 'Le dictionnaire et les termes', *Cahiers de lexicologie* 39/2: 79–104.

MEIJS, W. (1992), 'Computers and dictionaries', *in* Butler, C. (ed.), *Computers and Written Texts* (Oxford: Blackwell): 141–65.

MEL'ČUK, I. A. (1988*a*), 'Semantic description of lexical units in an explanatory combinatorial dictionary: Basic principles and heuristic criteria', *IJL* 1/3: 165–88.

—— (1988*b*), 'Paraphrase et lexique dans la théorie linguistique Sens-Texte', *in* Bès, G. G. and Fuchs, C. (eds), Lexique et Paraphrase, *Lexique*: 13–54.

—— (1992), 'Lexicon: an overview', *in* Bright, W. (ed.), *Encyclopedia of Linguistics* 2 (Oxford: OUP): 332–5.

—— (1998), 'Collocations and lexical functions', *in* Cowie (ed.) (1998*a*): 23–53.

—— and POLGUÈRE, A. (2007), *Lexique actif du français* (Bruxelles: de boeck)

——, CLAS, A. and POLGUÈRE, A. (1995), *Introduction à la lexicologie explicative et combinatoire* (Louvain-la-Neuve: Duculot).

MESCHONNIC, H. (1991), *Des mots et des mondes. Dictionnaires, encyclopédies, grammaires, nomenclatures* (Paris: Hatier).

MEYER, C. (2002), *English Corpus Linguistics: An Introduction* (Cambridge: CUP).

MICHIELS, A. (1982), *Exploiting a Large Dictionary Database*, Ph.D., U of Liège.

—— and NOËL, J. (1984), 'The pro's and con's of a controlled defining vocabulary in a learner's dictionary', *in* Hartmann (ed.): 385–94.

MICKLETHWAIT, D. (2000), *Noah Webster and the American Dictionary* (Jefferson, NC: McFarland).

MILES, E. A. (1991), 'William Allen and the Webster–Worcester Wars', *Dictionaries* 13: 1–15.

MILLER, C. and SWIFT, K. (1979), *Words and Women* (Harmondsworth: Penguin Books). 1st edn (1976) (London: Anchor Press).

MILLER, G. A. (1984), 'How to misread a dictionary', *in* Wilks, Y. (ed.), *Proceedings of Coling '84* (Morriston, NJ: Association for Computational Linguistics): 462.

—— and GILDEA, P. M. (1985), 'How to misread a dictionary', *AILA Bulletin*: 13–26.

—— and GILDEA, P. M. (1987), 'How children learn words', *Scientific American*, September: 94–9.

—— and LEACOCK, C. (2000), 'Lexical representations for sentence processing', *in* Ravin and Leacock (eds): 152–60.

MILLER, G. A., BECKWITH, R., FELLBAUM, C., GROSS, D., and MILLER, K. J. (1990), 'Introduction to WordNet: An on-line lexical database', *IJL* 3/4: 235–44. Also in Fontenelle 2008*a*.

MILLS, J. (1989), *Womanwords: A Vocabulary of Culture and Patriarchal Society* (Harlow: Longman).

MINSKY, M. A. (1975), 'A framework for representing knowledge', *in* Winston, P. E. (ed.) *The Psychology of Computer Vision* (New York: McGraw-Hill).

MITCHELL, E. (1983), *Search-Do Reading: Difficulties in Using a Dictionary* (Aberdeen: Aberdeen College of Education).

MITCHELL, L. C. (2005), 'Johnson among the early modern grammarians', *IJL* 18/2: 203–16.

MITTERAND, H. (1963), *Les Mots français* (Paris: PUF).

MOGENSEN, J. E., PEDERSEN, V. H., and ZETTERSTEN, A. (eds) (2000), *Symposium on Lexicography IX* (Tübingen: Niemeyer).

MOLLIER, J.-Y. and ORY, P. (eds) (1995), *Pierre Larousse et son temps* (Paris: Larousse).

MONDRIA, J.-A. (1993), 'The effects of different types of context and different types of learning activity on the retention of foreign-language words', Paper presented at the 10th AILA World Congress, Amsterdam.

MOON, R. (1987*a*), 'Monosemous words and the dictionary', *in* Cowie (ed.) (1987*a*): 173–82.

—— (1987*b*), 'The analysis of meaning', *in* Sinclair (ed.) (1987*a*): 86–103.

—— (1988), ' "Time" and idioms', *in* Snell-Hornby (ed.): 107–15.

—— (1989), 'Objective or objectionable: ideological aspects of dictionaries, or the subversive dictionary', *English Language Research* 3: 59–94.

—— (1998*a*), *Fixed Expressions and Idioms in English: A Corpus-Based Approach* (Oxford: Clarendon Press).

—— (1998*b*), 'On using spoken data in corpus lexicography', *in* Fontenelle *et al.* (eds): 347–55.

—— (1999), 'Needles and haystacks, idioms and corpora: Gaining insight into idioms, using corpus analysis', *in* Herbst and Popp (eds): 265–81.

—— (2000), 'Phraseology and early English dictionaries: the growth of tradition', *in* Heid *et al.* (eds): 507–16.

—— (2002), 'Dictionaries: Notions and expectations', *in* Braasch and Povlsen (eds): 629–36.

—— (2004*a*), 'On specifying metaphor: An idea and its implementation', *IJL* 17/2: 195–222.

—— (2004*b*), 'Cawdrey's A Table Alphabeticall: A quantitative approach', *in* Williams and Vessier (eds): 639–50.

MORTON, H. C. (1989), 'Gove's rationale for illustrative quotations in *Webster's Third New International*', *Dictionaries* 11: 153–64.

—— (1991), 'Philip Gove's formative years: From academe to the editorship of *Webster's Third New International Dictionary*', *Dictionaries* 13: 16–30.

—— (1994), *The Story of Webster's Third: Philip Gove's Controversial Dictionary and Its Critics* (Cambridge: CUP).

MOULIN, A. (1981), 'The treatment of "Dialect" and "Register" in dictionaries for advanced learners of English', *Gräzer Linguistiche Studien* 15: 166–83.

MUGGLESTONE, L. (ed.) (2000*a*), *Lexicography and the OED* (Oxford: OUP).

—— (2000*b*), '"Pioneers in the untrodden forest": The *New* English Dictionary', *in* Mugglestone (ed.): 1–21.

—— (2000*c*), '"An Historian not a Critic": The standard of usage in the *OED*', *in* Mugglestone (ed.): 189–206.

—— (2000*d*), 'Labels reconsidered: Objectivity and the *OED*', *Dictionaries* 21: 22–36.

—— (2004), 'Departures and returns: Writing the English dictionary in the eighteenth and nineteenth centuries', *in* O'Gorman, F. and Turner, K. (eds), *The Victorians and the Eighteenth Century: Reassessing the Tradition* (Aldershot: Ashgate): 144–62.

—— (2005), *Lost for Words, The Hidden History of the* Oxford English Dictionary (Yale: Yale U Press).

—— (2007), '"Decent reticence": Coarseness, contraception, and the first edition of the *OED*', *Dictionaries* 28: 1–22.

MULLER, C. (1975), 'Peut-on estimer l'étendue d'un lexique ?', *Cahiers de lexicologie* 27/2: 3–29.

MÜLLICH, H. (1990), *'Die Definition ist blöd!' Herübersetzen mit dem einsprachigen Wörterbuch. Das französische und englische Lernerwörterbuch in der Hand der deutschen Schüler* (Tübingen: Niemeyer).

MURPHY, L. (1991), 'Defining racial labels: Problems and promise in American dictionaries', *Dictionaries* 13: 43–64.

MURPHY, L. (1998), 'Defining people: Race and ethnicity in South African English dictionaries', *IJL* 11/1: 1–33.

—— (2003), *Semantic Relations and the Lexicon* (Cambridge: CUP).

MURRAY, J. (1993), 'The Romanes Lecture, 1900', *IJL* 6/2: 100–22.

MURRAY, K. M. E. (1977), *Caught in the Web of Words: James A.H. Murray and the Oxford English Dictionary* (New Haven, CT and London: Yale U Press).

NAGY, A. R. (2004), 'Life or lexicography: How popular culture imitates dictionaries', *Dictionaries* 25: 107–21.

NATION, I. S. P. (1990), *Teaching and Learning Vocabulary* (Boston: Heinle and Heinle).

NEEF, M. and VATER, H. (2006), 'Concepts of the lexicon in theoretical linguistics', *in* Wunderlich, D. (ed.), *Advances in the Theory of the Lexicon* (Berlin and New York: Mouton de Gruyter), 27–55.

NELSON, G. (1997), 'A study of the top 100 wordforms in ICE-GB text categories', *IJL* 10/2: 112–34.

NESI, H. (1984), 'Dealing with lexical errors', MSc., U of Aston.

—— (1994), 'The effect of language background and culture on productive dictionary use', *in* Martin *et al.* (eds): 577–85.

—— (1996a), 'The role of illustrative examples in productive dictionary use', *Dictionaries* 17: 198–206.

—— (1996b), 'For future reference? A review of current electronic learner's dictionaries', *System* 24/4: 537–57.

—— (1998), 'Defining a shoehorn: the success of learners' dictionary entries for concrete nouns', *in* Atkins (ed.): 159–78.

—— (1999a), 'A user's guide to electronic dictionaries for language learners', *IJL* 12/1: 55–66.

—— (1999b), 'The specification of dictionary reference skills in higher education', *in* Hartmann, R. R. K. (ed.), *Dictionaries in Language Learning* (www.fu-berlin.de/elc/Tnproductions/SP9dossier.doc).

—— (2000a), *The Use and Abuse of EFL Dictionaries: How Learners of English as a Foreign Language Read and Interpret Dictionary Entries* (Tübingen: Niemeyer).

—— (2000b), 'Electronic dictionaries in second language vocabulary comprehension and acquisition: the state of the art', *in* Heid *et al.* (eds): 839–47.

—— and MEARA, P. (1991), 'How using dictionaries affects performance in multiple-choice EFL tests', *Reading in a Foreign Language* 8/1: 631–43.

—— and MEARA, P. (1994), 'Patterns of misinterpretation in the productive use of EFL dictionary definitions', *System* 22/1: 1–15.

NEUBACH, A. and COHEN, A. D. (1988), 'Processing strategies and problems encountered in the use of dictionaries', *Dictionaries* 10: 1–19.

NEUBAUER, F. (1984), 'The language of explanation in monolingual dictionaries', *in* Hartmann (ed.): 117–23.

—— (1987), 'How to define a defining vocabulary' *in* Ilson (ed.) (1987c): 49–59.

—— (1989), 'Vocabulary control in the definitions and examples of monolingual dictionaries', *in* Hausmann *et al.* (eds) (1989/91): 899–905.

NIDA, E. A. (1997), 'The molecular level of lexical semantics', *IJL* 10/4: 265–74.

NIELSEN, S. (2008), 'The effect of lexicographical information costs on dictionary making and use', *Lexikos* 18: 170–89.

NORLING-CHRISTENSEN, O. and ASMUSSEN, J. (1998), 'The Corpus of the Danish dictionary', *Lexikos* 8: 223–42.

NORRI, J. (1996), 'Regional labels in some British and American dictionaries', *IJL* 9/1: 1–29.

—— (2000), 'Labelling of derogatory words in some British and American dictionaries', *IJL* 13/2: 71–106.

NORVIG, P. and LAKOFF, G. (1987), 'Taking: A study in lexical network theory', *in* Aske, J., Beery, N., Michaelis, L. A., and Filip, H. (eds), *Proceedings of the Thirteenth Annual Meeting of the Berkeley Linguistics Society* (Berkeley, CA: BLS): 195–206.

NUCCORINI, S. (1992), 'Monitoring dictionary use', *in* Tommola *et al.* (eds): 89–102.

NUNBERG, G. (1978), *The Pragmatics of Reference* (Bloomington: Indiana U Linguistics Club).

—— (1994), 'The once and future dictionary', paper read at The Future of the Dictionary Xerox Workshop, Uriage, France.

—— (1995), 'Transfers of meaning', *Journal of Semantics* 12: 109–32; also (1996) *in* Pustejovsky and Boguraev (eds).

—— and ZAENEN, A. (1992), 'Systematic polysemy in lexicology and lexicography', *in* Tommola *et al.* (eds): 387–95.

OGILVIE, S. (2004), 'From "Outlandish words" to "World English": The legitimization of global varieties of English in the *Oxford English Dictionary* (*OED*)', *in* Williams and Vessier (eds): 651–8.

—— (2008), 'Rethinking Burchfield and world Englishes', *IJL* 21/1: 23–59.

OOI, V. B. Y. (1998), *Computer Corpus Lexicography* (Edinburgh: Edinburgh U Press).

OSSELTON, N. (1958), *Branded Words in English Dictionaries Before Johnson* (Groningen: Wolters).

—— (1979), 'John Kersey and the Ordinary Words of English', *English Studies* 60: 555–61.

—— (1983), 'On the history of dictionaries. The history of English-language dictionaries', *in* Hartmann (ed.) (1983*c*): 13–21.

—— (1986), 'Dr Johnson and the English Phrasal Verb', *in* Ilson (ed.) (1986*e*): 7–16.

—— (1988), 'The dictionary label "figurative": Modern praxis and the origins of a tradition', *in* Hyldgaard-Jensen and Zettersten (eds) (1988*a*): 239–50.

—— (1989), 'The history of academic dictionary criticism with reference to major dictionaries', *in* Hausmann *et al.* (eds) (1989/91): 225–30.

—— (1990), 'English lexicography from the beginning up to and including Johnson', *in* Hausmann *et al.* (eds) (1989/91): 1943–53.

—— (1991), 'Review of Stein, *The English Dictionary before Cawdrey*', *IJL* 4/4: 316–18.

OSSELTON, N. (1993), 'Review of *The Oxford English Dictionary*, Second Edition', *IJL* 6/2: 124–31.

—— (1995), *Chosen Words. Past and Present Problems for Dictionary Makers* (Exeter: U of Exeter Press).

—— (1999), 'The history of academic dictionary criticism with reference to major dictionaries', *in* Hausmann *et al.* (eds): 225–30.

—— (2000), 'Murray and his European counterparts', *in* Mugglestone (ed.) (2000*a*): 59–76.

—— (2002), 'Review of Murray, *Caught in the Web of Words*', *IJL* 15/4: 332–3.

—— (2005), 'Review of Samuel Johnson, A Dictionary of the English Language on CD-ROM', *IJL* 18/4: 546–8.

—— (2006), 'Usage guidance in early dictionaries of English', *IJL* 19/1: 99–105.

—— (2007), 'Alphabet fatigue and compiling consistency in early English dictionaries', *in* Considine and Iamartino (eds): 81–90.

OSTLER, N. (2005), *Empires of the Word* (London, HarperCollins publishers).

—— (2007), *Ad Infinitum, A Biography of Latin* (New York: Walker and Company).

—— and ATKINS, B. T. S. (1992), 'Predictable meaning shift: Some linguistic properties of lexical implication rules', *in* Pustevosky, J. and Bergler, S. (eds), *Lexical Semantics and Knowledge Representation*, (Berkeley, CA: U of California): 76–87.

OSTYN, P. and GODIN, P. (1985), 'RALEX: An alternative approach to language teaching', *Modern Language Journal* 69/4: 346–55.

PADRON, Y. and WAXMAN, H. (1988), 'The effects of EFL students' perceptions of their cognitive strategies on reading achievement', *TESOL Quarterly* 22: 146–50.

PASCAL, B. (1667/1963), 'De l'esprit géométrique et de l'art de persuader', Opuscules, *Oeuvres completes* (Paris: Editions du Seuil).

PATON, B. (1995), 'New-word lexicography and the OED', *Dictionaries* 16: 79–89.

PAWLEY, A. and SYDER, F. H. (1983), 'Two puzzles for linguistic theory: nativelike selection and nativelike fluency', *in* Richards, J. C. and Schmidt, R. W. (eds), *Language and Communication* (London: Longman): 191–227.

PEETERS, B. (2000), 'Setting the scene: Some recent milestones in the lexicon–encyclopedia debate', *in* Peeters, B. (ed.), *The Lexicon–Encyclopedia Interface* (Amsterdam: Elsevier): 1–52.

PETERS, A. M. (1983), *The Units of Language Acquisition* (Cambridge: CUP).

PETERS, W. and KILGARRIFF, A. (2000), 'Discovering semantic regularity in lexical resources', *IJL* 13/4: 287–312.

PICKETT, J. (2007), 'Considered and regarded: Indicators of belief and doubt in dictionary definitions', *Dictionaries* 28: 48–67.

PICOCHE, J. (1986), *Structures sémantiques du lexique français* (Paris: Fernand Nathan).

PILARD, G. (2002), 'English, lingua franca, cultural imperialism and dictionaries', *in* Braasch and Povlsen (eds): 429–33.

PINKER, S. (1994), *The Language Instinct* (London: Allen Lane).

PIOZZI, H. L. (1925), *Anecdotes of the Late Samuel Johnson*. BCL 1 PR English Literature no. 535.

POLGUÈRE, A. (2003), *Lexicologie et sémantique lexicale* (Montréal: Presses de l'Université de Montréal).

POTTER, L. (1998), 'Setting a good example. What kind of examples best serve the users of learners' dictionaries?', *in* Fontenelle *et al.* (eds): 357–62.

POTTIER, B. (1965), 'La définition sémantique dans les dictionnaires', *Travaux de Linguistique et de Littérature* 3/1: 33–9.

PRAT ZAGREBELSKY, M. T. (ed.) (1989), *Dal dizionario ai dizionari* (Turin: Tirrenia Stampatori).

PRĆIĆ, T. (2004), 'Enter the "Big Fifth" EFL Dictionary: MACMILLAN ENGLISH DICTIONARY FOR ADVANCED LEARNERS', *Lexicographica* 20: 303–22.

—— (2008), 'Suffixes vs final combining forms in English: A lexicographic perspective', *IJL* 21/1: 1–22.

PRUVOST, J. (ed.) (1995), *Les Dictionnaires de langue, Méthodes et contenus* (Université de Cergy-Pontoise). Actes de la Journée des dictionnaires 1994.

—— (2000), *Dictionnaires et nouvelles technologies* (Paris: PUF).

—— (ed.) (2001*a*), *Les Dictionnaires de langue française: Dictionnaires d'apprentissage, Dictionnaires spécialisés de la langue, Dictionnaires de spécialité* (Paris: Champion).

—— (2001*b*), 'Les dictionnaires d'apprentissage monolingues de la langue française (1856–1999), Problèmes et méthodes', *in* Pruvost (ed.): 67–95.

—— (2002*a*), *Les Dictionnaires de langue française* (Paris: PUF).

—— (2002*b*), 'Les dictionnaires d'apprentissage monolingues du français langue maternelle: l'histoire d'une métamorphose, du sous-produit à l'heureux pragmatisme en passant par l'heuristique', *in* Braasch and Povlsen (eds): 55–84.

—— (2004), *La dent-de-lion, la Semeuse et le* Petit Larousse (Paris: Larousse).

—— (2006), *Les Dictionnaires français, outils d'une langue et d'une culture* (Paris: Ophrys).

PUSTEJOVSKY, J. (1995), *The Generative Lexicon* (Cambridge, MA: MIT Press).

—— and BOGURAEV, B. (1994), 'A richer characterization of dictionary entries: The role of knowledge representation', *in* Atkins and Zampolli (eds): 295: 311.

—— and BOGURAEV, B. (eds) (1996), *Lexical Semantics, The Problem of Polysemy* (Oxford: Clarendon Press).

PUTNAM, H. (1975), 'The meaning of meaning', *in* Putnam, H. (1975), *Mind, Language and Reality* (Cambridge: CUP): 215–71.

QUEMADA, B. (1968), *Les Dictionnaires du français moderne 1539–1863; étude de leur histoire, leurs types et leurs méthodes* (Paris: Didier).

—— (1972), 'Lexicology and lexicography', *in* Sebeok, T. A. (ed.), *Current Trends in Linguistics* IX/1 (The Hague: Mouton): 395–475.

—— (1983), 'Bases de données informatisée et dictionnaires', *Lexique* 2: 101–20.

—— (1987), 'Notes sur *lexicographie* et *dictionnairique*', *Cahiers de lexicologie* 51/2: 229–42.

QUINE, W. V. O. (1973), 'Vagaries of definition', *in* McDavid and Duckert (eds): 247–50.

QUIRK, R. (1972), *The English Language and Images of Matter* (Oxford: OUP).

——(1973), 'The social impact of dictionaries in the U.K.', *in* McDavid and Duckert (eds): 76–88. Also as 'The image of the dictionary' *in* Quirk, R. (ed.) (1974), *The Linguist and the English Language* (London: Edward Arnold): 148–63.

——(1986), 'Opening remarks', *in* Ilson (ed.) (1986e): 1–6.

——*et al.* (1985), *A Comprehensive Grammar of the English Language* (Longman: London).

RAMSON, W. S. (1987), 'The *Australian National Dictionary*: a foretaste', *in* Burchfield (ed.): 137–55.

——(2002), *Lexical Images. The Story of the* Australian National Dictionary (Oxford: OUP).

RAND HOARE, M. and SALMON, V. (2000), 'The vocabulary of science in the *OED*', *in* Mugglestone (ed.) (2000a): 156–71.

RASKIN, V. (1985), 'Linguistic and encyclopaedic knowledge in text processing', *Quaderni di semantica* 6: 92–102.

RAVIN, Y. and LEACOCK, C. (eds) (2000), *Polysemy, Theoretical and Computational Approaches* (Oxford: OUP).

READ, A. W. (1934), 'An obscenity symbol', *American Speech* 9/4: 264–78.

——(1936), 'American projects for an academy to regulate speech', *PMLA* 51/4: 1141–79.

——(1962), 'The labeling of national and regional variation in popular dictionaries', *in* Householder and Saporta (eds): 217–27.

——(1973a), 'Approaches to lexicography and semantics', *in* Sebeok, T. A. (ed.), *Current Trends in Linguistics* X/1 (The Hague: Mouton): 145–205.

——(1973b), 'The social impact of dictionaries in the United States', *in* McDavid and Duckert (eds): 69–75.

——(1979), 'The war of the dictionaries in the Middle West', *in* Congleton *et al.* (eds): 3–16.

——(1986), 'The history of lexicography', *in* Ilson (ed.) (1986e): 28–50.

——(1987), 'A dictionary of the English of England: Problems and findings', *Dictionaries* 9: 149–63.

——(1991), 'Review of *Dictionary of American Regional English*. Vol. 2. D–H', *Dictionaries* 13, 115–17.

——(2003), 'The beginnings of English lexicography', *Dictionaries* 24: 187–226.

REDDICK, A. (1990), *The Making of Johnson's Dictionary, 1746–1773*, rev. edn 1996 (Cambridge: CUP).

REIF, J. A. (1987), 'The development of a dictionary concept: an English learner's dictionary and an exotic alphabet', *in* Cowie (ed.) (1987a): 146–58.

RENOUF, A. J. (1987), 'Corpus development', *in* Sinclair (ed.) (1987a): 1–40.

REY, A. (1970a), 'Un texte compromettant: le dictionnaire', *Critique* 273: 163–81.

——(1970b), 'Typologie génétique des dictionnaires', *Langages* 19: 48–68.

——(1970c), *Littré, l'humaniste et les mots* (Paris: Gallimard).

—— (1970*d*), *La Lexicologie: Lectures* (Paris: Klincksieck).

—— (1972), 'Usages, jugements et prescriptions linguistiques', *Langue Française* 16: 4–28.

—— (1973/1976), *Théories du Signe et du Sens*, Tome 1 (1973); Tome 2 (1976) (Paris: Klincksieck).

—— (1977), *Le Lexique: images et modèles. Du dictionnaire à la lexicologie* (Paris: Armand Colin).

—— (1982), *Encyclopédies et Dictionnaires* (Paris: PUF).

—— (1985), 'La terminologie dans un dictionnaire général de langue française: le *Grand Robert*', *TermNet News* 14: 5–7.

—— (1987*a*), 'Le dictionnaire culturel', *Lexicographica* 3: 3–50.

—— (1987*b*), 'La notion de dictionnaire culturel et ses applications', *Cahiers de lexicologie* 51/2: 243–56.

—— (1990), 'Polysémie du terme définition', *in* Centre d'Etudes du Lexique (ed.): 13–22.

—— (1995), 'Du discours au discours par l'usage: pour une problématique de l'exemple', *Langue française* 106: 95–120.

—— (2003), 'La renaissance du dictionnaire de langue française au milieu du xxe siècle: une révolution tranquille', *in* Cormier *et al.* (eds): 88–99.

—— (2007), 'La notion de dictionnaire culturel et ses applications', *in* Lorente, M., Estopà, R., Freixa, J., Marti, J., and Tebé, C. *Estudis de lingüistica i de lingüistica aplicada en honor de M. Teresa Cabré Castellví* (Barcelona: Institut Universitari de Lingüística Aplicada, Universitat Pompeu Fabra): 91–103.

—— and DELESALLE, S. (1979), 'Problèmes et conflits lexicographiques', *Langue Française* 43: 4–26.

REY-DEBOVE, J. (1969*a*), 'Le dictionnaire comme discours sur la chose et discours sur le signe', *Semiotica* 1/2: 185–95.

—— (1969*b*), 'Les relations entre le signe et la chose dans le discours métalinguistique', *Travaux de Linguistique et de Littérature* 7/1: 113–29.

—— (1970*a*), 'Le domaine du dictionnaire', *Langages* 19: 3–34.

—— (ed.) (1970*b*), La Lexicographie, *Langages* 19 (Paris: Didier/Larousse).

—— (1971), *Etude linguistique et sémiotique des dictionnaires français contemporains* (The Hague: Mouton).

—— (1978), *Le Métalangage* (Paris: Le Robert).

—— (1989*a*), 'La métalangue lexicographique: formes et fonction en lexicographie monolingue', *in* Hausmann *et al.* (eds): 305–12.

—— (1989*b*), 'Le traitement analogique dans le dictionnaire monolingue', *in* Hausmann *et al.* (eds): 635–40.

—— (1989*c*), 'Les systèmes de renvois dans le dictionnaire monolingue', *in* Hausmann *et al.* (eds): 931–7.

—— (2001), 'De quelques utopies lexicographiques concernant l'apprentissage des langues', *in* Pruvost (ed.) (2001*a*): 97–103.

RICHARDS, J. C. (1976), 'The role of vocabulary teaching', *TESOL Quarterly* 10/1: 77–89.

—— and TAYLOR, A. (1992), 'Defining strategies in folk definitions', *Perspectives* (City U of Hong Kong), 4.

RIEGEL, M. (1987), 'Définition directe et indirecte dans le langage ordinaire: les énoncés définitoires copulatifs', *Langue Française* 73: 29–53.

ROBINS, R. H. (1987), 'Polysemy and the lexicographer', *in* Burchfield (ed.): 52–75.

ROBINSON, J. (1982), 'The dictionary as witness', *Dictionaries* 4: 110–17.

ROBINSON, R. (1954), *Definition* (Oxford: OUP).

RODRIGUEZ-ÁLVAREZ, A. and RODRIGUEZ-GIL, M. E. (2006), 'John Entick's and Ann Fisher's dictionaries: An eighteenth-century case of (cons)piracy?', *IJL* 19/3: 287–319.

ROE, K. (1982), 'A survey of the encyclopedic tradition in English dictionaries', *in* Hobar (ed.): 16–23.

ROLLINS, R. M. (1980), *The Long Journey of Noah Webster* (Philadelphia: U of Pennsylvania Press).

ROONEY, K. (1994), 'Review of *The Penguin Canadian Dictionary*', *IJL* 7/3: 254–6.

ROSCH, E. (1977), 'Human categorization', *in* Warren, N. (ed.), *Studies in Cross-Cultural Psychology*, vol. 1 (London: Academic Press): 1–49.

—— (1978), 'Principles of categorization', *in* Rosch, E. and Lloyd, B. B. (eds), *Cognition and Categorization* (Hillsdale: Lawrence Erlbaum): 27–48.

—— and MERVIS, C. B. (1975), 'Family resemblances: Studies in the internal structure of categories', *Cognitive Psychology* 7: 573–605.

RUHL, C. (1978), 'Two forms of reductionism', *in* Paradis, M. (ed.), *The Fourth LACUS Forum* (Columbia, SC: Hornbeam Press): 370–83.

—— (1979), 'Alleged idioms with *hit*', *in* Wölck, W. and Garvin, P. L. (eds), *The Fifth LACUS Forum* (Columbia, SC: Hornbeam Press): 93–107.

—— (1980), 'The semantic field of *break, cut* and *tear*', *in* McCormack, W. C. and Izzo, H. J. (eds), *The Sixth LACUS Forum* (Columbia, SC: Hornbeam Press): 200–14.

RUNDELL, M. (1988), 'Changing the rules: Why the monolingual learner's dictionary should move away from the native-speaker tradition', *in* Snell-Hornby (ed.): 127–37.

—— (1998), 'Recent trends in English pedagogical lexicography', *IJL* 11/4: 315–42. Also in Fontenelle 2008*a*.

—— (1999) 'Dictionary use in production', *IJL* 12/1: 35–53.

—— (2002), 'Good old-fashioned lexicography: Human judgment and the limits of automation', *in* Corréard (ed.): 138–55.

—— (2006), 'More than one way to skin a cat: Why full-sentence definitions have not been universally adopted', *in* Corino *et al.* (eds): 323–37. Also in Fontenelle 2008*a*.

—— and STOCK, P. (1992), 'The Corpus Revolution', *English Today* 30: 9–14; 31: 21–31; 32: 45–51.

SAGARIN, E. (1963), *The Anatomy of Dirty Words* (New York: Lyle Stuart).

SAPORTA, S. (1961), *Psycholinguistics: A Book of Readings* (New York: Holt, Rinehart and Winston).

SAPPLER, P. (1990), 'Der Index', in Hausmann et al. (eds) (1989/91): 1567–73.

SAUSSURE, F. DE (1968), Cours de linguistique générale (Paris: Payot).

SCHÄFER, J. (1980), Documentation in the O.E.D.: Shakespeare and Nashe as Test Cases (Oxford: Clarendon Press).

—— (1989), Early Modern English Lexicography (Oxford: Clarendon Press).

SCHELBERT, T. (1988), 'Dictionaries—Too many words?', in Snell-Hornby (ed.): 63–70.

SCHOLFIELD, P. J. (1979), 'On a non-standard dictionary definition schema', in Hartmann (ed.): 54–62.

—— (1982), 'Using the English dictionary for comprehension', TESOL Quarterly 16/2: 185–94.

—— (1999), 'Dictionary use in reception', IJL 12/1: 13–34.

SCHOLLER, H. and REIDY, J. (eds) (1973), Lexicography and Dialect Geography (Wiesbaden: Franz Steiner).

SCHULMAN, A. and LEPORE, J. (2008), Websterisms (New York: Free Press).

SCHUR, N. (1980), English English (Essex, CN: Verbatim).

SCOTT, F. S. (1986), 'Review of The New Zealand Pocket Oxford Dictionary', Dictionaries 8: 317–26.

SCOTT, M. (1999), WordSmith Tools (Oxford: OUP).

SEBEOK, T. A. (1962) 'Materials for a typology of dictionaries', Lingua 11: 363–74.

SHCHERBA, L. V. (1940), 'Towards a general theory of lexicography', English translation by Farina, Donna M.T.Cr., IJL 8/4: 314–50. Original text: 'Opyt obscej teorii leksikografii', Izvestija Akademii Nauk SSSR 3, 89–117. English summary in Word 3 (1947) by Garvin, P., 129–30. German translation by Wolski.

SHEIDLOWER, J.T. (1995), 'Principles for the inclusion of new words in college dictionaries', Dictionaries 16: 32–44.

—— (2000), 'Review of Oxford English Dictionary Additions Series, Volume 3', Dictionaries 21: 143–8.

SIEGEL, M. E. A (2007), 'What do you do with a dictionary? A study of undergraduate dictionary use', Dictionaries 28: 23–47.

SIEPMANN, D. (1998), 'Review of John Sinclair (ed.), Collins COBUILD English Collocations Dictionary on CD-ROM', Fremdsprachen und Hochschule 53: 134–7.

—— (2005), 'Collocation, colligation and encoding dictionaries'; 'Part I: Lexicological Aspects', IJL 18/4: 409–43; 'Part II: Lexicographical Aspects', IJL 19/1: 1–39.

SILVA, P. (2000), 'Time and meaning: Sense and definition in the OED', in Mugglestone (ed.) (2000a): 77–95.

—— (2005), 'Johnson and the OED', IJL 18/2: 231–42.

SIMES, G. (2005), 'Gay slang lexicography: A brief history and a commentary on the first two gay glossaries', Dictionaries 26: 1–159.

SIMPSON, J. A. (1988), 'Computers and the new OED's new words', in Snell-Hornby (ed.): 437–44.

—— (1990), 'English lexicography after Johnson to 1945', in Hausmann et al. (eds) (1989/91): 1953–66.

SIMPSON, J. A. (2003), 'The production and use of occurrence examples', *in* van Sterkenburg (ed.) (2003*a*): 260–72.

SINCLAIR, J. (ed.) (1987*a*), *Looking up: An account of the COBUILD project in lexical computing* (London: Collins ELT).

——(1987*b*), 'Grammar in the dictionary', *in* Sinclair (ed.) (1987*a*): 104–15.

——(1987*c*), 'The nature of the evidence', *in* Sinclair (ed.) (1987*a*): 150–9.

——(1991), *Corpus, concordance, collocation* (Oxford: OUP).

——(2003*a*), 'Corpora for lexicography', *in* van Sterkenburg (ed.) (2003*a*): 167–78.

——(2003*b*), 'Corpus processing', *in* van Sterkenburg (ed.) (2003*a*): 179–93.

——(2004*a*), 'In praise of the dictionary', *in* Williams and Vessier (eds): 1–11.

——(2004*b*), 'Meaning in the framework of corpus linguistics', *Lexicographica* 20: 20–32.

SINGH, R. A. (1982), *An Introduction to Lexicography* (Mysore, India: Central Institute of Indian Languages).

SINGLETON, D. (2000), *Language and the Lexicon, An Introduction* (London: Arnold).

SIVERTSEN, E. (ed.) (1958), *Proceedings of the Eighth International Congress of Linguists* (Oslo: Oslo U Press).

SLEDD, J. H. (1972), 'Dollars and dictionaries: The limits of commercial lexicography', *in* Weinbrot (ed.) (1972*b*): 119–37.

——and EBBITT, W. R. (eds) (1962), *Dictionaries and That Dictionary: A Casebook on the Aims of Lexicographers and the Targets of Reviewers* (Chicago: Scott, Foresman and Co).

——and KOLB, G. J. (1955), *Dr. Johnson's Dictionary: Essays on the Biography of a Book* (Chicago: U of Chicago Press).

SMITH, J. W. (1979), 'A sketch of the history of the dictionary of English usage', *in* Congleton *et al.* (eds): 47–58.

SMITH, R. N. (1986), 'Conceptual primitives in the English lexicon', *in* Frawley and Steiner (eds), vol. I: 99–137.

SNELL-ORNBY, M. (ed.) (1988), *ZüriLEX '86 Proceedings. Papers read at the EURALEX International Conference* (Tübingen: Francke).

SPARCK-ONES, K. (1986), *Synonymy and Semantic Classification* (Edinburgh: Edinburgh U Press).

SPEARS, R. A. (1995), 'Review of *Random House Historical Dictionary of American Slang*', *Dictionaries* 16: 186–203.

STANLEY, E. (2000), '*OED* and the Earlier History of English', *in* Mugglestone (ed.) (2000*a*): 126–55.

——(2004), 'Polysemy and synonymy and how these concepts were understood from the eighteenth century onwards in treatises, and applied dictionaries of English', *in* Coleman and McDermott (eds), 157–83.

STARK, M. P. (1999), *Encyclopedic Learners' Dictionaries: A Study of Their Design Features from the User Perspective* (Tübingen: Niemeyer).

STARNES, D. T. (1954), *Renaissance Dictionaries: English–Latin and Latin–English* (Austin: U of Texas Press).

—— (1965), 'John Florio reconsidered', *Texas Studies in Language and Literature* 6: 407–22.

—— and NOYES, G. E. (1946), *The English Dictionary from Cawdrey to Johnson (1604–1755)* (Chapel Hill: U of North Carolina Press). 2nd edn (1991) with introduction and new bibliography by G. Stein (Amsterdam: Benjamins).

STEIN, G. (1979), 'The best of British and American lexicography', *Dictionaries* 1: 1–23.

—— (1984*a*), 'Towards a theory of lexicography: principles and/vs practice in modern English dictionaries', *in* Hartmann (ed.): 124–30.

—— (1984*b*), '*Traditio delectat*: or no change at OUP', *Anglia* 102: 392–405.

—— (1985), *The English Dictionary before Cawdrey* (Tübingen: Niemeyer).

—— (1991*a*), 'Illustrations in dictionaries', *IJL* 4/2: 99–127.

—— (1991*b*), 'The phrasal verb type "*to have a look*" in Modern English', *IRAL* 29: 1–29.

—— (1999), 'Exemplification in EFL dictionaries', *in* Herbst and Popp (eds): 45–70.

—— (2002), *Better Words: Evaluating EFL Dictionaries* (Exeter: U of Exeter Press).

—— (2006), 'Richard Huloet as a Recorder of the English Lexicon', *in* McConchie, R. W. et al. (eds), *Selected Proceedings of the 2005 Symposium on New Approaches in English Historical Lexis (HEL-LEX)* (Somerville, MA: Cascadilla Proceedings Project): 24–33.

—— and QUIRK, R. (1991), 'On having a look in a corpus', *in* Aijmer, K. and Altenberg, B. (eds), *English Corpus Linguistics. Studies in Honour of Jan Svartvik* (London: Longman): 197–203.

STEINER, G. (1997), *Errata, an examined life* (New Haven and London: Yale U Press).

STEINER, R. J. (1980), 'Putting obscene words into the dictionary', *Maledicta* IV/1: 23–37.

—— (1984), 'Guidelines for reviewers of bilingual dictionaries', *Dictionaries* 6: 166–81.

STEVENSON, M. and WILKS, Y. (2000), 'Large vocabulary word sense disambiguation', *in* Ravin and Leacock (eds): 161–77.

STOCK, P. (1984), 'Polysemy', *in* Hartmann (ed.): 131–40. Also in Fontenelle 2008*a*.

—— (1992), 'The cultural dimensions in defining', *in* Tommola *et al.* (eds), 113–20.

STREVENS, P. (ed.) (1978), *In Honour of A. S. Hornby* (Oxford: OUP).

STUBBS, M. (1996), *Text and Corpus Analysis* (Oxford: Blackwell).

—— (2001), *Words and Phrases: Corpus Studies of Lexical Semantics* (Oxford: Blackwell).

SUMMERS, D. (1988), 'The role of dictionaries in language learning', *in* Carter and McCarthy (eds): 111–25.

—— (1993), 'Longman/Lancaster English Language Corpus—criteria and design', *IJL* 6/3: 181–208.

SVARTVIK, J. (ed.) (1990), *The London Corpus of Spoken English: Description and Research* (Lund: Lund U Press).

—— (ed.) (1992), *Corpus Linguistics* (Berlin: Mouton de Gruyter).

—— (1999), 'Corpora and dictionaries', *in* Herbst and Popp (eds): 283–94.

SVENSÉN, B. (1993), *Practical Lexicography: Principles and Methods of Dictionary-Making* (Oxford: OUP).

SWANEPOEL, P. (2001), 'Dictionary quality and dictionary design: A methodology for improving the functional quality of dictionaries', *Lexikos* 11: 160–90.

SWEET, H. (1899), *The Practical Study of Languages* (London: Dent). New edition (1964) (Oxford: OUP).

TAYLOR, J. R. (1995), *Linguistic Categorization* (Oxford: Clarendon Press), 2nd edn.

TEUBERT, W. (2004), 'Language and Corpus Linguistics', *in* Halliday *et al.* (eds): 73–112.

—— (2005), 'Corpus linguistics and lexicography: The beginning of a beautiful friendship', *Lexicographica* 20: 1–19.

—— and ČERMAKOVA, A. (2004), 'Directions in corpus linguistics', *in* Halliday *et al.* (eds): 113–65.

THOMAS, J. and SHORT, M. (eds) (1996), *Using Corpora for Language Research: Studies in Honour of Geoffrey Leech* (London: Longman).

THORNDIKE, E. L. and LORGE, I. (1944), *The Teacher's Word Book of 30,000 Words* (Columbia, SC: Columbia U Press).

THUMB, J. (2004), *Dictionary Look-up Strategies and the Bilingualized Learner's Dictionary: A Think-Aloud Study* (Tübingen: Niemeyer).

TICKOO, M. L. (ed.) (1989), *Learners' Dictionaries: State of the Art* (Singapore: SEAMEO Regional Language Centre).

TOGNINI-BONELLI, E. (2001), *Corpus Linguistics at Work* (Amsterdam: Benjamins).

TOMASZCZYK, J. (1979), 'Dictionaries: users and uses', *Glottodidactica* 12: 103–19.

—— and LEWANDOWSKA-TOMASZCZYK, B. (eds) (1990), *Meaning and Lexicography* (Amsterdam: Benjamins).

TOMMOLA, H. *et al.* (eds) (1992), *EURALEX '92 Proceedings* (Tampere: U of Tampere).

TONO, Y. (1984), 'On the dictionary user's reference skills', B.Ed. dissertation, U of Tokyo.

—— (1987), 'Which word do you look up? A study of dictionary reference skills', M.Ed. dissertation, U of Tokyo.

—— (1998), 'Interacting with the users: Research findings in EFL dictionary user studies', *in* McArthur and Kernerman (eds): 97–118.

—— (2001), *Research on Dictionary Use in the Context of Foreign Language Learning* (Tübingen: Niemeyer).

TOURNIER, J. (1985), *Introduction descriptive à la lexicogénétique de l'anglais contemporain* (Paris-Geneva: Champion-Slatkine).

TRENCH, R. C. (1857), *On Some Deficiencies in our English Dictionaries* (London: Transactions of the Philological Society); (1860), 2nd rev. edn (London: John W. Parker and Son).

TRUDEAU, D. (1992), *Les Inventeurs du bon usage* (Paris: Les Editions de Minuit).

TSOHATZIDIS, S. L. (ed.) (1990), *Meanings and Prototypes: Studies in Linguistic Categorization* (London: Routledge).

TYLER, A. and EVANS, V. (2001), 'Reconsidering prepositional polysemy networks: The case of *over*', *in* Nerlich, B., Todd, Z., Herman, V., and Clarke, D. (eds), *Polysemy: Flexible Patterns of Meaning in Mind and Language* (Berlin: Mouton de Gruyter): 95–160.

ULLMANN, S. (1962), *Semantics: An Introduction to the Science of Meaning* (London: Blackwell).

Urdang, L. (1963), 'Review of Householder and Saporta (eds), *Problems in Lexicography*', *Language* 39: 586–94.

—— (1979), 'Meaning: denotative, connotative, allusive', *in* Hartmann (ed.), 47–52. Also *in ITL: Review of Applied Linguistics* 45/46: 47–52.

—— (1993), 'Review of *The American Heritage Dictionary of the English Language*', *IJL* 6/2: 131–40.

—— (1996a), 'The uncommon use of proper names', *IJL* 9/1: 30–4.

—— (1996b), 'Review of *A Thesaurus Dictionary of the English Language*', *IJL* 9/1: 70–1.

—— (1997), 'Review of *Empire of Words, The Reign of the OED*', by John Willinsky', *IJL* 10/1: 75–82.

—— (2000), 'Review of Hartmann and James, *Dictionary of Lexicography*', *IJL* 13/1: 35–42.

van den Hurk, I. and Meijs, W. (1986), 'The dictionary as corpus: Analyzing *LDOCE*'s definition-language', *in* Aarts and Meijs (eds): 99–125.

van der Meer, G. (1999), 'Metaphors and dictionaries: the morass of meaning, or how to get two ideas for one', *IJL* 12/3: 195–208.

—— (2000a), 'Further ways to improve an active dictionary: collocations, non-morphological derivations, grammar', *in* Mogensen *et al.* (eds): 125–41.

—— (2000b), 'Core, subsense and the *New Oxford Dictionary of English* (NODE). On how meanings hang together, and not separately', *in* Heid *et al.* (eds): 419–31.

—— and Sansome, R. (2001), 'OALD6 in a linguistic and a language teaching perspective', *IJL* 14/4: 283–306.

van Hoof, H. (1994), *Petite histoire des dictionnaires* (Louvain-la-Neuve: Peeters).

van Sterkenburg, P. (ed.) (2003a), *A Practical Guide to Lexicography* (Amsterdam: Benjamins).

—— (2003b), '"The" dictionary: Definition and history', *in* van Sterkenburg (ed.) (2003a): 3–17.

Varantola, K. (2001), 'Review of Nesi, *The Use and Abuse of EFL Dictionaries*', *IJL* 14/3: 237–40.

Veisbergs, A. (2002), 'Defining political terms in lexicography: Recent past and present', *in* Braasch and Povlsen (eds): 657–67.

Vossen, P. (ed.) (1998), *EuroWordNet: A Multilingual Database with Lexical Semantic Networks* (Dordrecht/Boston/London: Kluwer Academic Publishers).

—— (2004), 'EuroWordNet: A multilingual database of autonomous and language-specific wordnets connected via an inter-lingual-index', *IJL* 17/2: 161–73.

Wagner, R.-L. (1967), *Les Vocabulaires français I. Définitions. Les Dictionnaires* (Paris: Didier).

—— (1975), 'Réflexions naïves à propos des dictionnaires', *Cahiers de lexicologie* 27: 81–106.

Weinbrot, H. D. (ed.) (1972a), *New Aspects of Lexicography* (Carbondale, IL: Southern Illinois U Press).

—— (1972b), 'Samuel Johnson's Plan and Preface to the *Dictionary*. The growth of a lexicographer's mind', *in* Weinbrot (ed.) (1972a): 73–94.

WEINER, E. S. C. (1986), 'The New *Oxford English Dictionary* and world English', *English Worldwide* 7: 256–66.

——(1987), 'The New *Oxford English Dictionary*: Progress and prospects', *in* Bailey (ed.): 30–48.

——(1994), 'The lexicographical workstation and the scholarly dictionary', *in* Atkins and Zampolli (eds): 413–38.

——(1997), 'The African dimension of the *Oxford English Dictionary*', *Lexikos* 7: 252–9.

WEINREICH, U. (1962), 'Lexicographic definition in descriptive semantics', *in* Householder and Saporta (eds), 25–44.

——(1964), '*Webster's Third*: a critique of its semantics', *International Journal of American Linguistics* 30/4: 405–9.

WELLS, R. A. (1973), *Dictionaries and the Authoritarian Tradition* (The Hague: Mouton).

WEST, M. (1936/1953), *A General Service List of English Words* (London: Longman).

WHITCUT, J. (1986), 'The training of dictionary users', *in* Ilson (ed.) (1986*e*): 111–22.

WHITTAKER, K. (1966), *Dictionaries* (London: Clive Bingley).

WIEGAND, H. E. (1984), 'On the structure and contents of a general theory of lexicography', *in* Hartmann (ed.): 13–30.

——(1998*a*), *Wörterbuchforschung. Untersuchungen zur Wörterbuchbenutzung, zur Theorie, Geschichte, Kritik und Automatisierung der Lexikographie* (Berlin: de Gruyter).

——(1999), *Semantics and Lexicography. Selected Studies (1976–1996)* (Tübingen: Niemeyer).

WIERZBICKA, A. (1972), *Semantic Primitives* (Frankfurt: Atheneum).

——(1982), 'Why can you have a drink when you can't *have an eat?*', *Language* 58: 753–99.

——(1985), *Lexicography and Conceptual Analysis* (Ann Arbor: Karoma Publishers Inc).

——(1993), 'Review of Tsohatzidis, *Meanings and Prototypes*', *IJL* 6/3: 215–21.

——(1996), *Semantics: Primes and Universals* (Oxford: OUP).

WILKS, Y. (1973), 'Preference Semantics', *in* Keenan, E. (ed.) *The Formal Semantics of Natural Language* (Cambridge: CUP): 329–48.

——, FASS, D. C., GUO, C.-M., MCDONALD, J. E., PLATE, T., and SLATOR, B. M. (1989), 'A tractable machine dictionary as a resource for computational semantics', *in* Boguraev and Briscoe (eds): 193–228.

WILKS, Y., SLATOR, B. M., and GUTHRIE, L. (1996), *Electric Words—Dictionaries, Computers and Meanings* (Cambridge, MA: MIT Press).

WILLIAMS, D. (2000), 'Mary Tudor's French Tutors', *Dictionaries* 21: 37–50.

WILLIAMS, G. and VESSIER, S. (eds) (2004), *Proceedings of the Eleventh EURALEX International Congress* (Université de Bretagne Sud).

WILLINSKY, J. (1994), *Empire of Words, The Reign of the* OED (Princeton: Princeton U Press).

WINCHESTER, S. (1998), *The Surgeon of Crowthorne* (London: Viking).

——(2003), *The Meaning of Everything, The Story of the* Oxford English Dictionary (Oxford: OUP).

WINGATE, U. (2002), *The Effectiveness of Different Learner Dictionaries* (Tübingen: Niemeyer).

WITTGENSTEIN, L. (1953), *Philosophical Investigations* (Oxford: Blackwell).

WRAY, A. (2002), *Formulaic Language and the Lexicon* (Cambridge: CUP).

XIAO, Z. (2007), 'Well-known and influential corpora', *in* Lüdeling, A. and Kyto, M. (eds), *Corpus Linguistics: An International Handbook* (Berlin: Mouton de Gruyter).

ZAENEN, A. (2002), 'Musings about the electronic dictionary', *in* Corréard (ed.): 230–44.

——and ENGDAHL, E. (1994), 'Descriptive and theoretical syntax in the lexicon', *in* Atkins and Zampolli (eds): 181–212.

ZAMPOLLI, A. (1994), 'Introduction', *in* Atkins and Zampolli (eds): 3–15.

ZAUNER, A. (1903), 'Die romanischen Namen der Körperteile. Eine onomasiologische Studien', *Romanische Forschungen* 15: 339–530.

ZGUSTA, L. (1971), *Manual of Lexicography* (The Hague: Mouton).

——(ed.) (1980), *Theory and Method in Lexicography. Western and Non-Western Perspectives* (Columbia, SC: Hornbeam Press).

——(1986a), 'Summation', *in* Ilson (ed.) (1986e): 138–46.

——(1986b), 'The lexicon and the dictionaries: some theoretical and historical observations', *in* Frawley and Steiner (eds): 67–81.

——(1989a), 'The role of dictionaries in the genesis and development of the standard', *in* Hausmann *et al.* (eds) (1989/91): 70–9.

——(1989b), 'The influence of scripts and morphological language types on the structure of dictionaries', *in* Hausmann *et al.* (eds) (1989/91): 296–305.

——(1989c), 'The *Oxford English Dictionary* and other dictionaries', *IJL* 2/3: 188–230.

——(ed.) (1992), *History, Language and Lexicographers* (Tübingen: Niemeyer).

——(2006), *Lexicography Then and Now* (Tübingen: Niemeyer).

——and FARINA, M. T. C. (1988), *Lexicography Today* (Tübingen: Niemeyer).

ZWICKY, A. and SADOCK, J. M. (1975), 'Ambiguity tests and how to fail them', *in* Kimball, J. P. (ed.), *Syntax and Semantics 4* (New York: Academic Press): 1–36.

INDEX

McEnery 349, 351–4, 357–8, 360–1
MacFarquhar and Richards 251
McGregor 197
McKean 159
McKeown 251
Mackintosh 277, 324
McLeod 156
Macmillan English Dictionary 186–9
McNamara and Miller 330
Mac Orlan 79
Macaulay 10
machine-readable dictionaries 376
macrostructure 11–4, 282–5; in
    LDOCE 173; in *COB* 178; in *CIDE* 185
Mahn 86
Maingay and Rundell 245, 252
Makkai 217, 267, 274, 313
Malkiel 23, 42
Malone 263, 268, 356
Manes 329
Manguel 92
March 21, 98
Marckwardt 85, 152, 154, 263, 265–6
Marello 46, 236
Martin 65, 76, 305
Mathews 120
Matoré 7, 8, 44, 61, 92, 229, 236, 238
Mazière 219
Meaning → Text theory 291, 338
Meijs 375
Mel'čuk 9, 22, 195, 285, 291, 308, 311, 314,
    338, 345, 356
menus in *LDOCE* 176; in *MEDAL* 187
Mérimée 92
Merman 133
Meschonnic 26–7, 203
metalexicographer, the word 9
metaphors in *MEDAL* 189
Meyer 349, 352–4, 358, 360–1, 364
Michiels 376
Michiels and Noël 172
Micklethwait 88

microstructure 11–4
Miller 249, 253, 261, 377
Miller and Gildea 246, 248–9, 253
Miller and Swift 202
Mills 213
Minor 98
Minsky 290
Mitchell 57, 81, 247
Mitterand 265
Mondria 254
monitor corpora 352, 364–5
monolingual 45
monosemy 286
Montaigne 56
Moon 2, 54, 56–7, 64–5, 203–6, 231, 233–4,
    269, 276, 288, 293–5, 306–7, 309, 313–4,
    340, 355
Moreri 61
morpheme 23
Morris 136,
Morton 26, 30, 64–5, 69, 74, 83–8, 109, 123,
    129–37, 139, 142, 147, 149, 152–3, 155, 208,
    293, 330, 345
Moulin 340
Mugglestone 31, 32, 69–70, 74, 83, 88,
    97–106, 108–9, 111, 113, 206, 210, 212, 232,
    288, 294
Mulcaster 56
Müllich 247–8
multiword items 17, 147, 249–50, 277–8,
    284, 308; ordering 315–6
Murphy 28, 207, 303, 307
Murray, James 7, 83, 98–9, 102, 104, 109,
    221, 232, 237, 268, 277, 279, 281, 288, 294
Murray, K. M. E. 109, 111
mutual information 314

Nagy 8
Nation 260
natural semantic metalanguage 333
necessary and sufficient conditions 303
Neef and Vater 30